# EUROPEAN UNION PUBLIC LA

Since                                        elf as
one                                       com-
preh                                      rings
toget                                     ional
law o                                    of the
Unio                                     ntext'
appr                                     col-
lectic                                   dents
conce                                    public la                                   text
inval

DAM                                      ol of
Econ                                     ts in
Euro                                     l, the
Univ                                     ). He
is cu

ADA                                      sgow.
His a                                    dom,
Nort                                     003),
Our                                      *Sixth*
Editi

Birmingham • Chester • Guildford • London • York

# EUROPEAN UNION
# PUBLIC LAW

## TEXT AND MATERIALS

DAMIAN CHALMERS

ADAM TOMKINS

CAMBRIDGE
UNIVERSITY PRESS

CAMBRIDGE UNIVERSITY PRESS
Cambridge, New York, Melbourne, Madrid, Cape Town, Singapore, São Paulo

Cambridge University Press
The Edinburgh Building, Cambridge CB2 8RU, UK

Published in the United States of America by Cambridge University Press, New York

www.cambridge.org
Information on this title: www.cambridge.org/9780521709026

First published 2007

Printed in the United Kingdom at the University Press, Cambridge

*A catalogue record for this publication is available from the British Library*

ISBN 978-0-521-88237-8 hardback
ISBN 978-0-521-70902-6 paperback

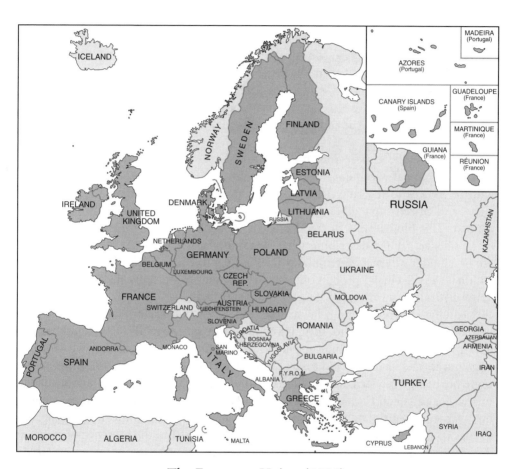

The European Union (2006)

# PREFACE

This book reprints the first ten chapters of the wider project *European Union Law: Text and Materials* (Cambridge University Press, 2006) that we co-wrote with Christos Hadjiemmanuil and Giorgio Monti. We would like to thank them for their support for this book. We decided to publish these chapters as a separate book partly as a response to a perceived demand by those who wish to study only the public law of the European Union. We also decided to publish them separately as they bring out issues which are present in all European Union law but are more openly contested in its public law.

First, whilst the Union does not aspire to be a state, it cannot avoid using the legal and political vocabulary of the state. European Union legal debates are replete with references to the rule of law, separation of powers, democracy, fundamental rights and citizenship – all terms developed within and associated with the national context. This bind results in traditional understandings of these terms never quite being satisfactory for describing what is taking place. Yet, on the other hand, there are no suitable alternative templates from which to draw. Evaluating the European Union is thus an elusive process but, also, an intriguing one, as it calls us to reconsider many central assumptions about law and government.

Secondly, European Union law cannot escape its political nature. The European Union has, on the one hand, little if any taken-for-granted authority. On the other, it is a big place of half a billion people in which any legal measure will generate large numbers of winners and losers. The calculus of the European Union is always therefore being contested. Many will go beyond this, arguing not only that a particular measure is unfair in that it imposes costs on them or unevenly distributes benefits, but that it is illegitimate in the deeper sense of lacking the authority to make the change in the first place. The absence of 'right answers' and the presence of constant debate about revisiting measures, we would suggest, are features of European Union law which provide new opportunities for democratisation by leading citizens more openly to question the nature of public power. The extent to which such opportunities are actually taken up is a different question, of course.

The third feature of the European Union is its continual, some would say obsessive, quest for justifications. This lack of authority leads it to work harder to legitimate itself, either through so-called 'input legitimacy' by opening its procedures or by 'output legitimacy' through continually re-evaluating the effects of its measures. This has made it a peculiar laboratory for public law where all kinds of measures are tested in the ongoing and sometimes apparently desperate search for an elixir.

Finally, European Union law is European. It institutionalises and carries forward, through invocation of the name, a particular view of Europe. At the heart of this view of Europe lies the nation state. It is impossible to conceive of the European Union without the nation states. Its procedures and norms would make no sense if one took them away. The European Union suggests equally, however, that Europe is something a little bit more than the nation states. It locates them in a wider environment of norms, procedures, symbols and values to which they must adapt. They can adapt by incorporating them or maybe rejecting them, but it is not open to them to ignore them. In that, it reminds us that public law is not just a set of formal procedures, and calls us continually to reconsider the nature of political community and public power.

These chapters appear, with only minor modifications, as they did in the earlier book. As then, we have endeavoured to state the legal position as at 30 September 2005.

DC and AT

# CONTENTS

PART II **Administrative law**

8 Accountability in the European Union 311

9 The enforcement of European law 348

# ABBREVIATIONS

| | |
|---|---|
| AFSJ | Area of Freedom, Security and Justice |
| BER | Block Exemption Regulation |
| BSE | bovine spongiform encephalopathy |
| CAP | Common Agricultural Policy |
| CESR | Committee of European Securities Regulators |
| CFI | Court of First Instance |
| CFSP | Common Foreign and Security Policy |
| COR | Committee of the Regions |
| COREPER | Committee of Permanent Representatives |
| CT | Constitutional Treaty |
| DCT | Draft Constitutional Treaty |
| DG | Directorate-General |
| EC | European Communities |
| ECB | European Central Bank |
| ECHR | European Convention on Human Rights |
| ECN | European Competition Network |
| ECSC | European Coal and Steel Community |
| ECtHR | European Court of Human Rights |
| ECU | European currency unit |
| EDC | European Defence Community |
| EDP | excessive deficit procedure |
| EEC | European Economic Community |
| EFSA | European Food Safety Authority |
| EMI | European Monetary Institute |
| EMS | European Monetary System |
| EMU | economic and monetary union |
| EO | European Ombudsman |
| ERDF | European Regional Development Fund |
| ERM | exchange rate mechanism |
| ERT | European Round Table |
| ESC | Economic and Social Committee |
| ESCB | European System of Central Banks |
| ESecC | European Securities Committee |

| | |
|---|---|
| ESF | European Social Fund |
| EUCFR | European Union Charter of Fundamental Rights |
| EURATOM | European Atomic Energy Community |
| EUROPOL | European Police Office |
| FSA | Financial Services Authority |
| FSAP | Financial Services Action Plan |
| IGC | intergovernmental conference |
| ISO | International Standards Organisation |
| JHA | Justice and Home Affairs |
| MiFiD | Markets in Financial Instruments Directive |
| NCA | national competition authority |
| NCB | national central bank |
| NGO | non-governmental organization |
| OHIM | Office for Harmonisation in the Internal Market |
| OLAF | European Anti-Fraud Office |
| OMC | open method of coordination |
| PJCC | police and judicial cooperation in criminal matters |
| QMV | qualified majority voting |
| SEA | Single European Act |
| SGEI | services of general economic interest |
| SIA | Schengen Implementing Agreement |
| SIS | Schengen Information System |
| TEU | Treaty on European Union |
| WTO | World Trade Organisation |

# ACKNOWLEDGMENTS

Every attempt has been made to secure permission to reproduce copyright material in this title and grateful acknowledgment is made to the authors and publishers of all reproduced material. In particular, the publishers would like to acknowledge the following for granting permission to reproduce material from the sources set out below:

A. Arnull, 'Private Applicants and the Action for Annulment under Article 173 of the EC Treaty' (1995) 40 *Common Market Law Review* 44–46 © 1995 Kluwer Law International. Reprinted with permission from Kluwer Law International; www.kluwerlaw.com.

E. Balibar, 'Europe as Vanishing Mediator' (2003) *Constellations* 312. Reprinted by permission of Blackwell Publishing.

A. Clapham, 'A Human Rights Policy for the European Community' (1990) *Yearbook of European Law* 309. Reprinted by permission of Oxford University Press.

H. Farrell and A. Héritier, 'Interorganizational Negotiation and Intraorganizational Power in Shared Decision Making: Early Agreements under Codecision and their Impact on the European Parliament and the Council' (2004) 37 *Comparative Political Studies* 1184. © 2004 by Sage Publications, pp. 1198–1199. Reprinted by permission of Sage Publications.

D. Grimm, 'Does Europe Need a Constitution?' (1995) 1 *European Law Journal* 218. Reprinted by permission of Blackwell Publishing.

C. Harlow, 'Public Law and Popular Justice' (2002) 65 *Modern Law Review* 1. Reprinted by permission of Blackwell Publishing.

D. Judge and D. Earnshaw, 'Weak European Parliament Influence? A Study of the Environment Committee of the European Parliament' (1994) *Government and Opposition* 262. Reprinted by permission of Blackwell Publishing.

M. Kumm, 'The Jurisprudence of Constitutional Conflict: Constitutional Supremacy in Europe before and after the Constitutional Treaty' (2005) 11 *European Law Journal* 262. Reprinted by permission of Blackwell Publishing.

N. MacCormick, 'The Maastricht Urteil: Sovereignty Now' (1995) 1 European Law Journal 259. Reprinted by permission of Blackwell Publishing.

S. Mazey and J. Richardson, 'Interest Groups and the Brussels Bureaucracy' in J. Hayward and A. Menon (eds.), *Governing Europe* (Oxford, Oxford University Press, 2003). Reprinted by permission of Oxford University Press.

D. Obradovic, 'Policy Legitimacy and the European Union' (1996) 34 *Journal of Common Market Studies* 191. Reprinted by permission of Blackwell Publishing.

M. Shapiro, 'The Problems of Independent Agencies in the United States and the European Union' (1997) 4(2) *Journal of European Public Policy* 276–277 (http://www.tandf.co.uk). Reprinted by permission of Taylor & Francis.

M. de la Torre, 'The Law Beneath Rights' Feet: Preliminary Investigation for a Study of the Charter of Fundamental Rights of the European Union' (2002) 8 *European Law Journal* 513. Reprinted by permission of Blackwell Publishing.

T. Tridimas, *The General Principles of EC Law* (Oxford, Oxford University Press, 1999). Reprinted by permission of Oxford University Press.

J. Weiler, 'The Transformation of Europe'. Reprinted by permission of The Yale Law Journal Company and William S. Hein Company from *The Yale Law Journal*, Vol. 100, pages 2403–2483.

J. Weiler, 'A Constitution for Europe? Some Hard Choices' (2002) 40 *Journal of Common Market Studies* 563. Reprinted by permission of Blackwell Publishing.

A. Williams, *EU Human Rights Policies: A Study in Irony* (Oxford, Oxford University Press, 2004). Reprinted by permission of Oxford University Press.

J. Zielonka, 'How New Enlarged Borders will Reshape the European Union' (2001) 39 *Journal of Common Market Studies* 507. Reprinted by permission of Blackwell Publishing.

# TABLE OF CASES

## European Court of Justice and Court of First Instance: cases in case number order

### European Court of Justice and Court of First Instance: cases in alphabetical order by party or common title

## National Courts

### Austria

### Belgium

### Benelux

### Denmark

### Finland

### France

### Germany

## Hungary

## Ireland

## Italy

## Netherlands

## Poland

## Portugal

## Spain

# TABLE OF TREATIES, INSTRUMENTS AND LEGISLATION

## Treaties and analogous instruments

*Note*: Article numbers are those introduced by the Treaty of Amsterdam. Earlier numbers are shown in square brackets. Where the only number given is in square brackets, it should be assumed that the Article in question has been deleted.

## EU legislation and policy documents

### Commission Communications

### Commission Decisions

### Commission Declarations

### Commission Notices/Guidelines

### Commission Regulations (EC)

## Council Framework Decisions

## Council Regulations/Council and Parliament Regulations

# TABLE OF EQUIVALENTS

## EC Treaty Article numbers and their pre-Amsterdam equivalents*

| Current Article number | Pre-Amsterdam Article number | Current Article number | Pre-Amsterdam Article number |
|---|---|---|---|
| 1 | 1 | 32 | 38 |
| 2 | 2 | 33 | 39 |
| 3 | 3 | 34 | 40 |
| 4 | 3a | 35 | 41 |
| 5 | 3b | 36 | 42 |
| 6 | 3c | 37 | 43 |
| 7 | 4 | 38 | 46 |
| 8 | 4a | 39 | 48 |
| 9 | 4b | 40 | 49 |
| 10 | 5 | 41 | 50 |
| 11 | 5a | 42 | 51 |
| 12 | 6 | 43 | 52 |
| 13 | 6a | 44 | 54 |
| 14 | 7a | 45 | 55 |
| 15 | 7c | 46 | 56 |
| 16 | 7d | 47 | 57 |
| 17 | 8 | 48 | 58 |
| 18 | 8a | 49 | 59 |
| 19 | 8b | 50 | 60 |
| 20 | 8c | 51 | 61 |
| 21 | 8d | 52 | 63 |
| 22 | 8e | 53 | 64 |
| 23 | 9 | 54 | 65 |
| 24 | 10 | 55 | 66 |
| 25 | 12 | 56 | 73b |
| 26 | 28 | 57 | 73c |
| 27 | 29 | 58 | 73d |
| 28 | 30 | 59 | 73f |
| 29 | 34 | 60 | 73g |
| 30 | 36 | 61 | 73i |
| 31 | 37 | 62 | 73j |

| Current Article number | Pre-Amsterdam Article number | Current Article number | Pre-Amsterdam Article number |
|---|---|---|---|
| 63 | 73k | 106 | 105a |
| 64 | 73l | 107 | 106 |
| 65 | 73m | 108 | 107 |
| 66 | 73n | 109 | 108 |
| 67 | 73o | 110 | 108a |
| 68 | 73p | 111 | 109 |
| 69 | 73q | 112 | 109a |
| 70 | 74 | 113 | 109b |
| 71 | 75 | 114 | 109c |
| 72 | 76 | 115 | 109d |
| 73 | 77 | 116 | 109e |
| 74 | 78 | 117 | 109f |
| 75 | 79 | 118 | 109g |
| 76 | 80 | 119 | 109h |
| 77 | 81 | 120 | 109i |
| 78 | 82 | 121 | 109j |
| 79 | 83 | 122 | 109k |
| 80 | 84 | 123 | 109l |
| 81 | 85 | 124 | 109m |
| 82 | 86 | 125 | 109n |
| 83 | 87 | 126 | 109o |
| 84 | 88 | 127 | 109p |
| 85 | 89 | 128 | 109q |
| 86 | 90 | 129 | 109r |
| 87 | 92 | 130 | 109s |
| 88 | 93 | 131 | 110 |
| 89 | 94 | 132 | 112 |
| 90 | 95 | 133 | 113 |
| 91 | 96 | 134 | 115 |
| 92 | 98 | 135 | 116 |
| 93 | 99 | 136 | 117 |
| 94 | 100 | 137 | 118 |
| 95 | 100a | 138 | 118a |
| 96 | 101 | 139 | 118b |
| 97 | 102 | 140 | 118c |
| 98 | 102a | 141 | 119 |
| 99 | 103 | 142 | 119a |
| 100 | 103a | 143 | 120 |
| 101 | 104 | 144 | 121 |
| 102 | 104a | 145 | 122 |
| 103 | 104b | 146 | 123 |
| 104 | 104c | 147 | 124 |
| 105 | 105 | 148 | 125 |

| Current Article number | Pre-Amsterdam Article number | Current Article number | Pre-Amsterdam Article number |
|---|---|---|---|
| 149 | 126 | 192 | 138b |
| 150 | 127 | 193 | 138c |
| 151 | 128 | 194 | 138d |
| 152 | 129 | 195 | 138e |
| 153 | 129a | 196 | 139 |
| 154 | 129b | 197 | 140 |
| 155 | 129c | 198 | 141 |
| 156 | 129d | 199 | 142 |
| 157 | 130 | 200 | 143 |
| 158 | 130a | 201 | 144 |
| 159 | 130b | 202 | 145 |
| 160 | 130c | 203 | 146 |
| 161 | 130d | 204 | 147 |
| 162 | 130e | 205 | 148 |
| 163 | 130f | 206 | 150 |
| 164 | 130g | 207 | 151 |
| 165 | 130h | 208 | 152 |
| 166 | 130i | 209 | 153 |
| 167 | 130j | 210 | 154 |
| 168 | 130k | 211 | 155 |
| 169 | 130l | 212 | 156 |
| 170 | 130m | 213 | 157 |
| 171 | 130n | 214 | 158 |
| 172 | 130o | 215 | 159 |
| 173 | 130p | 216 | 160 |
| 174 | 130r | 217 | 161 |
| 175 | 130s | 218 | 162 |
| 176 | 130t | 219 | 163 |
| 177 | 130u | 220 | 164 |
| 178 | 130v | 221 | 165 |
| 179 | 130w | 222 | 166 |
| 180 | 130x | 223 | 167 |
| 181 | 130y | 224 | 168 |
| 182 | 131 | 225 | 168a |
| 183 | 132 | 226 | 169 |
| 184 | 133 | 227 | 170 |
| 185 | 134 | 228 | 171 |
| 186 | 135 | 229 | 172 |
| 187 | 136 | 230 | 173 |
| 188 | 136a | 231 | 174 |
| 189 | 137 | 232 | 175 |
| 190 | 138 | 233 | 176 |
| 191 | 138a | 234 | 177 |

| Current Article number | Pre-Amsterdam Article number | Current Article number | Pre-Amsterdam Article number |
|---|---|---|---|
| 235 | 178 | 275 | 205a |
| 236 | 179 | 276 | 206 |
| 237 | 180 | 277 | 207 |
| 238 | 181 | 278 | 208 |
| 239 | 182 | 279 | 209 |
| 240 | 183 | 280 | 209a |
| 241 | 184 | 281 | 210 |
| 242 | 185 | 282 | 211 |
| 243 | 186 | 283 | 212 |
| 244 | 187 | 284 | 213 |
| 245 | 188 | 285 | 213a |
| 246 | 188a | 286 | 213b |
| 247 | 188b | 287 | 214 |
| 248 | 188c | 288 | 215 |
| 249 | 189 | 289 | 216 |
| 250 | 189a | 290 | 217 |
| 251 | 189b | 291 | 218 |
| 252 | 189c | 292 | 219 |
| 253 | 190 | 293 | 220 |
| 254 | 191 | 294 | 221 |
| 255 | 191a | 295 | 222 |
| 256 | 192 | 296 | 223 |
| 257 | 193 | 297 | 224 |
| 258 | 194 | 298 | 225 |
| 259 | 195 | 299 | 227 |
| 260 | 196 | 300 | 228 |
| 261 | 197 | 301 | 228a |
| 262 | 198 | 302 | 229 |
| 263 | 198a | 303 | 230 |
| 264 | 198b | 304 | 231 |
| 265 | 198c | 305 | 232 |
| 266 | 198d | 306 | 233 |
| 267 | 198e | 307 | 234 |
| 268 | 199 | 308 | 235 |
| 269 | 200 | 309 | 236 |
| 270 | 201a | 310 | 238 |
| 271 | 202 | 311 | 239 |
| 272 | 203 | 312 | 240 |
| 273 | 204 | 313 | 247 |
| 274 | 205 | 314 | 248 |

* No number is provided where earlier provisions have been deleted or for new Treaty provisions introduced by the Treaty of Nice which have no pre-Amsterdam equivalent.

**Treaty on European Union Article numbers and their Pre-Amsterdam equivalents**

| Current Article number | Pre-Amsterdam Article letter | Current Article number | Pre-Amsterdam Article letter |
|---|---|---|---|
| 1 | A | 28 | J.18 |
| 2 | B | 29 | K.1 |
| 3 | C | 30 | K.2 |
| 4 | D | 31 | K.3 |
| 5 | E | 32 | K.4 |
| 6 | F | 33 | K.5 |
| 7 | F.1 | 34 | K.6 |
| 11 | J.1 | 35 | K.7 |
| 12 | J.2 | 36 | K.8 |
| 13 | J.3 | 37 | K.9 |
| 14 | J.4 | 38 | K.10 |
| 15 | J.5 | 39 | K.11 |
| 16 | J.6 | 40 | K.12 |
| 17 | J.7 | 41 | K.13 |
| 18 | J.8 | 42 | K.14 |
| 19 | J.9 | 43 | K.15 |
| 20 | J.10 | 46 | L |
| 21 | J.11 | 47 | M |
| 22 | J.12 | 48 | N |
| 23 | J.13 | 49 | O |
| 24 | J.14 | 50 | P |
| 25 | J.15 | 51 | Q |
| 26 | J.16 | 52 | R |
| 27 | J.17 | 53 | S |

# ELECTRONIC WORKING PAPER SERIES

**ARENA Working Papers**: www.sv.uio.no/arena/

**Constitutionalism Web (CONWeb) Papers**:
www.qub.ac.uk/schools/SchoolofPoliticsInternationalStudiesandPhilosophy/
Research/PaperSeries/ConWEBPapers/

**Centre for the Advanced Study in Social Sciences (CEACS) Working Papers**:
www.march.es/ceacs/ingles/Publicaciones/working/working.asp

**Centre for Culture, Organization and Politics Working Papers**:
http://socrates.berkeley.edu/~iir/culture/papers.html

**Jean Monnet Papers**: www.jeanmonnetprogram.org/papers/index.html

**European Research Papers Archive**: http://olymp.wu-wien.ac.at/erpa/

**European Integration Online Papers**: http://eiop.or.at/eiop/

**EUI Online Papers**: www.iue.it/PUB/

**Federal Trust Constitutional Online Papers**:
www.fedtrust.co.uk/constitutionalpapers

**Ius Gentium Conimbrigae Working Papers**: www.fd.uc.pt/hrc/pages_en/papers.htm

**Lucas Pires Working Papers on Constitutionalism**: www.fd.unl.pt/je/work_pap.htm

**Max Planck Institut für Gesellschaftsforschung (MPIfG) Working Papers**:
www.mpi-fg-koeln.mpg.de/pu/workpapers_en.html

**Mannheim Zentrum für Europäische Sozialforschung (MZES) Working Papers**:
www.mzes.uni-mannheim.de/frame.php?oben=titel_e.html&links=
n_publikationen_e.php&inhalt=publications/wp/workpap_e.php

**Nuffield College Working Papers in Politics**: www.nuffield.ox.ac.uk/Politics/papers/

**Queens Papers on Europeanisation**:
www.qub.ac.uk/schools/SchoolofPoliticsInternationalStudiesandPhilosophy/
Research/PaperSeries/EuropeanisationPapers/

PART I

# Constitutional and Institutional Law

## 1

## European integration and the Treaty on European Union

## 1. Introduction

A book about European Union law is a book about the legal system of a particular organisation: the European Union. The name of this organisation was not chosen randomly from a handbook. It was chosen on the basis of the mission of that organisation, namely the realisation of two particular ideals, those of 'Europe' and 'Union', which each carry a legacy of rich, complex and contradictory associations.

Europe may be the territory which stretches from the Atlantic in the West to the Urals in the East, and Europeans, the people of that territory.[1] However, even this highly contested definition assumes shared traits which distinguish Europeans from non-Europeans, and their territory from other territories. These have evolved over the years, as the idea of Europe and European ideals have been invoked to justify a number of causes and beliefs, and, as a self-consciously European body, the European Union taps into and extends this heritage. Consider, for example, the Preamble of the 2004 Constitutional Treaty, which was to relaunch European integration and will be discussed in chapter 2. The opening words state that its authors are:

> DRAWING INSPIRATION from the cultural, religious and humanist inheritance of Europe, from which have developed the universal values of the inviolable and inalienable rights of the human person, freedom, democracy, equality and the rule of law,
>
> BELIEVING that Europe, reunited after bitter experiences, intends to continue along the path of civilisation, progress and prosperity, for the good of all its inhabitants, including the weakest and most deprived; that it wishes to remain a continent open to culture, learning and social progress; and that it wishes to deepen the democratic and transparent nature of its public life, and to strive for peace, justice and solidarity throughout the world

However, by wrapping itself in these ideals, the European Union cannot escape their contentiousness. Indeed, in this case, they are doubly so. They are contentious not only because some may disagree with them, but also because some may object to the European Union claiming ownership of them, seeing them as neither exclusively European, nor as justifying European-wide laws or government.

---

1 e.g. M. Gorbachev, *Perestroika* (London, Harper Collins, 1987) 197–8.

The European Union, however, also represents a break from this heritage, for it is a form of political union established to deal with a series of contemporary problems and realise a set of goals that individual states felt unable to manage alone. For these purposes, it comprises its own system of government and its own legal system. Nothing like it had existed previously nor has done so since its inception. It has been allocated a unique constellation of tasks, involves a unique set of institutions and has a unique political and legal identity. It is neither a state nor simply an international organisation. It is a peculiarly modern institution in that its daily practice focusses on the problems of the here and now, rather than dwelling on its position within European history. A consequence of this is that it is an institution in flux, as attitudes on what is to be accomplished and how this is to be done are constantly changing. As with any system of government, it has its own views on how economic and social relations are, and should be, conducted, and its own array of benefits, frustrations, mistakes, hierarchies and rivalries. All these need to be assessed in the light of the problems it is to address and how it has chosen to resolve those problems.

These two central agendas of the European Union – the development of European ideals and the government of the problems of contemporary Europe – are realised almost exclusively through EU law. Both sit at the heart of all EU law and elements of both permeate all the chapters of this book. In some areas there is a tension, imbalance or dysfunction between the two. In others, there is a dialectic between the two so that each is being revised in the light of concerns provoked by the other. In other fields, there is a healthy balance between the two. The balance is, however, never a static one. It is constantly changing as political beliefs change, the European Union's institutional settlement evolves and the challenges of the outside world alter. However, each development is not considered anew. It is considered in the light of a long legacy: be this the history of the European ideal, the institutional settlement of the European Union or a policy whose inception and development goes back many years. To understand EU law and its current goals and challenges, it is necessary, therefore, to trace both the development of the European ideal and that of the European Union itself.

## 2. The idea of 'Europe'

The most famous early reference to Europe is that found in Greek mythology. Europa is a Phoenician woman seduced by the Greek god, Zeus, to come from Lebanon to Crete.[2] Europa was also, however, a Phoenician word that referred to the setting sun. From this, Europe was associated in Ancient Greece with the idea of 'the West'. Originally used to designate the lands to the west of Greece, the usage shifted as the Ancient Greek territorial centre of gravity changed with their incursions into modern Turkey and Iran. In his wars, Alexander the Great used it to denote non-Persians and it became associated with the lands in Greece and Asia Minor (today's Turkish

2 D. De Rougemont, *The Idea of Europe* (New York, Macmillan, 1965) 6–19.

Mediterranean coastline). Following this, the term was to lie largely dormant for many centuries. The Roman Empire and Christianity dominated in the organisation of political life and neither had much use for the term. Europe re-emerged as an important political idea from the eighth century onwards. It became an expression of a siege mentality. The advance of Islam led to Europe being associated with resistance to the religion, which originated in the South and the East. Charlemagne styled himself as the father of Europe, whilst an army of Franks which fought against the Moors were referred to as a 'European army'. Resistance to Islam and the idea of 'the West' led to the association of Europe with Western Christianity. However, it was only from the twelfth century onwards that it was used to refer to a place whose inhabitants enjoyed a shared way of life based on Christian humanism, revolving around images of God and Christ portrayed as human.[3] Alongside particular religious beliefs, Europe also became associated with a particular form of political economy, namely that of rural trade. Increasingly, the rural town became the centre of the local economy. Trade relations between towns expanded across Europe, so that from the fifteenth century onwards, trade flourished between the Italian ports in the south and Flanders in the north, in which the role of the merchant was pivotal. The final feature of this European region was the persecution of non-Christians, be they pagans or followers of other faiths, such as Judaism or Islam. Those whose conduct offended the central values of Christianity were also maltreated, such as heretics and homosexuals, as were those perceived as socially unproductive, in particular, lepers.

Developments in the sixteenth and seventeenth centuries were to set the dominant institutional context for the subsequent evolution of the concept of Europe. The establishment of the modern nation-state consolidated power in centralised, impersonal bureaucracies and led to certain core policies, such as tax, law and order and foreign policy, being the exclusive competence of these bureaucracies.[4] This hegemony of the nation-state over political life led to Europe acquiring new associations in the eighteenth and nineteenth centuries. It became, increasingly, an 'aesthetic category, romantic and nostalgic', associated with utopian ideals. Authors such as Rousseau and Kant saw Europe as an expression of certain ideals: be it a social contract between nations, in the case of Rousseau, or as a form of perpetual peace, according to Kant. Europe was also considered to represent a shared aesthetic tradition:[5] be this

3 J. Le Goff, *The Birth of Europe* (Oxford, Blackwell, 2005) 76–80.
4 C. Tilly (ed.), *The Formation of Nation-States in Europe* (Princeton, NJ, Princeton University Press, 1975); G. Poggi, *The Development of the Modern State: A Sociological Introduction* (Stanford, CA, Stanford University Press, 1978); M. Mann, 'The Autonomous Power of the State: its Origins, Mechanisms and Results' (1984) 25 *European Journal of Sociology* 185; H. Spruyt, *The Sovereign State and its Competitors: an Analysis of Systems Change* (Princeton, NJ, Princeton University Press, 1994).
5 A. Chebel d'Appollonia, 'European Nationalism and European Union' and J. Tully, 'The Kantian Idea of Europe: Critical and Cosmopolitan Perspectives' in A. Pagden (ed.), *The Idea of Europe: From Antiquity to the European Union* (Cambridge, Cambridge University Press, 2002). Recent examples of this tradition are Z. Bauman, *Europe: An Unfinished Adventure* (Cambridge, Polity, 2004); U. Beck, *Cosmopolitan Europe* (Cambridge, Polity, 2005).

a common form of high culture, institutionalised through the growth of elite tourism in Europe at that time, or that of a historical civilisation, distinguishing it from the New World and justifying its colonialism.

The final twist came in the twentieth century and derives from the USA's involvement in Europe. The role of the USA in two World Wars, the Cold War, and in the regeneration of Europe after the Second World War, heavily influenced European identity.[6] The idea of Europe as a historically entrenched community has been reinforced. The other association has been of Europe as the Eastern borderlands of the USA. For those reverting to market democracy after forty-five years of communism, a 'return to Europe' means a turn to the West and to values that are associated unashamedly with the USA, namely those of free markets and constitutional democracy. In today's Western Europe, Europe has acquired an alternative meaning, in that its values are similar to, but different from, those of the USA. Although there is a shared commitment to markets and constitutional democracy, these take a different form from those in the USA. There is an emphasis on the social market and on supposedly 'European' values, such as opposition to the death penalty, which are not considered present in the USA:

---

**J. Habermas and J. Derrida, 'February 15, or, What Binds Europeans Together: Plea for a Common Foreign Policy Beginning in Core Europe' in D. Levy *et al.*, *Old Europe, New Europe, Core Europe: Transatlantic Relations after the Iraq War* (London, Verso, 2005) 5, 10–12**

[T]he spread of the ideals of the French revolution throughout Europe explains, among other things, why politics in both of its forms – as organizing power and as a medium for the institutionalization of political liberty – has been welcomed in Europe. By contrast, the triumph of capitalism was bound up with sharp class conflicts, and this fact has hindered an equally positive appraisal of free markets. That differing evaluation of politics and markets may explain Europeans' trust in the civilizing power of the state, and their expectations for it to correct market failures.

The party system that emerged from the French revolution has often been copied. But only in Europe does this system also serve an ideological competition that subjects the socio-pathological results of capitalist modernization to an ongoing political evaluation. This fosters the sensitivities of citizens to the paradoxes of progress. The contest between conservative, liberal and socialist agendas comes down to the weighing of two aspects: Do the benefits of a chimerical progress outweigh the losses that come with the disintegration of protective, traditional forms of life? Or do the benefits that today's processes of 'creative destruction' promise for tomorrow outweigh the pain of modernity's losers?

In Europe, those affected by class distinctions, and their enduring consequences, understood these burdens as a fate that can be averted only through collective action. In the context of workers' movements and the Christian socialist traditions, an ethics of solidarity, the

---

6 G. Delanty, *Inventing Europe: Idea, Identity, Reality* (Basingstoke, Macmillan, 1995) 115–55.

struggle for 'more social justice', with the goal of equal provision for all, asserted itself against the individualist ethos of market justice that accepts glaring social inequalities as part of the bargain.

Contemporary Europe has been shaped by the experience of the totalitarian regimes of the twentieth century and by the Holocaust – the persecution and annihilation of European Jews in which the National Socialist regime made the societies of the conquered countries complicit as well. Self-critical controversies about the past remind us of the moral basis of politics. A heightened sensitivity to injuries to personal and bodily integrity reflects itself, among other ways, in the fact both the Council of Europe and the EU made the ban on capital punishment a condition for membership.

### 3. The idea of 'European Union'

The unification of different regions within the nation-state led to its being perceived increasingly as a unitary political community. No such development occurred with regard to the idea of Europe. When independent proposals for a 'united Europe' emerged at the end of the seventeenth century, they were still firmly confederal in nature. Ultimate authority was vested in the state, with pan-European structures acting as little more than a fetter upon the autonomy of the states. In 1693, the English Quaker, William Penn, wrote *An Essay Towards the Present and Future Peace of Europe*. Penn suggested that a European Parliament should be established consisting of representatives of the Member States. The primary purposes of this Parliament would be to prevent wars breaking out between states and to promote justice. Its decisions would be binding upon states. A more far-reaching proposal was put forward by John Bellers in 1710. Bellers proposed a cantonal system based upon the Swiss model whereby Europe would be divided into 100 cantons, each of which would be required to contribute to a European army and send representatives to a European Senate.

The first proposal suggesting a Europe in which the state system was to be replaced by a system within which there was a sovereign central body, came from the Frenchman, Saint-Simon. In a pamphlet published in 1814, entitled *Plan for the Reorganisation of the European Society*, Saint-Simon took a romanticised view of the Middle Ages, which he considered to have been disrupted by the religious wars. He approved of the British parliamentary model and, therefore, considered that all European states should be governed by national parliaments, but that a European Parliament should be created to decide on common interests. This Parliament would consist of a House of Commons peopled by representatives of local associations and a House of Lords consisting of peers appointed by a European monarch. Saint-Simon's views enjoyed considerable attention during the first part of the nineteenth century. Mazzini, the *éminence grise* of Italian nationalism, allied himself with Proudhon and Victor Hugo in declaring himself in favour of a united Europe. Yet, the nineteenth century represented the age of the nation-state and the relationship between that structure and that of a united Europe was never fully explored. Much of the talk took place amongst academics and reflected only renewed interest in Europe's romanticised past or a wistful yearning for a utopian future, rather than anything concrete to be placed before decision-makers.

The balance was altered by the shock of the First World War, which acted as a stimulus for those who saw European union as the only means both to prevent war breaking out again between the nation-states and as a means of responding to increased competition from the USA, Argentina and Japan. Most prominent was the Pan-European movement set up in the 1920s by the Czech, Count Coudenhove-Kalergi.[7] This movement not only enjoyed considerable support amongst many of Europe's intellectuals and some politicians, but was genuinely transnational, having 'Economic Councils' both in Berlin and in Paris. During the 1920s, the idea of European unity received governmental support in the shape of the 1929 Briand Memorandum. This Memorandum, submitted by the French Foreign Minister to twenty-six other European states, considered the League of Nations to be too weak a body to regulate international relations and proposed a European Federal Union, which would better police states, whilst not 'in any way affect the sovereign rights of the States which are members of such an association'. This proposal, despite being strongly confederal in that it acknowledged the authority of the nation-states, was still regarded as too radical and received only a lukewarm response from the other states.

A further shock, in the form of the Second World War, was needed to arouse greater governmental interest in the idea of a united Europe. The coming into being and development of, first, the European Communities, followed by the European Union, are explored in greater depth in the rest of this chapter. It is useful to consider for a moment how the creation of this political organisation with law-making powers, with the idea of Europe as its justification and its purpose, changed the geo-political context in which the idea of Europe was formulated. On the one hand, it has led to the perception of an increasing opposition between the idea of Europe and nation communities. The European Union has become an independent centre in its own right for the generation of understandings about Europe and European values and symbols. The European Union has, therefore, tried to replicate the symbols and tools of nationhood at a pan-European level – be it through the (re)discovery of European flags, anthems, Cities of Culture or common passports.[8] This understanding of Europe, as a competing alternative to the nation-state, has been replicated by 'Eurosceptic' groups, who see Europe as a centralised, monolithic entity which crushes local communities and self-government.[9] On the other hand, the idea of Europe has become a justification for, and been associated with, government policy as the Union has become a vehicle through which national governments pursue and articulate

7 N. Coudenhove-Kalergi, *Pan-Europe* (New York, Knopf, 1926). An excellent discussion can be found in C. Pegg, *Evolution of the European Idea 1914–1932* (Chapel Hill, NC, University of North Carolina Press, 1983).
8 C. Shore, *Building Europe: The Cultural Politics of European Integration* (London/New York, Routledge, 2000).
9 A flavour is provided in M. Holmes (ed.), *The Eurosceptical Reader* (Basingstoke, Macmillan, 1996).

their understanding of the national interest. On such a view, Europe does not act as a competitor to the nation-state but, rather, as a vehicle through which nation-states articulate their understandings of themselves and their place in the world:

> ### M. Malmborg and B. Stråth, 'Introduction: The National Meanings of Europe' in M. Malmborg and B. Stråth (eds.), *The Meaning of Europe* (Oxford, Berg, 2002) 1, 9, 20
>
> Europe is understood as a discourse and an ideological programme not necessarily in opposition to the nation-State or as an alternative to it . . . In national political debates 'Europe' often enters as a dimension of national identity rather than a project of transnational unification. The universal pretensions are downloaded and nationalized. Rather than 'How shall Europe be united?', the questions dwelt upon in public debate have been 'How European is our nation?' 'How shall we relate ourselves to "Europe"?' 'To what extent should we be European, something else or simply ourselves?'

The authors then consider a number of examples, of which one, the Finnish case, is cited below.

> Finland's national history has been characterized by a strong awareness of being either on the brink of Europe or on the margins of Russia or somewhere in between . . . Meinander traces two basic conceptions of Finnish national identity: the Fennoman that stresses the indigenous features of Finnish culture and sees Finland as a cooperative borderland between the West and Russia, and the liberal that is akin to the Russian *zapadniki* in the sense that it prescribes close integration with the Western and European cultures. For the Fennomans, Russia was in a cultural sense never outside Europe, but the feeling of standing at the edge of Europe was reinforced by the Russian revolution, the Finnish civil war and the foundation of the Soviet Union, which effectively precluded any acknowledgement of the eastern layers of Finnish identity. The Finnish notion of Europe became increasingly polarized not least due to the experiences of Finland being left very much alone in the Second World War. Forced into a policy of friendly neutrality with the Soviet Union after the war Finland rediscovered its role as a mediator between East and West. The Finns began to admit that Russia, even in its Soviet manifestation, was a part of European civilization.
>
> The accession to the EU in 1995 was supported by a feeling that the Finns had at last found an answer to two centuries of uncertainty and identity-searching. Finland had, as it were, ultimately found a synthesis of its two historical roles, to be both on the brink of Western Europe and serve as a bridge-builder toward a Europe that stretched to include Russia and Slavonic Europe. EU membership implies both an improvement of national security and an emotional homecoming.[10]

## 4. The European Communities and their origins

### (i) From the Treaty of Paris to the Treaty of Rome

The origins of the European Union lie in a crisis provoked by the establishment of the Federal Republic of Germany in 1949. The Ruhr, which was then under the

---

10 H. Meinander, 'On the Brink or In Between? The Conception of Europe inFinnish Identity' in M. Malmborg and B. Stråth (eds.), *The Meaning of Europe* (Oxford, Berg, 2002).

administration of the International High Commission, was due to be handed back to the Federal Republic, along with the Saar. French fears of emerging German industrial might were compounded by Germany's increasing share of European steel production. The French response was a plan drafted by the French civil servant, Jean Monnet, which was known as the the Schuman Plan, after the French Finance Minister, Robert Schuman.[11]

### Robert Schuman, Declaration of 9 May 1950[12]

World peace cannot be safeguarded without the making of creative efforts proportionate to the dangers which threaten it.

The contribution which an organised and living Europe can bring to civilisation is indispensable to the maintenance of peaceful relations. In taking upon herself for more than 20 years the role of champion of a united Europe, France has always had as her essential aim the service of peace. A united Europe was not achieved and we had war.

Europe will not be made all at once or according to a single plan. It will be built through concrete achievements which first create a *de facto* solidarity. The coming together of the nations of Europe requires the elimination of the age-old opposition of France and Germany. Any action which must be taken in the first place must concern these two countries. With this aim in view, the French Government proposes that action be taken immediately on one limited but decisive point. It proposes that Franco-German production of coal and steel as a whole be placed under a common High Authority, within the framework of an organisation open to the participation of the other countries of Europe.

The pooling of coal and steel production should immediately provide for the setting up of common foundations for economic development as a first step in the federation of Europe, and will change the destinies of those regions which have long been devoted to the manufacture of munitions of war, of which they have been the most constant victims.

The solidarity in production thus established will make it plain that any war between France and Germany becomes not merely unthinkable, but materially impossible. The setting up of this powerful productive unit, open to all countries willing to take part and bound ultimately to provide all the member countries with the basic elements of industrial production on the same terms, will lay a true foundation for their economic unification.

This Plan formed the basis of the Treaty of Paris in 1951, which established the European Coal and Steel Community (ECSC).[13] This Treaty entered into force on 23 July 1952 and ran for fifty years.[14] It set up a common market in coal and steel, which was supervised by the High Authority, a body independent from the Member

---

11  W. Diebold, *The Schuman Plan: A Study in International Cooperation* (Oxford, Oxford University Press, 1959).

12  European Parliament, *Selection of Texts Concerning Institutional Matters of the Community for 1950–1982* (Luxembourg, OOPEC, 1982) 47.

13  On the negotiations see P. Gerbet, 'The Origins: Early Attempts and the Emergence of the Six (1945–52)' in R. Pryce (ed.), *The Dynamics of European Union* (London, Croom Helm, 1987); R. Bullen, 'An Idea Enters Diplomacy: the Schuman Plan, May 1950' in R. Bullen (ed.), *Ideas into Politics: Aspects of European History 1880–1950* (London, Croon Helm, 1984).

14  The ECSC expired on 23 July 2002. Decision of the representatives of the Member States meeting within the Council on the consequences of the expiry of the European Coal and Steel Community, OJ 2002 L194/35.

States and composed of international civil servants, which had considerable powers to determine the conditions of production and prices for coal and steel.[15] The High Authority was, in turn, supervised by a Council, which consisted of Member State representatives. The Treaty of Paris was signed by only six states – the BENELUX states (Netherlands, Belgium and Luxembourg), Italy, France and Germany. The United Kingdom had been invited to the negotiations, but refused to participate, as it opposed both the idea of the High Authority and the remit of its powers.[16]

The origins of the next step in European integration started in 1950, during nego-tiations for the Treaty of Paris. The Korean War began, and the USA, perceiving an increased threat from Stalin's Soviet Union, pressed for German rearmament and its entry into NATO, something which was inimical to the French.[17] As a response, the French Defence Minister, Pléven, proposed a European Defence Community, which would be structured along similar lines to the ECSC. There would be a European army under a European Minister of Defence, administered by a European Commissariat. Once again, Britain was invited to join, but it declined on the basis that it preferred an expansion of NATO to the establishment of a European Defence Community (EDC). Nevertheless, a treaty establishing a European Defence Community was signed between the same six states which had signed the ECSC in 1952. However, the EDC failed. A less integrationist French government under Mendès-France assumed power, and French reverses in South-East Asia made it wary about ceding military sovereignty. In 1954, the French National Assembly refused to ratify the treaty.[18]

The failure of the EDC marked a moment of considerable political fluidity. The BENELUX states were increasingly worried by the nationalist policies of the Mendès-France government in France, in particular, its attempt to upgrade bilateral relations with Germany. In 1955, the Belgian Foreign Minister, Henri-Paul Spaak, suggested that there should be integration in a limited number of sectors, notably transport and energy. This worried the Netherlands as it threatened to restrict its efficiencies, particularly in the transport sector. The Dutch government responded by reactivating the 1953 Beyen Plan, which proposed a common market that would lead to economic union. A meeting of Foreign Ministers was held in Messina, Italy, in 1955. The British were invited, in addition to the six ECSC Member States, but did no more than

---

15 A good history is D. Spiernburg and R. Poidevin, *The History of the High Authority of the European Coal and Steel Community: Supranationality in Operation* (London, Weidenfeld & Nicolson, 1994).

16 E. Dell, *The Schuman Plan and the British Abdication of Leadership in Europe* (Oxford, Clarendon, 1995); C. Lord, '"With But Not Of": Britain and the Schuman Plan, a Reinterpretation' (1998) 4 *Journal of European Integration History* 23.

17 T. Schwartz, 'The Skeleton Key: American Foreign Policy, European Unity, and German Rearmament, 1949–54' (1986) 19 *Central European History* 369.

18 On this ill-fated enterprise see E. Fursdon, *The European Defence Community: a History* (London, Macmillan, 1980); R. Cardozo, 'The Project for a Political Community (1952–4)' in R. Pryce (ed.), *The Dynamics of European Union* (London, Croom Helm, 1987); R. Dwan, 'Jean Monnet and the Failure of the European Defence Community' (2001) 1 *Cold War History* 141.

send a Board of Trade official. Despite considerable French scepticism, a Resolution was tabled, calling for an Intergovernmental Committee, under the chairmanship of Spaak, to be set up to examine the establishment of a common market. As a carrot to the French, it was agreed that this should be done in tandem with examining the possibility of integration in the field of atomic energy. British objections to the supranational elements required for a common market entailed that they were unable to participate in the project.

The Spaak Report, published in 1956, laid the basis for the Treaty Establishing the European Economic Community (EEC Treaty). The Report made a pragmatic distinction between matters affecting the functioning of the common market, which would require a supranational decision-making framework and some supranational supervision of Member States' compliance with their obligations, and more general matters of budgetary, monetary and social policy, which would remain within the reserved competence of the Member States. Where these policies had a significant effect on the functioning of the common market, however, Member States should endeavour to coordinate these policies. An intergovernmental conference was convened in Venice, in 1956. Its object was to use the Spaak Report as the basis for negotiations for a new treaty. The result was the signing of the Treaties of Rome in 1957 between the Six – Germany, France, Italy and the BENELUX states. Doubts about difficulties in French ratification led to two treaties being signed, one establishing the European Economic Community (EEC), the other the European Atomic Energy Community (EURATOM). The treaties duly entered into force on 1 January 1958.[19]

### (ii)   The EEC Treaty

The central aims of the EEC Treaty were set out in Article 2 EEC:

> by establishing a common market and progressively approximating the economic policies of Member States, to promote throughout the Community a harmonious development of economic activities, a continuous and balanced expansion, an increase in stability, an accelerated raising of the standard of living and closer relations between the States belonging to it.[20]

The common market can be divided into a number of different elements. The first was the customs union, which required the abolition of all customs duties or charges having equivalent effect on the movement of goods between Member States and the establishment of a common external tariff. Secondly, the common market

---

19 The literature on the negotiations is voluminous. See E. di Nolfo (ed.), *Power in Europe? Britain, France, Germany, Italy, and the Origins of the EEC, 1952–1957* (Berlin/New York, de Gruyter, 1992); E. Serra (ed.), *The Relaunching of Europe and the Treaties of Rome* (Baden Baden, Nomos, 1989).

20 Although it was formally called the EEC Treaty until the Treaty on European Union, the treaty will be referred to in the text from now on as the EC Treaty, the name given to it by the Treaty on European Union for purposes of cross-reference and simplicity.

extended beyond the customs union to include the 'four freedoms', so that restrictions on the movement of goods, workers, services and capital were also prohibited by the EC Treaty.[21] Furthermore, a procedure was put in place for harmonising national laws, where differences were preventing the establishment and functioning of the common market. Thirdly, a competition policy was set up to ensure that private market barriers and cartels did not undermine the prohibition on state barriers.[22] Fourthly, state intervention in the economy, such as that in the form of state aids and public undertakings, was closely regulated.[23] Fifthly, Member States' fiscal regimes on goods were regulated so that they could not discriminate against imports. Sixthly, a common commercial policy was established to regulate the Community's trade relations with third states. Finally, provision was made for more general cooperation in the field of economic policy in order that broader economic policy-making did not disrupt the common market.

A number of other policies were established. Arguably, the most famous is the Common Agricultural Policy. At the time, agriculture accounted for about 20 per cent of the European labour force and the memory of the severe deflation in the agricultural sector during the 1930s recession had led to considerable government intervention in the sector. A separate policy was, therefore, required in order to Europeanise the system of state intervention currently in place. A further policy included in the EEC Treaty was a common transport policy. As with agriculture, this required a separate heading due to the heavy intervention by states in their transport sectors. The EEC Treaty also contained a limited social policy. This owed its inclusion to the view that differing social policies would affect production costs, and hence distort competition.[24] Finally, an association policy was included to provide for the economic and social development of dependent or formerly dependent territories of the Member States.

The most remarkable feature of the EEC Treaty was the institutional arrangement set up to realise these objectives.[25] There were four central institutions. The Commission, a body independent from the Member States, was responsible, inter alia, for proposing legislation and checking that the Member States and other institutions complied with the Treaty and any secondary legislation. The Assembly, later to develop into the European Parliament, was composed, initially, of national parliamentarians. It had the right to be consulted in most fields of legislative activity and was the body responsible for holding the Commission to account. The Council was the body in which national governments were represented. It had the power of final decision in almost all areas of EEC activity. It voted by unanimity or, in only a few areas initially, by a weighted form of voting, known as qualified majority voting (QMV). Finally, the European Court of Justice was established to monitor compliance with the treaty.

21 These are discussed, respectively in *EUL*, chapters 15, 16, 17, 19 and 12.
22 On this see *EUL*, chapters 21, 22, 23 and 24.        23 This is analysed in more depth in *EUL*, chapter 25.
24 C. Barnard, 'The Economic Objectives of Article 119' in T. Hervey and D. O'Keeffe (eds.), *Sex Equality Law in the European Union* (Chichester, John Wiley, 1996) 321, 322–4.
25 This is discussed in chapter 3.

Matters could be brought before it, not only by the Member States, but also by the supranational Commission, or be referred to it by national courts.

## 5. Early development of the European Communities

### (i)   De Gaulle and the Luxembourg Accords

1958 marked not only the coming into force of the Treaties but also the establishment of Charles de Gaulle as President of France. De Gaulle was well known for his opposition to the development of any supranational organisation and for his support for a Europe of nation-states, based upon intergovernmental cooperation. As early as 1961, De Gaulle attempted to subvert the supranational qualities of the EEC Treaty through the Fouchet Plan. This proposed a European Political Community whose remit would cover not only economic, but also political and social affairs. It would be based on intergovernmental cooperation, with each state retaining a veto. This failed to gain the support of the other Member States.[26] Tensions were raised further in 1963 when De Gaulle vetoed the accession of the United Kingdom who, along with Denmark, Norway and Ireland, had applied for membership in 1961. De Gaulle justified his veto on the grounds that the British economy differed greatly from those of the Member States and the British Commonwealth links made it difficult for it to join. Undoubtedly, the fear that Britain might be a vehicle for further American influence within Europe had played a part. Yet the exercise of the veto on grounds relating to narrow national interests jarred with the ideals set out by the founders and with the interests of some of the other Member States.

Matters came to a head in 1965. The Commission had made proposals in three areas: increased powers for the Assembly, a system of 'own resources' so that the Communities were financially independent and not dependent on national contributions, and a series of financial regulations which would allow the Common Agricultural Policy to make progress. France favoured the third proposal, but was strongly opposed to the first two. The Commission insisted on a 'package deal', however, where Member States accepted either all or none. When negotiations broke down, the French walked out of the Council in June 1965, refusing to take part in further EEC business. De Gaulle came under considerable domestic criticism for this drastic move.[27] Yet, the Commission was also perceived as having adopted a very high-handed approach. The crisis was eventually diffused in January 1966 in Luxembourg, but in a way that would cast a shadow over the development of the EEC for the next twenty years. The Luxembourg Accords, as they came to be known, were an 'agreement to disagree'. If a

---

26  P. Gerbet, 'The Fouchet Negotiations (1960–2)' in R. Pryce, *Dynamics of Political Union* (London, Croom Helm, 1987); N. Ludlow, 'Challenging French Leadership in Europe: Germany, Italy and the Netherlands and the Origins of the Empty Chair Crisis of 1965' (1999) 8 *Contemporary European History* 231.

27  On De Gaulle's Europe see W. Loth (ed.), *Crises and Compromises: The European Project, 1963–9* (Baden Baden, Nomos, 2001); C. Parsons, *A Certain Idea of Europe* (Ithaca, NY, Cornell University Press, 2003).

Member State raised 'very important interests' before a vote in the Council was taken, it was agreed that the matter would not be put to a vote. In essence, it gave every Member State a veto in all fields of decision-making. Whilst this veto was developed at the behest of France, once in place, it was invoked equally freely by all the Member States.[28] 'Very important interests' were invoked at every turn, even where the interest in question was insignificant. Most notoriously, in 1985, Germany used the 'red card' to prevent a 1.8 per cent decrease in the price of colza.[29]

The Accords had the effect of suppressing the legislative process. There were other consequences. The Commission, aware that only proposals which had the assent of all the Member States had any prospect of becoming law, became a more passive body, reluctant to generate controversy. Because it was only by negotiating with all the Member States that legislation could be passed, the Commission focussed on its relations with the Council, thereby sidelining the Assembly. Also, the direction of integration was skewed. There was one institution unaffected by the Accords: the Court of Justice. In 1963 and 1964, the Court gave two of its most significant judgments. In *Van Gend en Loos*[30] and *Costa*,[31] the Court held that the Community was a sovereign legal order, which gave rise to rights that could be invoked before national courts and that in cases of conflict, Community law took precedence over national law. Throughout the 1960s and 1970s, the Court continued to give a series of integrationist judgments, expanding its 'constitutional' jurisprudence, developing treaty-making powers for the Community, expanding the treaty provisions on sex equality, the economic freedoms and the competition provisions. The activities of the Court, when juxtaposed with the inertia of the legislature, led to the development of an unplanned deregulatory bias under which national policies were prohibited or tightly restricted by the Court, without there being any substitute Community legislation available to take their place.[32]

Despite this, significant institutional developments did take place during this period. In 1957, three Communities existed – the European Economic Community, the European Atomic Energy Community and the European Coal and Steel Community – each with a separate set of institutions. It was feared that no single set of institutions would be taken seriously. Turf wars might break out over the responsibilities of the different institutions and there would be difficulties of coordinating the activities of the different Communities. At the signing of the Treaty of Rome, the Convention Relating to Certain Institutions Common to the European Communities was also signed. This established a single Court and a single Assembly for the three Communities. In 1963, it was agreed that the institutions would be merged pending

---

28 W. Nicholl, 'The Luxembourg Compromise' (1984) 23 *JCMS* 35.
29 M. Vasey, 'The 1985 Farm Price Negotiations and the Reform of the Common Agriculture Policy' (1985) 22 *CML Rev.* 649, 664–6.
30 Case 26/62 *Van Gend en Loos v Nederlandse Administratie der Belastingen* [1963] ECR 1.
31 Case 6/64 *Costa v ENEL* [1964] ECR 585.
32 F. Scharpf, 'Negative and Positive Integration in the Political Economy of European Welfare States' in G. Marks *et al.*, *Governance in the European Union* (London, Sage, 1996).

a review of a merging of the three Communities. Although the latter has never taken place, the Merger Treaty, which provided for a single Commission and a single Council for the three Communities, was signed in 1965.[33]

The next significant step was the establishment of the Community Budget, for, if many Community policies were to function at all, it was essential that there be resources in place to meet their needs. Initially, the Communities were financed by Member States' contributions, but this gave Member States a financial leverage over the Community institutions which undermined the latter's autonomy. Under Article 201 EC, the Commission was required to examine the conditions under which these contributions could be replaced by the Community's own system of revenue. The Commission's initial proposals, as we have seen, led, in part, to the crisis resulting in the Luxembourg Accords. The project had to wait until De Gaulle's death, in 1968, before it could be resurrected. At The Hague, in 1969, agreement was reached on the principle of 'Own Resources', in the form of the 1970 Own Resources Decision, which stipulated the sources of Community revenue.[34] The First Budgetary Treaty was also established, which increased the powers of the European Parliament in respect of Community expenditure. In 1975, a Second Budgetary Treaty further increased the Parliament's powers and set up the Court of Auditors, with the task of verifying the collection of revenue and the expenditure of Community resources.

The third principal institutional reform during the 1970s concerned the European Parliament. In 1957, as mentioned, the European Parliament consisted of representatives of national parliaments, but it was envisaged that in due course members would be directly elected. The Parliament duly submitted proposals in 1961, but for many years these encountered resistance in the Council. The Parliament modified its proposals in 1973 so that a uniform electoral procedure was not required for all Member States. This opened the way for agreement in the Council in 1976 for direct elections.[35] These were first held in 1979 and have since been held at five-year intervals.

### (ii)   The initial enlargements

The United Kingdom was all too aware that the establishment of a common market left it economically isolated. Therefore, from 1956 onwards, it pushed for the establishment of a free trade area with other European states, which culminated in its setting up the European Free Trade Area (EFTA) with Austria, Denmark, Norway, Sweden, Switzerland and Portugal in 1960. By 1961, however, states within the EEC were experiencing faster economic growth rates than Britain and its failure to prevent South Africa's expulsion from the Commonwealth, following the Sharpeville massacres, brought home Britain's relative decline on the international stage. As discussed earlier,[36] the French President, De Gaulle, vetoed the British entry in 1963.

33 P.-H. Houben, 'The Merger of the Executives of the European Communities' (1965) 3 *CML Rev.* 37.
34 Decision 70/243/EEC, OJ English Spec. Ed. 1970 (I) 224.     35 Decision 76/87/EEC, OJ 1976 L278/1.
36 See p. 13.

Four years later, the United Kingdom, plus Ireland, Denmark and Norway, reapplied. The British application was once again vetoed by De Gaulle. This use of the veto left France increasingly isolated and French policy changed in 1969 with the resignation of De Gaulle. The Six agreed in The Hague to open negotiations with the applicants, with a view to extending membership. The United Kingdom, Denmark and Ireland formally became members on 1 January 1973.[37] However, following a referendum, where 53 per cent voted against membership, Norway did not accede to the EEC.

The next state to join the EEC was Greece. Greece applied for membership in 1975, following its establishment of a democratic government. Accession was attractive for both parties. For the Greeks, accession was not only economically attractive, but symbolised modernisation and democratic stability. For the Member States, Greece was important geo-politically during the Cold War because of its strategic location in the Aegean. Membership was, therefore, seen as tying Greece more firmly to the West. The Greek Act of Accession was completed in 1979, with Greece becoming a member in 1981.

Like Greece, Spain and Portugal emerged from dictatorships and isolationism in the mid-1970s. They made applications to join the Communities only two years after Greece in 1977. Yet accession was more problematic in their cases. Whilst both saw the Community as a fulcrum through which to achieve economic modernisation and end their relative international isolation, the size of the agricultural sector in Spain resulted in initial French resistance to entry due to the likely negative effects on the French agricultural sector. It was, therefore, not until 1985 that an Act of Accession was signed, with Spain and Portugal becoming members in 1986.

## 6. The Single European Act and beyond

### (i)   Run-up to the Single European Act

The recession of the early 1980s, prompted by the oil crisis of 1978, led national governments in the EEC to confront their relative economic decline. Japan had emerged as the pre-eminent economic force within the world economy. Despite the world recession, the American economy continued to lose fewer jobs than that in Europe. Moreover, the raising of interest rates by the USA in 1980, which provoked a double dip recession, coupled with its increased defence expenditure, which many saw as a covert form of industrial policy for high-tech industries, increased the perception among European governments that the USA was an unreliable economic ally.

---

37 U. Kitzinger, *Diplomacy and Persuasion: How Britain Joined the Common Market* (London, Thames & Hudson, 1973); C. O'Neill, *Britain's Entry into the European Community: Report on the Negotiations of 1970–1972* (London, Frank Cass, 2000).

These circumstances prompted a *relance* of the integration process, as a way of combating this decline. A Solemn Declaration on European Union was adopted by the Heads of Government in 1983. This proposed little concrete reforms, but declared that there should be a 'renewed impetus towards the development of Community policies on a broad front', one of which was completion of the internal market, in particular the removal of obstacles to the free movement of goods, services and capital.[38] This Declaration occurred against the backdrop of a number of significant developments. 1983 marked the collapse of the Keynesian economic policies, which had been adopted in France. This collapse led to some convergence between national governments that economic policy-making had to focus on 'supply-side' measures which stimulated competition and trade. Market integration did both and, therefore, fitted this new consensus.[39] Alongside this, since the 1970s, transnational pressure groups had begun to locate themselves in Brussels. The number of these groups expanded in the early 1980s, leading to the growth of an organised industrial constituency that was increasingly rallying for European solutions.[40] From the early 1980s onwards, major industrialists mobilised through organisations such as the European Round Table (ERT) and UNICE. These groups lobbied aggressively across Europe, arguing for the completion of the common market as a means of promoting European competitiveness.[41] Finally, direct elections had also produced a more aggressive European Parliament. Under the chairmanship of Altiero Spinelli, it produced a draft Treaty on European Union which proposed a fully federal Europe with common foreign, macro-economic and trade policies and a developed system of central institutions.[42]

These developments all pressed towards further European integration, but were fragmented and uncoordinated. The final piece in the jigsaw fell into place with the appointment of a new Commission in late 1984, headed by the charismatic, former

---

38 Solemn Declaration on European Union, EC Bulletin 6–1983, 3.1.6. For critical comment see J. Weiler, 'The Genscher-Colombo Draft European Act: the Politics of Indecision' (1983) 6 *Journal of European Integration* 129.

39 On the convergence of national government preferences see K. Middlemas, *Orchestrating Europe: The Informal Politics of European Union 1973–1995* (London, Fontana, 1995) 115–35; A. Moravscik, *The Choice for Europe: Social Purpose and State Power from Messina to Maastricht* (Ithaca, NY, Cornell University Press, 1998) ch. 5; J. Gillingham, *European Integration 1950–2003: Superstate or New Market Economy* (Cambridge, Cambridge University Press, 2003) ch. 9.

40 N. Fligstein and J. McNichol, 'The Institutional Terrain of the European Union' in W. Sandholtz and A. Stone Sweet (eds.), *European Integration and Supranational Governance* (Oxford, Oxford University Press, 1998) 59, 75–80; N. Fligstein and P. Brantley, 'The Single Market Program and the Interests of Business' in B. Eichengreen and J. Frieden (eds.), *Politics and Institutions in an Integrated Europe* (Berlin, Springer, 1995).

41 W. Sandholtz and J. Zysman, '1992: Recasting the European Bargain' (1989) 42 *World Politics* 95, 116; M. Cowles, 'Setting the Agenda for a New Europe: The ERT and EC 1992' (1995) 33 *JCMS* 527; Middlemas, above n. 39, 136–40.

42 OJ 1984, C77/33. For comment, see R. Bieber *et al.*, *An Ever Closer Union: a Critical Analysis of the Draft Treaty Establishing the European Union* (Luxembourg, OOPEC, 1985).

French Finance Minister, Jacques Delors. Delors, in lobbying for the post, had already seized upon the goal of market unity as the principal task of the new Commission to be achieved by the end of 1992. In November 1984, he gave the national governments four choices for recapturing momentum: monetary policy, foreign policy and defence, institutional reform or the internal market.[43] All agreed that the internal market was the way forward.

The Commission was instructed by the Member States to consider the practical steps necessary to realise this. In truth, the idea of the internal market – a form of rebranded common market – had been kicking around the Commission for a few years. In 1981, the German Commissioner, Karl-Heinz Narjes, had looked into the idea of creating an 'internal market' in which there were no barriers to the exchange of goods, services and labour, but this had met with opposition from the French government in 1982.[44] The new British Commissioner, Lord Cockfield, took up Narjes' work, and in June 1985, presented the White Paper on Completion of the Internal Market to the Heads of Government at Milan.[45] The paper was a clever piece of work, suggesting that 279 measures were necessary to realise the internal market. Member States were not, therefore, committing themselves to an open-ended set of obligations, but to a finite and limited project. The project was also cast as largely a technical mission rather than one having broader panoramas of greater integration.[46] For all this, the goal of the internal market was unattainable whilst unanimity voting prevailed in the Council. This was firmly opposed by Britain, Denmark and Greece. By linking majority voting to market liberalisation, a goal supported by Britain, the Commission hoped to soften opposition. Notwithstanding this, when the Italian government called for a conference to amend the treaties, the British, Danes and Greeks all voted against the proposal. Despite their opposing stance, all three states attended. The result was the signing of the Single European Act in 1986.

### (ii)   The Single European Act

The principal achievements of the Single European Act (SEA) appeared limited and modest at the time. They were described as a victory for minimalism,[47] and both the Commission and the Parliament were cool about the Act.[48] The central reforms were sixfold.

---

43  Middlemas, above n. 39, 141.
44  N. Fligstein and I. Mara-Drita, 'How to Make a Market: Reflections on the Attempt to Create a Single Market in the European Union' (1996) 102 *American Journal of Sociology* 1, 11–13.
45  EC Commission, *Completing the Internal Market*, COM(85)310 final.
46  W. Sandholtz and J. Zysman, '1992: Recasting the European Bargain' (1989) 42 *World Politics* 95, 114–15.
47  G. Bermann, 'The Single European Act: A New Constitution for the European Community?' (1989) 27 *Columbia Journal of Transnational Law* 529; A. Moravscik, 'Negotiating the Single European Act' (1991) 45 *IO* 19.
48  C.-D. Ehlermann, 'The Internal Market Following the Single European Act' (1987) 24 *CML Rev.* 361.

The first was the establishment of the internal market by 31 December 1992. By that date, 'an area without internal frontiers' was to be realised 'in which the free movement of goods, persons, services and capital is ensured in accordance with the provisions of this Treaty'.[49] The project seemed, however, to be no more than a restatement of the old dream of establishing a common market. Moreover, the internal market looked a less ambitious project than the common market. In particular, it was unclear whether it extended to policies clearly caught by the common market, such as competition policy, commercial policy, non-discrimination and economic policy.[50]

The second was institutional reform. A new legislative procedure, the cooperation procedure, was introduced for the purposes of the internal market. This provided for qualified majority voting in the Council and increased powers for the European Parliament. The new voting procedure did not, however, apply to core areas such as taxation and freedom of persons. It was also difficult to see how amending the Treaties could affect the Luxembourg Accords as the latter had been concluded outside the Treaty framework. This was especially so, as the United Kingdom, Greece and Denmark insisted upon a Declaration being appended to the Single European Act, claiming that nothing within it affected Member States' rights to invoke the Accords.

Thirdly, formal recognition was also given to the European Council.[51] There had been regular summits between the Heads of Government from 1961 onwards. It was agreed in Paris, in 1974, that these should take place on a more formal footing, with the Heads of Government meeting twice a year to discuss internal difficulties within the European Communities and to engage in broader discussions about the future of European integration and the place of the European Communities in the world order. Although these were well established by the mid-1980s, it was not until the SEA that the European Council was made a formal institution of the European Communities.

The fourth development introduced by the Single European Act also promised to be little more than legal fluff. This was the extension of express Community competence to the fields of health and safety at work, economic and social cohesion, research and development and environmental protection. Yet, policies in all these areas had already been adopted under the general pre-existing Treaty provisions.

The fifth step provided for the laying down of foundations for greater economic and monetary integration through a provision stating that greater economic and monetary convergence was necessary for the development of the Community. However, the terms of the provision were very vague.

Finally, a Title was added to the Treaty on European Cooperation in the Sphere of Foreign Policy, although it amounted to little more than a codification of

---

49 This is now Article 14(2) EC.
50 P. Pescatore, 'Some Critical Remarks on the Single European Act' (1987) 24 *CML Rev.* 9, 11.
51 Article 2 SEA. On the early evolution of the European Council see S. Bulmer, 'The European Council's First Decade: Between Interdependence and Domestic Politics' (1985) 23 *JCMS* 89; S. Bulmer and W. Wessels, *The European Council* (London, Macmillan, 1987); J. Werts, *The European Council* (North Holland, Elsevier, 1992).

existing practice. It was, therefore, based almost exclusively upon intergovernmental cooperation, with there being no room provided for involvement by the supranational institutions.


### (iii)   The road to Maastricht

The Single European Act confounded expectations and brought about the most radical change in the history of the European Communities' fortunes. It changed both the legislative and political culture of the EC. In legislative terms, Member States became less tolerant of each others' attempts to invoke the Luxembourg Accords. This was reflected in the 1987 Council Decision on the 'vote to go to a vote', where it was agreed that if a simple majority of Member States voted to go to a formal vote, then a vote should be taken.[52]

The legislative processes became energised. By the end of 1990, all the measures contained in the White Paper had been formally proposed by the Commission.[53] By the end of 1992, almost 95 per cent of the measures had been enacted and 77 per cent had entered into force in the Member States.[54] Alongside this, the Commission had vastly understated the legislative output of the European Communities. Legislative output increased to 2,500 binding acts per year by 1994.[55] 53 per cent of the legislative measures adopted in France in 1991 were EC inspired and 30 per cent of all Dutch legislation during the 1990s implemented EC legislation.[56]

This transformation in law-making brought about a change in political culture. As the technical facade of the White Paper was exposed, highly divisive questions became more salient. These included such matters as the relationship between state and market, the role of central government actors, and the appropriate method to regulate non-economic public goods, such as public health or the environment:

### J. Weiler, 'The Transformation of Europe' (1991) 100 *Yale Law Journal* 2403, 2476–7

[T]he Community political culture which developed in the 1960s and 1970s led both the principal political actors and the political classes in Europe to an habituation of all political forces to thinking of European integration as ideologically neutral in, or ideologically transcendent over, the normal debates on the left-right spectrum. It is easy to understand how

---

52 Council Rules of Procedure, Article 5, OJ 1987 L291/27.
53 *Twenty Fourth Report on the General Activities of the European Communities 1990* (Luxembourg, OOPEC, 1991) 53. For an insight into how the Commission operated during this period see G. Ross, *Jacques Delors and European Integration* (London, Polity, 1995).
54 *Twenty Sixth General Report on the Activities of the European Communities 1992* (Luxembourg, OOPEC, 1993) 35.
55 W. Wessels, 'An Ever Closer Fusion? A Dynamic Macropolitical View on Integration Processes' (1997) 35 *JCMS* 267, 276.
56 G. Mancini, 'Europe: The Case for Statehood' (1998) 4 *ELJ* 29, 40.

this will have served the process of integration, allowing a nonpartisan consensus to emerge around its overall objectives.

1992 changes this in two ways. The first is a direct derivation from the turn to majority voting. Policies can be adopted now within the Council that run counter not simply to the perceived interests of a Member State, but more specifically to the ideology of a government in power. The debates about the European Social Charter and the shrill cries of 'Socialism through the back door', as well as the emerging debate about Community adherence to the European Convention on Human Rights and abortion rights are harbingers of things to come. In many respects this is a healthy development, since the real change from the past is evidenced by the ability to make difficult social choices and particularly by the increased transparency of the implications of the choice. At the same time, it represents a transformation from earlier patterns with obvious dysfunctional tensions.

The second impact of 1992 on ideological neutrality is subtler. The entire program rests on two pivots: the single market plan encapsulated in the White Paper, and its operation through the new instrumentalities of the Single European Act. Endorsing the former and adopting the latter by the Community and its Member States 'and more generally by the political class in Europe' was a remarkable expression of the process of habituation alluded to above. People were successfully called to rally behind and identify with a bold new step toward a higher degree of integration. A 'single European market' is a concept which still has power to stir. But it is also a 'single European *market*'. It is not simply a technocratic program to remove the remaining obstacles to the free movement of all factors of production. It is at the same time a highly politicized choice of ethos, ideology, and political culture, the culture of 'the market'. It is also a philosophy, at least one version of which 'the predominant version' seeks to remove barriers to the free movement of factors of production, and to remove distortion to competition as a means to maximise utility. The above is premised on the assumption of formal equality of individuals. It is an ideology the contours of which have been the subject of intense debate within the Member States in terms of their own political choices.

This led to tensions arising on three fronts. The first concerned the degree of regulation needed to complete the internal market. In a speech to the European Parliament, in July 1988, the Commission President, Jacques Delors, observed that it could lead to 80 per cent of Member State economic legislation being passed as Community law. The second concerned the social dimension of the Community. From 1986, the Commission tried to link the development of a Community social policy to the realisation of the internal market, on the grounds that some harmonisation of social legislation was necessary for the attainment of the latter. In May 1989, the Commission proposed a Community Charter of Fundamental Social Rights. This was adopted by all of the Member States, apart from Britain, at the Strasbourg European Council in December 1989.[57]

The third front was economic and monetary union. As early as 1987, the Commission indicated that due to the uncertainty generated by national currency stability, the gain anticipated for the single market could not be fully realised without some

---

57 Conclusions of Strasbourg European Council, EC Bulletin 12–1989, 1.1.1.

form of economic and monetary union.[58] Insofar as it was perceived to contribute to monetary stability, it also fitted in with the anti-inflationary policies adopted by most Member States.[59] Monetary union was also a Trojan horse. It fitted in with the aspirations of those, notably President Mitterand of France and President Kohl of Germany, who saw 1992 as being the cantilever to open the door to greater political integration. The question of economic and monetary union was, therefore, placed on the agenda of the Hanover Summit, in June 1988. At Hanover, the Heads of State asserted that 'the Single European Act confirmed the objective of progressive reali-sation of economic and monetary union'.[60] The Delors Committee, a committee of central bank governors chaired by the Commission President, Jacques Delors, was mandated to examine the concrete steps required to realise this goal. All three of these goals were opposed by the British government in particular, which perceived them as being interventionist and centralising. This opposition surfaced in a speech given by Mrs Thatcher, the British Prime Minister at the time, at the College of Europe, in Bruges, in September 1988, where she attacked the idea of a new European superstate emerging from Brussels.

In June 1989, the Delors Report on economic and monetary union was submitted to the Heads of State in Madrid.[61] This Report suggested a gradualist approach to monetary union, which was to be completed in three stages. The first stage should consist of achievement of the internal market, liberalisation of all capital movements and all states becoming members of the Exchange Rate Mechanism. The second stage required the establishment of an independent European Central Bank, convergence of national economies and a gradual assumption of the national central bank func-tions by the European Central Bank. The final stage would necessitate the European Central Bank fully taking over national central bank functions and assuming a monopoly over the money supply.[62] Faced with the opposition of all the other Mem-ber States and the threatened resignation of both her Chancellor of the Exchequer and Foreign Secretary, Mrs Thatcher grudgingly adopted the Report and it was agreed that the first stage should begin on 1 July 1990. The outmanoeuvring of Mrs Thatcher was completed at Strasbourg, where it was agreed that an intergovernmental confer-ence should be held to amend the treaties, with a view to economic and monetary union.

Presidents Kohl and Mitterand, the German and French Presidents, considered that economic and monetary union would not be sustainable without further political

---

58  T. Padoa-Schipoa *et al.*, *Efficiency, Stability and Equity: a Strategy for the Evolution of the Economic System of the European Community* (Oxford, Oxford University Press, 1987).

59  W. Sandholtz, 'Choosing Union: Monetary Politics and Maastricht' (1993) 47 *IO* 1.

60  EC Bulletin 6–1988 1.1.1–1.1.5.

61  Conclusions of Madrid European Council, EC Bulletin 6–1989, 1.1.11.

62  The German Central Bank, the Bundesbank, applied strong pressure for the Report to follow the German model of monetary policy-making as the price for its support. It was also adamant that the transition should be a gradual one. M. Artis, 'The Maastricht Road to Monetary Union' (1992) 30 *JCMS* 299.

integration, and launched an initiative to that effect in April 1990.[63] In Dublin, in June 1990, it was agreed that a separate conference should be held on political union.[64] The two parallel intergovernmental conferences opened on 13 December 1990.[65] They culminated in the signing of the Treaty on European Union, at the European Council in Maastricht, on 10 December 1991.

### 7. The Treaty on European Union

The Treaty on European Union (TEU) was a very different treaty from the Single European Act. If the latter required considerable legal integration, this was simply the byproduct of the establishment of an internal market. By contrast, the Treaty on European Union marked very definitely a change in tone. It created a new form of political project, which included, to be sure, an amount of arcane detail, but also marked out a new form of polity, which has its own set of political values and political communities.

---

**D. Obradovic, 'Policy Legitimacy and the European Union' (1996)**
**34 *Journal of Common Market Studies* 191, 208**

If the Union is defined as essentially a policy-generating process only, then it could be argued that the issue of how to maintain legitimacy rests with the participating member governments. What counts then is the choices made by those governments about when to take their policy problems to the Union level for resolution and when not to do this. Political loyalty in these circumstances lies at the Member State level, leaving the Union an object of approval or disapproval, not of political affiliation. But if the Union is defined as a partial polity, i.e. as an entity that might develop into a form of direct governance in its own right, the questions concerning the political identity, loyalty and affiliation attached to the Union level of governance, according to H.Wallace, become crucial.[66]

She emphasises that the debate on political union that surrounds the Union Treaty is precisely about the shift from policy to polity, and the broaching of metaphysical or basic political values. In other words, it is not merely a matter of adjusting institutional rules and procedures or legal powers to act, important though these are. On the contrary a political union needs a constitution which should be founded on some set of shared values and should

---

63 On the Franco-German role in the negotiations leading to Maastricht see C. Mazzucelli, *France and Germany at Maastricht: Politics and Negotiations to Create the European Union* (New York, Garland, 1997).

64 Conclusions of the Dublin European Council, EC Bulletin 6–1990, 1.11. Political union was added as an afterthought to economic and monetary union and negotiations were not as well prepared on it as they could have been. See R. Corbett, 'The Intergovernmental Conference on Political Union' (1992) 30 *JCMS* 271.

65 The most detailed analysis of the negotiations is F. Laursen and S. Vanhoonacker, *The Intergovernmental Conference on Political Union: Institutional Reforms, New Policies and International Identity of the European Community* (Dordrecht, Martijnus Nijhoff, 1992).

66 H.Wallace, 'Deepening and Widening: Problems of Legitimacy for the EC' in S. Garcia (ed.), *European Identity and the Search for Legitimacy* (London, Pinter, 1993), 95, 100.

express commitment to some form of collective identity. The delineation of some such values and identity would in itself provide some basis for legitimation required for the shift from policy to a more encompassing sociopolitical unit.

The newly emerging integration arrangement introduced by the Maastricht Treaty provides the constitutional basis for the evolving polity at the European level. Apart from economic and monetary union, the Maastricht Treaty expands Community competence proper in fields such as culture, education, health and consumer protection, as well as bringing foreign policy and security and home affairs within the Union structure. Thus the pillars of Maastricht involve areas at the heart of government. The current legitimacy dilemma in the Union concerns precisely the question of the altered polity context in which the decision-making process envisaged by the Union Treaty takes place.

This shift was reflected most clearly in the TEU's first two Articles:

### Article 1 TEU

This Treaty marks a new stage in the process of creating an ever closer union among the peoples in Europe, in which decisions are taken as closely as possible to the citizen.

The Union shall be founded on the European Communities, supplemented by the policies and forms of cooperation established by this Treaty. Its task shall be to organise, in a manner demonstrating consistency and solidarity, relations between the Member States and between their peoples.

### Article 2 TEU

The Union shall set itself the following objectives:

to promote economic and social progress which is balanced and sustainable, in particular through the creation of an area without internal frontiers, through the strengthening of economic and social cohesion and through the establishment of economic and monetary union, ultimately including a single currency in accordance with the provision of this Treaty;

to assert its identity on the international scene, in particular through the implementation of a common foreign and security policy including the eventual framing of a common defence policy, which might in time lead to a common defence;

to strengthen the protection of the rights and interests of the nationals of its Member States through the introduction of a citizenship of the Union;

to maintain and develop the Union as an area of freedom, security and justice, in which the free movement of persons is assured in conjunction with appropriate measures with respect to external border controls, asylum, immigration and the prevention and combating of crime;[67]

to maintain in full the 'acquis communautaire' and build on it with a view to considering to what extent the policies and forms of cooperation introduced by this Treaty may need to be revised with the aim of ensuring the effectiveness of the mechanisms and the institutions of the Community.

---

67 The provisions cited here are those currently in force. They are slightly different from those agreed in 1991. In particular, the sub-paragraph on the Area of Freedom, Security and Justice, to which this footnote is attached, was not present. It was added by the Treaty of Amsterdam in 1997.

> The objectives of the Union shall be achieved as provided in this Treaty and in accordance with the conditions and the timetable set out therein while respecting the principle of subsidiarity.

### (i)   Three pillars of the European Union

The Commission and the Parliament pressed for the European Union to be governed by a single institutional, supranational structure. In two fields, a practice of intergovernmental cooperation had emerged that was to prove difficult to displace. The first was foreign policy. This intergovernmental cooperation had been institutionalised by the SEA under the title of 'European Political Cooperation'. All Member States, other than the Belgians and the Dutch, wanted to keep it this way and were opposed to bringing foreign and defence policy within the EC supranational framework. The second field was that of Justice and Home Affairs; a ragbag field containing issues such as combating international crime, terrorism and immigration of non-EU nationals. In 1985 and 1990, two agreements were signed at Schengen, in Luxembourg, between all the Member States, excluding Ireland and the United Kingdom.[68] These Conventions provided for the abolition of frontier checks between parties and a common external frontier. To realise this, the 1990 Convention provided for intergovernmental cooperation in the fields of migration of non-EU nationals, crime and policing. Whilst many Member States wanted to see this brought within the EC framework, the British, Irish, Greeks and Danes were adamant that this was an area where the national veto should be maintained.

The Union was, therefore, to be composed of three pillars. The first is that of the European Community, the second, that of Common Foreign and Security Policy (CFSP) and the third, Justice and Home Affairs (JHA).[69] These three pillars were, in principle, to constitute a single institutional framework, at the centre of which stands the first pillar, the European Community:

### Article 3 TEU

The Union shall be served by a single institutional framework which shall ensure the consistency and the continuity of the activities carried out in order to attain its objectives while respecting and building upon the 'acquis communautaire'.

The Union shall in particular ensure the consistency of its external activities as a whole in the context of its external relations, security, economic and development policies. The Council and the Commission shall be responsible for ensuring such consistency. They shall ensure the implementation of these policies, each in accordance with its respective powers.

---

68 This is now to be found at OJ 2000, L239/19. Iceland and Norway are also associated members.

69 Allegedly, the idea was first suggested by a French negotiator, Pierre de Boissieu, and was constructed around the metaphor of a temple based on three pillars, Middlemas, above n. 39, 188.

The overarching, unitary provisions were weak, however. To be sure, there was a unitary legal framework in that any understanding of one pillar could only be had by reference to the TEU as a whole.[70] Beyond that, only two provisions united the three pillars.

The European Council was given a pre-eminent, coordinating role for all three pillars. Its position as the body with ultimate political authority and the body which was responsible for visioning and coordinating all EU activities was, for the first time, formalised:

### Article 4 TEU

The European Council shall provide the Union with the necessary impetus for its development and shall define the general political guidelines thereof.

In addition, the unique position of the Member States and the commitment to respect fundamental rights was recognised as a constituent element of each pillar:

### Article 6(1) TEU

1. The Union shall respect the national identities of its Member States, whose systems of government are founded on the principles of democracy.
2. The Union shall respect fundamental rights, as guaranteed by the European Convention for the Protection of Human Rights and Fundamental Freedoms signed in Rome on 4 November 1950 and as they result from the constitutional traditions common to the Member States, as general principles of Community law.

The institutional balance within each pillar was, however, very different. The Parliament and the Court of Justice were only minimally associated with either the second or third pillars.[71] If the EC pillar was characterised by some parliamentary and judicial controls, these were largely absent at either a national or Union level from the other pillars, and instead, these were to be dominated by executive government. Whilst the Commission was associated quite strongly with the work of the third pillar on Justice and Home Affairs, it was almost completely excluded from the second pillar. Even between the two intergovernmental pillars, there was a mismatch, with one being more clearly Europeanised than the other. The question of legal personality was also mixed. The EC had had legal personality since 1957, and retained this. By contrast, the European Union was to have no legal personality. Whilst the EC had treaty-making powers

---

70 A. v. Bogdandy and M. Nettesheim, 'Ex Pluribus Unum: Fusion of the European Communities into the European Union' (1996) 2 *ELJ* 267, 279–81; D. Curtin and I. Dekker, 'The EU as a Layered International Organization: Institutional Unity in Disguise' in P. Craig and G. de Búrca (eds.), *The Evolution of EU Law* (Oxford, Oxford University Press, 1999).
71 For a recent reassertion of this see Case C-160/03 *Spain v Eurojust*, judgment of 15 March 2005.

in its field of competence, there was no equivalent power in the fields of CFSP and JHA.[72]

## (ii)  The new competences

Relatively uncontroversially, the EC was granted express competencies in the fields of visas for third country nationals, education, culture, public health, consumer protection, the establishment of transEuropean networks in transport, energy and telecommunications, industrial policy and development cooperation. There were two fields which evoked particular controversy.

The first was economic and monetary union (EMU).[73] The Treaty followed the three stage structure of the Delors Report, with the third stage of economic and monetary union beginning on 1 January 1999.[74] Economic and monetary union allocated responsibility for various aspects of economic policy to different institutions. Monetary policy was to be the responsibility of an independent European Central Bank, now established in Frankfurt. It was exclusively responsible for authorising the issue of the new European currency, the euro, and therefore, for the setting of short-term interest rates. For states to participate in the euro, they were required to meet a set of arduous convergence criteria, which attempted to secure economic convergence and economic readiness between the participating states.[75] Monetary policy was the only policy to be completely centralised. Constraints were, however, to be placed on national fiscal policy through the limiting of the size of the deficits that governments could run. A procedure was established – the excessive deficit procedure – whereby governments participating in the euro could be heavily sanctioned if they ran an excessive deficit. The reason for this is that it is impossible to run simultaneously an expansive fiscal policy and a tight monetary policy. The former involves incurring a debt, which, at some point, must be monetised to be repaid (normally through inflation). This is inconsistent with a monetary policy which, through placing costs on borrowing, is trying to limit the amount of money in circulation. Other areas of economic policy-making were considered less potentially disruptive than fiscal policy

---

72  D. Curtin, 'The Constitutional Structure of the Union: A Europe of Bits and Pieces' (1993) 30 *CML Rev.* 17.

73  This is explored in greater detail in *EUL*, chapter 12.

74  It was initially envisaged that the third stage could begin as early as 31 December 1996 if the convergence criteria were met by sufficient Member States: Article 109j(3) EC. At the Cannes Summit, in 1995, it was agreed that the date for the third stage should be 1 January 1999: EU Bulletin 6–1995, I.11.

75  These criteria were as follows: inflation (a state's inflation should not be more than 1.5 per cent more than the best three performing states); avoidance of an excessive budgetary deficit (the planned or actual deficit exceeds 3 per cent of GDP or total government debt exceeds 60 per cent of GDP); stable long-term interest rates (these do not exceed by more than 2 per cent the average of the three Member States with the lowest rates of inflation) and currency stability (participation within the narrow margins of the Exchange Rate Mechanism for two years without devaluation or severe tensions): Protocol on the Convergence Criteria Referred to in Article 109j EC.

for monetary union. In these areas, it was agreed that there should be coordination of policy-making, with the Council providing guidelines to Member States on how they should manage their economies.

The other area to prove particularly problematic was that of Social Policy. There was strong support amongst all Member States, apart from Britain, for an extension of the Community social policy provisions. These already allowed for legislation in the fields of gender equality in the workplace and health and safety at work. There was a desire to extend Community competence to all areas of labour law and social protection for workers. The British government opposed this on the grounds that this was purely a matter of national concern and it did not fit in with that government's views of a deregulated labour market. The compromise reached was a Protocol to the EC Treaty, which authorised all the Member States, apart from the United Kingdom, to establish an Agreement on Social Policy that would bind only those Member States, but would allow them access to existing EC machinery and resources.

### (iii)   Recasting the institutional settlement and the quest for 'democracy'

Maastricht was the first conference where serious consideration was given to the 'democratic' nature of the European Union and its need to seek legitimacy. A variety of strategies were introduced.

The first was to increase parliamentary input into the legislative processes. A new legislative procedure was introduced, the co-decision procedure, which gave the European Parliament more powers by allowing it, in certain sectors, to veto legislation. The place of national parliaments was recognised for the first time, albeit in a fairly minimal manner. A Declaration was attached to the TEU committing governments to greater involvement of their national parliaments in the integration process and to ensuring these receive legislative proposals in good time. Alongside this, there was an attempt to pluralise the decision-making process. New stakeholders were introduced, most notably the Committee of the Regions which, whilst only being given consultative powers, created a voice for the European regions within the Community policy process.

The TEU was also concerned with administrative accountability.[76] To that end, an Ombudsman was established to consider acts of maladministration by the Union institutions. Provision was also made for considering whether the decision-making procedures could be made more transparent and, for the first time, the question of freedom of information was formally acknowledged.

Most symbolic of the sentiment that a new centre for democratic participation was being created, was the institution of European Union citizenship.[77] Citizens were granted new rights to free movement and to access to social benefits in other Member States. New possibilities for democratic participation at both local and European

---

76 This is discussed in further detail in chapter 8.     77 See *EUL*, chapter 13.

level were created. European citizenship also created new patterns of inclusion and exclusion between Europeans and non-Europeans, insofar as these rights were only granted to Member State nationals as European Union citizens. Most controversially, as citizenship has traditionally been used to foster new political allegiances, it suggests a common political identity between its members, which to some, seemed to compete with that claimed by the nation-state.

### (iv)  Division of power between the European Union and the Member States

The Preamble in the initial proposed draft to the TEU stated that the:

> Treaty marks a new stage in the process leading gradually to a Union with a federal goal.

This was opposed by the British government and was eventually removed from the TEU. British opposition was, in part, because such a statement implied a gradual accretion of macro-economic, defence and foreign policy under a single, central, European Union authority, as such powers were generally enjoyed by federal authorities. More generally, the British government opposed the implication that the allocation of politics and law-making was to be done from a pan-European perspective, in which the Union should have law-making powers and be capable of producing pan-Union benefits. The British vision was that allocation of law-making powers was, foremost, a matter of national choice.

This opposition reflected the increasing pressures placed on national, regional and local self-government by European integration. The European Union was churning out more legislation, more intensely, in more fields than ever before. To manage these tensions, a new principle was introduced – the subsidiarity principle. In areas where both it and the Member States had powers, the European Union was only to act if the objectives of the proposed action could not be sufficiently achieved by the Member States and by reason of its scale or effects the action could be better achieved by the Community. This principle still implied that there was a pan-Union answer to questions about the allocation of law-making responsibility. It could be decided in a unitary fashion whether national or Union law-makers should legislate in a particular area. Maastricht also witnessed the start of opt-outs for individual Member States, who clearly did not agree with the Community's allocation of law-making responsibility. We have already seen that the Protocol on Social Policy allowed the British not to participate in the Agreement on Social Policy. The United Kingdom and Denmark were also unwilling to give an outright commitment to the abolition of their currencies. Protocols were, therefore, attached to the treaty, allowing these states to notify the other Member States whether or not they wished to participate in the third stage of EMU. Alongside these, Member States began to ask for their national legislation to be ring-fenced from EC law. The Irish government insisted that a Protocol be added protecting their constitutional provisions prohibiting abortion.

The Danes obtained a similar instrument protecting their legislation on the ownership of second homes from the bite of EC legislation.

## 8. The 1990s: the decade of self-doubt

### (i)   Ratification of the Treaty on European Union

On 2 June 1992, the Danes voted narrowly against ratification of the TEU by 50.7 per cent to 49.3 per cent. Despite the Irish having voted conclusively in favour of ratification,[78] this shook the process to the core, as the Treaty could not enter into effect unless all Member States ratified it. To boost the credibility of the ratification process, President Mitterand decided to hold a referendum in France. Although an easy 'yes' vote had been predicted, it soon became a very close contest, with only 51 per cent of the vote being in favour of ratification. The Treaty was salvaged at Edinburgh, in December 1992. The other Member States considered the Treaty to be non-negotiable, but something had to be done to allow the Danish government to say that the treaty it was proposing for a second referendum was substantially different from the initial treaty. The route taken was a Decision 'interpreting' the Treaty,[79] which gave the Danish government the necessary breadth to hold a second referendum. This was duly held in May 1993, with 56 per cent voting in favour of ratification. However, the damage had been done. The political aura of inevitable integration and the assumption of popular support for it had been tarnished. The first Danish referendum signalled the beginning of a bitter legislative fight in the British Parliament, in which ratification was fought for by both the British Labour Party and a minority of the then ruling Conservative party. The legislation was only adopted in July 1993 – a year and a half after the Treaty had been agreed – and only after the government had put a gun to its rebels' heads, by passing it as a motion of confidence, with the consequence that if it had fallen, the government would have had to resign.[80] The drama of ratification of the Treaty having been played out in the streets and in parliaments was now re-enacted in the courts. Challenges to the Treaty were made before the British, French, Danish and Spanish courts.[81] It was the challenge before the German Constitutional Court, in October 1993, which was to have the most far-reaching consequences. A

---

78  69 per cent of the vote was in favour of ratification.
79  Conclusions of the Edinburgh European Council, EC Bulletin 12–1992, Annex 1, Part B. D. Howarth, 'The Compromise on Denmark and the Treaty on European Union: a Legal and Political Analysis' (1994) 31 CML Rev. 465.
80  R. Rawlings, 'Legal Politics: The United Kingdom and Ratification of the Treaty on European Union' (1994) PL 254, 367; D. Baker, A. Gamble and S. Ludlum, 'The Parliamentary Siege of Maastricht: Conservative Divisions and British Ratification' (1994) 47 Parliamentary Affairs 37.
81  R v Secretary of State for Foreign and Commonwealth Affairs ex parte Rees-Mogg [1994] QB 552 (Britain); Re Treaty on European Union (Decision 92–308), Journel Officiel de la République Française 1992, No. 5354 (France); Re Treaty on European Union [1994] 3 CMLR 101 (Spain).

German law professor challenged the ratification of the TEU by Germany on the grounds that excessive powers were being transferred to the European Union.[82] The German Constitutional Court stated this was not the case, but placed markers on the nature and limits of European integration. The German court ruled that democratic legitimacy is constituted at a national level, and rests most firmly in regional and national parliaments. Within this setting, the legitimacy of the European Union rests on its being an economic union with limited powers whose legitimacy derives from Member States choosing to grant it powers that they are no longer able to exercise effectively. Within these fields, the Community must still operate in a democratically accountable fashion. For the European Union to be acceptable to national constitutional courts, it must neither acquire new powers nor exercise them in a way that would fundamentally undermine national self-government, and it must strengthen its own democratic checks and balances with the advancement of the integration process.

The TEU entered into force on 1 November 1993. The environment was now more polarised than at Maastricht. Public support for the European Union had diminished[83] and deeper divisions had emerged between national governments about which direction to take.[84] Relations between the United Kingdom and the other Member States were also soured by the BSE crisis. On 20 March 1996, the British government announced that there was a possible link between bovine spongiform encephalopathy (BSE), a terminal disease which lodged in the nervous systems and brains of cattle, and Creutzfeld-Jakob disease, which manifested itself in a similar way in humans. Pushed by the other Member States, the Commission imposed an export ban on all cattle, beef and beef products from the United Kingdom. The British government, considering that the link was at best remote and that those parts which posed a risk had been removed from the food chain, lobbied for a reversal of the ban. When this was not forthcoming, it began a policy of non-cooperation, whereby it would exercise any veto powers it possessed indiscriminately. A deal was eventually done at Florence in June 1996, but the consequence was that little more than points of difference were identified during the first half of 1996. Negotiations only began in earnest in the latter half of 1996, with the Irish government presenting a draft treaty to the other Member States in December 1996.[85] The Treaty of Amsterdam was signed on 2 October 1997.

---

82 *Brunner v European Union Treaty* [1994] 1 CMLR 57.
83 Opinion polls showed that those who considered the European Union a 'good thing' had dropped from 72 per cent in 1990 to 48 per cent in Autumn 1996. EUROBAROMETER, *Public Opinion in the EU, Report No. 46, Autumn 1996* (Luxembourg, OOPEC, 1997).
84 A summary of all the positions taken by the Member States at the 1996 Intergovernmental Conference can be found at http://europa.eu.int/en/agenda/igc-home/ms-doc
85 Conference of the Representatives of the Governments of the Member States, *The European Union Today and Tomorrow: Adopting the European Union for the Benefit of its Peoples and Preparing it for the Future, a General Outline for a Draft Revision of the Treaties*, CONF 2500/96.

## (ii)   The Treaty of Amsterdam

### (a)   Area of Freedom, Security and Justice

If the central monuments of the SEA and the TEU were the internal market and EMU, respectively, then the Area of Freedom, Security and Justice occupied a similar place for the Treaty of Amsterdam.[86]

The Area of Freedom, Security and Justice (AFSJ) was a commitment to realise, within five years of the entry into force of the Treaty of Amsterdam, an area without internal border controls and with common external borders. This area was to include common measures in the fields of immigration, asylum and the rights of non-EU nationals. It was also to involve judicial cooperation in civil and criminal matters and police cooperation.

To realise the AFSJ, the Treaty of Amsterdam, first, integrated the Schengen Agreements into the legal framework of the TEU. As mentioned earlier, these agreements, signed in 1985 and 1990, committed all Member States, other than Ireland and the United Kingdom, to realising an area without internal border controls and with common external frontiers. A Protocol integrating the Schengen Acquis into the framework of the European Union was adopted, which made the Schengen Agreements and the implementing decisions taken under these agreements, part of Union law.

Secondly, the AFSJ reallocated decision-making between the EC and Justice and Home Affairs pillars. A new Title was added to the EC Treaty on visas, immigration and other policies related to free movement of persons. This had the effect of bringing immigration, asylum and the rights of non-EU nationals within EC legislative competencies, whilst all other aspects of the Area of Freedom, Security and Justice remained subject to the predominantly intergovernmental procedures of the third pillar. As the only policies remaining within the third pillar were now policing and judicial cooperation in criminal matters, that pillar has been renamed accordingly, so that is now Policing and Judicial Cooperation in Criminal Matters (PJCC).

Finally, the AFSJ reoriented the mission of the Union more strongly around the maintenance of certain political ideals. This was marked most strongly in the new Article 6 TEU, which stated that the Union was to be founded on the 'principles of liberty, democracy, respect for human rights and fundamental freedoms, and the rule of law'. These ideals were institutionalised in a couple of ways. The EC acquired legislative competence to combat discrimination based on sex, race or ethnic origin, religion or belief, disability, age or sexual orientation. A new provision was also added, which allowed for a Member State to have its rights suspended under the TEU or expelled from the European Union where it was deemed that the Member State had seriously and persistently breached its obligations under Article 6 TEU.

---

86 The Area of Freedom, Security and Justice has been much modified since the Treaty of Amsterdam. Its
   central elements are analysed further in *EUL*, chapter 14.

## (b) Amsterdam and the democratic deficit

The Treaty of Amsterdam led to a significant extension of qualified majority voting (QMV) to new fields. In quantitative terms, it led, for the first time, to the majority of EC law being passed by qualified majority, and the veto becoming the exception. There were 101 legal bases that provided for QMV, whilst only 76 retained the national veto.[87] Qualitatively, QMV was extended to important new fields, which included employment, countering social exclusion, equality of opportunity and treatment for men and women, public health, transparency, fraud and freedom of establishment. In terms of parliamentary accountability, it also led to a considerable extension of the European Parliament's powers. The scope of the co-decision procedure, which granted it a veto, was extended considerably. The European Parliament was also, for the first time, given some involvement in the third pillar. Alongside this, more attention was paid to the role of national parliaments within the integration process. A Protocol on National Parliaments was adopted, which extended their guarantees. All consultation documents would now be sent to them and there would be a six-week period between proposals being announced and their being placed on the EC legislative agenda, in order to allow national parliaments to consider them. Administrative accountability was strengthened by the principle of transparency being formally incorporated into the EC Treaty, with a qualified right of access to EC documents being granted to every citizen of the European Union and natural or legal person having its registered office in a Member State.

## (c) Differentiated integration

The Treaty of Amsterdam added few new competencies to the TEU. Outside of the Area of Freedom, Security and Justice, a new Title on Employment was added to the EC Treaty and, with a change in government, the United Kingdom decided to get rid of its opt-out from EC Social Policy. The Protocol on Social Policy was subsequently abolished, and social policy was placed on the same footing as all other policies governed by the EC Treaty. Amsterdam was rather noteworthy for reflecting the multiplicity of tensions surrounding the pace, direction and form of European integration that had emerged since Maastricht. A Protocol on the Application of the Principles of Subsidiarity and Proportionality was agreed, which entrenched in Treaty law the Declarations agreed at Edinburgh that had enabled Denmark to hold a second referendum on the Maastricht Treaty. The bigger problem, however, was not disagreement about the intensity of integration, but rather, deep disagreements about which fields the Union should be operating in and what legislation it should be adopting.

Provision was, therefore, made at Amsterdam for 'Enhanced Cooperation'.[88] Member States intending to establish closer cooperation between themselves could make use of the TEU institutions and mechanisms. This cooperation must only be used

---

87 A. Maurer, 'The Legislative Powers and Impact of the European Parliament' (2003) 41 *JCMS* 227, 229.
88 See pp. 155–8.

as a last resort, must involve at least a majority of the Member States and must not affect the competencies, rights and obligations of non-participating Member States. In areas covered by either the EC Treaty or PJCCA, prior authorisation is required, with a qualified majority of all Member States being in favour, before such cooperation can proceed.

More specific opt-outs also proliferated at Amsterdam. A number of states were wary about their immigration and asylum policies being governed by supranational processes. The Protocol on the Application of Certain Aspects of Article 14 EC Treaty to the United Kingdom and Northern Ireland allows the United Kingdom to retain its rights to verify those entering its territory and to deny permission to enter. As Ireland and the United Kingdom form a common travel area, an identical provision was made for Ireland. The relationship is one of reciprocity, in that other Member States are permitted to retain their border controls vis-à-vis persons entering from the United Kingdom or Ireland. Furthermore, a second Protocol, the Protocol on the Position of the United Kingdom and Ireland, allows the United Kingdom and Ireland neither to participate in the adoption of nor be bound by measures taken under the EC Title on visas, immigration, asylum and other policies related to free movement of persons. Denmark shared similar reservations to the United Kingdom, but is party to the Schengen Conventions. Therefore, a Protocol was attached, stating that Denmark would not participate in the adoption of and would not be bound by any measure adopted under this EC Title as a matter of EC law. However, Denmark would continue to be bound by such measures as a matter of international law.

A series of soft opt-outs were also negotiated. A Protocol had been adopted on Asylum for Nationals of Member States of the European Union. This established a presumption that all Member States were to be regarded as safe countries of origin for the purposes of asylum, implying that applications for asylum originating in these EU states should be presumed inadmissible. Belgium was unhappy with the Protocol, which it felt compromised the right to asylum. It adopted a Declaration suggesting it would not follow the presumption of safety of EU states but would treat each case on its merits. Germany, Luxembourg and Austria sought Declarations in a different field. These states were concerned that their systems of public banking might be compromised by EC competition law, and therefore sought Declarations to the contrary.

## 9. Recasting the borders of the European Union

During the 1990s, events outside the European Union's borders were as important as internal events for its development. The shape of the European Union was modified by two events at the end of the 1980s. The success of the Single European Act increased the potential benefits of membership and the costs of non-membership. Exclusion from the world's largest trading bloc posed significant economic risks for other European states. At the same time, communism collapsed in Central and Eastern Europe. Many states, previously antagonistic to the European Union, now embraced the market-orientated ideals it symbolised and saw membership as the anchor around which changes in their societies could be made.

The process of expansion began with the EFTA states (Norway, Sweden, Finland, Iceland, Austria, Liechtenstein and Switzerland). Formal relations went back to 1972 and 1973, where a series of bilateral free trade agreements had been signed between the European Community and these states. In 1984, the Luxembourg Declaration stated that economic cooperation between the EC and these states should be increased, leading to the creation of a 'European economic space'.[89] This concept was ill-defined and negotiations were stagnant until the onset of the Single European Act. In 1989, the European Community proposed that the existing bilateral relations between the EC and individual EFTA states be replaced by a single institutional arrangement. The result was the Treaty of Oporto of 1991, establishing the European Economic Area (EEA).[90] The EFTA states were required to adopt all EC legislation in the fields of the internal market, research and development policy, social policy, education, consumer protection and environmental protection. Whilst common institutions were set up, they were not built upon in any substantive form of reciprocity, as their purpose was to ensure the EEA regime complied with that of the EC. Whilst allowing EFTA states access to the internal market, it gave them no input in the political process through which the market was regulated. Therefore, the agreement was only politically sustainable if perceived as a stepping stone to membership negotiations.

At Lisbon, in June 1992, the Member States agreed that accession negotiations should immediately follow the signing of the Treaty on European Union. In Copenhagen, in June 1993, the European Council agreed that membership be offered to Austria, Finland, Sweden and Norway.[91] Referenda were necessary in all four states prior to accession. In Austria and Finland, comfortable majorities voted in favour of membership. However, that in Sweden was narrow. The Norwegians voted narrowly against membership. The three new Member States acceded to the TEU on 2 January 1995.

More challenging was the question of possible membership of the former communist states of Central and Eastern Europe. By the early 1990s, twelve of these states had applied for membership.[92] This would almost double the size of the Union, and

---

89 B. Hurni, 'EFTA-EC Relations: Aftermath of the Luxembourg Declaration' (1986) 20 *JWTL* 507.

90 Although Switzerland signed the treaty, following a referendum, it decided not to ratify it. In 2002, agreements were signed between the European Union and Switzerland in the fields of free movement of persons, agriculture, transport, public procurement, mutual recognition, scientific and technological cooperation, OJ 2002, L114/1. The most detailed analysis of the treaty can be found in T. Blanchet *et al.*, *The Agreement on the European Economic Area* (Oxford, Clarendon Press, 1994).

91 M. Jorna, 'The Accession Negotiations with Austria, Finland, Sweden and Norway: a Guided Tour' (1995) 20 *EL Rev.* 131; F. Granell, 'The European Union's Enlargement Negotiations with Austria, Finland, Norway and Sweden' (1995) 33 *JCMS* 117.

92 These were Bulgaria, Cyprus, the Czech Republic, Estonia, Hungary, Latvia, Lithuania, Malta, Poland, Romania, Slovenia and Slovakia.

would both necessitate institutional reform in order that the decision-making processes work effectively and involve a corresponding reduction of political influence
for existing Member States. It would create a financial burden on current members
as the applicants were poorer than the Western European states and many had large
agricultural populations, which could press claims for support from the Union budget. Nevertheless, in Lisbon 1992, the European Union stated that any European state
whose government was based on the principle of democracy could apply to accede.[93]
A year later, at Copenhagen, the European Union went a step further and agreed that
the states of Central and Eastern Europe could become members of the European
Union once able to satisfy the obligations of membership. These obligations required
new states to have:

- stability of institutions guaranteeing democracy, the rule of law, human rights and
  respect for and protection of minorities;
- the existence of a functioning market economy as well as the capacity to cope with
  competitive pressure and market forces within the Union;
- the ability to assume the obligations of membership, including adherence to the
  aims of political, economic and monetary union;
- the conditions for their integration through the adjustment of their administrative
  structures, so that EC legislation transposed into national legislation is implemented
  effectively through appropriate administrative and judicial structures.[94]

In 1994, it was agreed that a 'structured relationship' should be established forthwith between the European Union and the countries of Central and Eastern Europe
in order to prepare the latter for membership. In July 1997, following the Treaty
of Amsterdam, the Commission stepped up the process with the launch of its 2000
Agenda programme. In a 1,300 page document, it assessed how far the applicant
states met the criteria agreed in Copenhagen. On the basis of that progress report,
it recommended the opening of membership negotiations with the Czech Republic,
Poland, Hungary, Slovenia, Estonia and Cyprus, with a view to accession by 2003.
The discussions began in March 1998. However, limiting negotiations to a selection
of applicant states proved hopelessly divisive and in January 2000, Bulgaria, Romania, Latvia, Lithuania, Malta and Slovakia were also invited to participate. Between
1997 and 2002, the Commission published annual reports on each applicant and
in November 2002, recommended that all the applicant states, excluding Romania
and Bulgaria, be offered membership. In Copenhagen, in December 2002, the Member States agreed that these states should become members of the European Union
from 1 May 2004, bringing the size of the Union to twenty-five states. In addition, it
was agreed that 2007 should be anticipated as the date of membership for Bulgaria
and Romania, assuming they made satisfactory progress in meeting the Copenhagen

93 Conclusions of the Lisbon European Council, EC Bulletin 6–1992, I.4.
94 This last condition was added at Madrid in December 1995.

criteria. In June 2004, it was agreed to open accession negotiations with Croatia, with a view to possible membership in 2007. However, these were discontinued in March 2005, following Croatia's refusal to hand over General Gotovina to the War Crimes Tribunal in The Hague.

Enlargement is not simply a question of extending institutional arrangements and frontiers to accommodate new Member States. Enlargement also transforms the nature of the European Union's political community. New states bring with them their own conceptions of the relationship between the state and society, of civic responsibility and of the limits of political tolerance:

### J. Zielonka, 'How New Enlarged Borders will Reshape the European Union' (2001) 39 *Journal of Common Market Studies* 507, 513–15

From a formal point of view, all countries negotiating accession to the EU already meet the basic democratic requirement: they all revised their communist constitutions, putting in place a set of democratic institutions and guaranteeing civil and human rights. However, trust in these democratic institutions remains low across the region. Existing data show a very low level of support for political parties, in particular, but also for parliaments, trade unions and private enterprises. The applicant states are also more 'socialist' than current EU Member States in the sense that the average level of self-responsibility is low, whilst the solidarity level with the disadvantaged is strong. In contrast to the current Member States, the applicant states are also much less 'republican' in the sense that the level of 'civic engagement' and 'trust in others' is lower. True, some Western European states such as Spain and Finland also deviate from other EU Member States. (In Spain the rejection of violence is relatively low, while in Finland support for democracy is relatively low). Indeed the main dividing line in Europe in terms of democratic orientation of citizens runs not between the applicant and current EU members, but between these two groups and some countries further East and South. (In Albania and in the Slav successor states of the Soviet Union – Russia, Ukraine, Belarus and Moldova – there are fewer than 25 per cent of solid democrats which is two or even three times less than in countries such as the Czech Republic, Hungary or Slovenia.) That said, it is clear that admission to the EU of several new states from the east and southeast will only complicate the process of creating a European demos, usually seen as a precondition for creation and legitimization of a truly European state.

The ethnic composition of the applicant states also differs from current Member States with important implications for the cohesion of these countries and the EU itself. In Latvia and Estonia the Russian-speaking minority exceeds 30 per cent of the population and the official minority policy is confrontational. In four countries (Slovakia, Bulgaria, Romania and Lithuania) minorities comprise up to 25 per cent of the population, and the official policy towards them oscillates between open hostility and temporary accommodation. Four other countries (Poland, the Czech Republic, Slovenia and Hungary) have minority populations not exceeding 10 per cent of the population. However, Hungary and Poland have many co-nationals living outside their borders, which time and again have proved to be a matter of contention. For instance, as a result of the 1920 Trianon Treaty, about one-third of Hungarians found themselves outside Hungary's borders with serious political implications for both its domestic and international politics. Most EU Member States do not have similar types of ethnic minorities within their borders, but in contrast to Eastern Europe they are faced with large numbers of immigrants, which results in a specific type of multiculturalism. Recognition of cultural differences is also an Eastern European problem. For instance, the ethnically homogenous Czech Republic has witnessed many xenophobic incidents against a tiny Roma minority. However, as Liebich has pointed out,[95] the prime factor behind the minority problems in Eastern Europe is a different conception of the state. If the state is perceived as the exclusive state of the titular majority, minorities (national or cultural alike) will be viewed as peripheral, if not illegitimate.

All the above-mentioned evidence could be interpreted in several ways, but there is no doubt that accession of several countries from the East and Southeast will increase internal diversity within the EU and make it more difficult for it to provide an overlap between its various functional and territorial boundaries. However, this is not to demonize divergence. The argument here is not that divergence is bad in itself and that therefore the EU would be well advised to forget about enlargement because of the expected impact of divergence. The argument here, let us repeat, is that enlargement makes it less likely for the EU to become a Westphalian type of state. One does not need to be a disciple of Max Weber to acknowledge that ambitious projects of political, economic and military integration can only work in a relatively homogenous environment. Common laws with administrative regulations cannot cope well with a high degree of diversity, and so various complicated opt-outs and multi-speed arrangements ensue.

These tensions crystallised in the debate about possible Turkish membership of the European Union. Formal EU-Turkey relations go back over forty years to the signing of an Association Agreement in 1963. In 1987, Turkey applied for membership of the European Union. This application lay dormant, largely due to the antipathetic reaction it received from a number of Member States. Fears over alienating Turkey led to a rapprochement in the mid-1990s, which resulted in the establishment of a customs union between Turkey and the European Union, in 1995. It was clear that this was likely to be insufficient, and in 1999, in Helsinki, the Member States recognised Turkey's eligibility for membership and agreed this should be assessed, as with other applicants, according to the Copenhagen Criteria. Formally at least, the most problematic of the criteria, from the Member States' perspective, has been whether or not Turkey can meet the political criteria, namely the attainment of stable democratic institutions and respect for the rule of law and human rights. Turkey was pressed to bring in reform of its Criminal Code, strengthen its judiciary, secure the rights of association, expression and religion more effectively and reduce the role of the military in the government of the country.[96] In December 2004, it was agreed that Turkey had made the necessary political reforms and that accession negotiations would open in October 2005.

Turkey would be the largest state to join the European Union since 1957. It would be the first predominantly Islamic state and would extend the Union's borders far into Asia. As a state with high levels of poverty and agriculture relative to other Member

95 A. Liebich, *Ethnic Minorities and Long-term Implications of EU Enlargement* (Fiesole, EUI Working Paper 98/49 EUI, 1998).
96 Turkey was also pressed to contribute to the resolution of the conflict in Cyprus.

States, the pressures on the Union budget and on other Member State labour markets would increase. Accession would, therefore, transform the Union[97] and public opinion in Austria, Denmark, Germany and France has been extremely hostile to Turkish accession.[98] On the basis of this, notwithstanding the prior agreement to open talks, the Austrian government indicated in September 2005 that it would not support Turkish membership on the grounds that public opinion was so sceptical, with the consequence that the opening of talks had to be postponed.

Opposition to Turkish membership is based on the idea that any political community should have a common standard of political values which, possibly, are not shared by the Turkish state. Even if this were true, it has been argued that this misinterprets the nature of the political community being created by the European Union. The European Union exists precisely because of the differences and oppositions already present within the Union. The only alternative to the Union would be conflict, either overt or frozen. Because the Union is not a traditional political community, it takes its inherent diversity as an opportunity for common action and for the realisation of common goods, such as free and fair trade, protection of the environment and the securing of fundamental rights:

### E. Balibar, 'Europe as Vanishing Mediator' (2003)
### *Constellations* 312, 332–3

([T]he idea of a 'Euro-Mediterranean' ensemble (or alliance)) does not say that there are no 'faultlines' and no vested hostilities around them; it says that political institutions (the 'city' and 'civility') arise precisely when hostility becomes a focal point for the elaboration of common interests and historic compromises. Such common interests express the 'complementarity of enemies' . . . and this is what makes them politically significant.

Recent debates – sometimes virulent – about the possible admission of Turkey into the EU, which followed the electoral victory of the 'Party of Justice and Development' (AKP) (a party that defines itself as 'conservative' and is depicted by political scientists as 'moderate Islamic'), prompted by (former French president and current Chair of the European Constitutional Convention) Giscard d'Estaing's declarations that Turkey was 'non-European' and its admission would ruin the European project, have had at least one good effect: they have manifested a reality that does not belong to utopia or a distant future, but is fast approaching. Whatever the (probably very great) diversity of institutional solutions, ranging from formal inclusion to close association, Turkey will not remain an isolated case. The whole of the south shore of the Mediterranean will be progressively involved in the construction of a common space of interdependence, a laboratory for new relationships between 'developed' and 'developing' countries, and between cultures with religious roots in antithetical versions of the same monotheistic theology – provided, of course, that the political conditions are consciously and tenaciously forged.

---

97 EC Commission, *Staff Working Paper on Issues Arising from Turkey's Membership Perspective*, COM(2004) 656.
98 K. Hughes, *The Political Dynamics of Turkish Accession to the European Union: a European Success Story or the EU's Most Contested Enlargement* (Stockholm, SIEPS, 2004).

> If such an ensemble were to come into being, it would become at once an instrument to correct inequalities in the rates of development, an intermediary structure making it easier for Europeans to effectively influence world affairs and a powerful aegis for democratizing Arab-Islamic regimes of the Middle East. This is the real way to overcome the old patterns of opposition between 'Occidental' and 'Oriental' cultures, which are only one way of understanding the history of humankind, but still cast their shadow on contemporary thought and politics.

## 10. The Treaty of Nice and beyond

### (i)   Fin-de-siècle *decay: from Amsterdam to Nice*

Amsterdam was less concerned with grand questions about the European Union's political and legal identity, and more with making the Union work efficiently and consensually. This managerialism was evinced most strongly in the renumbering of the TEU.[99] More significant matters, such as the institutional pressures that would be generated by possible enlargement of the Union to twenty-seven states, were too divisive to be discussed. Fewer areas were subject to qualified majority voting than had been anticipated.[100] The consequence was a further postponement of the day of reckoning. A Protocol was signed, agreeing that an intergovernmental conference (IGC) be convened at least one year before membership of the European Union reached twenty, to carry out a comprehensive review of the composition and functioning of the institutions.

The Treaty of Amsterdam came into force relatively easily on 1 May 1999. The first official discussions for the next IGC began in the same month. It was agreed that negotiations should not be concerned with redefining the status of the Union or granting new powers, but be directed towards recasting the institutional settlement so that it would function more efficiently and accommodate new states who might join the Union. This task was, however, a challenging one, as it was essentially redistributive. Any reallocation of votes or influence within the EU institutions meant that for every winner, there must be a loser. The situation was further complicated by its having being agreed that the twelve states which had applied to join the Union could participate in the negotiations.

The climate of negotiation was then poisoned by two events. The European Parliament had been concerned for some time at the Commission's poor management of the Union's financial resources. In January 1999, the Parliament appointed a Committee of Independent Experts to examine this. The Report of the Committee was

---

99 The current treaty numbers date from that treaty.
100 K. Hughes, 'The 1996 Intergovernmental Conference and EU Enlargement' (1996) 72 *International Affairs* 1; A. Teasdale, 'The Politics of Qualified Majority Voting in Europe' (1996) *Political Quarterly* 101, 110–15.

damning.[101] It found poor financial controls, a culture of poor oversight and some cronyism by individual Commissioners. Faced with a damning vote in the European Parliament, the Commission resigned en masse in March 1999.[102] A new Commission was appointed immediately, but it led to the institution, which had historically been a mediator between Member States, being politically enfeebled. It also changed the nature of institutional debate at the IGC. Reform was no longer merely directed at preparing the Union for enlargement. It was equally directed at managing internal dissatisfaction with the performance of the EU institutions.

Despite its limited formal agenda, these wider objectives of preparation for enlargement and management of internal reform posed a real challenge for the IGC, for they had not been addressed satisfactorily by previous IGCs. Attempts to deal with them were disrupted by the attitude of the French government during the second half of 2000. As host of the summit, the French government was responsible for chairing treaty negotiations and proposing drafts. The French government made clear that it would use its position to redress the imbalance that had arisen in its view between the power of small states and that of the large states. In June 2000, in a manner that antagonised many smaller states, France decided to begin negotiations 'with a clean sheet', ignoring previous discussions. The Treaty of Nice was finally signed on 11 December 2000, after over ninety hours of acrimonious, direct negotiations between the Heads of Government.[103]

### (ii)   The Treaty of Nice and its aftermath

The Treaty of Nice was mainly concerned with the minutiae of institutional reform. It extended qualified majority voting into thirty-one new areas.[104] Most of these new areas were procedural, however, and were concerned with the appointment of EU officials. Beyond this, it addressed the composition of the institutions. Reforms were made to the Community judicature. It was agreed that there should be no more than one Commissioner from each Member State from 2005 onwards. The method for allocation of seats in the European Parliament was altered. Most contentiously, the distribution of votes between national governments within the Council for the purposes of QMV was recalculated and the voting rules were altered. Finally, the rules governing enhanced cooperation were relaxed to enable Member States to engage in this more easily.

Even within governmental confines, Nice was seen as a disappointment. The Treaties were now a confusing and in coherent mess. The political and legal

101 Committee of Independent Experts, *First Report on Allegations Regarding Fraud, Mismanagement and Nepotism in the European Commission*, 15 March 1999.
102 P. Craig, 'The Fall and Renewal of the Commission: Accountability, Contract and Administrative Organisation' (2000) 7 *ELJ* 98; L. Metcalfe, 'Reforming the Commission' (2000) 38 *JCMS* 817.
103 M. Gray and A. Stubb, 'The Treaty of Nice: Negotiating a Poisoned Chalice?' (2001) 39S *JCMS* 5.
104 The current legislative situation is discussed in chapter 4.

identity of the European Union, raised at Maastricht, had been left unaddressed and was left in a form of limbo. The Union had now a bewildering and confusing gamut of competencies, governed by an array of legislative procedures, producing a range of legal instruments, many with very different legal effects. There were thirty-eight combinations of 'possible voting modalities in the Council and participation opportunities of the European Parliament of which twenty-two are "legislative".[105] Such a thicket obscured the democratic values and mission of the Union.

The lack of vision was apparent to public opinion. In June 2001, the Irish voted 53.87 per cent against ratification of the Treaty of Nice. Turnout was low, at 34.79 per cent, and the central reason given for voting 'No' was lack of information about the Treaty of Nice. In short, whilst there did not seem to be many strong reasons to vote against the Treaty of Nice, the Union had reached an impasse where there did not seem to be many reasons to vote for it.[106] The matter was considered in June 2002 by all the national governments. A Declaration was added that nothing in the TEU affected Irish military neutrality, something that had been raised as a concern amongst a small number of Irish voters. On the basis of this Declaration, a second referendum was held in September 2002, and the Treaty of Nice was approved by 62.89 per cent of the vote.[107]

The loss of way was already clear to the governments at Nice. They announced that there would be yet another IGC in 2004. There was a realisation that incremental reform and last minute bargains were producing an unwieldy institutional settlement whose mission was increasingly unclear:

---

### 23. Declaration on the Future of the Union

3. Having thus opened the way to enlargement, the Conference calls for a deeper and wider debate about the future of the European Union. In 2001, the Swedish and Belgian Presidencies, in cooperation with the Commission and involving the European Parliament, will encourage wide-ranging discussions with all interested parties: representatives of national parliaments and all those reflecting public opinion, namely political, economic and university circles, representatives of civil society, etc. The candidate States will be associated with this process in ways to be defined . . .

5. The process should address, inter alia, the following questions: how to establish and monitor a more precise delimitation of powers between the European Union and the Member States, reflecting the principle of subsidiarity; the status of the Charter of Fundamental Rights of the European Union, a simplification of the Treaties with a view to making them clearer and better understood without changing their meaning; the role of national parliaments in the European architecture.

---

105  K. Gilland, 'Ireland's (First) Referendum on the Treaty of Nice' (2002) 40 *JCMS* 527.
106  The Treaty of Nice came into force on 2 February 2003.
107  The Treaty of Nice came into force on 2 February 2003.

The Declaration suggested two themes. First, the ideals and justifications underpinning the European Union had to be, if not reconsidered, then at least brought out more clearly. There should be clear answers to the question 'What is the European Union for?' Alongside this, there would need to be consideration of wide-ranging institutional reform, which could provide an institutional settlement that addressed these ideals and tasks more clearly. Such a large-scale reform required some overall ideal, which could be used both to justify a new institutional settlement and to stabilise and institutionalise debate and resources around some long-term goal. This ideal was constitutionalism, and it is to the constitutional debate that we turn, in chapter 2.

### Further reading

E. Balibar, *We, the People of Europe? Reflections on Transnational Citizenship* (Princeton, NJ, University of Princeton Press, 2003)

Z. Bauman, *Europe: An Unfinished Adventure* (Oxford, Polity, 2004)

G. Delanty, *Inventing Europe: Idea, Identity, Reality* (Basingstoke, Macmillan, 1995)

K. Dyson and K. Featherstone, *The Road to Maastricht* (Oxford, Oxford University Press, 1999)

J. Gillingham, *European Integration 1950–2003: Superstate or New Market Economy* (Cambridge, Cambridge University Press, 2003)

J. Le Goff, *The Birth of Europe* (Oxford, Blackwell, 2005)

D. Levy *et al.*, *Old Europe, New Europe, Core Europe: Transatlantic Relations after the Iraq War* (London, Verso, 2005)

M. Malmborg and B. Stråth (eds.), *The Meaning of Europe* (Oxford, Berg, 2002)

K. Middlemas, *Orchestrating Europe: The Informal Politics of European Union 1973–1995* (London, Fontana, 1995)

A. Milward, *The Reconstruction of Western Europe 1945–51* (London, Methuen, 1984)

A. Moravscik, *The Choice for Europe: Social Purpose and State Power from Messina to Maastricht* (Ithaca, NY, Cornell University Press, 1998)

D. O'Keeffe and P. Twomey (eds.), *Legal Issues of the Maastricht Treaty* (Chichester, John Wiley/Chancery, 1994)

D. O'Keeffe and P. Twomey (eds.), *Legal Issues of the Amsterdam Treaty* (Oxford, Hart, 1999)

A. Pagden (ed.), *The Idea of Europe: From Antiquity to the European Union* (Cambridge, Cambridge University Press, 2002)

F. Scharpf, *Governing in Europe: Effective and Democratic?* (New York, Oxford University Press, 1999)

C. Shore, *Building Europe: The Cultural Politics of European Integration* (London/New York, Routledge, 2000)

# 2

# Constitutionalism and the 'failure' of the Constitutional Treaty

| CONTENTS | |
|---|---|

## 1. Introduction

The previous chapter surveyed the development of the European Union by tracing the making of its various Treaties, summarising both the original Treaty of Rome and its subsequent amendments through the Single European Act, the Maastricht Treaty on European Union and the Treaties of Amsterdam and Nice. The story told in the previous chapter was not supposed to end with the unsatisfactory compromises and loose ends of the Treaty of Nice: it was supposed to end with a new Constitutional Treaty for the European Union. The Constitutional Treaty (CT) was drafted by a grand and grandly named 'Convention on the Future of Europe', which sat from early 2002 until the summer of 2003. Its Draft Constitutional Treaty (DCT) was initially rejected by the European Council, with Spain and Poland leading the objections, concerned as they were with the reduction of their voting power in the Council of Ministers that the DCT would have entailed.[1] After further deliberation and a change of government in

---

1 For the rules on 'qualified majority' voting in Council, see chapter 3.

Spain the Heads of State and Heads of Government meeting as the European Council in Rome finally signed the CT in October 2004. Ratification of the CT was a matter for each Member State. About ten Member States proposed to hold popular referenda; the remainder would allow ratification through national parliaments. The first of the referendums was held in Spain, where the CT was approved by 72 per cent of those who voted. However, in the next referendums, held in France (on 29 May 2005) and in the Netherlands (three days later, on 1 June 2005), the CT was roundly rejected, with 55 per cent voting against it in France and 62 per cent voting against it in the Netherlands. As a consequence of these referendum results the ratification process was halted and both the immediate and longer-term future of the CT remain, at the time of writing, unclear.[2]

The second part of this chapter explores the thinking behind the Constitutional Treaty and something of the reasons for its apparent failure. Why it was felt necessary to 'constitutionalise' the Treaties, what the 'constitutionalisation' of the Treaties would have meant in practice, the work of the Convention on the Future of Europe and the changes that would have been effected by the CT had it come into force, are all outlined and discussed later in this chapter. First, however, we need substantially to rewind – for the turn to constitutionalism and the CT cannot be understood without first having a sense of what EU law already provided by way of its own constitutional self-understanding. If one thing is clear it is that the constitutional law and theory of the European Union is not limited to the Constitutional Treaty.

## 2. Constitutional law and the Court of Justice

### (i)   *What makes the European Union different*

The European Union is not like other international organisations. This is true as a matter of political reality but, more importantly for our purposes, it is also true as a matter of law. What makes the EU different *politically* is the extent of its involvement in and influence over governance and regulation within nation-states. States frequently make Treaties – binding international agreements with other states – in which they promise to do or to refrain from doing certain things. They promise to cut carbon emissions by a particular date, or they undertake not to violate certain human rights standards, for example. Clearly, the European Union is politically more ambitious

---

2 The European Council declared on 18 June 2005 that 'We have noted the outcome of the referendums in France and the Netherlands. We consider that these results do not call into question citizens' attachment to the construction of Europe. Citizens have nevertheless expressed concerns and worries which need to be taken into account. Hence the need for us to reflect together on this situation . . . The recent developments do not call into question the validity of continuing with the ratification processes. We are agreed that the timetable for the ratification in different Member States will be altered if necessary in response to these developments and according to the circumstances in these Member States. We have agreed to come back to this matter in the first half of 2006 to make an overall assessment of the national debates and agree on how to proceed.'

than this: such Treaties are 'single issue', whereas the range of the EU's activities is far greater. The single issue may be important – environmental protection and human rights are not exactly trivial – but Treaties such as the Kyoto Protocol to the Framework Convention on Climate Change or the UN Convention against Torture are nonetheless narrowly focused on particular problems. The European Union's scope is broader. But it is not only the breadth of the European Union's coverage that marks it out as different: it is also its depth. The European Union is certainly not the only international organisation in the world, nor is it the only such in Europe. Both the United Nations and the Council of Europe, for example, cover an array of subject areas, just as the EU does. But neither is able to reach anything like as deeply into the way nation-states govern and regulate themselves and their societies as the European Union does. For sure, the United Nations may intervene when its Security Council considers that a state has violated a core provision of the UN Charter. Equally, UN aid and development agencies may frequently intervene in the developing world to help governments reduce poverty and tackle its desperate consequences. But a more developed state will not feel so much as the breath of the United Nations, never mind the military might wielded in its name by the members of its Security Council, on its territory without first having seriously breached the rules of international law. This is not so with the European Union. You cannot so much as shop, sell, buy, produce, manufacture, transport, distribute or trade in any goods or services anywhere in the European Union without being touched by EU law.

What makes the European Union different *legally* are the effects that EU law has in the domestic legal systems of its Member States. Such legal effects are the products of EU law itself, not the results of national law, and they arise because of certain key rulings of the European Union's highest court, the European Court of Justice, rather than by virtue of the Treaties. These legal effects of EU law make it significantly and substantially different from the ways in which international law ordinarily operates. The special legal effects of EU law are known as the doctrines of *supremacy* and *direct effect*. Both will be discussed in more detail in later chapters: supremacy in chapter 5 and direct effect in chapter 9. For now, all that is needed is an outline. The doctrines of supremacy and direct effect are the core principles of the European Union's constitutional law as it has been fashioned by the Court of Justice. Any attempt to understand constitutionalism in the European Union must commence with these doctrines.

The doctrine of supremacy is the claim that EU law is supreme over conflicting norms of national law, even over conflicting norms of national constitutional law. This is a claim not only in abstract legal theory seeking to locate European law in a hierarchy of legal norms, but in hard practice, containing as it does the injunction that all courts in the European Union (including national courts) must apply and give effect to EU law even where it conflicts with norms of national law. It is to be noted that it is not only the Treaties themselves that the Court of Justice has ruled to be supreme over domestic law: the doctrine extends also to secondary legislation made by the institutions under the Treaties.[3] The doctrine of direct effect provides that provisions of EU law may be invoked and relied on by parties in legal proceedings before national courts. The question of whether provisions of international law may be invoked and relied on by parties in legal proceedings before national courts is normally a matter for each national legal system to determine but, in 1963, the Court of Justice ruled in its seminal judgment in *Van Gend en Loos* that, for the European Union (as it now is; then the EEC), this was a matter for European law to determine, its determination being binding on all the Member States, no matter what their national legal systems would have provided.

### (ii)   Van Gend en Loos

*Van Gend en Loos* is arguably the Court's single most important judgment to date. In terms of the ways in which it tears European law away from the conventional model of international law it is both radical and revolutionary. The judgment is critical in the development of both supremacy and direct effect. As such, it is critical in the development of European constitutional law. The facts which gave rise to the legal dispute in the case were as follows. Van Gend en Loos was charged an import duty on chemicals imported from Germany by the Dutch authorities. It considered this to be in breach of Article 25 EC, which prohibited customs duties or charges having equivalent effect being placed on the movement of goods between Member States. It sought to invoke Article 25 EC in legal proceedings before a Dutch tax court, the Tariefcommissie. The question for the European Court of Justice was whether a party could invoke and rely on provisions of Community law in proceedings before a national court: in other words, does Community law have direct effect? The Court's answer was that it does – Van Gend en Loos could invoke and rely on Article 25 EC in proceedings before the Tariefcommissie:[4]

---

**Case 26/62 *Van Gend en Loos v Nederlandse Administratie der Belastingen* [1963] ECR 1**

The first question of the Tariefcommissie is whether Article [25] of the Treaty has direct application in national law in the sense that nationals of Member States may on the basis of this Article lay claim to rights which the national court must protect.

To ascertain whether the provisions of an international Treaty extend so far in their effects it is necessary to consider the spirit, the general scheme and the wording of those provisions.

The objective of the EEC Treaty, which is to establish a common market, the functioning of which is of direct concern to interested parties in the community, implies that this Treaty

---

3  See further on the various institutions, chapter 3; law-making by the institutions is discussed in chapter 4, the doctrine of supremacy is considered in detail in chapter 5.

4  Here we are concerned with what *Van Gend en Loos* tells us about European constitutional law in broad terms. The details of the Court's rulings as regards supremacy and as regards direct effect are considered more fully in chapters 5 and 9, respectively.

is more than an agreement which merely creates mutual obligations between the contracting States. This view is confirmed by the Preamble to the Treaty which refers not only to governments but to peoples. It is also confirmed more specifically by the establishment of institutions endowed with sovereign rights, the exercise of which affects Member States and also their citizens. Furthermore, it must be noted that the nationals of the States brought together in the Community are called upon to cooperate in the functioning of this Community through the intermediary of the European Parliament and the Economic and Social Committee.

In addition the task assigned to the Court of Justice under Article [234 EC[5]] the object of which is to secure uniform interpretation of the Treaty by national courts and tribunals, confirms that the States have acknowledged that Community law has an authority which can be invoked by their nationals before those courts and tribunals. The conclusion to be drawn from this is that the Community constitutes a new legal order of international law for the benefit of which the States have limited their sovereign rights, albeit within limited fields, and the subjects of which comprise not only Member States but also their nationals. Independently of the legislation of Member States, Community law therefore not only imposes obligations on individuals but is also intended to confer upon them rights which become part of their legal heritage. These rights arise not only where they are expressly granted by the Treaty, but also by reason of obligations which the Treaty imposes in a clearly defined way upon individuals as well as upon the Member States and upon the institutions of the Community.

Four aspects of this short passage should be noted for what they reveal about the constitutional perspective of the Court of Justice – even as early in the development of the Community as 1963. The first is its reference to the so-called 'teleological' reasoning of the Court, one of its most famous features. In the second paragraph of the extract the Court states that in answering the questions before it, 'it is necessary to consider the spirit, the general scheme and the wording' of the Treaty. The Court continues, in the next sentence, to refer to an 'objective' of the Treaty, namely, the establishment of the common market.[6] What these phrases make clear is that the Court of Justice does not consider its role to be one of interpreting only the bald text of the Treaties. For sure, the wording of the Treaties will play a role, sometimes a leading and determinative role, in the interpretation and development of European law, but the bare words of the Treaties will not be the Court's only source. The Court will also consider more amorphous sources, such as the 'spirit' and the 'general scheme' of the Treaties. Teleological reasoning is reasoning that is driven by a *telos*, or a goal. The Court first identifies what the goal of European law is and then interprets (in this case) Article 25 EC in conformity with that goal. Thus, in *Van Gend en Loos* the Court held that a goal of the European Community was to establish a common market, that the establishment of the common market entailed the conferral of rights on private parties such as Van Gend en Loos, who were engaged in the business of cross-border trade, and that such parties ought, therefore, to be able to invoke and

5 Article 234 EC (formerly Article 177 of the EC Treaty) is the provision of the Treaty that enables national courts and tribunals to refer questions of the interpretation of Community law to the Court of Justice. The relationships between national courts and the Court of Justice are considered in detail in chapter 7.
6 The Court did not invent this as an objective: it is enshrined in what is now Article 2 EC.

rely on provisions of Community law in proceedings before national courts. Making provisions of Community law directly effective enhances the ability of parties to have national courts enforce Community law, which in turn aids the establishment of the common market, realising a central goal of the European Community. Adopting a teleological approach to reasoning frees the Court of Justice from the confines of the text of the Treaties and allows the Court to supplement the law as it is found in the Treaties with a living jurisprudence, tailored to meet the European Union's changing needs, as the Court sees them. The Court has made use of its teleological approach in developing several constitutional principles: not only direct effect, but also the principles governing how national courts should interpret national law in the light of European law and the principles governing remedies in EU law.[7]

The second notable feature of this extract is the reference in the third paragraph 'not only to governments but to peoples'. In that paragraph the Court asserts that European law is 'more than' an agreement that creates mutual obligations between states. In this sense, European law is something more than simply *international law* – law that governs relations between states *inter se*. European law is something that, in addition to doing this, also governs relations between states and other parties – the peoples of Europe, the citizens of the Member States. In the conventional model of international law, the subjects of international law (that is, those who owe the obligations imposed by, and those who enjoy the rights conferred by, international law) are the states who sign and ratify international Treaties. Private parties, whether individuals or corporations such as Van Gend en Loos, are not normally subjects of international law. Individuals may indirectly benefit from the obligations entered into by states (cutting carbon emissions, for example) but they are not generally able to enforce those obligations in court. The major exception to this in international law is in the field of human rights, where individuals are under some Treaties able to enforce their rights before international human rights courts. This is true, for example, of the European Court of Human Rights (ECtHR) in Strasbourg.[8] The judgment of the Court of Justice in *Van Gend en Loos* makes the important constitutional statement that European law is not like conventional international law in that it recognises private parties, citizens and corporations, as well as Member States, as being its subjects.

But it is not just a question of European law recognising private parties as subjects – it is not only a question of what European law may do for private parties. It is a matter also of what private parties may do for European law. For there is a sense in this passage that the Court of Justice considers that European law derives something of

---

7 See Case 14/83 *Von Colson and Kamann v Land Nordrhein-Westfalen* [1984] ECR 1891 and Joined Cases C-6 and 9/90 *Francovich and Bonifaci v Italy* [1991] ECR I-5357. See further chapter 9.

8 This Court is not to be confused with the European Court of Justice, which is in Luxembourg. The sole task of the ECtHR is to enforce the European Convention on Human Rights. This international Treaty is not part of EU law. See further on human rights in the European Union, chapter 6.

its authority from the fact that the Treaties are proclaimed to be of the 'peoples' of Europe and not merely of the 'governments' of Europe. It is as if European law is seen by the Court to gain a degree of its legitimacy from the fact that it recognises private parties as subjects of its legal system. Somewhat abstract as it may seem, from a constitutional perspective this is a point of enormous significance. It suggests that at least something of the authority and legitimacy of European law is derived directly from the peoples of Europe rather than from the governments of the Member States. In other words, it suggests that the constituent power of the European Union resides at least in part in the peoples of Europe themselves. That constituent power may use the intermediary of the state to confer authority on the European Union, but it does not necessarily have to. The Court in *Van Gend en Loos* does not say this explicitly, but it clearly suggests that the founding myth of the European Union may be legally constructed so that the European Union may be seen as an agreement between the peoples of Europe that binds their governments, and not simply as an agreement between the governments of Europe that binds its peoples. Even if that is not in fact what happened when the EEC was created, it is what the Court of Justice suggests European law should regard as having happened.[9] Looking at European law in this way, it is not so much international law as *supra*national law.

The third aspect of the Court's judgment in *Van Gend en Loos* to note, closely related to the previous point, is the Court's statement that Community law is intended to confer 'rights' on 'individuals', rights which 'become part of their legal heritage' and which arise 'not only where they are expressly granted by the Treaty'. This reinforces the Court's view that there is a direct relationship between European law on the one hand and private parties on the other and that the Member States are not in complete control of that relationship. For sure, that relationship may *start* with what Member States write into the Treaties but what is 'expressly granted by the Treaty' is simply a starting point, and no more. What is determinative of the rights which private parties enjoy under European law is not the text of the Treaties but the interpretation of EU law given by the Court of Justice and, as we have seen, such interpretation relies not only on the wording of the Treaties but also on their spirit and their general scheme. Frequently, the rights conferred by EC law will be rights that private parties enjoy against the state in which they are based. *Van Gend en Loos* is a case in point – the right (to be able to import goods from another Member State free of customs duties) was to be enjoyed by the Van Gend en Loos company against the Dutch customs authorities. This right is expressly written into the Treaty: Article 25 EC. What the Court did in *Van Gend en Loos* was to supplement this express right with another, which was not written into the text of the Treaty: namely, the right to invoke and to rely on the protections conferred by Article 12 EEC in proceedings before the national court, enabling Article 12 EEC to be enforced against the Dutch authorities by the national court. This again is a clear break from the conventional model of international law.

---

9 These claims of sovereignty are explored further in chapter 5, where we also consider the responses of the Member States to the constitutional position sketched here by the Court of Justice.

Under European law, national courts are required to enforce European law, against the state, at the instigation of private parties.

The final feature to note is the Court's famous sentence in the middle of the final paragraph of the extract, which sums up much of what we have already said about the case: 'the Community constitutes a new legal order of international law for the benefit of which the States have limited their sovereign rights, albeit within limited fields'. Indeed. The EC *is* a new legal order. There has never before been anything quite like it anywhere in the world. Its claims to sovereignty are stronger than the claims of any other international law. The directly effective nature of much of its law marks it out as strikingly different from the norm. Its constitutional fundamentals of supremacy and direct effect mean that the European Union has encroached upon the sovereignty of its Member States more profoundly than any other international organisation has done:

---

**A. Moravcsik, 'The European Constitutional Compromise and the Neofunctionalist Legacy' (2005) 12 *Journal of European Public Policy* 349**

Over the past half-century the European Union has evolved until its policies and institutions are of a scope and significance without parallel among international organisations. Within Europe, tariffs, quotas, and most customs barriers have been all but eliminated. In regulatory areas such as environmental policy, competition, agricultural and industrial standardisation policy, the EU is a dominant regional and global force. Similarly the EU is a bona fide superpower in the area of global trade. The European Court of Justice has established the supremacy of EU law, the right of individuals to file suits, and constitutional review for consistency with the Treaty of Rome, which is binding through the near-uniform acceptance of its decisions by domestic courts.[10] Taken as a whole, its policies make Europe a 'quiet superpower' with power that matches or exceeds that of the US in almost every area except the deployment of high-intensity military force.

---

The last line of this extract is slightly misleading for, as Moravcsik goes on to discuss at more length later in his article, there is one other significant difference between the European Union and a state. This is that, unlike states, the European Union has very limited powers to tax and spend. As Moravcsik puts it, 'the EU, broadly speaking, does not tax, spend, implement, coerce or, in most areas, monopolise public authority. It has no army, police, and intelligence capacity, and a miniscule tax base'.[11] Nonetheless, the point remains: the European Union is no ordinary international organisation.

### (iii) Legitimacy of the 'new legal order'

The fact that the European Union is a new legal order means not only that, from the state's perspective, it is more invasive than are most international organisations.

---

10 'Near uniform acceptance' is a slight exaggeration: see chapter 5.

11 A. Moravcsik, 'The European Constitutional Compromise and the Neofunctionalist Legacy' (2005) 12 *JEPP* 349, 370.

It also and more importantly means that there is no precedent, no clear model on which the EU is based. The European Union is *sui generis* – of its own kind, peculiar and unique in the world. This is as true today as it has been throughout its fifty-year history. There is no map that sets the constitutional contours of the European Union. On the contrary, the European Union has been constitutionally making it up as it goes along; it has been doing this for half a century and it will, no doubt, continue to do so for the foreseeable future. European constitutionalism is, in this vein, dynamic and evolutionary. The fundamentals of supremacy and direct effect have not been significantly reworked since the early 1960s, but they have been supplemented, as human rights, notions of citizenship and principles of federalism, among other matters, have been added to the expanding matrix of European constitutional law.[12]

The fact that the European Union is constitutionally *sui generis* has caused problems as well as opportunities. While the EU has been relatively free to develop along lines that suit it, rather than being constrained by preconceived and ill-fitting models, a difficulty arises when it comes to seeking to explain what makes the European Union legitimate. The above analysis of *Van Gend en Loos* highlighted the various ways in which the Court of Justice sought in that case to distinguish the EU from ordinary international law. The European Union, the Court insisted, was a '*new* legal order of international law'. This means that the ways in which international organisations are usually legitimated are likely to be unavailable in the case of the EU. Yet, as the Court pointed out, and as the extract from Moravcsik's article amplifies, the European Union, for all its newness and exceptionalism, remains an 'order *of international law*'. The one thing the EU clearly is *not* is a state. This means, of course, that the ways in which states are usually legitimated are likewise likely to be unavailable in the case of the EU.

Yet an organisation with the range and depth of powers enjoyed by the European Union surely needs to be legitimated in some way. It would be a disaster for the European project if its supporters were unable convincingly to refute allegations that the EU was somehow illegitimate. That said, however, the lesson of our analysis of *Van Gend en Loos* is that finding an adequate theory of legitimacy for the European Union might not be straightforward. For that analysis shows how the legitimacy of the EU veers uncomfortably between the ill-fitting model of international organisations and the equally ill-fitting model of the state. International organisations derive their legitimacy from the fact that they are created through the voluntary acts of national governments (those governments, in a democracy, being accountable either to a parliament or directly to the people, or both). We can call this model 'Treaty-based legitimacy'. States derive their legitimacy from the constitutional compact that governs the legal and political relationship between the government and the governed. 'We the people' of the USA, the US Constitution proclaims, for example, 'do ordain

12 See, respectively, chapters 6 and 5.

and establish this Constitution',[13] so allowing the American people to be governed in accordance with the principles and procedures the Constitution then proceeds to lay down. We can call this model 'constitutional legitimacy'.

Neither model fits the European Union. The model of Treaty-based legitimacy does not fit the EU for precisely the reasons set out in the previous section: the Court of Justice has never retreated from the view it set out in its earliest jurisprudence that the Treaties are but one source of the EU's authority. Perhaps the central point in *Van Gend en Loos* and in the constitutionalism it has spawned, is that the authority of the European Union does not derive solely from its Treaties. Yet the model of constitutional legitimacy does not fit the EU either. For all the Court's rhetoric, it was not the peoples of Europe that founded the European Union: it was the governments of the Member States. Constitutional legitimacy is shorthand for what Dieter Grimm has described as 'the popular legitimation of the legal act constituting the Union, and the associated self-determination of Union citizens as to the form and content of their political unity'.[14] For as long as it is Member States and not citizens directly who 'determine the form and development of the Union', the model of constitutional legitimacy cannot be made to apply to the European Union, Grimm suggests.[15]

Four solutions to this legitimacy conundrum suggest themselves. First, the Court of Justice could reformulate its *Van Gend en Loos* conception of the constitutional basis of the European Union, returning the EU to the fold of regular international organisations, thereby allowing the model of Treaty-based legitimacy to fit. This solution has been commended by Trevor Hartley, who has argued that 'it is possible to rebuild the bridge between Community law and international law, a bridge that once existed but was deliberately destroyed in the early days of the Community by over-zealous judges and lawyers who believed they were laying the foundations of a new superstate, some kind of United States of Europe'.[16] Most EU lawyers would be inclined to agree (sometimes reluctantly but more often probably not) with Neil Walker's assessment that Hartley's views represent 'an obdurately defensive internationalism'.[17] In political terms Hartley's position has commended itself to few, other than to some of Britain's notoriously hard-line Euro-sceptic Conservatives.

At the other extreme lies the second solution, which entails a reformation of the European Union such that the model of constitutional legitimacy may fit it snugly. In other words, make the EU into a state. This solution was perhaps most famously advocated by Mancini, at the time a judge on the European Court of

---

13 These words are taken from the Preamble to the US Constitution (1787).

14 D. Grimm, 'Does Europe Need a Constitution?' (1995) 1 *ELJ* 282, 298.          15 *Ibid.*

16 T. Hartley, 'The Constitutional Foundations of the European Union' (2001) 117 *LQR* 225, 245.

17 N. Walker, 'Postnational Constitutionalism and the Problem of Translation' in J. Weiler and M. Wind (eds.), *European Constitutionalism Beyond the State* (Cambridge, Cambridge University Press, 2003) 29.

Justice, albeit that he made his arguments in his personal capacity and not from the bench:

> ### F. Mancini, 'Europe: the Case for Statehood' (1998) 4 *European Law Journal* 29, 39–42[18]
>
> [I]f, as promised by the Treaties . . . the march towards an ever closer union between the peoples of Europe is to continue and if, in the course of this march, the peoples of Europe are to preserve the constellation of values informing their ways of life, then Europe needs those well-tested institutions and procedures which only statehood can provide . . .
>
> Forced with their backs to the wall by a world economy which they cannot control, some of our nation states are at a loss to manage the aftermaths of the upheaval which globalisation has brought about without resorting to coercion. A European state, by contrast, were it only because of the broader vision and the single-mindedness which it could bring to the exercise of Europe's vast economic power, would probably be able to influence the global market . . .
>
> Forceful as this argument is, however, it is not the most cogent one which can be advanced in support of statehood for Europe. It is in fact based on the social rights of the European citizens, while something even more precious is at stake: their political rights or, in one word, democracy . . .
>
> Today's European Union presupposes democracy as a heritage of values and institutions shared by its Member States in all of which the representatives of the people control the action of the executive branch; but it is not itself democratic . . . [D]emocracy will elude Europe as long as its form of government includes rules and legitimises practices moulded on those of the international community.

In other words, the European Union needs to become a state, first in order for there to be any effective European influence over the global market, and secondly in order for there to be democracy in the EU. It is what remains of the intergovernmental diplomacy in the European Union that makes it undemocratic; the further it moves from the intergovernmental model of Treaty-based legitimacy and the more it embraces constitutional legitimacy, the more effective the European Union will be and the more democratic it will be able to become, according to Mancini. We shall return to both aspects of Mancini's argument later in this chapter.

The third solution rejects the notion that the European Union should be recast so that the models of Treaty-based or of constitutional legitimacy can be made to fit it and suggests, alternatively, that what is needed is a new model of legitimacy – a model that fits the EU as it is. Pleas of this nature are found over and again in the literature on the European Union. Yves Mény, for example, has argued that what is needed is 'a major intellectual shift, comparable to the one that took place at the time of the American and French Revolutions', in which 'new paradigms' are invented. He goes on immediately to lament that 'as nobody has yet been able to propose

---

18  See also Weiler's response: 'Europe: the Case Against the Case for Statehood' (1998) 4 *ELJ* 43. Weiler's views are considered below.

a credible and acceptable solution, progress can only result – at least for the time being – from adjustments, tentative explorations, trials and errors'.[19] Larry Siedentop has written in a similar vein, a central theme of his widely read book *Democracy in Europe* being to complain that, in comparison with the great constitutional thinkers (and doers) of the American founding, Madison and Hamilton especially, turn of the millennium Europeans have shown themselves to be 'such pygmies' when it comes to constitutional questions.[20] Modern Europeans have demonstrated considerable ingenuity in inventing new means of economic regulation, but have allowed the 'withering of the ambition of political thought' to proceed so far that 'sometimes it seems as if economic growth is the *only* criterion of public policy'.[21] Questions of liberty, democracy and constitutionalism have been overlooked, their importance denied, in the quest for that Holy Grail of the European Union – economic integration. This is all very well, but it does not take us very far. It is one thing to moan that someone needs to come up with a 'major intellectual shift' in the history of constitutional ideas, but it is quite another actually to do it. In the meantime, this solution turns out not to solve very much. As Mény concedes, until the new paradigm is invented the European Union will just have to carry on muddling along.[22]

The fourth solution seeks to use apparent adversity to European advantage. A number of scholars have suggested that 'muddling along', as we have just put it, is not what the European Union has been doing. On the contrary, they insist, the status of the EU as a sort of halfway-house mismatch between Treaty-based legitimacy and constitutional legitimacy is quite deliberate. Moreover, such scholars maintain, it is not only deliberate but is no less than the constitutional *genius* of the European Union that it has a blurred sense of the roots of its authority and a hazy notion of its legitimacy. It is precisely here that the constitutional strength of the EU lies, according to this view. Without doubt, the best known and most influential exponent of this view is Joseph Weiler, who has coined the term 'the principle of constitutional tolerance' to describe what he considers to be the European Union's unique model of legitimacy:

> ### J. Weiler, 'In Defence of the Status Quo: Europe's Constitutional Sonderweg' in J. Weiler and M. Wind (eds.), *European Constitutionalism Beyond the State* (Cambridge, Cambridge University Press, 2003) 18–22
>
> Europe was built on the ashes of the Second World War, which witnessed the most horrific alienation of those thought of as aliens, an alienation which became annihilation. What we should be thinking about is not simply the prevention of another such carnage: that is the easy part . . . More difficult is dealing at a deeper level with the source of these attitudes.

---

19 Y. Mény, '*De la Démocratie en Europe*: Old Concepts and New Challenges' (2002) 41 *JCMS* 1, 11.
20 L. Siedentop, *Democracy in Europe* (London, Penguin, 2000) xi.        21 *Ibid.* 37.
22 If nothing else, Mény's position shows that constitutional pragmatism is not the unique preserve of the British!

In the realm of the social, in the public square, the relationship to the alien is at the core of such decency. It is difficult to imagine something normatively more important to the human condition and to our multicultural societies.

There are, it seems to me, two basic strategies for dealing with the alien . . . One strategy is to remove the boundaries. It is the spirit of 'come, be one of us'. It is noble since it involves, of course, elimination of prejudice, of the notion that there are boundaries that cannot be eradicated. But the 'be one of us', however well intentioned, is often an invitation to the alien to be one of us, by being us. Vis-à-vis the alien, it risks robbing him of his identity. Vis-à-vis oneself, it may be a subtle manifestation of both arrogance and belief in my superiority as well as intolerance. If I cannot tolerate the alien, one way of resolving the dilemma is to make him like me, no longer an alien. This is, of course, infinitely better than the opposite: exclusion, repression, and worse. But it is still a form of dangerous internal and external intolerance.

The alternative strategy of dealing with the alien is to acknowledge the validity of certain forms of non-ethnic bounded identity but simultaneously to reach across boundaries. We acknowledge and respect difference, and what is special and unique about ourselves as individuals and groups; and yet we reach across differences in recognition of our essential humanity. What is significant in this are the two elements I have mentioned. On the one hand, the identity of the alien, as such, is maintained. One is not invited to go out and, say, 'save him' by inviting him to be one of us. One is not invited to recast the boundary. On the other hand, despite the boundaries which are maintained, and constitute the I and the Alien, one is commanded to reach over the boundary and accept him, in his alienship, as oneself. The alien is accorded human dignity. The soul of the I is tended to not by eliminating the temptation to oppress but by learning humility and overcoming it.

The European current constitutional architecture represents this alternative, civilizing strategy of dealing with the 'other'. Constitutional Tolerance is encapsulated in that most basic articulation of its meta-political objective in the preamble to the EC Treaty . . . : 'Determined to lay the foundations of an ever closer union among the *peoples* of Europe'. No matter how close the Union, it is to remain a union among distinct peoples, distinct political identities, distinct political communities. An ever closer union could be achieved by an amalgam of distinct peoples into one which is both the ideal and/or the de facto experience of most federal and non-federal states. The rejection by Europe of that One Nation ideal or destiny is . . . intended to preserve the rich diversity, cultural and other, of the distinct European peoples . . .

[I]n the Community, we subject the European peoples to constitutional discipline even though the European polity is composed of distinct peoples. It is a remarkable instance of civic tolerance to accept being bound by precepts articulated not by 'my people' but by a community composed of distinct political communities . . .

Constitutional actors in the Member States accept the European constitutional discipline not because, as a matter of legal doctrine, as is the case in the federal state, they are subordinate to a higher sovereignty and authority attaching to norms validated by the federal people, the constitutional demos. They accept it as an autonomous voluntary act, endlessly renewed on each occasion, of subordination, in the discrete areas governed by Europe, to a norm which is the aggregate expression of other wills, other political identities, other political communities. Of course, to do so creates in itself a different type of political community, one unique feature of which is that very willingness to accept a binding discipline which is rooted in and derives from a community of others. The Quebecois are told: in the name of the people of Canada, you are obliged to obey. The French or the Italians or the Germans are told: in the name of the peoples of Europe, you are invited to obey . . .

> This process operates also at Community level. Think of the European judge or the European public official who must understand that, in the peculiar constitutional compact of Europe, his decision will take effect only if obeyed by national courts, if executed faithfully by a national public official with whom he belongs to a national administration which claims from them a particularly strong form of loyalty and habit. This, too, will instil a measure of caution and tolerance.

Weiler's is, in many respects, an attractive argument, but as he has himself acknowledged, in making it he is fighting 'a rearguard and losing battle'.[23] For a range of reasons which we shall explore in the next section of this chapter, the tide of political opinion across Europe was, at the turn of the millennium, increasingly in favour of the view that the European Union needed a new constitutional settlement. It is the attempt to refound the European Union on the basis of a new constitutional agreement that we can now examine. We call this attempt 'the constitutional turn'.

### 3. The Constitutional Treaty

#### (i)  Explaining the constitutional turn

Talk of creating a constitution for the European Union began in the mid-1970s but it was at that time a stuttering discussion at best. There were some federalists, such as the then Italian Commissioner, Alfiero Spinelli, who even at that time saw the European Communities as an incipient federation:

> It [the European Community] is . . . a political entity with its own personality, superior in certain aspects to the States, possessing its own organisation, producing decisions which must be accepted by the Member States and respected by the citizens. Thus, that for which the States is a Treaty, is for the Community its own constitution; that which for the States is a revision of the Treaty is for the Community a revision of its constitution.[24]

These views were not influential. Instead, the origins of modern European constitutionalism lay more in the idea that the EC should be an autonomous organisation with its own values and procedures, which could not be rearranged at whim by the Member States. The Court of Justice, building on its earlier case law of *Van Gend en Loos*, thus moved in that period from describing the European Union as a 'new legal order of international law' to describing it as a new legal order *simpliciter*.[25] The other institutions used similar language. Leo Tindemans, author of the Tindemans

---

23 J. Weiler and M. Wind, 'Introduction' in J. Weiler and M. Wind (eds.), *European Constitutionalism Beyond the State* (Cambridge, Cambridge University Press, 2003) 4. This was his verdict in late 2002. Subsequent events might mean that his position is able to regain some ground.

24 A. Spinelli, *The European Adventure* (London, Knight, 1972) 26.

25 See J. Weiler and U. Haltern, *The Autonomy of the Community Legal Order: Through the Looking Glass*, Jean Monnet Working Paper 10/96.

Report, the most influential report on reform of the Community institutions during the period, stated that:

> To achieve European Union we must henceforth be able to find in the different European institutions the authority needed to define a policy, the efficiency needed for common action and the legitimacy needed for democratic control. It also implies that the institutions should have that coherence of vision and of action which alone will allow them to define and then pursue a policy.[26]

All these debates were concerned with organisational reform. It was only following the first direct elections of the European Parliament that there was a move to more explicit constitutional language. In the 1980s and 1990s the European Parliament twice put forward proposals for a European Constitution, the first drafted by Spinelli, who was by then an MEP.[27] The Court of Justice followed this lead when in 1986 it described the EC Treaty for the first time as a 'constitutional charter'.[28]

Significant though these developments were, a more decisive moment came with a speech by Joschka Fischer, the German Foreign Minister, at the Humboldt University in Berlin in 2000. Fischer's speech was concerned with a number of matters. He considered that European integration had to have a '*finalité*', an end point, but that, at the moment, it was a very imperfect project. Most of the European Union's citizens, he claimed, were antipathetic to it; it had failed to make a mark on international affairs; and its political structures were not ready for enlargement:

> These three reforms – the solution of the democracy problem and the need for fundamental reordering of competences both horizontally, i.e. among the European institutions, and vertically, i.e. between Europe, the nation-state and the regions – will only be able to succeed if Europe is established anew with a constitution. In other words: through the realisation of the project of a European Constitution centred around basic, human and civil rights, an equal division of powers between the European institutions and a precise delineation between European and nation-state level. The main axis for such a European Constitution will be the relationship between the Federation and the nation-state.[29]

A number of Heads of Government picked up on this theme. Within two months Jacques Chirac, the French President, had also talked of a 'first European Constitution'. Tony Blair, the British Prime Minister, suggested that there should be a new

---

26  This is quoted from M. Burgess, *Federalism and European Union: The Building of Europe 1950–2000* (London, Routledge, 2000) 111. On this subject more generally, see *ibid.* ch. 4.

27  Draft Treaty on European Union, OJ 1984 C77/33; the Herman Report (1994), EP Docs. A3/31/94 and A3/64/94.

28  Case 294/83 *Parti écologiste 'Les Verts' v European Parliament* [1986] ECR 1339, para. 23.

29  'From Confederacy to Federation: Thoughts on the Finality of European Integration', speech by Joschka Fischer at the Humboldt University in Berlin, 12 May 2000: see www.auswaertiges-amt.de/www/de/infoservice/download/pdf/reden/redene/r000512b-r1008e.pdf

statement of principles about the Union. And in June 2000 Paavo Lipponen, the Finnish Prime Minister, suggested that a special Convention be established to launch a 'constitutionalisation process'.[30]

We saw in the previous chapter that, at the end of the rather unsatisfactory Nice Intergovernmental Conference (IGC), a Declaration was made on the future of the European Union. The Declaration called for a wide-ranging debate to reconsider a range of constitutional issues. Where should the line be drawn between the powers of the European Union and those reserved to the various Member States? Should the Treaties include a Bill of Rights for the EU? And what should be the role of national parliaments in the European architecture? These were among the issues specifically referred to in that Declaration. A year after Nice, in December 2001, the Member States meeting at Laeken in Belgium decided that a sort of constitutional convention, known as the 'Convention on the Future of Europe', would be established to discuss these issues further and to draw up a document that could be used as the basis for discussion at the next IGC, scheduled for 2004. The Laeken Declaration is a critical statement in the shaping of the debates about the European Union's constitutional order and needs to be set out at some length. As we shall see, it identifies four sets of reasons that help to explain why the EU took a turn for the constitutional at the opening of the twenty-first century:

> **European Council, Laeken Declaration on the Future of the European Union (2001)**
>
> *Europe at a Crossroads*. The European Union is a success story. For over half a century now, Europe has been at peace. Along with North America and Japan, the Union forms one of the three most prosperous parts of the world. As a result of mutual solidarity and fair distribution of the benefits of economic development, moreover, the standard of living in the Union's weaker regions has increased enormously . . . Fifty years on, however, the Union stands at a crossroads, a defining moment in its existence. The unification of Europe is near. The Union is about to expand to bring in more than ten new Member States, predominantly Central and Eastern European . . . [This is] a real transformation clearly calling for a different approach from fifty years ago, when six countries first took the lead.
>
> *The Democratic Challenge facing Europe*. At the same time, the Union faces twin challenges, one within and the other beyond its borders. Within the Union, the European institutions must be brought closer to its citizens. Citizens undoubtedly support the Union's broad aims, but they do not always see a connection between those goals and the Union's everyday action. They want the European institutions to be less unwieldy and rigid and, above all, more efficient and open. Many also feel that the Union should involve itself more with their particular concerns, instead of intervening, in every detail, in matters by their nature better left to Member States' and regions' elected representatives. This is even perceived by some

---

30 P. Norman, *The Accidental Constitution: The Story of the European Convention* (Brussels, Gazelle, 2003) 11–24. For academic comment on the Fischer statement see C. Joerges, Y. Meny and J. Weiler (eds.), *What Kind of Constitution for What Kind of Polity? Responses to Joschka Fischer* (Florence, Robert Schuman Centre, 2000).

as a threat to their identity. More importantly, however, they feel that deals are all too often cut out of their sight and they want better democratic scrutiny.

*Europe's New Role in a Globalised World.* Beyond its borders, in turn, the European Union is confronted with a fast-changing, globalised world. Following the fall of the Berlin Wall, it looked briefly as though we would for a long while be living in a stable world order, free from conflict, founded upon human rights. Just a few years later, however, there is no such certainty. September 11 has brought a rude awakening. The opposing forces have not gone away: religious fanaticism, ethnic nationalism, racism and terrorism are on the increase, and regional conflicts, poverty and underdevelopment still provide a constant seedbed for them . . .

Now that the Cold War is over and we are living in a globalised, yet also highly fragmented world, Europe needs to shoulder its responsibilities in the governance of globalisation. The role it has to play is that of a power resolutely doing battle against all violence, all terror and all fanaticism, but which also does not turn a blind eye to the world's heartrending injustices. In short, a power wanting to change the course of world affairs, in such a way as to benefit not just the rich countries but also the poorest. A power seeking to set globalisation within a moral framework, in other words to anchor it in solidarity and sustainable development.

*The Expectations of Europe's Citizens.* The image of a democratic and globally engaged Europe admirably matches citizens' wishes. There have been frequent calls for a greater EU role in justice and security, action against cross-border crime, control of migration flows and reception of asylum seekers and refugees from far-flung war zones. Citizens also want results in the fields of employment and combating poverty and social exclusion, as well as in the field of economic and social cohesion. They want a common approach on environmental pollution, climate change and food safety, in short, all transnational issues which they instinctively sense can only be tackled by working together . . .

At the same time, citizens also feel that the Union is behaving too bureaucratically in numerous other areas. In co-ordinating the economic, financial and fiscal environment, the basic issue should continue to be proper operation of the internal market and the single currency, without this jeopardising Member States' individuality . . . What citizens . . . expect is more results, better responses to practical issues and not a European superstate or European institutions inveigling their way into every nook and cranny of life.

In short, citizens are calling for a clear, open, effective, democratically controlled Community approach, developing a Europe which points the way ahead for the world. An approach that provides concrete results in terms of more jobs, better quality of life, less crime, decent education and better health care. There can be no doubt that this will require Europe to undergo renewal and reform.

As we saw in the previous chapter, by the end of the Nice IGC it had become clear to everybody that the European Union had lost its way. The Laeken Declaration signals the way in which the Member States intended to revive the Union – to rescue it from the doldrums of Nice. Four key themes for the future of the European Union can be seen to underpin the Declaration. These are: the European Union's success to date, its enlargement, its democratic challenge, and its roles in and policies for a globalised world. Each of these themes reveals a set of reasons that, together, explain why it was felt necessary to embark on a process of 'constitutionalising' the Treaties. Accordingly, we will use these four themes to structure our discussion of the lead-up to the Constitutional Treaty.

## (a)   Success

The first theme is that of the European Union's success to date. The opening statement of the extract above is that the 'European Union is a success story'. Thus, the first and immediate suggestion is that, no matter how difficult and disappointing the Nice IGC, we should by no means give up on the European project. It may readily be accepted that the European Union has, overwhelmingly, succeeded in delivering its core objectives. There has been an unbroken and unprecedented period of peace between its Member States – one has only to compare the first fifty years of the twentieth century with its second fifty years to appreciate just how significant an achievement this is. Peace has been accompanied by what is, in historical terms, an astonishing degree of economic and, indeed, monetary union. It would not be an exaggeration to say that, on these bases, the European Union has a strong claim to being the most successful experiment in transnational governance that the world has seen in the modern era. Even if the turn of the millennium was not the brightest period in the short history of the European Union, there is no reason to despair at its future prospects, or so the Laeken Declaration claims.

And yet there is another sense in which we may be more sceptical about claims of the EU's success. From a *constitutional* point of view, how successful has the European Union been? For sure, the EU has helped to secure peace in (Western) Europe and it has established deep economic integration among its Member States but, since Maastricht, the European Union has claimed to be a political union as well as an economic one. To what extent have its *political* ambitions been realised? Is it not the case that the Community's economic successes have been enjoyed *despite* the political and constitutional structures and values of the EU rather than because of them? It is not only that intellectuals and commentators have struggled to come up with convincing accounts of the European Union's legitimacy: it is also that the last fifteen years have been peppered with popular, political and legal challenges to the authority of the EU – challenges that in some cases seem to have gone largely unanswered. As we saw in the previous chapter, the Maastricht Treaty was initially rejected in a referendum in Denmark, as the Treaty of Nice was initially rejected by referendum in Ireland. Both results were reversed by subsequent votes, but the initially negative results surely suggest at least a degree of popular resistance to ever closer union. The ignominious resignation of the Santer Commission in 1999, after a report of independent experts stated of it that 'it is becoming difficult to find anyone who has even the slightest sense of responsibility',[31] was a shocking moment that revealed the depths of mismanagement and maladministration to which the Commission had sunk. And the German Constitutional Court, clearly unhappy about the way in which successive Treaty reforms had sought to push integration forward without it being accompanied by adequate constitutional standards, checks and balances, laid down

---

31 Committee of Independent Experts, *First Report on Allegations of Fraud, Mismanagement and Nepotism in the European Commission* (15 March 1999), para. 9.4.25. See further on this, chapter 8.

in its judgment in the *Brunner* case a series of markers seeking to limit the growth of European power. With these events in mind, it is difficult unambiguously to accept the Laeken Declaration's statement that the European Union is a success story. From a political or a constitutional point of view, its success has been mixed.

## (b)   Enlargement

The second theme is enlargement. As we saw in the previous chapter, the development of the European Union can be marked out as two, sometimes related, series of events: Treaty amendments on the one hand (Rome, the Single European Act, Maastricht, Amsterdam, Nice) and gradual expansion of membership on the other (the founding Six, growing to nine, ten, twelve, fifteen and, with effect from 2004, twenty-five Member States). The most recent enlargement, from fifteen to twenty-five, was, in all sorts of ways, the most significant to date. Not only was it the biggest, with ten new Member States joining simultaneously, but it was also the most ambitious in terms of the nature of the new Members. Eight of the ten are Eastern European states from the former communist and Soviet bloc. The symbolic, even ideological, importance of this can be seen in the Laeken Declaration, with its reference to the 'unification of Europe' being 'near'. A function of the European Union in the post-Cold War world, it seems, is to facilitate the unification of a continent that has been divided for almost all of its past. In the 1950s and 1960s, the project was to accommodate the formerly fascist nations of Germany and Italy into the European mainstream. In the 1980s, the European Union expanded to welcome the Mediterranean nations of Greece, Spain and Portugal into the fold, all of which had only shortly before their accession emerged from periods of dictatorship. Now the EU's mission is to accommodate the formerly communist nations of Central and Eastern Europe.

As well as being ideologically important, the 2004 enlargement was also significant in terms of its sheer size. Never before had as many as ten new Member States joined at once. The number of Member States has direct consequences for the composition of the various institutions of the European Union – the Commission, the Council and the European Parliament.[32] Traditionally, for example, each Member State has had at least one of its nationals on the Commission. While this was relatively unproblematic in a Union of fifteen, it is not obvious that there is an administrative need for as many as twenty-five Commissioners. Similarly in the European Parliament: each Member State elects Members of the European Parliament (MEPs) in proportion to their various populations. But just how big should the European Parliament be allowed to become before it is simply too big to function cohesively as a single chamber? These matters are considered in more depth in chapter 3. For now, all that needs to be grasped is a sense that the enlargement of the European Union required a serious rethink about its institutional structure: a central question for any constitution.

As with the theme of success, however, a critical note should be sounded. We may readily acknowledge that enlargement poses questions for the detail of institutional

---

32 See, in more detail, chapter 3.

structure. We may even concede that the questions may sometimes be politically very difficult – Member State governments are not likely to want to give up the expectation that there will be one Commissioner from each Member State without getting something back in return, for example. But it is less evident that enlargement necessarily requires any deeper constitutional rethinking than this. Important as institutional restructuring may be, it is not the same thing as writing a new constitution. Yet the Laeken Declaration suggests that enlargement does require more than mere institutional restructuring. Enlargement is described as bringing about a 'real transformation' that 'clearly call[s] for a different approach'. This is curious. Beyond the institutional rejigging required by the growth in the European Union's membership, what is it about the EU that needs now to be done differently? The curiosity is deepened when it is remembered that institutional restructuring is one of the things that the Amsterdam and Nice IGCs did manage to achieve. For all their other faults, even the least ambitious IGCs have managed this task. So why turn to an extraordinary Convention when the usual means of the IGC has shown itself to be capable of delivering, on this issue at least?

In a valuable analysis, Neil Walker reveals something of the answer. The reality, he suggests, was that a 'debate on institutional reform was unavoidable regardless of enlargement' and that 'enlargement merely served to increase its urgency'.[33] This is true not only for the detailed debate on institutional reform: it is true for the entirety of the constitutional turn. The coupling of enlargement and constitutionalisation was a diplomatic device, almost a smokescreen, if you like. It is not that enlargement required the European Union to embark upon a constitutional rethink. The EU needed to do this in any event (for the reasons, principally, to which we are about to turn). Enlargement offered a convenient cover: it was much easier for the Member States to say that the European Union needed a new constitution because of enlargement than it would have been for them to say that the EU needed a new constitution because its old one was not very good. In this sense, 'enlargement concentrated the minds on [the] vital issue of constitutional reform . . . when agreement on the terms of the debate might otherwise have been unavailable'.[34] Enlargement was a pretext, and an enormously valuable one, but it was not the true reason for the European Union's constitutional turn.[35]

(c)   The democratic challenge

If the first two themes of the Laeken Declaration were meant by its authors to be positive for the European Union, the next two are markedly more cautious. Indeed, the Declaration refers to them as the 'twin challenges' that face the EU. The first of

33 N. Walker, 'Constitutionalising Enlargement, Enlarging Constitutionalism' (2003) 9 *ELJ* 365, 375.
34 Walker, *ibid.* 377.
35 Weiler has put it more bluntly: 'there is something, indeed more than one thing, deceptive in the juxtaposition of enlargement and Constitution'. See J. Weiler, 'A Constitution for Europe? Some Hard Choices' (2002) 40 *JCMS* 563, 564.

these – our third theme – is the challenge of democracy. The Laeken Declaration is replete with references to problems, or perceived problems, with European governance: the institutions of the European Union must be 'brought closer to its citizens', who want the EU to be 'less unwieldy and rigid' and 'more efficient and open'. Similarly, the European Union's constant intervention in matters of detail that would be better left for the various Member States is perceived to be a threat to the very identity of particular states, regions or groups of individuals. There are also references to how certain matters should be left to people's nationally or regionally 'elected representatives' and not run directly from Brussels. The broad aims of the European Union are generally supported, we are told, but there is apparently little affection for its detailed workings, for its everyday action.

These references touch on two matters that have been central to the way the EU has been criticised in recent years. We may refer to these by their familiar labels: 'competence creep' on the one hand and the 'democratic deficit' on the other. A little more can be said here about both of these. 'Competence creep' is a term frequently used to describe the way in which the European Union is perceived to have extended the reach of its powers and, particularly, its law-making powers (also called the EU's competences). Certain Member States and regional authorities within Member States (most notably the *Länder* – the German regions) have become concerned that the European Union has trespassed too far into law-making territory that ought properly to be reserved to national or domestic authorities. A key component of this complaint is a concern that EU law, as it is currently structured, is unable to act as an effective brake on the EU's competence creep and that, as such, significant law reform in this area is required. Consideration of competence creep brings us into the stormy waters of federalism in the European Union – a key theme, it will be recalled, of Joschka Fischer's Humboldt speech in 2000. Federalism is the constitutional doctrine that divides power between the centre and others. The question of what the EU should be responsible for and what should be left for the Member States is, in constitutional terms, a question of federalism. The topic is a big one and is considered in detail in chapter 5.

'Democratic deficit' is a term coined in 1979 by the British political scientist (and campaigner for liberal constitutional reform) David Marquand.[36] Democratic *deficit* is a wonderfully apt economic term to describe a feature of what was then the European Economic Community. The idea is simple: given the extent of its legislative and executive powers, the institutions of the European Union are insufficiently democratic in character. This is an argument which closely relates to some of the issues concerned with the EU's legitimacy that we considered in the previous section of this chapter: Mancini, for example, referred explicitly to democracy in Europe as part of his 'case for

---

36 See D. Marquand, *Parliament for Europe* (London, Cape, 1979). For a short and valuable appraisal of the argument, see Y. Mény, '*De la Démocratie en Europe*: Old Concepts and New Challenges' (2002) 41 *JCMS* 1.

Statehood'.[37] The democratic deficit argument is a criticism of the European Union which is often understood to refer principally to the lack of *representative* democracy in the *law-making* institutions of the Union. While this is one part of the argument about the democratic deficit, however, the problem should not be seen as being confined either to representative democracy or to law-making alone.[38] Let us explain. Democracy as a modern political theory comprises many elements. One such is, of course, that political decisions should be taken by those who are elected to do so by a people or, in Greek, a *demos*. In a democracy we elect representatives to make political decisions on our behalf. And just as we may elect our representatives so too may we unelect them – remove them from office – if we choose to do so. But democracy, properly understood, requires more than mere elections and representatives. It also requires decision-making procedures to be open and responsive to popular or public participation. Participatory democracy enables citizens and interest groups actively to take part in policy-making that affects their interests. For some, democracy also requires that decisions are made deliberatively – on the basis of reasoned discussion – and that decisions and the reasons for political decisions are made transparent and open. As well as comprising many elements, democracy is a theory of government that applies to a variety of bodies. It is not only legislation (or law-making) which should be performed democratically, but also the administration and execution of the laws – the tasks that traditionally are for the executive, or government, rather than for the legislature. Some go further and insist that adjudication should likewise be conducted democratically, that prosecutors and judges should be, if not directly then at least indirectly, accountable democratically. This, however, is a position more widespread in the USA than it is in Europe. In short, then, democracy in Europe may be seen as requiring that both legislative and executive bodies are representative, participatory, deliberative and transparent. To the extent that the institutions of the European Union fail to meet these criteria, it may be said that there is a democratic deficit in the EU – or so the argument runs.[39]

It is important to appreciate that whether the European Union really suffers from a democratic deficit has always been sharply contested. One issue is what the appropriate comparator should be. When assessing democracy in the EU should we compare the Union with other international organisations (the United Nations, for example) or with nation-states? When compared with the United Nations the EU may seem considerably more democratic than it might if compared with certain nation-states. Think, for example, about the composition and democratic accountability of the

---

37 See p. 54.
38 The democratic deficit as it relates to law-making in the European Union is considered in more detail in chapter 4.
39 Douglas-Scott similarly sees the democratic deficit as comprising four main elements: ineffective parliamentary oversight of executive action, secretive decision-making, lack of transparency and inadequate citizen participation: see S. Douglas-Scott, *Constitutional Law of the European Union* (London, Longman, 2002) 131.

UN Security Council or even of the UN General Assembly. Advocates of the democratic deficit argument may respond to the effect that it would be inappropriate to compare the European Union with other international organisations, as the range and depth of the EU's regulatory powers is clearly and substantially greater. Others have objected that within the democratic deficit argument there is an inescapable, if implicit, comparison being made between the European Union and nation-states and that this comparison is just as inappropriate. The most famous articulation of this view came in an important essay by Andrew Moravcsik, one of the USA's leading commentators on the EU.

## A. Moravcsik, 'In Defence of the "Democratic Deficit": Reassessing Legitimacy in the European Union' (2002) 40 *Journal of Common Market Studies* 603, 605, 607–9, 613

[I]f we adopt reasonable criteria for judging democratic governance, then the widespread criticism of the EU as democratically illegitimate is unsupported by the existing empirical evidence. At the very least, this critique must be heavily qualified. Constitutional checks and balances, indirect democratic control via national governments, and the increasing power of the European Parliament are sufficient to ensure that EU policy-making is, in nearly all cases, clean, transparent, effective and politically responsive to the demands of European citizens . . .

Much is . . . excluded from the EU policy agenda. Absent concerns include taxation and the setting of fiscal priorities, social welfare provision, defence and police powers, education policy, cultural policy, non-economic civil litigation, direct cultural promotion and regulation, the funding of civilian infrastructure, and most other regulatory policies unrelated to cross-border economic activity . . . Even within the core functions of the EU, governments are allowed to exempt themselves to maintain high regulatory protection . . . or to act unilaterally where the EU has not effectively legislated . . .

It is not coincidental that the policies absent from the EU's policy portfolio – notably social welfare provision, defence, education, culture and infrastructure – require high government expenditure. The ability to tax and spend is what most strikingly distinguishes the modern European state from its predecessors, yet the EU's ability to tax is capped at about 2–3 per cent of national and local government spending (1.3 per cent of GDP) and is unlikely to change soon. The disbursement of these funds, moreover, is explicitly directed to a small range of policies – the common agricultural policy, structural funding and development aid – that must periodically be renewed by unanimous consent of the Member States. The EU is thereby rendered a 'regulatory polity' – a polity with legal instruments but little fiscal capacity . . .

[Further,] the EU implements very few of its own regulations. With the exceptions of monetary policy, competition policy and the conduct of, though not ultimate control over, external trade negotiations, the powers of the EU to administer and implement are, in fact, exceptionally weak . . . Except in a few areas, the task of legally or administratively implementing EU regulations falls instead to national parliaments and administrations . . .

Of course the lack of administrative clout, and even perhaps of fiscal discretion, would be of less consequence if the EU technocracy could act unhampered by procedural constraints. Yet the EU's ability to act, even in those areas where it enjoys clear competence, is constrained by institutional checks and balances, notably the separation of powers, a multi-level structure of decision-making and a plural executive. This makes arbitrary action (indeed, any action) difficult . . .

Accordingly, the EU has developed over the past two decades only by focusing on core areas of exceptionally broad consensus . . .

It might be objected that the EU sometimes . . . relies overly on autonomous technocrats in the Commission or constitutional court judges to resolve essentially political questions involving the apportionment of cost, benefit and risk. Yet there is little that is distinctively 'European' about [this] pattern . . . The late twentieth century has been a period of the 'decline of parliaments' and the rise of courts, public administrations and the 'core executive' . . .

The critical point for the study of the EU is this: within the multi-level governance system prevailing in Europe, EU officials . . . enjoy the greatest autonomy *in precisely those areas* – central banking, constitutional adjudication, criminal and civil prosecution, technical administration and economic diplomacy – in which many advanced industrial countries, including most of the Member States of the EU, insulate themselves from direct political contestation. The apparently 'undemocratic' nature of the EU as a whole is largely a function of this selection effect.

Moravcsik goes on to note that the apparent lack of citizen participation in EU policy-making is also directly connected to the selection of subject-areas governed at the EU level. He suggests that 'Of the five most salient issues in most west European democracies – health care provision, education, law and order, pension and social security policy, and taxation – none is primarily an EU competence'.[40]

Moravcsik attempts in this essay to weave together a series of arguments explaining why, in his view, the apparent democratic deficit in the European Union is of less concern than commentators such as Marquand and Mancini would have us believe. For Moravcsik, ample checks and balances are already in place in the European architecture, particularly considering that, for all its powers, the EU still falls far short of what a nation-state can do; it has very little coercive power and it does not tax and spend. Rule by technocrats and constitutional court judges may be a prominent feature of European governance, but it is not distinctive to the EU. Many states similarly rely on bureaucrats and experts, insulated from regular processes of democratic accountability, particularly in the sorts of areas in which the European Union acts. Any lack of citizen involvement in – even interest in – European affairs may be explained, Moravcsik suggests, through the fact that the issues that polls consistently reveal to be of principal concern to voters (health care, education, law and order, social security and taxation) continue to be governed by states and not by the EU.

This is a measured and powerful critique, which should be taken seriously. Yet surely the Member States were right to draw attention in their Laeken Declaration to the fact that, for all Moravcsik's objections, citizens throughout the European Union routinely perceive there to be deep problems with the lack of democracy in the way the

---

40 A. Moravcsik, 'In Defence of the "Democratic Deficit": Reassessing Legitimacy in the European Union' (2002) 40 *JCMS* 603, 615.

EU conducts its business. For sure we may concede that the EU is not commensurate with a nation-state. For sure we may agree that the EU is not democratically hopeless; there are degrees of accountability and there are, of course, periodic elections (albeit elections from which no government is formed and, as a result of which, no government ever falls). But, equally, there remains great force in the critique Moravcsik seeks to address. The European Union does *suffer* from its lack of effective parliamentary oversight of executive action, from its secretive decision-making, from its lack of transparency and from its inadequate citizen participation.[41] These issues do contribute to the EU's difficulties in seeking a persuasive account of its own legitimacy. The Member States did the EU a tremendous service at Laeken in recognising that there is a *perceived* democratic deficit in the EU and, even more so, in citing this as an impediment to the continued success of the Union. Addressing the various elements of the democratic deficit (and, indeed of the competence creep to which it is related) was a large part of the reason for the European Union's constitutional turn.

### (d)   Roles and policies

The fourth theme of the Laeken Declaration (and the second of the European Union's 'twin challenges') concerns the EU's role in a globalised world. What should the EU do, for example, in the face of the challenge of the international terrorism unleashed in New York and elsewhere on 11 September 2001, only three months before Laeken and therefore fresh in the memory at the time of the Declaration? A range of issues is referred to in the Declaration: the European Union's role in 'justice and security', its action against 'cross-border crime' and its 'control of migration' among them. What powers should the EU possess in these fields? And what policies should it adopt? How should the common foreign and security policy, the EU's second pillar introduced at Maastricht, be developed? And what should become of police and judicial cooperation in criminal matters and of the area of freedom, security and justice that the EU has laboured to take forward?

It is not just a question of security policy. The Laeken Declaration refers in numerous places to other, critical, policy matters for the European Union. It refers, for example, to its social policies and to its roles in promoting international trade and development. There are references to 'combating poverty and social exclusion', to 'solidarity and sustainable development', to 'environmental pollution' and 'climate change' and, perhaps most interestingly of all, to being 'a power wanting to change the course of world affairs in such a way as to benefit not just the rich countries but also the poorest'. All these, it seems, are ambitions which the Member States would like the EU, building on its past successes, to work towards. The political content of these goals is striking. An obvious contrast is with the USA of George W. Bush. While

---

41 See Douglas-Scott, above n. 39.

in the context of security and international terrorism the sense is that the European Union needs to work with the USA, in the contexts of combating poverty, promoting sustainable development and preventing or reducing environmental damage, the priorities for the EU are quite different from, and not necessarily compatible with, those of the current American administration. It is as if the Member States are seeking to promote the European Union as an international power that can complement and in some areas do better than the USA. Taking the best of the European welfare state and seeking to strengthen it within the EU while promoting its adoption in the developing world is being strongly signalled here as a key component of the EU's future mission, it seems. This is an aspect of Mancini's argument for a European state, but it has been most forcefully articulated as a reason underpinning the constitutional turn by the influential German philosopher and commentator, Jürgen Habermas.

### J. Habermas, 'Why Europe Needs a Constitution' (2001) 11 *New Left Review* 5, 6, 12, 14

[T]he challenge before us is not to *invent* anything but to *conserve* the great democratic achievements of the European nation-state, beyond its own limits. These achievements include not only formal guarantees of civil rights, but levels of social welfare, education and leisure that are the precondition of both an effective private autonomy and of democratic citizenship . . .

A European constitution would enhance the capacity of the Member States of the Union to act jointly, without prejudicing the particular course and content of what policies it might adopt. It would constitute a necessary, not a sufficient condition for the kind of policies some of us are inclined to advocate. To the extent that European nations seek a certain re-regulation of the global economy, to counterbalance its undesired economic, social and cultural consequences, they have a reason for building a stronger Union with greater international influence . . .

From this perspective, the European project can be seen as a common attempt by the national governments to recover in Brussels something of the capacity for intervention that they have lost at home.

Here we have the final set of reasons for the European Union's constitutional turn. As this last theme amply demonstrates, the EU is not short of ambition! The Laeken Declaration envisages a Europe that can represent itself to the world as 'the continent of humane values', no less. The single market may have been established, but there remains an enormous amount for the EU to do, ranging from security and international justice to environmental development and ending world poverty. The European Union has ambitions, in short, to rival the USA as one of the world's superpowers, albeit that in the European version values of social welfare would continue to be placed front and centre. The constitutional turn was, in part, a way of seeking a governmental framework within which these ambitions may be realised.

## 4. Drafting of the Constitutional Treaty

### (i)    *The Convention on the Future of Europe*

We have seen that the Laeken Declaration set out a formidable agenda: improving European governance, enhancing the European Union's global role and taking forward its substantive policies are enormous tasks. The Member States took the view at Laeken that the agenda as set out in their Declaration was too big for the regular processes of the IGC to deal with adequately. After all, the last two IGCs had managed to produce only relatively minor reforms, as reflected in the Amsterdam and Nice Treaties. The Member States needed help – especially in preparing the ground so that a future IGC might be able to tackle some of the ambitious items on the agenda more success-fully than had their predecessors. Accordingly, an extraordinary process was called for.

---

**European Council, Laeken Declaration on the Future of the European Union (2001)**

In order to pave the way for the next Intergovernmental Conference as broadly and openly as possible, [it has been] . . . decided to convene a Convention composed of the main parties involved in the debate on the future of the Union. In the light of the foregoing, it will be the task of that Convention to consider the key issues arising for the Union's future development and try to identify the various possible responses.

[We have] appointed Mr V. Giscard d'Estaing as Chairman of the Convention and Mr G. Amato and Mr J. L. Dehaene as Vice-Chairmen.

*Composition.* In addition to its Chairman and Vice-Chairmen, the Convention will be composed of fifteen representatives of the Heads of State or Government of the Member State (one from each Member State), thirty members of national parliaments (two from each Member State), sixteen members of the European Parliament and two Commission representatives. The accession candidate countries will be fully involved in the Convention's proceedings. They will be represented in the same way as the current Member States (one national government representative and two national parliament members) . . . The Presidium of the Convention will be composed of the Convention Chairman and Vice-Chairmen and nine members drawn from the Convention . . .

*Forum.* In order for the debate to be broadly based and involve all citizens, a Forum will be opened for organisations representing civil society (the social partners, the business world, non-governmental organisations, academia, etc.). It will take the form of a structured network of organisations receiving regular information on the Convention's proceedings. Their contributions will serve as input into the debate. Such organisations may be heard or consulted on specific topics in accordance with arrangements to be established by the Presidium.

---

This was not the first time such a Convention had been established in the EU. The law of the European Union does not include a Bill of Rights. For a long time a number of campaigners argued that the EU should accede to the terms of the European Convention on Human Rights, incorporating the rights protected by that Convention into EU law.[42] However, in 1996 the Court of Justice ruled that the EU lacked the legal competence to do so.[43] Attention turned, therefore, to the prospect of the European Union developing its own Bill of Rights. The Member States, meeting at Cologne in 1999, agreed that an EU 'Charter of Fundamental Rights' should be established cataloguing such rights 'to make their overriding importance and relevance more visible to the Union's citizens', as they put it. One of the most innovative features about the Charter was the body that was appointed to develop it. Instead of it being left to intergovernmental negotiations, a special Convention was established.[44] Chaired by Roman Herzog, formerly the German President (and before that the President of Germany's Constitutional Court), the Convention was composed of fifteen representatives of national governments, thirty representatives of national parliaments, sixteen representatives of the European Parliament and one representative of the Commission (a total of sixty-two). It met in open session, decided upon matters by consensus rather than by voting, and received extensive representations from civil society. Parliamentarians were not only more numerous in the Convention than government representatives, but also more vocal. A total of 805 amendments were put forward by parliamentarians whilst only 356 were put forward by government representatives.[45] It constituted a move away from negotiations between governments to a new form of deliberative decision-making.

It was also successful in terms of its outcome: the Convention drafted and adopted a Charter of Rights that was widely welcomed for its inclusive and forward-looking content.[46] The Charter was adopted by the Convention in October 2000. There followed, however, a period of sustained disagreement about what legal status it should be granted. The matter was discussed at the Nice IGC, but there was no agreement. The consequence was that the Charter was 'proclaimed' at Nice but it was not formally incorporated into the EU's Treaties. As the law currently stands the Charter of Fundamental Rights, while frequently *referred to* by courts, may not be judicially *enforced*. Thus, for the time being, it remains the case that EU law does not include an enforceable Bill of Rights.[47]

The Convention on the Future of Europe established at Laeken was consciously modelled on the Convention that had drafted the Charter of Fundamental Rights. As can be seen from the above extract, the Convention was chaired by Valéry Giscard d'Estaing, the former French President, with Giuliano Amato and Jean-Luc Dehaene,

---

42  See further chapter 6, which is concerned with the topic of fundamental rights in EU law.

43  Opinion 2/94 *Accession to the ECHR* [1996] ECR 1759. See further chapter 5.

44  See G. de Búrca, 'The Drafting of the EU Charter of Fundamental Rights' (2001) 26 *EL Rev.* 126.

45  A. Maurer, 'The Convention, the IGC 2004 and European System Development: a Challenge for Parliamentary Democracy' in *Democracy and Accountability in the Enlarged European Union*, Joint Conference of SWP and the Austrian Academy of Sciences, 7–8 March 2003, see www.swp-berlin.org/common/get_document.php?id=585

46  See further chapter 6.

47  All of this is discussed further in chapter 6. The legal position of the Charter would have been changed by the Constitutional Treaty, had it come into force: see further below.

the former Italian and Belgium Prime Ministers, as his deputies. There were 105 members of the Convention but, in reality, it was rather bigger than this, as everybody apart from the Chairman and the two Vice-Chairmen had an 'alternate' who could participate in their place if they were not present. The Convention met in plenary session, with all members present, once a month. It was the final decision-making body, responsible for adopting any agreed text. Its decisions were taken by consensus rather than by vote. A number of bodies helped to structure the debates within the Convention. The Forum, referred to in the above extract, sought to 'connect' the debate to European citizenry and civil society. The most important body, however, was the Presidium. It was the responsibility of this body, which met twice a month, to draft agendas for the Convention and to organise the Forum. Informally, it acted as an interlocutor between national governments and the Convention, finding out what was acceptable to the Member States and what was not. Alongside it, there was a small Secretariat, providing administrative assistance, summarising debates and preparing discussion papers.

The Convention opened in February 2002 and closed in July 2003. Its output was the Draft Constitutional Treaty for the European Union. There was nothing inevitable about this outcome. It would be a mistake to assume that the EU was fixed on a course that led inexorably to a new constitutional settlement. We saw earlier that, following the Nice IGC, the tide of political opinion across Europe was moving in that direction. But tides ebb as well as flow, and even at Laeken it was not clear that the result of the Convention would necessarily be a constitution. The Laeken Declaration, it will be recalled, talked of the Convention preparing the ground for the 2004 IGC, to consider the key issues, and 'try to identify the *various* possible responses'. Notwithstanding the political mood of the time, and notwithstanding the precedential weight of the Convention that had drafted the Charter of Fundamental Rights, the Convention on the Future of Europe was not explicitly instructed at Laeken to draft a constitution. It was instructed to identify a variety of possible responses to the issues that faced the Union. This is all very well, but the weight of expectation when the Convention first met bore precious little relation to the measured tone of the Laeken Declaration. As Paul Magnette, an authoritative commentator on the Convention, noted:

> Knowing that a vast majority of the Convention was willing to reach an ambitious agreement, Giscard affirmed during the first session they should try to achieve 'broad consensus on a single proposal . . . [that] would thus open the way towards a Constitution for Europe'. The idea that its role would be limited to identifying options, which would then be settled by the IGC, was abandoned from the very beginning.[48]

Amid much pomp and fanfare Giscard d'Estaing presented the Draft Constitutional Treaty to the Member States on 18 July 2003. The fanfare fell flat with remarkable

---

48 P. Magnette, 'In the Name of Simplification: Coping with Constitutional Conflicts in the Convention on the Future of Europe' (2005) 11 *ELJ* 432, 436.

speed, however, as the Member States initially rejected the Draft. Spain and Poland were particularly unhappy about the voting rights accorded in the European law-making process to countries of their size[49] (neither is quite as big in terms of population as Germany, France, Italy and the United Kingdom, but both have considerably bigger populations than the next largest Member State, which is the Netherlands). However, after a change of government in Spain and a series of small but important amendments to the text, the Member States changed their position and signed the Constitutional Treaty, at a ceremony in Rome, in October 2004. The Treaty needed to be signed *and ratified*, however, before it could come into force. As we saw at the beginning of this chapter, the question of how the Member States would ratify the Constitutional Treaty was left for the each state to determine for itself. About ten of the twenty-five elected to hold popular referendums, and it was the negative results in the French and Dutch referendums, in May and June 2005, that stalled the ratification process and that led to the current impasse.

### (ii)   Process at the Convention

The process of drafting the Constitutional Treaty was curious. The presence of the Forum and the taking of decisions by consensus and in open session marked a more deliberative *form* of decision-making.[50] But although it was formally populist, the Convention was in practice constrained by the nature of its membership and by the complexity of the issues from being an exercise in genuinely 'popular constitution making'.[51] Most members of the Convention were inclined to take existing levels of integration as a starting point and to consider what further could be done at the EU level. The Convention, thus, had an integrationist tilt, which alienated some members, who felt that the adoption of decisions by consensus did not protect Euro-sceptic positions sufficiently.[52] The Convention was also unrepresentative in other ways. Women were poorly represented, accounting for only seventeen of the 105 members.[53] The blizzard of proposals provided to the Convention made it

---

49 The law-making process and the voting rights of Member States are considered in more detail in chapters 3 and 4.

50 The literature on this is voluminous. In addition to that which is discussed below, it includes: C. Closa, *Improving Constitutional Politics? A Preliminary Assessment of the Convention*, CONWEB Paper No. 1/2003; J. Wouters, 'Exit the Convention, Come the IGC: Some Reflections on the Convention as a Method for Constitutional Change in the EU' (2003) 10 *MJ* 225; K. Lenaerts and M. Desomer, 'New Models of Constitution-Making in Europe' (2002) 39 *CML Rev.* 1217; J. Shaw, 'Process, Responsibility and Inclusion in European Union Constitutionalism: the Challenge for the Convention on the Future of the Union' (2003) 8 *ELJ* 45 and M. Rosenfeld, 'The European Convention and Constitution-Making in Philadelphia' (2003) 2 *ICON* 373.

51 On the inevitable elitism of such models see C. Skach, 'We the Peoples? Constitutionalising the European Union' (2005) 43 *JCMS* 149.

52 An alternative Constitution was therefore presented by Euro-sceptic members of the Convention. On the integrationist tilt by a non-Euro-sceptic member of the Convention see G. Stuart, *The Making of Europe's Constitution* (London, Fabian Society, 2003) 19–24.

53 M. Léon *et al.*, *Engendering the Convention: Women and the Future of Europe*, Federal Trust Constitutional Paper 6/03.

difficult for individual members to be anything other than reactive, as they struggled to cope with the demands placed on them. This, in turn, allowed the Chairman, the Vice-Chairmen and the Secretariat considerable leeway in steering debate. There was also a marked lack of cohesion among the national parliamentarians. Numerically the largest group, they were split by considerable political differences.[54]

Nonetheless, there are those who saw in the Convention process a tremendous solution to the alleged democratic deficit of the European Union. Its openness and transparency, the closeness of its relationship with civil society and its deliberative decision-making style, have all been celebrated as means of doing constitutional business that are far preferable to the relatively closed, secretive and negotiation-driven processes of regular IGCs.[55] More reflective commentary, however, has been more cautious in its appraisal. For one thing, such commentary has emphasised the need to see the Convention and the IGC that followed it as two parts of the same overall process. For all Giscard's early rhetoric, whatever the Convention recommended, its recommendations would be made to the Member States in the IGC, not directly to the people(s) of Europe. In this sense, attempts to exaggerate the differences between the Convention process and the IGC process are flawed. With this in mind, how democratic was the Convention? Was this really an exercise in open and deliberative constitution-making, or is that too rosy a picture? In a penetrating analysis, Fossum and Menéndez conclude that 'when compared to the standard IGC model, the Convention cannot but be seen as a major step in the direction of constitutionalisation of Treaty amendment procedures. The explicit character of the signalling, and the transparent and open way in which most of the work of the Convention was conducted have increased (even if modestly) the inclusivity of the process.'[56] However, care should be taken not to overstate the point.

---

**J. Fossum and A. Menéndez, 'The Constitution's Gift? A Deliberative Democratic Analysis of Constitution Making in the European Union' (2005) 11 *European Law Journal* 380, 403**

[T]he Convention was set up to meet on an intermittent rather than on a continuous basis. The secretariat, and the president and two vice-presidents, were full-timers. All the others held other full-time tasks . . . The full-timers, concentrated in the Presidium and secretariat, which were closest to the Council [ie closest to the Member States], obviously were also able to influence and guide the process far better than were the part-timers . . . [I]t was predictable that government representatives would be equipped with a strict mandate that would prevent them from revising their preferences in view of the arguments put forward by other Convention members. By assigning a central role to those national government

---

54 G. Beck, 'The British Parliament and the Convention on the Future of Europe' (2005) 30 *EL Rev.* forthcoming.

55 See e.g., O. Duhamel, 'Convention versus IGC' (2005) 11 *EPL* 55.

56 J. Fossum and A. Menéndez, 'The Constitution's Gift? A Deliberative Democratic Analysis of Constitution Making in the European Union' (2005) 11 *ELJ* 380, 407.

representatives, the Council reduced the deliberative potential of the Convention, which was even further reduced once many Member States replaced their initial representatives with their Foreign or European Ministers.

Fossum and Menéndez are not alone in this view. Magnette and Nicolaïdis have argued in a similar vein.

### P. Magnette and K. Nicolaïdis, 'The European Convention: Bargaining in the Shadow of Rhetoric' (2004) 27 *West European Politics* 381, 382

We argue that there has . . . been a Convention paradox. On the one hand, the negotiations within and around the Convention did not fundamentally differ from previous treaty reform. In spite of the Convention's formal independence from the governments that had given birth to it, the broader range of actors participating in the process, and the public character of their deliberations, there is little doubt that the work of the Convention took place above all 'in the shadow of the IGC' with the familiar patterns of interests and strategies. And yet, on the other hand, the final result of the Convention would not have been imaginable as the output of an IGC. This outcome, we argue, was due to two contradictory factors: the 'constitutional ethos' pervading the proceedings of the Convention and the special brand of 'forceful leadership' to which it gave rise.

The two 'classic cleavages' that 'dominated' debate in the Convention were identical to those which have dogged recent IGCs, according to Magnette and Nicolaïdis. These are the differences of view between supranationalists and intergovernmentalists (or between federalists and non-federalists) on the one hand, and the differences of perspective between big states and little states on the other.[57] Whatever the process adopted, it seems, these are issues that the European Union simply cannot avoid.

### N. Walker, 'The Legacy of Europe's Constitutional Moment' (2004) 11 *Constellations* 368, 376

Many constituencies historically opposed to the idea of the European Constitution as an inspiration towards and mark of European political community became in the pre-Convention phase converted to the constitutional process *not* as a polity-making or polity-consolidating device, but as a polity-limiting device. Groups such as the German *Länder*, with their commitment to a strong competence catalogue or the various other Eurosceptic voices who supported the Charter of Rights as a power-constraining rather than a power-enabling device, became strategically reconciled to the constitutional process as a way of advancing a Eurosceptical agenda rather than as a mark of their conversion to the idea of the EU Constitution as *constitutive* of a robust self-standing polity.

---

57 P. Magnette and K. Nicolaïdis, 'The European Convention: Bargaining in the Shadow of Rhetoric' (2004) 27 *WEP* 381, 390.

It may be, however, that reluctance to see the Convention as an unambiguously successful experiment in deliberative and democratic decision-making lies less in these matters, important as they are, and more in the role played in the Convention by the Presidium and, especially, by its Chairman, Giscard d'Estaing. As Magnette and Nicolaïdis report, 'while the Convention was supposed to remain "sovereign" . . . the Presidium acted as the interpreter of the dominant view and was the sole drafter of the actual text presented to the floor'.[58]

---

**P. Magnette and K. Nicolaïdis, 'The European Convention: Bargaining in the Shadow of Rhetoric' (2004) 27 *West European Politics* 381, 398–9**

These tactics worked in reaching a 'consensus' which might have eluded a traditional IGC. But they also left a definite 'bad taste' among many delegates, which in the end might have deprived the [proposals] of the kind of legitimacy that a more thoroughly negotiated text would have. By debating in absolute secrecy, without displaying the textual basis for its own sessions, the Presidium conveyed the idea that the grounds for its decisions were not purely normative. Moreover, within the Presidium itself, the Chair ruled with an iron fist, controlling relations with the secretariat and often submitting proposals to his twelve colleagues a few hours before discussion . . .

The so-called 'consensus' arrived at in the Convention, without real deliberations and by overlooking the strong opposition of two medium States and the great lack of enthusiasm of all small States, proved very fragile to say the least . . .

[D]espite the originality of its composition and procedures, the European Convention did not substantially differ from the previous rounds of Treaty reform in the EU.

---

## 5. The Constitutional Treaty: a brief summary

So much for the process of making the Constitutional Treaty. What now of the content of the Constitutional Treaty? What substantive differences would it have made, had it come into force, to the law and constitution of the European Union?

Detailed consideration of the terms of the Constitutional Treaty (CT) is given throughout this book, as and when the issue arises. Thus, for example, discussion of what the CT would have changed in the law and practice of subsidiarity is included within our discussion of the current law and practice of subsidiarity (in chapter 5). Similarly, the ways in which the CT would have changed the composition of the various institutions of the European Union are examined in our discussion of the institutions (in chapter 3), and so on. However, it may be helpful to list in this section – without offering a great deal in terms of commentary and analysis – what the CT would have changed, so that readers may find in one place a convenient summary of its main points. It should be emphasised that what follows is only an outline. References to more detailed consideration, elsewhere in the book, are given in the notes.

The Constitutional Treaty was divided into four parts. Part I (Articles I-1 to I-60) contained provisions on the objectives, the law-making powers and the finances of

---

58 *Ibid.* 396–7.

the European Union, on fundamental rights, citizenship and democracy, and on the EU's institutional framework. Part II (Articles II-61 to II-114) contained the text of the Charter of Fundamental Rights, to which the CT would have granted some legal effect. Part III (Articles III-115 to III-436), by far the longest part, contained the detailed provisions on the EU's various policy areas. Part IV (Articles IV-437 to IV-448) contained a small number of closing provisions, the detail of which need not concern us here. In addition, 36 Protocols were added, providing a further 190 pages to go along with the 202 pages of the CT itself.[59] Part I contained much that had not previously been written into the Treaties, but relatively little that was not, one way or another, already part of EU law. There were innovations and novelties, for sure, and we shall come to them in a moment, but the bulk of it set out principles and practices which already existed. Likewise, a great deal of Part III was lifted from the current Treaties. Of the four parts, it was Part III that read most like the Treaties that presently govern the EU.

A principal feature of the CT was its attempt to abolish the three-pillar structure erected at Maastricht. While the distinction between the European Community and the European Union would formally have been abandoned, however, many of the differences between the powers (especially the law-making powers) of the first pillar on the one hand and the second pillar on the other would have been maintained. As it is now, European law-making in the fields of foreign and defence policy would have remained notably more intergovernmental and less supranational than it is in respect of the first pillar, meaning that the more supranational institutions (Commission, European Parliament and Court of Justice) would have continued, as now, to play relatively minor roles in these fields. Several commentators have suggested that the three-pillar structure would in many ways have merely disappeared 'underground'.[60] This is something of an overstatement, as the structures of the first pillar, particularly the legislative ones, were extended over the fields of the third pillar, policing and judicial cooperation in criminal matters. These would have been as subject to supranational disciplines and procedures as traditional fields of Community law. Related to the formal abolition of the three pillars, however, was an important change in nomenclature, as the names of the various species of European laws would have been changed. Thus, Regulations would have become 'European laws' and Directives would have become 'European framework laws'.[61]

One of the first things to say about the Constitutional Treaty is that there is a great deal of EU law that it would not have changed.[62] The core *activities* of the European

---

59 As printed in the *Official Journal*: see OJ 2004 C310. If you add the Annexes as well, the total page count comes in at 474.

60 See J. Shaw, 'Europe's Constitutional Future' [2005] *PL* 132, 139. Shaw attributes the notion to Kalypso Nicolaïdis.

61 Articles I-33 to I-39. See chapter 4.

62 This is a point strongly made by Jo Shaw, who has argued that the European Union's constitutional future is no less than 'dominated by' the weight of its past: see J. Shaw, 'Europe's Constitutional Future' [2005] *PL* 132.

Union would have remained much as they are now: the free movement of persons, of services, of goods and of capital – the four so-called 'fundamental freedoms' of the single market – would have remained central,[63] as would matters of competition policy,[64] social and environmental law,[65] the single currency[66] and agriculture and fisheries. These policy areas together would have continued to take up the vast bulk of the EU's resources, as they do now. In addition, the European Union would have continued to complement the Member States in fields of criminal justice and foreign policy.[67] Moreover, the *institutions* of the EU would have continued more or less as they are now, at least in terms of their functions.[68] European laws, as now, would have been made principally by the Council of Ministers (comprising ministers from national governments) and the directly elected European Parliament. The Commission would have continued, as now, to have the right to initiate legislation – that is, the right to suggest what laws and policies the EU should adopt. All of this would have continued to be subject to financial review by the European Court of Auditors[69] and to judicial review by the European Court of Justice.[70]

While the tasks of the institutions would have changed relatively little, however, the rules governing their composition and functioning would have been more substantially reformed.[71] Thus, the European Parliament would have been limited to no more than 750 MEPs;[72] the principle whereby the Commission includes at least one member from each Member State would have been abandoned, albeit not until 2009.[73] Most importantly, perhaps, the rules governing decision-making in the Council of Ministers would have been altered so that more decisions could have been made by 'qualified majority' (rather than requiring unanimity), while the all-important definition of what counts as a qualified majority would also have been revised.[74] The most significant institutional innovations are the changes that would have been made to the Presidency of the Council and the establishment of the new EU Minister for Foreign Affairs. As things stand the Presidency of the Council rotates every six months among the twenty-five Member States. The CT would have established a new two-and-a-half year term.[75] The Minister for Foreign Affairs (who would have been a member, indeed a Vice-President, of the Commission) would have been a new office. The Minister for Foreign Affairs would have been responsible for 'conducting' the European Union's foreign policy, although that policy would continue to have been set by the Council, which (as now) would have to act unanimously in this area, preserving each Member State's veto.[76]

---

63 See *EUL*, chapters 11 and 15–19.     64 See *EUL*, chapters 21–25.     65 See *EUL*, chapters 12 and 20.
66 See *EUL*, chapter 12.     67 See *EUL*, chapter 14.     68 See chapter 3.     69 See chapter 8.
70 See chapter 10.     71 Again, see further chapter 3.     72 Article I-20 CT.     73 Article I-26 CT.
74 Article I-25 CT. This is the matter, more than any other, that caused Spain's and Poland's objections to lead to the European Council rejecting the Draft Constitutional Treaty when it was first presented to it in 2003. See further chapter 3.
75 Article I-22 CT.     76 Articles I-40 and III-300 CT.

Two of the most significant changes of substance were the incorporation of the Charter of Rights in Part II of the CT and the provisions concerning subsidiarity and the role of national parliaments in the first two Protocols to the CT. As we saw above, the Charter of Rights was 'proclaimed' at Nice in 2001, but as a statement of policy, not of law. Part II of the Constitution would have changed this, making the Charter formally recognised as a part of the constituent Treaties for the first time.[77] The doctrine of subsidiarity was introduced into EU law at Maastricht. The doctrine means that action should be taken at the European level only when it cannot sensibly be taken at the national level. It is a principle of federalism, ensuring that sovereignty remains with the Member States except where they cannot act as effectively as the Community.[78] At least, that is the theory. In practice it has not worked well. This is because the bodies responsible for enforcing the doctrine have been strongly pro-European. Had it come into force, the Constitution would have made national parliaments responsible for policing subsidiarity. At the moment national parliaments play no role in making European law; they are frequently required to make national law in order to implement European Directives, but they play no role in making the Directives themselves. Protocols 1 and 2 to the CT would have required national parliaments to be given copies of all draft European laws so that they could be examined in order to make sure they comply with the principle of subsidiarity. The European institutions would have been required to take account of the views of national parliaments and, in some cases, to review their draft laws in the light of their views.

The law-making powers of the European Union would have been explicitly listed ('catalogued' is the term more often used). While making little difference to the substance of EU law, this would have enabled interested parties quickly to identify the areas in which the EU may make law.[79] There was no corresponding catalogue of the law-making powers that remain with the Member States, although one provision of the CT did list a number of 'essential state functions'.[80] The CT included a number of other, constitutionally symbolic provisions. The principle of the primacy of EU law over that of the Member States – long recognised by the Court of Justice as a matter of EU law – was brought into the Treaty text for the first time.[81] New provisions declaring the European Union's commitment to representative and participatory democracy were included, although the extent to which these would have been judicially enforceable remained open to doubt.[82] A new provision was inserted stating that 'Any Member State may decide to withdraw from the Union in accordance with its own constitutional requirements'.[83] The 'symbols of the Union' were listed – its flag, its anthem (Beethoven's *Ode to Joy*), its motto ('united in diversity')

---

77 Articles II-61 to II-114 CT. Curiously, the CT would also have provided that 'the Union shall accede' to the European Convention on Human Rights: Article I-9. See further chapter 6.

78 See chapter 5.     79 Articles I-11 to I-18. These provisions are discussed in detail in chapter 5.

80 Article I-5.     81 Article I-6. See chapter 5.     82 Articles I-45 to I-48.     83 Article I-60.

and its day ('Europe Day' is, apparently, to be celebrated 'throughout the Union' on 9 May).[84]


## 6. Overview and assessment

The central reason for the constitutional turn was, as we have seen, somehow to resolve the legitimacy deficit at the heart of the Union. Anchoring the Union in a formal constitution was, it was argued, necessary for a common political culture to emerge. Without central constitutional symbols and a constitutionally framed European political sphere, it would be impossible for shared political values or a strong sense of solidarity between Europeans to emerge.[85] Without these, the European Union would be impeded from ever taking effective or legitimate action.[86] Viewed in such terms, the Constitutional Treaty was an exercise in polity-building, an invitation to EU citizens to revisit their values and their sense of political community and to recast them in explicitly European terms.[87]

It was an exercise fraught with risks. It was never clear that the citizenry would be likely to accept the terms of this invitation. Debate about the European Union's future could no longer be confined simply to the technical – to the merits or otherwise of particular Treaty amendments introduced by various IGCs – but became, inevitably, a more fundamental argument about the very foundations of the Union. Items previously taken somewhat for granted, such as the desirability of enlargement, the sovereignty of EU law, the benefits of the single market, and so forth, were placed centre-stage. And we know what the result was: rejection at the hands of the French and Dutch electorates. That the ratification process was suspended following these verdicts is surely indicative that the governments of other Member States in which referendums were scheduled were, to say the least, doubtful of the likelihood of the Constitutional Treaty being accepted by the electorates of their countries. The reaction to the Danish 'no' over Maastricht and the Irish 'no' over Nice was, in both cases, the deeply patronising (not to say undemocratic) one that the well-meaning Danish and Irish voters had simply misunderstood the question or somehow got the answer wrong and that they should, at the earliest opportunity, be asked to revise their view. The reaction to the French and Dutch 'no' votes, by contrast, was to recognise that 'citizens have . . . expressed concerns and worries which need to be taken into account'[88] and to pause to allow for reflection on what to do next. This is a practical question. The difficulties identified since the Treaty of Nice are still present, and the question

---

84 Article I-8.      85 See Grimm, above n. 14.

86 See J. Habermas, 'Why Europe Needs a Constitution' (2001) 11 *New Left Review* 5. For a more critical view see J. Weiler, 'On the Power of the Word: Europe's Constitutional Iconography' (2005) 3 *ICON* 173.

87 See N. Walker, 'Europe's Constitutional Momentum and the Search for Polity Legitimacy' (2005) 3 *ICON* 211.

88 European Council, 18 June 2005: see above n. 2.

remains what do about them. It seems that the European Union has a number of options.

### C. Closa, *Sisyphus Revisited: Options for the EU's Constitutional Future*, US-Europe Analysis Series (Brookings Institution, Washington, DC, July 2005) 1–5

The proposed Constitution was designed precisely as a response to the perceived shortcomings and defects of the Nice Treaty. The solution (i.e. the Constitution) has failed, but this does not mean that the problems have disappeared. On the contrary, it is logical to assume that they persist and like Sisyphus, the EU must once again begin to push the boulder up the hill. What are the current options for reforming the EU and which ones make the most sense?

*Option 1. Selective application of parts of the Constitution within the framework of Nice.* Some recent proposals suggest implementing some of the constitutional novelties . . . Some of these reforms could be realised with no additional juridical structure . . . Some others, such as the Charter of Fundamental Rights, could presumably be added to the existing Treaties without much opposition even if they would require national ratifications. Yet the political and juridical difficulties in implementing some of the constitutional reforms (for instance, including the Minister of Foreign Affairs as part of the Commission) limit the ability to use this mechanism extensively. Moreover, the Constitution is a complete package that includes various interconnected compromises by the Member States that cannot be easily deconstructed.

*Option 2. Incremental reform (i.e. partial and progressive constitution building).* Andrew Moravcsik [see below] advocates a return to the old-fashioned incremental reform procedure. Paradoxically, the process for creating the Constitution began because of the exhaustion of this method; a return to it would mark the abandonment of the constitutional objectives (e.g. simplification and codification, the attempt to delineate EU responsibilities, and the creation of a clearer system of norms). Incrementalism is not a recipe for success. Former rounds of reform were characterised by a diminishing will of national governments to compromise and, hence, agreements were reached on increasingly smaller packages of reforms. This outcome caused frustration among politicians and political elites and triggered discontent and calls for radical changes in the mechanism of reform.

*Option 3. Restarting the process: renegotiation of the Constitution.* Some politicians (such as the Danish Eurosceptic Peter Bonde) and academics have argued that a new constitutional round should start to accommodate the demands voiced by the citizens in the referendums. The objections to this option are quite clear. First, there would be a problem of identification of demands – just what do EU citizens want? Secondly, there would be a problem of congruency between these demands – citizens in different countries appear to want different and indeed opposing reforms of the EU. But even if those obstacles could be overcome and agreement reached, the process of ratification would have to start again. If countries again resorted to referendums (and they would be difficult to avoid), the same situation would probably be repeated.

*Option 4. Keep the ratification process open.* Declaration 30 of the Constitutional Treaty implicitly commits national governments to complete ratification in order to verify whether 20 or more Member States are able to do so and, then, decide accordingly. Obviously, the negative votes in France and the Netherlands transformed the significance of ratification of other states. The EU Constitution is technically a reform of the Treaty of Nice, and thus, according to Article 48 of the Treaty on European Union, requires unanimous approval.

Under these conditions, ratification by any number of other Member States will not suffice
to bring the Constitution into force . . .

There are, though, good reasons for keeping the process going: opinions of parliaments
and citizens in the Member States that have not yet voted should be heard so that they are
put on a similar footing. Since the 'no' votes in France and the Netherlands, Latvia, Cyprus,
Malta and Luxembourg (through a referendum) have all ratified the Constitution. But some
observers . . . consider these ratifications essentially meaningless from the point of view of
'reviving' the Constitution (even though they mean that 13 Member States comprising both
a majority of states and population have ratified it).

Strategically, it makes sense to have a cooling-down period or an extended ratification
period that goes beyond the initial target of November 2006. This would smooth the ride for
certain governments, but for France and the Netherlands a different solution would have to
be engineered. Since ratification requires unanimity, the remainder of the process is invalid
until a second successful ratification in these two countries happens. Hence, it is up to the
governments of these countries to identify what would be satisfactory for them . . .

**Option 5**. *We are seafarers and we must rebuild the ship at sea*. Rebuilding the ship at high-
seas means that both the Constitution and the ratification process have to be adapted on the spot
to the current circumstances and an eventual mechanism has to be improvised. The starting
point is a correct diagnosis of the factors that triggered rejection. A number of reasons for the
"no" vote have been identified (fear of globalization, protest against enlargement, nationalism,
anti-Turkish feeling, anti-government sentiment, etc.) . . . However, a more precise diagnosis
of the rejection would note that the Constitution was not the source of these fears but, rather,
the repository of fears nurtured over many years and which the EU only provoked in part.
The referendums merely provided an outlet for expressing a more general malaise. In any
case, the constitutional blockage came about not so much because of the referendums but
because of their combination with unanimity . . .

A mini-IGC could reform Article 48 of the Treaty of European Union and remove the unanimity requirement. At the same time, a similar reform of Article 477 of the EU Constitution
(i.e. removal of unanimity for its entering into force) would be required. Since the resulting
Constitution would technically be a new one, it would require a new round of ratification.

The choice of route, however, begs a bigger question about what the European Union
is about and what the meaning and purpose of the constitutional turn was.

### N. Walker, 'The Legacy of Europe's Constitutional Moment' (2004) 11 *Constellations* 368, 373–4

Europe is caught in a tragic cycle of constitutional inflation. The more that the breadth and
depth of European power and the lack of a common popular basis for exercising that power is
exposed . . . the more that the myth and ceremony of constitutional performance is invoked to
resolve the impasse. But since each successive constitutional performance merely dramatises
the continuing absence of the consensual social foundations for a lasting settlement, its failure,
paradoxically, merely feeds the demand for a bigger and better version of the same – a yet
grander and more aspirationally conclusive constitutional moment. The law of diminishing
returns applies its remorseless logic and at the end of the cycle, to which we may be coming
perilously close with the first self-styled 'Constitutional' Treaty, lies the unnerving prospect
of documentary constitutionalism as a busted flush.

If the constitutional turn was fraught with risks, there is also a sense in which it was infected with a dangerous ambivalence. What was it, precisely, that the constitutional turn was designed to accomplish? Was the aim to reconstitute the present European Union, or to constitute a new European Union? The only plausible answer to this question is that it was both. Whether you consider the Laeken Declaration, the Convention, or the Constitutional Treaty itself, throughout the process there was a persistent tension between these two aims. What the Laeken Declaration says about the success of the EU and about enlargement suggests that the aim was to reconstitute the present Union – to put more or less what we already have on a new constitutional footing. But what was said at Laeken about the democratic challenge and about the future role and policies of the EU suggests something quite different – that the constitutional turn was designed to constitute a new European Union, a Union that was founded on democracy rather than on diplomacy and on openness and deliberation rather than on closed intergovernmental bargaining. One of the reasons for the 'failure' of the Constitutional Treaty may lie in the Convention's inability – or unwillingness, perhaps – to resolve this tension either way.

The result continued the ambivalence which lies at the heart of the way in which the European Union is currently legitimated. The Constitutional Treaty was neither one thing nor another. The 'failure' of the Constitutional Treaty was its failure to choose clearly which one of the four potential solutions to the legitimacy conundrum outlined above the EU should adopt. While the extreme positions of Hartley and Mancini were rejected, in that the CT would have transformed the EU neither into an ordinary international organisation nor into a state, there is nothing in the Constitutional Treaty to satisfy the likes of Siedentop and others who think that the European Union needs a new constitutional vision as breathtaking and bold as that of the American founding fathers. The result was a Treaty that claimed to be a Constitution[89] and a Constitution that took the legal form of a Treaty. As such, it *continued* rather than resolved the hazy legitimacy of the EU, drawing as it does partly on the constitutional tradition that legitimates states and partly on the Treaty-based tradition that legitimates international organisations. Weiler, as so often, has put the matter most clearly. For the Constitutional Treaty to have been able to claim the hallmarks of a true constitution, it would have to have provided for at least one of the following: *either* that it could be ratified and amended by a majority (or supermajority) of states, abandoning the requirement of unanimity that is the hallmark of internationalism, not constitutionalism; *or* that it could be ratified and amended by a majority (or supermajority) vote in a single Europe-wide referendum.[90] For as long as these remain

---

89 We have taken care throughout this chapter to refer to the Constitutional Treaty as that, and not to refer to it as 'the Constitution'. The text of the CT itself does not do this, but refers to itself throughout as 'this Constitution', not 'this Constitutional Treaty'. See e.g., the opening sentence of Article I-1.

90 See J. Weiler, 'A Constitution for Europe? Some Hard Choices' (2002) 40 *JCMS* 563, 565–6.

steps too far, the European Union's search for 'legitimation-through-constitution' will remain a search in vain.

Given this, perhaps the European Union would be better advised to abandon the search. Such is the intriguing argument of Ulrich Haltern. With remarkable prescience, Haltern argued in 2003 that those who aim to construct for the EU what he has called 'foundation narratives' of the constitutional sort 'will be prone to making a laughing-stock of themselves rather than serving the Union's purpose'.[91] Rather than attempting in vain to clothe the EU in the ill-fitting garb of state constitutionalism, the European Union should be celebrated for what it is: a 'shallow' and 'superficial' entity engineered for the 'privileging of the commercial' over all else.[92] The EU is a project born not from visionary belief or shared sacrifice, but from relentlessly modern rationality.[93] Its symbol is the world of Brussels' office towers, 'a world of xeroxed working documents and greyish-greenish office furniture, of simultaneous translators in soundproof cabins featuring multi-channel cables'.[94] Its *zeitgeist* is one of 'skyscrapers, autobahns and nuclear power stations'.[95] It is, in other words, a dull technocracy that should remain in the hands of dull technocrats, its purpose being to make Europeans richer, so that they stop trying to kill one another. Haltern is not joking, and nor is he being pejorative. He means to call the European Union what it is: an experiment in transnational governance that is designed to preserve and advance the interests – mainly the economic interests – of the states and peoples of Europe. Such an entity is not to be legitimated by conferring upon it a constitution. Such an entity is to be legitimated by recognising it for the shallow, superficial and, in economic terms, overwhelmingly successful thing that it is.

While he would by no means agree with all of Haltern's views, Andrew Moravcsik has come to a similar conclusion that has echoes in it not only of Haltern's bluntness but also of Joseph Weiler's 'principle of constitutional tolerance', which we encountered earlier.[96]

### A. Moravcsik, 'Europe Without Illusions', *Prospect*, July 2005, 25–6

The unique genius of the EU is that it locks in policy co-ordination while respecting the powerful rhetoric and symbols that attach to national identity . . . [A] constitutional order that preserves national democratic politics for the issues most salient to citizens, but delegates to more indirect democratic forms those issues that are of less concern, or on which there is an administrative, technical or legal consensus, is highly appealing. The EU's distinctive system of multi-level governance is the only new form of state organisation to emerge and prosper since the rise of the welfare state at the turn of the twentieth century. Now it is a mature constitutional order, one that no longer needs to move forward to legitimate its past and present successes. Left behind must be the European centralisers and democratisers for

---

91  U. Haltern, 'Pathos and Patina: the Failure and Promise of Constitutionalism in the European Imagination' (2003) 9 *ELJ* 14, 43.
92  *Ibid*. 19.      93  *Ibid*. 25.      94  *Ibid*. 26.      95  *Ibid*.      96  See p. 55.

whom 'ever closer union' remains an end in itself. They will insist that the answer to failed democracy is more democracy and the answer to a failed constitution is another constitution. But Europe has moved beyond them. Disowning this well-meaning, even admirable, band of idealists may seem harsh, but it is both necessary and just. On this basis, Europeans can develop a new discourse of national interest, pragmatic co-operation and constitutional stability – a discourse that sees Europe as it is.

This is one view of 'where next?'. It suggests that the ratification of the Constitutional Treaty should not be stalled as much as dropped altogether and that the attempt to seek greater – or perhaps just clearer – legitimacy for the European Union through the means of constitutionalism, laudable as it may have been, should be abandoned. Whether, if this now happens, it will mean (as the likes of Mancini and Habermas have suggested) that European nation-states find it ever more difficult to hold on to their values of social welfare in a global economy dominated by the USA and China, remains to be seen.

### Further reading

J. Fossum and A. Menéndez, 'The Constitution's Gift? A Deliberative Democratic Analysis of Constitution Making in the European Union' (2005) 11 *ELJ* 380

D. Grimm, 'Does Europe Need a Constitution?' (1995) 1 *ELJ* 282

J. Habermas, 'Why Europe Needs a Constitution' (2001) 11 *New Left Review* 5

U. Haltern, 'Pathos and Patina: The Failure and Promise of Constitutionalism in the European Imagination' (2003) 9 *ELJ* 14

T. Hartley, 'The Constitutional Foundations of the European Union' (2001) 117 *LQR* 225

P. Magnette and K. Nicolaïdis, 'The European Convention: Bargaining in the Shadow of Rhetoric' (2004) 27 *West European Politics* 381

F. Mancini, 'Europe: the Case for Statehood' (1998) 4 *ELJ* 29

Y. Mény, '*De la Démocratie en Europe*: Old Concepts and New Challenges' (2002) 41 *JCMS* 1

A. Moravcsik, 'In Defence of the "Democratic Deficit": Reassessing Legitimacy in the European Union' (2002) 40 *JCMS* 603

J. Shaw, 'Europe's Constitutional Future' [2005] *Public Law* 132

N. Walker, 'The Legacy of Europe's Constitutional Moment' (2004) 11 *Constellations* 368

N. Walker, 'Europe's Constitutional Momentum and the Search for Polity Legitimacy' (2005) 3 *International Journal of Constitutional Law* 211

J. Weiler, 'Europe: the Case Against the Case for Statehood' (1998) 4 *ELJ* 43

J. Weiler, *The Constitution of Europe* (Cambridge, Cambridge University Press, 1999)

J. Weiler, 'A Constitution for Europe? Some Hard Choices' (2002) 40 *JCMS* 563

J. Weiler, 'In Defence of the Status Quo: Europe's Constitutional Sonderweg', in Weiler and Wind, below

J. Weiler and U. Haltern, *The Autonomy of the Community Legal Order: Through the Looking Glass*, Jean Monnet Working Paper 10/96

J. Weiler and M. Wind (eds.), *European Constitutionalism Beyond the State* (Cambridge, Cambridge University Press, 2003)

# 3

## The EU Institutions

<table>
<tr><td colspan="2" align="center">CONTENTS</td></tr>
</table>

## 1. Introduction

A feature of the European Union is that, unlike other international organisations, its business is not carried out through diplomacy and ad hoc negotiation. Instead, the European Union is characterised by a number of institutions and procedures. Even a brief account of the European Union must discuss at least six central institutions: the

Council, the Parliament, the Commission, the European Council, the Court of Justice and the European Central Bank. Yet the European Union's institutional settlement is an unusual one. Its organising principle is not the separation of powers between legislature, executive and judiciary. Instead, its central concern is to secure the representation of different interests and a balance between them. Each institution has to be viewed in terms of the interests it represents, and the balance between institutions has also to be considered in terms of the balance between these different interests.[1] Put crudely, in areas where national sovereignty is valued, one would expect the interests of national governments to be emphasised. In areas where extensive Community action is sought, one would suppose supranational institutions to be more influential.

Even if the Union's institutional settlement has to accommodate a particularly broad array of interests, it still legislates, administers and adjudicates. The legitimacy of these processes also has to be assessed according to the same standards that one would apply to any government. There is, thus, a second level of analysis that must be applied to the institutions, namely that of more general standards of legitimacy. Yet, legitimacy also has a number of dimensions. Input-oriented legitimacy looks at the opportunity for participation and representation offered by the institutions. It looks at how open the settlement is to civil society and how plural and representative it is. The other is output-oriented legitimacy. This looks at how effectively the institutions carry out their tasks, their independence of judgment, consistency, expertise, accountability and fairness.[2] In considering both the input and output legitimacy of the Union, it makes sense to consider these both in relation to each institution and its place in the overall scheme of things, and in relation to the institutional settlement as a whole.

## 2. The Commission

### (i)  The Commission bureaucracy

The Commission is often described in unitary terms, as a single body with the single agenda of promoting European integration. The reality is more complex. It employs more than 24,000 people, performs a wide number of tasks and has a wide array of relationships with a multiplicity of actors. Whilst in legal terms, it is a single body, it is best to see the Commission as composed of three tiers: the College of Commissioners, the Directorates-General and the Cabinets.

### (a)  College of Commissioners

Formally, the Commission consists of twenty-five Commissioners, with one Commissioner from each Member State.[3] These twenty-five Commissioners make up the

---

1 G. Majone, *Dilemmas of European Integration: The Ambiguities and Pitfalls of Integration by Stealth* (Oxford, Oxford University Press, 2005) 47.
2 F. Scharpf, *Governing in Europe: Effective and Democratic?* (Oxford/New York, Oxford University Press, 1998) 6–23.
3 Article 213(1) EC as amended by the Protocol on Enlargement.

College of Commissioners. The Commission is appointed for a five-year term. Once appointed, the Commissioners are allocated portfolios by the President.[4] Each Commissioner is then the primary person responsible for all the work of the Commission that falls within that policy area. The Commissioners are to be persons whose 'independence is beyond doubt'. They are required not to seek or take instructions from any government or any other body and a duty is imposed on Member States to respect this principle. In addition, Commissioners must not find themselves in a position where a 'conflict of interest' arises. They must not, therefore, engage in any other occupation during their period of office. If any Commissioner fails to observe these rules, the Court of Justice may, on application by either the Council or the Commission, compulsorily retire that Commissioner. This independence must be seen in relative terms. Commissioners are the political face of the Commission. Chosen because of distinguished and well-connected prior careers, they have a list of professional and political contacts:

> Usually, they are members – and appointees – of the major parties in their member state and continue some involvement with national politics after becoming Commissioners. Frequent trips to speak before (and to lecture to) national audiences are common. Again, the metaphor of gate-keeping is perhaps most useful: Commissioners are an easy and efficient way for the Commission to maintain a link with member state governments and domestic political systems. They will know what legislative proposals are politically acceptable in national capitals, while at the same time being in an ideal position to communicate to national elites the requirements of efficient European policy-making.[5]

The other feature of the College is the principle of *collegiality*. The Commission is collectively responsible for all decisions taken and all Commission decisions should be taken collectively. In principle, these decisions should take place at the weekly meetings of the Commission by a simple majority vote of the College. Meetings of each Commissioner's Cabinet (staff) occur two days before the weekly meeting. If there is agreement, it will be formally adopted as an 'A' item and there will be no formal discussion of the matter at the meeting. However, the reality is that there is little discussion within the College about the majority of the Commission's business. According to the Commission's own figures, the Commission, between 2000 and

---

4 The portfolios for the 2004–2009 Commission are Institutional Relations and Communication Strategy; Enterprise and Industry; Transport; Administrative Affairs and Anti-fraud; Justice, Freedom and Security; Information Society, Environment; Economic and Monetary Affairs; Regional Policy; Fisheries; Budget; Science and Research; Education and Culture; Health and Consumer Protection; Enlargement; Development and Humanitarian Aid; Taxation and Customs Union; Competition; Agriculture and Rural Development; External Relations and European Neighbourhood Policy; Internal Market and Services; Employment, Social Affairs and Equal Opportunities; External Trade; and Energy.
5 T. Christiansen, 'Tensions of European Governance: Politicised Bureaucracy and Multiple Accountability in the European Commission' (1997) 4 *JEPP* 73, 82; A. Smith, 'Why Commissioners Matter' (2003) 41 *JCMS* 137, 143–5.

2003, took 1,344 decisions. A vote was taken on only eleven of these decisions (less than 1 per cent) and on less than 3 per cent was there any discussion.[6]

In the interests of administrative expediency, the Commission has found two procedures for conducting the majority of its business. The first is the 'written procedure'. Under this procedure, a proposal, a *greffe*, is adopted by the Commissioner responsible for the relevant portfolio. After the proposal has been approved by the Legal Service and associated Directorates-General, it is then circulated to the Cabinets of the other Commissioners. If there is no objection, the proposal is adopted as a Commission decision. The 'ordinary' written procedure gives the Cabinets five working days to consider the proposal. The expedited written procedure must be authorised by the President. In such circumstances, the Cabinets are only given three working days. The second procedure is internal delegation. The Commission can delegate a straightforward 'act of management' to particular members.[7] What constitutes such an act is not self-evident. A decision requiring undertakings to submit to a Commission investigation into anti-competitive practices was considered to be an act of management which could be delegated. By contrast, a decision finding a violation of EC competition law was not considered to be administrative in nature and was considered to be too wide a power to be delegated.[8]

**The President**    The only Commissioner without a portfolio, the President, is the most powerful of all the Commissioners.[9] He is involved, first, in the appointment of the other Commissioners. After his appointment by the national governments is approved by the European Parliament, he nominates the other Commissioners, in consultation with the Heads of Government. These are then subject to a collective vote of approval by the European Parliament and then appointed by the Council. Secondly, he decides on the internal organisation of the Commission. This involves not only the allocation of individual portfolios at the beginning of the term, but the President can also shift the portfolios of Commissioners during their term of office. Thirdly, individual Commissioners are responsible to him. The President can request individual Commissioners to resign, who are obliged to do so should the College agree with the request.[10] Fourthly, the President is responsible for providing 'political guidance' to the Commission. At its most formal, this involves chairing and setting the agenda for the weekly meetings of the Commission. More substantively, it means proposing the political priorities of the Commission through pushing forward one proposal rather than another for adoption by the Commission. Fifthly, the President has a roving policy brief. Although this can cause tensions with the individual Commissioner

---

6 EC Commission, *A Constitution for the Union*, COM(2003)548 final, Annex I.
7 This practice was upheld in Case 5/85 *AKZO v Commission* [1986] ECR 2585.
8 Case C-137/92P *Commission v BASF* [1994] ECR I-2555.
9 The current President is a Portuguese national, Manuel Barroso.
10 Article 213(4) EC. The Constitutional Treaty would have removed the requirement that the College agree, giving the President a unilateral power to sack individual Commissioners: Article I-27(3) CT.

concerned, the President may seek to take over a particular issue and drive Commission policy on that issue. This may be because the issue is of such seminal importance to that term of the Commission or because there is strong disagreement between the Commissioner and the President over an issue. In the early 1990s, for example, Jacques Delors worked closely with the British Commissioner, Lord Cockfield, on the internal market because it was so central to the Commission's work at that time. He also intervened extensively, however, on social and environmental issues because he was unhappy with the work of the two Commissioners in those fields.[11] The President can also reserve important policy issues for himself. For example, in the mid-1990s, President Santer decided that he would assume responsibility for institutional reform. Finally, the President has an important representative role. He represents the Commission at meetings involving the Heads of Government and must account before other institutions when there is a questioning of the general conduct of the institution or a particular issue raises broader questions.

**Size of the Commission**    A College with too many Commissioners is seen to pose a number of problems. It would be increasingly difficult to find meaningful jobs for individual Commissioners or ones that did not involve substantial overlap between portfolios. An oversized Commission might also compromise the collegial nature of the Commission. The College would no longer be a small corpus of officials, all of whom know each other well and interact regularly, but would become a deliberative assembly, where meetings would resemble parliamentary debates. Finally, such a Commission would be difficult for the President to manage. It would be easier for fiefdoms and cliques to emerge. Commissioners would be specialised and know more about their area and less about other areas. At the Treaty of Nice, it was agreed that when the Union reached a size of twenty-seven states, the number of Commissioners would become less than the number of Member States. The number of Commissioners would be decided by the Council on the accession of the twenty-seventh state, but there would be a rotation principle so that all Member States would be treated equally in terms of their right to have one of their own nationals as a Commissioner. Notwithstanding that not all Member States would have a national in any one College, any College would be reflective of the demographic and geographic range of all the Member States of the Union.[12]

This issue was revisited at the Future of Europe Convention. The proposal of the Convention was that, from 1 November 2009, the Commission should comprise a national from each Member State. There would, however, be a distinction between voting and non-voting Commissioners. A College of fifteen Commissioners could vote and take decisions. There would be a rotation of nationality for this College, but it would be required to be geographically and demographically representative. The other

---

11 G. Ross, *Jacques Delors and European Integration* (Oxford/New York, Oxford University Press, 1995).
12 Protocol on Enlargement of the European Union, Article 4.

Commissioners might have portfolios, but they would not form part of the College.[13] This proposal was highly contentious. The Commission, in particular, opposed it.[14] It was argued that the proposal violated the principle that all Commissioners be equal because it made a distinction between voting and non-voting Commissioners. A more substantial objection was that the proposal blurred managerial accountability. If a non-voting Commissioner were to be allocated responsibility for a portfolio, the relationship between her and the voting Commissioner, within whose broad umbrella it fell, would be unclear. It was uncertain who would have the final say and who would be responsible if an error were to be made. Notwithstanding this, the distinction between senior and junior ministers exists in many Member States.

The proposal was also opposed by a large number of the smaller Member States, who saw Commissioners as important sources of prestige and influence and were worried by the possibility that one of their nationals might not be in the College.[15] The IGC rejected the proposal and approved an alternative solution:

---

### Article I-26 (5) CT

The first Commission appointed under the provisions of the Constitution shall consist of one national of each Member State . . .

6. As from the end of the term of office of the Commission referred to in paragraph 5, the Commission shall consist of a number of members . . . corresponding to two-thirds of the number of Member States, unless the European Council, acting unanimously, decides to alter this number.

The members of the Commission shall be selected from among the nationals of the Member States on the basis of a system of equal rotation between the Member States. This system shall be established by a European decision adopted unanimously by the European Council and on the basis of the following principles:

(a) Member States shall be treated on a strictly equal footing as regards determination of the sequence of, and the time spent by, their nationals as members of the Commission; consequently, the difference between the total number of terms of office held by nationals of any given pair of Member States may never be more than one;

(b) subject to point (a), each successive Commission shall be so composed as to reflect satisfactorily the demographic and geographical range of all the Member States.

---

Under this system, the College would house between sixteen and eighteen Commissioners. Smaller than the current College, this would be easier to manage and more coherent. However, it is not linked to the number of policy fields managed by the Commission and it seems to be an unsatisfactory half-way house between the need for representativeness and the desire to reduce the size of the College.

---

13 Article I-25(3) DCT.
14 EC Commission, *A Constitution for the Union*, COM(2003)548 final.
15 P. Craig, *The Constitutional Treaty: Legislative and Executive Power in the Emerging European Constitutional Order*, EUI Working Paper 2004/7 (Fiesole, EUI, 2004).

## (b)   The Directorates-General

The majority of Commission employees work for the Directorates-General (DG), which are the administrative arms of the Commission. Directorates-General are the equivalent of ministries within a national government. In the current Commission, there are twenty-seven Directorates-General.[16] In addition, there are a number of specialised services, such as the European Anti-Fraud Office, EUROSTAT (the Commission statistical office), the Joint Research Centre, the Internal Audit Service and the EuropeAid Cooperation Office. Finally, there are a number of overarching services, most notably the Legal Service and the Secretariat-General, which provides support to the President. Historically, the portfolios allocated to individual Commissioners did not necessarily equate with a particular Directorate-General. The initial purpose was to emphasise the collegiality of the Commission and to allow the College to coordinate between Directorates-General. As the Commission grew, the mismatch came to be seen as a source of inefficiency.[17] This mismatch has been reduced with the current Commission, so that the portfolio of most Commissioners is synonymous with a particular Directorate-General. However, the fit is still not perfect. Energy and Transport, for example, are dealt with by Commissioners, but only one Directorate-General.

The variety of fields and roles in which the Commission is engaged results in there being little cohesion between the different Directorates-General.[18] Put simply, the interests, backgrounds and values of those officials working for the Environment DG are likely to be very different from those working in the Competition DG. In addition to this, the work of each DG may focus on very different tasks. The bulk of the work of the Environment DG will be concentrated around the proposal and enforcement of legislation. By contrast, in the fields of education and culture the Community has no law-making powers. The work of officials in that DG focuses on the development of programmes, administration of Community funding and bringing different public and private actors together. This leads to different DGs having quite distinct cultures. This distinctiveness is reinforced by poor central coordinating mechanisms, which lead, arguably, to insufficient exchange between the DGs and to poor policy coherence because different DGs are often working in very different directions.[19]

---

16 They are Press and Communication; Economic and Financial Affairs; Enterprise and Industry; Competition; Employment, Social Affairs and Equal Opportunities; Agriculture and Rural Development; Energy and Transport; Environment; Research; Information Society and Media; Fisheries and Maritime Affairs; Internal Market and Services; Regional Policy; Taxation and Customs Union; Education and Culture; Health and Consumer Protection; Justice, Freedom and Security; External Relations; Trade; Development; Enlargement; Humanitarian Aid; Personnel and Administration; Informatics; Budget; Interpretation; Translation.

17 P. Ludlow, 'The European Commission' in R. Keohane and S. Hoffmann, *The New European Community: Decision Making and Institutional Change* (Boulder, Westview Press, 1991), 85, 91–3.

18 L. Cram, 'The European Commission as a Multi-Organization: Social Policy and IT Policy in the EU' (1994) 1 *JEPP* 195.

19 L. Hooghe, *The European Commission and the Integration of Europe* (Cambridge, Cambridge University Press, 2001) 201–5.

The other noteworthy feature of the Commission is the extent to which it is shaped by external influences. A study found that Commission officials were not zealots working towards some goal of a united Europe, but that their views were most strongly shaped by their prior professional backgrounds, their nationality and their party political views.[20] More importantly, it found that Commission officials spend 38 per cent of their time on policy-related matters with people from outside of the Commission.[21] This is an organisation aware of its weak public image and is particularly porous to external influence. The problem is frequently not that it does not listen, but rather to whom it listens.

### (c)   The Cabinets

As we have shown, the College of Commissioners represents very much the political arm of the Commission, while the DGs represent the administrative arm. Between them, sit the Cabinets. Formally appointed by the President, each Cabinet is the Office of a Commissioner. Composed of six officials,[22] the Cabinets act, first, as the interface between the Commissioner and the DGs under her aegis. They enable liaison between the two, and they help the Commissioner with formulating priorities and policies. They also act as the eyes and ears for the Commissioner, keeping her informed about what is happening elsewhere in the Commission. Finally, they combine with other Cabinets to prepare the weekly meetings for the College of Commissioners.

These seemingly administrative tasks place the Cabinets in a very strong position within the Commission. The preparation of the meetings between the Commissioners forecloses a great deal of debate in the College, because in reality, much is negotiated between the Cabinets. Similarly, by acting as the interface between the Commission and the DG, they inevitably become gate-keepers to the Commissioner, who must be negotiated with by DG officials wishing to put forward particular ideas. Their role is, thus, controversial. DGs have seen them at times as Machiavellian, bypassing normal procedures and sabotaging perfectly acceptable proposals.[23] The dividing line between their responsibilities and those of the DGs is often unclear, with a grey line being drawn by the Prodi Commission between the formulation of policy, for which Cabinets were responsible, and its implementation, for which DGs were responsible.[24]

### (ii)   Powers of the Commission

### (a)   Legislative and quasi-legislative powers

The Commission has direct legislative powers in only two limited fields. It can issue Directives to ensure that public undertakings comply with the rules contained in the

---

20 *Ibid.* ch. 8.     21 *Ibid.* 41.     22 The President's Cabinet is larger, with ten officials.
23 J. Peterson, 'The Santer Era: The European Commission in Normative, Historical and Theoretical Perspective' (1999) 6 *JEPP* 46.
24 N. Nugent, *The European Commission* (Basingstoke, Palgrave, 2001) 127–31.

Treaty[25] and can issue Regulations determining the conditions under which Community nationals may reside in another Member State after having worked there.[26] It has more significant powers in the field of delegated legislation. Under Article 202 EC, the Council can confer quasi-legislative powers upon the Commission. This provision is reciprocated by Article 211 EC, which imposes corresponding duties on the Commission to exercise the powers delegated to it. The remit of the quasi-legislative powers capable of being delegated has been interpreted very broadly. Whilst the Council cannot delegate the essential elements of a policy to the Commission, it can delegate any other legal powers. The implications of this were spelt out in *Afrikanische Fruchtcompanie*. This case revolved around the importation of bananas into the Union. Two million were allowed in without having to pay tariffs. Prior to 1993, the determination of the criteria for which bananas could benefit from this quota were determined by the Council. It delegated this responsibility to the Commission, but stated that it had to have regard to traditional trade flows. When the Commission used slightly different criteria, a German importer sued, claiming that the Council had delegated powers which were too wide.

> ### Joined Cases T-64/01 and T-65/01 *Afrikanische Fruchtcompanie v Council* [2004] ECR II-521
>
> 118. Under [Article 211 EC], the Commission, with a view to ensuring the proper functioning and development of the common market, is to exercise the powers conferred on it by the Council for the implementation of the rules laid down by the latter. According to settled case-law, it is clear from the Treaty context in which that article must be placed and also from practical requirements that the concept of implementation must be given a wide interpretation. Since only the Commission is in a position to keep track of agricultural market trends and to act quickly when necessary, the Council may confer on it wide powers in that sphere. Consequently, the limits of those powers must be determined by reference amongst other things to the essential general aims of the market organization . . . Thus, the Court has held that, in matters relating to agriculture, the Commission is authorised to adopt all the implementing measures which are necessary or appropriate for the implementation of the basic legislation, provided that they are not contrary to such legislation or to the implementing legislation adopted by the Council . . .
>
> 119. The Court of Justice has also held that a distinction must be drawn between rules which, since they are essential to the subject-matter envisaged, must be reserved to the Council's power, and those which, being merely of an implementing nature, may be delegated to the Commission . . . It stated that only those provisions which are intended to give concrete shape to the fundamental guidelines of Community policy can be classified as essential . . . The Court of Justice also stated that since the Council has laid down in its basic regulation the essential rules governing the matter in question, it may delegate to the Commission general implementing power without having to specify the essential components of the delegated power; for that purpose, a provision drafted in general terms provides a sufficient basis for the authority to act.

25  Article 86(3) EC.      26  Article 39(3)(d) EC.

The delegation of quasi-legislative powers to the Commission is very widespread. Provision for delegation is present in about 20 per cent of all legislation enacted since 1987. The figure is still higher where legislation either authorises expenditure or was adopted by qualified majority voting, with it being used in 66 per cent of all expenditure-authorising legislation and in 67 per cent of legislation adopted under the single market procedures.[27] Highly significant matters have also been delegated. The measure prompting the BSE crisis, the prohibition on the export of beef and bovine products from the United Kingdom, was instigated under powers granted to the Commission to make veterinary and zootechnical checks on live animals and products with a view to the completion of the internal market.[28] The measure had huge implications for animal welfare, public health, public finances and the livelihood of farmers across the European Union. These were so big that they prompted a political crisis across the Union.[29]

Such widespread delegation raises questions of democratic accountability.[30] One justification is that the laborious nature of the primary law-making procedures can result in pressing decisions not being taken sufficiently quickly. Another is policy credibility. Primary legislatures may neither have the expertise nor be able to take a sufficiently long-term view of matters, because of fears about electoral accountability. Finally, it can be argued that the grant of legislative powers to the Commission in highly technical areas liberates other institutions, allowing them to spend more time on what 'matters'. Yet, even if these were accepted, they should not provide a blank cheque to the Commission to legislate in so many areas.[31] The absence of a requirement to justify why delegation is taking place is a striking failure of the EU system of governance.

Since the early 1960s, the exercise of these powers has been monitored by committees composed of representatives of the national governments. In certain circumstances, these committees can refer a matter to the Council, one of the primary legislative bodies in the Union, to overrule the Commission. This process, known as comitology, is dealt with in more detail in chapter 4.[32] It is sufficient to note here that members of these committees represent governmental interests and, insofar as they are experts, also monitor the technical quality of the Commission's work. Even to secure these interests, these are quite modest controls, with an eschewal of the

27 R. Dogan, 'Comitology: Little Procedures with Big Implications' (1997) 20 *WEP* 36. Similar findings are made in F. Franchino, 'Delegating Powers in the European Community' (2004) 34 *BJPS* 269.

28 The measure was Decision 96/239/EC, OJ 1996 L78/47. The principal basis for it was Directive 90/425/EEC, OJ 1990 L224/29, Article 10(4).

29 See p. 31.

30 M. Cini, 'The Commission: an Unelected Legislator?' (2002) 8(4) *Journal of Legislative Studies* 14.

31 G. Majone, 'Two Logics of Delegation: Agency and Fiduciary Relations in EU Governance' (2001) 2 *EUP* 103; F. Franchino, 'Efficiency or Credibility? Testing the Two Logics of Delegation to the European Commission' (2002) 9(5) *JEPP* 1; M. Pollack, *The Engines of European Integration: Delegation, Agency and Agenda-Setting in the EU* (Oxford, Oxford University Press, 2003) 101–7.

32 See pp. 159–67.

more rigorous types of control that are present in the USA to control similar delegated powers.[33] More broadly, they do not secure other values one would expect in a mature polity, such as value pluralism, transparency or due process.

Some awareness of the unsatisfactory state of affairs permeated into the debate on the Constitutional Treaty. The consequence was that it was proposed that increased judicial powers of scrutiny be put in place where the Commission was exercising its delegated powers. Individuals could challenge these acts, known as Regulations, in the Constitutional Treaty. Primary legislation was described as laws or framework laws under the Constitutional Treaty[34] and could be challenged by any individual if they were to be directly concerned. This would be the case wherever it directly prejudiced her legal rights.[35] The consequence would have been that it would have been much easier for a wide variety of private parties to challenge Commission quasi-legislation, and that delegated legislation would have been much more heavily scrutinised by the Community courts.

### (b)   Agenda-setting

The Commission has responsibility for initiating the policy process in a number of ways. It, first, decides the legislative programme for each year.[36] Secondly, it has a monopoly over the power of legislative initiative under the EC Treaty. It can make proposals under the CSFP[37] and PJCC.[38] It also has the power of financial initiative. The Commission starts the budgetary process by placing a draft budget before the Parliament and the Council.[39] Finally, the Commission is responsible for stimulating policy debate more generally. The most celebrated example of this was the White Paper on Completion of the Internal Market, which set out an agenda and timetable for completing the internal market by the end of 1992.[40]

Very few proposals are at the Commission's own initiative.[41] It enjoys, instead, a gate-keeper role, where different interests – national governments, industry, NGOs – come to it with legislative suggestions. This results in the Commission being far more politicised than traditional civil service, as it transforms it into a market-place for the development of ideas and accommodation of interests, with a variety of parties, both public and private, seeking to influence it.[42] The matter will be assigned to the DG within whose field the proposal seems to fall most clearly. The DG will appoint a senior official as rapporteur. This rapporteur will be responsible

---

33 These include time limits on delegation, appeal procedures, public hearings and requirements for explicit legislative approval. F. Franchino, 'Delegating Powers in the European Community' (2004) 34 *BJPS* 269.
34 Article I-33(1) CT.
35 Case C-486/01P *Front National v Parliament*, judgment of 29 June 2004.
36 For 2005, see EC Commission, *Commission Work Programme for 2005*, COM(2005)15.
37 Article 22(1) TEU.        38 Article 34(2) TEU.        39 Article 272(2) EC.        40 COM(85)doc310 final.
41 Only 5–10 per cent of proposals are put as own initiative proposals. N. Nugent, *The European Commission* (Basingstoke, Palgrave, 2001) 236–7.
42 G. Peters, 'Agenda-Setting in the European Community' (1994) 1 *JEPP* 9.

to a 'management board' of senior officials within the DG. He is responsible for internal consultation with other interested DGs and for external consultation with outside parties. The external consultation will take place in expert committees, consisting of national officials and experts and advisory committees composed of different sectional interests (e.g. industry, consumer and environmental groups and trade unions). The proposal has then to be vetted by the Commission Legal Service for its legality. It will then be adopted by a lead Commissioner with responsibility for the portfolio, who will choose whether to put it before the other Commissioners.

These powers of proposal are significant because they make the Commission both an agenda-setter and a veto-player. Nothing can happen without the Commission deciding to make a proposal in the first place and it can frame the terms of debate and legislation. It also gives the Commission significant influence in the subsequent debates. Because it can withdraw a proposal at any time, parties cannot ignore its views even after the proposal has been made. However, the power should not be over-estimated. Its influence depends upon a number of variables. Central, is institutional context. In areas where a unanimity vote by Member States is not required, the Commission can act as a broker between some actors and to outmanoeuvre others.[43] In some areas, it can induce other institutions to adopt its proposal as the 'lesser evil', by threatening other powers at its disposal, such as bringing a Member State before the Court of Justice, which would lead to more draconian consequences.[44] There is also a temporal dimension. If the Commission is impatient, its influence is weakened as it has to accept more readily the views of the other institutions. The reverse is true if the other institutions are impatient for a measure to be adopted.[45]

The traditional justification for the Commission's powers was that its autonomy would result in its being best able to represent the common European interest.[46] Over time, this justification has come to carry less weight. The transfer of competences to the European Union has not always resulted in a corresponding transfer of powers to the Commission. It shares its power of initiative in the second and third pillars with the Member States. Increasingly, national governments have taken an interest in agenda-setting and limiting the Commission's discretion.[47] The Council, through its Presidency, sets out legislative timetables of six months each, which the Commission is expected to follow. More wide-ranging, in 2002, the European Council agreed to

43  S. Schmidt, 'Only an Agenda-Setter? The Commission's Power over the Council of Ministers' (2000) 1 *EUP* 37.

44  S. Schmidt, 'The European Commission's Powers in Shaping Policies' in D. Dimitrakopoulos (ed.), *The Changing Commission* (Manchester, Manchester University Press, 2004).

45  M. Pollack, 'Delegation, Agency and Agenda Setting in the European Community' (1997) 51 *IO* 99, 121–4.

46  K. Featherstone, 'Jean Monnet and the "Democratic Deficit" in the European Union' (1994) 32 *JCMS* 149, 154–5.

47  G. Majone, *Dilemmas of European Integration: The Ambiguities and Pitfalls of Stealth by Integration* (Oxford, Oxford University Press, 2005) 51–3.

be far more hands-on in determining the legislative agenda of the Union, agreeing and revising annual and tri-annual legislative programmes every year.[48]

### (c)   Executive powers

The Commission is responsible for ensuring that the EC's revenue is collected and passed on by national authorities and that the correct rates are applied. It is also responsible for overseeing and coordinating a large part of Community expenditure. There are four important funds: the European Social Fund (ESF), the European Regional Development Fund (ERDF), the European Agricultural Guidance and Guarantee Fund, Guidance Section (EAGFF) and the Financial Instrument for Fisheries (FIFG). In addition, it is responsible for administering Community aid to third countries. Thirdly, the Commission exercises a supervisory role over 'frontline' policy implementation. Whilst national administrations are responsible for Customs and Excise and Agricultural Intervention Boards, the Commission will check to ensure that there is a degree of uniformity. Fourthly, the Commission represents the EC in its external trade relations with third states and in international organisations. It thus represents the European Union in the WTO and participates in the work of the United Nations,[49] the Council of Europe[50] and the OECD.[51] In addition, the Commission handles applications for membership of the European Union by carrying out an investigation of the implications of membership and submitting an opinion to the Council.

### (d)   Supervisory powers

The Commission acts as the 'conscience of the Community'. First, it may bring Member States before the Court of Justice for breaching EC law.[52] It uses this power extensively. At the end of 2003, for example, the Commission had instigated proceedings in 3,927 cases.[53] Of these, only very few actually resulted in Court judgments. In 2003, there were only eighty-six judgments.[54] The Commission is also responsible for monitoring compliance by Member States with judgments of the Court of Justice. It can bring those Member States, which it considers to have failed to comply, back before the Court to have them fined. At the end of 2003, there were sixty-nine such cases outstanding.[55] The Commission can also bring other EU institutions before the Court for failure to comply with EC law.[56] Finally, the Commission enjoys certain regulatory powers. It can declare illegal state aids provided by Member States[57] or measures enacted in favour of public undertakings which breach the Treaty.[58] It has also been granted powers to declare anti-competitive practices by private undertakings

---

48  This is discussed below.       49  Article 302 EC.       50  Article 303 EC.
51  Article 304 EC.       52  Article 226 EC.
53  EC Commission, *Twenty First Annual Report on Monitoring the Application of Community Law*, COM(2004)839, 4.
54  *Annual Report of the Court of Justice 2003* (OOPEC, 2004) 221.
55  EC Commission, *Twenty First Annual Report*, above n. 53, 4.
56  Article 230(1) EC.       57  Article 88 EC.       58  Article 86(3) EC.

illegal and to fine those firms,[59] as well as the power to impose duties on goods coming from third states, which are benefiting from 'unfair' trade practices, such as dumping or export subsidies.[60]

### (iii)  Regulatory agencies and the Commission

The concentration of so many functions in the Commission has placed pressure on its resources. Its executive and supervisory functions are particularly time-consuming. Starting in the early 1970s, but gathering pace in the mid-1990s, a preference emerged for delegating specialised and time-consuming tasks to independent agencies and offices rather than for using the Commission as a repository for further regulatory competencies.[61] Three agencies have significant powers. The Office for Harmonisation in the Internal Market has the power to register the Community trademark and the Community Plant Variety Office has a similar power for Community plant variety rights, whilst the Agency for Evaluation of Medicinal Products provides a technical evaluation for the authorisation of new medicines. These tasks were, however, very confined. All other agencies did little more than provide information. This delegation took on a new urgency following the mismanagement scandals of the Santer Commission; a Task Force for Administrative Reform was established in 1999. One of the recommendations of this Task Force was that the Commission was administering too much, and more needed to be delegated to specialised agencies.[62] This theme was taken up a year later in the Commission's White Paper on Governance, which advocated:

> The creation of further autonomous EU regulatory agencies in clearly defined areas will improve the way rules are applied and enforced across the Union. Such agencies should be granted the power to take individual decisions in application of regulatory measures. They should operate with a degree of independence and within a clear framework established by the legislature. The regulation creating each agency should set out the limits of their activities and powers, their responsibilities and requirements for openness.[63]

Since the White Paper, a further six agencies have been created, with a further two proposed.[64] These 'New Regulatory Agencies' are much more directly engaged

---

59 Regulation 1/2003/EC, OJ 2001 L1/1, Articles 7 and 23 respectively.
60 In relation to dumping see Regulation 384/96/EC, OJ 1996 L56/1, especially Articles 7–9.
61 These are the European Centre for the Development of Vocational Training; European Foundation for the Improvement of Living and Working Conditions; European Environment Agency; European Training Foundation; European Monitoring Centre for Drugs and Drug Addiction; European Agency for the Evaluation of Medicinal Products; Office for Harmonisation in the Internal Market (Trade Marks and Designs); European Agency for Health and Safety at Work; Community Plant Variety Office; European Centre for Monitoring Racism and Xenophobia; European Agency for Reconstruction; Translation Centre for the Bodies of the European Union.
62 EC Commission, Reforming the Commission, COM(2000)200, Part I, 6.
63 EC Commission, European Governance: A White Paper, COM(2001)428, 24.
64 These are the European Food Safety Authority; European Maritime Safety Agency; European Aviation Safety Authority; European Network and Information Security Agency; European Railway Agency;

in policy formulation and implementation than the earlier agencies. The various agencies have differing powers. Perhaps the most wide-ranging are those enjoyed by the European Food Safety Authority (EFSA).[65] The central power of this agency is to issue scientific opinions on which food and animal feed is safe. Whilst the Commission is not bound by these opinions in adopting legislation or authorising the marketing of food, it must consult the EFSA before doing this.[66] It can depart from EFSA's opinions on grounds of safety only where it can provide an alternative, equally authoritative, contradictory opinion. This is difficult and, in practice, the Commission has always followed EFSA's opinions. The consequence has been that the latter has become the central institution for determining which food may be marketed in the European Union. The disadvantages of using agencies are set out below.

> ## M. Shapiro, 'The Problems of Independent Agencies in the United States and the European Union' (1997) 4 *Journal of European Public Policy* 262, 281–2
>
> The standard, overt rationale for the creation of EU agencies is that they ought to be partially or wholly independent of the Commission because they are 'managerial', perform 'technical' tasks or are engaged in 'information' gathering and analysis only . . .
>
> Is all this managerial-technical-informational talk simply a smoke screen for the more fundamental argument that, because Europeans don't like the technocrats in Brussels and fear concentrating even more governance there, if we want more EU technocrats, we need to split them up and scatter them about Europe? I think the answer to this question is largely yes but not entirely.
>
> A second motive is, I believe, a kind of 'neo-functionalism'. If currently direct routes to further political integration of the Union are blocked, following Haas's old arguments about the World Health Organisation and the UN, further growth can be achieved indirectly through the proliferation of small, limited jurisdictions, allegedly 'technical agencies' that will appear politically innocuous. That is why it is not enough to say that the agencies are not in Brussels. It must also be said that they are merely technical or informational.
>
> A third motive is about technocracy. The Member State composed management boards were no doubt a political necessity. But by stressing the technical and informational functions of these agencies, by making each highly specialised to a particular technology and by incorporating large components of scientific personnel, there is undoubtedly the hope that the technocrats will take over these agencies from the politicians. And the technocrats for each of these agencies, it is hoped, will create Europe-wide epistemic communities whose technical truths transcend intergovernmental politics. As Americans say 'there is no Republican or

European Centre for Disease Prevention and Control. The proposals are for a Chemicals Agency and External Frontiers Agency. EC Commission, Proposal for a European Chemicals Agency, COM(2003)644; EC Commission, Proposal for a European Agency for the Management of Operational Cooperation at the External Frontiers, COM(2003)687. The most wide-ranging analysis is D. Geradin and N. Petit, 'The Development of Agencies at EU and National Levels: Conceptual Analysis and Proposals for Reform' (2004) 14 *YBEL* 137.

65  The central powers of EFSA are set out in Regulation 178/2002/EC, OJ 2002 L31/1.
66  Case T-13/99 *Pfizer v Council* [2002] ECR II-3305. See *EUL*, pp. 484–6.

Democratic way to pave a street', Europeans may be able to say there is no French or Greek way. Thus, while the proffered technocratic rationales do not really explain why the agencies should be independent of the Commission, they do explain why the agencies should each take a small slice of allegedly technical-informational activity. That kind of organisation is most likely, over time, to assure the internal dominance within each agency of its transnational technocrats over its national politicians.

### 3. The Council of Ministers

#### (i)   Powers and workings of the Council

The Council comprises a minister from each Member State, who is authorised to commit the government of that state.[67] The Council's powers are fivefold. First, in areas of policy where responsibility lies with the Member States, such as general economic policy, foreign and security policy, justice and home affairs, it acts as a forum within which Member States can consult with each other and coordinate their behaviour. Secondly, the Council can take the other institutions before the Court, either for actions which contravene EC law[68] or for failing to act when required by Community law.[69] Thirdly, the Council can request the Commission to undertake studies or submit legislative proposals.[70] Fourthly, the Council can delegate legislative powers to the Commission. The fifth and most influential role is the power of final decision on the adoption of legislation in most areas of EU policy. This power of assent bolsters the Council's influence at earlier stages in the decision-making process because the other institutions are aware that a proposal will only become law if it has the Council's approval and, thus, tailor their actions accordingly.

The ministers representing each Member State are those equipped to represent the government on that matter. Environment Ministers will sit in the Environmental Council and agriculture or fisheries ministers in the Agriculture and Fisheries Council. Since 2002, it has been agreed that more than one minister from each Member State may sit in a Council meeting, particularly where an issue crosses different ministerial portfolios.[71] Most Councils meet formally between once a month and once every two months. The Council sits in nine configurations:

- General Affairs and External Relations;
- Economic and Financial Affairs;
- Justice and Home Affairs;
- Employment, Social Policy and Consumer Affairs;
- Competitiveness;
- Transport, Telecommunications and Energy;

---

67 Article 203 EC.     68 Article 230 EC.     69 Article 232 EC.     70 Article 208 EC.

71 The rules for the Council are set out in Decision 2002/682/EC, EURATOM adopting the Council's Rules of Procedure, OJ 2002 L230/7.

- Agriculture and Fisheries;
- Environment;
- Education, Youth and Culture.

Special mention must be made of the General Affairs and External Relations Council. Composed of Foreign Ministers, this Council sits in two different forms of session. As the External Relations Council, it decides on the Union's foreign and security policy. It has a very different role when it sits as the General Affairs Council. There, it has a number of functions. It deals with dossiers affecting more than one of the Union's policies, such as enlargement or preparation of the Budget. It prepares and follows up meetings of the Heads of Government in the European Council. Finally, it coordinates the work of the other Councils. The strengthening of the General Affairs Council in 2002 was designed to counter a number of features, which were weakening the cohesion of the Council. Decision-making was fragmented by the specialised nature of the different Council configurations. Furthermore, the floating membership of each Council, with the constant changing of ministers and governments, and its occasional nature, namely that it only met once a month, were felt to weaken any sense of collective identity.

At the 'Future of Europe' Convention, there was doubt as to whether the General Affairs Council managed to remedy these defects. The Convention proposed the establishment of a permanent General and Legislative Affairs Council, which would sit over all the other Council formations.[72] When this sat as the General Affairs Council, its responsibility was to prepare and follow up the work of the Heads of Government in the European Council. When it sat as the Legislative Affairs Council, its function was to create a monopoly within the Council over the adoption of legislation. The idea was, therefore, to create a corpus of semi-permanent Ministers of Europe, who would deal with all the legislative responsibilities of the Council and its relations with the Heads of Government. The idea was rejected at the IGC. It was felt there would be too great a concentration of power in this new Council. It would act as an alternative base of power that might 'go native' – start acting on behalf of the supranational interest rather than representing national interests. There were also concerns about creating a hierarchy of Councils, with the role of other Council formations becoming increasingly unclear. Instead, the status of the General Affairs Council was formalised and its role entrenched. It was not to have overarching legislative functions but, in keeping with current practice, it was to ensure consistency in the tasks of the other Council configurations and to continue to prepare and follow up the work of European Councils.[73]

### (ii)  Decision-making within the Council

The first form of voting is the *simple majority* vote. Under this system, each member of the Council has one vote, and thirteen votes are required for a measure to be adopted.

72 Article I-23(1) DCT.      73 Article I-24(2) CT.

This procedure is used in only a few areas, principally procedural ones, as it fails to protect national interests and undue weight is given to the interests of small states at the expense of larger ones. The only area of real significance that is subject to a simple majority vote is the decision to convene an intergovernmental conference to amend the TEU.[74] The converse of simple majority voting is voting by *unanimity*. Every Member State has a veto on any legislation being considered. It must actively vote against a measure for it to be vetoed; abstention is insufficient. Unanimity voting is used in those areas of the TEU which are more politically sensitive. Its requirement is still widespread in the Treaty.[75] The final form of voting frequently used is that of *qualified majority voting* (QMV). This is a weighted system of voting, under which each Member State is allocated a number of votes. If the measure is proposed by the Commission, it requires 232 out of 321 possible votes to be adopted and at least thirteen states must vote for it. In the rare circumstances where a measure is not proposed by the Commission, it requires 232 votes, but at least two-thirds of the Member States must vote for it. In either case, any Member State can ask to verify that states representing at least 62 per cent of the total EU population supported it. The respective votes and population sizes are shown in Table 3.1.

The way in which the votes are weighted aims to achieve a delicate balance between preserving individual national voice and reflecting the different population sizes of the Member States. Since the 2004 enlargement, however, the majority of EU Member States are 'small', with populations of less than 10 million. One has the perverse situation where the fifteen smallest Member States have a combined population of 57.6 million citizens, about two-thirds of the German population, but combined, they have 102 votes, almost four times the number of votes of Germany. This is not the only anomaly, as each state's voting strength depended as much upon its perseverance in the negotiations at the Treaty of Nice as on anything else. France insisted, therefore, upon equal votes to Germany, despite having a population only two-thirds the size of the latter. Belgium made a similar demand with regard to the Netherlands, despite similar proportions. The concession eventually made was that the Netherlands would have one more vote. The most overrepresented states, however, are Poland and Spain. These were each given only two votes less than Germany, despite having populations less than half the size of that of Germany.

This question was revisited at the Convention, where it was proposed that a QMV should be a majority of Member States, representing at least three-fifths of the population of the Union.[76] This was opposed by both the smaller Member States, Poland and Spain, who argued that this allowed any three of the four largest Member States

---

74 Article 48 TEU. The others are adoption of the Council's own rules of procedure (Article 207(3) EC); extension of time limits for the legislative procedures (Articles 251(7) EC and 252(g) EC); request for the Commission to undertake studies or submit proposals (Article 208 EC).

75 The Annex at the end of this book contains a list of the different legislative competences of the Union and the procedures and voting requirements used.

76 Article 24(1) DCT.

Table 3.1. *Qualified majority voting: Member States' votes and population size*

| State | Votes | Population (million) |
|---|---|---|
| Germany | 29 | 82 |
| United Kingdom | 29 | 59.4 |
| France | 29 | 59.1 |
| Italy | 29 | 57.7 |
| Spain | 27 | 39.4 |
| Poland | 27 | 38.6 |
| Netherlands | 13 | 15.8 |
| Greece | 12 | 10.6 |
| Czech Republic | 12 | 10.3 |
| Belgium | 12 | 10.2 |
| Hungary | 12 | 10 |
| Portugal | 12 | 9.9 |
| Sweden | 10 | 8.9 |
| Austria | 10 | 8.1 |
| Slovakia | 7 | 5.4 |
| Denmark | 7 | 5.3 |
| Finland | 7 | 5.2 |
| Lithuania | 7 | 3.7 |
| Ireland | 7 | 3.7 |
| Latvia | 4 | 2.4 |
| Slovenia | 4 | 2 |
| Estonia | 4 | 1.4 |
| Cyprus | 4 | 0.8 |
| Luxembourg | 4 | 0.4 |
| Malta | 3 | 0.4 |

to come together to veto a measure. Despite an absence of evidence that this has ever happened,[77] a new formula was devised at the IGC:

> ### Article I-25(1) CT
>
> A qualified majority shall be defined as at least 55 per cent of the members of the Council, comprising at least fifteen of them and representing Member States comprising at least 65 per cent of the population of the Union.
>
> A blocking minority must include at least four Council members, failing which the qualified majority shall be deemed attained.

---

[77] M. Mattila and J. Lane, 'Why Unanimity in the Council? A Roll-Call Analysis of Council Voting' (2001) 2 *EUP* 31.

Poland and Spain were still dissatisfied with this formula, as their voting influence was reduced considerably. To meet this concern, it was agreed that the new arrangements would not enter into force until 31 October 2009.[78] A further Declaration was also added. This stated that if Member States representing three-quarters of the population or a sufficient number of Member States necessary to block a measure indicated their opposition, there would be further discussion.[79] In other words, no vote would be taken. This further relaxation would allow Poland and Spain to form blocking minorities of four states with any combination of the six largest Member States.

Traditionally, the distinction between unanimity and QMV has been seen as influencing the climate of negotiation. Under unanimity, it is argued that Member States, aware of their veto, are inclined to have a heightened sense of self-interest and to look for matching concessions.[80] In circumstances where Member States do not have a veto, they are aware of the possibility of outmanoeuvring. A climate of problem-solving prevails, with Member States looking far more towards constructing common solutions and being less protective of their initial positions.[81] Whilst these differences in style may exist on occasion, more recent, empirical studies have suggested the differences to be less stark. Votes were taken in the Council in only about 25 per cent of matters discussed, even under QMV.[82] The majority of voting is concentrated, moreover, in two sectors, agriculture and fisheries. Studies suggest that there is a desire to realise consensus, with states not wishing to exercise their veto or marginalise other states. The key dynamic, a study by Beyers and Dierickx suggests, is not the form of vote taken, but the presence of central players and smaller players.[83] The central players tend to be the large Member States and the Commission, which acts as mediator. Other states see themselves as having to mediate with these, and rarely negotiate with other partners. Negotiations are, thus, principally driven within the Council by a few key players.

This focus on consensus has led to concerns about the quality of debate in the Council. In 2002, it was agreed that where the co-decision legislative procedure was used, parts of Council meetings should be open to the public. This would include the

---

78  Protocol to the Constitutional Treaty on Transitional Provisions relating to the Institutions and Bodies of the Union, Article 2. For further analysis see D. Cameron, 'The Stalemate in the Constitutional IGC over the Definition of a Qualified Majority' (2004) 5 *EUP* 373.

79  Declaration 5 on Article I-25, Article 2.

80  F. Scharpf, 'The Joint Decision Trap: Lessons from German Federalism and European Integration' (1988) 66 *Public Administration* 239. Contra, B. Peters, 'Escaping the Joint Decision Trap: Repetition and Sectoral Politics in the European Union' (1997) 20 *WEP* 22. A good introduction to the different types of interaction in the Council is H. Wallace, 'The Council: An Institutional Chameleon?' (2002) 15 *Governance* 325.

81  F. Hayes-Renshaw and H. Wallace, *The Council of Ministers* (Basingstoke, Macmillan, 1997) 256–8.

82  M. Mattili, 'Contested Decisions: Empirical Analysis of Voting in the Council of Ministers' (2004) 43 *EJPR* 29; F. Hayes-Renshaw, W. van Aken and H. Wallace, 'When and Why the Council of Ministers of the EU Votes Explicitly', paper presented at Austin, Texas, 1 April 2005.

83  J. Beyers and G. Dierickx, 'The Working Groups of the Council of the European Union: Supranational or Intergovernmental Negotiations?' (1998) 36 *JCMS* 289.

initial presentation of the proposal by the Commission to the Council, the ensuing debate and the votes and explanation of votes. The form of public access was, however, of a limited kind, as it involved only the provision of a room in which the public could watch via live feed.[84] This was taken a step further in the Constitutional Treaty, where it was decided that all Council meetings, where a vote was to be taken on a legislative act, should be held in public.[85] This may go ahead, notwithstanding the non-ratification of the Constitutional Treaty, as there is a strong desire that the Council be more open and accountable. This approach is not without risks. It may lead to grandstanding by individual ministers for the benefit of their home constituencies, thereby obstructing problem-solving. Furthermore, as it would only be the formal meetings that are made public, there is a fear that the real decision-making processes will be driven elsewhere, out of sight, with the Council becoming no more than a ratifying body designed, more than anything else, for public show.

### (iii)   Management of the Council: the Presidency, the Secretariat and COREPER

The Presidency of the Council rotates between the Member States for six months at a time. The Presidency has a number of duties:

- it arranges and chairs Council meetings and sets the agenda for them;[86]
- it represents the Council both before the other EU institutions and in the world more generally;
- it acts as a 'neutral broker' between other Member States in order to secure legislation;
- it sets the legislative agenda for its six-month term of office; this will be done in consultation with the Commission and the Presidencies preceding and succeeding it.

There is some debate about the power of the Presidency. It has been argued that the short term of office and the need not to appear too partisan restrict it to an essentially clerical role.[87] Certainly, these features prevent the Presidency from hijacking the agenda of the Council to further national priorities. Nevertheless, in a study of eight Presidencies, Bailleul and Versluys found that whilst these had to stay within the mandates set by their predecessors or the Commission, they have a soft power in the form of discretion to steer or shape these agendas.[88] If they had been given only a vague mandate to realise a task, they could choose, instead, to make it a priority for their Presidency. Unanticipated events, such as September 11, also provide opportunities

---

84 Decision 2002/682/EC, EURATOM, above n. 71, Article 8(1).        85 Article I-24(6) CT.

86 Decision 2002/682/EC, EURATOM, above n. 71, Article 20.

87 A sceptical review of this literature is to be found in J. Tallberg, 'The Agenda-Shaping Powers of the EU Council Presidency' (2003) 10 *JEPP* 1.

88 E. Bailleul and H. Versluys, 'The EU Rotating Presidency: "Hostage Taker" of the European Agenda?', paper presented at EUSA Conference, 30 March 2005.

for agenda-setting. As they require new forms of response from the Union, reliance is placed on the Presidency to organise that response and set out the framework for future action.

Whilst the Presidency sets out the overall framework for Council meetings, the mundane details are carried out by the Secretariat.[89] Based in Brussels, the central functions of the Secretariat are conference organisation and committee servicing. It produces documents, arranges translation, takes notes and organises meeting rooms. It also provides advice to the Council on the legality of its actions and will represent the Council before the other institutions. It will thus be the Council Secretariat who will litigate on behalf of the Council in the Court of Justice or represent the Council before European Parliament Committees.[90]

However, the central body in the preparation of Council meetings is the Committee of Permanent Representatives (COREPER). The formal duties of COREPER are merely to prepare the work of the Council and carry out any tasks assigned to it.[91] It has no power to take formal decisions other than ones on Council procedure.[92] It is divided into COREPER I, which is composed of deputy permanent representatives and is responsible for issues such as the environment, social affairs, the internal market and transport. COREPER II consists of permanent representatives of ambassadorial rank responsible for the more sensitive issues, such as economic and financial affairs and external relations. Each meets weekly. Successive reports have recognised COREPER as essential to the functioning of the Council. It both alleviates the general workload of the Council and coordinates the work of the specialised Councils.[93]

The heart of COREPER's power lies in its setting the agenda for Council meetings and its dividing that agenda into 'A' and 'B' matters. 'A' items are technical matters on which there is agreement. These are nodded through in the Council meeting, without discussion. 'B' items, by contrast, are considered more contentious, requiring discussion. COREPER, therefore, decides on what the Council is to decide on. An 'A' item is effectively decided by COREPER and a 'B' item by the Council of Ministers. In this, the overwhelming majority of items are 'A' items. A study in the early 1990s found that of 500 items placed on the Agricultural Council agenda, ministers discussed only 13 per cent of them.[94]

In this, COREPER does not act as a loose cannon, but as a conduit for informing national capitals of the work of the European Union and for enabling national positions to be properly defended.[95] It is, thus, assisted by about 250 Working Groups

---

89  Article 207(2) EC.

90  F. Hayes-Renshaw and H. Wallace, *The Council of Ministers* (Basingstoke, Macmillan, 1997) ch. 4.

91  Article 207(1) EC.        92  Case C-25/94 *Commission v Council* [1996] ECR I-1469.

93  *Report on the European Institutions by the Committee of Three to the European Council* (Tindemans Report) (Brussels, EC Council, 1979) 49–54; *Report from the Ad Hoc Committee on Institutional Affairs to the European Council* (Dooge Report), EC Bulletin 3–1985, 3.5.1.

94  M v. Schendelen, '"The Council Decides": Does the Council Decide?' (1996) 34 *JCMS* 531.

95  F. Hayes-Renshaw, C. Lequesne and P. Lopez, 'The Permanent Representatives of the Member States of the European Union' (1989) 28 *JCMS* 119, 129–31.

of national civil servants. A Commission proposal is first passed to these Groups for analysis. These Groups provide Reports which set the agenda for COREPER meetings by indicating points on which there has been agreement within the Working Group (Roman I points) and points which need discussion within COREPER (Roman II points). It is best to see COREPER as the tip of complex networks of national administrations working together to agree legislation.[96] Even in this light, COREPER raises some concerns. It is not a strong guarantor of different ideological perspectives or strongly held national interests, as it is a body concerned with solving problems and reaching agreement, wherever possible.[97] The other concern raised by COREPER is government by 'moonlight'. Meetings of the COREPER are not public. Its minutes are not published and it is not accountable to any parliamentary assembly. To be sure, many decisions taken in any national government are taken by civil servants, but it is the unprecedented extent of COREPER's influence that raises particular concerns about accountability and transparency.

## 4. The European Council

The European Council comprises the Heads of Government of the Member States and the President of the Commission, and is a separate institution from the Council of Ministers. It was agreed in 1961 in Bonn that the Heads of Government should meet at regular intervals and this practice of 'summitry' was institutionalised in 1974 when it was agreed that they should meet at least three times a year. The European Council was not formally recognised until the Single European Act.[98] Its tasks were not fully articulated until the TEU.

---

**Article 4 TEU**

The European Council shall provide the Union with the necessary impetus for its development and shall define the general political guidelines thereof.

The European Council shall bring together the Heads of State or of Government of the Member States and the President of the Commission. They shall be assisted by the Ministers for Foreign Affairs of the Member States and by a member of the Commission. The European Council shall meet at least twice a year, under the chairmanship of the Head of State or of Government of the Member State which holds the Presidency of the Council.

The European Council shall submit to the European Parliament a report after each of its meetings and a yearly written report on the progress achieved by the Union.

---

Although the TEU provides that the European Council is only to meet twice a year, it was agreed in 2002 that the European Council would meet at least four times a year and, if necessary, could meet in extraordinary session beyond that. The TEU is

---

96 D. Bostock, 'COREPER Revisited' (2002) 40 *JCMS* 215, 231–2.
97 J. Lewis, 'National Interests: COREPER' in J. Peterson and M. Shackleton (eds.), *The Institutions of the European Union* (Oxford, Oxford University Press, 2002).
98 Article 2 SEA.

also rather oblique about the Council's responsibilities. These can be understood to involve roughly four duties.

First, the European Council makes decisions about the future institutional shape and new tasks of the European Union. Questions about whether to initiate or conclude treaty reform or enlargement are discussed and it is the defining body on these questions.

Secondly, the European Council plays an important role in the development of Community policy. Heads of Government have the domestic authority to resolve issues which have reached an impasse within the Council of Ministers. This role is not merely a problem-solving role, but also an agenda-setting one. The European Council will, frequently, agree programmes of legislation that must be agreed within a set time-frame. A good example of the type of programme that can be agreed is 'The Hague' programme, agreed by the European Council in November 2004. The objectives of this programme include:

• to improve the common capability of the European Union and its Member States to guarantee fundamental rights, minimum procedural safeguards and access to justice;
• to provide protection in accordance with the Geneva Convention on Refugees and other international treaties to persons in need;
• to regulate migration flows and to control the external borders of the Union;
• to fight organised cross-border crime and repress the threat of terrorism;
• to carry further the mutual recognition of judicial decisions and certificates in civil and in criminal matters, and to eliminate legal and judicial obstacles in litigation in civil and family matters with cross-border implications.[99]

Having set out the broad principles for the programme, the European Council asked the Commission to develop an Action Plan to implement these principles and to develop a scoreboard so that progress could be monitored. A division of labour takes place, in which the European Council sets the overall framework for policy-making, but the content and timing is dictated largely by the Commission.

Thirdly, the European Council has a particularly prominent role in the second pillar – Common Foreign and Security Policy (CFSP). Traditionally, the external relations of the European Union have taken up a considerable proportion of this institution's time, and, in this field, it has been more concerned with day-to-day detail. In addition to being responsible for defining the principles and general guidelines for a common foreign and security policy, it is also responsible for deciding on common strategies to be pursued in areas where Member States have important interests in common.[100]

---

99 Conclusions of the Presidency of the European Council 4/5 November 2004, Council Doc. 14292/1/04, Annex I.
100 Article 13(1) and (2) TEU.

Fourthly, the European Council has the pre-eminent institutional role in the so-called 'Lisbon process', and one of its annual four meetings, the Spring meeting, is dedicated exclusively to this. In 2000, at Lisbon, the European Union committed itself to becoming, by 2010, 'the most competitive and dynamic knowledge-based economy in the world, capable of sustainable economic growth with more and better jobs and greater social cohesion'.[101] To do this, it recognised it would have to carry out a number of tasks that did not fall within standard Community legislative competencies, most notably in the fields of welfare reform and macro- and micro-economic policy. To that end, it created a new form of legislative procedure, known as the open method of coordination (OMC), which is discussed in more detail in chapter 4. The European Council sits at the heart of this procedure and is central to both policy formulation and policy monitoring under it. Every year it sets guidelines combined with specific timetables for achieving the short, medium and long-term goals set in each of the fields in which OMC applies. Alongside this, it reviews the progress of individual Member States towards meeting the specific commitments they have made towards realising these goals. The workload is considerable. At the end of 2004, the process comprised 28 main objectives and 120 sub-objectives, with 117 different indicators. The reporting system for 25 Member States added up to 300 annual reports.[102]

Whilst the European Council has the resources to set priorities for the European Union, it is less clear that it can discharge the more extensive responsibilities demanded of it under both CFSP and the Lisbon process. To that end, in 2002, it was agreed that the General Affairs and External Relations Council would perform a similar role to COREPER. It would set an agenda for the European Council, agreeing items that could be adopted without discussion and those that needed further debate. If the item required discussion, the General Affairs and External Relations Council would prepare an outline paper, setting out the issues to be discussed and the options available.[103] This process, in turn, puts pressures on the General Affairs and External Relations Council, which comprises Foreign Ministers and which cannot be expected to manage well the gamut of issues that touch on matters other than foreign policy.

This was recognised in the Constitutional Treaty. The General Affairs Council would continue to prepare the work of the European Council. In addition, it was decided that the European Council would elect a President by qualified majority. This person would not be a national office holder, and would be elected for a term of two and a half years, renewable once. The central duties of the President would be to manage the business of the European Council. To that end, she would chair and drive forward its work, ensure that its meetings were prepared and seek to ensure consensus between its members.[104] There was widespread agreement amongst the Member

---

101  Conclusions of the Presidency, EU Bulletin 3–2000, I.5.
102  See http://europa.eu.int/growthandjobs/index_en.htm
103  Decision 2002/682/EC, EURATOM, above n. 71, Article 2(3).
104  Article I-22 CT.

States that this was a desirable reform. It is yet to be seen whether or not it will be introduced, notwithstanding the uncertainties surrounding the Constitutional Treaty.

## 5. The European Parliament

### (i)   Composition of the European Parliament

The European Parliament was initially set up as the European Assembly and was only formally recognised as a parliament in the SEA.[105] Prior to 1979, it consisted of representatives from national assemblies or parliaments. Since then, Members of the European Parliament (MEPs) have been elected by direct universal suffrage at five yearly intervals.[106] There are a number of features which distinguish the European Parliament from its national counterparts.

The seats are not evenly distributed on the basis of population.[107] The Parliament is composed of 732 members, but citizens in smaller Member States are better represented than citizens in larger Member States. Luxembourg, with a population of 400,000 citizens, has one MEP for roughly every 65,550 citizens. Germany, by contrast, with a population of 82 million citizens, has one MEP for approximately every 828,000 citizens. This lack of equal representation was exacerbated by a lack of uniform election procedures. In 2002, common procedures were established and were used for the first time in the 2004 elections. MEPs are elected on the basis of proportional representation. However, states can decide on the particular system of proportional representation they wish to use. They can establish constituencies as they see fit and can require parties to achieve 5 per cent of the vote before they are allocated seats.[108]

The other distinctive feature of the European Parliament is that there are no European political parties. Although the importance of European political parties in forming a 'European awareness' was recognised at Maastricht,[109] MEPs are elected as representatives of national political parties. This has made elections 'second order national contests'.[110] Voters vote on domestic issues and turnouts tend to be lower than for national elections, with only 45 per cent of the electorate voting in the 2004 elections. The lists of candidates, chosen by national parties, for these elections are frequently

---

105  Article 3 SEA.
106  Decision 76/787/EEC, OJ 1976 L278/1. On the history of the European Parliament since the establishment of the Common Assembly in the ECSC see B. Rittberger, *Building Europe's Parliament: Democratic Representation Beyond the Nation-State* (Oxford, Oxford University Press, 2005) chs 3–6.
107  The respective numbers are Austria 18, Belgium 24, Czech Republic 24, Cyprus 6, Denmark 14, Estonia 6, Finland 14, France 78, Germany 99, Greece 24, Hungary 24, Ireland 13, Italy 78, Latvia 9, Lithuania 13, Luxembourg 6, Malta 5, the Netherlands 27, Poland 54, Portugal 24, Slovakia 14, Slovenia 7, Spain 54, Sweden 19, United Kingdom 78.
108  Decision 2002/772/EURATOM/EC, concerning the election of the members of the European Parliament by direct universal suffrage, OJ 2002 L283/1.
109  Article 191 EC.
110  S. Hix, *The Political System of the European Union* (2nd edn, Basingstoke, Palgrave, 2005) 192–6.

influenced by narrow domestic issues and commentators suggest that this has had an influence on the behaviour of MEPs who, with a view to renomination, have an eye on what is going on back home.[111] Although there are no European political parties, the parties sit in European party groupings.[112] There are eight groupings, of which the two largest are the European Peoples Party (right of centre parties) and the Party of European Socialists (left of centre parties).[113] These groupings are important in the organisation of the Parliament.[114] Studies have shown that these groupings affect voting behaviour, with MEPs within groupings acting reasonably cohesively.[115] That said, with 129 national delegations represented within the European Parliament, voting behaviour is still considerably less cohesive than in national parliaments and they are unable to affect the way national delegations cast their votes in key votes.[116] Their real influence is exerted in determining the composition of the European Parliament Committees. Although Committee membership is intended to reflect the ideological and territorial composition of the full Parliament, the groups can usually secure membership for their MEPs on the more influential committees and the Chairs of the Committees are determined by negotiation between the groups.[117]

These traits indicate ambivalence on the part of both national governments and the general public about the democratic credentials of the European Parliament. There are concerns about both its representative and deliberative capacities. The concerns about the former lie in the argument that a representative democracy depends upon the presence of a 'people' (*demos*), or collective sense of 'Us', to represent.[118] Without this common sense of 'Us', Scharpf has argued, there is no reason for losers of any vote to accept the view of the majority, for they do not see themselves as part of a common political community with whose decisions they must comply.[119] Within the European Union, this is significant because most citizens do not see themselves

111 M. Abélès, 'Political Anthropology of a Transnational Institution: The European Parliament' (1993) 11 *French Politics and Society* 1, 11–17; J. Brzinski, 'Political Group Cohesion in the European Parliament, 1989–1994' in C. Rhodes and S. Mazey, *The State of the European Union*, vol. 3, *Building a European Polity* (Harlow, Longman, 1995) 135, 143–4.

112 On the evolution of these see A. Kreppel, *The European Parliament and the Supranational Party System* (Cambridge, Cambridge University Press, 2002).

113 For the 2004–2009 Parliament, the groupings are European Peoples Party (266 MEPs); Party of European Socialists (201 MEPs); Alliance of Liberals and Democrats for Europe (89 MEPs); the Greens and European Free Alliance (42 MEPs); European United Left and Nordic Green Left (41 MEPs); Independence and Democracy Group (35 MEPs); Europe of the Nations (27 MEPs). There are 27 MEPs who belong to no groups.

114 Membership of a grouping also entitles a national party to funding. Regulation 2004/2003/EC on the regulations governing political parties at European level and the rules regarding their funding, OJ 2003 L297/1.

115 S. Hix, A. Noury and G. Roland, 'Power to the Parties: Cohesion and Competition in the European Parliament' (2005) 35 *BJPS* 209.

116 D. Judge and D. Earnshaw, *The European Parliament* (Basingstoke, Palgrave, 2003) 149–55.

117 S. Bowler and D. Farrell, 'The Organizing of the European Parliament: Committees, Specialization and Co-ordination' (1995) 25 *BJPS* 219.

118 J. Weiler, 'Does Europe Need a Constitution? Reflections on Demos, Telos and the German Maastricht Decision' (1995) 1 *ELJ* 219, 225.

119 F. Scharpf, *Governing in Europe: Effective and Democratic?* (Oxford, Oxford University Press, 1999) 7–20.

as part of a 'European people', but as nationals of their own Member States. The concerns about the latter stem from political parties, media and civil society all being organised along predominantly national lines. This prevents a debate which is plural, transparent and vigorous.

### D. Grimm, 'Does Europe Need a Constitution' (1995) 1 *European Law Journal* 282, 293–4, 296–7

The democratic nature of a political system is attested not so much by the existence of elected parliaments . . . as by the pluralism, internal representativity, freedom and capacity for compromise of the intermediate area of parties, associations, citizens movements and communication media. Where a parliament does not rest on such a structure, which guarantees constant interaction between people and State, democratic substance is lacking even if democratic forms are present . . .

At European level, though, even the prerequisites are largely lacking. Mediatory structures have hardly been even formed here yet. There is no Europeanised party system, just European groups in the Strasbourg parliament, and a part from that, loose cooperation among programmatically related parties. This does not bring any integration of the European population, even at the moment of European elections. Nor have European associations or citizens' movements arisen, even though cooperation among national associations is further advanced than with parties. A search for European media, whether in print or broadcast, would be completely fruitless. This makes the European Union fall far short not just of ideal conceptions of a model democracy but even of the already deficit situation in Member States . . .

The absence of a European communication system, due chiefly, to language diversity, has the consequence that for the foreseeable future there will be neither a European public nor a European political discourse. Public discourse instead remains for the time bound by national frontiers, while the European sphere will remain dominated by professional and interest discourses conducted remotely from the public. European decisional processes are accordingly not under public observation in the same way as national ones. The European level of politics lacks a matching public. The feedback to European officials and representatives is therefore only weakly developed, while national politicians orient themselves even in the case of Council decisions to their national publics, because effective sanctions can come only from them. These circumstances give professional and technical viewpoints, particularly of an economic nature, excessive weight in European politics, while the social consequences and side-effects remain in the dark. This shortcoming cannot be made up for even by growing national attention to European policy themes, since the European dimension is just what is lacking there.

If this is true, the conclusion may be drawn that the full parliamentarisation of the European Union on the model of the national constitutional State will rather aggravate than solve the problem. On the one hand it would loosen the Union's ties back to the Member States, since the European Parliament is by its construction not a federal organ but a central one. Strengthening it would be at the expense of the Council and therefore inevitably have centralising effects. On the other hand, the weakened ties back to the Member States would not be compensated by any increased ties back to the Union population. The European Parliament does not meet with any European mediatory structure in being: still less does it constitute a European popular representative body, since there is yet no European people. This is not an argument against any expansion of Parliament's powers. That might even enhance participation opportunities in the Union, provide greater transparency and create a counterweight to the dominance of technical and economic viewpoints. Its objective ought not, however, to be full parliamentarisation on the national model, since political decisions would otherwise move away to where they can be only democratically accountable.

The suspicion that this assessment is a front for the idea that democracy is possible only on the basis of a homogenous 'Volksgemeinschaft' [ethnic community] is, after all that, baseless. The requirements for democracy are here developed not out of the people, but out of the society that wants to constitute itself as a political unit. It is true that this requires a collective identity, if it wants to settle its conflicts non-violently, accept majority rule and practise solidarity. But this identity need by no means be rooted in ethnic conflict, but must also have other bases. All that is necessary is for the society to have formed an awareness or belonging together that can support majority decisions and solidarity efforts, and for it to have the capacity to communicate about its goals and problems discursively. What obstructs democracy is accordingly not the lack of cohesion of Union citizens as a people, but their weakly developed collective identity and low capacity for transnational discourse. This certainly means that the European democracy deficit is structurally determined. It can therefore not be removed by institutional reforms in any short term. The achievement of the democratic constitutional State can for the time being be adequately recognised only in the national framework.

### (ii)   Powers of the European Parliament

Most people consider parliaments as law-makers and their influence is often measured by their power over the making of policy and legislation. Strong parliaments are responsible for making policy and law, whilst weaker parliaments can only influence them.[120] Parliaments also exercise power over the executive. In stronger parliamentary systems, executive power is derived from the legislature. The legislature appoints the executive and sets the conditions for the exercise of its powers.[121] In weaker systems, parliaments exercise powers of scrutiny over the executive and it is accountable to them. Finally, parliaments traditionally have powers over the finances of a state. Once again, these vary according to the strength of the parliament, with the stronger parliaments having control over both revenue (money coming in) and expenditure (money going out).

### (a)   Legislative powers of the European Parliament

The legislative powers of the European Parliament vary according to the legislative procedure adopted and this will depend on the policy field in question. There are two dominant ones: the consultation procedure and the co-decision procedure. Under the former, the Parliament is consulted on a proposal and has the right to propose amendments. Under the latter, in addition to these rights, the Parliament can veto any proposal. It also has the power to negotiate joint texts in a committee, the Conciliation Committee, with the Council. Bald statements of its powers do not capture the significance of its input and this has to be considered in relation to the legislative powers and influence of the other institutions, which is addressed in chapter 4.

120  P. Norton, *Legislatures* (Oxford, Oxford University Press, 1990) 179.
121  P. Raworth, 'A Timid Step Forwards: Maastricht and the Democratisation of the European Community' (1994) 19 *EL Rev.* 16, 17.

Parliament does have, however, informal, general powers of agenda-setting. It can request the Commission to submit a proposal where it considers this is necessary to implement EC Treaty objectives.[122] This power is significant, as since 1982, the Commission has agreed that it will, in principle, pursue any parliamentary proposal. Where it does not, it will appear before the Parliament to provide reasons.[123] The route for preparing a parliamentary proposal is through its 'Own Initiative' reports. The relevant Committee of the Parliament will draw up a report. The Parliament will then vote on it in plenary session, adopting a Resolution requesting the Commission to act. As the extract below indicates, this power has been used by the Parliament not merely to stimulate debate, but to control the legislative agenda.

---

### D. Judge and D. Earnshaw, 'Weak European Parliament Influence? A Study of the Environment Committee of the European Parliament' (1994) 29 *Government and Opposition* 262, 264–6

In using these procedures the Environment Committee again sought to involve itself at the *pre-legislative* stage through a conscious strategy of agenda-setting. There are several dimensions to this strategy. One was to use 'Rule 63' reports to encourage action on the part of the Commission. On many occasions the Commission might already have been considering such action, and so the intention of the Committee was either to accelerate this process, and so advance the issue up the Commission's overcrowded agenda, or to focus the Commission's attention upon an issue and so determine the priorities and relative policy-making of the Commission. Aware, for example, that the Commission was formulating proposals on waste management, the Environment Committee initiated its own investigation in the subject with the intention of 'guiding' the Commission's own internal deliberations. The influence of the Committee's report is partially observable in the Commission's eventual proposals on the incineration of hazardous waste and on landfill of waste. Rather than simply waiting, therefore, to react to formal Commission proposals as part of the consultation process, the Environment Committee engaged in a proactive strategy of articulating its own policy concerns to the Commission. Exactly how much direct influence this strategy had upon the final Commission proposal is difficult, if not impossible, to assess; but the Committee itself would probably claim no more than that it sought to articulate the concerns of the EP at the formative stage of legislation alongside other interested parties considered by the Commission.

On occasion, however, EP initiatives have been openly acknowledged by the Commission's Directorate General for Environment, Nuclear Safety and Civil Protection (DG XI) as being of importance in prompting action or changing its own priorities. Perhaps the clearest, and most publicly acknowledged, example was the genesis of the Commission's *Green Paper on the Urban Environment*. In the preface to the Green Paper the then Commissioner, Ripa di Meana, openly recorded that the paper was a 'practical response to the resolution tabled in December 1988 by a Member of the European Parliament, Ken Collins, urging that the problems facing the urban environment be studied in greater detail'. Rarely is the influence of MEPs proclaimed in such a public manner. As a consequence, the informal dimension of agenda-setting and initiation are often overlooked in standard texts on, and 'guides' to the EC decision-making process.

---

122 Article 192(2) EC.
123 D. Earnshaw and D. Judge, *The European Parliament* (Basingstoke, Palgrave, 2002) 211–13.

This extract also illustrates the astute use of Committees by the European Parliament. The bulk of the Parliament's legislative work is done by Committees. These write the legislative reports and suggest amendments to Commission proposals. This specialisation allows Parliament to garner its resources effectively and target its comments more incisively. There are currently twenty-one Committees and the number of MEPs sitting on each Committee varies (for the 2004 Parliament) between thirty-four (Budgetary Control) and seventy-seven (Foreign Affairs). Their levels of activity differ. Thus, Earnshaw and Judge note that between 1999 and 2002, five Committees wrote nearly 50 per cent of all reports.[124] Their degree of influence also varies. Based on a number of case studies, Judge, Earnshaw and Cowan suggest a number of factors will affect influence:[125]

- *Type of policy*: low-visibility policies, such as agriculture, characterised by a high degree of cooperation between the Commission, industry and the Member States, set up a relatively closed and interconnected world with little room for parliamentary access. There is greater room for parliamentary influence in the case of regulatory policies, environmental protection being an example, which are seen as affecting a less specialised, less closed group of actors.
- *Intergovernmentalism*: in some areas where unanimity is required in the Council, parliamentary influence is diminished both by national resistance to Community intrusion and by there being no possibilities for Parliament to exploit divisions between the Member States.
- *Inter-institutional relations*: these exist at a formal level, depending upon the particular legislative procedure used. They also exist at an informal level. The authors thus noted the manner in which Parliament had been able to increase its pre-legislative influence by ensuring that a Rapporteur for a Committee was appointed once the Commission's Annual Programme was announced rather than later when the formal proposal for a legislative measure was announced. This allowed it to influence the content of the Commission's legislative proposal.
- *Institutional resources*: the quality of personnel involved with any measure affected parliamentary influence. It was noted, therefore, that the existence of an expert in biochemistry on the Environmental Committee of the Parliament had undoubtedly increased its influence in the field of biotechnology.

### (b)   Powers over the Executive

**Powers of appointment and dismissal**    There is no general right for the Parliament to hire and fire at will any of the other institution representatives. It does, however,

---

124 *Ibid.*, 184–6.
125 D. Judge, D. Earnshaw and N. Cowan, 'Ripples or Waves: the European Parliament in the European Community Policy Process' (1994) 1 *JEPP* 27.

have a significant influence over the appointment and dismissal of the members of two institutions.

The Parliament is exclusively responsible for appointing the European Ombudsman.[126] Whilst the Ombudsman is completely independent, it is the Parliament that can apply for her to be dismissed by the Court of Justice if she no longer fulfils the conditions required for the performance of her duties or is guilty of serious misconduct.[127]

Of greater political significance are the Parliament's powers over the appointment of the Commission. The Parliament has a double power of approval. It must approve the President of the Commission who has been nominated by the Heads of Government. If the nomination is accepted, it must also approve the College of Commissioners nominated by the President of the Commission and the Heads of Government.[128] Since 1999, the term of the Commission has been synchronised with that of the Parliament. This has allowed the Parliament to use its powers of assent extremely effectively. All prospective Commissioners are subject to questioning by Parliamentary Committees before assent is given to their appointment. They must answer questions about their professional past, their views on European integration and their legislative agenda for their term in office. That Parliament will use its power of assent if it is not satisfied with the views of individual Commissioners, was shown by the events of 2004. The Parliament was unhappy with three nominees, in particular. It disapproved of the Italian nomination, Rocco Buttiglione, because of his views on women and homosexuality. It was also unhappy with the Latvian nominee, Ingrida Udre, because of allegations surrounding corruption in her party. Finally, it was unconvinced that the Hungarian nominee, László Kovács, knew sufficient about the Energy portfolio allocated to him. When it became clear that there was not a majority for the Commission because of these nominations, Barroso, the Commission President, had to arrange for the Italian and Latvian nominations to be replaced, and Kovács was allocated the Taxation and Customs Union portfolio instead.

The Parliament also has important powers to dismiss the Commission. If a motion of censure is passed by a two-thirds majority of the votes cast representing a majority (i.e. more than 365) of the members of the European Parliament, the Commission is obliged to resign as a body.[129] This is an 'all or nothing' power. It does not allow the Parliament to criticise or dismiss individual Commissioners. Nevertheless, it was threatened against the Santer Commission in 1998 following allegations of corruption and maladministration against some of its members.[130] The Commission resigned the day before a vote would have been taken sacking the entire College. Following this, there was debate about whether the Parliament should have the power to make individual Commissioners resign. This has not happened.

---

126 Article 195(1) EC.       127 Article 195(2) EC.       128 Article 214(2) EC.       129 Article 201 EC.
130 D. Judge and D. Earnshaw, 'The European Parliament and the Commission Crisis: a New Assertiveness?'
   (2002) 15 *Governance* 345.

**Powers of inquiry**   Since 1953, EU citizens and residents of the Union have been entitled to petition the Parliament.[131] In 1987, the Parliament set up a Committee of Petitions, consisting of MEPs, to consider the petitions.[132] In 2003, a typical year, the Committee received 1,313 petitions.[133] These petitions either express views on an issue, such as human rights or animal welfare, or seek redress for a particular grievance, which may have been caused by a Community institution, national authority or private body. The process serves a number of functions. In cases where a political issue is raised, it allows the possibility for a hearing to be organised by the European Parliament, thereby securing a voice for parties who might otherwise be disenfranchised. In cases where maladministration by a Community institution is alleged, the Parliament may take the matter up itself. In cases where a failure of a Member State is alleged, it will ask the Commission to take the matter up with the Member State concerned.

**Powers to hold to account**   Parliament has the power to ask questions of or receive reports from most of the Community institutions. The powers vary according to the institution in question.

**The Commission**   The Commission is required to submit an Annual Report, which is debated and voted on by the Parliament[134] and is required to reply to questions put by parliamentary members.[135]

**The European Council**   The European Council is required, by Article 4 TEU, to submit a report to Parliament after each of its meetings and an annual written report on the progress of the Union.

**The Council of Ministers**   Formally, the Council of Ministers is the least accountable of all the Community institutions to the Parliament. However, the need for inter-institutional dialogue has resulted in a limited accountability. It is customary for the President of the Council to present the proposed work of the Council for the Presidency before the Parliament. Secondly, a convention has grown whereby the Council will answer questions put to it by members of the Parliament. A corollary of this is that the Council has a right to be heard by the Parliament.[136]

**The European Central Bank (ECB)**   The European Central Bank must submit an Annual Report to all the institutions including the Parliament.[137] In addition, the President of the ECB and members of the Executive Council may, at the request

131  This is now formally recognised in Article 194 EC.
132  This Committee has been given a formal basis in Article 193 EC.
133  European Parliament, *Report on the Deliberations of the Committee Petitions during the Parliamentary Year 2003–2004*, A6–0040/2005. The Report gives a good idea of the types of issue raised by petitioners.
134  Article 200 EC.        135  Article 197(3) EC.        136  Article 197(3) EC.        137  Article 113(3)(1) EC.

of the European Parliament, or on their own initiative be heard by the competent Committees of the Parliament.[138]

### (c)  Powers of litigation

The final route for the Parliament to hold other institutions to account is to take them before the Court of Justice. It has unlimited powers to challenge the acts of the other Community institutions before the Court as well as their failure to act where they are legally required to do so.[139] This is a relatively new power because, prior to the Treaty of Nice, legal acts could only be challenged where they transgressed on the Parliament's prerogatives. Parliamentary litigation focussed around securing greater institutional powers for itself. It would, therefore, litigate to try to secure legal procedures, which ensured it the greatest amount of influence, challenging legislation which was either based on procedures where it had little voice or which delegated significant law-making powers to the Commission.[140] That strategy continues, but since the Treaty of Nice, Parliament has used its unlimited *locus standi* to develop an alternative strategy. It will challenge those acts, which it cannot veto in the legislative process, where it is unhappy with the policy being adopted. A good example of this is the Agreement made between the European Union and the USA allowing the American authorities to have access to the passenger name records of air carriers flying to and from the USA.[141] These records would include features such as credit card details and e-mail addresses. The Parliament considers this to be a violation of the right to respect for privacy and has challenged the Agreement before the Court of Justice.[142]

### (d)  Financial powers of the European Parliament

Parliament's central financial power is, acting by a majority of its members and two-thirds of the votes cast, to reject the draft Budget if there are 'important reasons' for doing so and ask for a new draft to be submitted to it by the Commission.[143] Parliament also has important powers over the control of expenditure. In this regard, a distinction is made between non-compulsory and compulsory expenditure, with the latter being considered to be expenditure that the EC is obliged to enter into in order to meet its legal obligations.[144] With regard to the former, the Parliament can propose modifications to the draft Budget, but the final say remains with the Council. With regard to non-compulsory expenditure, the Parliament not only can propose

138 Article 113(3)(2) EC.      139 Articles 230(2) EC and 232(1) EC.

140 On this strategy see M. McCowan, 'The European Parliament before the Bench: ECJ Precedent and EP Litigation Strategies' (2003) 10 *JEPP* 974.

141 Decision 2004/496/EC on the conclusion of an Agreement between the European Community and the United States of America on the processing and transfer of PNR data by air carriers to the United States Department of Homeland Security, Bureau of Customs and Border Protection, OJ 2004 L183/83.

142 Joined Cases C-317/04 and C-318/04 *Parliament v Commission*, OJ 2004 C228/31.

143 Article 272(8) EC.

144 Joint Declaration by the Community Institutions on 30 June 1982 on the Community Budgetary Procedure, OJ 1982 C194/1.

modifications, but, within limits, also has the final word.[145] The distinction between these heads of expenditure is an unhappy one. There is little rationale for the distinction and it has led to jockeying between the institutions as to the head under which a particular item of expenditure should fall. In 1999, an Inter-Institutional Agreement was reached in which each budgetary heading was classified with an agreement that any future disputes should be mediated on the basis of this classification.[146]

The Parliament's final say in relation to non-compulsory expenditure has also to be put into perspective. The amount by which the Parliament can increase expenditure is limited. The Commission establishes a maximum rate of increase for Community expenditure,[147] which Parliament cannot exceed unless through agreement with the Council.[148] Alongside this, Parliament's powers to raise revenue do not match its powers in the field of expenditure. It is the Council which determines the EC's revenue system of own resources for financing the Budget.[149] This imposes an additional constraint because revenue and expenditure must be balanced.[150]

## 6. The Court of Justice and the Court of First Instance

### (i)   Jurisdiction of the Court of Justice

The duty of the Court of Justice is to ensure that in the interpretation and the application of the Treaty, 'the law is observed'.[151] Its power is restricted by limits on its jurisdiction, which prevent it ruling on certain parts of the TEU and the rules on *locus standi*, which determine the circumstances in which parties can bring actions before the Court.

Whilst the Court has full jurisdiction to consider any matter which falls within the EC pillar, [152] it is excluded from ruling on the second pillar, CFSP. The position is most complicated with regard to the third pillar. It has no general jurisdiction to rule on this pillar, but can adjudicate upon secondary legislation adopted under it. Its powers depend, however, upon the type of secondary act in question. It has the power to interpret and rule on the validity of framework decisions and decisions, but only has the power to interpret conventions and cannot declare these invalid.[153] In

---

145 Article 272(5) EC.
146 This is now consolidated in Decision 2003/429/EC, on the Inter-Institutional Agreement between the European Parliament, the Council and the Commission on budgetary discipline and improvement of the budgetary procedure, OJ 2003 L147/25.
147 This maximum rate is based on the trend in GNP within the Community, budgetary increases within the Member States and increase in the cost of living.
148 There is an exception, where the Council establishes a draft Budget which has further increased expenditure as a whole by over one and a half times the maximum rate. Parliament is entitled to propose amendments to non-compulsory expenditure which allow for a further increase of up to one half the maximum rate: Article 272(9) EC.
149 The period for 2000–2006 is governed by Decision 2000/597/EC/EURATOM on the system of own resources, OJ 2000 L253/42. There is considerable contention over the system to replace it.
150 Article 268 EC.       151 Article 220 EC.       152 Article 46(a) TEU.
153 Articles 46(b) and 35(1) TEU.

any judgment given under this pillar, the Court is further restricted in that it has no power to review the validity or proportionality of operations carried out by the police or enforcement agencies of a Member State or the exercise of national responsibilities with regard to the maintenance of law and order and the safeguarding of internal security.[154] Finally, there are some general provisions in the TEU on which the Court can rule, most notably the procedures for entry and expulsion of a Member State from the Union and the procedures for amending the treaties.[155]

At the 'Future of Europe' Convention, the President of the Court of Justice expressed dissatisfaction, arguing that these uneven powers were leading to disrespect for the rule of law:

> The rule of law is an essential part of any constitutional system and it is the Court's responsibility to ensure that it is observed . . . In this regard, the current situation is not entirely satisfactory. One can point to the fact the transition from the European Communities to the European Union did not entail a corresponding extension of the guarantees of the observance of the law. Instead, it resulted in a situation in which the mechanisms for judicial protection vary.[156]

This view was adopted in the Constitutional Treaty. The Court of Justice was given full jurisdiction over the Constitutional Treaty and a single set of procedures were to apply to all fields,[157] subject to two exceptions. It was still excluded from ruling on the Common Foreign and Security Policy.[158] It would also continue to have no jurisdiction to review the validity of operations carried out by the police or other law enforcement agencies, or review the exercise of national responsibilities with regard to the maintenance of law and order and internal security.[159] It is difficult to know what to make of this in the light of the non-ratification of the Constitutional Treaty. The comments of the Court of Justice and the proposals suggested by the Constitutional Treaty amount to a damning indictment of the current arrangements, particularly in the third pillar, but in the absence of a Treaty amendment, they are likely to persist. It is possible that the Court will try to expand its jurisdiction incrementally here, aware that there may not be too much resistance from the Member States.[160]

Within its field of jurisdiction, matters can come before the Court in a variety of ways:

- *Preliminary references from national courts*:[161] a point of EC law is raised before a national court that is necessary to enable it to decide the dispute. It may, or in some cases must, refer the point of EC law to the Court of Justice. The Court of Justice

154 Article 35(5) TEU.      155 Article 46(e) and (f) TEU.

156 Oral presentation by Gil Carlos Rodriguez Iglesias to the 'discussion circle' on the Court of Justice, CONV 572/03, 1–2.

157 Article I-29(3) CT.      158 Article III-376 CT.      159 Article III-377 CT.

160 The Court has thus interpreted its powers under Article 35(1) TEU widely in Case C-105/03 *Pupino*, judgment of 16 June 2005.

161 Article 234 EC.

will give judgment on the point of EC law, which the national judge will apply to the dispute in hand.

• *Enforcement actions brought by the Commission or Member States against other Member States:*[162] the Commission, or in rare cases another Member State, can bring a Member State before the Court of Justice for a Declaration that the latter is in breach of EC law.

• *Sanctions for failure to comply with Court judgments:*[163] if a Member State fails to comply with a Court of Justice judgment, the Commission can bring it back before the Court in order to have it fined for its behaviour.

• *Judicial review of EC institutions:*[164] as we will see below, private parties seeking judicial review of behaviour of the EU institutions must bring their action before the Court of First Instance. However, if a Member State or EU institution is seeking judicial review of such behaviour, it brings the action before the Court of Justice.

• *Opinions on the conclusion of international agreements:* the Council, Parliament, Commission or any Member State can ask for an Opinion of the Court as to whether the EC has lawfully concluded a draft treaty. The reason for this exceptional procedure is that international agreements, being binding upon the international plane, cannot be annulled as easily as internal acts. If the Court rules that the international agreement is illegal, it can only enter into force if the Treaty is first amended.[165]

• *Appeals from the Court of First Instance:*[166] these procedures are discussed in far more detail in subsequent chapters in this book. Combined, they make a substantial docket. In 2004, the Court of Justice disposed of 665 cases and gave 375 judgments.[167] Despite this considerable output, it struggles to cope with the number of cases that are submitted to it: 840 cases were still pending at the end of 2004. The average wait for a preliminary reference was 23.5 months.[168] These pressures have led to a number of difficulties: most notably, delay for litigants, the Court working under strong time pressures and increased resort to the Chamber system.[169]

### (ii)   Composition and working methods of the Court of Justice

The Court is made up of twenty-five judges, one from each Member State. These are appointed for a renewable period of six years[170] and are required to be persons whose independence is beyond doubt and who are either suitable for the highest judicial office in their respective countries or 'jurisconsults of recognised competence'.[171] Concern has been raised about the politicisation of appointments, as judges are appointed by

---

162 Articles 226 and 227 EC.       163 Article 228(2) EC.
164 Articles 230(2) EC, 232(1) EC.          165 Article 300(6) EC.          166 Article 225(1) and (3) EC.
167 *Annual Report of the Court of Justice 2004* (Luxembourg, OOPEC, 2005) 168–9.
168 *Ibid.,* 174.          169 These are discussed in more detail in chapter 7. See pp. 303–4.
170 This is done on a three-yearly cycle, so that every three years half the Court is replaced: Article 223(2) EC.
171 Article 223 EC.

the 'common accord' of the national governments.[172] This concern was addressed in the Constitutional Treaty, which would have established a Panel comprising former members of the Court of Justice and members of national supreme courts to rule on the suitability of candidates,[173] and governments could only appoint candidates after consulting this Panel.[174] Fears have also been expressed that the ability to renew the term of office might compromise the independence of the judges. In 1993, the European Parliament proposed that judges should be elected by the Parliament for a non-renewable term of nine years, a suggestion endorsed by the Court of Justice.[175] In practice, this has not posed a problem, possibly because the Court works under the principle of collegiality. A single judgment will be given, with there being no possibility for either dissenting or concurring opinions. This protects the anonymity of the judges and thereby their independence. It has also been considered to enhance the authority of the Court as Member States are unable to point to sympathetic dissenting opinions or the views of their national judge as a means of undermining the authority of a particular judgment. Members of the Court have argued that considerable intellectual dynamism is generated by the debate leading to a single judgment, as it allows for a considerable exchange of views and differing national legal traditions to filter through to the judgment.[176] This has been countered by some observers, who argue that because the judgment is built on compromise, this affects the quality of its reasoning, with the Court often seeming not to counter a point or consider a question.[177]

The Court is assisted by eight Advocates General.[178] The same procedure and conditions of appointment apply to these as to judges of the Court of Justice. The job of the Advocate General is to make, in open court, impartial and independent submissions on any case brought before the Court.[179] She acts not as a legal representative of one of the parties, but as a legal representative of the public interest. These Opinions are published in advance of the judgment to allow the Court sufficient time to

---

172 *Ibid.* On this debate see P. Kapteyn, 'Reflections on the Future of the Judicial System of the European Union after Nice' (2001) 20 *YBEL* 173, 188–9.

173 Article III-357 CT.        174 Article III-355 CT.

175 The Rothley Report, European Parliament Session Doc. A3–0228/93. The Court of Justice's view are in *Report of the European Court of Justice for the 1996 Intergovernmental Conference*, Proceedings of the Court 15/95, 11.

176 T. Koopman, 'The Future of the Court of Justice of the European Communities' (1991) 11 *YBEL* 15, 24; P. Kapteyn 'The Court of Justice of the European Communities after the Year 2000' in D. Curtin and T. Heukels (eds.), *Institutional Dynamics of European Integration: Liber Amicorum Schermers*, vol. 1 (Dordrecht, Martijnus Nijhoff, 1994) 135, 139; F. Jacobs, 'Advocates General and Judges in the European Court of Justice: Some Personal Reflections' in D. O'Keeffe and A. Bavasso (eds.), *Judicial Review in European Union Law: Liber Amicorum Lord Slynn*, vol. 1 (The Hague/Boston/London, Kluwer Law International, 2000).

177 W. Bishop, 'Price Discrimination under Article 86: Political Economy in the European Court' (1981) 44 *MLR* 282, 294–5.

178 On the Advocates General see K. Borgschmidt, 'The Advocate General at the European Court of Justice: a Comparative Study' (1988) 13 *EL Rev.* 106; T. Tridimas, 'The Role of the Advocate General in Community Law: Some Reflections' (1997) 34 *CML Rev.* 1349.

179 Article 222 EC.

consider them. From a lawyer's perspective, the Opinions are interesting as they often provide a more detailed analysis of the context and the argument than is found in the judgment of the Court itself. However, they are not binding on the Court, although they are increasingly referred to by the Court of Justice in its judgments. Even when the conclusions reached are similar, it is difficult to know whether the reasoning is the same, given that the Opinion is often discursive in nature, whilst the judgment itself is very terse.

For reasons of workload, cases are rarely decided by the full Court. Indeed, it is only to sit in full session in cases of 'exceptional importance' or where it is to rule that a senior Community official (e.g. Commissioner, Ombudsman, or member of the Court of Auditors) is to be deprived of office for not meeting the requisite conditions.[180] In 2004, only 0.24 per cent of all cases were assigned to the full Court. [181] Instead, the majority of cases are heard by Chambers of either three or five judges, with 34.18 per cent of the cases being heard by Chambers of three judges, and 54.03 per cent by Chambers of five judges in 2004. The central exception to this is the Grand Chamber. A Member State or Community institution party to the proceedings can request a case to be heard by a Chamber of thirteen judges. This occurred in only 6.48 per cent of cases in 2004.[182] The consequence of all this is that the Court has become increasingly fragmented and specialised, with individual judges acquiring increased significance in the judgments upon which they rule. It has also increased the influence of the President. The judges elect the President from amongst themselves for a three-year term.[183] Her central responsibility is to determine the case list and allocate cases to different Chambers,[184] thereby selecting which cases each judge will decide.

### (iii)   The Court of First Instance

Established in 1989, the Court of First Instance (CFI) is comprised of twenty-five judges. Unlike the Court of Justice, it is not confined to a single judge from each Member State, but must comprise at least one judge from each Member State.[185] The CFI can sit in full court if it considers the circumstances require or because of the importance of the case.[186] It almost always sits in Chambers of three or five judges. Of the 361 judgments given in 2004, Chambers of three accounted for 276 and Chambers of five for 64 judgments.[187] Although no Advocates General are assigned to it, one of the judges will act as Advocate General. A single judge can give judgments in actions

---

180 Statute of the Court of Justice, Article 16.
181 *Annual Report of the Court of Justice 2004* (Luxembourg, OOPEC, 2005) 181.        182 *Ibid.* 170.
183 Article 223(3) EC. The current President Greek, Judge Skouris.
184 The President also chairs the Grand Chamber, and is responsible for interim measures.
185 Article 224 EC.
186 Rules of Procedure of the Court of First Instance, article 14(1). The consolidated text is to be found at www.curia.eu.int/en/instit/txtdocfr/txtsenvigueur/txt7.pdf
187 *Annual Report*, above n. 181, 197.

brought by private parties, but the circumstances in which this can occur are extremely restricted. The case must raise only questions already clarified by established case law, and must not cover certain fields, notably state aids, competition, mergers, agriculture and trade with non-EU states.[188] In 2004, there were only fourteen judgments given by a single judge.[189]

The CFI started with a relatively limited jurisdiction but, over the years, this has expanded and it now has the power to receive the following cases:

- actions by private parties challenging Community action or inaction or seeking damages from the Communities;
- matters referred to the Court of Justice under an arbitration clause;[190]
- actions brought by Member States against acts of the Council where it is exercising delegated powers or is authorising state aids;[191]
- appeals from decisions of the Office for Harmonisation in the Internal Market (OHIM).[192] This agency is responsible for the grant of the Community trade mark and anyone adversely affected by its decisions can appeal these to the CFI.

The jurisdiction over these matters results in the CFI being the central Community court for a number of fields. It is the central administrative court, as it is the first port of call for all challenges of administrative acts of Community institutions. It has thus become the central court for developing administrative principles of due process and powerful in developing the case law on fundamental rights. Much administrative case law in EC law involves either competition and merger law or EC external trade law. The reason for this is that the Commission enjoys direct regulatory powers in these fields and it is in these fields that most Community administration is challenged. The CFI has, thus, also become the dominant competition and external trade court. Finally, whilst Community intellectual property is expanding, the most litigated legislation is the Community trade mark. The CFI's influence in intellectual property law is, if not dominant, at least significant.

In 2004, private actions against Community institutions accounted for 43.47 per cent of cases before the CFI. Trade mark cases accounted for 20.52 per cent and arbitration for 1.31 per cent.[193] The CFI is struggling even more than the Court of Justice to keep up with its docket. At the end of 2004, 1,174 cases were still pending and the duration of proceedings was 17.3 months for trade mark cases and 22.6 months for actions against the Community institutions.[194] Notwithstanding this, there was a

---

188 Rules of Procedure of the Court of First Instance, article 14(2).
189 *Annual Report 2004*, above n. 181.  190 For both this and the above heading see Article 225(1) EC.
191 Statute of the Court of Justice, article 51(a).
192 Regulation 40/94/EC on the Community trade mark, Article 63.
193 *Annual Report*, above n. 181, 193. The preponderance of the remainder was staff cases, which have now been transferred to the European Civil Service Tribunal.
194 *Annual Report*, above n. 181, 191, 198. These delays are so serious that they have led to decisions being overturned on the grounds that they were not heard within a reasonable period. In *Baustahlgewerbe*, the proceedings lasted five years and six months. The Court ruled this to be too long: Case C-185/95P *Baustahlgewerbe v Commission* [1998] ECR I-8417.

move at the Treaty of Nice to expand the CFI. We have already mentioned the provision
made for more judges. There was also provision for the CFI to receive preliminary
rulings in fields to be specified.[195] As yet, no field has been transferred under this
heading to the CFI. The provision is important for what it promises. For it suggests
that over the years, the jurisdiction and size of the CFI could be expanded so that it
becomes the central court for handling the case law, with the Court of Justice dealing
with only the most significant preliminary references.

There is a right to appeal from the CFI to the Court of Justice within two months
of notification of the decision. The appeal must be on points of law,[196] but this right
to appeal exists not just for parties to the dispute but also for Member States and
EC institutions.[197] In 2004, out of a possible 241 CFI acts susceptible to challenge,
53 were appealed. This figure was not dissimilar from previous years: in 2003, there
were 254 acts open to challenge, but only 67 were appealed to the Court of Justice.
The success rate for appeals is low. Even if the Court of Justice finds that the CFI has
misapplied Community law, it will only uphold an appeal if the mistake of law relates
to the operative part of the judgment. Even if Community law is misapplied in the
operative part of the judgment, the appeal will not be successful if the operative part
is shown to be well-founded for other legal reasons.[198] In 2004, the Court of Justice
considered 94 appeals of which only 15 were partially or totally successful.[199] These
statistics are a little misleading, as it is often on the most significant and controversial
areas of law that differences have emerged between the two courts.[200]

If the Court of Justice finds the appeal to be well-founded, it will quash the decision
of the CFI. It then has the discretion to give the final judgment or to refer the matter
back to the CFI. If it adopts the latter course of action, the CFI is bound by the Court
of Justice's decision on the point of law.[201] The CFI takes the view that it is only
bound by the judgments of the Court where its decision has been quashed by the
Court of Justice and the matter is referred back, or where the principle of *res judicata*
operates, that is to say, a dispute involving the same parties, the same subject-matter
and the same cause of action had already been decided by the Court of Justice.[202]
Nevertheless, the circumstances in which the CFI will not follow judgments of the
Court of Justice will be rare, as this would generate considerable instability. This
would stem not merely from the increased unpredictability in the CFI's judgments,
but also from the systemic conflict it would create between the two Courts, whereby

---

195 Article 224(3) EC.       196 Statute of the Court of Justice, article 58.       197 *Ibid.* article 56.
198 Case C-30/91P *Lestelle v Commission* [1992] ECR I-3755; Case C-226/03P *José Martí Peix v Commission*,
    judgment of 2 December 2004.
199 *Annual Report*, above n. 181, 203.
200 There have been strong differences, for example, over the rules on *locus standi* of private parties to chal-
    lenge Community acts (Case T-177/01 *Jégo-Quéré v Commission* [2002] ECR II-2365; Case C-263/02P
    *Commission v Jégo-Quéré*, [2004] ECR I-3425) and over the status of public international law in Com-
    munity law (Case T-115/94 *Opel Austria v Council* [1997] ECR II-39; Case C-162/96 *Racke* [1998] ECR
    I-3655).
201 Statute of the Court of Justice, article 54.
202 Case T-162/94 *NMB France v Commission* [1996] ECR II-427.

the CFI would take one decision reversing established Court of Justice case law, only to have it reaffirmed by the Court of Justice on appeal.

### (iv)   Judicial Panels

The anticipation of increased work for the CFI at the Treaty of Nice led to a decision to transfer some of the more mundane and fact-intensive of the CFI's work to Judicial Panels. The rules on the organisation for each Panel are likely to be different, as this will be governed by the Decision establishing each Panel. In all cases, members must be independent and fit for judicial office. There must also be the possibility of appeal to the Court of First Instance. To date, only one Panel has been established, European Union Civil Service Tribunal, which will hear disputes between employees of the Community institutions and the institutions themselves.[203]

## 7. Other institutions

### (i)   European Central Bank

The European Central Bank is considered in more detail in chapter 12. The central and most well-known power of the ECB is the exclusive right to authorise the issue of euros.[204] By doing this, it sets the short-term interest rates for the twelve states who have the euro as their currency. The ECB also has powers to adopt legislation in a number of fields: most notably, the definition and implementation of Community monetary policy, minimum reserves to be held by credit institutions and regulation of clearing and payments systems.[205] Finally it also has certain enforcement powers. It can bring national central banks, who fail to comply with their obligations under EC law, before the Court of Justice.[206] In addition, it has the power to impose fines and penalty payments on undertakings which do not comply with its regulations or decisions.[207]

The ECB has two decision-making bodies. The first is the Executive Board, which consists of the President and Vice-President of the European Central Bank and four other members. The other is the Governing Council. This consists of members of the Executive Board plus the governors of the national central banks of those Member States participating in the third stage of monetary union.[208] The President of the Council and a member of the Commission may participate in its meetings but do not have the right to vote.[209] The Governing Council is responsible for developing policy (such as the setting of interest rates or the adoption of legislation), whilst the Executive Board is responsible for implementing it. The Executive Board is responsible

---

203 Decision 2004/752/EC, EURATOM establishing the European Union Civil Service Tribunal, OJ 2004
      L333/7.
204 Article 106 EC.        205 Article 110(1) EC.        206 Article 237(d) EC.
207 Article 110(3) EC. These are set out in Regulation 1999/4, OJ 1999 L264/21.
208 Article 112(1) and (2) EC.        209 Article 113 EC.

for implementing these guidelines and giving the necessary instructions to national central banks.


### (ii)   Court of Auditors

The Court of Auditors consists of twenty-five members, who are appointed for a term of six years by the Council, acting by QMV after having consulted the Parliament.[210] The duty of the Court of Auditors is to audit the revenue and expenditure of the EC.[211] The audit is to be based on the records of the EC and if necessary, performed on the spot on the premises of any body that manages Community revenue or receives any payments from the Community Budget.[212] Despite these investigative powers, it has no powers to prosecute for fraud, but is obliged to report any irregularity to the appropriate body. For these purposes, the Court of Auditors is required to liaise with national audit bodies or, where appropriate, with national departments. The Court of Auditors can submit observations or deliver opinions on specific matters at the request of the other Community institutions and it can also assist the Parliament and the Council in exercising their powers of control over the implementation of the Community Budget. However, its greatest voice comes from the Annual Report it publishes on the finances of the EC at the end of each financial year.[213] The Parliament can only give a discharge to the Commission in respect of implementation of the Budget on the basis of this Report.[214] These Reports have been trenchant in their criticism of the management of the Community finances and, for ten years consecutively, up to 2004, the Court of Auditors has refused to give assurances that there are no irregularities in the management of the Budget.[215]


### (iii)   Economic and Social Committee

The Economic and Social Committee (ESC) both represents civil society within the EU decision-making processes and acts as the intermediary between civil society and the decision-making processes. There are 317 members appointed by the Council for a four-year renewable term[216] and these are divided into three Groups. Group I comprises employers; Group II consists of employees and trade unions; Group III represents variable interests: this is a heterogeneous group representing farmers, small businesses, the crafts, the professions, cooperatives and non-profit associations, consumer and environmental organisations, associations representing the family, women, persons with disabilities and the academic community.

---

210 B. Laffan, 'Becoming a "Living Institution": the Evolution of the European Court of Auditors' (1999) 37
  JCMS 251.
211 Article 246 EC.        212 Article 248 EC.        213 Article 248(4) EC.        214 Article 276(1) EC.
215 The Annual Report for 2003 is at OJ 2004, C293/7.        216 Articles 257–259 EC.

One function of the ESC is to provide opinions on legislative initiatives. In some fields, consultation with the Committee is compulsory,[217] whilst in others it is optional. The Committee can also provide 'own initiative' opinions on any topic of its choosing. There is some controversy about its role here, with some authors considering its role to be minor, whereas others think it helps the quality of the drafting process.[218] Since 2001, another function has become more significant as the Community has tried to broaden the possibilities for participation in its decision-making processes. The ESC has been used as an intermediary for this and a Protocol was signed between the ESC and the Commission in September 2001, agreeing a more proactive role for the ESC, in which it would be 'an indispensable intermediary between the EU institutions and organised civil society' and would organise many consultations on behalf of the Commission.[219] To this end, the mandate of the ESC has, increasingly, been to establish 'structured cooperation' rather than ad hoc consultations. In 2004, it established a Liaison Group between itself and an 'Organised European Civil Society' consisting of pan-European organisations that articulate the different interests it represents. This meets three to four times a year to discuss and provide input on the overall work of the ESC.

### (iv)    The Committee of the Regions

Established to give regional authorities greater input in the decision-making process, the Committee has 317 members, appointed by the Council acting by QMV on proposals from the Member States, for a four-year renewable term.[220] The Committee has merely an advisory status. Furthermore, whilst the Council, Parliament and Commission can consult it whenever they wish,[221] the circumstances in which they are obliged to do so are limited.[222] There still remain a number of areas, such as the internal market, competition, industrial policy and consumer protection, which have an important regional dimension and for which no consultation is required. It has been relatively unsuccessful as an institution. Evidence suggests that its opinions carry limited weight with the other institutions[223] and that the most powerful regions of the Union prefer to deal with the other institutions directly, rather than act through the Committee.[224]

---

217 Articles 40, 44(1), 52(1), 71(1) and (3), 75(3), 80(2), 93, 94, 95(1), 128(2), 129, 137(2), 140, 141(3), 144, 148, 149(4), 150(4), 152(4), 153(4), 156, 157(3), 159, 161, 162, 166(4), 172, 175(2) and (3) EC.
218 Cf. S. Weatherill and P. Beaumont, *EC Law: The Essential Guide to the Legal Workings of the European Community* (3rd edn, Harmondsworth, Penguin, 1999) 169; D. Gordon-Smith, 'The Drafting Process in the European Community' (1989) 10 *Statute Law Review* 56.
219 See the joint statement by the President of the European Commission and the President of the European Economic and Social Committee of 24 September 2001 (CES 1235/2001).
220 Article 263 EC.       221 Article 265 EC.
222 Articles 128(2), 129, 137(2), 148, 149(4), 150(4), 151(5), 152(4), 156, 159, 161, 162, 175(2) and (3) EC.
223 R. McCarthy, 'The Committee of the Regions: an Advisory Body's Tortuous Path to Influence' (1997) 4 *JEPP* 439.
224 T. Borzel, *States and Regions in the European Union* (Cambridge, Cambridge University Press, 2002) 73.

## Further reading

A. Arnull, *The European Union and its Court of Justice* (Oxford, Oxford University Press, 1999)

N. Brown and F. Jacobs, *The Court of Justice of the European Communities* (5th edn by N. Brown and T. Kennedy, London, Sweet & Maxwell, 2000)

G. de Búrca and J. Weiler (eds.), *The European Court of Justice* (Oxford, Oxford University Press, 2001)

R. Dehousse, *The European Court of Justice* (Basingstoke, Macmillan, 1998)

D. Earnshaw and D. Judge, *The European Parliament* (Basingstoke, Palgrave, 2003)

F. Hayes-Renshaw and H. Wallace, *The Council of Ministers* (Basingstoke, Macmillan, 1996)

L. Hooghe, *The European Commission and the Integration of Europe* (Cambridge, Cambridge University Press, 2001)

G. Majone, *Dilemmas of European Integration: The Ambiguities and Pitfalls of Integration by Stealth* (Oxford, Oxford University Press, 2005)

N. Nugent, *The European Commission* (Basingstoke, Palgrave, 2001)

B. Rittberger, *Building Europe's Parliament: Democratic Representation Beyond the Nation-State* (Oxford, Oxford University Press, 2005)

# 4

# Community law-making

## CONTENTS

## 1. Introduction

The European Union has no general law-making power. Instead, its legislative powers are to be found in specific Treaty provisions which authorise it to make laws in certain fields. This system enabled the designers of the Treaty to strike a delicate balance between the EU institutions and the Member States, with the types of instrument and legal procedure varying according to the field in question. As the Treaty has expanded, both in terms of its competencies and its institutions, so the number of legal bases has become ever more voluminous and the institutional settlement ever more complex.[1] All this raises a question about the coherence of Community law-making, namely whether the principles for determining which procedure is used and which type of law is adopted strike an appropriate balance between the different fields of Community

---

1 The legal bases are set out in the Annex to this chapter.

activity, respect the prerogatives of the different institutions and sufficiently imbue the system with a sense of rationality and clarity.

The second question addressed in this chapter is that of the law-making procedures themselves. There are three main law-making procedures, but they cover only a small fraction of the laws adopted by the Community. The majority of Community laws are adopted under procedures whereby initial legislation delegates the Commission law-making powers, which it exercises in liaison with committees of national representatives in a system known as comitology. Laws adopted under comitology are often as significant as those adopted under the primary legislative procedures. Another complication is that the institutions do not follow the legislative procedures passively. Individual institutions will act in the shadow of these procedures, operating them to secure maximum informal influence for themselves. Alongside this, all institutions have an interest in making the system work efficiently and as one in which the good faith of the institutions is accepted by all. After all, all the institutions want the procedures to enable the passing of laws each considers to be important. To accommodate these features, informal practices and *modi operandi* have emerged within the procedures. These are central to the government and operation of the procedures, but result in the distribution of legislative powers in ways very different from that intended by the drafters of the relevant provisions.

The third question considered in this chapter is that of addressing the democratic legitimacy of the procedures. Once again, there is a complication. A simple majoritarian principle does not work for Community law-making. Southern Europe, for example, would not accept laws if they were to be voted for exclusively by Northern Europe. Excluded states would feel that laws were being imposed by a 'foreign bloc'. Other measurements have to be found. These might include the role of elected representative institutions in the law-making process, the degree of pluralism and participation in the law-making procedures and the level and quality of public debate surrounding these procedures.

## 2. EU legislation

Most EU law-making is carried out within the Community pillar. Article 249 EC sets out the central types of legal instrument in Community law:

### Article 249 EC

In order to carry out their tasks and in accordance with the provisions of this Treaty, the European Parliament acting jointly with the Council, the Council and the Commission shall make regulations and issue directives, take decisions, make recommendations or deliver opinions.

> A regulation shall have general application. It shall be binding in its entirety and directly applicable in all Member States.
>
> A directive shall be binding as to the result to be achieved, upon each Member State to which it is addressed, but shall leave to the national authorities the choice of form and methods.
>
> A decision shall be binding in its entirety upon those to whom it is addressed.
>
> Recommendations and opinions shall have no binding force.

The provision is not exhaustive. International agreements with non-EU states are not mentioned in Article 249 EC, but are regarded as secondary legislation, binding both the Community and the Member States.[2]

**Regulations**   Regulations are the most centralising of all Community instruments and are used wherever there is a need for uniformity. One distinguishing feature is that they are to have general application, so they do not apply to individual sets of circumstances, but to an 'objectively determined situation and produce(s) legal effects with regard to categories of persons described in a generalised and abstract manner'.[3] The other hallmark of regulations is their direct applicability. They enter into force either twenty days after publication in the Official Journal or on the date specified in the regulation.[4] From that date they are automatically incorporated into the domestic legal order of each Member State and require no further transposition. Indeed, it is normally illegal for a Member State to adopt implementing legislation because such measures might contain changes which affect the uniform application of the regulation[5] or obscure from citizens the fact that the Regulation is the direct source of the rights and obligations in question.[6] However, in some cases, Regulations will require national authorities to adopt implementing measures. If there is such a requirement, a failure to implement the Regulation will be a breach of Community law.[7]

**Directives**   The Directive is binding as to the result to be achieved. It leaves the choice as to form and methods used to implement it to the discretion of Member States. Whilst a Directive will come into force 20 days after publication or on the date stipulated in the Directive,[8] it will give a deadline – usually 18 or 24 months after publication – by which Member States must transpose its obligations into national law.

**Decisions**   Decisions are binding upon those to whom they are addressed. For this reason the addressee must be notified of any decision.[9] The majority of Decisions are

2 Article 300(7) EC.     3 Joined Cases 789 and 790/79 *Calpak v Commission* [1980] ECR 1949.
4 Article 254 EC.     5 Case 39/72 *Commission v Italy* [1973] ECR 101.
6 Case 34/73 *Variola v Amministrazione delle Finanze* [1973] ECR 981.
7 Case 128/78 *Commission v United Kingdom* [1978] ECR 2429.
8 Article 252 EC.     9 Article 254(1) EC.

addressed to Member States, with only a small number addressed to private parties with almost all of the latter being in the field of competition law, where the Commission can impose fines on parties or require them to desist from certain practices. Decisions addressed to particular parties can be distinguished from Decisions which have no addressee ('Beschluss'). Although the latter are not addressed to particular parties, they are intended to be binding. They bind the Union as an organisational entity and Member States, as part of that entity, are bound by them. However, as they are not addressed to private parties, they cannot impose obligations on them.[10]

***Framework Decisions***   These are used for the harmonisation of legislation. They are binding upon the Member States as to the result to be achieved, but leave the form and method of implementation to national authorities. They are analogous to Directives, although they cannot generate independent rights capable of being invoked in national courts.[11]

***Decisions***   These are to be adopted for all purposes other than harmonisation of legislation. A good example of what this means is Decision 98/701/JHA on common standards for filling in the residence permit for non-EU nationals.[12] These would appear to be harmonising procedures for administrative officials on how to fill in residence permits. A Framework Decision was not chosen, however, as the measure was intended to be purely administrative, and was not intended to affect the competence of Member States relating either to the recognition of states or to passports from these states. Decisions adopted under the third pillar are analogous to first pillar decisions in that they are binding. Like Framework Decisions, however, they cannot generate independent rights to be invoked before national courts.

**International agreements**   Agreements entered into by the Community with non-EU states are regarded as a source of Community law. The agreement will only have legal effects within Community law for that part of the agreement that falls within Community competence. Its legal effects will depend upon how it has been phrased. If it imposes precise obligations, these will not require implementation by either Member States or the Community Institutions. More vaguely phrased provisions will necessitate implementation. Interpretation of the provisions of an international agreement will be carried out in the light of the object and purpose of that agreement. Provisions identically worded to Community law provisions may be interpreted differently, on the ground that the objective of the agreement differs from that of the EC Treaty.[13]

10 A. v. Bogdandy, F. Arndt and J. Bast, 'Legal Instruments in European Union Law and their Reform: a Systematic Approach on an Empirical Basis' (2004) 23 *YBEL* 91, 103–6.
11 Whilst Framework Decisions cannot be invoked directly in national courts, national measures must be interpreted in the light of them: Case C-105/03 *Pupino*, judgment of 16 June 2005. See pp. 194–5.
12 OJ 1998 L333/8.
13 The seminal case on international agreements is Case 104/81 *Hauptzollamt Mainz v Kupferberg* [1982] ECR 3641.

Alongside these must be placed the legislative instruments of the third pillar.[14] Article 34(2) TEU sets out three forms of legislative measure.[15]

**Conventions**   These are similar to international agreements. They generate commitments between the Member States and the Union, but their effects upon the internal legal order of Member States is unclear. For the Union can only recommend to the Member States that they be adopted within a time limit in accordance with national constitutional requirements. They tend to be adopted in areas of particular national sensitivity, a good example being the Convention on Jurisdiction and the Recognition and Enforcement of Judgments in Matrimonial Matters.[16] This allowed mutual recognition of divorce arrangements and marriages, but addresses highly charged matters such as judicial procedure and the nature of the family in modern societies. A Convention was, therefore, seen as the best way to proceed.

A recent study found Community legislation accounted for about 99 per cent of all EU legislation. Regulations were most widely used, accounting for 31 per cent of all legislation. Decisions addressed to a party accounted for a further 27 per cent, with Decisions not addressed to anybody accounting for 10 per cent of all measures. Directives and international agreements each accounted for 9 per cent of all legislation.[17] There is not only a wide array of legislative instruments, but they also appear to be substitutable for one another. One finds Regulations which substitute for Decisions in that they apply to individual sets of circumstances rather than generally.[18] There are, conversely, Directives which look like Regulations because they are so detailed that they vitiate the discretion granted to Member States and must be transposed into national law verbatim.[19] Finally, Decisions without addressees act as a substitute for Directives in that they require Member States to realise certain results without specifying the means. In no instance has any of this been declared illegal on the grounds that one instrument is being used wrongly in place of another. The other difficulty is that there is no hierarchy of norms, where one type of instrument is taken to trump another. This is particularly problematic as the majority of Regulations, 69 per cent, are delegated legislation, adopted by the Commission under powers granted to it by the other institutions.[20] The Community legal system does not identify these as delegated legislation nor establish a clear relationship between these acts, which are essentially executive, and other legislation.

---

14 Although the European Union can take a variety of measures under the second pillar (Article 14 TEU), their legal status is unclear and has not been addressed.

15 Article 34(2) TEU lists 'common positions' as a measure that can be adopted. These define the approach of the European Union to a particular matter, but cannot be considered legislation as it is not clear what legislative effects these have.

16 OJ 1998 C221/1.    17 v. Bogdandy, Arndt and Bast, above n. 10, 97.

18 e.g. Joined Cases 41–4/70 *International Fruit Company v Commission* [1971] ECR 411.

19 Case 38/77 *ENKA v Inspecteur der Invoerrechten* [1977] ECR 2203.

20 v. Bogdandy, Arndt and Bast, above n. 10, 99.

The Laeken Declaration asked the 'Future of Europe' Convention to consider whether the European Union's instruments should be better defined and their number reduced.[21] The Constitutional Treaty brought all legislative acts into an integrated framework in which there would only be four types of binding act.

> ### Article I-33(1) CT
>
> To exercise the Union's competences the institutions shall use as legal instruments . . . European laws, European framework laws, European regulations, European decisions, recommendations and opinions.
>
> A European law shall be a legislative act of general application. It shall be binding in its entirety and directly applicable in all Member States.
>
> A European framework law shall be a legislative act binding, as to the result to be achieved, upon each Member State to which it is addressed, but shall leave to the national authorities the choice of form and methods.
>
> A European regulation shall be a non-legislative act of general application for the implementation of legislative acts and of certain provisions of the Constitution. It may either be binding in its entirety and directly applicable in all Member States, or be binding, as to the result to be achieved, upon each Member State to which it is addressed, but shall leave to the national authorities the choice of form and methods.
>
> A European decision shall be a non-legislative act, binding in its entirety. A decision which specifies those to whom it is addressed shall be binding only on them.
>
> Recommendations and opinions shall have no binding force.

The provision parallels Article 249 EC in many ways. The European Law is clearly analogous to the current EC Regulation, the European Framework Law to the Community Directive and the European Decision to the current EC Decision. The central reform proposed by Article I-33 CT was the introduction of a new form of legal act, the European Regulation, which would be adopted whenever secondary legislation was used. This was because the 'Future of Europe' Convention felt that the functions of primary legislation and delegated legislation were different.[22] The function of the former should be to set out the essential elements of an area, whilst the latter's role was to fill in the detail. This was not simply for the sake of legislative clarity, but also to enable a clear separation of powers. The legislature should be focussed exclusively on the central policy choices, whilst the executive should be responsible for administering the technical detail. This distinction is dogmatic and certainly open to question,[23] yet, viewed as a critique of the current system, it is quite damning. It suggests that the substitutability of the different types of Community law is leading not merely to legal confusion, but also to a blurring of institutional roles. Without

21 European Council, Declaration on the Future of the European Union, N 300/1/01 Rev. 1.
22 *Final Report of Working Group IX on Simplification*, CONV 424/02.
23 For a strong discussion see E. Vos, 'The Role of Comitology in European Governance' in D. Curtin and R. Wessel (eds.), *Good Governance and the European Union: Concept, Implications and Applications* (Antwerp, Intersentia, 2005).

clear parameters, primary legislation adopted by the Council and Parliament can, on occasions, micro-manage, through being excessively detailed and rigid. By contrast, the lack of confines on delegated legislation leads to the opposite danger in relation to the Commission. Adopting laws like any other institution can lead it, under that guise, to make significant political choices which would be better left to the other institutions.

### 3. Soft law

Recommendations and Opinions are mentioned in Article 249 EC, but have no binding force. They must be viewed alongside a variety of other instruments, which include Resolutions and Declarations, action programmes and plans, decisions of the representatives of the Member States meeting in Council, guidelines issued by institutions as to how they will exercise their powers and inter-institutional arrangements. These measures all come under the generic of 'soft law'; 'rules of conduct which, in principle, have no legally binding force but which nevertheless may have practical effects'.[24] These instruments are an integral part of the Union legal order, accounting for 13 per cent of all EU law.[25] These instruments are used for a variety of purposes.

**Commitments about the conduct of institutions** These are commonly used to organise the relations between the institutions. A good example is the Joint Declaration on Practical Arrangements for the New Co-Decision Procedure, which sets out the *modus vivendi* for one of the main Community legislative procedures and the institutions' understanding of their rights and duties under it.[26]

**Commitments to respect certain values** Soft law, most notably Declarations, are used to commit Union institutions to pursuing certain values. Declarations are not merely commitments to future conduct, but also seek to redefine the political identity of the Union. The most obvious example is the Joint Declaration by the European Parliament, the Council and the Commission on Fundamental Rights, where the institutions were asserting for the first time that observance of fundamental rights norms was a goal of the Union's institutions, thereby admitting that it was not merely concerned with economic integration, but also had an incipient civil identity.[27]

**Programming legislation** The instrument, *par excellence*, for this is the action plan. Action plans set out objectives and timetables for particular EU policies, which are used to justify specific legislation and which provide a wider background against which this legislation is understood and interpreted. A good example is the Commission

---

24 F. Snyder, 'The Effectiveness of European Community Law: Institutions, Processes, Tools and Techniques' (1993) 56 *MLR* 19, 32.
25 v. Bogdandy, Arndt and Bast, above n. 10, 97.     26 OJ 1999 C148/1.     27 OJ 1977 C103/1.

Action Plan for European Renewal in the field of Freedom, Security and Justice, adopted in 2005.[28] The Action Plan identifies ten priorities for freedom, security and justice for the period up to 2010. These include developing policies for fundamental rights and citizenship, the establishment of a common asylum area, managing migration and developing an integrated management of the external borders of the European Union. It also lists over 200 measures, some legislative and others administrative, some binding and others not, to be adopted to meet these priorities.

**Regulatory instrument**   In areas such as nuclear energy and competition, the Commission will issue opinions as an informal way of indicating to undertakings whether they are complying with Community law. It will also issue notices, setting out its general enforcement policy on what infractions it will or will not pursue.[29]

The most controversial use of soft law is for 'model law-making', where guidelines or recommendations setting out best practice are adopted. In some areas of Community law, most notably economic policy, employment policy, education, culture and public health, soft law is even envisaged as the primary form of law-making.[30] The Secretariat at the 'Future of Europe' Convention identified three circumstances where binding legislation is unlikely to be adopted and soft law preferred:

- where the area of work is closely connected with national identity or culture;
- where the instruments for implementing national policies are so diverse and/or complex that harmonisation seems disproportionate in relation to the objectives pursued;
- where there is no political will for EC legislation amongst the Member States, but there is a desire to make progress together.[31]

Soft law exploded in 2000. At Lisbon, the European Union set itself the objective of becoming by 2010 'the most competitive and dynamic knowledge-based economy in the world, capable of sustainable economic growth with more and better jobs and greater social cohesion'.[32] Recognising that traditional Community law-making alone would not be suitable for realising these ambitious goals, the European Council set out a new procedure of soft law-making, known as the open method of coordination (OMC), to cover a number of areas that lay either outside, or at the periphery of, Community competence. Over time, the procedure has been applied to the following

---

28  COM(2005)184.
29  e.g. Commission Notice on agreements of minor importance which do not appreciably restrict competition, OJ 2001 C368/13. The use of this has been criticised on the grounds that it allows the Commission to enshrine a particular interpretation of Community law without proper judicial control: S. Lefevre, 'Interpretative Communications and the Implementation of Community Law at National Level' (2004) 29 *EL Rev.* 808.
30  Articles 99(2), 128(2), 149(4), 151(5), 152(4) EC.
31  European Convention, *Coordination of National Policies: the Open Method of Coordination*, WG VI WD015 (Brussels, 26 September 2002).
32  EU Bulletin 3–2000, I.5.5.

fields: the information society, research policy, enterprise, pensions, education and vocational training, combating social exclusion and sustainable development.[33] Although the procedure varies according to sector, the central features of the OMC have been described by Sabel and Zeitlin:

- joint definition by the Member States (usually acting as the European Council) of initial objectives (general and specific), indicators and, in some cases, guidelines;
- the development of national reports or action plans by Member States which assess performance in light of the objectives and metrics, and propose reforms accordingly;
- peer review of these plans by the other Member States, including mutual criticism and exchange of good practices, backed up by recommendations in some cases;
- re-elaboration of the individual plans and, at less frequent intervals, of the broader objectives and metrics in light of the experience gained in their implementation.[34]

There has been a recent fierce debate over the value of soft law in the light of the growth of this method. The arguments of each side have been well set out by Trubek, Cottrell and Nance.[35] Some of the criticisms of soft law they observe are that:

- it lacks the clarity and precision needed to provide predictability and a reliable framework for action;
- soft law cannot really have any effect, but is a covert tactic to enlarge the European Union's legislative hard law competence;
- soft law bypasses normal systems of accountability;
- soft law undermines EU legitimacy because it creates expectations, but cannot bring about change.

They argue, however, that soft law has some advantages over traditional law:

- hard law tends toward uniformity of treatment while many current issues demand tolerance for significant diversity among Member States;
- hard law presupposes a fixed condition based on prior knowledge while situations of uncertainty may demand constant experimentation and adjustment;
- hard law is very difficult to change yet in many cases frequent change of norms may be essential to achieve optimal results;
- if actors do not internalise the norms of hard law, enforcement may be difficult; if they do, it may be unnecessary.

---

33 Details can be found at www.europa.eu.int/growthandjobs/index_en.htm
34 C. Sabel and J. Zeitlin, 'Active Welfare, Experimental Governance, and Pragmatic Constitutionalism: the New Transformation of Europe' (2003) cited in D. Trubek, P. Cottrell and M. Nance, 'Soft Law', 'Hard Law', and European Integration: toward a Theory of Hybridity, Jean Monnet Working Paper 02/05, 19.
35 Ibid. 6–7. There is also an excellent literature review at ibid. nn. 3–5.

From this, it would appear that much depends on the nature of the field. In areas where uniformity is not important and there is a need for experimentation, soft law would seem to have important attributes. Yet even in these fields, the criticisms of soft law still persist, namely the manner in which it has been used to expand EU competencies and its lack of concern with asymmetries of power, so that compliance with soft law only tends to occur when it suits vested interests.

## 4. Legal bases for Community legislation

Each piece of EU legislation must be grounded upon a legal base set out in the Treaty. The legal base has the following roles: first, it enables the Community to legislate in the given field and sets out the scope for Community legislation in the area. Secondly, the legal base determines the legislative procedures and the types of laws that can be adopted. In turn, this determines the respective powers and influences of the different EU institutions and the influence of national governments within the law-making process.[36] Often, it will be possible for the European Union to choose between two or more different legal bases for a piece of legislation, with the different institutions seeking to use the legal basis that provides the procedure most advantageous to them. Unsurprisingly, as different procedures privilege different institutions, this has led to both Community institutions and Member States vigorously litigating the choice of legal base.[37]

The relationship between the first pillar, the Community pillar, and the other two pillars, Common Foreign and Security Policy and Policing and Judicial Cooperation, was analysed for the first time in *Environmental Crimes*. The Council adopted a Framework Decision on protection of the environment through criminal law, Framework Decision 2003/80/JHA, under the third pillar. The measure set out a number of environmental offences that Member States undertook to criminalise. The Commission challenged this, arguing that, as the purpose of the measure was to protect the environment, the measure should have been adopted under the legal provision in the Community pillar, Article 175 EC, which was concerned with protection of the environment.

---

**Case C-176/03 *Commission v Council* ('Environmental Crimes'), judgment of 13 September 2005**

38. Article 47 EU provides that nothing in the Treaty on European Union is to affect the EC Treaty. That requirement is also found in the first paragraph of Article 29 EU, which introduces Title VI of the Treaty on European Union.

---

36 R. Barents, 'The Internal Market Unlimited: Some Observations on the Legal Basis of Community Legislation' (1993) 30 *CML Rev.* 85, 92.
37 H. Cullen and H. Charlesworth, 'Diplomacy by Other Means: the Use of Legal Basis Litigation as a Political Strategy by the European Parliament and Member States' (1999) 36 *CML Rev.* 1243.

39. It is the task of the Court to ensure that acts which, according to the Council, fall within the scope of Title VI of the Treaty on European Union do not encroach upon the powers conferred by the EC Treaty on the Community . . .

40. It is therefore necessary to ascertain whether Articles 1 to 7 of the framework decision affect the powers of the Community under Article 175 EC inasmuch as those articles could, as the Commission maintains, have been adopted on the basis of the last-mentioned provision . . .

46. As regards the aim of the framework decision, it is clear both from its title and from its first three recitals that its objective is the protection of the environment. The Council was concerned 'at the rise in environmental offences and their effects which are increasingly extending beyond the borders of the States in which the offences are committed', and, having found that those offences constitute 'a threat to the environment' and 'a problem jointly faced by the Member States', concluded that 'a tough response' and 'concerted action to protect the environment under criminal law' were called for.

47. As to the content of the framework decision, Article 2 establishes a list of particularly serious environmental offences, in respect of which the Member States must impose criminal penalties. Articles 2 to 7 of the decision do indeed entail partial harmonisation of the criminal laws of the Member States, in particular as regards the constituent elements of various criminal offences committed to the detriment of the environment. As a general rule, neither criminal law nor the rules of criminal procedure fall within the Community's competence.

48. However, the last-mentioned finding does not prevent the Community legislature, when the application of effective, proportionate and dissuasive criminal penalties by the competent national authorities is an essential measure for combating serious environmental offences, from taking measures which relate to the criminal law of the Member States which it considers necessary in order to ensure that the rules which it lays down on environmental protection are fully effective.

49. It should also be added that in this instance, although Articles 1 to 7 of the framework decision determine that certain conduct which is particularly detrimental to the environment is to be criminal, they leave to the Member States the choice of the criminal penalties to apply, although, in accordance with Article 5(1) of the decision, the penalties must be effective, proportionate and dissuasive.

50. The Council does not dispute that the acts listed in Article 2 of the framework decision include infringements of a considerable number of Community measures, which were listed in the annex to the proposed directive. Moreover, it is apparent from the first three recitals to the framework decision that the Council took the view that criminal penalties were essential for combating serious offences against the environment.

51. It follows from the foregoing that, on account of both their aim and their content, Articles 1 to 7 of the framework decision have as their main purpose the protection of the environment and they could have been properly adopted on the basis of Article 175 EC.

The judgment does not say that there should be a relationship of balance and comity between the three pillars in which none encroach excessively upon the fields of the other. Instead, it adopts a one-sided logic, which raises questions both about the balance of the TEU and the limits on Community powers. For it suggests there is no field that can be governed *a priori* by the other two pillars. Measures can only be adopted under these insofar as they do not correspond to the very broad purposes of the EC.

*Environmental Crimes* is the first case of its type. Conflicts internal to the Community pillar are more common. A recent example is the *Recovery of Indirect Taxes* litigation. The Commission and Parliament challenged the adoption of Directive 2001/44/EC, which provided for mutual assistance between Member States in the recovery of unpaid indirect taxation. The Council had adopted it under Article 93 EC, which concerned harmonisation of indirect taxes, and Article 94 EC, the common market provision, rather than under Article 95 EC, the internal market provision. The latter requires the use of the co-decision procedure, which provides for QMV in the Council and a greater role for the Parliament in the legislative process. The others, by contrast, provide for a unanimity vote in the Council and a reduced role for the Parliament. If tax measures could be agreed by QMV, recalcitrant states could be outmanoeuvred and bargained down. If the process was subject to a veto, fiscal integration would be held hostage to the wishes of the least integrationist Member State.

### Case C-338/01 *Commission v Council* ('Recovery of Indirect Taxes') [2004] ECR I-4829

54. . . . the choice of the legal basis for a Community measure must rest on objective factors amenable to judicial review, which include in particular the aim and the content of the measure.

55. If examination of a Community measure reveals that it pursues a twofold purpose or that it has a twofold component and if one of these is identifiable as the main or predominant purpose or component whereas the other is merely incidental, the act must be based on a single legal basis, namely that required by the main or predominant purpose or component.

56. By way of exception, if it is established that the measure simultaneously pursues several objectives which are inseparably linked without one being secondary and indirect in relation to the other, the measure must be founded on the corresponding legal bases.

57. However, no dual legal basis is possible where the procedures laid down for each legal basis are incompatible with each other.

58. In the present case, the procedures set out under Articles 93 EC and 94 EC, on the one hand, and that set out under Article 95 EC, on the other, mean that the latter article cannot be applied in conjunction with one of the other two articles mentioned above in order to serve as the legal basis for a measure such as Directive 2001/44. Whereas unanimity is required for the adoption of a measure on the basis of Articles 93 EC and 94 EC, a qualified majority is sufficient for a measure to be capable of valid adoption on the basis of Article 95 EC. Thus, of the provisions cited above, Articles 93 EC and 94 EC alone may provide a valid dual legal basis for the adoption of a legal measure by the Council.

59. So far as concerns the scope of Article 95 EC, which the Commission and Parliament argue ought to have been used as the legal basis for the adoption of Directive 2001/44, it must be pointed out that it is clear from the very wording of Article 95(1) EC that that article applies only if the Treaty does not provide otherwise.

60. It follows that, if the Treaty contains a more specific provision that is capable of constituting the legal basis for the measure in question, that measure must be founded on such provision. That is, in particular, the case with regard to Article 93 EC so far as concerns the harmonisation of legislation concerning turnover taxes, excise duties and other forms of indirect taxation.

61. It must also be pointed out that Article 95(2) EC expressly excludes certain areas from the scope of that article. This is in particular the case with regard to 'fiscal provisions', the approximation of which cannot therefore take place on the basis of that article . . .

67. The words 'fiscal provisions' contained in Article 95(2) EC must be interpreted as covering not only the provisions determining taxable persons, taxable transactions, the basis of imposition, and rates of and exemptions from direct and indirect taxes, but also those relating to arrangements for the collection of such taxes . . .

76. . . . it must be held that Directive 2001/44 does relate to 'fiscal provisions' within the meaning of Article 95(2) EC, with the result that Article 95 EC cannot constitute the correct legal basis for the adoption of that directive.

In determining the predominant purpose of a measure, the Court will look at the principles on which it is based and its ideological content rather than its effects. In *Framework Directive on Waste*,[38] the Commission challenged the adoption of the Directive under Article 175(1) EC, the environmental base, arguing that it should have been based on Article 95 EC, the internal market provision. The Court disagreed. It noted that the central tenets of the Directive were those of environmental management. Instead of securing the internal market objectives of free movement of waste, the Directive implemented the ecological principles that environmental damage should be rectified at source and that waste should be disposed of as close as possible to the place of production in order to keep transport to a minimum.

If two objectives are so inextricably and equally associated that the Court cannot ascertain the predominant purpose of a measure, it moves to a different test in which it operates a formal hierarchy between the different legal bases, looking to the relationship specified in the EC Treaty between each. The agricultural provision, Article 37 EC, has, therefore, been held to take precedence over the single market provisions, Articles 94 and 95 EC, on the grounds that Article 32(2) EC stated that the common market rules applied 'save as otherwise provided in Articles 33 to 38'.[39] By contrast, the internal market provision, Article 95 EC, enjoys a similar precedence over Article 175(1) EC, the environmental provision. In *Titanium Dioxide*,[40] the Court deduced this hierarchy between the two bases from Article 175(2) EC, which provided that 'environmental protection requirements shall be a component of the EC's other policies', thereby implying that environmental measures could be adopted under other legal bases, and from Article 95(3) EC, which required internal market legislation to take a high level of environmental protection, suggesting that measures adopted under Article 95 EC could pursue environmental objectives. Finally, at the bottom of the pecking order sits Article 308 EC, the provision that allows the EC to take measures to meet its objectives where no other legal base provides the requisite power. As this provision is only applicable in these circumstances, all other legal bases enjoy precedence over it.[41]

---

38 Case C-155/91 *Commission v Council* [1993] ECR I-939.
39 Case 68/86 *United Kingdom v Council* [1988] ECR 855. See R. Barents, 'Hormones and the Growth of Community Agricultural Law' (1989/2) *LIEI* 1.
40 Case 300/89 *Commission v Council* [1991] ECR I-2867.
41 Case C-295/90 *Parliament v Council* [1992] ECR I-4193.

However, it will be rare that a measure pursues inextricably and equally associated objectives. In *Linguistic Diversity in the Information Society*, the Court had to consider a Decision which set up a programme to promote linguistic diversity in the information society. It had been adopted under Article 130 EC, the legal base for industrial policy. The Parliament challenged this, arguing that it should have been based on Article 128 EC, the legal base for culture. The Court stated that the fact that a measure had twin objectives was insufficient to bring it outside the 'predominant purpose' rule. Each component had to be equally essential to the Directive and had to be indissociable. In this instance, the predominant purpose was industrial. The beneficiaries of the programme were, almost exclusively, small and medium-sized enterprises, who might lose competitiveness because of the costs associated with linguistic diversity.[42]

Neither rule is easy to apply to particular sets of circumstances. The 'predominant purpose' rule assumes each legal base is characterised by a distinctive set of principles, which it is possible to identify in all legislation founded on it.[43] This is rarely the case and the Court has to engage in highly selective analysis to justify a particular legal base for a measure. The 'inextricably associated' rule, if applied literally, is so narrow that it is almost meaningless. Yet it has been applied in some cases, suggesting that sometimes, for ulterior motives, the Court simply wishes to discard the 'predominant purpose' rule. It is wise not to be too critical of the Court. While differing legal bases exist, uncertainty will persist and result in continued litigation. Weatherill has observed that this is a problem which is likely to remain whatever test is adopted by the Court. The underlying difficulty is the Byzantine structure of the Treaty with its proliferation of legal bases and legislative procedures.[44]

## 5. Community primary legislative procedures[45]

Although it is possible to identify twenty-two different legislative procedures in EU law,[46] the overwhelming majority of primary law-making is governed by three legislative procedures.[47]

---

42  Case C-42/97 *Parliament v Council* [1999] ECR I-869.
43  D. Chalmers, 'The Single Market: from Prima Donna to Journeyman' in J. Shaw and G. More (eds.), *New Legal Dynamics of the European Union* (Oxford, Clarendon, 1995), 55, 69–71.
44  S. Weatherill, 'Regulating the Internal Market: Result Orientation in the House of Lords' (1992) 17 *EL Rev.* 299, 312–13.
45  These are sometimes referred to as Treaty-derived procedures because the 'primary law' is the Treaty. This is true, but the Treaty is not a law-making procedure. We have used primary legislation, therefore, as a more elegant term.
46  European Convention, *Legislative Procedures (including the Budgetary Procedure): Current Situation*, CONV 216/02, Annex I.
47  Calculations by Andreas Maurer suggest that since the Treaty of Nice, these procedures account for 90 per cent of all EU law-making: A. Maurer, 'The Legislative Powers and Impact of the European Parliament' (2003) 41 *JCMS* 227, 232.

### (i)   Council legislation without consultation of the Parliament

Under this procedure, the Council adopts the measure, acting on a proposal from the Commission, usually by QMV, but depending on the legal base, sometimes by unanimity. This procedure tends to be used in fields which are politically sensitive for the Member States (such as emergency measures for immigration or free movement of capital), in fields where the EC is making soft law and in some fields where the legislation is performing an 'implementing' role, notably implementing agreements made in social policy by the social partners.[48]

It is not merely the powers of the European Parliament that are weak here, but also the powers of national parliaments. Both the Commission and the Council are executive-dominated and the current safeguards for national parliamentary input are limited.[49] Consequently, the allocation of policy-making to these procedures makes it the preserve of the executive. There is still the question of which 'executive' holds the balance of power in these procedures. Everything hinges on the vote required in the Council. If a unanimity vote is required, power would seem to remain in the hands of individual national governments, as any government can veto the measure. However, the position is more complicated. Twenty-four national governments do not have the power to push through a measure if one national government resists it. Power is, therefore, concentrated in the government that is most resistant to the measure, as it holds the decision on whether or not to go forward.[50]

The position is very different where QMV is used. This is because of Article 250 EC, which is a general provision, but whose effects are particularly apparent with this procedure:

---

**Article 250(1)EC**

Where in pursuance of this Treaty, the Council acts on a proposal from the Commission, unanimity shall be required for an act constituting an amendment to that proposal . . .

2. As long as the Council has not acted, the Commission may alter its proposal at any time during the procedures leading to the adoption of a Community act.

---

In areas of QMV, the first paragraph of this provision means it is always easier for the Council to accept the Commission proposal rather than to amend it. Not only must all Member States agree that the Commission proposal is deficient, but they must also all agree on the merits of a new text. The second paragraph further increases the power of the Commission by giving it an important mediatory role. It has the freedom to adjust its text right up until the moment of adoption by the Council, and to tweak it to the minimum necessary for the requisite votes.

---

48 A list of the different procedures is set out in the Annex to this chapter.      49 See pp. 137–8.

50 On this see *Report by the Ad Hoc Group Examining the Question of Increasing the Parliament's Powers* (the Vedel Report) EC Bulletin Supplt. 4/72; Committee of Three, *Report on the European Institutions* (Luxembourg, OOPEC, 1980) 74–5.

The procedure gives rise to three concerns. The first is the lack of parliamentary involvement. The second concerns the balance of power. Where a unanimity vote is used, power is concentrated in the hands of the most resistant party. In the case of QMV, power seems to rest very strongly with the enthusiastic proponent of the proposal, the Commission. The sheer lack of balance in either case is disturbing. Finally, there are concerns about the lack of structure in the process. It is, ultimately, a Commission–Council negotiation rather than a structured legislative procedure. As with any negotiating procedure, there is a danger of lack of transparency and fluidity about proceedings, with important stakeholders not being aware of latest proposals or the state of play.

### (ii)   Consultation procedure

The consultation procedure follows three stages:

(a) the Commission submits a proposal to the Council;
(b) the Council consults the Parliament;
(c) the Council adopts the measure, either by qualified majority or by unanimity, depending upon the field in question.

The most salient feature of the consultation procedure is the duty to consult the Parliament. In *Roquette Frères*, the Court stated that consultation was an expression of the cardinal principle of institutional balance:

> [Consultation] . . . allows the Parliament to play an actual part in the legislative process of the Community, such power represents an essential factor in the institutional balance intended by the Treaty. Although limited, it reflects at Community level the fundamental democratic principle that the peoples should take part in the exercise of power through the intermediary of a representative assembly. Due consultation of the Parliament in the cases provided for by the Treaty therefore constitutes an essential formality disregard of which means that the measure concerned is void.[51]

From this principle of institutional balance, the Court has crafted a number of mutual obligations between the Parliament and the Council. On the one hand, the Council is obliged to reconsult the Parliament if the text is amended so that the one adopted by the Council differs substantially from the one on which the Parliament has been consulted. In *Cabotage II*, Parliament was consulted on a proposal which gave non-resident hauliers an unlimited right to operate road haulage services within another Member State. The final Regulation adopted did not provide for full liberal-isation. Instead, it established a system whereby a limited number of hauliers could

---

51 Case 138/79 *Roquette Frères v Council* [1980] ECR 3333.

apply for an authorisation to run road haulage services in another Member State for a limited period of time.

---

### Case C-65/90 *Parliament v Council* ('Cabotage II') [1992] ECR I-4593

16. . . . the duty to consult the European Parliament in the course of the legislative procedure, in the cases provided for by the Treaty, includes the requirement that the Parliament be reconsulted on each occasion when the text finally adopted, viewed as a whole, departs substantially from the text on which the Parliament has already been consulted, except in cases where the amendments essentially correspond to the wishes of the Parliament itself . . .

19. A comparison between the Commission's original proposal and the contested regulation shows that temporary authorization within the framework of a Community quota has been substituted for the principle of freedom of cabotage in Member States for carriers established in another Member State. Those amendments affect the very essence of the instrument adopted and must therefore be regarded as substantive. They do not correspond to any wish of the Parliament. On the contrary, in its opinion of 12 September 1986 the Parliament favoured greater liberalization, proposing that a paragraph should be added to Article 1, ensuring that Member States in which authorization to carry out national transport operations is subject to quantitative restrictions should increase the number of authorizations appropriately in order to allow carriers from other Member States to participate in domestic transport operations when additional authorizations are issued.

---

By contrast, the Parliament must not abuse its right of consultation. In 'General Tariff Preferences',[52] the Council sought to consult the Parliament on a proposal to extend the Regulation on general tariff preferences, which gave preferential tax treatment to imports from less developed countries, to the states which had emerged from the collapse of the Soviet Union. The request was made in October 1992 and was termed 'urgent'. The matter was debated in November 1992, but full decision was postponed until a further debate in January 1993 on the grounds that the Parliament's Committee on Development was not sure that these states were sufficiently poor to justify inclusion. The Council adopted the Regulation in December 1992, without further consultation on the grounds that the matter was urgent. This was challenged by the Parliament:

---

### Case C-65/93 *Parliament v Council* ('General Tariff Preferences') [1995] ECR I-693

21. The first point to note is that due consultation of the Parliament in the cases provided for by the Treaty constitutes an essential procedural requirement, disregard of which renders the measure concerned void. The effective participation of the Parliament in the legislative process of the Community, in accordance with the procedures laid down by the Treaty,

---

52 Case C-65/93 *Parliament v Council* [1995] ECR I-643.

represents an essential factor in the institutional balance intended by the Treaty. Such power reflects the fundamental democratic principle that the people should take part in the exercise of power through the intermediary of a representative assembly . . .

22. Furthermore, observance of the consultation requirement implies that the Parliament has expressed its opinion and the requirement cannot be satisfied by the Council's simply asking for the opinion . . . In an emergency, it is for the Council to use all the possibilities available under the Treaty and the Parliament's Rules of Procedure in order to obtain the preliminary opinion of the Parliament.

23. However . . . inter-institutional dialogue, on which the consultation procedure in particular is based, is subject to the same mutual duties of sincere cooperation as those which govern relations between Member States and the Community institutions . . .

26. However, the documents before the Court show that, notwithstanding the assurances thereby given to the Council, the Parliament decided, pursuant to Article 106 of its Rules of Procedure, to adjourn the plenary session of 18 December 1992 at the request of 14 Members, without having debated the proposal for the regulation. It appears, moreover, that that decision was based on reasons wholly unconnected with the contested regulation and did not take into account the urgency of the procedure and the need to adopt the regulation before 1 January 1993.

27. By adopting that course of action, the Parliament failed to discharge its obligation to cooperate sincerely with the Council. That is so especially since the Council was unable to avail itself of the possibility open to it under Article 139 of the Treaty, the information obtained by the Council from the President of the Parliament having made it clear that it was impossible for practical reasons to convene an extraordinary session of the Parliament before the end of 1992.

28. In those circumstances, the Parliament is not entitled to complain of the Council's failure to await its opinion before adopting the contested regulation of 21 December 1992. The essential procedural requirement of parliamentary consultation was not complied with because of the Parliament's failure to discharge its obligation to cooperate sincerely with the Council.

To be sure, by forcing itself to be consulted properly, the Parliament can ensure that its arguments are heard. The presence of parliamentary hearings also brings greater transparency to the process and provides an arena for actors, whose voice might otherwise have been excluded, to express their views. However, these features exert only a limited effect upon the broader institutional settlement, which revolves around the Commission-Council axis. The procedure is thus very much subject to the same criticisms as the procedure where the Parliament is not consulted.

The Council is not required to take account of the Parliament's views or to give reasons for rejecting them. The lack of leverage over the Council also harms the Parliament's relations with the Commission. As the Parliament's views count for so little, there are no incentives for the Commission to coordinate or even consult with it. This marginalisation is further increased by the Council not being required to wait until the Parliament has been consulted before it considers a proposal, with the Court even stating that the Council is making good use of time if it considers the matter pending consultation of the Parliament.[53] Political agreement is thus often reached within the Council before the Parliament's opinion has been heard.[54]

### (iii) Co-decision procedure

### (a) Central features of the co-decision procedure

The TEU added a further legislative procedure, the co-decision procedure, which was refined at the Treaty of Amsterdam. It is contained in Article 251 EC.

---

**Article 251(2) EC**

The Commission shall submit a proposal to the European Parliament and the Council.

The Council, acting by a qualified majority after obtaining the opinion of the European Parliament,

– if it approves all the amendments contained in the European Parliament's opinion, may adopt the proposed act thus amended;
– if the European Parliament does not propose any amendments, may adopt the proposed act;
– shall otherwise adopt a common position and communicate it to the European Parliament. The Council shall inform the European Parliament fully of the reasons which led it to adopt its common position. The Commission shall inform the European Parliament fully of its position.

If, within three months of such communication, the European Parliament:

(a) approves the common position or has not taken a decision, the act in question shall be deemed to have been adopted in accordance with that common position;
(b) rejects, by an absolute majority of its component members, the common position, the proposed act shall be deemed not to have been adopted;
(c) proposes amendments to the common position by an absolute majority of its component members, the amended text shall be forwarded to the Council and to the Commission, which shall deliver an opinion on those amendments.

3. If, within three months of the matter being referred to it, the Council, acting by a qualified majority, approves all the amendments of the European Parliament, the act in question shall be deemed to have been adopted in the form of the common position thus amended; however, the Council shall act unanimously on the amendments on which the Commission has delivered a negative opinion. If the Council does not approve all the amendments, the President of the Council, in agreement with the President of the European Parliament, shall within six weeks convene a meeting of the Conciliation Committee.

4. The Conciliation Committee, which shall be composed of the members of the Council or their representatives and an equal number of representatives of the European Parliament, shall have the task of reaching agreement on a joint text, by a qualified majority of the members of the Council or their representatives and by a majority of the representatives of the European Parliament. The Commission shall take part in the Conciliation Committee's proceedings and

---

53 Case C-417/93 *Parliament v Council* [1995] ECR I-1185.
54 M. Westlake, *The Commission and the Parliament* (London, Butterworths, 1994) 34.

shall take all the necessary initiatives with a view to reconciling the positions of the European Parliament and the Council. In fulfilling this task, the Conciliation Committee shall address the common position on the basis of the amendments proposed by the European Parliament.

5. If, within six weeks of its being convened, the Conciliation Committee approves a joint text, the European Parliament, acting by an absolute majority of the votes cast, and the Council, acting by a qualified majority, shall each have a period of six weeks from that approval in which to adopt the act in question in accordance with the joint text. If either of the two institutions fails to approve the proposed act within that period, it shall be deemed not to have been adopted.

6. Where the Conciliation Committee does not approve a joint text, the proposed act shall be deemed not to have been adopted.

7. The periods of three months and six weeks referred to in this Article shall be extended by a maximum of one month and two weeks respectively at the initiative of the European Parliament or the Council.

The length of this provision makes the procedure look intimidating. It is best to think of the procedure as a series of noteworthy features.

**Joint agreement**    The procedure provides for the joint adoption of legislation, co-decision, by the Council and the Parliament. This can happen at three junctures during the procedure.

It can happen after the first reading by the Parliament. In this scenario, the Commission makes a proposal. The Parliament issues an opinion on it (the first reading). The Council can adopt the act by QMV if either the Parliament has made no amendments or it agrees with its amendments.

The second juncture occurs after the second reading by the European Parliament. If there is no agreement between the Parliament and the Council, after the first reading by the Parliament, the Council can adopt a 'common position'. If it is adopting the Commission proposal, it does this by QMV. If it makes amendments of its own, it does this by unanimity. This common position is referred back to the Parliament for a second reading. If the Parliament does nothing for three months or agrees with the common position, the measure is adopted. Alternately, it may propose amendments. If the amendments have been approved by the Commission, they may be adopted by the Council by QMV. If, however, the Commission expressed a negative view of the Parliament's amendments, these have to be adopted by unanimity in the Council.

The final juncture comes after the third reading. If there is no agreement following the second reading, a Conciliation Committee is established. This comprises twenty-five members from the Council and twenty-five MEPs. It has six weeks to approve a joint text. This text must be adopted within six weeks, by both the Council, by QMV, and the Parliament to become law.

**Double veto of the Parliament**    The co-decision procedure grants the Parliament a veto over legislation. The veto can either be exercised at the second reading, where the Parliament decides to reject the common position of the Council. The other possibility is at the third reading, after the Conciliation Committee has provided a joint text on which it must vote. Technically speaking, it is not a veto that is being exercised here, but parliamentary assent. The Parliament does not need to reject the measure. It must positively agree to it at this point for it to become law.

**Assent of the Council**  A measure will only become law if the Council agrees to it. The number of votes required will either be QMV or unanimity. If the measure has been approved by the Commission – be it either the original proposal or amendments suggested by the Parliament – or by the Conciliation Committee, it will be QMV.[55] In cases where the Council is proposing on its own amendments, it must act by unanimity to adopt those amendments.

**The Conciliation Committee**  This is convened following the Parliament's second reading, where the Council is unable to accept the amendments proposed by the Parliament. Modelled on the Mediations Committee present in the German legislative system,[56] its task is to agree a joint text within six weeks where the Council has been unable to accept amendments proposed by the Parliament. In the Committee, the Council members vote by QMV and the MEPs by simple majority. Since 1995, the Conciliation Committee has been preceded by trilogues, which prepare its work for it.[57] The use of the trilogue grew out of the enlargement of the European Union. Prior to the 2004 enlargement, there would typically be 100 people in a Conciliation Committee meeting. This was too many for meaningful negotiation. The trilogue is composed of three parties – two or three MEPs, normally from the respective committee, a Deputy Permanent Representative, normally from the state holding the Presidency, and a senior Commission official. The job of the trilogue is to act as a forum where each side can explain its position to the other and, if possible, where agreement can be reached in advance of the formal meeting of the Conciliation Committee. If agreement is reached, the matter is noted as an 'A' point and adopted without discussion by the Committee.

(b)   Legislative practice under the co-decision procedure

Looking at the European Parliament, the most dramatic power it enjoys appears to be the veto. However, it has made only limited use of this. Between 1 May 1999 and 1 May 2004, Parliament only used the veto twice in 403 procedures; less than 0.5 per cent.[58] There are a number of reasons for this. The veto can bring the worst outcome

---

55  There are a limited number of fields where unanimity is required in the Council. See pp. 180–1.
56  N. Foster, 'The new Conciliation Committee under Article 189b' (1994) 19 *EL Rev.* 185.
57  On the trilogue see M. Shackleton, 'The Politics of Codecision' (2000) 38 *JCMS* 325, 334–6; M. Shackleton and T. Raunio, 'Codecision since Amsterdam: a Laboratory for Institutional Innovation and Change' (2003) 10 *JEPP* 171, 177–9.
58  European Parliament, *Activity Report for 5th Parliamentary Term*, PE 287.644, 10.

because, often, from the Parliament's perspective, imperfect Community legislation is better than no legislation. Regular exercise of the veto would also be bad politics. Other parties will not communicate with the Parliament if, in the end, its position is black or white. This will be true not just of the Commission and the Council, but also of lobbyists, such as those in industry and NGOs.

For the Parliament, it is not the veto which is important, but the shadow of the veto. By threatening to thwart other parties' objectives, it can secure input for itself. They have to listen to its policy preferences and it can secure influence for itself in a positive way in order to realise outcomes it desires. This role is reinforced by a quirk in the legislative procedure. If the Commission agrees with the Parliament, it is easier for the Council to accept parliamentary amendments than to produce its own. Acceptance of amendments proposed by the Parliament only requires a QMV in the Council, whilst it requires unanimity to produce its own. To be sure, the Commission must agree with the Parliament's suggestions but, importantly, it cannot propose amendments of its own without withdrawing the proposal and starting again. The Parliament is the only institution that has the opportunity to 'improve' the text. This has led to a number of authors talking of its being a 'conditional agenda-setter': provided it sticks within the limit of what is acceptable to the other two institutions, it can seize the agenda.[59] Statistics seem to bear this out. A high number of parliamentary amendments are accepted by both Council and Commission. As of 1 May 2004, 23 per cent of parliamentary amendments were accepted by both institutions in an unqualified form. A further 60 per cent were accepted in some compromise form. In other words, 83 per cent of parliamentary suggestions are taken on in some form in the legislation.[60] There are, however, different forms of amendment. Some just 'dot is'. Others radically change policy. Research by Kreppel suggests parliamentary amendments are more likely to be successful where they are not suggesting a substantial change in policy to the Commission proposal, but are just clarifying or perfecting legislation.[61] If that is so, it may be that the role of the European Parliament is analogous to parliamentary committees in domestic legislatures. Its central role is proposing commonsense amendments to legislation that are rarely ideologically contentious. To be sure, this is a significant role, but it is not that of an aggressive agenda-setter.

The position of the Commission under the co-decision procedure is interesting. On the face of things, its influence diminishes as the procedure continues. As it plays no active role in the Conciliation Committee, it would be possible for the Council and the

---

59 G. Tsebelis, 'The Power of the European Parliament as a Conditional Agenda Setter' (1994) 88 *American Political Science Review* 128; G. Tsebelis and G. Garrett, 'Legislative Politics in the European Union' (2000) 1 *EUP* 9; G. Tsebelis, C. Jensen, A. Kalandrakis and A. Kreppel, 'Legislative Procedures in the European Union: an Empirical Analysis' (2001) 31 *BJPS* 573.

60 European Parliament, *Activity Report for 5th Parliamentary Term*, PE 287.644, 14.

61 A. Kreppel, 'Moving beyond Procedure: an Empirical Analysis of European Parliament Legislative Influence' (2002) 35 *Comparative Political Studies* 784.

Parliament to rearrange its proposals at that point.[62] In practice, its influence remains significant. This is because only 22 per cent of proposals require conciliation.[63] In the majority of instances, agreement is reached at first or second reading. At this point in the procedure, the Commission influence is considerable. Both the Council and the Parliament are working off its proposal and, in practice, it is very difficult for them to deviate from the proposal without the Commission's acquiescence. Almost all successful parliamentary amendments require the Commission's agreement. Very few are adopted by the Council where there has not been prior approval by the Commission. The evidence suggests that there is an 88 per cent probability that a Parliament amendment will be rejected by the Council if the Commission rejects it, whilst there is an 83 per cent probability that it will be accepted if the Commission approves it.[64]

The third counter-intuitive feature of the procedure is the effectiveness of the Conciliation Committee. The Committee would appear to have little mandate, as any decision requires the subsequent approval of both the Parliament and the Council and it might be thought that, by the time it meets, institutional positions would be so entrenched there would be little possibility of movement and agreement. Yet, until 1 May 2004, in eighty-four out of eighty-six procedures,[65] the Committee had been able to propose a joint text accepted by both the Parliament and the Council. This might be, in part, because of the trilogues, which allow for intensive interinstitutional dialogue. It might also be that the Council is able to behave more proactively and recapture the agenda within the Committee, as it is able to make its own amendments and accept amendments by QMV.[66] A final reason given has been that, as parties are aware of each others' positions, negotiation is easier. New amendments are not continually being thrown in, but there are a stable set of issues on which discussion can proceed.[67] Whatever the reason, the effect is an increase in the influence of COREPER, as it is members of COREPER, not Council ministers, who sit in the Conciliation Committee. COREPER is not just preparing the meeting here, but also adopting the joint text.

All this suggests a picture significantly different from that provided by a simple reading of Article 251(2) EC, which would emphasise the role of the parliamentary veto and the assent of the Council. Yet, even this understates the extent to which the balance of power is determined by a shared legislative culture, which has emerged with the evolution of the co-decision procedure. In 1999, following the entry into force of

---

62 C. Crombez, 'The Codecision Procedure in the European Union' (1997) 22 *Legislative Studies Quarterly* 97.

63 European Parliament, *Activity Report for 5th Parliamentary Term*, PE 287.644, 12.

64 Tsebelis *et al.*, above n. 59. For a case study see C. Burns, 'Codecision and the European Commission: a Study of Declining Influence?' (2004) 11 *JEPP* 1.

65 See above n. 63.

66 G. Tsebelis, 'Maastricht and the Democratic Deficit' (1997) 52 *Aussenwirtschaft* 26, 43–5.

67 A. Rasmussen and M. Shackleton, 'The Scope for Action of European Parliament Negotiators in the Legislative Process: Lessons of the Past and for the Future', paper presented at Ninth Biennial EUSA Conference, 31 March 2005.

the Treaty of Amsterdam, the institutions adopted a Joint Declaration on practical arrangements for the new co-decision procedure. The central provision stated:

> The institutions shall cooperate in good faith with a view to reconciling their positions as far as possible so that wherever possible acts can be adopted at first reading.[68]

The commitment to adopt legislation at first reading of the Parliament has been partially realised. Between 1999 and 2004, 115 legislative proposals, 28 per cent of the total, were agreed at first reading, 10 per cent without amendments to the Commission proposal and 18 per cent with amendments. Out of 200 legislative proposals, 50 per cent were agreed at second reading, with the remaining 22 per cent agreed following conciliation.[69] Most importantly, it has led to an intensification of contacts between the Council and the Parliament, so that these meet in trilogue immediately after the formal Commission proposal. These trilogues shape everything that follows.

### H. Farrell and A. Héritier, 'Interorganizational Negotiation and Intraorganizational Power in Shared Decision Making: Early Agreements under Codecision and their Impact on the European Parliament and the Council' (2004) 37 *Comparative Political Studies* 1184, 1198–9

Typically, an informal trilateral meeting is held soon after the Parliament and Council have individually gone through a Commission proposal. This meeting may be followed by others, in which the two sides report back in broad terms about the progress of discussions within Council and Parliament and seek both to reach agreement where possible and to identify possible areas of contention. As the vote in the relevant parliamentary committee approaches, the two sides begin to exchange compromise texts, and then arrange a trilogue proper where there is a clear possibility of agreement being reached. 'Apart from a few extremely formal encounters, we have reached the point of almost weekly informal meetings.' . . .

Early informal negotiations in small groups built mutual confidence. As one Council staff member describes it:

> They [informal trilogues] make it possible to speak more frankly and to explain what the underlying reasons are. You can also say: here is a real problem – we cannot go any further on this, please recognize this, but we will yield in another issue, this 'give and take' becomes possible.

This requires a feeling both for the sensitivities of the other organization and the sensitivities of actors in one's own organization in negotiating its own position. Thus a Presidency of Council member points out that:

> we have to be careful not to come out of a Council meeting with a fixed text which would not allow us to take on board the amendments of the Parliament. At the same time we need a text which is clear enough to unite the member states.

---

68 OJ 1999 C148/1.
69 European Parliament, *Activity Report for 5th Parliamentary Term*, PE 287.644, 12–13.

'We are looking from the very beginning at what Parliament thinks, and we try to incorporate. And we are delaying political agreements if Parliament is not ready' (interview, Council Secretariat, October 2001). Or as one representative of the Council said, 'We are aware of the opinion of the rapporteur/the shadow rapporteur. We have an idea of what could be their position and we try to take this into account' (interview, Permanent National Representations C, January 2001). In other words, Council and Parliament do not confront each on the basis of preagreed positions; 'it is another ballgame' (interview COREPER, October 2001). Decisions are not taken beforehand on the Council and Parliament side. Rather, selected figures of the two bodies engage with each other before either has reached a formal position (interview, COREPER, October 2001). In consequence, it is much easier for Parliament to influence deliberations within the Council, and vice versa.

The growth of the trilogue has implications for the balance of power between institutions. In instances where the trilogue is successful, the Parliament and COREPER are acting as genuine co-legislators. It also has implications for the democratic quality of law-making within co-decision. The trilogue is the biggest challenge to democratic legitimacy, for it centralises power in those actors who represent the Council and the Parliament at the trilogue. Farrell and Héritier note, therefore, that small parties within the European Parliament are excluded by the trilogue, as they are never represented at it and the committee structure and its attendant public debates within the European Parliament are bypassed. They also noted that trilogues reinforce the power of COREPER, as they result in even less being decided by the Council of Ministers.[70] There is, in all this, a sidelining of checks and balances and a lack of formality and transparency. A division is made between formal and substantive decision-making, with the locus of substantive decision-making being hidden away. Whilst formal decision-making takes place in the Council or in Parliament committees, in many instances substantive decisions are vested in these informal arrangements. The formal procedures do no more than rubber stamp the agreements. Only very well connected actors have the opportunity to lobby these informal processes because only they can know where they are taking place or who is important within them. Furthermore, only they will have the resources to arbitrage between these centres of power, lobbying both central protagonists in the trilogue and other important actors in the Council, the Parliament and the Commission.

## 6. Law-making and Enhanced Cooperation

Enhanced Cooperation grew out of a debate that emerged prior to the Treaty of Amsterdam, where it became clear that there were deep-seated differences between Member States about both the pace and extent of integration. It was agreed that some Member States should not be held back from developing common laws between

70 H. Farrell and A. Héritier, 'Interorganizational Negotiation and Intraorganizational Power in Shared Decision Making: Early Agreements under Codecision and their Impact on the European Parliament and the Council' (2004) 37 *Comparative Political Studies* 1184, 1200–4.

themselves, should they so wish. Enhanced Cooperation was established to enable this. It allows Community laws to be developed by as few as eight states where there is not a sufficient voting threshold for general legislation. Lowering the threshold in this way intrudes on general Community law-making as it raises the possibility of a 'hard-core Europe', which develops laws for itself, excluding other Member States and creating a two-tier Community.[71] To prevent this, the provisions on Enhanced Cooperation put in place a number of safeguards. Enhanced Cooperation was only to take place if a number of conditions, set out in Articles 43 and 43a TEU, were met.

### Article 43 TEU

Member States which intend to establish enhanced cooperation between themselves may make use of the institutions, procedures and mechanisms laid down by this Treaty and by the Treaty establishing the European Community provided that the proposed cooperation:

(a) is aimed at furthering the objectives of the Union and of the Community, at protecting and serving their interests and at reinforcing their process of integration;
(b) respects the said Treaties and the single institutional framework of the Union;
(c) respects the *acquis communautaire* and the measures adopted under the other provisions of the said Treaties;
(d) remains within the limits of the powers of the Union or of the Community and does not concern the areas which fall within the exclusive competence of the Community;
(e) does not undermine the internal market as defined in Article 14(2) EC Treaty, or the economic and social cohesion established in accordance with Title XVII of that Treaty;
(f) does not constitute a barrier to or discrimination in trade between the Member States and does not distort competition between them;
(g) involves a minimum of eight Member States;
(h) respects the competences, rights and obligations of those Member States which do not participate therein;
(i) does not affect the provisions of the Protocol integrating the Schengen *acquis* into the framework of the European Union;
(j) is open to all the Member States, in accordance with Article 43b.

### Article 43a TEU

Enhanced cooperation may be undertaken only as a last resort, when it has been established within the Council that the objectives of such cooperation cannot be attained within a reasonable period by applying the relevant provisions of the Treaties.

These constraints appear considerable. Combined, they would suggest Enhanced Cooperation can only take place in very limited circumstances. However, Articles 43 and 43a TEU are not justiciable, so it is difficult to know how stringently they will be

71 On the debate see A. Stubb, 'The 1996 Intergovernmental Conference and the Management of Flexible Integration' (1997) 4 *JEPP* 37; F. Tuytschaever, *Differentiation in European Union Law* (Oxford/Portland, Hart, 1999) 1–48; E. Phillipart, 'From Uniformity to Flexibility: the Management of Diversity and its Impact on the EU System of Governance' in G. de Búrca and J. Scott (eds.), *Constitutional Change in the EU: from Uniformity to Flexibility?* (Oxford, Hart, 2000).

enforced. Additional procedural constraints have been put in place for each pillar of the TEU.[72] For Community legislation, these are set out in Article 11 EC.

### Article 11 (1) EC

1. Member States which intend to establish enhanced cooperation between themselves in one of the areas referred to in this Treaty shall address a request to the Commission, which may submit a proposal to the Council to that effect. In the event of the Commission not submitting a proposal, it shall inform the Member States concerned of the reasons for not doing so.

2. Authorisation to establish enhanced cooperation as referred to in paragraph 1 shall be granted, in compliance with Articles 43 to 45 TEU, by the Council, acting by a qualified majority on a proposal from the Commission and after consulting the European Parliament. When enhanced cooperation relates to an area covered by the procedure referred to in Article 251 of this Treaty, the assent of the European Parliament shall be required. A member of the Council may request that the matter be referred to the European Council. After that matter has been raised before the European Council, the Council may act in accordance with the first subparagraph of this paragraph.

3. The acts and decisions necessary for the implementation of enhanced cooperation activities shall be subject to all the relevant provisions of this Treaty, save as otherwise provided in this Article and in Articles 43 to 45 TEU.

This procedure would seem to grant vetoes to a number of actors: the Commission who must propose it, the Parliament who must assent to it, and other Member States who can refer it to the European Council. In reality, it is unclear how significant these will be. It will be difficult for non-participating states to prohibit practices occurring on the territories of other states. And, if they did, these would simply adopt forms of cooperation outside the formal treaty arrangements.

Enhanced Cooperation also puts in place certain participatory safeguards. Non-participating Member States must be able to participate in the deliberations that lead up to the adoption of legislation under these procedures, even if they cannot vote.

### Article 44(1) TEU

For the purposes of the adoption of the acts and decisions necessary for the implementation of enhanced cooperation referred to in Article 43, the relevant institutional provisions of this Treaty and of the Treaty establishing the European Community shall apply. However, while all members of the Council shall be able to take part in the deliberations, only those representing Member States participating in enhanced cooperation shall take part in the

---

72 For the second pillar, these are set out in Article 27a(2) TEU. Enhanced Cooperation cannot relate to matters having military or defence implications. The decision is taken only by the Council, albeit that the Commission can express an opinion. The Council will act by QMV, although if a Member State declares that for important and stated reasons of national policy it intends to oppose the cooperation, no vote will be taken.

The procedure for the third pillar is set out in Article 40a TEU. The Commission will make a proposal, which the Council will vote on by QMV. The Parliament is only to be consulted.

adoption of decisions. The qualified majority shall be defined as the same proportion of the weighted votes and the same proportion of the number of the Council members concerned as laid down in Article 205(2) EC, . . . Unanimity shall be constituted by only those Council members concerned. Such acts and decisions shall not form part of the Union *acquis*.

The final safeguards are those preventing non-exclusion. Non-participant states are not to be excluded from adopting any legislation and participating in any procedures at any future date, provided that they comply with what has already been agreed.

### Article 43b TEU

When enhanced cooperation is being established, it shall be open to all Member States. It shall also be open to them at any time, in accordance with Articles 27e and 40b of this Treaty and with Article 11a of the Treaty establishing the European Community, subject to compliance with the basic decision and with the decisions taken within that framework. The Commission and the Member States participating in enhanced cooperation shall ensure that as many Member States as possible are encouraged to take part.

### Article 11a EC

Any Member State which wishes to participate in enhanced cooperation established in accordance with Article 11 shall notify its intention to the Council and to the Commission, which shall give an opinion to the Council within three months of the date of receipt of that notification. Within four months of the date of receipt of that notification, the Commission shall take a decision on it, and on such specific arrangements as it may deem necessary.

For all the energy devoted to Enhanced Cooperation, there is yet to be a measure adopted under these procedures. There has only been a Commission 'non-paper' on a common consolidated EU corporate tax base for enterprises with establishments in two or more Member States, which suggests that if this cannot be realised within a reasonable period of time in all Member States, the Enhanced Cooperation provisions should be used.[73] There are reasons for this. The procedures are cumbersome and in a European Union of fifteen Member States, the difference between QMV and eight Member States is not immense.

The position is different in a European Union of twenty-five Member States. Such a Union is subject to more diverse pressures and preferences. There is, consequently, a greater case for differentiation. In addition, the gap between the number of states necessary for Enhanced Cooperation and the voting thresholds is now considerable: being unanimity or a QMV for twenty-five states, on the one hand, and eight states, on the other. There is not only a likelihood of increased use of the procedure, but its use is likely to be further threatened. General law-making is likely to operate in the shadow of Enhanced Cooperation and it is the interaction between the two that is particularly significant. In such a scenario, the relative costs imposed by Enhanced Cooperation

---

73  EC Commission, 'A Common Consolidated EU Corporate Tax Base', 7 July 2004, Commission non-paper to informal Ecofin Council, 10 and 11 September 2004. For discussion see M. O' Brien, 'Company Taxation, State Aid and Fundamental Freedoms: Is the Next Step Enhanced Co-operation?' (2005) 30 *EL Rev.* 209.

become significant. There may be costs of inclusion, whereby participating states find that by cooperating, they have to shoulder some regulatory burden not borne by non-participants. These are likely to be areas such as environment or social regulation, where the legislation is placing additional costs on industry. By contrast, there may be legislation which creates costs of exclusion for non-participants. This is likely to be the case where a single regime reduces the costs or increases the competitiveness of industry within participating states vis-à-vis non-participating states. This might occur where common fiscal, corporate or intellectual property regimes are introduced, which allow multinational companies operating in these states to rationalise their structures. In instances where there are costs of inclusion, one would expect Enhanced Cooperation to have little effect on general law-making. States will not credibly threaten Enhanced Cooperation as they are aware that they place themselves at a disadvantage with regard to non-participating states. By contrast, the Enhanced Cooperation provisions are likely to have a significant effect on law-making where they impose high exclusion costs. In such circumstances, states agnostic about further integration have to countenance the second-best option of participation in an arrangement with which they are not happy about the higher costs of exclusion. In such areas, the Enhanced Cooperation provisions exert strong integrationist pressures.

## 7. Comitology

Most discussions of Community law-making focus on the primary legislative procedures. These often set out only the essential elements of a policy, delegating to the Commission powers to enact more detailed legislation.[74] However, we also saw that, in many instances, it was not merely 'technical', but highly significant questions that were delegated to the Commission.[75] This delegation is also widespread: 69 per cent of all Regulations and 16 per cent of all Directives are adopted under these delegated procedures.[76] These must, therefore, be seen, as a central part of the law-making process. The Commission does not have complete freedom under these procedures. It must adopt laws under a set of procedures, known as comitology, in which it works in tandem with a committee of national representatives. At the end of 2003, there were 256 Committees in operation.[77] The role of the committee varies according to the procedure used, and is set out in Decision 1999/468/EC.[78] Comitology establishes three central procedures, the advisory procedure, the management

74 Joined Cases T-64/01 and T-65/01 *Afrikanische Fruchtcompanie v Council*, judgment of 10 February 2004.
75 See pp. 94–6.        76 v. Bogdandy, Arndt and Bast, above n. 10, 99.
77 Commission Report on the Working of the Committees 2003; OJ 2005 C65/E/05.
78 OJ 1999 L184/23. For discussion see K. Lenaerts and A. Verhoeven, 'Towards a Legal Framework for Executive Rule-making in the EU? The Contribution of the New Comitology Decision' (2000) 37 *CML Rev.* 645. There is a further procedure, the safeguard procedure, which operates in the field of external trade, *ibid.* article 6. Only two committees have been established under it, however, and it is not discussed further here. Four regulations were adopted in 2003 to align all existing committees under this Decision. These were Regulation 806/2003/EC, OJ 2003 L122/1; Regulation 807/2003/EC, OJ 2003 L122/36; Regulation 1105/2003/EC, OJ 2003 L158/3; Regulation 1882/2003/EC, OJ 2003 L284/1.

procedure and the regulatory procedure. At the end of 2003, 31 advisory procedures, 74 management procedures and 100 regulatory procedures were in operation.[79] The criteria for determining which procedure is to be used is set out in Article 2.

---

### Article 2

The choice of procedural methods for the adoption of implementing measures shall be guided by the following criteria:

(a) management measures, such as those relating to the application of the common agricultural and common fisheries policies, or to the implementation of programmes with substantial budgetary implications, should be adopted by use of the management procedure;

(b) measures of general scope designed to apply essential provisions of basic instruments, including measures concerning the protection of the health or safety of humans, animals or plants, should be adopted by use of the regulatory procedure; where a basic instrument stipulates that certain non-essential provisions of the instrument may be adapted or updated by way of implementing procedures, such measures should be adopted by use of the regulatory procedure;

(c) without prejudice to points (a) and (b), the advisory procedure shall be used in any case in which it is considered to be the most appropriate.

---

The procedure where the Commission has the most freedom on paper is the advisory procedure. Under this procedure, the role of the Committee is to 'advise' the Commission, with the Commission required to take 'utmost account' of the view of the Committee but, having done that, it is ultimately free to disregard it.

---

### Article 3

1. The Commission shall be assisted by an advisory committee composed of the representatives of the Member States and chaired by the representative of the Commission.

2. The representative of the Commission shall submit to the Committee a draft of the measures to be taken. The committee shall deliver its opinion on the draft, within a time-limit which the chairman may lay down according to the urgency of the matter, if necessary by taking a vote.

3. The opinion shall be recorded in the minutes; in addition, each Member State shall have the right to ask to have its position recorded in the minutes.

4. The Commission shall take the utmost account of the opinion delivered by the committee. It shall inform the committee of the manner in which the opinion has been taken into account.

---

In the case of the management and regulatory procedures, the Committee has a fire-warning role. It has to decide whether or not the Commission draft should be referred to the Council. With the management procedure, the Committee, if it is unhappy with a Commission draft, can, by QMV, refer the matter to the Council. It

---

79 See above n. 77, E/06.

needs a QMV in favour of referral. The Council then has up to three months to adopt another decision.

### Article 4

1. The Commission shall be assisted by a management committee composed of the representatives of the Member States and chaired by the representative of the Commission.

2. The representative of the Commission shall submit to the committee a draft of the measures to be taken. The committee shall deliver its opinion on the draft within a time-limit which the chairman may lay down according to the urgency of the matter. The opinion shall be delivered by [qualified majority].

3. The Commission shall, without prejudice to Article 8, adopt measures which shall apply immediately. However, if these measures are not in accordance with the opinion of the committee, they shall be communicated by the Commission to the Council forthwith. In that event, the Commission may defer application of the measures which it has decided on for a period to be laid down in each basic instrument but which shall in no case exceed three months from the date of such communication.

4. The Council, acting by qualified majority, may take a different decision within the period provided for by paragraph 3.

There was concern that the majority of Committee members could disapprove of the Commission draft, but it would still be adopted. To that end, the Commission issued a Declaration on adoption of the Decision stating that, with regard to the management procedure, it would never go against 'any predominant position which might emerge against the appropriateness of an implementing measure'.[80]

This danger does not exist in the regulatory procedure, where the Committee must positively agree to the Commission draft by QMV. If it fails to do this, the draft is referred to the Council, which has up to three months to take a decision of its own.

### Article 5

1. The Commission shall be assisted by a regulatory committee composed of the representatives of the Member States and chaired by the representative of the Commission.

2. The representative of the Commission shall submit to the committee a draft of the measures to be taken. The committee shall deliver its opinion on the draft within a time-limit which the chairman may lay down according to the urgency of the matter. The opinion shall be delivered by [qualified majority.]

3. The Commission shall . . . adopt the measures envisaged if they are in accordance with the opinion of the committee.

4. If the measures envisaged are not in accordance with the opinion of the committee, or if no opinion is delivered, the Commission shall, without delay, submit to the Council a proposal relating to the measures to be taken and shall inform the European Parliament.

80 OJ 1999 C103/1.

5. If the European Parliament considers that a proposal submitted by the Commission pursuant to a basic instrument adopted in accordance with the procedure laid down in Article 251 of the Treaty exceeds the implementing powers provided for in that basic instrument, it shall inform the Council of its position.

6. The Council may, where appropriate in view of any such position, act by qualified majority on the proposal, within a period to be laid down in each basic instrument but which shall in no case exceed three months from the date of referral to the Council. If within that period the Council has indicated by qualified majority that it opposes the proposal, the Commission shall re-examine it. It may submit an amended proposal to the Council, resubmit its proposal or present a legislative proposal on the basis of the Treaty. If on the expiry of that period the Council has neither adopted the proposed implementing act nor indicated its opposition to the proposal for implementing measures, the proposed implementing act shall be adopted by the Commission.

A danger with both the management and regulatory procedures is that, if the matter is referred to the Council, the voting thresholds can make it extremely difficult for it to rewrite the Commission draft. Both require a QMV to be adopted in the Council on another draft within a relatively short timescale. This provides the possibility that a draft may become law, albeit that all the Member States are dissatisfied with it, as they do not have sufficient time to reach consensus on an alternative draft. In practice, this has not happened because almost no referrals occur. In 2003, the Commission adopted 2,768 instruments under comitology, and the committees gave 2,981 opinions,[81] but not one reference was made to the Council. The Commission's Report notes that comitology works under a high degree of consensus, with Commission drafts normally approved by the committees. In practice, a process of give and take occurs, where committee suggestions are taken on by the Commission.

In pioneering work in the field of EC food safety law, Joerges and Neyer studied the interaction between the Commission and two such committees, the Standing Committee on Food Stuffs (StCF) and the Scientific Committee on Foodstuffs (SCF). They found that comitology did not consist of national checks on Commission decision-making but was, rather, a more fluid settlement centred around deliberative problem-solving.

### C. Joerges and J. Neyer, 'Transforming Strategic Interaction into Deliberative Problem-solving: European Comitology in the Foodstuffs Sector' (1997) 4 *Journal of European Public Policy* 609, 618–20

Whereas the comitology system in the foodstuffs sector is far too small an arena to allow generalization, it is nevertheless indicative of how this relationship can work in practice and what its deficiencies might be. Three elements are of particular importance:

81 See above n. 77, E/07.

(a) The proposals which the Commission presents to the StCF are in general the result of extensive consultations with individual national administrations and independent experts. Particularly in committees like the StCF which act under qualified majority voting, proposals not only reflect the Commission's interest but also what it assumes to be in the interest of *more than a qualified majority* of the other parties involved. This becomes of crucial importance as the effectiveness of any measure adopted depends on Member States transposing the measure adequately into their national legal systems without leaving too many opportunities for evasion and – more importantly – not invoking safeguard procedures. However, in an institutional environment without effective means of hierarchical enforcement, this is only likely to happen if delegates see their own legitimate concerns acknowledged and protected in decision-making.

(b) The importance of the SCF in supporting certain arguments does not derive from any formal power to decide issues of conflict (it has only an advisory status) but from the legal fiction of its scientific expertise and neutrality. To be sure, Member States are well aware that the SCF is sometimes used by the Commission as an instrument for furthering its interests and, furthermore, that its experts do not always comply with the norm of objectivity. Moreover, the bovine spongiform encephalopathy (BSE) case has highlighted the fact that even scientific institutions can easily be captured by certain interest groups and instrumentalized for political purposes by the Commission. The Scientific Veterinary Committee was not only chaired by a British scientist; the available records of attendance also show the preponderance of UK scientists and officials, meaning that the Committee tended to reflect current thinking at the British Ministry of Agriculture, Fisheries and Food. Why do Member State delegates nevertheless adhere to the fiction of objective science? To understand this, one needs to consider the functions of legal fictions: scientific findings are supposed to be accepted by all the parties concerned; science-based discourses have the power to discipline arguments; and they allow a clear distinction between legitimate and illegitimate arguments in cases of conflict over competing proposals. Therefore, the fact that the opinions of the SCF have never been seriously challenged by the StCF may be grounded less in the objectivity of its opinions than in the function of scientific discourses as a mechanism that is helpful in overcoming politically constituted preferences by relying on the fiction of objective science.

(c) International negotiations concerning common solutions to problems of interdependence generally involve two modes of interaction: strategic bargaining to maximize particular utilities at the expense of others and deliberative problem-solving to maximize collective utilities. Empirically, it is important to realize that the relative intensity of both modes may vary, and identify the conditions which influence them. Whereas the mainstream literature on international negotiations does not acknowledge the possibility of deliberative problem-solving but conceptualizes international negotiations as a pursuit of domestic policy goals by different means, recent contributions to the literature on epistemic communities highlight conditions where the grip which national politicians have on delegates is rather weak. The most prominent conditions mentioned are uncertainty about the distributive effects of certain policies, long-term interaction among delegates, as well as their mutual socialization into a community with common problem definitions and collectively shared approaches to dealing with them.

Under such conditions governments may be unaware of what their preferences are, or delegates, perceiving themselves as part of a transnational problem-solving community, may be able to change their governments' perceptions of interests or even simply bypass them. The condition of high uncertainty about the distributional effects of certain policies is surely not always met; often governments have clear perceptions of the costs that certain policy options might impose on them. However, in negotiations in the StCF – and even more so in the SCF – the particular economic costs of policies cannot be explicitly discussed, and information is primarily provided on non-distributional issues. *Ceteris paribus*, therefore, the knowledge of delegates about adequate problem-solving strategies will increase with the duration of negotiations, whereas their *relative* knowledge about economic effects will decline. This change in the perceptions and preferences of delegates becomes increasingly important for shaping national preferences as their informational advantage over their national administration increases over time. It is also important to note that negotiations sometimes last for years among nearly the same set of delegates. Moreover, delegates have frequent contacts outside the sessions of the Standing Committee, and have often previously met working on the preparation of a legislative proposal in negotiations about its adoption in Council working groups. During the course of this collaboration, delegates not only learn to reduce differences between national legal provisions but also to develop converging definitions of problems and philosophies for their solution. They slowly proceed from being representatives of national interests to being representatives of a Europeanized interadministrative discourse characterized by mutual learning and an understanding of each other's difficulties in the implementation of specific solutions. For the same reason, even the intergovernmental Committee of Permanent Representatives (COREPER) is jokingly referred to as the 'Committee of Permanent Traitors' in the German administration. It is also telling that delegates in the StCF often neither know nor seem to care according to which procedure they are actually negotiating; in practice, it often does not matter whether the Commission has the right or the obligation to take their concerns into account.

Subsequent studies have reaffirmed this characterisation. A study of Scandinavian officials found that whilst the overwhelming majority of those sitting on the committees saw themselves as government representatives, there was also a strong perception of themselves both as independent experts and as persons acting on behalf of the collective European interest. Above all, there was a strong *esprit de corps* and loyalty to the committee and other members of the committee, which was particularly marked amongst those who participated most intensively on the committee.[82]

Understandings of comitology as an interactive network of administrators and experts rather than as a check on the Commission's powers have provoked a fierce debate about its democratic qualities.[83] There have been two central concerns. One is that its language is too technocratic. Delicate political and social questions are reduced to questions of expertise and risk assessment.[84] The other is that its make-up is insufficiently pluralistic. Administrators may 'up their game' by having to respond to other administrators' arguments but, as Gerstenberg and Sabel artfully put it, this

82 J. Trondal, 'Beyond the EU Membership-Non-Membership Dichotomy? Supranational Identities among National EU Decision-makers' (2002) 9 *JEPP* 468.

83 R. Dehousse, 'Comitology? Who Watches the Watchmen' (2003) 10 *JEPP* 798.

84 J. Weiler, 'Epilogue: "Comitology" as Revolution – Infranationalism, Constitutionalism and Democracy' in C. Joerges and E. Vos (eds.), *EU Committees: Social Regulation, Law and Politics* (Oxford/Portland, Hart, 1999) 339, 345–6.

may only 'improve government performance and renovate the role of the bureaucrat without much changing the role of the citizen'.[85] The rights of audience or participation of private parties before these committees, for example, is notoriously unclear.[86] Joerges has observed, in defence of the processes, that they contain many checks and balances that are generally unappreciated.

> ### C. Joerges, 'Deliberative Supranationalism: A Defence' (2001) 5(8) *European Integration online Papers 8–9*
>
> . . . comitology . . interested us because of its links not just with the bureaucracies but also with the polities of the Member States, because of its complex internal structure in which government representatives, the representatives of social interests and 'the' economy all interact. Risk regulation in the internal market seemed to us to document the weaknesses of expertocratic models adequately, because the normative, political and ethical dimensions of risk assessments resist a merely technocratic treatment. Admittedly, in the debates about the tensions between the ideals of democracy and the constraints of the 'knowledge society', Columbus' egg has not been sighted so far. My mere status as a citizen does not qualify me for a qualitatively convincing (to me at least) technical decision, nor can it be seen how 'all' the citizens affected by such decisions are really to participate in them. What is true of risk policy is present as a problem in practically every corner of modern law. And what is true of risk policy in an EU Member State in which (relatively) dense communicative processes guarantee the ongoing political debate is true *a fortiori* for such a polymorphic entity as the EU.
>
> The much-maligned comitology has the advantage over agencies of the American pattern in that it structures risk policy pluralistically, that national bureaucracies have to face up to the positions of their neighbour states, and that interests and concerns in Member States cannot be filtered out. Committees can be observed closely by the wider public and such politicisation has proved to be effective. This seems to be the situation: any conceivable argument can be brought to bear in the committee system. It tends to offer *fora* for pluralistic discussions. Its links with the broader public do, however, remain dependent on the attention that an issue attracts and on the insistence of the actors concerned on public debate.

Nevertheless, some of these pressures were felt at the time of adoption of Decision 1999/468/EC. The procedure was, therefore, made more transparent. Public access to the documents and discussions of the committees was to be granted on the same basis as to the Commission.[87] The Commission was also to establish a register of any draft measures placed before the committees and of the agendas and voting records of the committee.[88]

---

85 O. Gerstenberg and C. Sabel, 'Directly-Deliberative Polyarchy: an Institutional Ideal for Europe' in C. Joerges and R. Dehousse (eds.), *Good Governance in Europe's Integrated Market* (Oxford, Oxford University Press, 2002) 289, 320.

86 F. Bignami, 'The Democratic Deficit in European Community Rulemaking: a Call for Notice and Comment in Comitology' (1999) 40 *Harvard International Law Journal* 451.

87 See above n. 78, article 7(2). On public access to the work of the Commission see pp. 316–29.

88 *Ibid.* article 7(5).

Provision was also made for some input by the European Parliament in the process. The Commission was to inform the Parliament of committee proceedings on a regular basis and of any referrals to the Council. It was also to be informed of any implementing measures submitted to a committee, where the parent instrument was adopted under the co-decision procedure.[89] Finally, if the Parliament considered that a draft implementing measure exceeded the implementing measures provided for in a parent instrument adopted under co-decision, it could ask the Commission to re-examine the measure.[90] The Commission might do so if it wished, but was not constrained by the view of the Parliament.[91] The role of the Parliament could still be felt to be insufficient. No formal provision was made for general consultation of it and it had no power to veto any measure.

In the light of these continuing concerns about comitology, the Commission proposed, in 2002, amendments to the procedures. These amendments focussed on reform of the regulatory procedure, which was seen as both the most significant of the procedures and as the one raising most concern.[92]

The first proposed reform was to place the regulatory committee procedure more clearly at the centre of comitology.[93] Its place as the procedure to be used where there are significant concerns was, therefore, enhanced. In areas where the parent instrument was to be adopted under the co-decision procedure, the management procedure was not to be available. Instead, the advisory procedure was to be applied whenever the executive measures had an individual scope or for procedural arrangements. If the executive measures were implementing essential aspects of the parent legislation or adapting it, the regulatory procedure was to be used. In other words, wherever the procedures were to be used for quasi-legislation, under co-decision, the regulatory committee procedure was to be used.

The proposed reforms, secondly, recast the relationship between the Commission and the Committee in the regulatory committee procedure. If the Committee did not agree to the Commission draft by QMV, the Commission was to withdraw the draft and present a new one, taking account of the views of the Committee. The Committee would express views on the new draft before it was adopted by the Commission.[94] The reforms made the Commission far more accountable to the Committee, as it was legally required to incorporate the objections of the Committee. This high degree of accountability suggests that, ultimately, what was being encouraged is the joint drafting

---

89 *Ibid.* article 7(3).

90 The Commission has agreed also to apply this procedure to measures which, although not adopted under co-decision, are of particular importance to the Parliament. Agreement between the Parliament and the Commission on Procedures for Implementing Decision 1999/468/EC, OJ 2000 L256/19.

91 See above n. 78, article 8.

92 EC Commission, Proposal for a Council Decision amending Decision 1999/468/ EC, COM(2002)719, as amended by COM(2004)324.

93 See above n. 78, article 2a.        94 *Ibid.* article 5a(3).

of the measure by the Committee and the Commission with each having an almost co-equal status.

Finally, the Parliament was proposed to be placed on an equal footing with the Council in the regulatory committee procedure.[95] If the matter was referred by the Committee, both the Council and the Parliament had one month to object.[96] If either objected, the Commission was to take one of four actions:

- make a proposal for ordinary legislation under the co-decision procedure;
- withdraw the draft;
- amend the draft;
- adopt the original draft.

The Commission had to take account of both the Council and the Parliament's positions in making its choice but, ultimately, could ignore them. In all cases, it had to explain to both institutions the action it intended to take on their respective objections and its reasons for doing so.

The new procedure reduced the Council's power to replace a Commission draft with its own measure. This was always an illusory threat, however. Instead, the proposal would increase Commission accountability to the Parliament and the Council. In terms of its relationship with the Council and Parliament, the proposal allowed an analogy to be drawn between the executive and the legislature. The Commission, as executive, was ultimately responsible for the adoption of the legislation, but it paid a heavy price politically in terms of its accountability to the legislature if it ignored the latter's wishes.

## 8. The 'democratic deficit' and the legislative process

The question of democratic legitimacy, the 'democratic deficit' in Euro-speak, has dominated debate surrounding the Community legislative processes. Such debate typically critiques the democracy of Community law-making in three ways. First, there are concerns about the quality of representative democracy. Such concerns focus both on the parliamentary input in the processes and the extent to which Community law-making undermines parliamentary democracy at a national and regional level. Secondly, there are concerns about the quality of participatory democracy. Community law-making has been accused of being insufficiently plural, of not listening to enough interested parties and of giving too great weight to some interests. Finally, concerns have been expressed about the quality of deliberative democracy – the quality of public debate that surrounds and informs the law-making processes. Concerns have been expressed that Community law is too much characterised by negotiation between interests rather than public debate between citizens.

95 *Ibid.* article 5a(5).    96 This period may be further extended by one month if either requests.

### (i)   Representative democracy and national parliaments

The concern over representative democracy is that the transfer of powers from the Member States to the EC has resulted in a loss of law-making powers for national parliaments, but this has not been accompanied by a corresponding transfer to the European Parliament.[97] Community law-making is dominated by bureaucrats. Comitology is clearly governed exclusively by officials, but they predominate also in the primary law-making processes. It is the Commission which proposes legislation. The proposal is negotiated amongst national officials in COREPER, and it is adopted by government ministers in the Council. The solution does not seem to be to increase the powers of the European Parliament, as it is not a body that can lay claim to the allegiances of most of the European Union's citizens.[98] The 'representative deficit' has focussed in recent years, instead, on the role of national parliaments in the law-making processes.[99]

Involvement of national parliaments in Community law-making processes has been extremely tortuous. Prior to the TEU, there was no formal requirement for these to be involved, and only the United Kingdom and Denmark had any mechanisms for parliamentary consideration of Commission proposals and the national position on these proposals prior to Council meetings. In 1989, the Conference of Community and European Affairs Committees of Parliaments of the European Union (COSAC) was established. COSAC is a forum in which national parliaments and the European Parliament meet, initially biannually, to discuss the business of the forthcoming Presidency. A Declaration was attached to the TEU, at Maastricht, stating that contacts and exchange of information between national parliaments and the European Parliament should be stepped up and that national parliaments should receive Commission proposals for legislation in good time for information or examination.[100] Alongside this, all Member States established parliamentary committees on EU affairs in the early 1990s.

The position of national parliaments was still poorly sketched out. At Amsterdam, a Protocol was adopted which set out in far more detail the role of parliaments in Community law-making.[101] The Protocol stated that all Commission consultative documents should be forwarded to national parliaments.[102] In addition, national governments should make all Commission proposals available in good time to their national parliaments, so that these can express an opinion before the matter is discussed at Council.[103] In the case of third pillar proposals, it was suggested that this

---

97  J.-C. Piris, 'After Maastricht, are the Community Institutions More Efficacious, More Democratic, More Transparent?' (1994) 19 *EL Rev.* 449, 462.

98  See pp. 111–14.

99  A. Maurer and W. Wessels (eds.), *National Parliaments on their Ways to Europe: Losers or Latecomers?* (Nomos, Baden Baden, 2001); A. Maurer, *National Parliaments in the European Architecture*, Federal Trust Online Paper 06/02.

100  Declaration 13 TEU.

101  Protocol to the TEU on the Role of National Parliaments in the European Union.        102  *Ibid.* para. 1.

103  *Ibid.* para. 2.

should take place six weeks before the matter is put on the legislative agenda.[104] In principle, these provisions would make the Council more a proxy of national parliaments and allow for greater public debate of Commission proposals. If ministers deviated from their parliament's wishes in Council, they would subsequently be accountable to it. By having to debate a Commission proposal, national parliaments would not be presented with a *fait accompli*, but would have time to consider its strengths and weaknesses and be able to express an opinion on the latter.

Two forms of parliamentary procedure have emerged in the Member States. One is the *document-based* model. This model was first adopted by the UK Parliament, but has since been followed by the Irish, French, Czech, Dutch, Maltese and Italian parliaments:

> The system does not in general focus on proceedings at individual Council meetings, nor does it seek to mandate Ministers formally or informally . . . The principal feature of a document-based approach is a sift of EU documents at the early stages of the decision-making procedure. Typically, the responsible committee will report to its chamber on the political and legal importance of each EU document, determining which documents require further consideration. Often these systems are accompanied by a *scrutiny reserve* which provides that Ministers should not agree to EU proposals in the Council until parliamentary scrutiny has been completed.[105]

The other is the *mandate-based* system, whereby the national parliament authorises the government to take a position and the national government cannot deviate from that. There are two forms of mandate used: systematic and selective:

> The Danish, Estonian, Finnish, Latvian, Lithuanian, Polish (Sejm), Slovakian, Slovenian and Swedish national parliaments belong to the first group, where the European Affairs Committee systematically mandates the government. The governments in these countries are all in principle obliged to present a negotiation position – in writing or orally – to the committees on all pieces of draft legislation to be adopted by the Council. However, the parliaments have different ways of filtering the proposals, so as to avoid spending time on proposals which are considered less important. Whereas the Danish European Affairs Committee mandates ministers on all proposals of 'greater importance' to be adopted by the Council, the Lithuanian Parliament has asked its sectoral committees to divide the different EU proposals into three categories: 'very relevant', 'relevant' and 'moderately relevant'. These are normally referred to as 'red', 'yellow' and 'green' issues. On 'red' and 'yellow' issues the government is obliged to submit its negotiation 'position' on all EU proposals to the Seimas within 15 days from the receipt of the proposals. 'Green' issues are those classified by the committees as being of minor or no interest to the Parliament.

---

104 *Ibid.* para. 3.
105 COSAC, *Third Biannual Report: Developments in European Union Procedures and Practices relevant to Parliamentary Scrutiny* (Luxembourg, 2005) 10.

On the other hand, in parliaments such as those in Austria and Hungary the mandating power is used less frequently. Here, legislative proposals are only put on the agenda of the European Affairs Committee if requested by the government or by members of the committee. In Austria the committee does not systematically receive information on the position of the government on EU documents. Nevertheless, the European Affairs Committees in these parliaments have the capacity on behalf of their parliaments to adopt positions which are binding for their governments . . .

In most national parliaments where there is a mandating system, the mandates given to governments are politically binding and are reported to be in general strictly observed by governments. In parliaments such as the Finnish, Hungarian and the Polish, the governments may deviate from the mandate under certain circumstances, but in such cases the governments have to explain their actions to the European Affairs Committees of the parliaments. In Denmark the government would need to reconsult the committee to obtain a new mandate. In the Austrian system a minister is legally bound by the position of the National Council as laid down in article 23e of the Austrian Constitution. However, the government may deviate from the opinion of the parliament but only for compelling reasons and only after having approached the National Council again. If the government still decides to deviate from the opinion of the National Council, it must inform the parliament of its reasons for doing so.[106]

In both systems, a number of difficulties have emerged. First, national governments often pass the proposals to national parliaments late or pass on insufficient information about the proposals. Secondly, it is often difficult for national parliaments to formulate a position, as they have few supporting staff, contacts with the relevant minister and ministry might be minimal and the matter might be considered by the European Affairs Committee rather than a sectoral committee with greater knowledge of the field. Finally, the interest of national parliamentarians is highly variable.[107] Sitting on a European Affairs Committee is not a route to professional advancement. These committees often contain disgruntled or mediocre politicians, whose interest is not exclusively directed at obtaining the best legislation possible.

The Laeken Declaration suggested that one of the matters to be addressed by the 'Future of Europe' Convention was how to enhance the role of national parliaments within the law-making process.[108] The Working Group on this had a number of ideas:

- to secure time for parliamentary consideration, there should be no preliminary agreements within COREPER until the six-week period for consultation of national parliaments had elapsed, except in urgent cases;

---

106  *Ibid.* 12–13.
107  For criticisms see Final Report of Working Group IV on the Role of National Parliaments, CONV 353/02, 4–5.
108  European Council, Declaration on the Future of the European Union, N 300/1/01 Rev. 1.

- parliament scrutiny reserves be given clearer status within the Council's rules of procedure, so that it would be clearer where parliaments had been consulted;
- the Commission should simultaneously transmit all legislative proposals and consultative documents to national parliaments, the Council and the European Parliament;
- COSAC should draft a code of conduct on desirable parliamentary scrutiny.[109]

Much more modest amendments were incorporated into the Constitutional Treaty. Draft legislative acts would have to be sent directly to national parliaments.[110] Save in cases of urgency, a six-week period should elapse between this time and its being placed on the provisional agenda of the Council for all draft legislative proposals, not just those adopted under the third pillar.[111] The agendas of Council meetings would also be sent directly to national parliaments.[112] It is likely that these reforms will be adopted, whatever the fate of the Constitutional Treaty, as they do not require Treaty reform for their implementation. Bolder reforms have been eschewed. These would have only allowed Council members to vote on a mandate from a national parliament, which had been clearly signalled to other Council members, or would have placed a moratorium on COREPER negotiations for six weeks. It is clear that these were not agreed in order to preserve negotiating flexibility within the Council. Without them, however, it is clear that there is no strong outlet for representative democracy within the European Union.

### (ii) Participatory democracy and republicanism

From the early 1990s onwards, it became clear that the European Union was not going to become a 'superstate' and replicate the features of the nation-state at a pan-European level. A corollary of this was that the same measurements of democratic legitimacy could not be applied to the European Union as to nation-states. It was not a single political community, which could lay claim to the primary political allegiances of its members in the same way as the nation-state. Unlike states, it is also a community of states. It consists of states who are admitted as members to the European Union and who have sovereign rights over certain fields of authority, which are not to be challenged by EU law.[113] This 'mixed nature' of the European Union makes it more suited to models of republican or associative democracy that are concerned with instilling democracy in polities which are not centred around one

---

109 See above n. 107, 8–9.
110 Protocol to the Constitutional Treaty on the Role of National Parliaments in the European Union, Article 2. Most of the new powers for national parliaments granted by the Constitutional Treaty revolve around the vetting of the subsidiarity principle. On this see pp. 228–30.
111 *Ibid.* Article 4.      112 *Ibid.* Article 5.
113 K. Nicolaïdis, 'We, the Peoples of Europe . . .' (2004) 83(6) *Foreign Affairs* 97.

political community, but around a 'community of communities'. Advocates of these models point to three sources of democratic legitimation in the EU set-up.[114]

First, the European Union institutionalises a principle of 'constitutional tolerance'.[115] It leads nationals of Member States to accept and acknowledge a shared destiny with strangers and the values of strangers without trying to change them. The European Union requires the British citizen to recognise her interdependence with the French citizen, that the French citizen has rights and interests that she must not impinge upon, and that the French citizen brings something different, but equally valuable, to the European Union political community. Secondly, the European Union is built around the creation of common institutions to realise shared projects (e.g. the single market, the area of freedom, security and justice, a common environmental policy). These institutions have an elevating effect, as they require citizens to come together to realise common goods; to act and negotiate in the public interest recognising each other's needs and arguments rather than acting in a self-interested manner. They require citizens to act in a public rather than a private manner.[116] Thirdly, the complex institutional settlements of the European Union prevent concentrations of power and foster pluralism.[117] Power is not centred in any one set of institutions, but is spread across the supranational institutions and national governments. Each has its own constituencies and each represents different interests. In a polity, where there is no single dominant community, this institutional settlement allows a voice to be given to a variety of identities and interests. These views have been articulated by a number of authors, but the most careful analysis of the Community's practice has been carried out by Adrienne Héritier.

> ### A Héritier, 'Elements of Democratic Legitimation in Europe: an Alternative Perspective' (1999) 6 *Journal of European Public Policy* 269, 273–7
>
> . . . there are other structural and process elements to muster support for European policies and enhance democratic legitimation which are inherent in the features of the European polity

---

114 It can be argued that such divisions are present in nation-states and have not stopped national democracy: J. Lacroix, 'For a European Constitutional Patriotism' (2002) 50 *Political Studies* 944.

115 J. Weiler, *The Constitution of Europe* (Cambridge, Cambridge University Press, 1999) especially 332–48; M. Poiares Maduro, *We, the Court: the European Court of Justice and the European Economic Constitution* (Oxford, Hart, 1998) 166–74; K. Nicolaïdis, *The New Constitution as European Democracy*, Federal Trust Working Paper 38/03.

116 On the ethic of participation see R. Bellamy and R. Warleigh, 'From an Ethics of Integration to an Ethics of Participation' (1998) 27 *Millennium* 447. See also P. Magnette, 'European Governance and Civic Participation: Beyond Elitist Citizenship?' (2003) 51 *Political Studies* 1.

117 N. McCormick, 'Democracy, Subsidiarity and Citizenship in the European Commonwealth' (1997) 16 *Law and Philosophy* 331. K. Nicolaïdis, 'Conclusion: the Federal Vision Beyond the Federal State' in K. Nicolaïdis and R. Howse (eds.), *The Federal Vision: Legitimacy and Levels of Governance in the United States and the European Union* (Oxford, Oxford University Press, 2001).

itself, that is, the diversity of its actors and the fragmented nature of its architecture. These elements are mutual horizontal control and 'distrust', bargaining democracy and the presence of multiple authorities in a 'composite polity'.

### Mutual horizontal control and 'distrust'

At each step of the European policy process, from the first tentative drafts to the formal decision-making process, policy-making is characterized by a distrustful and circumspect observation of the mutual policy proposals made by the involved actors. The participants controlling each other are generally experts and/or decision-makers from the different Member States, responding to each other's policy proposals with counterproposals backed up by expertise. The mutual distrust signifies an enormous potential for control and a chance to hold actors accountable for individual policy moves which need to be defended in substantive terms. This is the virtuous side of the slowness, and indeed potential deadlock, inherent in the European decisional process. This phenomenon is so widespread, permeating virtually the entire fabric of the decision-making process across issue areas, that individual policy examples are superfluous. . .

The dark side of mutual control and distrust is – considering that European decision-making does not usually rely on the majority principle – of course stalemate, where a decisional process is stalled because the participants are exclusively engaged in controlling and fending-off policy initiatives presented by other actors involved. 'Distrust leads to foregone opportunities' unless it is overcome by constructive bargaining.

### Bargaining democracy

Fortunately, bargaining constitutes the complementary side of mutual horizontal control and distrust. It is present in all aspects of European policy-making, given the presence of actors with diverse interests and a concrete need for consensual decision-making. Consensus is achieved through negotiating in the course of which compromises are formulated, compensation payments made, and package deals struck.

Actors negotiating may be representatives from territorial units or delegates from functional organizations, such as associations. Thus, in negotiating sectoral questions, such as in regional and social policy under the 'partnership principle', delegates from functional organizations are predominantly involved. During the input phase bargaining mostly takes place at the supranational level. If legislative details need to be specified during the output phase they occur at the national/subnational level as well. Bargaining democracy creates input-legitimation since it prevents individual interests from being outvoted and thereby forces actors to take multiple interests into account. This is reflected in the more equitable outcomes of bargaining processes. By virtue of precisely this fact it also constitutes a source of output-legitimation. The underlying process mechanism is consensus-building with the help of compromises, compensation payments, and package deals.

### Pluralistic authorities in a 'composite polity'

The multiple political and jurisdictional authorities which exist in the European Union at the vertical and horizontal level have generated more opportunities for individual citizens and corporate actors to address an authority and voice their concern in the case of a specific policy issue. In practice, this means the opportunity to exit from a specific avenue of decision-making which has proved less than promising and to test prospects in another arena. Thus, a citizen or corporate actor may address his or her representative in parliament at the national or European level, the national or the European Ombudsman, and the national courts or the

European Court of Justice. These increased opportunities at the European Union level – as compared with their nation state counterparts – create leverage to press for political action . . .

However, the new opportunities on the part of individual citizens and corporate actors have a price. The more fragmented a polity, the greater the difficulty of reaching an overall definition of the general welfare of the society subject to this segmented and intersecting structure of authority. The body responsible for defining the 'common weal', the parliament, will tend to lose power as a result of competition among those laying claim to authority. There will consequently be less room for debate and deliberation as to the general direction in which a society as a whole is to develop. If, for instance, political goals are achieved through litigation in court instead of going through parliament, no attempt will be made to build a social consensus by debating various possibilities and then coming to a compromise in the parliamentary arena. As a consequence the policy goals which are pursued become more and more particularistic. Another problematic consequence may be decisional deadlock. Under conditions of joint decision-making, stalemate may ensue because one of the implicated authorities does not come forward with a decision. In the case of separate decision- making there is a risk that the responsibility for unpopular decisions is simply shifted to another authoritative body. Hence, while the presence of competing authorities in a composite polity such as the European Union offers more opportunities for voicing criticism and exercising influence and thereby enhances input-legitimation, it may also be detrimental to the overall welfare of a society in terms of policy outputs and favour decisional stalemate.

The republican model is an alluring project, but it is an ideal and, as such, risks mischaracterising and oversimplifying the practice of the European Union. Often, elements considered by it to be positive can have a negative underbelly. For each of its positive claims about Community law-making, a counter-argument can be found.

We turn, first, to the question of constitutional tolerance. Republicans argue that the European Union requires nationals to recognise the rights and identities of foreigners. This may be true, but, in practice, this notion may only apply to foreigners 'like us' rather than genuine outsiders. The European Union can be characterised as a cartel of elites, who act together to disenfranchise others' subjects within their respective territories or other foreigners (e.g. non-EU nationals).[118] This latter view is also too simplistic, but it is notable that, of 1,450 EU interest groups recognised by the EU institutions in 2001, almost two-thirds, 950, represented industry, with only 299 representing the public sector or public interests.[119] The mutual recognition taking place is, therefore, a highly selective one in which similar types of interests in the different Member States talk to one another.

Similarly, it is argued that the European Union induces parties to act in a public-spirited manner to realise public projects. However, there is something speculative in this statement. The art of lobbying is a black art, indeed, and Brussels is full of

---

118  This is the essence of the consociational model. P. Taylor, *International Organization in the Modern World: the Regional and the Global Process* (London, Pinter, 1993) ch. 1. For a more radical form of recognition see J. Shaw, 'Postnational Constitutionalism in the European Union' (1999) 6 *JEPP* 579.

119  C. Lahusen, 'Commercial Consultancies in the European Union: the Shape and Structure of Professional Interest Mediation' (2002) 9 *JEPP* 695.

lobbyists who are acting exclusively to realise their clients' interests.[120] It is difficult to see what public spirit is being realised here. More substantively, as Héritier points out, republican models, concerned with day-to-day checks and balances, are not well designed to setting out, with much strategic vision, common goals. These are often poorly defined – be they the common market, Community environment policy or the subsidiarity principle – and subject to the vicissitudes of daily politics. The idea of the single market, for example, has become what the lobbyists have made it, rather than being so noble an ideal that it structures their behaviour.

Finally, the argument that the European Union diffuses power and encourages pluralism can be turned on its head. De Areilza has noted that institutional differentiation only diffuses power where different constituencies are confined to specific institutional settings. Otherwise, it benefits two kinds of powerful interest. One type is that which can arbitrage between different institutional settings: lobbying MEPs, lunching with a Commissioner, visiting the office of national governments or litigating before national courts. The transnational nature of the European Union means that these are likely to be actors that are well-resourced, well-connected and transnational in scope. The other is locally vested interests, who can act as veto-players: blocking something in the Council that will undoubtedly be for the greater good, but does not favour their narrow interests. It can thus act to concentrate power and, in many circumstances, make the process more opaque.[121]

### (iii)   Deliberative democracy and the European public sphere

The final perspective through which the Community legislative procedures have been analysed is that of deliberative democracy. The central protagonist for this is Jürgen Habermas. According to him, democracy enables strangers to come together to decide matters of common interest as free and equals. Individuals accept legal restrictions in democracies precisely because they have had the opportunity to participate in the debate that led to the adoption of that law.[122] This requires not only that all individuals participate in the debate, but that individuals deliberate rather than negotiate. They should only put forward arguments that 'would count as a good reason for all others involved'.[123] By this standard, the measure of Community democracy is the quality of deliberation that leads to Community law, and the public institutions that allow such debate to flourish (the public sphere):

---

120 On the daily practice see R. van Schendelen, *Machiavelli in Brussels: the Art of Lobbying the EU* (Amsterdam, University of Amsterdam Press, 2002).

121 J. de Areilza, *Enhanced Cooperations in the Treaty of Amsterdam: Some Critical Remarks*, Jean Monnet Working Paper 13/98.

122 J. Habermas, *Between Facts and Norms* (Oxford, Polity, 1996) especially 360–79.

123 S. Benhabib, 'Towards a Deliberative Model of Democratic Legitimacy' in S. Benhabib (ed.), *Democracy and Difference: Contesting the Boundaries of the Political* (Princeton, NJ, Princeton University Press, 1994) 67, 71–2.

from a normative perspective, there can be no European federal state worthy
of the name of a democratic Europe unless a European-wide integrated public
sphere develops in the ambit of a common political culture: a civil society with
interest associations; non-governmental organisations; citizens' movements,
etc; and naturally a party system appropriate to a European arena. In short, this
entails public communication that transcends the boundaries of the until now
limited national public spheres.[124]

The institutional conditions for deliberative democracy are clearly not present
within the European Union, either at all or to the same extent as in nation-states.
However, Eriksen has observed that there are elements of deliberative democracy in
some areas, with the problem being not the absence of debate, but its fragmented
nature.

### E. Eriksen, 'Conceptualizing European Public Spheres: General, Segmented and Strong Publics', ARENA Working Paper 3/04 (Oslo, ARENA, 2004) 16–19

. . . a general public in Europe is not totally absent as there are new European audio-visual
spaces – newspapers, television, Internet, and English maybe as a bound to be first language –
and new social movements and identity politics across borders. The poly-lingual TV-channel
'Euro-News' operates on a large scale. In addition the *Financial Times, International Her-
ald Tribune, The Economist*, BBC World, ARTE, The European Voice, Deutsche Welle
(broadcasting in English), *Le Monde Diplomatique* with editions in most major European
languages – and certainly not least the Internet – create audio-visual spaces in Europe. Many
of these efforts are market driven, but such communicative spaces are not restricted to economic issues. Many NGOs, such as ATTAC, keep Internet pages in several languages and thus
facilitate transnational European debate. Some media operate as a motor for Europeanization . . . There are also traits of a Europeanized public debate: The 'Haider Affair' reveals that
even though transnational events are still viewed through national lenses they lead to common and simultaneous types of debates within the different national public spheres. There is
in other words a Europeanization of events. The same can be said about Joschka Fischer's
famous speech in May 2000, which was widely reflected and commented upon by journalists
in 12 newspapers of six EU Member States. We should also not forget the large demonstra-
tions that took place in all major European cities against the war in Iraq during the winter
of 2003. In Europe there is a potential space for the creation of collective identity through
pan-European press and media based on English as lingua franca. But there is a long way
from the kind of debate and information dissemination taking place nowadays in Europe, to
the kind of committed public deliberation needed for collective opinion and will-formation,
viz. the requirement of a general, supranational public sphere revolving on identical topics
and policy proposals throughout Europe, rendering collective decision-making possible on
the background of a broad mobilization of public support effectively sluiced into the governmental complex by intermediate organizations and political parties. A general supranational

---

124 J. Habermas, 'Remarks on Dieter Grimm's "Does Europe Need a Constitution?"' (1995) 1 *ELJ* 303,
    307.

public required by a fully democratic government is for the time being more of a potential that an actuality, even though the European Greens now – February 2004 – have been formed, as the first European wide party.

### Segmented publics

Common communicative systems of mass-media facilitating real public debates conducive to collective will-formation are to a large degree lacking at the European level. However, there are transnational public spheres emanating from the policy networks of the Union. Networks are joint problem sites based on common issue orientations and knowledge – epistemic communities. Such issue communities constituted on the common interests of actors in certain issue areas fluctuate, grow and shrink, sometimes in cycles. In Europe, networks of transnational regulation are conducive to Europeanization of policies and deliberative governance beyond the nation state. Networks represent the *institutional software* for the reflective treatment of discourses. They take the form of publics as far as there is a coupling between the collective actors and the audience in the sense that the actors do not only communicate among themselves but are also heard by others. As far as the communication can be heard by an 'undetermined audience' – a public – this takes the shape of *transnational resonance*. Scandals and campaigns are vehicles of such . . . *Scandals and campaigns* are the legitimating and delegitimating functions of the silent and speaking publics respectively. The public sphere effects of (the criticism of) Schengen, of the European campaigns against racism, of the BSE, of the charges of corruption and fraud in the Commission which developed into a scandal in the eyes of the public, are examples of events creating transnational but segmented public spheres. These cases show that not one unifying form of discourse develops but discourses that vary according to the issue fields and reflecting the institutional structure of the EU. The ability to manipulate or homogenize the European public discourse is rather limited. The bare suspicion of manipulation in fact leads to a delegitimising critique and is conducive to the broadening and pluralisation of public communication. Still it is a form of elite communication, where the experts and the well-educated speak to one another and stage communicative noise and protest. It surely falls short of reaching a level of mass communication in a homogenized political public sphere. But segmented publics also fall far short of complying with the democratic proviso of openness and equal access.

The European public space is currently fragmented, differentiated and in flux. In the place of the sovereign people, there is the noise of anarchic and pluralistic communication. The public sphere nevertheless has effects on governance as it subjects the decision-makers to protests and 'communicative noise' – *Kommunikativer Lärm*. Such 'noise' can be anticipated and thus discipline decision-makers ex ante.

The informal and unruly stream of communication that characterizes the European public debate takes place in scattered fora and arenas. From a democratic viewpoint the lingering problem pertains to the lack of ability to form collective identities on an equal basis in order to facilitate collective decision-making as well as solving the problem of (de facto) holding the rulers to account. But what about the deliberative and democratic qualities of the *institutional 'hardware'* of the EU?

### Strong publics in the EU

The EU is a highly complex institution possessing many points of access and sites for negotiation and deliberation. It displays a conglomerate of organization forms geared towards integrating policy-fields and establishing consensus ranging from the hard core decision-making units like the Council, the EP and the ECJ, via the nexus of adjacent committees – expert committees, COREPER, Comitology, COSAC – to the two Conventions on constitutional matters. The deliberative mark on these varies but some amount to strong publics as a brief look at three of the institutional forms renders clear: there are (a) open deliberative spaces (b) in which deliberation takes place prior to decision-making and (c) decision-makers are held to account.

## Further reading

F. Bignami, 'The Democratic Deficit in European Community Rulemaking: a Call for Notice and Comment in Comitology' (1999) 40 *Harvard International Law Journal* 451

A. v. Bogdandy, F. Arndt and J. Bast, 'Legal Instruments in European Union Law and their Reform: a Systematic Approach on an Empirical Basis' (2004) 23 *Yearbook of European Law* 91

C. Burns, 'Codecision and the European Commission: a Study of Declining Influence? (2004) 11 *Journal of European Public Policy* 1

R. Dehousse, 'Comitology? Who Watches the Watchmen' (2003) 10 *Journal of European Public Policy* 798

H. Farrell and A. Héritier, 'Formal and Informal Institutions under Codecision: Continuous Constitution Building in Europe' (2003) 16 *Governance* 577

O. Gerstenberg and C. Sabel, 'Directly-Deliberative Polyarchy: an Institutional Ideal for Europe' in C. Joerges and R. Dehousse (eds.), *Good Governance in Europe's Integrated Market* (Oxford, Oxford University Press, 2002)

C. Joerges and E. Vos (eds.), *EU Committees: Social Regulation, Law and Politics* (Oxford/Portland, Hart, 1999)

A. Kreppel, 'Moving beyond Procedure: an Empirical Analysis of European Parliament Legislative Influence' (2002) 35 *Comparative Political Studies* 784

A. Maurer and W. Wessels (eds.), *National Parliaments on their Ways to Europe: Losers or Latecomers?* (Baden Baden, Nomos, 2001)

M. Shackleton and T. Raunio, 'Codecision since Amsterdam: a Laboratory for Institutional Innovation and Change' (2003) 10 *Journal of European Public Policy* 171

D. Trubek, P. Cottrell and M. Nance, *'Soft Law', 'Hard Law,' and European Integration: toward a Theory of Hybridity*, Jean Monnet Working Paper 02/05

F. Tuytschaever, *Differentiation in European Union Law* (Oxford/Portland, Hart, 1999)

## Annex

### *Community legal bases where Council acts on Commission proposal without Parliamentary input (unanimity unless noted)*

Article 14(3) guidelines for internal market (QMV)

Article 26 fixing of common customs tariff duties (QMV)

Article 57(2) restrictions on movement of capital from non-EU states involving direct investment (QMV)

Article 59 restrictions on movement of capital from non-EU states causing serious difficulties for EMU (QMV)

Article 64 emergency measures restricting immigration of non-EU nationals (QMV)

Article 75 harmonisation of conditions for carriage of goods (QMV)

Article 96 eliminating distortions of competition in the common market (QMV)

Article 99(2) guidelines for economic policies of Member States (QMV)

Article 99(4) recommendations to Member States in breach of economic policy guidelines (QMV)

Article 100 measures dealing with severe difficulties in supply of products (QMV)

Article 111(2) general orientations for exchange rate policy (QMV)

Article 111(3) foreign exchange agreements (QMV)

Article 128(4) recommendations to Member States on employment (QMV)

Article 133(2) implementation of common commercial policy (QMV)

Article 133(3) international agreements in common commercial policy (QMV/unanimity if internal policies require unanimity)

Article 139(2) implementation of labour agreements between social partners (QMV/unanimity if these concern legislation that requires unanimity)

Article 151(5) recommendations on culture

Article 152(4) recommendations on public health (QMV)

Article 187 rules for association of overseas territories with European Union

Article 296(2) protection of essential national security interests associated with arms trade

Article 301 sanctions against non-EU states (QMV)

### *Legal Bases Covered By Consultation Procedure (Unanimity unless noted)*

Article 11 authorisation of Enhanced Cooperation (QMV)

Article 13(1) non-discrimination on grounds of sex, racial or ethnic origin, religion or belief, disability, age or sexual orientation

Article 19 voting rights for municipal and European Parliament elections

Article 22 extension of EU citizenship

Article 37(2) implementation of Common Agricultural Policy (QMV)

Article 52(1) liberalisation of specific service sectors (QMV)

Article 62(2)(b)(i) non-EU states whose nationals require visas (QMV)

Article 62(2)(b)(iii) format of visas (QMV)

Article 63(3)(a) residence permits, long-term visas and family reunion

Article 63(4) residence of long-term non-EU national residents in other Member States

Article 83 competition (QMV)

Article 89 state aids (QMV)

Article 93 indirect taxation

Article 94 common market

Article 104(14) amendment of excessive deficit procedure

Article 111(1) adjustment of central exchange rates of the European Currency Unit (ECU).

Article 128(2) employment guidelines (QMV)

Article 133(7) extension of common commercial policy to intellectual property

Article 137(2) social security and social protection of workers, protection of workers
after termination of contract, collective defence of workers' interests, conditions
of employment for non-EU nationals

Article 166(4) adoption of specific research and development programmes (QMV)

Article 172 establishment of joint research undertakings (QMV)

Article 175(2) environmental taxes, resource management, town and country planning, measures significantly affecting choice of energy sources

Article 300(3) international agreements (QMV)

*Legal bases covered by co-decision (QMV unless noted)*

Article 12 prohibition of any discrimination on grounds of nationality

Article 13(2) new anti-discrimination measures

Article 18 citizenship: right of citizens to move and reside freely within the territory
of the Member States

Article 40 freedom of movement for workers

Article 42 freedom of movement for workers: social security of migrant workers in
the Community (unanimity required in Council)

Article 44 right of establishment

Article 46 right of establishment: special treatment for foreign nationals

Article 47(1) taking up and pursuing activities as self-employed persons, training and
conditions of access to professions: mutual recognition of diplomas

Article 47(2) measures concerning the self-employed: amendment of national legislation (unanimity required in Council)

Article 55 right of establishment: services

Article 62(1), (2)(a), (3) border controls

Article 62(2)(b)(ii), (iv) border controls: issuing of visas; rules on uniform visas

Article 63(1)(a), (b), (c) asylum measures

Article 63(1)(d) asylum measures: minimum standards for granting or withdrawing
refugee status

Article 63(2)(a) measures on refugees and displaced persons: temporary protection
to displaced persons from third countries

Article 63(2)(b) promoting a balance of effort between Member States in receiving
refugees and displaced persons

Article 63(3)(b) illegal immigration, illegal residence and repatriation of illegal
residents

Article 65 judicial cooperation in civil matters (except family law)

Article 71(1) transport: common rules applicable to international transport, conditions under which non-resident carriers may operate transport services within a
Member State, measures to improve transport safety

Article 80(2) sea and air transport

Article 95(1) harmonisation of the internal market

Article 129 employment: incentive measures

Article 135 customs cooperation

Article 137(1)–(2) social policy: workers' health and safety, working conditions, information and consultation of workers, equality between men and women, measures to encourage cooperation in fight against social exclusion

Article 141 social policy: equal opportunities and pay

Article 148 Social Fund: implementing decisions

Article 149(4) education: incentive measures

Article 150(4) vocational training: measures to contribute to the achievement of objectives

Article 151(5) incentive measures in respect of culture (unanimity required in Council)

Article 152(4) public health: minimum standards of quality and safety of organs and substances of human origin, blood and blood derivatives, measures in the veterinary and phytosanitary fields designed to protect public health, action to improve public health

Article 153(4) consumer protection

Article 156 trans-European networks: establishment, funding

Article 157(3) specific support measures in the industrial sphere

Article 159(3) specific actions for economic and social cohesion outside the Structural Funds

Article 162 European Regional Development Fund (implementing decisions)

Article 166 framework programme for research and technical development

Article 172(2) research: adoption of programmes

Article 175(1), (3) environment: measures, adoption and implementation of programmes

Article 179 development cooperation

Article 191 regulations governing political parties at European level and the rules regarding their funding

Article 255 transparency: general principles and limits on access to documents

Article 280 measures to counter fraud

Article 285 statistics

Article 286 protection of data: establishment of an independent supervisory body

# 5

## Sovereignty and federalism: the authority of EU law and its limits

## CONTENTS

## 1. Introduction

This chapter covers some of the most fiercely contested territory of EU law. Sovereignty and federalism are as politically sensitive as they are legally central to the European project. Both terms – sovereignty and federalism – are subjects on which there is vast literature in legal theory and political science. The definitions and implications of the terms are examined from dozens of angles and at exhaustive length.[1] The good news is that we are not especially concerned with sovereignty or federalism as general concepts in politico-legal studies. We are not seeking a mastery of the myriad meanings these terms may be said to possess. Rather, we are concerned simply with the doctrine and practice of sovereignty and federalism as principles of EU law. As such, in the present context, *sovereignty* concerns the authority enjoyed by EU law over the law, including the constitutional law, of the Member States. In this chapter we explore, first, the claim that the European Court of Justice has made

---

1 The following may be recommended as starting points for further reading: N. Walker (ed.), *Sovereignty in Transition* (Oxford, Oxford University Press, 2003) and K. Nicolaïdis and R. Howse (eds.), *The Federal Vision: Legitimacy and Levels of Governance in the United States and the European Union* (Oxford, Oxford University Press, 2000).

for the sovereignty of European law. Then we turn to consider the reaction of the Member States. *Federalism* concerns the constitutional relationship between the central authorities and the constituent parts of the European Union. In this chapter we focus, in particular, on the relationship as it is manifested in the allocation of law-making powers between the institutions on the one hand and the Member States on the other.

As well as being controversial, both sovereignty and federalism in the European Union must be understood as remaining somewhat fluid. The territory we navigate in this chapter is changing and is likely to continue to do so as the European Union develops and takes on new challenges. We may be dealing with fundamental, even constitutional, doctrines here, but there is little, even in the fundament of the European Union, that is fixed. This should not necessarily be seen as a cause for concern – either from the perspective of the European citizen or from that of the student of EU law. On the contrary, the ongoing European debates about how much of their national sovereignty Member States should 'pool' (as the Court of Justice describes it) for the sake of 'ever closer Union' and about where the lines should be drawn between what the European Union should regulate and what should be left to the governments of Member States, go to the very heart of the matter. There is no preconceived end-point to be reached. Both the destination of the European project and its route there remain, emphatically, matters for negotiation and argument. That is what makes the study of European law so fascinating. Where should sovereignty lie in the European Union? How should we even conceive of sovereignty in twenty-first century Europe? What powers, if any, should be reserved uniquely to the Member States? Where should the federal lines be drawn between European and national law-making and who should protect them? These are the key issues we explore in this chapter and, as we shall see, there are no settled answers. This should strike citizens and students alike less as a frustration and more as an opportunity.

## 2. Sovereignty of EU law: primacy and the Court of Justice

When states come together to make treaties, even where the international law made by those treaties binds the states that agree to (or ratify) them, states remain sovereign. As a matter of international law, they may have to exercise their sovereignty subject to the international obligations they have created, but the domestic legal effects of any such obligations will be a matter for the national legal orders of each state to determine. At the inception of the EC Treaties, it was widely assumed that this, the traditional model of international law, would apply to the European Communities. The EC Treaties were just like any other treaties in international law, or so it was thought. Under this model, it is the states who are masters of the treaties, and not the other way around. This means that, collectively, states may change the EC's powers, interpret its effects or even extinguish it if they so desired. It also means that, individually, the EC could not trump states' domestic, sovereign legal processes.[2] In 1962, a House of Lords Committee, asked to report on the legal implications of British membership of the European Communities, explicitly applied this model when it stated as follows:

> The transfer of legislative power . . . does not of course mean, from the point of view of the constitutional law of the United Kingdom, a surrender of any part of the ultimate sovereignty of Parliament. An Act of Parliament applying the Treaties can be repealed by a subsequent Act, and if this happens, the Treaties will cease to be law in this country and the power of the European Council to make regulations having effect as law in this country will come to an end. If we did this without the agreement of other member countries, we would be in breach of our international obligations and would be liable to proceedings under public international law.[3]

In two judgments in the early 1960s, the Court of Justice moved dramatically to overturn these assumptions. It considered the EC Treaty to be different from other treaties. First, it ruled in *Van Gend en Loos* that the EC Treaty did not merely regulate mutual obligations between Member States, but established what the Court called a 'new legal order of international law for the benefit of which the states have limited their sovereign rights'.[4] *Van Gend en Loos* is considered in more detail in chapters 2 and 9. What the Court of Justice stated in that case about the sovereignty of European law was taken further in *Costa v ENEL*, decided shortly afterwards. *Costa* concerned an Italian Law that sought to nationalise the electricity production and distribution industries. Costa, a shareholder of Edison Volta, a company affected by the nationalisation, claimed that it breached Community law. The Italian government claimed that the matter was one of Italian law as the Italian legislation post-dated the EC Treaty and, for that reason, should be held to be the applicable law.

### Case 6/64 *Costa v ENEL* [1964] ECR 585

By contrast with ordinary international treaties, the EEC Treaty has created its own legal system which, on the entry into force of the Treaty, became an integral part of the legal systems of the Member States and which their courts are bound to apply.

By creating a Community of unlimited duration, having its own institutions, its own personality, its own legal capacity and capacity of representation on the international plane and, more particularly, real powers stemming from a limitation of sovereignty or a transfer of powers from the States to the Community, the Member States have limited their sovereign rights, albeit within limited fields, and have thus created a body of law which binds both their nationals and themselves.

---

2 See J. Weiler and U. Haltern, 'The Autonomy of the Community Legal Order: Through the Looking Glass' (1996) 37 *Harvard International Law Journal* 411, 417–19.
3 Public Record Office LCO 29/108.
4 Case 26/62 *Van Gend en Loos v Nederlandse Administratie der Belastingen* [1963] ECR 1. See pp. 47–8.

The integration into the laws of each Member State of provisions which derive from the Community, and more generally the terms and the spirit of the Treaty, make it impossible for the States, as a corollary, to accord precedence to a unilateral and subsequent measure over a legal system accepted by them on a basis of reciprocity. Such a measure cannot therefore be inconsistent with that legal system. The executive force of Community law cannot vary from one State to another in deference to subsequent domestic laws, without jeopardizing the attainment of the objectives of the Treaty set out in Article [10(2)] and giving rise to the discrimination prohibited by Article [12].

The obligations undertaken under the Treaty establishing the Community would not be unconditional, but merely contingent, if they could be called in question by subsequent legislative acts of the signatories. Wherever the Treaty grants the States the right to act unilaterally, it does this by clear and precise provisions . . . Applications by Member States for authority to derogate from the Treaty are subject to a special authorization procedure . . . which would lose their purpose if the Member States could renounce their obligations by means of an ordinary law.

The precedence of Community law is confirmed by Article [249], whereby a regulation 'shall be binding' and 'directly applicable in all Member States'. This provision, which is subject to no reservation, would be quite meaningless if a state could unilaterally nullify its effects by means of a legislative measure which could prevail over Community law.

It follows from all these observations that the law stemming from the Treaty, an independent source of law, could not, because of its special and original nature, be overridden by domestic legal provisions, however framed, without being deprived of its character as Community law and without the legal basis of the Community itself being called into question.

The transfer by the States from their domestic legal system to the Community legal system of the rights and obligations arising under the Treaty carries with it a permanent limitation of their sovereign rights, against which a subsequent unilateral act incompatible with the concept of the Community cannot prevail.

It would be difficult to overstate the radicalism of *Costa*. The claim that EC law enjoys some form of sovereignty means that the EC's powers cannot be seen as deriving from the Member States, but must be understood instead as being somehow autonomous and original. An essential property of the legal concept of sovereignty is that it is *constitutive* in character:

> in the context of the internal structure of a political society, the concept of sovereignty has involved the belief that there is an absolute power within the community. Applied to problems which arise in the relations between political communities, its function has been to express the antithesis of this argument – the principle that internationally, over and above the collection of communities, no supreme authority exists.[5]

The claim that EU law is sovereign has three main implications. The first concerns the *primacy* of EU law. EU law governs the conditions of its application; unless it expressly provides, it cannot be disapplied in favour of any other form of law. The second concerns *competence*. EU law determines the limits of its own authority; it is

5 F. Hinsley, *Sovereignty* (Cambridge, Cambridge University Press, 1986) 158.

for EU law to determine the extent of the European Union's law-making powers (or competences) and what legal effects the existence and exercise of these competences bring. The third concerns *fidelity*. The sovereignty of EU law establishes a rule of law to which all public institutions within the Member States are subject, including national courts. This involves specifying a series of institutional duties setting out what such institutions must do to make the Union work as a fully effective legal system.

Of these, the first, primacy, is perhaps the most straight-forward. It is neatly illustrated by the decision of the Court of Justice in *Internationale Handelsgesellschaft*, in which the Court famously ruled that EU law takes precedence over all forms of national law, including national Constitutional law. The claimant brought an action before a German administrative court challenging the validity of an EC Regulation. The German court considered that the Regulation violated certain provisions of the German Constitution. The view of the Court of Justice was uncompromising.

---

### Case 11/70 *Internationale Handelsgesellschaft v Einfuhr- und Vorratstelle für Getreide und Futtermittel* [1970] ECR 1125

3. Recourse to the legal rules or concepts of national law in order to judge the validity of measures adopted by the institutions of the Community would have an adverse effect on the uniformity and efficacy of Community law. The validity of such measures can only be judged in the light of Community law. In fact, the law stemming from the Treaty, an independent source of law, cannot because of its very nature be overridden by rules of national law, however framed, without being deprived of its character as Community law and without the legal basis of the Community itself being called in question. Therefore the validity of a Community measure or its effect within a Member State cannot be affected by allegations that it runs counter to either fundamental rights as formulated by the constitution of that State or the principles of a national constitutional structure.

---

It is not only with regard to primacy that the Court of Justice has taken a strong line when it comes to matters of sovereignty. The toughness of its overall approach was encapsulated in the Court's judgment in *Simmenthal*. The case concerned an Italian system of fees for veterinary inspections of beef imports. The system had already been held by the Court of Justice to breach Community law. An Italian magistrate asked the Court whether he was required to disapply the relevant Italian law, a power which at that time was enjoyed only by the Italian Constitutional Court.

---

### Case 106/77 *Amministrazione delle Finanze dello Stato v Simmenthal* [1978] ECR 629

17. . . . in accordance with the principle of the precedence of Community law, the relationship between provisions of the Treaty and directly applicable measures of the institutions on the one hand and the national law of the Member States on the other is such that those provisions and measures not only by their entry into force render automatically inapplicable

any conflicting provision of current national law but – in so far as they are an integral part of, and take precedence in, the legal order applicable in the territory of each of the Member States – also preclude the valid adoption of new national legislative measures to the extent to which they would be incompatible with Community provisions.

18. Indeed any recognition that national legislative measures which encroach upon the field within which the Community exercises its legislative power or which are otherwise incompatible with the provisions of Community law had any legal effect would amount to a corresponding denial of the effectiveness of obligations undertaken unconditionally and irrevocably by Member States pursuant to the Treaty and would thus imperil the very foundations of the Community . . .

21. . . . . every national court must, in a case within its jurisdiction, apply Community law in its entirety and protect rights which the latter confers on individuals and must accordingly set aside any provision of national law which may conflict with it, whether prior or subsequent to the Community rule.

22. Accordingly any provision of a national legal system and any legislative, administrative or judicial practice which might impair the effectiveness of Community law by withholding from the national court having jurisdiction to apply such law the power to do everything necessary at the moment of its application to set aside national legislative provisions which might prevent Community rules from having full force and effect are incompatible with those requirements which are the very essence of Community law.

This is all very well but matters are not, in reality, quite as straightforward as a bald reading of *Internationale Handelsgesellschaft* and *Simmenthal* might suggest. While these cases show that there is, as Weiler has put it, a 'hierarchy of norms' in which 'Community norms trump Member States' norms', the hierarchy of norms 'is not rooted in a hierarchy of normative authority or in a hierarchy of real power'.[6] What Weiler refers to as 'real power' in the European Union remains firmly with the Member States. It must always be remembered that the European Union has very little ability to execute the laws it makes. The execution or administration of EU law is overwhelmingly a matter for domestic authorities and national governments within Member States. Moreover, the European Union possesses very little in the way of direct means of enforcement – it has only limited mechanisms to deal with a 'disobedient' state.[7] For the primacy of EU law to remain effective, therefore, it generally needs to retain the goodwill of the Member States. If EU law is deemed unreasonable, states have the means to evade its requirements. If states unreasonably seek to evade measures of EU law, however, they risk the censure of other states (and even of their own citizens) for disrespect of a legal text. In this sense, sovereignty in the European Union may be seen as circular or at least paradoxical. EU law needs to justify itself as reasonable, while a state seeking to disapply EU law must likewise justify its action as reasonable. This cycle of justification, where,

6 J. Weiler, 'Federalism without Constitutionalism: Europe's Sonderweg' in K. Nicolaïdis and R. Howse (eds.), *The Federal Vision: Legitimacy and Levels of Governance in the United States and the European Union* (Oxford, Oxford University Press, 2000) 57.

7 See further chapter 9.

ideally, power is never taken for granted, but where its exercise must always be justified is, for Weiler, one of the most distinctive and one of the most civilising features of EU law.

Thus far, we have considered the first major implication of the sovereignty of EU law: primacy. Now we turn to consider the second and third implications: competence and fidelity.

### (i)   Pre-emption and the allocation of competences

The sovereignty of EU law requires not only that it take precedence over national law, but that EU law, alone, determine its legal effects. It is a matter for EU law to determine which fields it governs,[8] and what legal effects it has in those areas. These questions are anchored in the doctrine of pre-emption.[9] This doctrine sets out the conditions under which Member States are prohibited or 'pre-empted' from legislating by virtue of an EU law-making power. These powers, or competences, come in four main varieties. The four varieties are exclusive competence, shared competence, minimum harmonisation and competence to take supporting, coordinating or complementary action. Where the EC has exclusive competence to legislate, the mere existence of such competence is sufficient to pre-empt Member State laws. Where the EC has shared competence, its law-making power must actually have been exercised for the Member States to be pre-empted. In the context of minimum harmonisation, Member States may adopt legislation, on condition that it is more protective than any overlapping Community legislation. Where the European Union has the power to take only supporting, coordinating or complementary action, the presence of EU legislation does not prevent Member States taking measures, although these will have to be interpreted in the light of any relevant EU measures. We will now consider each of these in more detail.

### (a)   Exclusive competence

From the perspective of the Member States, the most draconian fields are those in which the EC has exclusive competence. Exclusive competence involves a complete surrender of law-making power by the Member States to the European Union. It is, therefore, unsurprising that only a small number of fields of Community competence are exclusive. One is the common commercial policy. The effects of exclusivity in this field were illustrated by the Court in Opinion 1/75. An Opinion was sought on whether the EC was exclusively competent under Article 133 EC (the provision on the common commercial policy) to conclude an OECD Understanding on a Local Costs Standard.

---

8 See Opinion 1/91 *Re European Economic Area* [1991] ECR I-6079.
9 See M. Waelbroeck, 'The Emergent Doctrine of Community Pre-emption: Consent and Re-delegation' in T. Sandalow and E. Stein (eds.), *Courts and Free Markets: Perspectives from the United States and Europe,* vol. II (Oxford, Oxford University Press, 1982) and E. Cross, 'Pre-emption of Member State Law in the European Economic Community: a Framework for Analysis' (1992) 29 *CML Rev.* 447.

Under the Understanding, participating governments agreed not to provide credit to undertakings for more than 100 per cent of the value of the goods or services exported to other participating states.

> **Opinion 1/75 *Re Understanding on a Local Costs Standard* [1975] ECR 1355**
>
> [Article 133 EC is conceived] in the context of the operation of the Common Market, for the defence of the common interests of the Community, within which the particular interests of Member States must endeavour to adapt to each other.
>
> Quite clearly, however, this conception is incompatible with the freedom to which the Member States could lay claim by invoking a concurrent power, so as to ensure that their own interests were separately satisfied in external relations, at the risk of compromising the effective defence of the common interests of the Community.
>
> In fact any unilateral action on the part of the Member States would lead to disparities in the conditions for the grant of export credits, calculated to distort competition between undertakings of the various Member States in external markets. Such distortion can be eliminated only by means of a strict uniformity of credit conditions granted to undertakings in the Community, whatever their nationality.
>
> It cannot therefore be accepted that, in a field such as that governed by the Understanding in question, which is covered by export policy and more generally by the common commercial policy, the Member States should exercise a power concurrent to that of the Community, in the Community sphere and in the international sphere. The provisions of Articles [133 and 134] concerning the conditions under which, according to the Treaty, agreements on commercial policy must be concluded show clearly that the exercise of concurrent powers by the Member States and the Community in this matter is impossible.
>
> To accept that the contrary were true would amount to recognizing that, in relations with third countries, Member States may adopt positions which differ from those which the Community intends to adopt, and would thereby distort the institutional framework, call into question the mutual trust within the Community and prevent the latter from fulfilling its task in the defence of the common interest.

The issue of what should be classified as falling within the EC's exclusive competence has been fiercely contested. Even now there is no legally authoritative list. In a valuable analysis, de Búrca reported that the Commission:

> has argued that when the Community is under a duty to act and has been given the responsibility to take action in a particular field, it has exclusive competence in that sphere, which includes not only the free movement core of the internal market, but also the common commercial policy, agriculture, competition, transport and fisheries conservation. No sooner is this list considered, however, than it is apparent that these policy areas cannot be entirely outside the scope of Member State competence.[10]

This is an issue that would have been resolved by the Constitutional Treaty, Article I-13 of which provided as follows:

---

10 G. de Búrca, *Reappraising Subsidiarity's Significance after Amsterdam*, Jean Monnet Working Paper 7/99.

1. The Union shall have exclusive competence in the following areas:
   (a) customs union;
   (b) the establishing of the competition rules necessary for the functioning of the internal market;
   (c) monetary policy for the Member States whose currency is the euro;
   (d) the conservation of marine biological resources under the common fisheries policy;
   (e) common commercial policy.
2. The Union shall also have exclusive competence for the conclusion of an international agreement when its conclusion is provided for in a legislative act of the Union or is necessary to enable the Union to exercise its internal competence, or insofar as its conclusion may affect common rules or alter their scope.

It is submitted that this, considerably shorter, list is broadly reflective of the present legal position and that the Commission's ambition to extend the category of the EC's exclusive competence to the internal market, competition, agriculture and the like should be firmly rejected.[11] In any event, the principle of exclusivity has in practice proved to be too absolutist. There would be a danger of regulatory gaps emerging if Member States were barred from regulating a matter where no substitute EU legislation was in place. To prevent this, in all fields where the European Union has exclusive powers, national measures are permitted, provided that prior authorisation has been granted by one of the EU institutions and that there is no Community legislation already in place.[12]

### (b)   Shared competence

Areas of shared competence include the following: the internal market, social policy, structural policy and cohesion policy, agriculture and fisheries, excluding the conservation of marine biological resources (which is exclusive to the European Union), the environment, consumer protection, transport, transEuropean networks, immigration, asylum and visas, police and judicial cooperation in criminal matters,[13] certain matters of public health,[14] research and development and development cooperation.[15]

---

11 As it has been: see Case C-377/98 *Netherlands v European Parliament and Council* ('Biotechnology Directive') [2001] ECR I-7079 and Case C-491/01 *R v Secretary of State for Health ex parte British American Tobacco* [2002] ECR I-11453. See further A. Dashwood, 'The Relationship between the Member States and the European Union/European Community' (2004) 41 *CML Rev.* 355, 369–73.

12 Case 41/76 *Donckerwolcke v Procureur de la République* [1976] ECR 1921; Case 70/77 *Simmenthal v Italian Finance Administration* [1978] ECR 1453; Case 804/79 *Commission v United Kingdom* [1981] ECR 1045. See also Article I-12(1) CT.

13 This is in the third pillar and is not subject to the automatic jurisdiction of the Court of Justice. The European Union does have power to adopt harmonising measures which bind the Member States, however: see Article 34(2)(b) TEU.

14 These are standards for the quality and safety of organs of human origin and blood, and veterinary and phytosanitary measures, which have public health as their direct object.

15 Article I-14(2)–(4) CT.

In these fields, Member States retain a power to regulate matters falling within the respective EU competence, but they must not create a conflict with the rules adopted by the European Union.

In some of these fields, most notably the internal market, agriculture and fisheries, and transport, Member States can exercise competence only to the extent that the EC has not exercised or has ceased to exercise competence. Known as 'field occupation', everything depends on whether the issue at hand is regulated by Community law or not. In *Commission v United Kingdom*, for example, the Commission brought an action against a British requirement that cars could be driven on British roads only if they were equipped with dim-dip lights.[16] The relevant EC Directive did not impose this as a requirement and, furthermore, it provided that any car which met its stipulations should be able to be driven on the roads. The Court of Justice found the British requirement to be illegal. It stated that the intention of the Directive was to regulate exhaustively the conditions for lighting devices on cars. As this was now exhaustively regulated by EC law, Member States were prohibited from imposing additional requirements.

Within the context of the internal market, such a rule is particularly important. The maintenance of differing national regimes would lead to distortions of competition and trade restrictions, with the consequence that the harmonisation process would be robbed of much of its effect. It creates, however, a regime which is both monolithic and inflexible. It is impossible to maintain national provisions that impose higher standards and the only way of adapting legislation to new risks and technologies is through amending the EU legislation, which can be an arduous and time-consuming process.[17] The Court has been particularly concerned about circumstances where Community legislation fails to protect public interests that were previously safeguarded by national legislation. It has, on occasion, interpreted EU legislation narrowly so that it is not deemed to regulate the field covered by national law, thereby allowing the national legislation to remain in place.[18] If this is not possible, in extreme circumstances the Court will refuse to disapply the national legislation. *Commission v Germany* is an example. Member States were required by Article 4(1) of Directive 79/409/EEC to designate the most suitable habitats in their territory for certain species of wild bird. Under Article 4(4), once designated, these habitats were to be preserved and appropriate steps taken to prevent their deterioration. The Directive envisaged no circumstances in which measures could be taken to reduce the size of the special protection areas. Germany wished to build a dyke across one of its designated areas in the Leybucht region. It argued this was necessary because, otherwise, the coast would be washed away.

---

16 Case 60/86 *Commission v United Kingdom* [1988] ECR 3921.
17 S. Weatherill, 'Beyond Preemption? Shared Competence and Constitutional Change in the European Community' in D. O'Keeffe and P. Twomey (eds.), *Legal Issues of the Maastricht Treaty* (Chichester, Chancery, 1994) 13, 18–19.
18 Examples of this include Case C-11/92 *R v Secretary of State for Health ex parte Gallaher Ltd* [1993] ECR I-3545. This is dealt with in more detail in *EUL*, chapter 11.

> ### Case C-57/89 *Commission v Germany* [1991] ECR I-883
>
> 20. Although the Member States do have a certain discretion with regard to the choice of the territories which are most suitable for classification as special protection areas pursuant to Article 4(1) of the Directive, they do not have the same discretion under Article 4(4) of the Directive in modifying or reducing the extent of the areas, since they have themselves acknowledged in their declarations that those areas contain the most suitable environments for the species listed in Annex I to the Directive . . .
>
> 21. . . . It follows that the power of the Member States to reduce the extent of a special protection area can be justified only on exceptional grounds.
>
> 22. Those grounds must correspond to a general interest which is superior to the general interest represented by the ecological objective of the Directive . . .
>
> 23. With regard to the reason put forward in this case, it must be stated that the danger of flooding and the protection of the coast constitute sufficiently serious reasons to justify the dyke works and the strengthening of coastal structures as long as those measures are confined to a strict minimum and involve only the smallest possible reduction of the special protection area.

As EU competences have expanded, another doctrine has become significant in areas of shared competence: namely, that of minimum harmonisation. Under this doctrine, Community laws are seen as creating a 'bed of rights'. Member States are not prevented from enacting more restrictive provisions, although frequently there will be a procedural requirement that such national measures be notified to the Commission.[19] In a number of fields, the EC Treaty provides that the EC may engage only in minimum harmonisation: these include the environment, consumer protection, public health, and health and safety at work.[20] In other areas, secondary legislation may provide that it is setting only minimum standards. Indeed, at the Edinburgh European Council in 1992, the European Council stated that attention should always be given to whether minimum harmonisation is possible and, only where this would conflict with the objectives of the Treaty or would defeat the purpose of the measure, should it not be used.[21]

Minimum harmonisation allows national authorities to take only measures that are more stringent or more protective than the EU measure. Litigation in this area has tended to focus on this requirement. In *Deponiezweckverband Eiterköpfe*, for example, a landfill operator was refused permission to fill two sites with waste.[22] The reason was that the waste exceeded German limits on the proportion of organic waste that could be disposed of in landfill sites. By contrast, the Directive (on which the German law was based) set limits only for biodegradable organic waste. The operator argued that the national legislation was, therefore, unlawful. The Court of Justice disagreed. It stated that what was central was that the German legislation pursued the same objective as the Directive, namely the limitation of waste going into landfill. Insofar

---

19 See e.g., Article 176 EC.     20 Articles 176 EC; 153(3) EC; 152(4)(a) EC and 137(5) EC respectively.

21 Conclusions of the Edinburgh European Council, Annex I to Part A: EC Bulletin 12-1992, 15.

22 Case C-6/03 *Deponiezweckverband Eiterköpfe v Land Rheinland-Pfulz* [2005] ECR I-2753.

as it set limits for a wider range of waste, it was more stringent than the EU Directive and was, therefore, permissible.

### (c) Supporting, coordinating and complementary action

The final type of EU competence is where the field remains one of national competence, but in respect of which the European Union may take supporting, coordinating or complementary action. These areas include industry, culture, employment, education, youth and vocational training, economic policy coordination and general public health measures.[23] In such fields, the European Union is excluded from taking harmonising measures that might restrict national competence and the measures which can be adopted by the European Union are usually confined to the issuing of recommendations or guidelines. Whilst these cannot be invoked directly in national courts, they can still have some interpretive force. National courts are to have regard to them when interpreting national legislation, implementing them, or when interpreting binding EU measures which supplement them, for example.[24]

### (ii) Fidelity principle

The sovereignty of EU law requires more of Member States than merely that they refrain from breaching EU law. Such a limited obligation on the part of the Member States would be unlikely to be sufficient to secure the full effectiveness of the EU legal system. All legal systems confer responsibilities upon public bodies to ensure that the law is generally applied, policed, accessible and that there are sufficient remedies for breach of the law. Known in the USA as the 'fidelity principle', the requirement is that 'each level and unit of government must act to ensure the proper functioning of the system of governance as a whole'.[25] In EU law, the principle is set out most explicitly in Article 10 EC:

> **Article 10 EC**
>
> Member States shall take all appropriate measures, whether general or particular, to ensure fulfilment of the obligations arising out of this Treaty or resulting from action taken by the institutions of the Community. They shall facilitate the achievement of the Community's tasks.
>
> They shall abstain from any measure which could jeopardise the attainment of the objectives of this Treaty.

Although, on paper, this provision falls only within the EC pillar of the European Union and is addressed only to Member States, the Court of Justice has expanded

---

23 Articles 157(3) EC; 151(5) EC; 129 EC; 149(4) EC; 99 EC; 152(4)(c) EC.
24 Case 322/88 *Grimaldi v Fonds des Maladies Professionelles* [1989] ECR 4407.
25 D. Halberstam, 'The Political Morality of Federal Systems' (2004) 90 *Virginia Law Review* 101, 104.

its scope so as to transform it into an overarching principle 'drawing all relevant institutions into the job of effectively sustaining Community policy'.[26] It has, therefore, been held to apply not only to the Member States, but also to the EU institutions, who must cooperate with national bodies to secure the full effectiveness of EU law.[27]

In *Pupino*, the Court ruled that the principle of fidelity applies throughout EU law and is not confined to the EC pillar. Pupino was charged with using physical violence against a number of young boys whom she taught. Under Italian criminal law, evidence may be submitted which does not have to be subject to cross-examination in court, if either the victim is susceptible to violence or for sexual offences involving minors. The prosecution wanted to use this procedure for the children, a number of whom were under five years old, on grounds that cross-examination would cause psychological trauma. Pupino argued that this was not permitted by Italian law. Framework Decision 2001/220/JHA required Member States to provide special protection from the effects of giving evidence in open court to the most vulnerable victims, by enabling them to testify through alternative means. The Italian court asked whether it was required to interpret Italian law in the light of this Framework Decision.

### Case C-105/03 *Pupino*, judgment of 16 June 2005

41. The second and third paragraphs of Article 1 of the Treaty on European Union provide that that Treaty marks a new stage in the process of creating an ever closer union among the peoples of Europe and that the task of the Union, which is founded on the European Communities, supplemented by the policies and forms of cooperation established by that Treaty, shall be to organise, in a manner demonstrating consistency and solidarity, relations between the Member States and between their peoples.

42. It would be difficult for the Union to carry out its task effectively if the principle of loyal cooperation, requiring in particular that Member States take all appropriate measures, whether general or particular, to ensure fulfilment of their obligations under European Union law, were not also binding in the area of police and judicial cooperation in criminal matters, which is moreover entirely based on cooperation between the Member States and the institutions . . .

43. In the light of all the above considerations, the Court concludes that the principle of interpretation in conformity with Community law is binding in relation to framework decisions adopted in the context of Title VI of the Treaty on European Union. When applying national law, the national court that is called upon to interpret it must do so as far as possible in the light of the wording and purpose of the framework decision in order to attain the result which it pursues.

The fidelity principle requires national institutions to secure legal certainty for EU law. The Court of Justice has stated that Member States must implement their obligations 'with unquestionable binding force, and with the specificity, precision and clarity necessary to satisfy that principle'.[28] Mere administrative practice will not

---

26 Weatherill, above n. 17, 31. For a description of the forms these obligations can take see J. Temple Lang, 'Community Constitutional Law: Article 5 EEC Treaty' (1990) 27 *CML Rev.* 645.

27 See Case 2/88 *Zwartveld* [1990] ECR I-3365.

28 Case C-159/99 *Commission v Italy* [2001] ECR I-4007.

be enough to meet a state's obligations: measures must be in place which, whilst not necessarily legislation, are sufficiently binding that they cannot be changed at will. Such measures must be public so that citizens are able to identify their rights.[29]

In addition, Member States must actively police EC law. In *Commission v France*, French farmers launched a violent campaign targeting the importation of Spanish strawberries.[30] Their action involved threatening shops, burning lorries carrying the goods and blockading roads. The French government took almost no action either to stop these protests or to prosecute offences committed as a result of them. While the acts stopping the import of Spanish strawberries were performed by *private* actors – the farmers – and while the relevant provision of EU law, Article 28 EC, imposed obligations only on *states* not to prevent the free movement of goods, the Court ruled that France had breached EC law.[31] The state was required to adopt all appropriate measures to guarantee the full scope and effect of Community law. In taking measures that were manifestly inadequate, France had failed to do this. The requirement to police EC law, however, is not an absolute one: a Member State does not have to police EC law if this would result in public disorder which it could not contain. Similarly, it must not police EC law in such a way that it violates fundamental rights and civil liberties.[32]

The fidelity principle also requires that Member States penalise infringements of EC law under conditions, both procedural and substantive, that are analogous to those applicable to infringements of national law of a similar nature and importance.[33] As we have already seen, EC law must be able to be invoked in national courts, which must be empowered to review and disapply national legislation and national administrative measures where these conflict with EC law.[34] In addition, national courts must ensure that, irrespective of the situation for breaches of national law, penalties for breach of EC law are effective, proportionate and dissuasive.[35] In *Berlusconi*,[36] Advocate General Kokott set out what these criteria mean:

> 88. Rules laying down penalties are *effective* where they are framed in such a way that they do not make it practically impossible or excessively difficult to impose the penalty provided for and, therefore, to attain the objectives pursued by Community law.

---

29 Case C-313/99 *Mulligan and others v Minister for Agriculture and Food, Ireland* [2002] ECR I-5719. The principle of legal certainty also requires that if Member States amend a law to comply with EU law, the amending measure must have the same legal force as the original measure so as to enable citizens to identify their rights with sufficient certainty: see Case C-33/03 *Commission v United Kingdom*, judgment of 10 March 2005.

30 Case C-265/95 *Commission v France* [1997] ECR I-6959.　　31 On Article 28 EC see *EUL*, chapter 15.

32 Case C-112/00 *Schmidberger v Republic of Austria* [2003] ECR I-5659.

33 These matters are explored in more detail in chapter 9.　　34 See *Simmenthal*, pp. 186–7.

35 Case 68/88 *Commission v Greece* [1989] ECR 2965; Case C-326/88 *Anklagemyndigheden v Hansen & Son* [1990] ECR I-2911; Case C-167/01 *Kamer van Koophandel en Fabrieken voor Amsterdam v Inspire Art* [2003] ECR I-10155.

36 Joined Cases C-387/02, C-391/02 and C-403/02 *Berlusconi and others* [2005] ECR I-3565.

89. A penalty is *dissuasive* where it prevents an individual from infringing the objectives pursued and rules laid down by Community law. What is decisive in this regard is not only the nature and level of the penalty but also the likelihood of its being imposed. Anyone who commits an infringement must fear that the penalty will in fact be imposed on him. There is an overlap here between the criterion of dissuasiveness and that of effectiveness.

90. A penalty is *proportionate* where it is appropriate (that is to say, in particular, *effective* and *dissuasive*) for attaining the legitimate objectives pursued by it, and also necessary. Where there is a choice between several (equally) appropriate penalties, recourse must be had to the least onerous. Moreover, the effects of the penalty on the person concerned must be proportionate to the aims pursued.

It may be seen from the above that the claim of sovereignty for EU law, while relatively simple to state, has a number of implications. Having set these out from the perspective of the European Union, and particularly the Court of Justice, we now turn to examine the reaction of the Member States.

### 3. Contesting EU legal sovereignty: primacy and the national courts

#### (i) Case law of the national courts

In the previous section, we saw that the sovereignty of EU law is essentially concerned with securing the primacy of EU legal norms in national courts and with ensuring that such courts enforce the application of EU law by other actors. As it is, above all, a series of injunctions to national courts, it is critically important to understand the extent to which the sovereignty of EU law has been accepted by national courts. For, unless it is so accepted, the claims in *Costa, Internationale Handelsgesellschaft* and the rest that EU law is sovereign remain just claims, and rather hollow ones at that. One of the most striking features of the EU legal system is that national courts across the European Union, despite being the ostensible guardians of their respective *national* constitutional settlements, have been generally willing to apply EC law at the expense of national law.

---

**B. de Witte, 'Direct Effect, Supremacy, and the Nature of the Legal Order' in P. Craig and G. de Búrca (eds.), *The Evolution of EU Law* (Oxford, Oxford University Press, 1999) 196–8**

Among the original Six, no special efforts were required from the courts in the Netherlands and Luxembourg, where the supremacy of international treaty provisions over national legislation was accepted prior to 1957. Of the other four countries, the courts in Belgium reacted most promptly and loyally to the European Court's injunctions. A model of what national courts can achieve in the absence of clear constitutional guidelines is the 1971 judgment of the Belgian Cour de Cassation in the *Franco-Suisse Le Ski* case. Although the Belgian Constitution was silent on the domestic effect of international or European law (or precisely because of this absence of written rules) the Supreme Court adopted the principle of primacy as it had been formulated in *Costa*, and based on the nature of international law and (a fortiori) of EC law. The other Belgian courts soon followed the same line. In France, although the text of Article 55 of the Constitution recognised the priority of international treaties even over later French laws, the courts were surprisingly slow to accept that this constitutional provision could actually be used as a conflict rule in real cases and controversies. The Cour de Cassation taking the lead of all ordinary courts decided to cross the Rubicon in the 1975 *Cafés Jacques Vabre* judgment. The Conseil d'Etat (and the administrative courts subject to its authority) followed suit much later with the *Nicolo* decision (1989), after what must have been a very painful revision of established truths. One may note that one of the arguments used by the *commissaire* Frydman, when advising the Conseil in *Nicolo* to change its views on the supremacy of EC law, was that the supreme courts of surrounding countries (even those with ingrained dualist traditions) had long recognised this supremacy.

In Italy and Germany, the actual duties imposed on national courts by *Costa* went well beyond what the mainstream constitutional doctrine, at that time, was prepared to accept in terms of the domestic force of international treaty law. Yet the European Court suggested, by cleverly distinguishing EEC law from 'ordinary' international law, that the German and Italian courts might, with some creativity, find the constitutional resources needed for recognising the primacy of Community law. The message, in *Costa*, was primarily addressed to the Italian Constitutional Court. This court has gradually come to recognise the supremacy of Community law over national legislation, on the basis of its special nature which distinguishes it from other international treaties. A similar evolution took place in Germany . . .

Greece and Ireland, when they joined, had put their constitutions in order. Article 28 of the Greek Constitution, adopted prior to accession, recognises the primacy of international conventions over any national legislation. In Ireland, given the inability of the dualist constitutional tradition to cope with the demands of membership, a special EC clause was added to the Constitution (and adapted to later Treaty revisions) vouchsafing the direct effect and primacy of Community law.

In the United Kingdom, the supremacy question floated around for many years, until the *Factortame II* judgment, where the House of Lords for the first time disapplied a later Act of Parliament for being inconsistent with the EEC Treaty . . .

So, by and large, 'ordinary' supremacy of Community law, that is, supremacy over national legislation and sources of national law lower in rank than legislation, seem to be accepted in most Member States (primacy over national constitutional law is quite another matter . . .). But there are lingering doubts, even concerning 'ordinary' supremacy, in a long-standing Member State like Denmark. That country's Constitution contains no rules on the relation between Community law and national law, and the doctrine of the primacy of EC law has never been expressly accepted by the courts. Indeed, it seems that there has not been, in the twenty-five years of Danish membership, a single court case involving a conflict between EC law and a later Danish Act of Parliament.

Acceptance of the primacy of EC law by national courts has been facilitated by the fact that only a small proportion of EU law has, in practice, been invoked before domestic courts. One study found that just five areas of law – taxation, sex discrimination, free movement of goods, free movement of workers and intellectual property – accounted for 61 per cent of all reported litigation in the United Kingdom, and that just five Directives accounted for 73 per cent of the Directives that were invoked in British courts.[37] It has also been facilitated by national courts finding ways of accepting the primacy of EC law on terms and conditions drawn from their national constitutional settlements. The case law of Europe's constitutional courts reveals that three broad approaches are available for national courts to take. Space precludes a detailed consideration of the reception of EU law in all twenty-five Member States. In what follows, therefore, we have had to be selective. The three approaches may be called 'European constitutional sovereignty', 'unconditional national constitutional sovereignty' and 'constitutional tolerance'. Of these, it is the third which has been most widely followed, as we shall see. Each of the three can now be illustrated with reference to decisions of various national constitutional courts. A decision of the Spanish Constitutional Court represents the first approach (European constitutional sovereignty), a decision of the Polish Constitutional Court represents the second approach (unconditional national constitutional sovereignty) and a famous and critically important decision of the German Constitutional Court represents the third approach (constitutional tolerance).

### (a)   European constitutional sovereignty

The first approach is where a constitutional court of a Member State unconditionally accepts the standpoint of the Court of Justice with the consequence that EU law is seen as being supreme, even over the national constitution. This position has not yet been definitively taken by any national constitutional court. Perhaps the closest such a court has come to accepting this position, is in Spain. In the following case the Spanish Constitutional Court was asked to rule on whether the Constitutional Treaty was compatible with the Spanish Constitution. The court was, in particular, concerned with Article I-6 CT, which sought to write the claims of *Costa* as to the primacy of EU law into the Treaty.[38]

> ### Re EU Constitutional Treaty and the Spanish Constitution (Spanish Constitutional Court) [2005] 1 CMLR 981
>
> 52. The status of the Constitution as the supreme statute law under the Spanish legal system is a matter which, although not expressly stated in any of its provisions, is undoubtedly derived from many of them . . . and is consubstantial with its status as a fundamental law: the Constitution has supremacy over or ranks superior to any other law, and more specifically over international treaties . . . Now the declaration of the primacy of Union law by Article I-6 of the Treaty does not contradict the supremacy of the Constitution.
>
> 53. Primacy and supremacy are categories that operate in different areas of the law. Primacy operates in the application of valid laws; supremacy in legislative processes. Supremacy

---

37 D. Chalmers, 'The Positioning of EU Judicial Politics within the United Kingdom' (2000) 23 *WEP* 169, 178–83.

38 Article I-6 CT would have provided that 'The Constitution and law adopted by the institutions of the Union in exercising their competences conferred on it shall have primacy over the law of the Member States'.

is founded on the hierarchical superiority of a law which is, therefore, the source of validity of all lower-ranking laws, with the result that the latter are invalid if they conflict with it. Primacy, on the other hand, is not necessarily based on hierarchy, but rather on the distinction between areas of application of different laws, on valid principles, one or more of which will nevertheless have the capacity to displace others by virtue of their prior or prevalent applicability for various reasons. In principle any supremacy implies primacy . . . unless the Supreme Law itself has displaced it or rendered it inapplicable in one field or another. The supremacy of the Constitution is, therefore, compatible with rules of application that give priority to the rules of a system other than Spanish law, provided that the Constitution itself has so provided, which is exactly what occurs with the provision contained in Art. 93, according to which it is possible to assign powers derived from the Constitution to an international institution constitutionally so empowered to legislate on matters hitherto reserved for the existing internal powers, and to apply the said legislation to those internal powers. In summary, the Constitution itself has accepted, by virtue of Art. 93, the primacy of Union law in the areas covered by that Law, as is now expressly acknowledged in Art. I-6 of the Treaty.

54. And this relationship has existed since Spain became a member of the European Communities in 1986. At that time, an independent legislative system was integrated into Spanish law; it had specific rules of applicability, based on the principle that the provisions thereof should prevail over any internal laws with which they might conflict. This principle of primacy, built on case law, formed part of the Community *acquis* incorporated by means of Organic Law 10/1985, of August 2, authorising the adhesion of Spain to the European Union because it derives from the doctrine created by the Court of Justice of the European Communities in its Decision of July 15, 1964.

### (b)   Unconditional national constitutional sovereignty

The second available approach is the opposite of the first in that it insists upon the continuing and unconditional sovereignty of the national constitutional order. Whilst acknowledging that EU law may make special claims for itself, the second approach denies that EU law is any different from other forms of international law.

### *Polish Membership of the European Union (Accession Treaty)* (Polish Constitutional Court), judgment K18/04 of 11 May 2005

6. It is insufficiently justified to assert that the Communities and the European Union are 'supranational organisations' – a category that the Polish Constitution, referring solely to an 'international organisation', fails to envisage. The Accession Treaty was concluded between the existing Member States of the Communities and the European Union and applicant States, including Poland. It has the features of an international agreement, within the meaning of Article 90(1) of the Constitution. The Member States remain sovereign entities – parties to the founding treaties of the Communities and the European Union. They also, independently and in accordance with their constitutions, ratify concluded treaties and have the right to denounce them under the procedure and on the conditions laid down in the Vienna Convention on the Law of Treaties 1969. The expression 'supranational organisation' is not mentioned in the Accession Treaty, nor in the Acts constituting an integral part thereof or any provisions of secondary Community law.

7. Article 90(1) of the Constitution authorises the delegation of competences of State organs only 'in relation to certain matters'. This implies a prohibition on the delegation of all competences of a State authority organ or competences determining its substantial scope of activity, or competences concerning the entirety of matters within a certain field.

8. Neither Article 90(1) nor Article 91(3) authorise delegation to an international organisation of the competence to issue legal acts or take decisions contrary to the Constitution, being the 'supreme law of the Republic of Poland' (Article 8(1)). Concomitantly, these provisions do not authorise the delegation of competences to such an extent that it would signify the inability of the Republic of Poland to continue functioning as a sovereign and democratic State.

9. From an axiological perspective of the Polish Constitution, the constitutional review of delegating certain competences should take into account the fact that, in the Preamble of the Constitution, emphasising the significance of Poland having reacquired the possibility to determine her fate in a sovereign and democratic manner, the constitutional legislator declares, concomitantly, the need for 'cooperation with all countries for the good of a Human Family', observance of the obligation of 'solidarity with others' and universal values, such as truth and justice. This duty refers not only to internal but also to external relations.

10. The regulation contained in Article 8(1) of the Constitution, which states that the Constitution is the 'supreme law of the Republic of Poland', is accompanied by the requirement to respect and be sympathetically predisposed towards appropriately shaped regulations of international law binding upon the Republic of Poland (Article 9). Accordingly, the Constitution assumes that, within the territory of the Republic of Poland – in addition to norms adopted by the national legislator – there operate regulations created outside the framework of national legislative organs.

11. Given its supreme legal force (Article 8(1)), the Constitution enjoys precedence of binding force and precedence of application within the territory of the Republic of Poland. The precedence over statutes of the application of international agreements which were ratified on the basis of a statutory authorisation or consent granted (in accordance with Article 90(3)) via the procedure of a nationwide referendum, as guaranteed by Article 91(2) of the Constitution, in no way signifies an analogous precedence of these agreements over the Constitution.

12. The concept and model of European law created a new situation, wherein, within each Member State, autonomous legal orders co-exist and are simultaneously operative. Their interaction may not be completely described by the traditional concepts of monism and dualism regarding the relationship between domestic law and international law. The existence of the relative autonomy of both, national and Community, legal orders in no way signifies an absence of interaction between them. Furthermore, it does not exclude the possibility of a collision between regulations of Community law and the Constitution.

13. Such a collision would occur in the event that an irreconcilable inconsistency appeared between a constitutional norm and a Community norm, such as could not be eliminated by means of applying an interpretation which respects the mutual autonomy of European law and national law. Such a collision may in no event be resolved by assuming the supremacy of a Community norm over a constitutional norm. Furthermore, it may not lead to the situation whereby a constitutional norm loses its binding force and is substituted by a Community norm, nor may it lead to an application of the constitutional norm restricted to areas beyond the scope of Community law regulation. In such an event the Nation as the sovereign, or a State authority organ authorised by the Constitution to represent the Nation, would need to decide

on: amending the Constitution; or causing modifications within Community provisions; or, ultimately, on Poland's withdrawal from the European Union.

14. The principle of interpreting domestic law in a manner 'sympathetic to European law' . . . has its limits. In no event may it lead to results contradicting the explicit wording of constitutional norms or being irreconcilable with the minimum guarantee functions realised by the Constitution. In particular, the norms of the Constitution within the field of individual rights and freedoms indicate a minimum and unsurpassable threshold which may not be lowered or questioned as a result of the introduction of Community provisions.

Unconditional national constitutional sovereignty emphasises national self-determination and the need to put in place an active system of constitutional checks and balances on the development of EU law. It has only really been adopted by Poland. This is, in part, because unconditional national constitutional sovereignty inaccurately describes institutional practice. It is not simply that the Court of Justice has developed the filaments of a new constitutional order in its case law; it is that these doctrines have been applied, albeit pragmatically, by the overwhelming majority of national courts. To describe EU law as merely another form of international law is to dismiss not merely the views of the Court of Justice, but of the broader European judicial community.[39] It is also a normatively contentious position, as it privileges the idea of the state unquestioningly.

### (c) Constitutional tolerance

The third approach is that of constitutional tolerance. This posits that while the authority and reach of EU law is ultimately for national constitutional courts to decide, such courts commit themselves to recognise the special status of EU law and to give it a constitutional validity, but that they do so on the condition that it does not violate certain constraints of national constitutional law. Of the three approaches available to national constitutional courts, this is the position that has (thus far) been most frequently taken. Its most famous articulation came in the decision of the German Constitutional Court in *Brunner*. A challenge was mounted to the TEU on the ground that it violated the German Constitution, in particular its Article 38. This provision entitled all Germans to participate in the election of deputies for the German Bundestag. The complainants argued that the transfer of so many powers to the European Union violated this provision as the Bundestag was deprived of a substantial part of its decision-making competence. The Constitutional Court considered that the Treaty did not violate the German Constitution, but placed clear constraints on the further development of European integration.

---

39 Weiler and Haltern, above n. 2, 420–3; N. Walker, 'The Idea of Constitutional Pluralism' (2002) 65 *MLR* 317, 321–3.

### *Brunner v European Union Treaty* (German Constitutional Court) [1994] 1 CMLR 57

39. The European Union is, according to its understanding of itself as a union of the peoples of Europe . . . , a federation of democratic States whose objectives include a dynamic development . . . If the Union carries out sovereign powers for those purposes, it is first and foremost the national peoples of the Member States who, through their national parliaments, have to provide the democratic legitimation for its so doing . . .

43. . . . What is decisive is that the democratic bases of the European Union are built up in step with integration, and that as integration proceeds a thriving democracy is also maintained in the Member States. An excess weight of functions and powers within the responsibility of the European federation of States would effectively weaken democracy at national level, so that the parliaments of the Member States could no longer adequately provide the legitimation for the sovereign power exercised by the Union.

44. If the peoples of the individual States provide democratic legitimation through the agency of their national parliaments (as at present) limits are then set by virtue of the democratic principle to the extension of the European Communities' functions and powers. Each of the peoples of the individual States is the starting point for a state power relating to that people. The States need sufficiently important spheres of activity of their own in which the people of each can develop and articulate itself in a process of political will-formation which it legitimates and controls, in order thus to give legal expression to what binds the people together (to a greater or lesser degree of homogeneity) spiritually, socially and politically.

45. From all that it follows that functions and powers of substantial importance must remain for the German Bundestag.

46. . . . The exercise of sovereign power through a federation of States like the European Union is based on authorisations from States which remain sovereign and which in international matters generally act through their governments and control the integration process thereby. It is therefore primarily determined governmentally. If such a community power is to rest on the political will-formation which is supplied by the people of each individual State, and is to that extent democratic, that presupposes that the power is exercised by a body made up of representatives sent by the Member States governments, which in their turn are subject to democratic control . . .

49. . . . What is decisive is that Germany's membership and the rights and duties that follow there from (and especially the immediately binding legal effect within the national sphere of the Communities' actions) have been defined in the Treaty so as to be predictable for the legislature and are enacted by it in the Act of Accession with sufficient certainty. That also means that subsequent important alterations to the integration programme set up in the Union Treaty and to the Union's powers of action are no longer covered by the Act of Accession to the present Treaty. Thus, if European institutions or agencies were to treat or develop the Union Treaty in a way that was no longer covered by the Treaty in the form that is the basis for the Act of Accession, the resultant legislative instruments would not be legally binding with the sphere of German sovereignty. The German state organs would be prevented for constitutional reasons from applying them in Germany. Accordingly the Federal Constitutional Court will review legal instruments within the limits of the sovereign rights conferred on them or transgress them.

50. The Union Treaty satisfies the above-stated requirements in so far as it falls to be scrutinised in the present proceedings . . .

54. The competences and powers which are granted to the European Union and the Communities belonging to it remain essentially the activities of an economic union in so far as they

are exercised through the implementation of sovereign rights. The central areas of activity of the European Community in this respect are the customs union and the free movement of goods, the internal market, the assimilation of laws to ensure the proper functioning of the common market, co-ordination of the Member States' economic policies, and the development of a monetary union. Outside the European Communities, co-operation stays on an inter-governmental basis; that applies particularly in the case of foreign and security policy and the fields of justice and home affairs.

55. The Federal Republic of Germany, therefore, even after the Union Treaty comes into force, will remain a member of a federation of States, the common authority of which is derived from the Member States and can only have binding effects within the German sovereign sphere by virtue of the German instruction that its law be applied. Germany is one of the 'Masters of the Treaties', which have established their adherence to the Union Treaty concluded 'for an unlimited period' . . . with the intention of long-term membership, but could also ultimately revoke that adherence by a contrary act. The validity and application of European law in Germany depend on the application-of-law instruction of the Accession Act. Germany thus preserves the quality of a sovereign State in its own right and the status of sovereign equality with other States . . .

107. Any further development of the European Union cannot escape from the conceptual framework set out above. The legislature in amending the Constitution took that into account in connection with this Treaty by the insertion of Article 23 into the Constitution, since express mention is made there of the development of the European Union, which is subject to the principles of democracy and the rule of law, social and federal principles, and the subsidiarity principle. What is decisive, therefore, from the viewpoint both of the Treaties and of constitutional law, is that the democratic bases of the Union will be built up in step with the integration process, and a living democracy will also be maintained in the Member States as integration progresses.

Similar reasoning has been adopted by other national courts: notably in Denmark, Belgium, the United Kingdom and Hungary.[40] Some commentators have argued that, with its assertions that sovereignty vests ultimately in national constitutions and that national constitutional courts have the final say on the authority of EU law within their territories, *Brunner* is a bald restatement of national constitutional sovereignty and that, as such, it stands in direct opposition to *Costa*.[41] It is not clear, however, that this is what was actually asserted in *Brunner*. After all, the judgment states that *limited sovereign* powers have been transferred to the European Union. This is a statement that EU law has some kind of sovereign authority, albeit not of an absolute sort.

40 See *Carlsen v Rasmussen* [1999] 3 CMLR 854 (Denmark); Case No 12/94 *Ecole Européenne*, CA, 3 February 1994, B6 (Belgium); *R v MAFF ex parte First City Trading Treaty* [1997] 1 CMLR 250; *Marks & Spencer v CCE* [1999] 1 CMLR 1152 (United Kingdom); Judgment 30 of the Hungarian Constitutional Court invalidating Article 62 of the 1994 Europe Agreement between Hungary and the European Union, judgment of 25 June 1998.
41 T. Schilling, 'The Autonomy of the Community Legal Order: an Analysis of Possible Foundations' (1996) 37 *Harvard International Law Journal* 389; T. Hartley, 'The Constitutional Foundations of the European Union' (2001) 117 *LQR* 225.

It is to enjoy day-to-day authority, which will be lost only if it transgresses certain predetermined limits. These limits seem to be threefold.[42]

First, EU law must not violate fundamental rights as set out in national constitutions. In two judgments, in the early 1970s, both the German and the Italian Constitutional Courts indicated that they would not apply provisions of EU law that failed to respect the fundamental rights and values set out in their respective national constitutions.[43] These threats have remained latent. Indeed, the German Constitutional Court has since stated that, as EU law now contains sufficient fundamental rights guarantees of its own, it will not actively review EU legislation provided this general level of protection is maintained.[44] Other courts have begun, however, to review EU legislation against national systems of fundamental rights. A taste was provided in 1997 when an EC regime, which imposed a 200 per cent duty on bananas imported from Central America in excess of a certain quota, was referred by the German Administrative Court to the German Constitutional Court. In the view of the former, the EC regime violated the German Constitution, notably the right to property and the principle of equality. The German Constitutional Court reaffirmed its position that it would not strike down the EC legislation, as EC law now provided sufficient guarantees.[45] A different position, however, was taken in Hungary. In 2004, the Hungarian Constitutional Court struck down a Hungarian statute that had been expressly required by a Commission Regulation on transitional measures regarding agricultural products. The Regulation concerned the accumulation of surplus stocks by speculators prior to Hungarian accession to the European Union. It was found to violate the principle of non-retroactivity in that it did not take account of transactions reducing stocks in the five months prior to accession.[46] The Constitutional Court claimed that it was merely striking down national legislation, but this argument is unconvincing because the legislation largely replicated the Regulation and the latter had no force without the implementing measures.[47]

Secondly, the European Union is to have only limited powers. If legislation is enacted (or a Court of Justice judgment adopted) that breaches this principle, a national constitutional court could declare it to be invalid. No national court has (yet) done this. It was perhaps most explicitly threatened by the English High Court

---

42 M. Kumm, 'The Jurisprudence of Constitutional Conflict: Constitutional Supremacy in Europe before and after the Constitutional Treaty' (2005) 11 *ELJ* 262, 264 *et seq.*

43 See, respectively, *Internationale Handelsgesellschaft v Einfuhr-und Vorratsstelle für Getreide und Futtermittel* [1974] 2 CMLR 540 and *Frontini v Ministero delle Finanze* [1974] CMLR 386.

44 See (1986) 73 BVerfGE 339 ('Solange II').

45 U. Everling, 'Will Europe Slip on Bananas? The Bananas Judgement of the Court of Justice and National Courts' (1996) 33 *CML Rev.* 401; S. Kupfer, 'How the European Community Banana Regulation Brought Back Solange II' (2001) 7 *Colum. JEL* 307; M. Aziz, 'Sovereignty Lost, Sovereignty Regained? Some Reflections on the Bundesverfassungsgericht's Bananas Judgment' (2002) 9 *Colum. JEL* 109.

46 Case 17/04 AB.Hat, Constitutional Court of the Republic of Hungary, 25 May 2004.

47 See A. Sajo, 'Learning Co-operative Constitutionalism the Hard Way: the Hungarian Constitutional Court Shying Away from EU Supremacy' (2004) 3 *Zeitschrift für Staats- und Europawissenschaften* 351.

in *First City Trading*. In this case, a beef exporter challenged the compensation scheme that had been established in the light of the BSE crisis. Only those exporters who had slaughterhouses were eligible for compensation. The applicant did not have one and argued that the scheme unlawfully discriminated against him and was, therefore, in breach of a general principle of Community law. His argument was rejected by the High Court, which considered that such principles applied in the national context only where Member States were compelled to do something by force of EC law and not where their actions merely touched upon interests regulated by EC law. In response to the suggestion that this might not be the view of the Court of Justice, Laws J, the English judge, stated as follows:

> Like any statute law containing orders or prohibitions, the Treaty is *dirigiste*: it is law in the shape of command. Law of this kind may intrude into areas previously altogether free of any legal controls, because of the sovereign force of the legislation. It may open a new jurisdiction. But it is to be sharply distinguished from law which is made by a court of limited jurisdiction, such as the Court of Justice. The legitimacy of that law depends upon its being elaborated by the court within the confines of the power with which it is already endowed. Its writ cannot run where it could not run before. The position is, or may be, different in the case of a court whose powers are inherent and original, not conferred by any legislation. But the Court of Justice has no inherent jurisdiction. Its authority is derived solely from the Treaties. Although . . . its decisions are as a matter of English law supreme, its supremacy runs only within its appointed limits. Although of course I am being asked to apply the Community principle of equal treatment as a domestic judge, I must decide whether to do so by having regard to the lawful confines of the power of the Court of Justice, since it is a function of that Court's internal law, its common law, which is relied on.[48]

Thirdly, national courts might not apply EU law where there appears to be a conflict between it and specific provisions that, whilst not protecting fundamental rights, form part of the national constitutional order. This category is slightly different from the previous two, in that national courts are less willing to confront EU law explicitly. Instead, they tend to adopt minimalist interpretations of EU law so as to secure its conformity with national constitutions. A good example is the decision of the French Constitutional Court on the compatibility of the Constitutional Treaty with the French Constitution. Article 1 of the French Constitution provides that France is a secular republic. This has been interpreted as banning any display of religious symbols in schools, including the wearing of the cross or the veil by pupils. Article II-70 CT would have provided that anybody may manifest his religious belief in public. There seemed, therefore, to be a straightforward conflict. The French Constitutional Court stated that Article II-70 CT was intended to have the same scope and meaning

---

48 *R v MAFF ex parte First City Trading* [1997] 1 CMLR 250, 268.

as Article 9 ECHR, which allows restrictions to be imposed on the display of religious belief on grounds, inter alia, of public policy. This has been interpreted to give considerable weight to the principle of secularism in national constitutional traditions, leaving national authorities a considerable margin of discretion as to how to reconcile freedom of religion with secularism. On this basis, the Constitutional Court considered there to be no conflict between the Constitutional Treaty and the French Constitution.[49]

### (ii)   Academic commentary

Academic commentators have adopted two types of argument to seek to make sense of questions of sovereignty in the European Union. Some have put forward arguments from pluralism and others have suggested arguments from principle. Among the strongest advocates of the former is MacCormick.

> ### N. MacCormick, 'The Maastricht Urteil: Sovereignty Now' (1995)
> ### 1 *European Law Journal* 259, 264–5
>
> . . . the most appropriate analysis of the relations of legal systems is pluralistic rather than monistic, and interactive rather than hierarchical. The legal systems and their common legal system of EC law are distinct, but interacting systems of law, and hierarchical relations of validity within criteria of validity proper to distinct systems do not act up to any sort of all-purpose superiority of one system over another. It follows also that the interpretative power of the highest decision-making authorities of the different systems must be, as to each system, ultimate. It is for the European Court of Justice to interpret in the last resort and in a finally authoritative way the norms of Community law. But, equally, it must be for the highest constitutional tribunal of each Member State to interpret its constitutional and other norms, and hence to interpret the interaction of the validity of EC law with higher level norms of validity in the given state system. Interpretative competence-competence is a feature of the highest tribunal of any normative system . . .
>
> What this indicates is that acceptance of a pluralistic conception of legal systems entails acknowledging that not all legal problems can be solved legally. The problem in principle is not that of an absence of legal answers to given problems, but of a superfluity of legal answers. For it is possible that the European Court interprets Community law so as to assert some right or obligation as binding in favour of a person within the jurisdiction of the German court, while that court in turn denies the validity of such a right or obligation in terms of the German Constitution. In principle, the same conflict is possible as between any Member State system and EC law. The problem is not logically embarrassing, because strictly the answers are from the point of different systems. But it is practically embarrassing to the extent that the same human beings are said to have and not to have a certain right. How shall they act? To which system are they to give their fidelity in action?

---

49 *Re EU Constitutional Treaty and the French Constitution* (French Constitutional Court) [2005] 1 CMLR 750. For a similar style of reasoning by the Greek Constitutional Court, albeit in relation to the public status of universities, see M. Maganaris, 'Greece: the Principles of Supremacy of Community Law – the Greek Challenge' (1998) 23 *EL Rev.* 179.

Resolving such problems, or more wisely still, avoiding their occurrence in the first place is a matter for circumspection and for political as much as legal judgment. The European Court of Justice ought not to reach its interpretative judgments without regard to their potential impact on national constitutions. National courts ought not to interpret laws or constitutions without regard to the resolution of their compatriots to take full part in European Union and European Community. If despite this conflicts come into being through judicial decision-making and interpretation, there will necessarily have to be some political action to produce a solution.

The advantages and disadvantages of a pluralistic approach lie in its intellectual elasticity. The dispute about the sovereignty of EC law has been used by some authors as evidence that legal authority is no longer something exclusively vested in the state, but is now enjoyed by a number of different institutions. These include the European Union and states, but also include international organisations, such as the WTO or the United Nations, regional government and even private organisations with strong norm-setting powers, such as professional or standardisation bodies. In such a world, there are possibilities for more diverse forms of self-government and greater checks and balances, with each order limiting the excesses of the other. Such accounts, however, overemphasise the similarities between these different types of legal authority. Just as an elephant and a mouse are mammals but are, nonetheless, very different, so these various types of law may work in diverse ways and may be quite different beasts. Furthermore, pluralist accounts tend to be weak on explaining the relationship between these legal orders. Mutual accommodation is all very well, but there must be certain norms of mutual recognition and certain criteria for determining when it would be possible for one legal order to trump another.[50]

Other writers have argued that this indeterminacy entails that the question cannot be left to pragmatism. They argue instead that there are certain transcendent principles, recognised by all these legal orders, which should be seen as governing relations between them. Eleftheriadis, for example, has argued that conflicts should be resolved through resort to 'cosmopolitan law': a code of universal human rights.[51] Laws failing to respect the rights of individuals should give way to those which do. Cosmopolitan law is, however, both very libertarian – little is said about collective goods, such as protection of the environment – and very thin. It would not give strong indicators of which norms to choose in complex areas of market regulation. A more

50 See C. Richmond, 'Preserving the Identity Crisis: Autonomy, System and Sovereignty in European Law' (1997) 16 *Law and Philosophy* 377; M. la Torre, 'Legal Pluralism as an Evolutionary Achievement of Community Law' (1999) 12 *Ratio Juris* 182; N. Walker, 'The Idea of Constitutional Pluralism' (2002) 65 *MLR* 317; N. Walker, 'Late Sovereignty in the European Union' in N. Walker (ed.), *Sovereignty in Transition* (Oxford, Oxford University Press, 2003). For a response, see M. Loughlin, 'Ten Tenets of Sovereignty' in *ibid.* and D. Kostakopoulou, 'Floating Sovereignty: a Pathology or Necessary Means of State Evolution?' (2002) 22 *OJLS* 135.
51 P. Eleftheriadis, 'The European Constitution and Cosmopolitan Ideals' (2001) 7 *Colum. JEL* 21.

sophisticated test has been proposed by Kumm, who has argued that a common idea of constitutionalism informs both the law of the Member States and EU law. He has identified four tenets central to this idea of constitutionalism. These are commitment to the rule of law, protection of fundamental rights, federalism and a commitment to valuing the specific nature of the national community. It is these tenets, he suggests, which should be used to resolve disputes.

---

### M. Kumm, 'The Jurisprudence of Constitutional Conflict: Constitutional Supremacy in Europe before and after the Constitutional Treaty' (2005) 11 *European Law Journal* 262, 299–300

The *first* principle is formal and is connected to the *idea of legality*. According to the principle of the effective and uniform enforcement of EU law, further strengthened by the recent explicit commitment by Member States to the primacy of EU law, national courts should start with a strong presumption that they are required to enforce EU law, national constitutional provisions notwithstanding. *The presumption for applying EU law can be rebutted, however, if, and to the extent that, countervailing principles have greater weight.* Here there are three principles to be considered. The first is *substantive*, and focuses on the effective *protection of fundamental rights of citizens*. If, and to the extent that, fundamental rights protection against acts of the EU is lacking in important respects, than that is a ground to insist on subjecting EU law to national constitutional rights review. If, however, the guarantees afforded by the EU amount to structurally equivalent protections, then there is no more space for national courts to substitute the EU's judgment on the rights issue with their own. Arguably the EU, and specifically the Court of Justice, has long developed substantially equivalent protections against violations of fundamental rights. At the very least the Constitutional Treaty, with its elaborate Charter of Fundamental Rights should finally put an end to this issue. Even if some doubt that the Court of Justice can be trusted as an institution to take rights seriously, if the Charter of Fundamental Rights becomes the law of the land after ratification the guarantees it provides may not fall below the guarantees provided by the European Convention of Human Rights as interpreted by the ECHR. The second of the counter-principles is *jurisdictional*. It protects national communities against unjustified usurpations of competencies by the European Union and undermines the legitimate scope of self government by national communities. Call this principle the principle of *subsidiarity*. Here the question is whether there are sufficient and effective guarantees against usurpation of power by EU institutions. Much will depend on how the procedural and technical safeguards of the Constitutional Treaty will work in practice once the Treaty has been ratified. If the structural safeguards will succeed in establishing a culture of subsidiarity carefully watched over by the Court of Justice, then there are no more grounds for national courts to review whether or not the EU has remained within the boundaries established by the EU's constitutional charter. Lastly, there is the *procedural* principle of *democractic legitimacy*, the third counter-principle. Given the persistence of the democratic deficit on the European level – the absence of directly representative institutions as the central agenda-setters of the European political process, the lack of a European public sphere, and a sufficiently thick European identity even if the Constitutional Treaty will be ratified – national courts continue to have good reasons to set aside EU law *when it violates clear and specific constitutional norms that reflect essential commitments of the national community.*

The principles elaborated by Kumm provide a nuanced and, on the whole, more convincing matrix for resolving disputes between national constitutional courts and the Court of Justice. However, no solution is without its costs. He treats the state as something of a black box in which there is a single constitutional order whose role is to allocate decision-making powers between different levels of government and to protect fundamental rights. Pluralists would argue that within any territory there are a number of different sources of legal authority. Treating the matter in terms simply of national court versus EU court struggles to capture this complexity and diversity. Thus, many of the popular challenges to EU law, be they objections to using metric measurements in the United Kingdom, regulation of the football transfer market by EU law, or requirements that pasta need not be made exclusively from durum wheat in Italy, raise broader sociological questions, such as the extent to which regulation of the market can be used as a basis for getting rid of local traditions or justifying bureaucratic intrusion. Insofar as these questions are unaddressed, there is likely to be continuing resistance to EU law when individuals are told to cease with established ways of doing things or to put up with new administrative restrictions simply for the sake of the uniformity of EU law.

## 4. Federal limits of EU law

Even to the extent that Member States and national constitutional courts have allowed the European Union to assert and to exercise sovereign power – however it may be defined and analysed – such sovereignty is, *as a matter of EU law*, limited by the federal nature of the European Union. Three fundamental principles of EU law serve to delimit its federal reach: these are the principles of conferred powers, of subsidiarity and of proportionality. These principles draw the lines between what the Union may do and what is left for the governments of Member States.

### Article 5 EC

The Community shall act within the limits of the powers conferred upon it by this Treaty and of the objectives assigned to it thereto.

In areas which do not fall within its exclusive competence, the Community shall take action, in accordance with the principle of subsidiarity, only if and insofar as the objectives of the proposed action cannot be sufficiently achieved by the Member States and can therefore, by reason of the scale and effects of the proposed action, be better achieved by the Community.

Any action by the Community shall not go beyond what is necessary to achieve the objectives of this Treaty.

Subsidiarity and proportionality concern the proper *exercise* of the EC's powers, while the principle of conferred powers concerns the *existence* of powers. The former will be breached where the EC's powers are improperly or inappropriately exercised, whereas the principle of conferred powers will be breached where the EC purports to exercise a power that it does not possess. Article 5 EC pertains only to the EC. An analogous provision, Article 2 TEU, governs the second and third pillars.

### Article 2 TEU

The objectives of the Union shall be achieved as provided in this Treaty and in accordance with the conditions and the timetable set out therein while respecting the principle of subsidiarity as defined in Article 5 of the Treaty establishing the European Community.

These provisions are broadly reflective of the political philosophy of self-government. Article 1 TEU captures the idea by stating that decisions should be taken 'as closely as possible to the citizen'. Local decisions are, in principle, better than regional ones and national decisions are, likewise, better than international ones. This is because the closer to the people decisions are made, the more the people will be able to participate and the more responsive to the people's concerns the decisions will be.[52] The principles enshrined in Article 5 EC and Article 2 TEU can be seen as being intimately connected with the theory and practice of democracy. Similar principles are to be found in the German Basic Law, Article 72(2) of which provides as follows:

### German Basic Law 72(2)

In this field the [federal authorities] will have the right to legislate if federal legal regulation is needed:

(1) because a matter cannot be settled effectively by the legislation of the individual *Länder* [regions], or
(2) because the regulation of a matter by the law of a *Land* [region] could affect the interests of other *Länder* or the community as a whole, or
(3) to safeguard legal or economic unity, and in particular, to safeguard the homogeneity of the living conditions beyond the territory of a *Land*.

With this in mind, the ambit of EU law has to be considered not simply in terms of how far it encroaches upon *national* competences. Its impact on *regional* and *local* self-government must also be considered. Indeed, much of the anxiety about the extent of the European Union's powers has come in recent years from the German *Länder* (its regions) rather than from any state's central government.[53]

---

52 For discussion, see N. Barber, 'The Limited Modesty of Subsidiarity' (2005) 11 *ELJ* 308.
53 For the views of the *Länder* see A. v. Bogdandy and J. Bast, 'The European Union's Vertical Order of Competences: the Current Law and Proposals for its Reform' (2002) 39 *CML Rev.* 227 and G. de Búrca and B. de Witte, 'The Delimitation of Powers between the EU and its Member States' in A. Arnull and D. Wincott (eds.), *Accountability and Legitimacy in the European Union* (Oxford, Oxford University Press, 2002) ch. 12.

Article 5 EC suggests that there are three sorts of concern that must be met if self-government is to be preserved within the European Union. The first concerns the *extent* of EU legislation. The European Union should not be able to put political and legal demands over everything. There are some areas that are to be governed only within states. In such areas, national or regional authorities should be as free as possible to adopt the measures their constituents wish. This freedom is to be preserved by the European Union's competence being confined to specific tasks: such is the task of the doctrine of conferred powers. The second concern is with the *density* of EU law. Legislation might cover only a narrowly focussed field but, if it is extensive and exhaustive, it can squeeze out all other legislation in the field, with a consequent loss of possibility for local democracy within that field. That danger is confronted by the subsidiarity principle. The final danger for local democracy is where EU legislation is too *intrusive*. If it pervades every nook and cranny of daily life, individuals will not be free to escape its incessant demands. This danger is confronted by the proportionality principle. All EU actions and decisions must satisfy the requirements of proportionality: the principle applies not only to law-making but to all administrative decision-making in the European Union. As such, it is a 'general principle of law' that is central to the law of judicial review in the European Union. This is considered in detail in chapter 10. The remainder of this chapter is concerned with a detailed examination of the principles of conferred powers and subsidiarity.

### (i)   Principle of conferred powers

The principle of conferred powers expresses two complementary ideals. One is that of limited government: the European Union is to operate only in specific, confined fields. It has no general law-making power. The other is derived government: the European Union has only such powers as are assigned to it by the treaties. It is the treaties, rather than any other consideration, that ultimately determine what the EU can and cannot do.

The first pressure point on these ideals comes from the doctrine of implied powers. This holds that the European Union possesses not only those powers that are expressly granted to it by the treaties but also, implicitly, such further powers as are necessary to the achievement of its broader objectives. Article 140 EC, for example, empowers the Commission to 'encourage cooperation between the Member States and facilitate the coordination of their action in all social policy fields'. Under this Article, the Commission is specifically empowered to make studies on, to deliver opinions about and to arrange consultations on relevant common problems. In 1985, the Commission adopted a decision *requiring* Member States to inform it of draft measures they proposed to take in certain of these fields. A number of Member States claimed the decision was unlawful on the ground that under Article 140 the Commission had no power to adopt a binding act. The Court of Justice disagreed:

## Joined Cases 281, 283–5 and 287/85 *Germany and others v Commission* [1987] ECR 3203

27. . . . it must be considered whether the second paragraph of Article [140 EC], which provides that the Commission is to act, *inter alia*, by arranging consultations, gives it the power to adopt a binding decision with a view to the arrangement of such consultations.

28. In that connection it must be emphasized that where an Article of the EEC Treaty – in this case Article [140] – confers a specific task on the Commission it must be accepted, if that provision is not to be rendered wholly ineffective, that it confers on the Commission necessarily and *per se* the powers which are indispensable in order to carry out that task. Accordingly, the second paragraph of Article [140] must be interpreted as conferring on the Commission all the powers which are necessary in order to arrange the consultations. In order to perform that task of arranging consultations the Commission must necessarily be able to require the Member States to notify essential information, in the first place in order to identify the problems and in the second place in order to pinpoint the possible guidelines for any future joint action on the part of the Member States; likewise it must be able to require them to take part in consultations.

29. Indeed, the collaboration between Member States required by Article [140] is only possible within the framework of organized consultations. In the absence of any action to initiate it that collaboration might remain a dead letter, even though provision is made for it in the Treaty. Since the Commission was specifically given the task of promoting such collaboration and arranging it, it is entitled to initiate consultation procedures within the social field referred to in Article [140].

30. It must be borne in mind that that power of the Commission must be confined to arranging a procedure for the notification of information and consultation and that in the present stage of development of Community law the subject-matter of the notification and consultation falls within the competence of the Member States. It must also be pointed out that the power which the Commission seeks to exercise under Article [140] is simply a procedural one to set up the notification and consultation machinery which is to result in the adoption of a common position on the part of the Member States.

A further and more significant pressure point comes from the fact that the Treaties contain numerous examples of powers which have been expressly conferred upon the European Union, but in extraordinarily wide and undefined terms. Article 95 EC, for example, which has been of central importance in the making of the internal market, allows the EC to adopt measures for the approximation of national laws, which have as their object the 'establishment and functioning of the internal market'.[54] Similarly, Article 175 EC allows for an astonishingly broad array of measures to be adopted in the field of environmental protection. Article 13 EC allows measures to be taken to combat discrimination based on sex, racial or ethnic origin, religion or belief, disability, age, or sexual orientation 'within the limits of the powers conferred . . . upon the Community' (whatever that last phrase means). The most problematic of these provisions, however, is Article 308 EC.

---

54 This provision has generated considerable case law, which is considered at *EUL*, pp. 470–5.

## Article 308 EC

If action by the Community should prove necessary to attain, in the course of the operation of the common market, one of the objectives of the Community and this Treaty has not provided the necessary powers, the Council shall, acting unanimously on a proposal from the Commission and after consulting the European Parliament, take the appropriate measures.

The Court of Justice has interpreted this provision so broadly that it can be used to justify almost any legislation.

## J. Weiler, *The Constitution of Europe* (Cambridge, Cambridge University Press, 1999) 55, n. 120

Broadly speaking, two principal conditions must be fulfilled to invoke Article [308]. The measure must be 'necessary', in the course of the operation of the common market, to attain one of the objectives of the Treaty. In addition, Article [308] may be used when the Treaty does not provide the 'necessary' powers. The Court addressed both conditions liberally in the leading case of the early period, Case 8/73 *Haupzollamt Bremerhaven v Massey Ferguson* [1973] ECR 897 . . . Regarding the second, the Court was explicit. In an action for annulment of [a] regulation adopting . . . [a] Community customs-valuation regime, the Court had to decide whether reliance on Article [308] as an exclusive basis was justified. While acknowledging that a proper interpretation of the alternative legal bases in the EC Treaty . . . would provide an adequate legal basis, and thus, under a strict construction, render Article [308] not 'necessary', the Court, departing from an earlier statement, none the less considered that the Council's use of Article [308] would be 'justified in the interest of legal certainty' (at 908). Legally, this might have been an unfortunate formulation since an aura of uncertainty almost *ipso facto* attaches to a decision to make recourse to Article [308]. Politically, it must have been wise, for a more rigid interpretation could have thwarted the desire of the Member States, consonant with the Treaty objectives, to expand greatly the areas of activity of the Community, even if by the dubious use of Article [308] . . . Taking their cue from this case, Community institutions henceforth made liberal use of Article [308] without exhaustively considering whether other legal bases existed.

The generosity of the Court's approach to the expanded use of Article 308 has been considerable, but it has not been altogether unlimited. The Court reviewed its position in Opinion 2/94. The Council asked the Court whether the EC enjoyed the legal competence to accede to the European Convention on Human Rights.

## Opinion 2/94 *Accession to the ECHR* [1996] ECR I-1759

27. No Treaty provision confers on the Community institutions any general power to enact rules on human rights or to conclude international conventions in this field.

28. In the absence of express or implied powers for this purpose, it is necessary to consider whether Article [308] of the Treaty may constitute a legal basis for accession.

29. Article [308] is designed to fill the gap where no specific provisions of the Treaty confer on the Community institutions express or implied powers to act, if such powers appear none the less to be necessary to enable the Community to carry out its functions with a view to attaining one of the objectives laid down by the Treaty.

30. That provision, being an integral part of an institutional system based on the principle of conferred powers, cannot serve as a basis for widening the scope of Community powers beyond the general framework created by the provisions of the Treaty as a whole, and in particular, by those that define the tasks and the activities of the Community. On any view, Article [308] cannot be used as a basis for the adoption of provisions whose effect would, in substance, be to amend the Treaty without following the procedure which it provides for that purpose . . .

34. Respect for human rights is . . . a condition of the lawfulness of Community acts. Accession to the Convention would, however, entail a substantial change in the present Community system for the protection of human rights in that it would entail the entry of the Community into a distinct international institutional system as well as integration of all the provisions of the Convention into the Community legal order.

35. Such a modification of the system for the protection of human rights in the Community, with equally fundamental institutional implications for the Community and for the Member States, would be of constitutional significance and would therefore be such as to go beyond the scope of Article [308]. It could be brought about only by way of Treaty amendment.

The European Union's political institutions have been happy to exploit the leeway given to them by Article 308 EC and have used it to adopt a very wide array of measures.

### J. Weiler, *The Constitution of Europe* (Cambridge, Cambridge University Press, 1999) 39–40, 42–3, 53–6

In most federal polities the demarcation of competences between the general polity and its constituent units is the most explosive of 'federal' battlegrounds. Traditionally, the relationship in non-unitary systems is conceptualised by the principle of enumerated powers. The principle has no fixed content and its interpretation varies from system to system; in some it has a stricter and in others a more relaxed construction. Typically, the strength by which this principle is upheld (or, at least, the shrillness of the rhetoric surrounding it) reflects the strength of the belief in the importance of preserving the original distribution of legislative powers as a defining feature of the polity . . .

In the 1970s and early 1980s, the principle of enumerated powers as a constraint on Community *material* jurisdiction (absent Treaty revision) was substantially eroded and in practice virtually disappeared. Constitutionally, no core of sovereign state powers was left beyond the reach of the Community . . .

In the period from 1958 to 1973, Article [308] was used by Community institutions relatively infrequently and, when used, was usually narrowly construed. Under the restrictive view, shared by all interpretative communities at the time, the function of Article [308] was to compensate *within an area of activity explicitly granted by the Treaty* for the absence of an explicit grant of legal power to act . . .

> [F]rom 1973 until the entry into force of the Single European Act, there was not only a very dramatic quantitative increase in the recourse to Article [308], but also a no less dramatic understanding of its qualitative scope. In a variety of fields, including for example, conclusion of international agreements, the granting of emergency food aid to third countries, and creation of new institutions, the Community made use of Article [308] in a manner that was simply not consistent with the narrow interpretation of the Article as a codification of the implied-powers doctrine in its instrumental sense. Only a truly radical and 'creative' reading of the Article could explain and justify its usage as, for example the legal basis for granting emergency food aid to non-associated states. But this wide reading, in which all political institutions partook, meant that it would become virtually impossible to find an activity which could not be brought within the 'objectives of the Treaty' . . .
>
> There is no single event, no landmark case, that could be called the focal point of the mutation . . . Instead, there was a slow change of climate and ethos whereby strict enumeration was progressively, relentlessly, but never dramatically, eroded.

To put a figure on just how 'relentless' the erosion has been, de Búrca and de Witte reported, in 2002, that Article 308 EC had, by that date, served as the legal basis for about 700 EC legal acts.[55] This has caused considerable political concern. In the debate prior to the Treaty of Amsterdam, for example, the German *Länder* expressed strong reservations about the manner in which Article 308 EC had generated a persistent 'competence creep' on the part of the European Union. They suggested that the lists of woolly and broadly worded objectives contained in Articles 2 to 3 EC and Article 2 TEU should be replaced with new lists of specific and precisely enumerated competences.[56] These demands became more shrill at the negotiations leading to the Treaty of Nice, a treaty which the *Länder* said they would not be inclined to ratify unless the competence issue was placed on the agenda for the 2004 IGC. When the European Council met at Laeken in December 2001, it accepted that 'a better division and definition of competence' was required for the European Union. Accordingly, it made the reorganisation of the European Union's competences a key task for the Convention on the Future of Europe.[57]

## European Council, Laeken Declaration on the Future of the European Union (2001)

A first series of questions that needs to be put concerns how the division of competence can be made more transparent. Can we thus make a clearer distinction between three types of competence: the exclusive competence of the Union, the competence of the Member States

55 de Búrca and de Witte, above n. 53, 217.
56 See *Forderungen der Länder zur Regierungskonferenz 1996*, Drucksache 667/95 (Beschluß), 15 December 1995, 12–21.
57 See F. Mayer, *Competences – Reloaded? The Vertical Division of Powers in the EU after the New European Constitution*, Jean Monnet Working Paper 05/04 and U. Di Fabio, 'Some Remarks on the Allocation of Competences between the European Union and its Member States' (2002) 39 *CML Rev.* 1289.

and the shared competence of the Union and the Member States? At what level is competence exercised in the most efficient way? . . . And should we not make it clear that any powers not assigned by the Treaties to the Union fall within the exclusive competence of the Member States? . . .

The next series of questions should aim . . . to determine whether there needs to be any reorganisation of competence . . .

Lastly, there is the question of how to ensure that a redefined division of competence does not lead to a creeping expansion of the competence of the Union or to encroachment upon the exclusive areas of competence of the Member States and, where there is provision for this, regions. How are we to ensure at the same time that the European dynamic does not come to a halt? In the future as well the Union must continue to be able to react to fresh challenges and developments and must be able to explore new policy areas. Should Articles 95 and 308 of the Treaty be reviewed for this purpose?

The central response of the Convention was to write into Part I of its Draft Constitutional Treaty a catalogue of the European Union's competences. In the Constitutional Treaty subsequently agreed by the European Council, the main provisions were as follows.[58]

## Article I-11 CT

1. The limits of Union competences are governed by the principle of conferral. The use of Union competences is governed by the principles of subsidiarity and proportionality.

2. Under the principle of conferral, the Union shall act within the limits of the competences conferred upon it by the Member States in the Constitution to attain the objectives set out in the Constitution. Competences not conferred upon the Union in the Constitution remain with the Member States.

## Article I-12 CT

1. When the Constitution confers on the Union exclusive competence in a specific area, only the Union may legislate and adopt legally binding acts, the Member States being able to do so themselves only if so empowered by the Union or for the implementation of Union acts.

2. When the Constitution confers on the Union a competence shared with the Member States in a specific area, the Union and the Member States may legislate and adopt legally binding acts in that area. The Member States shall exercise their competence to the extent that the Union has not exercised, or has decided to cease exercising, its competence.

3. The Member States shall coordinate their economic and employment policies within arrangements as determined by Part III, which the Union shall have competence to provide.

4. The Union shall have competence to define and implement a common foreign and security policy, including the progressive framing of a common defence policy.

---

58  See S. Weatherill, 'Competence Creep and Competence Control' (2004) 23 *YEL* 1 and P. Craig, 'Competence: Clarity, Conferral, Containment and Consideration' (2004) 29 *EL Rev.* 323. The subsequent provisions, Articles I-13 to I-17 CT, catalogued the substantive policy areas in which the European Union enjoyed each of its forms of competence. These reflected existing understandings of the different forms of competence, as described above.

5. In certain areas and under the conditions laid down in the Constitution, the Union shall have competence to carry out actions to support, coordinate or supplement the actions of the Member States, without thereby superseding their competence in these areas. Legally binding acts of the Union adopted on the basis of the provisions in Part III relating to these areas shall not entail harmonisation of Member States' laws or regulations.

6. The scope of and arrangements for exercising the Union's competences shall be determined by the provisions relating to each area in Part III.

It is to be noted that the provisions of the Constitutional Treaty did not include a list of competences that were to be ring-fenced as matters for the Member States. There was just a general commitment on the part of the European Union to 'respect' the 'essential functions' of the nation-state.

## Article I-5 CT

The Union shall respect the equality of Member States before the Constitution as well as their national identities, inherent in their fundamental structures, political and constitutional, inclusive of regional and local self-government. It shall respect their essential State functions, including ensuring the territorial integrity of the State, maintaining law and order and safeguarding national security.

Even if the Constitutional Treaty were to be ratified, this provision appears to be too open-ended to be much of an obstacle to competence creep. It is not clear, for example, that it could be used as a basis for judicial review. Indeed, it is unlikely that the Constitutional Treaty would have done much to prevent further competence creep. Article 308 EC was retained in the form of Article I-18 CT, its so-called 'flexibility clause'.[59] There is nothing to suggest that the old problems of Article 308 would not have continued.[60] More broadly, it does not appear that the catalogue of competences contained in the Constitutional Treaty would have applied to soft law, such as the open method of coordination, or to the judgments of the Court of Justice.

Notwithstanding the fact that the focus in recent years has been on attempting to catalogue or, more precisely, to enumerate the European Union's competences, it is to be doubted that such a strategy would of itself ever be sufficient to arrest the onward creep of the European Union's powers. Mayer has suggested, for example, that more valuable than even a well-drafted and thorough catalogue of competences is a sensitivity on the part of the different levels of government to the interests and priorities of each other.[61] Others have argued that it is not constitutional text that we should look to in attempting to demarcate EU competence from what is left for

---

59 Article 95 EC likewise made its way into the Constitutional Treaty, as Article III-172.
60 There would have been one small difference: under Article I-18(3) the European Union would have been barred from using the flexibility clause in fields where it has competence only to support, coordinate or supplement the actions of the Member States.
61 See Mayer, above n. 57.

Member States, but process. This is reminiscent of Weiler's observation about the paradox of sovereignty in the European Union: that the hierarchy of norms which gives primacy to EU law does not reflect the hierarchy of what he calls 'real power' in the European Union, in respect of which the Member States remain at the top.[62] In an important contribution by one of the USA's leading scholars of federalism, Ernest Young has suggested that, if the American experience is anything to go by, the strategies recently adopted in the European Union to attempt to stop its competence creep might not be the most effective ones. Young has particular doubts over the likely effectiveness of attempting more precisely to catalogue the European Union's competences. 'While a meaningful federalism jurisprudence probably cannot afford to ignore substantive limits on central power altogether', he suggests, 'substantive limits . . . are exceedingly difficult for courts to define and enforce in a way that convincingly maintains the distinction between judging and policy-making'.[63] Courts in the USA, he reports, have struggled to confine Congress to its constitutionally 'enumerated powers', just as the Court of Justice has struggled to restrict competence creep in the European Union. 'True protection for state autonomy must be sought elsewhere', he insists.[64]

Rather than place our faith in tightly drawn catalogues of competence or lists of enumerated powers, Young urges us to rely on techniques of *process* to seek more effective limits to the centralisation of law-making. In the USA, in his analysis, the key ingredient in the protection of the various states against the legislative powers of the national government is the extreme difficulty of the process of passing federal law. Obtaining the agreement of the President and of sufficient numbers of Senators and Congressmen is, most of the time, far from straightforward. The most effective curb on excessive national law-making in the USA lies in the simple fact that national law-making is normally so very hard to do. In the European Union, he suggests, the most effective check on excessive law-making may well lie in the fact that the vast bulk of EU law is administered, not by a European executive bureaucracy, but by national and regional authorities within Member States.[65]

---

**E. Young, 'Protecting Member State Autonomy in the European Union: Some Cautionary Tales from American Federalism' (2002) 77 *New York University Law Review* 1612, 1736**

The separation and allocation of powers and functions within the central government has profound implications for federalism. If political safeguards for federalism are to function, then law-making at the central authority must be channelled through the particular institutions of

---

62  See above, text at n. 6.

63  E. Young, 'Protecting Member State Autonomy in the European Union: Some Cautionary Tales from American Federalism' (2002) 77 *NYU L Rev.* 1612, 1736.

64  *Ibid.* 1676.

65  As George Bermann has suggested, 'the real institutional safeguard . . . in the Community is that, in most areas, the implementation of Community policy ultimately lies in the hands of Member States and local officials'. See G. Bermann, 'Taking Subsidiarity Seriously: Federalism in the European Community and the United States' (1994) 94 *Colum. L Rev.* 331, 399 (cited by Young, above n. 63, at 1708).

> that authority in which the . . . Member States are represented. Division of powers also checks central authority simply by multiplying the barriers to central law-making and enhancing the force of legislative inertia; where [in a field of shared competence Europe] fails to act, after all, the field is left open to regulation by the [Member States] . . .
>
> [Further], there are distinct advantages to being a 'complete' government – that is, one with its own enforcement powers, resource base, and convincing claims to democratic legitimacy. To the extent that the Community lacks these things, it is unlikely to be a successful competitor to Member State governments for the loyalties of the people. Conversely, solutions to such problems as a democratic deficit or a lack of resources at the Community level may give rise to new problems of State autonomy. In some ways, the better the Community institutions work on their own, the more trouble the Member States will find themselves in.

The message that commentators such as Weiler and Young are seeking to convey is that, no matter how counter-intuitive it may be to lawyers, we should worry rather less about judicial statements of sovereignty and written catalogues of competence (even when they are written into the text of a constitution) and focus rather more on the vast extent to which the European Union, no matter what its powers are on paper, continues to rely on the Member States to make, to implement, to give effect to and even to enforce its laws and on the substantial room for manoeuvre which Member States continue to enjoy in seeking to avoid such consequences of EU law as they perceive to be undesirable.

### (ii)   Principle of subsidiarity

Whereas the principle of conferred powers was contained in the original Treaty of Rome, subsidiarity was inserted as a general principle only at Maastricht. This is not to say, however, that there were no suggestions before 1991 that subsidiarity ought to be a principle of Community law. Indeed, the idea goes back as far as the mid-1970s.[66] As we saw above, the potential threat to self-government may come not only from the European Union having too many powers, but also from the possibility that it might legislate too sweepingly *within* its established fields of competence. Pressure for the principle of subsidiarity to be applied more stringently has tended to increase when the pace of EU legislative activity has picked up. In the 1980s, for example, the EC began to legislate intensively in the field of environmental protection so that, by the late 1980s, there was a considerable body of EC environmental legislation in force. This led to the first explicit recognition of the subsidiarity principle in the treaties: the new Title on the Environment introduced by the Single European Act provided that the EC was to legislate on the environment only insofar as environmental objectives could be better attained at Community level than at the level of the Member States.[67]

The end of the 1980s – the period preceding and following the entry into force of the SEA – witnessed explosive growth in the quantity of European legislation. Estimates vary, but all agree that the pace of legislative activity at least trebled between 1984 and

---

66 See the *Tindemans Report on European Union*, Supplement 1/76, Bull. EC.      67 Article 130r(4) EEC.

1992. Fligstein and McNichol estimate that just under 400 binding acts were adopted in 1984, while nearly 2,500 were adopted in 1992.[68] Estella, more conservatively, estimates that 254 binding acts were adopted in 1984 and 752 in 1992.[69] Whatever the true figures, it is clear that the increase was not merely sudden, but also dramatic. By the time of Maastricht, EC legislation accounted for a significant proportion of the legislation in force in any Member State. Studies found, for example, that 53 per cent of the legislative measures adopted in France in 1991 were EC-inspired and that 30 per cent of Dutch legislation adopted that year was passed in order to implement EC Directives.[70]

As we saw above, what is now Article 5(2) EC, introduced at Maastricht, provides that 'in areas which do not fall within its exclusive competence, the Community shall take action, in accordance with the principle of subsidiarity, only if and insofar as the objectives of the proposed action cannot be sufficiently achieved by the Member States and can therefore, by reason of the scale and effects of the proposed action, be better achieved by the Community'. It is important to recognise that there are two limitations inherent in this wording. First, the principle of subsidiarity in Article 5 regulates only the relationship between the EC and the Member States. It says nothing about any other units of power – in particular it says nothing about regions within Member States (Scotland, for example, or Catalonia or the German *Länder*). Neither the relationship between the EC and sub-national regions nor the relationship between Member States and sub-national regions is governed, in Community law, by the principle of subsidiarity. Secondly, Article 5 makes plain that subsidiarity is not a *universal* principle that always governs the relationship between the EC and the Member States. Rather, it applies only to areas that do not fall within the EC's 'exclusive competence'. One of the problems with evaluating the impact of subsidiarity has been that, at least prior to the Constitutional Treaty,[71] there was no authoritative list of what falls within the EC's exclusive competence and what falls within the competence that is 'shared' between the EC and the Member States.[72] This issue was explored above.[73]

### (a)   Subsidiarity and judicial review

Although the principle of subsidiarity can be invoked before the Court of Justice as the basis for the striking down of EC legislation, the Court has been persistently reluctant to second-guess the political institutions on this question. It has yet to annul a measure

---

68  N. Fligstein and J. McNichol, 'The Institutional Terrain of the European Union' in W. Sandholtz and A. Stone Sweet (eds.), *European Integration and Supranational Governance* (Oxford, Oxford University Press, 1998) 76.

69  A. Estella, *The EU Principle of Subsidiarity and its Critique* (Oxford, Oxford University Press, 2002) 20.

70  See G. Mancini, 'Europe: the Case for Statehood' (1998) 4 *ELJ* 29, 40.

71  See Article I-13 CT, considered above.

72  See G. de Búrca, *Reappraising Subsidiarity's Significance after Amsterdam*, Jean Monnet Working Paper 7/99.

73  See pp. 188–90.

for breach of the principle of subsidiarity. An illustration of the lightness of its touch is found in the judgment below, which concerns a Directive that required Member States to ensure that biotechnological inventions were protected by patents.[74] Bear in mind when considering this case that Article 295 EC stipulates that nothing in the EC Treaty should prejudice national rules governing the system of property ownership.

---

### Case C-377/98 *Netherlands v European Parliament and Council* ('Biotechnology Directive') [2001] ECR I-7079

1. . . . the Netherlands brought an action under Article [230] EC for annulment of Directive 98/44/EC of the European Parliament and of the Council of 6 July 1998 on the legal protection of biotechnological inventions . . .

2. The Directive was adopted on the basis of Article [95] EC, and its purpose is to require the Member States, through their patent laws, to protect biotechnological inventions, whilst complying with their international obligations.

3. To that end the Directive determines inter alia which inventions involving plants, animals or the human body may or may not be patented . . .

30. The applicant submits that the Directive breaches the principle of subsidiarity laid down by Article [5] EC and, in the alternative, that it does not state sufficient reasons to establish that this requirement was taken into account . . .

32. The objective pursued by the Directive, to ensure smooth operation of the internal market by preventing or eliminating differences between the legislation and practice of the various Member States in the area of the protection of biotechnological inventions, could not be achieved by action taken by the Member States alone. As the scope of that protection has immediate effects on trade, and, accordingly, on intra-Community trade, it is clear that, given the scale and effects of the proposed action, the objective in question could be better achieved by the Community.

33. Compliance with the principle of subsidiarity is necessarily implicit in the fifth, sixth and seventh recitals of the Preamble to the Directive, which state that, in the absence of action at Community level, the development of the laws and practices of the different Member States impedes the proper functioning of the internal market. It thus appears that the Directive states sufficient reasons on that point.

---

The difficulties in applying the principle of subsidiarity stem, in part, from the inherent limits of judicial review. For the Court of Justice to strike down a measure under Article 5(2) EC, it would have to come to a different conclusion on the need for that measure from the view already taken by the Commission, the European Parliament and the Council. At such a late stage in the process, after all three political institutions had indicated their support for a measure, it would be difficult for the Court to tell them that they were all wrong. Commentators have, therefore, suggested a variety of institutional innovations to compensate for this. Weiler, for example, has argued for the creation a European Constitutional Court, presided over

---

74 See to similar effect Case C-491/01 *R v Secretary of State for Health ex parte British American Tobacco* [2002] ECR I-11453, paras. 181–3 and Joined Cases C-154/04 and C-155/04 *R v Secretary of State for Health ex parte Alliance for Natural Health*, judgment of 12 July 2005, paras. 99–108.

by the President of the European Court of Justice and comprising judges drawn from the constitutional courts or their equivalents in the various Member States.[75] He considers that only a body comprising the most senior judges in the European Union would have the authority and confidence to police the limits of Community powers. Others think the task should not be in the hands of judges. In 1994, the then British Commissioner, Leon Brittan, proposed the creation of a chamber of national parliamentarians who would vet the European Union's legislative proposals on grounds of subsidiarity before they became law.[76] This proposal was repeated, without success, by Tony Blair in 2000, when he proposed creating a second chamber of the European Parliament that would be composed of national parliamentarians.[77]

A further difficulty for the Court of Justice lies in the internal contradictions within the principle itself. The standard of review was set out in more detail by the Treaty of Amsterdam.

### Protocol on Subsidiarity and Proportionality (1997)[78]

5. For Community action to be justified, both aspects of the subsidiarity principle shall be met: the objectives of the proposed action cannot be sufficiently achieved by Member States' action in the framework of their national constitutional system and can therefore be better achieved by action on the part of the Community.

The following guidelines should be used in examining whether the above-mentioned condition is fulfilled:

– the issue under consideration has transnational aspects which cannot be satisfactorily regulated by action by Member States;
– actions by Member States alone or lack of Community action would conflict with the requirements of the Treaty (such as the need to correct distortion of competition or avoid disguised restrictions on trade or strengthen economic and social cohesion) or would otherwise significantly damage Member States' interests;
– action at Community level would produce clear benefits by reason of its scale or effects compared with action at the level of the Member States . . .

7. Regarding the nature and the extent of Community action, Community measures should leave as much scope for national decision as possible, consistent with securing the aim of the measure and observing the requirements of the Treaty. While respecting Community law, care should be taken to respect well established national arrangements and the organisation and working of Member States' legal systems. Where appropriate and subject to the need for proper enforcement, Community measures should provide Member States with alternative ways to achieve the objectives of the measures.

---

75 J. Weiler, 'The European Union Belongs to its Citizens: Three Immodest Proposals' (1997) 22 *EL Rev.* 150, 155–6.
76 L. Brittan, *The Europe We Need* (London, 1994).
77 Speech to the Polish Stock Exchange, 6 October 2000; see www.number-10.gov.uk/output/Page3384.asp
78 Protocol 30 annexed by the Treaty of Amsterdam to the EC Treaty.

The trouble with subsidiarity is that its two constituent tests are difficult to reconcile. The first test, that the objectives of the proposed action cannot be sufficiently achieved by Member States' action, is a test of local self-government. The British decision to drive on the left-hand side of the road is concerned to ensure road safety, but is also an expression of quirky Britishness. Left is chosen rather than right because that is the tradition within the United Kingdom and this tradition asserts British distinctiveness. The second test, that a measure can be better achieved by Community action, is a test of comparative efficiency. It looks at the efficiency gains that may be made from having a single Community law. In the example above, arguments could be made that Community legislation would allow a more integrated car industry, as the design and manufacture of cars would not have to be adjusted for the different national markets, and might lead to road safety gains, as there would be no problems with drivers having to adjust to driving on the other side of the road when they crossed borders. The logic of each test slides past the other. Scharpf has talked, therefore, of the subsidiarity principle putting in place a bipolar constitutional logic.[79] Judicial review must look equally to the concerns of central government (the European Union) and of local government (the Member States). The aim is not for the one to displace the other, but to secure mutual compatibility. To come down one way or the other is exceptionally difficult to do in individual cases. This is particularly so in the European Union, perhaps, as EU law contains no explicit specification of reserved national or regional interests that can be weighed against those of the EC.

The Court of Justice has an additional function in the context of subsidiarity. De Búrca has suggested that one of the 'significant legal functions' of subsidiarity is what she calls 'the imposition of a certain onus of justification – a kind of public reason requirement – on the various EU institutions when they act'.[80] Paragraph 4 of the Amsterdam Protocol on Subsidiarity and Proportionality provides as follows:

> For any proposed Community legislation, the reasons on which it is based shall be stated with a view to justifying its compliance with the principles of subsidiarity and proportionality; the reasons for concluding that a Community objective can be better achieved by the Community must be substantiated by qualitative or, wherever possible, quantitative indicators.

The quality of the justification provided by the political institutions – whether the reasons given are consistent, properly considered and accurately reflected the legal text – is something the Court of Justice ought to be able relatively easily to monitor. Crucial, however, is the extent to which the Court has the will to examine the detail of the reasons offered by the political institutions. In the case below, Germany argued that the Deposit Guarantee Directive should be annulled because the explanation

---

79 F. Scharpf, 'Community and Autonomy: Multi-level Policy Making in the European Union' (1994) 1 *JEPP* 219, 225–6.
80 de Búrca, above n. 72.

given that it satisfied the requirement of subsidiarity was cursory. The Court did not accept Germany's arguments and the Directive survived.

> ### Case C-233/94 *Germany v European Parliament and Council* ('Deposit Guarantee Directive') [1997] ECR I-2405
>
> 22. The German Government claims that the Directive must be annulled because it fails to state the reasons on which it is based . . . It does not explain how it is compatible with the principle of subsidiarity . . .
> 23. As to the precise terms of the obligation to state reasons in the light of the principle of subsidiarity, the German Government states that the Community institutions must give detailed reasons to explain why only the Community, to the exclusion of the Member States, is empowered to act in the area in question. In the present case, the Directive does not indicate in what respect its objectives could not have been sufficiently attained by action at Member State level or the grounds which militated in favour of Community action . . .
> 26. In the present case, the Parliament and the Council stated in the second recital in the Preamble to the Directive that 'consideration should be given to the situation which might arise if deposits in a credit institution that has branches in other Member States became unavailable' and that it was 'indispensable to ensure a harmonized minimum level of deposit protection wherever deposits are located in the Community'. This shows that, in the Community legislature's view, the aim of its action could, because of the dimensions of the intended action, be best achieved at Community level. The same reasoning appears in the third recital, from which it is clear that the decision regarding the guarantee scheme which is competent in the event of the insolvency of a branch situated in a Member State other than that in which the credit institution has its head office has repercussions which are felt outside the borders of each Member State.
> 27. Furthermore, in the fifth recital the Parliament and the Council stated that the action taken by the Member States in response to [a] Commission Recommendation has not fully achieved the desired result. The Community legislature therefore found that the objective of its action could not be achieved sufficiently by the Member States.
> 28. Consequently, it is apparent that, on any view, the Parliament and the Council did explain why they considered that their action was in conformity with the principle of subsidiarity and, accordingly, that they complied with the obligation to give reasons . . . An express reference to that principle cannot be required.

The Court's treatment of subsidiarity-based arguments has been perfunctory. In substantive terms, as the *Biotechnology Directive* judgment illustrates, it seems, that all the institutions have to do to show that a measure complies with the principle of subsidiarity is to demonstrate that an EU competence to legislate exists. While this may be understandable, the Court's failure to take seriously Germany's arguments in the *Deposit Guarantee Directive* judgment is more worrying. That case suggests that the procedural requirements will be held to have been complied with even where there is no evidence to suppose that the institutions actually considered whether the measure satisfied the principle of subsidiarity and notwithstanding the fact that no part of the measure in question specifically refers to it. As Dashwood has concluded, the Court has shown that 'while the justiciability of the principle cannot any longer be doubted, the case law indicates equally clearly that annulment of a measure on the ground that it offends against subsidiarity is likely to occur only in extreme circumstances'.[81]

### (b)   Subsidiarity: changing the European Union's legislative culture?

It is not only the Court of Justice that has responsibility under the Treaties for policing subsidiarity. Political institutions, too, are under a legal obligation to consider their legislative proposals in its light. Indeed, to the extent that subsidiarity has force as a principle within EU law, it is to be found less in the case law of judicial review and more in the law-making process, as the Commission, the European Parliament and the Council negotiate the positions that European measures should adopt. To that end, the Commission is required to publish an annual report on the application of the principle in the law-making process.[82] These reports demonstrate that the Commission considers subsidiarity to have had a significant effect on European law-making.[83] In its 2003 Report, for example, it noted that Commission proposals for legislative acts declined in number from 787 in 1990 to 371 in 2002. However, bald figures such as these are not especially informative. Surges in legislative activity can occur because the EC is allocated a mandate to carry out a programme, such as completion of the single market, over a particular time-frame. They do not tell one whether the EC is generally inclined to legislate less or not. Thus, no reason is given as to why 371 proposals were made in 2002 while 'only' 316 were made in 2001.[84] Such statistics also reveal little about the *type* and *intrusiveness* of the legislation being adopted. More instructive are the case studies summarised in some of the reports, as they disclose something of the way in which the Commission understands and seeks to apply the principle of subsidiarity. The following extracts give a flavour of its approach.

---

### European Commission, *Better Lawmaking 2002*, COM(2002)715

*Safety of transport*. Following the attacks which occurred on 11 September 2001 in the United States, there was felt to be a need to further reinforce the safety of citizens, particularly in the field of air transport. The Commission has identified a major risk in this area associated with

---

81 A. Dashwood, 'The Relationship between the Member States and the European Union/European Community' (2004) 41 *CML Rev.* 355, 368.

82 Amsterdam Protocol on Subsidiarity and Proportionality (1997), para. 9.

83 This view is shared by a number of national governments: see e.g. the study by the German government quoted in A. Verges Bausili, *Rethinking the Methods of Dividing and Exercising Powers in the EU: Reforming Subsidiarity and National Parliaments*, Jean Monnet Working Paper 09/02, n. 23. A similar view is held by the British government: see House of Lords European Union Committee, *Strengthening National Parliamentary Scrutiny of the EU: the Constitution's Subsidiarity Early Warning Mechanism* (Session 2004–05, 14th Report) para. 80.

84 European Commission, *Better Lawmaking 2003*, COM(2003)770, 31.

deficiencies in Member States' procedures with regard to carriers from third countries. Not all the Member States actually subject them to the same checks, creating a risk to the safety of passengers and a distortion of competition, with certain carriers being able to decide to use certain airports rather than others because of the less stringent regulations. After receiving the opinion of the High Level Group of aviation safety experts, therefore, the Commission proposed a European Parliament and Council Directive on the safety of third countries' aircraft using Community airports in order that on-the-ground inspections, in particular, be[ing] carried out by some Member States on non-Community aircraft be extended to the whole of the Community.

In order to achieve the proposal's objective most effectively, the Commission had to define the appropriate legislative instrument in the light of the recommendations made in the Protocol [see Article 6]. The Commission proposal sets out general objectives and procedures to guarantee harmonisation, but leaves the responsibility for transposing monitoring principles and structures, based on detailed common standards, up to the Member States. The choice of framework directive was therefore ruled out in favour of a directive and in the explanatory memorandum, the Commission explains why it is impossible to use a framework directive.

*Sustainable development and development co-operation.* Sustainable development is a concept which cuts across several areas, including the environment. The proposal for a European Parliament and Council Directive on environmental liability applies the principle that the polluter should pay . . . This proposal establishes a framework for the prevention and remedying of environmental damage. It was felt necessary to take action at Community level because of the existence of contaminated sites, water pollution and damage to biodiversity, and because not all the Member States have set up a liability system for environmental damage. The aim is to ensure that in the future those who contaminate clean up the damage or bear the costs . . . In the absence of a common legislative framework, economic operators could exploit the difference between the Member States to escape liability . . .

The concept of sustainable development is also included in the Commission's legislative initiatives in the field of transport and energy, in particular in the *oil and gas stocks package*, the main aim of which is to safeguard the security of energy supply. The Commission decided to make legislative proposals in this field for several reasons: inadequate harmonisation and co-ordination of national legislation at Community level may lead to distortions in the internal market for petroleum products; in addition, it is necessary to accompany the opening up of the internal market for energy with measures which will guarantee the security of supplies and, finally, to define a new framework for energy programmes associated with a European strategy for sustainable development.

Community action was felt to be necessary, given that the issues raised clearly have transnational aspects and action taken by the Member States seems insufficient on the basis of the present lack of co-ordination.

The 2002 Report also summarised the Commission's view of the way in which the European Parliament and the Council had sought that year to apply the principles of subsidiarity and proportionality:

> As the representative of the Member States and guarantor of their powers, the Council takes particular care to ensure respect of the principles of subsidiarity and proportionality in the Commission's legislative proposals. The discussions within the Council are evidence of this. Now and then they illustrate the diversity of appraisal of these principles between the national delegations and between

the delegations and the Commission. Far from hampering the decision-making process, these discussions on the contrary more often than not help to establish a satisfactory balance with regard to these principles, respecting the prerogatives of each of the institutions.

Thus, the proposal for a Directive . . . relating to the compulsory use of safety belts was discussed several times within the Council . . . During the discussions, some said that the directive was too prescriptive and did not respect the principle of subsidiarity and that legislation on the subject should remain within the competence of the Member States, and that the Community should restrict itself to adopting framework legislation laying down general principles. This position . . . which was reaffirmed on many occasions, was always challenged by the Commission. The Council finally accepted the Commission's approach, recognising, as the Commission claimed, that road safety had an indisputable transnational impact, given the very high mobility in this sector, and that, furthermore, in order to guarantee a uniform level of protection, Community action was more relevant than action by the Member States. This important, legitimate discussion within the Council did not prevent a unanimous political agreement from being reached on this subject with a view to formal adoption of the directive . . .

While the European Parliament also closely examines whether or not the principles of subsidiarity and proportionality are respected in the Commission's proposals, its approach differs from that of the Council and is geared more towards preserving the Community's powers . . . Here too, inter-institutional dialogue makes it possible to find a balanced solution in most cases.

As the above extracts demonstrate, the Commission considers itself to be somewhere in the middle between the Parliament's pushing for more European regulation and the Council's pulling back for less. This is somewhat misleading. As we saw in chapter 3, few of the Commission's legislative proposals are concocted by it alone. A 2001 study found, for example, that about 80 per cent originated from the Council or from a Member State.[85] The Commission's reports vary widely in quality. The 2004 Report is both glib and thin, amounting to a mere five-and-a-half pages. The reports for 2002 and 2003 are considerably better.[86] Not only are they longer (twenty-two and forty-one pages, respectively), they are also more detailed in their analysis of the strengths and limitations of the way in which subsidiarity has operated as a constraint on EC law-making. Even in the most comprehensive of its reports, however, the Commission discusses only a fraction of the legislative proposals that have been considered in any one year. It is particularly disturbing that the *quality* of the 'public reason' offered in justification for European legislation is generally

85  See G. Grevi, *Beyond the Delimitation of Competences: Implementing Subsidiarity* (Brussels, European Policy Centre, 2001).
86  See *Better Lawmaking 2002*, COM(2002)715; *Better Lawmaking 2003*, COM(2003)770; *Better Lawmaking 2004*, COM(2005)98.

extremely weak. The Commission does no better on this front than does the Court of Justice.

### (c)   Subsidiarity and process: national parliaments as guardians of EU law-making

The policing of subsidiarity would have been substantially amended by the Constitutional Treaty, had it come into force. The Treaty included a new Protocol on the Application of the Principles of Subsidiarity and Proportionality, the central innovation of which was the establishment of an 'Early Warning Mechanism' whereby national parliaments could ask the Commission to rethink measures they believed to be in breach of subsidiarity.[87]

---

**Constitutional Treaty, Protocol 2**

5. Draft European legislative acts shall be justified with regard to the principles of subsidiarity and proportionality. Any draft European legislative act should contain a detailed statement making it possible to appraise compliance with the principles of subsidiarity and proportionality . . . The reasons for concluding that a Union objective can be better achieved at Union level shall be substantiated by qualitative and, wherever possible, quantitative indicators . . .

6. Any national parliament or any chamber of a national parliament may, within six weeks from the date of transmission of a draft European legislative act, send to the Presidents of the European Parliament, the Council and the Commission a reasoned opinion stating why it considers that the draft in question does not comply with the principle of subsidiarity. It will be for each national parliament or each chamber of a national parliament to consult, where appropriate, regional parliaments with legislative powers . . .

7. The European Parliament, the Council and the Commission . . . shall take account of the reasoned opinions issued by national parliaments or by a chamber of a national parliament. Each national parliament shall have two votes, shared out on the basis of the national parliamentary system. In the case of a bicameral parliamentary system, each of the two chambers shall have one vote. Where reasoned opinions on a draft European legislative act's non-compliance with the principle of subsidiarity represent at least one-third of all the votes allocated to the national parliaments . . . the draft must be reviewed. This threshold shall be a quarter in the case of a draft European legislative act submitted on the basis of Article III-264 of the Constitution on the area of freedom, security and justice . . . After such review . . . [the institutions] may decide to maintain, amend or withdraw the draft. Reasons must be given for this decision.

8. The Court of Justice of the European Union shall have jurisdiction in actions on grounds of infringement of the principle of subsidiarity by a European legislative act, brought . . . by Member States, or notified by them in accordance with their legal order on behalf of their national parliament or a chamber of it.

---

In addition to this Early Warning Mechanism, the position of national parliaments to monitor subsidiarity was strengthened in two further ways. The annual report

---

87 For commentary, see N. Barber, 'Subsidiarity in the Draft Constitution' (2005) 11 *EPL* 197.

prepared by the Commission on the application of the subsidiarity principle would also have been required to be sent to national parliaments[88] and national parliaments would have been given extra powers in certain areas considered to be particularly sensitive. They were to be informed whenever Article I-18, the replacement for Article 308 EC, was used as a legal base[89] and they were to be involved, alongside the European Parliament, in the evaluation of the EU bodies responsible for cooperation in policing and combating criminality – EUROPOL and Eurojust.[90] The Protocol made it clear that the policing of subsidiarity by national parliaments was to be in addition to, and not a replacement for, its monitoring by the Commission, the Council and the European Parliament and its enforcement by the Court of Justice.[91]

The reforms were a welcome recognition that neither the European Union's political institutions nor the Court of Justice have been able to perform the task of monitoring subsidiarity adequately. Although the Constitutional Treaty has not been ratified, there is a good chance that these reforms may nonetheless be implemented, as they do not require a formal treaty amendment, but merely a change in institutional practice. National parliaments would seem to have a particularly important role in the process. It is the powers of national and regional parliaments that are most encroached upon by EU legislation. As those most directly affected by the growth of EU legislation, they would seem to be among the biggest stakeholders in determining where its limits should be set. National and regional parliaments are also frequently seen as the guardians of representative democracy within the European Union. If the European Union wishes to take concerns about democracy and self-government seriously, it would seem axiomatic that it place the institutions best equipped to articulate what that means at the very centre of the decision-making process.

That said, these reforms were not as innovative as they might have been. Inclusion of regional assemblies in the process was only optional[92] and the powers of national parliaments were curtailed in several important respects. They could issue only a 'yellow card' to the Community legislature, requiring it to reconsider a proposal. They had no power to issue a 'red card', requiring the Community legislature to abandon (or even requiring it to amend) legislation, even where a significant number of national parliaments considered that it would breach the principle of subsidiarity. Further, it was not clear how national parliaments would have secured their prerogatives under the procedures as they would not have been entitled to bring annulment actions before the Court of Justice – they would have had to have relied on national governments to do this. This seems odd.[93] As Weatherill has suggested:

---

88 Article 9 of the Protocol.      89 Article I-18(2) CT.      90 Articles III-273(1) and III-276(2) CT.
91 See, respectively, Articles 1 and 8 of the Protocol.
92 For criticism, see House of Lords European Union Committee, *Strengthening National Parliamentary Scrutiny of the EU*, above n. 83, paras. 183–203.
93 A. Maurer, *National Parliaments in the European Architecture*, Federal Trust Online Paper, 6/02, 24–5.

it would be logical to supplement the *ex ante* procedural niche carved for national parliaments by allowing them an independent right to bring a challenge before the Court in respect of matters covered by the *ex ante* reasoned opinion procedure. It is unfortunate that while the door to the political institutions has been opened to the national parliaments the door to the Court has been left shut.[94]

In addition to these deficiencies, there are wider reasons to be concerned about the likely effectiveness of the Early Warning Mechanism. The resources available to national parliaments vary considerably and are rarely sufficient to allow for detailed analysis of anything other than the most salient Commission proposals.[95] The Early Warning Mechanism would have required parliaments from one-third or one-quarter of Member States to present reasoned objections before the EU institutions could be required to reconsider a proposal. This would have been difficult to achieve. Typically, EU legislation will not violate some bright red line drawn by all national parliaments. Most will be equivocal about a proposal, but it will threaten some tradition, which is cherished in a particular Member State, be this measures prohibiting the use of snuff in Sweden, imperial weights and measures in the United Kingdom, or measures allowing cheese to be marketed as feta not from Greece or beer to be marketed in Germany despite not being in accordance with German purity laws. A feature of all these examples is that are idiosyncratic. Their value is deeply felt in the state in question, but much less so elsewhere. It would have been difficult, in such circumstances, for the national parliament of that state to persuade the parliaments in other states that there had been a breach of subsidiarity.

### Further reading

A. Albi, *EU Enlargement and the Constitutions of Central and Eastern Europe* (Cambridge, Cambridge University Press, 2005)

A. v. Bogdandy and J. Bast, 'The European Union's Vertical Order of Competences: the Current Law and Proposals for its Reform' (2002) 39 *CML Rev.* 227

G. de Búrca, *Reappraising Subsidiarity's Significance after Amsterdam*, Jean Monnet Working Paper 7/99

G. de Búrca and B. de Witte, 'The Delimitation of Powers between the EU and its Member States' in A. Arnull and D. Wincott (eds.), *Accountability and Legitimacy in the European Union* (Oxford, Oxford University Press, 2002) ch. 12

---

94  S. Weatherill, 'Better Competence Monitoring' (2005) 30 *EL Rev.* 23, 40. In addition, the new powers were poorly drafted, apparently excluding from review by national parliaments matters which the Convention on the Future of Europe had seemingly intended to include. Thus, national parliaments would have been entitled to review all legislation based on Article I-18 (the equivalent of Article 308 EC) but not that based on Article III-172 (the equivalent of Article 95 EC). This was despite the fact that in both the Laeken Declaration and in much of the work of the Convention, these Articles were quite deliberately coupled together. Their apparent decoupling in the Constitutional Treaty, it seems, was a drafting slip and was not intended. See Weatherill, *ibid.* 35.

95  This was discussed in chapter 4. See further A. Maurer and W. Wessels (eds.), *National Parliaments on their Ways to Europe: Losers or Latecomers?* (Baden-Baden, Nomos, 2001).

A. Dashwood, 'The Relationship between the Member States and the European Union/European Community' (2004) 41 *CML Rev.* 355

A. Estella, *The EU Principle of Subsidiarity and its Critique* (Oxford, Oxford University Press, 2002)

D. Halberstam, 'The Political Morality of Federal Systems' (2004) 90 *Virginia Law Review* 101

D. Kostakopoulou, 'Floating Sovereignty: a Pathology or Necessary Means of State Evolution' (2002) 22 *Oxford Journal of Legal Studies* 135

M. Kumm, 'The Jurisprudence of Constitutional Conflict: Constitutional Supremacy in Europe before and after the Constitutional Treaty' (2005) 11 *European Law Journal* 262

F. Mayer, 'Competences – Reloaded? The Vertical Division of Powers in the EU after the New European Constitution' (2005) 3 *International Journal of Constitutional Law* 493

N. Walker, 'The Idea of Constitutional Pluralism' (2002) 65 *MLR* 317

N. Walker (ed.), *Sovereignty in Transition* (Oxford, Oxford University Press, 2003)

S. Weatherill, 'Better Competence Monitoring' (2005) 30 *European Law Review* 23

J. Weiler, 'Federalism without Constitutionalism: Europe's Sonderweg' in K. Nicolaïdis and R. Howse (eds.), *The Federal Vision: Legitimacy and Levels of Governance in the United States and the European Union* (Oxford, Oxford University Press, 2000)

E. Young, 'Protecting Member State Autonomy in the European Union: Some Cautionary Tales from American Federalism' (2002) 77 *NYU L Rev.* 1612

# 6

# Fundamental rights

## CONTENTS

## 1. Introduction

The original EEC Treaty contained no system of fundamental rights protection. A bill of fundamental rights would have given the EC state-like characteristics which, at the time, were not anticipated for it. Furthermore, the relatively limited scope of the EEC Treaty, with its focus on instituting a common market, provided limited opportunities for possible conflicts between EC acts and fundamental rights. If conflicts did arise, states expected their national constitutions to be the best guarantee of protection of fundamental rights. The early case law of the European Court of Justice reflected this line of thinking. In a series of judgments through to the mid-1960s, it refused to countenance arguments that the EC institutions had violated some right protected in national constitutions.[1] The Treaties contained no reference to these fundamental rights, and, in the light of this, the Court resisted implying that it and other EC institutions were responsible for the protection of these fundamental rights. These assumptions were changed by *Van Gend en Loos* and *Costa v ENEL*.[2] The supremacy of EC law meant that national constitutional provisions could no longer be used to safeguard fundamental rights in all circumstances, as any EC legal provision took precedence over them. These judgments not only created this lacuna in protection, but also begged the question as to why this should be so. Even if the common market, the central aim of the original EEC Treaty, were to bring many benefits to the citizens of Europe, these were certainly not sufficient to legitimate the Treaty to such a degree that its citizens would be willing for it to exercise constitutional authority over them.[3] Human rights could provide such a justification as they have, since the Second World War, acquired 'symbolic pre-eminence' as an instrument for polity legitimation. Human rights were also a particularly powerful symbol in the context of European integration, for they were something archetypically European. They represented a common heritage, with the European Communities, being a European organisation, as the natural guardian of that heritage.[4]

The gradual establishment of fundamental rights in EU law, first by the Court of Justice and then by the other EU institutions, which we discuss in this chapter, therefore touches on a number of issues. First, it is concerned with legitimating the European Union. If the Union respects fundamental rights, it becomes more difficult to challenge its exercise of power. Secondly, it is also about state-building and giving the European Union a more explicitly political identity. If EU institutions are determining fundamental values, they are, by definition, determining matters which are integral to the way we live our lives, and which characterise our political identity. The development of fundamental rights in EU law should not, however, only be seen in such cold, instrumental terms. The enjoyment of these rights is seen as central to human dignity and freedom, as individuals are seen as incapable of living a decent life without these guarantees. Therefore, thirdly, the European Union's ability to provide and protect these rights is a mark of the quality of its government, the quality of life that it offers to its subjects, and the quality of the political community that it aspires to establish.

---

1  Case 1/58 *Stork v High Authority* [1959] ECR 17; Joined Cases 36, 37, 38 and 40/59 *Geitling v High Authority* [1960] ECR 423; Case 40/64 *Sgarlata v Commission* [1965] ECR 215.
2  Case 26/62 *Van Gend en Loos v Nederlandse Administratie der Belastingen* [1963] ECR 1; Case 6/64 *Costa v ENEL* [1964] ECR 585.
3  A. Williams, *EU Human Rights Policies: a Study in Irony* (Oxford, Oxford University Press, 2004) 139.
4  *Ibid.*, 133–4.

## 2. Development of fundamental rights protection in the EC legal order

### (i)   Incorporation of fundamental rights into EC law by the Court of Justice

Awareness of the difficulties of the absence of human rights safeguards in EC law, following *Costa*, led to a softening of the Court's case law towards the end of the 1960s. In *Van Eick*, the Court stated that EC institution staff disciplinary procedures were 'bound in the exercise of [their] powers to observe the fundamental principles of the law of procedure'.[5] The Court was more explicit in *Stauder*.[6] The Commission adopted a Decision designed to reduce Community butter stocks by allowing butter to be sold at a lower price to people who were on certain social welfare schemes. In order to claim the butter, the beneficiaries had to produce a coupon which, in the German and Dutch version of the Decision, had to indicate their name, whereas this was unnecessary in the French and Italian versions. *Stauder*, a German national, challenged the requirement that his name be on the coupon, claiming that it violated his right to respect for privacy. The Court indicated that the more liberal French and Italian version should be adopted because in this way the Decision would not prejudice the 'fundamental human rights enshrined in the general principles of Community law and protected by the Court'. In other words, if there were two legitimate interpretations of a Community law provision, the Court would adopt the one that did not violate fundamental rights.

Human rights still occupied no more than a second-order status in EC law. *Van Eick* and *Stauder*, whilst stressing the consonance between EC law and established notions of fundamental rights, did not grant these fundamental rights an organic status which would allow them to be used both as a basis for steering the actions of EC authorities and as a ground for judicial review. National courts were still, therefore, left with a choice between refusing to apply EC law or forsaking fundamental liberties enshrined in their national constitutions.[7] The matter came to the fore in the *Internationale Handelsgesellschaft* litigation. In this case, an EC Regulation had awarded Internationale Handelsgesellschaft, a German trading concern, a licence to export maize on condition that it set down a deposit which would be forfeited if it failed to export the maize within the time stipulated in the licence. The latter failed to export the maize and, upon forfeiture of the deposit, challenged the Regulation before the Administrative Court in Frankfurt. The court considered that the Regulation violated the provisions in the German Constitution, which protected the freedom to trade and required all public action to be proportionate.

---

5  Case 35/67 *Van Eick v Commission* [1968] ECR 329.
6  Case 29/69 *Stauder v City of Ulm* [1969] ECR 419.
7  U. Scheuner, 'Fundamental Rights in European Community Law and in National Constitutional Law' (1975) 12 *CML Rev.* 171, 173–4.

## Case 11/70 *Internationale Handelsgesellschaft v Einfuhr- und Vorratstelle für Getreide und Futtermittel* **[1970] ECR 1125**

3. Recourse to the legal rules or concepts of national law in order to judge the validity of measures adopted by the institutions of the Community would have an adverse effect on the uniformity and efficacy of Community law. The validity of such measures can only be judged in the light of Community law. In fact, the law stemming from the Treaty, an independent source of law, cannot because of its very nature be overridden by rules of national law, however framed, without being deprived of its character as Community law and without the legal basis of the Community itself being called in question. Therefore the validity of a Community measure or its effect within a Member State cannot be affected by allegations that it runs counter to either fundamental rights as formulated by the constitution of that State or the principles of a national constitutional structure.

4. However, an examination should be made as to whether or not any analogous guarantee inherent in Community law has been disregarded. In fact, respect for fundamental rights forms an integral part of the general principles of law protected by the Court of Justice. The protection of such rights, whilst inspired by the constitutional traditions common to the Member States, must be ensured within the framework of the structure and objectives of the Community.

The Court went on to rule that there had been no violation of the fundamental right to trade, but the decision establishes that fundamental rights form an integral part of EC law. Any act by an EC institution which violates these fundamental rights is illegal. However, the genesis of EC law on fundamental rights was tainted due to its emergence within the context of a dispute about the supremacy of EC law. Disgruntled, Internationale Handelsgesellschaft pursued the matter further, before the German Constitutional Court.

## *Internationale Handelsgesellschaft v Einfuhr- und Vorratstelle für Getreibe und Futtermittel* **(German Constitutional Court) [1974] 2 CMLR 540**

23. The part of the Constitution dealing with fundamental rights is an inalienable essential feature of the valid Constitution of the Federal Republic of Germany and one which forms part of the constitutional structure of the Constitution. Article 24 of the Constitution does not without reservation allow it to be subjected to qualifications. In this, the present state of integration of the Community is of crucial importance. The Community still lacks a democratically legitimated parliament directly elected by general suffrage which possesses legislative powers and to which the Community organs empowered to legislate are fully responsible on a political level; it still lacks in particular a codified catalogue of fundamental rights, the substance of which is reliably and unambiguously fixed for the future in the same way as the substance of the Constitution and therefore allows a comparison and a decision as to whether, at the time in question, the Community law standard with regard to fundamental rights generally binding in the Community is adequate in the long term measured by the standard of the Constitution with regard to fundamental rights (without prejudice to

possible amendments) in such a way that there is no exceeding the limitation indicated, set by Article 24 of the Constitution. As long as this legal certainty, which is not guaranteed merely by the decisions of the European Court of Justice, favourable though these have been to fundamental rights, is not achieved in the course of the further integration of the Community, the reservation derived from Article 24 of the Constitution applies. What is involved is, therefore, a legal difficulty arising exclusively from the Community's continuing integration process, which is still in flux and which will end with the present transitional phase.

24. Provisionally, therefore, in the hypothetical case of a conflict between Community law and a part of national constitutional law or, more precisely, of the guarantees of fundamental rights in the Constitution, there arises the question of which system of law takes precedence, that is, ousts the other. In this conflict of norms, the guarantee of fundamental rights in the Constitution prevails as long as the competent organs of the Community have not removed the conflict of norms in accordance with the Treaty mechanism . . .

35. The result is: as long as the integration process has not progressed so far that Community law also receives a catalogue of fundamental rights decided on by a parliament and of settled validity, which is adequate in comparison with the catalogue of fundamental rights contained in the Constitution, a reference by a court in the Federal Republic of Germany to the Bundesverfassungsgericht in judicial review proceedings, following the obtaining of a ruling of the European Court under [Article 234 EC], is admissible and necessary if the German court regards the rule of Community law which is relevant to its decision as inapplicable in the interpretation given by the European Court, because and in so far as it conflicts with one of the fundamental rights in the Constitution.

This challenge to the supremacy of Community law was supported by the Italian Constitutional Court. When the latter finally accepted the supremacy of Community law in *Frontini*,[8] it simultaneously held that supremacy of Community law will not occur where Community law violates fundamental principles of the Italian Constitution (including fundamental rights).[9] The decisions of the German and Italian Constitutional Courts allowed for a dialectic to develop, which would eventually lead to the development of a body of EC law on fundamental rights. The German Constitutional Court justified its authority to review EC acts on the basis that the European Communities were not a democratic regime and did not contain a catalogue of fundamental rights similar to that of the German Constitution. The implication was that if EC law, and more particularly, the Court of Justice, was to develop sufficiently a fundamental rights doctrine of its own, the threat of the German Constitutional Court would recede. In 1986, in *Solange II*,[10] the German Constitutional Court reversed its approach to the review of Community acts in light of fundamental rights. Though no catalogue of fundamental rights had yet been established in Community law, the German Constitutional Court considered that the protection of fundamental rights granted by the Court of Justice had reached a level that substantially coincided with

8  *Frontini v Ministero Delle Finanze* [1974] 2 CMLR 372.
9  See M. Cantabia, 'The Italian Constitutional Court and the Relationship between the Italian Legal System and the European Union' in A.-M. Slaughter, A. Stone Sweet and J. Weiler (eds.), *The European Courts and National Courts: Doctrine and Jurisprudence* (Oxford, Hart, 1998).
10  Decision of the Bundesverfassungsgericht of 22 October 1986, [1987] 3 CMLR 225.

that granted by the German Constitution. As long as that would be the case, the German Constitutional Court would no longer review the validity of specific Community acts in light of national fundamental rights. Fundamental rights protection, as a conditional element of EC law, was still central to acceptance of its authority by the German Court. What changed was the assessment of the protection of fundamental rights now available in the Community legal order. The German Constitutional Court started from the presumption that it was willing to give EC law the benefit of the doubt, with this only being removed on the presentation of hard evidence to the contrary.

### (ii)    Types of EC fundamental rights

Some have accused the Court of Justice of developing a fundamental rights doctrine to temper national resistance to market integration.[11] Member States concerned about the liberalisation of the economy were to be soothed by the parallel development of a culture of rights in Community law. However, this analysis should be seen sceptically. When a panoramic view of the Court's practice is taken, there is little evidence to support this view.[12] Whatever the motivations, the Court of Justice has developed fundamental rights in Community law according to an autonomous logic of its own. It looks, therefore, at sources other than national constitutions to determine the content of fundamental rights in EC law. In *Nold*, the Court stated that international human rights treaties were another source of fundamental rights in EC law.[13] Following *Nold*, the Court has recognised a number of human rights treaties as being sources of EC fundamental rights law. Most importantly, in *Rutili*, it referred to the European Convention for the Protection of Human Rights and Fundamental Freedoms (ECHR).[14] Since then, the Court has indicated that this treaty has a particular status as a source of law.[15] It has also referred to other international human rights treaties as sources of fundamental rights, most notably the International Covenant on Civil and Political Rights of the United Nations.[16] Among the other sources to which the Court of Justice (and also the CFI) makes reference, are the sources of social rights protection, such as the 1989 Community Charter of Fundamental Social Rights of Workers and the 1962 European Social Charter.[17] The Court has, consequently, recognised a number of categories of different right.

---

11 J. Coppell and A. O'Neill, 'The European Court of Justice: Taking Rights Seriously' (1992) 29 *CML Rev.* 669.

12 J. Weiler and N. Lockhart, '"Taking Rights Seriously" Seriously: the European Court and Fundamental Rights Jurisprudence, Part I' (1995) 32 *CML Rev.* 51; J. Weiler and N. Lockhart, '"Taking Rights Seriously" Seriously: the European Court and Fundamental Rights Jurisprudence, Part II' (1995) 32 *CML Rev.* 579.

13 Case 4/73 *Nold v Commission* [1974] ECR 491.

14 Case 36/75 *Rutili v Ministre de l'Intérieur* [1975] ECR 1219.

15 Case C-299/95 *Kremzow v Austria* [1997] ECR I-2629.

16 Case 374/87 *Orkem v Commission* [1989] ECR 3283.

17 Case 24/86 *Blaizot v Belgium* [1988] ECR 379; Case 149/77 *Defrenne II* [1978] ECR 1365.

**Civil rights**    These include: the  right to respect for family and private life,[18] freedom
of religion,[19] freedom of trade union activity,[20] freedom of expression,[21] protection
of personal data,[22] equality,[23] protection from discrimination on grounds of sexual
orientation,[24] the right to free and informed consent before any medical procedure
and the right to human   dignity.[25]

**Economic rights**    Normally subject to provisos which may be placed in the public
interest and which restrict their exercise, these include: the right to trade,[26] the right
to own property,[27] the right to carry out an economic activity.[28]

**Rights of defence**    These include: the right to an effective judicial remedy,[29] the right
to legal assistance and the right to all lawyer-client communications prepared for the
purpose of defending oneself to be confidential[30] the right to be heard in one's own
defence before any measure is imposed[31] and protection from self-incrimination.[32]

In *Internationale Handelsgesellschaft*, the Court of Justice indicated these were to
be interpreted according to an autonomous Community reasoning, whereby their
exact meaning would be determined in the light of broader Community objectives.
There has been extensive debate about the logic supporting this reasoning. Some
authors have argued that it should be centred around the Western liberal tradition
of protecting individual autonomy. EC law should opt for the standard which would
provide the individual with as high a level of protection as that offered by any of
the Member States.[33] Others have argued that this is too formal and individualistic
a conception of fundamental rights.[34] Fundamental rights articulate basic choices

18  Case 136/79 *National Panasonic v Commission* [1980] ECR 2033; Case C-249/86 *Commission v Germany*
    [1989] ECR 1263.
19  Case 130/75 *Prais v Council* [1976] ECR 1589.
20  Case 175/73 *Union Syndicale v Council* [1974] ECR 917.
21  Case C-260/89 *ERT v DEP* [1991] ECR I-2925.
22  Case C-101/01 *Lindqvist* [2003] ECR I-12971; Joined Cases C-465/00, C-138/01 and C-139/01 *Rechnungshof*
    *v Österreichisches Rundfunk* [2003] ECR I-4919.
23  Case C-43/75 *Defrenne v Sabena* [1976] ECR 455.
24  Case C-117/01 *KB v National Health Service Pensions Agency* [2004] ECR I-541.
25  Case C-377/98 *Netherlands v Parliament and Council* [2001] ECR I-7079.
26  Case 240/83 *Procureur de la République v Association de défense des brûleurs d'huiles usagées* (*ADBHU*)
    [1985] ECR 531.
27  Case 44/79 *Hauer v Land Rheinland-Pfulz* [1979] ECR 3727.
28  Case 230/78 *Eridania v Minister of Agriculture and Forestry* [1979] ECR 2749.
29  Case 222/84 *Johnston v RUC* [1986] ECR 1651.
30  Case 155/79 *AM & S v Commission* [1982] ECR 1575.
31  Case 17/74 *Transocean Marine Paint v Commission* [1974] ECR 1063.
32  Case 374/87 *Orkem v Commission* [1989] ECR 3283.
33  L. Besselink, 'Entrapped by the Maximum Standard: On Fundamental Rights, Pluralism and Subsidiarity
    in the European Union' (1998) 35 *CML Rev.* 629.
34  J. Weiler, 'Fundamental Rights and Fundamental Boundaries: On Standards and Values in the Protection of
    Human Rights' in N. Neuwahl and A. Rosas, *The European Union and Human Rights* (The Hague, Martijnus
    Nijhoff, 1995) 51, 52–3; M. Avbelj, *The European Court of Justice and the Question of Value Choices*, Jean
    Monnet Working Paper 6/04.

about the structure of state and society. The European Union should develop its own model according to EU conceptions of right and wrong. Commentary on what a distinctive European model of fundamental rights would involve is disappointingly vague. It has been argued that one feature might be a greater insistence on social rights and more scepticism of 'market rights' than in the USA.[35] Others have suggested that Europe's history of tragic events, most notably the Holocaust, would involve the development of a common set of choices concerned to avoid the suffering and pain associated with Europe's past and to give a voice to those suffering equivalent injustices today.[36]

In practice, the Court of Justice has eschewed these approaches. Its reasoning is a curious mix of universalism and pragmatism, with its findings tempered by awareness of the institutional scheme of the Treaty and the practice of the other institutions.[37] In *Omega*, Omega ran a game under a franchise from a British company, Pulsar, whereby competitors attempted to shoot each other with laser guns. Sensory tags in jackets worn by competitors picked up whether they had been shot and, indeed, 'killed' under the rules of the game. The Bonn police authority issued a prohibition order against Omega, on the grounds that the game simulated murder, and therefore constituted an affront to human dignity under paragraph 1(1) of the German Basic Law. Omega argued before the German court that the prohibition violated Article 49 EC, the provision on the freedom to provide services. The view of the German court was that the order would not, if it protected the right to human dignity. It therefore asked the Court of Justice as to the meaning of this right in Community law.

---

**Case C-36/02 *Omega Spielhallen- und Automatenaufstellungs v Oberbürgermeisterin der Bundesstadt Bonn* [2004] ECR I-9609**

33. It should be recalled in that context that, according to settled case-law, fundamental rights form an integral part of the general principles of law the observance of which the Court ensures, and that, for that purpose, the Court draws inspiration from the constitutional traditions common to the Member States and from the guidelines supplied by international treaties for the protection of human rights on which the Member States have collaborated or to which they are signatories. The European Convention on Human Rights and Fundamental Freedoms has special significance in that respect.

34. . . . the Community legal order undeniably strives to ensure respect for human dignity as a general principle of law. There can therefore be no doubt that the objective of protecting human dignity is compatible with Community law, it being immaterial in that respect that, in Germany, the principle of respect for human dignity has a particular status as an independent fundamental right.

---

35 C. Leben, 'Is there a European Approach to Human Rights?' in P. Alston (ed.), *The EU and Human Rights* (Oxford, Oxford University Press, 1999).

36 K. Günther, 'The Legacies of Injustice and Fear: a European Approach to Human Rights and their Effects on Political Culture' in P. Alston (ed.), *The EU and Human Rights* (Oxford, Oxford University Press, 1999).

37 I. Ward, 'Making Sense of Integration: a Philosophy of Law for the European Community' (1993) 17 *Journal of European Integration* 101, 128–9 and 132–3.

35. Since both the Community and its Member States are required to respect fundamental rights, the protection of those rights is a legitimate interest which, in principle, justifies a restriction of the obligations imposed by Community law, even under a fundamental freedom guaranteed by the Treaty such as the freedom to provide services.

36. However, measures which restrict the freedom to provide services may be justified on public policy grounds only if they are necessary for the protection of the interests which they are intended to guarantee and only in so far as those objectives cannot be attained by less restrictive measures . . .

37. It is not indispensable in that respect for the restrictive measure issued by the authorities of a Member State to correspond to a conception shared by all Member States as regards the precise way in which the fundamental right or legitimate interest in question is to be protected. Although . . . the Court referred to moral, religious or cultural considerations which lead all Member States to make the organisation of lotteries and other games with money subject to restrictions, it was not its intention, by mentioning that common conception, to formulate a general criterion for assessing the proportionality of any national measure which restricts the exercise of an economic activity.

38. On the contrary, as is apparent from well-established case-law subsequent to Schindler, the need for, and proportionality of, the provisions adopted are not excluded merely because one Member State has chosen a system of protection different from that adopted by another State . . .

39. In this case, it should be noted, first, that, according to the referring court, the prohibition on the commercial exploitation of games involving the simulation of acts of violence against persons, in particular the representation of acts of homicide, corresponds to the level of protection of human dignity which the national constitution seeks to guarantee in the territory of the Federal Republic of Germany. It should also be noted that, by prohibiting only the variant of the laser game the object of which is to fire on human targets and thus 'play at killing' people, the contested order did not go beyond what is necessary in order to attain the objective pursued by the competent national authorities.

*Omega* represents very much the paradox of the Court of Justice's case law on fundamental rights. It is making genuinely fundamental judgments about the nature of the human condition in Europe – what it means to have respect for human dignity – and about the organisation of society and politics within the European Union. The substance of its judgments is, however, quite empty. In *Omega,* the Court discusses human dignity, but fails to create a positive vision of it. Williams has argued that it is precisely this lack of substance and intellectual vacuity which is having powerful delegitimatting effects. For it is reducing the language of fundamental rights to a series of empty labels.

### A. Williams, *EU Human Rights Policies: a Study in Irony* (Oxford, Oxford University Press, 2004) 159–60

As the concern of the Community's institutions was to stave off criticism on the one hand and gain authenticity on the other, the phrase 'human rights' was used without regard to its full meaning or possibilities. Using the language of rights as a mythic construct was considered

> sufficient to justify the potential detractors of the Community and its Project. The resulting indeterminacy of human rights, the repeated failure to constitutionalise any definition of the term, ensured that the field was open to interpretation. Thus, the possibility of different human rights discourses, practices and definitions emerging in different arenas inspired by different sources of law and philosophy became apparent. The most significant demonstration of the potential for variance was at the external/internal divide. In both realms, the failure to define what the Community meant by human rights or how they should be applied and promoted in any coherent fashion determined that other forces could influence their evolution . . .
> the mythic nature of the narrative has presented a debilitating factor in any attempt to rectify a perceived bifurcation. Due to its lack of substance, its lack of certainty, the narrative of founding principle has become a vapid construction, a wistful statement repeated as law without any certain content or appreciation of practice. It ignores the 'considerable differences' between the attitudes of the Member States to rights. It has been incapable of providing a framework for any kind of consistent human rights activity. Instead, the myth has lost its vitality and relevance and has left human rights to the vagaries of context and inherent discrimination.

It would seem that Community law has reached a position where it recognises a very wide variety of rights as fundamental. Yet the reasons for recognising these rights in this way has been left undetermined. This has led to a great deal of uncertainty about the effectiveness and meaning of these rights, as well as to confusion about their relationship to each other. As there is no clear underpinning logic, the circumstances when one will be preferred to the other are completely unclear.

## 3. Development of fundamental rights by the political institutions of the European Union

### (i) Non-violation and fundamental rights

In 1977, the other three EC institutions gave support to the Court's case law by adopting a Joint Declaration on Fundamental Rights, in which they undertook to respect the European Convention on the Protection of Human Rights in the exercise of their powers.[38] This commitment, nevertheless, saw fundamental rights as enjoying a limited role. They were to act as a constraint on the activities of the institutions, but were not to become a central mission of the European Communities, pivotal to fashioning their political identities, or orienting their activities. The first institution to move to change this was the European Parliament. In the Spinelli Report, it suggested, in Article 4:

> 1. The Union shall protect the dignity of the individual and grant every person coming within its jurisdiction the fundamental rights and freedoms derived in particular from the common principles of the Constitutions of the

---

38 OJ 1977 C103/1.

Member States and from the European Convention for the Protection of Human Rights and Freedoms.

2. The Union undertakes to maintain and develop, within the limits of its competences, the economic, social and cultural rights derived from the Constitutions of the Member States and from the European Social Charter.

Over the next decade, the European Parliament sought to anchor the integration process around the realisation of these rights, most notably, through reports which catalogued these rights.[39] The other institutions were willing to see fundamental rights as no more than a basis for review of acts of the EC institutions. This vision was pre-eminent in the first explicit incorporation of fundamental rights into substantive provisions of the treaties at Maastricht:

---

### Article 6 TEU

The Union shall respect fundamental rights, as guaranteed by the European Convention for the Protection of Human Rights and Fundamental Freedoms signed in Rome on 4 November 1950 and as they result from the constitutional traditions common to the Member States, as general principles of law.

---

This provision did no more than confirm fundamental rights as a constraint on EU action. It did not establish them as a purpose of EU action. In Opinion 2/94, the Court of Justice ruled the EC had no competence to accede to the European Convention on Human Rights, as it did not have any general human rights competence.[40] The logic was that fundamental rights only existed in EC law as a constraint on other substantive policies and not as a positive agenda in its own right. Alston and Weiler have characterised the approach of non-violation as negative integration, in that it indicates only a bald commitment not to breach fundamental rights rather than an affirmative programme to realise them.[41] They criticised this as inadequate because it leads to a gap between rhetoric and reality, whereby the European Union affirms the importance of many rights, but does little to secure any of them. They also argued that it was marked by two further features: an inadequate information base, so that there was no real knowledge of what rights were being violated, and excessive reliance on judicial remedies. The latter was particularly problematic with regard to fundamental rights protection in the second and third pillars of the TEU, where judicial involvement was minimal.[42] More generally, there were difficulties where individuals either had

---

39 See the De Gucht Report, OJ 1989 C120/51, and the Hermann Report, OJ 1994 C61/155. On this see R. Rack and S. Lausegger, 'The Role of the European Parliament: Past and Future' in P. Alston (ed.), *The EU and Human Rights* (Oxford, Oxford University Press, 1999).

40 Opinion 2/94 *Re Accession of the Community to the European Human Rights Convention* [1996] ECR I-1759.

41 P. Alston and J. Weiler, '"An Ever Closer Union" in need of a Human Rights Policy' (1998) 9 *EJIL* 658, 665–9.

42 Article 46 TEU.

limited access to courts, or courts were marked by problems of legitimacy, thereby impeding their development of fundamental rights.[43]

### (ii)   Fundamental rights and the external relations of the European Union

In the absence of a general human rights competence, positive measures to promote human rights could only be incorporated in a piecemeal manner. The TEU, therefore, introduced a second standard of human rights protection in external relations. From the early 1990s, the European Communities had begun to include human rights references in its trade and aid policies.[44] This was formalised in Article 177(2) EC, which committed EC development policy to contribute to 'the general objective of developing and consolidating democracy and the rule of law, and to that of respecting human rights and fundamental freedoms'. From the mid-1990s onwards, all trade and cooperation agreements had clauses committing both parties to respect human rights.[45] For example, the General Scheme of Preferences, which allows for certain goods from less developed countries to be imported free from customs duties or at lower tariffs, could also be suspended where beneficiary states failed to respect fundamental rights or basic labour standards.[46] Provision is also made for Community development projects which contribute to the promotion of human rights.[47] For all this, the impact of these provisions appears slight. In the case of the General Scheme of Preferences, for example, the European Communities have only suspended benefits once, in the case of Myanmar in 1997.[48]

More significant was the decision to apply human rights norms to the enlargement process. In 1993, the Copenhagen Criteria were adopted, setting out the basis on which applicant states could apply for membership. The first were so-called political criteria, which required states to have 'stable institutions guaranteeing democracy, the rule of law, human rights and the respect for and protection of minorities'.[49] These criteria became the basis for Commission reports evaluating the state of human rights in all

---

43  Cf. A. v. Bogdandy, 'The European Union as a Human Rights Organization? Human Rights and the Core of the European Union' (2000) 27 *CML Rev.* 1307, 1319–20.

44  A. Brandtner and A. Rosas, 'Human Rights and the External Relations of the European Community: an Analysis of Doctrine and Practice' (1998) 9 *EJIL* 468. Most recently, see EC Commission, *The European Union's Role in Promoting Democratisation in Third Countries*, COM(2001)252.

45  E. Riedel and M. Will, 'Human Rights Clauses in External Agreements' in P. Alston (ed.), *The EU and Human Rights* (Oxford, Oxford University Press, 1999).

46  These are now set out in Regulation 1853/2004/EC, OJ 2004 L323/11.

47  Regulation 975/1999/EC laying down the requirements for the implementation of development cooperation operations which contribute to the general objective of developing and consolidating democracy and the rule of law and to that of respecting human rights and fundamental freedoms, OJ 1999 L120/1.

48  Regulation 552/97/EC temporarily withdrawing access to generalised tariff preferences from the Union of Myanmar, OJ 1997 L85/8.

49  EC Bulletin 6–1993, I.13.

the applicant countries.[50] These reports have proved wide-ranging in their criticism of applicant state practices.[51] There has, however, been dissatisfaction with their use. It has been argued that it has been hypocritical for the European Union to apply standards of scrutiny to other states that it does not apply to its own Member States.[52] It has also been argued that it has been applied in a highly selective and uneven manner, and that negative opinions have often had counter-productive consequences.[53]

### (iii)    Development of an internal fundamental rights policy

A third standard of fundamental rights emerged at the Treaty of Amsterdam. A number of Member States pushed both for full incorporation of a European bill of rights into the TEU and for EU accession to the ECHR.[54] Whilst there was resistance from other Member States, the Turin European Council, in March 1996, called on the IGC to study whether it was possible to strengthen fundamental rights and improve their protection within the TEU. The consequence was a number of significant amendments. For the first time, the European Union made protection of fundamental rights a central mission.[55]

---

### Article 6(1) TEU

The Union is founded on the principles of liberty, democracy, respect for human rights and fundamental freedoms, and the rule of law, principles which are common to the Member States.

---

50 M. Nowak, 'Human Rights "Conditionality" in relation to Entry to, and Full Participation in, the European Union' in P. Alston (ed.), *The EU and Human Rights* (Oxford, Oxford University Press, 1999); A. Williams, 'Enlargement and Human Rights Conditionality: a Policy of Distinction?' (2000) 25 *EL Rev.* 601; C. Pinelli, 'Conditionality and Enlargement in Light of EU Constitutional Developments' (2004) 10 *ELJ* 354.

51 Slovakia was initially denied pre-accession status in 1997 on the grounds of the quality of its political regime, and was then subject to sustained monitoring and criticism by the Commission. See e.g. EC Commission, *2002 Regular Report on Slovakia's Progress Towards Accession*, COM(2002)700. In its 2004 Recommendation on Turkish progress towards accession, the Commission stated that further reform of Turkey's Criminal Code and further improvement in prohibiting torture, promoting women's, minority and trade union rights, as well as progress in freedom of expression and religion, would be required. EC Commission, *Recommendation on Turkey's Progress Towards Accession*, COM(2004)656.

52 This is the central thesis of A. Williams, *European Union Human Rights Policy* (Oxford, Oxford University Press, 2004).

53 e.g. The treatment of Turkey during the 1990s, which led it to suspend relations with the European Union. See K. Smith, 'The Evolution and Application of EU Member State Conditionality' in M. Cremona (ed.), *The Enlargement of the European Union* (Oxford, Oxford University Press, 2003).

54 This was the position of Belgium, Finland, Italy, Spain and the German *Länder*. European Parliament, *White Paper on the 1996 Intergovernmental Conference*, vol. II (Brussels, European Parliament, 1997).

55 D. McGoldrick, 'The EU After Amsterdam: an Organisation with General Human Rights Competence?' in D. O'Keeffe and P. Twomey (eds.), *Legal Issues of the Amsterdam Treaty* (Oxford, Hart, 1999).

The European Union was more explicit still in a Declaration adopted on the fiftieth anniversary of the Universal Declaration on Human Rights:

> The universality and indivisibility of human rights and the responsibility for their protection and promotion, together with the promotion of pluralistic democracy and effective guarantees for the rule of law, constitute essential objectives for the European Union as a union of shared values and serve as a fundamental basis for our action.
>
> The human being is at the centre of our policies. Ensuring the human dignity of every individual remains our common goal.[56]

Only one new competence was added at the Treaty of Amsterdam to institutionalise this shift. Article 7 TEU allows a Member State's rights under the TEU to be suspended if it is found to be responsible for serious and persistent breaches of the rights set out in Article 6 TEU. In 2000, however, when the other fourteen Member States had concerns about the entry of the explicitly racist Freedom party into the Austrian government, these procedures were not used. Instead, the fourteen Member States entered into an extra-legal agreement, in which they would have no bilateral contacts with the Austrian government. The matter was only resolved six months later, when a 'Committee of Wise Men' found both that the sanctions had inflamed nationalist feelings in Austria and that the Austrian government had a relatively good human rights record.[57] The Report did suggest that an EU human rights agency should be set up to monitor the human rights situation in the Member States.

Despite doubts about its competence, the Commission and Parliament have tried to push the idea that, on the basis of Article 6 TEU, the European Union has a monitoring role in the field of fundamental rights, which allows it to report on the situation in all the Member States. In 2002, following a Recommendation from the Parliament, the Commission established a Network of Independent Experts, who publish annual reports, assessing the general fundamental rights situation in all Member States and publish opinions on particular issues, such as same sex marriages. The idea of common EU monitoring of fundamental rights gained popularity, and in December 2003, the Member States agreed, in principle, to establish a Fundamental Rights Agency to monitor the human rights situation in the different Member States.[58] Some have gone on to suggest that the European Union could act as a launch-pad for a system of benchmarking, peer review and mutual learning. National practices are assessed in the light of best practice from other Member States, positive and negative experiences

---

56 Declaration of the European Union on the occasion of the 50th Anniversary of the Universal Declaration on Human Rights, Vienna, 10 December 1998, http://europa.eu.int/comm/external_relations/human_rights/doc/50th_decl_98.htm

57 For discussion see M. Merlingen, M. Mudde and U. Sedelmeider, 'The Right and the Righteous? European Norms, Domestic Politics and the Sanctions against Austria' (2001) 39 *JCMS* 59.

58 The legal base for the Agency and the scope of its power is still subject to consultation. EC Commission, *The Fundamental Rights Agency*, COM(2004)693.

are shared and Member States are 'named and shamed' where they engage in mal-practice.[59] The success of such a scheme would depend upon how much weight is given to reporting, how well it is resourced, the wider dissemination amongst the general public of negative reports, and the extent to which Member States feel obliged to justify themselves in the light of reports by foreign officials. In this regard, it has to be said that there is little evidence to suggest any of this is present. The reports by the Network of Independent Experts have passed largely unnoticed.

There are two views of the triple standard. A critical view is that the tentative and differentiated development of human rights policy has led to ambiguity in relation to the extent of the policy and a lack of consistency between internal and external policies, as well as across the different pillars. It has prevented a culture of human rights developing, in which the EU institutions commit themselves to the realisation of human rights objectives, in the same way as to other policy goals. Moreover, a public sphere, in which non-governmental organisations and the European Parliament can enter a meaningful debate about what sort of common values the European Union should realise, is lacking.[60] Another view is that there is no 'one size fits all' approach to human rights. A differentiated approach reflects more realistically the different demands imposed by the wide variety of rights recognised in EU law.[61] This debate reflects deeper tensions about the ends and means of an EU human rights policy. The former view emphasises that many rights are equally important for realising a 'good life' for the citizens of the European Union. A right is deemed fundamental precisely because it is central to this goal. The latter view, by contrast, notes that increasing numbers and varieties of rights are becoming important. Even if all are equally important, the institutional machinery cannot be the same for all by virtue of their diversity.

## 4. The European Union Charter of Fundamental Rights

### (i)    Development of the Charter

In 1998, the Directorate-General for Employment of the Commission expressed a wish to incorporate social rights more strongly within the fundamental rights debate. It commissioned an independent report (the Simitis Report) to consider the estab-lishment of 'social rights as a constitutional element of the European Union'.[62] The Committee interpreted its brief widely, writing on the status of fundamental rights

---

59 O. de Schutter, *The Implementation of the EU Charter of Fundamental Rights through the Open Method of Coordination*, Jean Monnet Working Paper 7/04.
60 P. Alston and J. Weiler, '"An Ever Closer Union" in need of a Human Rights Policy' (1998) 9 *EJIL* 658, 675.
61 A. v. Bogdandy, 'The European Union as a Human Rights Organization? Human Rights and the Core of the European Union' (2000) 27 *CML Rev.* 1307, 1319–20.
62 Report of the Expert Group on Fundamental Rights, *Affirming Fundamental Rights in the European Union: Time to Act* (Brussels, EC Commission, 1999).

in general. It stated that the lack of visibility of EU fundamental rights and the lack of justiciability was diminishing their worth. To that end, it proposed a European bill of rights at the next IGC. More innovatively, the Committee argued that it was no longer sufficient for these rights merely to mirror the ECHR. They must reflect more fully the 'Union experience' in order to deal with phenomena such as the information society, justice and home affairs, and biotechnology. This small acorn of an initiative was fortunate in its timing. Its publication, in early 1999, coincided with the German Presidency, which was attracted by the idea of developing a Charter of Fundamental Rights, which would both make EU fundamental rights more visible and act as a forum for debate about the type of rights which should be recognised at the end of the millennium. At the Cologne European Council, in June 1999, it was agreed that:

> Protection of fundamental rights is a founding principle of the Union and an indispensable prerequisite for her legitimacy. The obligation of the Union to respect fundamental rights has been confirmed and defined by the jurisprudence of the European Court of Justice. There appears to be a need, at the present stage of the Union's development, to establish a Charter of fundamental rights in order to make their overriding importance and relevance more visible to the Union's citizens.[63]

The European Council believed that this Charter should be an amalgam of rights. It should include the rights contained in the ECHR, those present in the constitutional traditions common to the Member States. It should also include the rights set out in the EU citizenship provisions and economic and social rights as contained in the European Social Charter and the Community Charter of the Fundamental Social Rights of Workers. In the view of the European Council, a draft of a Charter of Fundamental Rights of the European Union should be elaborated by a body composed of representatives of the Heads of State and Government and of the President of the Commission as well as of members of the European Parliament and national parliaments. Representatives of the European Court of Justice should participate as observers. Representatives of the Economic and Social Committee, the Committee of the Regions and social groups, as well as experts, should be invited to give their views. Secretariat services should be provided by the General Secretariat of the Council.

The Charter was also to be drafted according to a novel method. It was not to be formulated through intergovernmental negotiation, but through a Convention, which more closely represented a parliamentary assembly. For this Convention was to comprise one representative from each of the then fifteen governments, a representative from the Commission, sixteen MEPs and two representatives from each national parliament. Of its sixty-two members, forty-six were, therefore, parliamentary. Its working method was, moreover, to be deliberative in nature. Human rights

---

63 Conclusions of the Presidency, EU Bulletin 6–1999, I.64.

groups, regional bodies, trade unions and wider civil society were invited to make contributions.[64]

The draft of the Charter was adopted by the Convention in October 2000, and was unanimously approved by the European Council at the Biarritz European Council. There was, however, considerable disagreement about the status of the Charter. At the Nice European Council, the Charter was 'proclaimed' by the Council, the Commission and the Parliament, but its final status was to be resolved by the Constitutional Treaty. This left a host of ambiguities, for if a number of justifications could be given for full incorporation of the Charter, opposition to the Charter was strong:

> Some saw the Charter as a potential threat to national interests and economic growth. Others saw it as an undesirable example of the creeping constitutional-ization of Europe. Yet others worried about the effects of the Charter on other organizations and systems, in particular that of the European Convention on Human Rights. Some considered it as intending to give, by stealth, greater com-petence to European institutions in areas from which they had previously been excluded. Arising from these concerns, several limits emerged in the drafting of the Charter. The Charter should adequately reflect existing national con-stitutional traditions. The Charter should respect the need for subsidiarity. The Charter should recognise the desirability of diverse conceptions of human rights. The Charter should not be legally binding. The Charter should not threaten the ECHR system. The Charter should not expand the range of rights protections already guaranteed. The Charter should not place unacceptable limits on the need to continue the liberalisation of the European and national economies.[65]

Into this vacuum stepped the European judiciary. Advocates General mentioned the Charter on at least twenty occasions in the following two years.[66] Though they did not always attribute it the same importance, a pattern emerged where the Advocates General recognised that the Charter had no formal binding force, but then noted its value as an expression of consensus among Member States and the EU institutions on what constitutes a shared set of fundamental rights and values. One of the first instances of this was *BECTU*. BECTU, the largest British trade union in the broad-casting sector, brought an action against the British government on the grounds that it had failed to transpose Directive 93/104/EC on the organisation of working time. Article 7 of the Directive entitled everybody to at least four weeks' annual leave a year. Under British law, entitlements did not begin to accrue until somebody had been with

---

64 For discussion and criticism of the method see G. de Búrca, 'The Drafting of the EU Charter of Fundamental Rights' (2001) 26 *EL Rev.* 126; O. de Schutter, 'Europe in Search of its Civil Society' (2002) 8 *ELJ* 198, 206–12.

65 C. McCrudden, *The Future of the EU Charter of Fundamental Rights,* Jean Monnet Working Paper 13/01

66 For a detailed analysis of the early judicial references see J. Morijn, *Judicial Reference to the EU Fundamental Rights Charter: First Experiences and Possible Prospects,* Working Paper 1 Ius Gentium Conimbrigae Institute; A. Menéndez, *Chartering Europe: the Charter of Fundamental Rights of the European Union,* Lucas Pires Working Papers on European Constitutionalism, WP 2001/03.

the same employer for at least thirteen weeks. The question arose whether it should be interpreted in the light of Article 31(2) of the Charter which grants every worker the right to limitation of working hours and to an annual period of paid leave. The Court made no reference to the Charter but it was addressed by the Advocate General.

### Case C-173/99 *R v Secretary of State for Trade and Industry ex parte BECTU* [2001] ECR I-4881, Advocate General Tizzano

26. Even more significant, it seems to me, is the fact that that right is now solemnly upheld in the Charter of Fundamental Rights of the European Union, published on 7 December 2000 by the European Parliament, the Council and the Commission after approval by the Heads of State and Government of the Member States, often on the basis of an express and specific mandate from the national parliaments. Article 31(2) of the Charter declares that: 'Every worker has the right to limitation of maximum working hours, to daily and weekly rest periods and to an annual period of paid leave.' And that statement, as expressly declared by the Presidium of the Convention which drew up the Charter, is inspired precisely by Article 2 of the European Social Charter and by paragraph 8 of the Community Charter of Workers' Rights, and also took due account of Directive 93/104/EC concerning certain aspects of the organisation of working time.

27. . . . the Charter of Fundamental Rights of the European Union has not been recognised as having genuine legislative scope in the strict sense. In other words, formally, it is not in itself binding. However, without wishing to participate here in the wide-ranging debate now going on as to the effects which, in other forms and by other means, the Charter may nevertheless produce, the fact remains that it includes statements which appear in large measure to reaffirm rights which are enshrined in other instruments. In its Preamble, it is moreover stated that 'this Charter reaffirms, with due regard for the powers and tasks of the Community and the Union and the principle of subsidiarity, the rights as they result, in particular, from the constitutional traditions and international obligations common to the Member States, the Treaty on European Union, the Community Treaties, the European Convention for the Protection of Human Rights and Fundamental Freedoms, the Social Charters adopted by the Community and by the Council of Europe and the case-law of the Court of Justice of the European Communities and of the European Court of Human Rights'.

28. I think therefore that, in proceedings concerned with the nature and scope of a fundamental right, the relevant statements of the Charter cannot be ignored; in particular, we cannot ignore its clear purpose of serving, where its provisions so allow, as a substantive point of reference for all those involved – Member States, institutions, natural and legal persons – in the Community context. Accordingly, I consider that the Charter provides us with the most reliable and definitive confirmation of the fact that the right to paid annual leave constitutes a fundamental right.

Both the Spanish Constitutional Court[67] and Italian Constitutional Court[68] were also quick to make reference to the Charter as an authoritative source of fundamental rights. The Court of First Instance also appears ready to attribute a powerful value

---

67 Decision 292/2000 of 30 November 2000, www.tribunalconstitucional.es/STC2000/STC2000-292.htm
68 Decision 135/2002 of 11 April 2002, para. 2.1, www.cortecostituzionale.it/pron/rp_m/pr_02/pr_02_m/pron_h_02.htm

to the Charter as an indirect source for the determination of what constitutes a fundamental right in the EU legal order. The CFI has also made use of the Charter. Most notably, in *Jégo-Quéré*,[69] it invoked Article 47 of the Charter, which sets out the right to an effective judicial remedy, in order to change the traditional rules of standing in annulment proceedings.[70] The Court of Justice, by contrast, recognising the political difficulties of pre-empting the Member States by commenting on the Charter before any decision was made in the Constitutional Treaty, has preferred to acknowledge the substance of the rights without referring to the Charter explicitly. This was significant because the Charter does not merely codify the Court's case law, but incorporates rights that had not hitherto been discussed or acknowledged by the Court of Justice.[71]

A good example of this practice is the *Dutch Biotechnology* judgment in which the Netherlands challenged Directive 98/44/EC, which provides for the patenting of biotechnological inventions. One of the grounds of the challenge was that the Directive violated the right of the patient to free and informed consent, in that she might not know whether any medical treatment administered to her involved biotechnology or whether any part of her body was to be used for biotechnological procedures. The Charter recognises the right to free and informed consent in Article 3(2), but it had never previously been recognised as a fundamental right in EU law. Whilst holding that the Directive did not violate any fundamental right, both the Advocate General and the Court went on to discuss this right in detail.

> ### Case C-377/98 *Netherlands v Parliament and Council* [2001] ECR I-7079, Advocate General Jacobs
>
> 210. It is of course clearly desirable that no element of human origin should be taken from a person without their consent. That principle is expressed at the forefront of the EU Charter of Fundamental Rights; it is also enshrined in Chapter II of the Council of Europe Convention on human rights and biomedicine, which provides that an intervention in the health field may only be carried out after the person concerned has given free and informed consent to it.
>
> 211. In my view, however, although the requirement of consent to all potential uses of human material may be regarded as fundamental, patent law is not the appropriate framework for the imposition and monitoring of such a requirement. A patent, as discussed above, simply confers the right to prevent others from using or otherwise exploiting the patented invention; how the grantee of the patent uses or exploits that invention is regulated not by patent law but by national law and practice governing the field concerned.
>
> 212. Moreover to make evidence of such consent a condition of granting a biotechnological patent – presumably by way of the morality principle – to my mind risks being unworkable.

69 Case T-177/01, *Jégo-Quéré v Commission* [2002] ECR II-2365.
70 This is discussed in more detail in chapter 10. See pp. 429–30.
71 L. Besselink, 'The Member States, the National Constitutions and the Scope of the Charter' (2000) 8 *MJ* 71; P. Eeckhout, 'The EU Charter on Fundamental Rights and the Federal Question' (2002) 39 *CML Rev.* 945, 951.

Biotechnological inventions may derive from research on possibly thousands of blood or tissue samples, possibly pooled and almost certainly anonymous at the time of analysis. I do not consider that it is reasonable to expect patent examiners to satisfy themselves that the chain of consent with regard to each sample is unbroken and evidenced. It is rather the responsibility of the medical or research staff taking the samples to ensure that consent is given; that responsibility, together with the form and scope of the consent, will be imposed by national regulations, codes of practice etc. outside the patent arena. That approach is not inconsistent with recital 26, which refers to national law. Patentability on the other hand is to be assessed only on the basis of the nature of the product or process itself, or on the ground that any commercial or industrial application would be objectionable.

213. Thus in my view the Directive is not the proper place for rules governing the consent of the donor or of the recipient of elements of human origin. Indeed such questions of consent arise more generally with regard to any use of human substances, such as transplants, organ donation, etc. That supports the view that the issues are not to be resolved by patent law, and in particular by patent law as it applies in this specific sector.

214. The Netherlands also submits that the Directive, by failing to require that a patient must consent to receiving medical treatment involving material which has been processed or obtained by biotechnological means, infringes fundamental rights. That argument is in my view misconceived. The conditions of exploitation or use of patented inventions are . . . outside the scope of patent legislation, falling to be controlled by other means. That is clearly spelt out by recital 14: it is not for substantive patent law, which merely entitles the holder to prohibit third parties from exploiting his inventions for industrial and commercial purposes, to replace ethical monitoring of research or the commercial use of its results. Similarly, as the Council points out, the Directive contains no provision requiring that the recipient of biotechnologically processed matter must be informed simply because it does not and cannot seek to regulate the use or commercialisation of such matter.

215. I therefore reach the conclusion that the Directive does not, either by what it provides or by what it fails to provide, infringe, in itself, fundamental rights recognised in Community law. The possibility cannot of course be excluded that a particular application of the Directive within a Member State may infringe fundamental rights, although it contains provisions designed to avoid that consequence. But the conclusion is clear in my view that the Directive does not in itself infringe fundamental rights.

## European Court of Justice

78. The second part of the plea concerns the right to human integrity, in so far as it encompasses, in the context of medicine and biology, the free and informed consent of the donor and recipient.

79. Reliance on this fundamental right is, however, clearly misplaced as against a directive which concerns only the grant of patents and whose scope does not therefore extend to activities before and after that grant, whether they involve research or the use of the patented products.

80. The grant of a patent does not preclude legal limitations or prohibitions applying to research into patentable products or the exploitation of patented products, as the 14th recital of the Preamble to the Directive points out. The purpose of the Directive is not to replace the restrictive provisions which guarantee, outside the scope of the Directive, compliance with certain ethical rules which include the right to self-determination by informed consent.

The exact legal status of the Charter remained contentious. The Working Group established by the Convention on the Future of Europe was excluded from considering the questions of whether the European Union should incorporate the Charter or accede to the ECHR, but was given the more technocratic task of considering the procedures and techniques for incorporation and their consequences, should this be what was decided.[72] The solution adopted in the Constitutional Treaty was to formalise the position adopted in 'Dutch Biotechnology Directive' by recognising the authoritative force of the Charter as a description of the fundamental rights binding the European Union:

## Article I-7 CT

The Union shall recognise the rights, freedoms and principles set out in the Charter of Fundamental Rights which constitutes Part II of the Constitution.

The Charter is, however, not given any constitutive force of its own. Instead, the Constitutional Treaty sees it as merely being a statement of certain deeper principles, whose authority precedes that of the Charter. This was particularly significant in the light of the non-ratification of the Constitutional Treaty. For it suggests a view that the Constitutional Treaty does no more than codify existing practice. For that reason, the provisions in the Constitutional Treaty are significant here, as they express an institutional position which may endure, notwithstanding the non-ratification of the Constitutional Treaty.

## Article II-111(1) CT

1. The provisions of this Charter are addressed to the Institutions, bodies and agencies of the Union with due regard for the principle of subsidiarity and to the Member States only when they are implementing Union law. They shall therefore respect the rights, observe the principles and promote the application thereof in accordance with their respective powers and respecting the limits of the powers of the Union as conferred on it in the other Parts of the Constitution.

2. This Charter does not extend the field of application of Union law beyond the powers of the Union or establish any new power or task for the Union, or modify powers and tasks defined in the other Parts of the Constitution.

## Article II-112(2) CT

Rights recognised by this Charter for which provision is made in other Parts of the Constitution shall be exercised under the conditions and within the limits defined by these relevant Parts.

Reactions to the Charter were mixed. There are those who consider that it does not go far enough. A Platform of European Social NGOs and the European Trade Unions, for example, called for the Charter to be a fully established bill of rights capable of being invoked in all circumstances against both the EU institutions and

72 Mandate of the Working Group on the Charter, CONV 72/02.

the Member States.[73] Others viewed the Charter more positively. It has been argued that the Charter marks out new directions and aspirations for the EU institutions. Fundamental rights are to act as 'regulative ideas', which the institutions must not only not violate, but which they must act to realise. This has a powerful legitimating force for the European Union because fundamental rights have a wider role to play in a system like the Union's, with its weak parliamentary controls.[74] It also transforms the political identity of the Union. It can no longer be viewed as an instrument to realise certain common ends, such as the common market, but is now 'an entity built upon the individual, her freedom and her well-being'.[75] Other authors have argued forcefully against the Charter.

> ## J. Weiler, 'A Constitution for Europe? Some Hard Choices' (2002) 40 *Journal of Common Market Studies* 563, 576–7
>
> The current system of looking to the common constitutional traditions and to the ECHR as a source of rights protected in the Union is, it is argued, unsatisfactory and should be replaced by a formal document listing such rights. But would clarity actually be added? Examine the text. It is, appropriately, drafted in the magisterial language characteristic of our constitutional traditions: human dignity is inviolable, etc. There is much to be said for this tradition, but clarity is not part of it. When it comes to the contours of the rights included in the Charter, I do not believe that it adds much clarity to what exactly is protected and what is not.
>
> Note, however, that by drafting a list and perhaps one day fully incorporating it into the legal order, we have jettisoned, at least in part, one of the truly original features of the pre-Charter constitutional architecture in the field of human rights – the ability to use the legal system of each of the Member States as an organic and living laboratory of human rights protection, which then, case by case, can be adapted and adopted for the needs of the Union by the European Court in dialogue with its national counterparts. The Charter may not thwart that process, but it runs the risk of inducing a more inward-looking jurisprudence and chilling the constitutional dialogue.

### (ii)  The rights and freedoms recognised in the Charter

The Charter is divided into six headings. Each heading contains a number of rights and principles, of which the central ones are set out below.

**Rights to human dignity**   Right to life; integrity of the person; prohibition of torture or inhuman and degrading treatment; prohibition of slavery or forced labour; prohibition on cloning or eugenics (Articles 1–5).

**Freedoms**   Right to liberty and security; respect for private and family life; protection of personal data; right to marry and found a family; freedom of thought, conscience

---

73 CHARTE 4286/00, 12 May 2000.
74 C. Engel, 'The European Charter of Fundamental Rights: a Changed Political Opportunity Structure and its Normative Consequences' (2001) 7 *ELJ* 151, 159.
75 E. Eriksen, 'Why a Charter of Fundamental Human Rights?' in E. Eriksen *et al.* (eds.), *The Chartering of Europe: the Charter of Fundamental Rights in Context* (Oslo, ARENA, 2001) 29, 41–2.

and religion; freedom of expression and information; freedom of assembly; freedom of the arts and sciences; right to education; freedom to choose an occupation and right to engage in work; freedom to conduct a business; right to asylum; right to property (Articles 6–19).

**Equality**   Equality before the law; non-discrimination on sex, race, colour, ethnic or social origin, genetic features, language, religion or belief or political opinion, disability, sexual orientation, birth; cultural, religious and linguistic diversity; equality between men and women; rights of the elderly, integration of persons with disabilities (Articles 20–26).

**Solidarity**   Workers' right to information and consultation; right of collective bargaining; protection in the event of unfair dismissal; right to placement services; fair and just working conditions; prohibition on child labour; right to social security; right to health care; protection of the family; high level of environmental and consumer protection; access to services of general economic interest (Articles 27–38).

**Citizen's Rights**   Right to vote and stand in municipal and European Parliament elections; right to good administration; right to access to documents; right to refer matters to European Parliament and petition Ombudsman; freedom of movement and residence; right to diplomatic protection (Articles 39–46).

**Justice**   Right to an effective remedy and a fair trial; presumption of innocence; right not to be tried or punished twice for same offence; principle of legality and proportionality of criminal offences (Articles 47–50).

Few of these rights are absolute, and many are conditioned by exceptions. Article 52(1) of the Charter sets out limits on how these exceptions may be invoked:

> Any limitation on the exercise of the rights and freedoms recognised by this Charter must be provided for by law and respect the essence of those rights and freedoms. Subject to the principle of proportionality, limitations may be made only if they are necessary and genuinely meet objectives of general interest recognised by the Union or the need to protect the rights and freedoms of others.

The rights were taken from three sources: rights recognised in the TEU, rights recognised in the constitutions of the Member States and international human rights treaties concluded by the Member States.[76] Even though it incorporates a wider array of rights and freedoms than any other human rights treaty, the Charter might appear to be no more than a rearticulation of the status quo. There are, however, some noteworthy features about the Charter.

---

76 CHARTE 4473/00, 11 October 2000.

First, it serves to amplify these rights. Many Member States had not signed up to the international conventions embodying many of these rights. All Member States are now committed to observe them. In the case of many of these rights, the commitment to observe existed at no higher a level than that of general international law, with limited mechanisms for monitoring or sanctioning non-observance. These rights now exist as a matter of EU law, which has a far wider array of administrative procedures and judicial sanctions to secure their observance.

Secondly, the Charter reformulates many of these rights.[77] They are expressed in a different fashion from the original source. This means, inevitably, that these rights may be interpreted differently in due course. In some cases, this is because the language has been adapted to the needs of modern society. Article 8(1) ECHR talks of the right to 'respect . . . for correspondence'. Article 7 of the Charter talks of the right to 'respect . . . for communications', which takes into account the growth of electronic communications. In other cases, this is because a particular right has been derived from multiple sources. The prohibition on discrimination on grounds of gender, racial or ethnic origin can be found in some constitutions, the ECHR and other international human rights treaties. In such circumstances, it is not possible to refer to any one source without excluding others. EU law will have to develop its own means of interpretation.

Thirdly, the Charter suggests the indivisibility of these rights. Social, civil, political and environmental rights should all be treated equally as fundamental rights. In this, as the piece below suggests, the Charter marks a fundamentally new political identity for the European Union.

---

**M. de la Torre, 'The Law Beneath Rights' Feet: Preliminary Investigation for a Study of the Charter of Fundamental Rights of the European Union' (2002) 8 *European Law Journal* 513, 533–5**

. . . in the Charter the rights concerned are both the specific ones of the European citizen (a status, we would recall, introduced by the Maastricht Treaty and confirmed and extended by the Amsterdam Treaty) and those of human beings in general, a category that thus covers not just citizens of Member States but also residents in them, and still more generally anyone who happens to be living or staying in the territory of the Member States. Civil, political and social rights are accordingly brought together in the single figure of fundamental rights. This has two consequences: (a) On one side the fundamental rights – since citizenship rights are reserved to Member State nationals – are pushed up towards the universal category of human rights. If, as the European Commission says, the Charter asserts the principle of indivisibility of rights, it will be increasingly hard to accept that a subject bearing civil and social rights (generic human rights) does not also enjoy political rights (fundamental rights in the strict sense), unless, of course, one wished to deny the foreigner (the non-citizen) the totality of social and civil rights, and ultimately any enjoyment whatever of human rights. (b) On the other side – and this is the point that most interests us here – if the rights are indivisible, there cannot be

---

77 K. Lenaerts and E. de Smijter, 'A "Bill of Rights" for the European Union' (2001) 38 *CML Rev.* 273, 281–3.

abstraction of political rights from them in any area. What I mean is that since the political rights (citizenship, above all), assign to individuals positive freedom, that is, a competence to intervene in the production of positive legal norms, and since these political rights are seen as inseparable in principle from those others that instead grant negative freedom, guarantees in relation to excesses by the public powers, then the fundamental rights (always, on this view, connected with political rights) can no longer be conceived of as mere limits on the activity of the public authorities. The political rights are first and foremost intervention positions within the public power. Fundamental rights and political and legislative activity are thus not 'armed against each other', as the romantic or disenchanted defender of the legislator's absolute will would have it. The legislator – on the view we have arrived at thanks to the discussion done in the foregoing sections, and on the view, consistent with it, manifested in the interpretation of the Charter itself – is constituted through the exercise of fundamental rights, which are, however, not just political but also civil (freedoms, essentially) and social (rights to specific performance by the authorities). Negative freedom and positive freedom, liberalism and democracy, fundamental rights and public powers, law and politics, finally, thus seem here to find a synthesis and a strong connection, referring reciprocally to each other. This, if taken seriously, cannot fail to have serious repercussions on the European constitutional model itself.

Once fundamental rights are affirmed and the indivisibility of such rights proclaimed, any project for a mixed constitution is devoid of legitimacy. Here I call a 'mixed constitution' one that maintains the idea of various institutional spheres within the Union, of which only one – Parliament (without true legislative powers) – would be the expression of citizenship rights, while in relation to the other spheres only guarantee rights (the civil rights) would apply. In other words, the 'mixed constitution', by some called 'regulatory model', is the one where legislation is distinct from the exercise of citizenship, and the latter ends by being reduced to a guarantee right in relation to norms to the production of which there is no access. This production is reserved to 'independent' authorities, since it is held that 'deliberation' can come about only away from representative and majority pressures. Deliberation and representation are thus separated, and entrusted to distinct bodies. The same happens to citizenship and (political) expertise, so that we are confronted with a revived duplication of political rights in passive (the ones of simple citizens) and active (the ones of experts, of a post-modern kind of statesmen). Statesmanship is consequently sharply severed from citizenship.

Criticism has been levelled at the content of the Charter. Some have argued that it might lead to a deterioration of human rights protection, with concentration focussing on rights included in the Charter, and a corollary abandonment of other rights and freedoms.[78] The right to nationality, the right to decent pay, the right to work and the right to housing are not included in the Charter.[79] The consequence, particularly in the field of social rights, is that the Charter looks patchy and arbitrary, with certain key rights seen to be missing.[80] Certain other rights (for example, the

78 J. Weiler, 'A Constitution for Europe? Some Hard Choices' (2002) 40 *JCMS* 563, 576.
79 Albeit that the right to 'housing assistance' is provided for in Article 34(3) (Article II-94(3) CT).
80 J. Kenner, 'Economic and Social Rights in the EU Legal Order: the Mirage of Indivisibility' in T. Hervey and J. Kenner (eds.), *Economic and Social Rights under the EU Charter of Fundamental Rights* (Oxford, Hart, 2003) 1, 16–18.

right to marry, the right to collective bargaining, the right of workers to information and consultation, the right to protection against unfair dismissal, the right to social security and health care) are to be recognised only in accordance with the rules laid down by national or Community laws. National laws are to determine the content of these rights so that instead of acting as a basis for review of EU and national practices, these are turned around to justify even egregious practices.[81]

Another concern centres on the distinction made between principles and rights, which was introduced on the incorporation of the Charter into the Constitutional Treaty.

### Article II-112(5) CT

The provisions of this Charter which contain principles may be implemented by legislative and executive acts taken by Institutions, bodies, offices and agencies of the Union and by acts of Member States when they are implementing Union law, in the exercise of their respective powers. They shall be judicially cognisable only in the interpretation of such acts and in the ruling on their legality.

To be sure, the Constitutional Treaty has not entered into force. Notwithstanding this, this view of the Charter, given the authority of the national government, may well enter subsequent interpretations. On one view, this distinction suggests that some of the provisions may be protected more absolutely by the judiciary than others. However, another view is that the sheer breadth of the Charter prevents a 'one size fits all' approach to protection of the entitlements granted by it. Courts are not well suited to determining when a right to sustainable development warrants protection, or when the level of health provision is so low that it violates the right to access to health care. More partial judicial control might be a price worth paying for having these recognised. Moreover, even there, courts have a useful role to play.

A more telling criticism is that such a distinction would generate legal uncertainty. It is unclear which provisions articulate rights and which articulate principles. Three provisions explicitly use the word 'principle'. Article 37 refers to the principle of sustainable development. Article 23 refers to the principle of equality between men and women. Yet, it must be read alongside Article 21, which sets out the right, inter alia, to non-discrimination on grounds of sex. If the principle of equality is non-justiciable in a free-standing manner, then it must be wider than the right to non-discrimination. Finally, the principles of legality and proportionality of criminal offences are set out in Article 49. Alongside these, it would seem that those provisions, whose content is dependent upon their realisation by national or EU law, would be considered to be

---

81 D. Ashiagbor, 'Economic and Social Rights in the European Charter of Fundamental Rights' (2004) 1 *European Human Rights Law Review* 62.

principles.[82] Yet, many of the provisions to be implemented by national law describe themselves as 'rights'.[83] There are also provisions where the European Union commits itself to respect certain values in its policies, such as a high level of environmental protection or consumer protection or respect for services of a general economic interest.[84] These provisions would not seem to confer free-standing rights, but act merely to orient the policy in question. Yet, the question is surrounded by ambiguity.

### (iii)   Interpretation of the Charter

Concerns emerged during the negotiations over the Constitutional Treaty that the wide ambit of many of the rights provided insufficient safeguards against judicial activism by the Court of Justice or national courts. These might use the Charter to impose a wide variety of demands or constraints on either EU or national legislatures. A proviso was therefore introduced which might influence future interpretations of the Charter:

### Article II-112(7) CT

The explanations drawn up by way of providing guidance in the interpretation of the Charter of Fundamental Rights shall be given due regard by the courts of the Union and the Member States.[85]

This would appear to undercut the judicial role in developing the Charter, as it is confined by the interpretations set out by the Secretariat to the Convention establishing the Charter. It is unclear how significant, in practical terms, this will be, as whilst it does indicate the inspiration for each right, the document is remarkably silent on the scope of each right. A problem which is likely to be more significant is that this provision encourages adjudicators to be backward-looking in their interpretation of the Charter. For the explanations invariably seek to locate individual provisions as simply the culmination of the existing case law of the Court of Justice or existing international treaties. Over time there is thus a real danger that undue prominence will be given to retrospective and dated interpretations, rather than to interpretations that meet the demands of an evolving society.

---

82  e.g. the right to marry (Article 9), the right to found educational establishments (Article 14(3)), the workers' right to information and consultation within their undertaking (Article 27), the right to collective bargaining (Article 28), the right to protection in the event of unjustified dismissal (Article 30), the right to health care (Article 35). Article 34 of the Charter recognises the right to entitlements to social and housing assistance in accordance with EU and national law.

83  All the provisions mentioned below n. 84, with the exception of Article 34, do this.

84  Article 37 Charter (Article II-97 CT); Article 38 Charter (Article II-98 CT).

85  Initially in CHARTE 4487/00 CONVENT 50, this is now set out in the Declaration concerning the Explanations relating to the Charter of Fundamental Rights.

In addition, the Charter is not to undermine the protections offered to the individual either by international treaties, notably the European Convention on Human Rights, or by national constitutions:

### Article 53

Nothing in this Charter shall be interpreted as restricting or adversely affecting human rights and freedoms as recognised, in their respective fields of application, by Union law and international law and by international agreements to which the Union or all the Member States are party, including the European Convention on Human Rights and Fundamental Freedoms, and by the Member States' constitutions.

To this end, the Charter also imposes certain duties of interpretation and alignment between it and the ECHR:

### Article 52(3)

Insofar as this Charter contains rights which correspond to rights guaranteed by the Convention for the Protection of Human Rights and Fundamental Freedoms, the meaning and scope of those rights shall be the same as those laid down by the said Convention. This provision shall not prevent Union law providing more extensive protection.

Amendment was made by the Constitutional Treaty for a similar provision in respect of national constitutions:

### Article 112(4) CT

Insofar as this Charter recognizes fundamental rights as they result from the constitutional traditions common to the Member States, those rights shall be interpreted in harmony with those traditions.

The force of these provisions is unclear. The earlier discussion suggests that it is not so easy to make statements about one level of protection being higher than the other.[86] Decisions often reflect choices between conflicting value claims: freedom of expression versus privacy in libel cases; freedom of expression versus respect for religion in blasphemy cases etc. One cannot talk of a baseline of protection that moves ever upwards without having a hierarchy of values, so that freedom of expression will trump freedom of religion etc.[87] The Charter does not provide any such hierarchy, and indeed, insofar as it suggests the rights within it are indivisible, seems to preclude it. The position is further complicated by the Charter having to respect the level of protection offered by a number of sources – national constitutions, the ECHR and

---

86 See pp. 238–41.
87 R. García, 'The General Provisions of the Charter of Fundamental Rights of the European Union' (2002) 8 *ELJ* 492, 508.

other international treaties. It is not clear what 'level' of protection should be offered where these conflict. Nevertheless, these provisions point to there being a certain core protection offered by the ECHR and national constitutions which the Charter should not undermine. If all national constitutions and the ECHR prohibit a particular state activity, it does not seem open for the Charter to allow it. The trick will be discovering when this is the case. For there will clearly be incentives for litigating lawyers to argue for a particular interpretation on the grounds that it is protected by constitutional courts across the European Union. If that is so, the Charter could become a vehicle for developing a common constitutional law of Europe, with national provisions and practices, and the ECHR being compared and synthesised before the Court of Justice and its building a common interpretation on the back of these.

The other question is whether these other sources will have too much effect. One concern is that these provisions will undermine the autonomy of EU law. Too much weight may now be given to the ECHR in rulings by the EU Courts.[88] It is notable that in recent years, the Court of Justice has stated that the ECHR has a special status in EC law. The consequence has been a reticence in the Court's case law here. Its recent judgments do not articulate new principles or values, but are characterised instead by a 'cut-out and paste' reliance on the case law of the European Court on Human Rights (ECtHR).[89] This might reflect an undue faith in the latter's decision-making processes and judgment. The ECHR covers forty-six states. It is committed to a less intense form of political integration and governs a more diverse array of situations than the European Union. It is not clear that the judgments of a court, such as the ECtHR, operating in that context, should be accepted almost unquestioningly. A more preferable arrangement would be one of mutual justification. The EU Courts treat any judgment given by the ECtHR as a persuasive suggestion. If the latter's judgment is not considered adequate to protect either the individual freedom or collective interest in question, then they can depart from it, but must give reasons for their choice.

The other concern is where an EU measure comes before a national or EU Court and it appears to conflict with a national constitutional provision. The Charter binds EU institutions and Member States when they are implementing EU law.[90] Article 112(4) CT would imply that the content of the Charter right, in such a scenario, should be the same as the national constitutional provision. The threat to the supremacy of EU law would look quite compelling.[91] On the other hand, Article 112(4) CT only talks

---

88 For discussion see R. García, *ibid.* 501–2.
89 e.g. Case C-109/01 *Akrich v Home Office* [2003] ECR I–9607; Case C-245/01 *RTL v Niedersächsische Landesmedienanstalt für privaten Rundfunk* [2003] ECR I-12489; Case C-117/01 *KB v National Health Service Pensions Agency* [2004] ECR I-541; Case C-71/02 *Karner v Troostwijk* [2004] ECR I-3025.
90 Article 51(1).
91 J. Liisberg, 'Does the EU Charter of Fundamental Rights Threaten the Supremacy of Community Law' (2001) 38 *CML Rev.* 1171, 1191. This article also provides an excellent summary of a parallel debate that took place at the time of the adoption of the Charter.

of the Charter being interpreted in harmony with national constitutional traditions. It might be argued, therefore, that Charter rights need only be convergent with, but not identical to, national constitutional provisions. Even this is a problematic interpretation, however, because if the Charter is interpreted as either granting or precluding individual rights articulated by a constitutional court, it is difficult to deny a conflict between the case law of the Charter and a national constitutional tradition.

### 5. Fundamental rights and the institutional scheme of the European Union

#### (i)   Fundamental rights and the EU institutions

Respect for fundamental rights is a condition for the legality of any Community instrument. Fundamental rights, therefore, act, in the first place, as a basis for review. To that end, following proclamation of the Charter, the Commission sought to mainstream fundamental rights more into the administrative practice of the Union.

> **EC Commission, *Application of the Charter of Fundamental Rights of the European Union*, SEC(2001)380/3**
>
> Any proposal for legislation and any draft instrument to be adopted by the Commission will . . . as part of the normal decision-making procedures, first be scrutinised for compatibility with the Charter. Moreover, legislative proposals or draft instruments which have a specific link with fundamental rights will incorporate the following recital as a formal statement of compatibility:
>
> > 'This act respects the fundamental rights and observes the principles recognised in particular by the Charter of Fundamental Rights of the European Union.'
>
> When certain rights and/or individual principles of the Charter are specifically involved, a second sentence may be added:
>
> > 'In particular, this [act] seeks to ensure full respect for [right XX] and/or to promote the application of [principle YY] / [Article XX and/or Article YY of the Charter of Fundamental Rights of the European Union].'

It is yet to be seen whether this pre-commitment by the Commission will be given legal bite by the Court, so that measures can be struck down, not merely where they violate a fundamental right, but also where it appears that the EU institutions have failed to give due consideration to whether or not a measure potentially violates a fundamental right. In the absence of this, commentators have suggested that it may be no more than a paper requirement, used to legitimise dubious practices through the suggestion that they have been evaluated for their implications for fundamental rights.[92] More generally, the number of successful actions is very small. There is no

---

92 G. de Búrca and J. Aschenbrenner, 'The Development of European Constitutionalism and the Role of the EU Charter of Fundamental Rights' (2003) 9 *CJEL* 355, 366–8.

instance in recent times of a Council Regulation or Directive being struck down because it violates fundamental rights. Instead, fundamental rights are increasingly having an interpretive function, where they are to be used to guide interpretation of EU acts. A good example is *Osterreichischer Rundfunk*. Under a 1997 law, the Austrian Court of Auditors required from all local authorities and public bodies details of the salaries and pensions of senior officials for the annual report that it submitted to the Austrian Parliament. It argued this was necessary to keep state finances in check. A number of these refused to submit the information, arguing that it violated Directive 95/46/EC on the protection of individuals with regard to the processing of personal data. In interpreting the obligations set out by the Directive, the Court was eager to interpret them in the light of Article 8 ECHR, upholding the right to respect for private life.

---

### Joined Cases C-465/00, C-138/01 and C-139/01 *Österreichischer Rundfunk* [2003] ECR I-4989

68. It should also be noted that the provisions of Directive 95/46, in so far as they govern the processing of personal data liable to infringe fundamental freedoms, in particular the right to privacy, must necessarily be interpreted in the light of fundamental rights, which, according to settled case-law, form an integral part of the general principles of law whose observance the Court ensures . . .

69. Those principles have been expressly restated in Article 6(2) EU, which states that [t]he Union shall respect fundamental rights, as guaranteed by the [Convention] and as they result from the constitutional traditions common to the Member States, as general principles of Community law.

70. Directive 95/46 itself, while having as its principal aim to ensure the free movement of personal data, provides in Article 1(1) that Member States shall protect the fundamental rights and freedoms of natural persons, and in particular their right to privacy with respect to the processing of personal data. Several recitals in its Preamble, in particular recitals 10 and 11, also express that requirement.

71. In this respect, it is to be noted that Article 8 of the Convention, while stating in paragraph 1 the principle that the public authorities must not interfere with the right to respect for private life, accepts in paragraph 2 that such an interference is possible where it is in accordance with the law and is necessary in a democratic society in the interests of national security, public safety or the economic well-being of the country, for the prevention of disorder or crime, for the protection of health or morals, or for the protection of the rights and freedoms of others.

72. So, for the purpose of applying Directive 95/46, in particular Articles 6(1)(c), 7(c) and (e) and 13, it must be ascertained, first, whether legislation such as that at issue in the main proceedings provides for an interference with private life, and if so, whether that interference is justified from the point of view of Article 8 of the Convention . . .

91. If the national courts conclude that the national legislation at issue is incompatible with Article 8 of the Convention, that legislation is also incapable of satisfying the requirement of proportionality in Articles 6(1)(c) and 7(c) or (e) of Directive 95/46. Nor could it be covered by any of the exceptions referred to in Article 13 of that directive, which likewise requires compliance with the requirement of proportionality with respect to the public interest

objective being pursued. In any event, that provision cannot be interpreted as conferring legitimacy on an interference with the right to respect for private life contrary to Article 8 of the Convention.

The judgment uses interpretation to displace review. If there is an interpretation that can render the measure lawful from a fundamental rights perspective, that interpretation must be chosen. The danger, in such circumstances, is that courts will look for mutual compatibility. They will not merely interpret EU secondary legislation in the light of fundamental rights norms, but will also interpret fundamental rights norms in the light of the legislation being challenged, with the possibility of the safeguards offered by the latter being adjusted downwards to protect the legislation in question.

The principle also serves to allocate risks between EU institutions and Member States. In adjusting their legislation to apply or comply with EU measures, Member States must adopt interpretations of those measures which comply with EU fundamental rights norms. If they fail to do this, as *Österreichischer Rundfunk* shows, it is the Member State which is held accountable, not the EU legislature. This has the advantage that national administrations become guarantors of fundamental rights norms. To avoid being the targets of litigation, they will need to ensure that the legislation is not applied in any way that violates their understandings of fundamental rights. The judgment does, however, leave them between a rock and a hard place. They are left in a situation where they have to choose between the apparent textual intent of a particular provision and compliance with an EU fundamental right. Adoption of either path is likely to leave them susceptible to legal challenge by individuals.

### (ii) Fundamental rights and the Member States

In the early years, fundamental rights litigation only involved challenges directed at acts of the Community institutions. If the doctrine were confined to this arena, then there was little to concern Member State governments directly. Fundamental rights acted as a constraint on the functioning of the Community institutions. If anything, they slowed down the process of political integration as they could be used to challenge and prevent Community action. The position would be radically altered, however, if the doctrine was extended to cover Member State action. The autonomy of national governments and legislatures would be reduced. Equally significantly, the EC would be given a stronger civil and political identity, as action occurring within the national sphere would not be struck down simply because it violated economic norms, but also for infringing civil liberties. Unsurprisingly, the Court was initially reticent about holding Member State action to be bound by fundamental rights. There were a number of instances in which fundamental rights were alluded to as an interpretive tool, so that they were used to determine the reach of EC legal provisions addressed to Member States.[93] The general position, however, was that they could not be used to review national action. In *Cinéthèque*, a judgment involving a challenge to French legislation prohibiting the marketing of any film shown in a cinema for a period between six and eighteen months after release, the Court stated that it had no jurisdiction to assess the compatibility of national law with the European Convention on Human Rights.[94]

This position posed difficulties. Most administration regulated by EC law was carried out by national authorities. Clearly, the coherence and unity of the Community legal order would be compromised if the EC institutions were subject to a regime in which they were bound by fundamental rights, and the national authorities were subject to another, in which they were not, or if different national authorities were subject to different regimes.[95] This anomaly was particularly apparent in those circumstances where national authorities were implementing EC obligations.[96]

In *Wachauf*, a German tenant farmer, upon expiry of his tenancy, requested compensation for the discontinuance of the production of milk for sale. German legislation, implementing an EC Regulation, provided that a milk producer could apply for compensation if he undertook to discontinue milk production definitively within a period of six months from the grant of the compensation. However, if the person making that application was a tenant of a farm, he was required to have the lessor's written consent to apply for compensation. Since Wachauf's landlord had withdrawn this consent, Wachauf was not able to receive the compensation. Wachauf argued that the German law violated his right to property, as the compensation was something he had built up through working the land during his lease.

---

### Case 5/88 *Wachauf v Germany* [1989] ECR 2609

17. The Court has consistently held . . . that fundamental rights form an integral part of the general principles of law, the observance of which is ensured by the Court. In safeguarding those rights, the Court has to look to the constitutional traditions common to the Member States, so that measures which are incompatible with the fundamental rights recognised by the

---

93 Case 36/75 *Rutili v Minister for the Interior* [1975] ECR 1219; Case 118/75 *Watson and Belmann* [1976] ECR 1185; Case 222/84 *Johnston v Chief Constable of the RUC* [1986] ECR 1651. For discussion see A. Drzemczewski, 'The Domestic Application of the Human Rights Convention as European Community Law' (1981) 30 *ICLQ* 118.

94 Joined Cases 60 and 61/84, *Cinéthèque v Fédération Nationale des Cinémas Français* [1985] ECR 2605. See also Case 12/86 *Demirel v Stadt Schwabisch Gmund* [1987] ECR 3719.

95 K. Lenaerts, 'Fundamental Rights to be Included in a Community Catalogue' (1991) 16 *EL Rev.* 367, 368; J. Temple Lang, 'The Sphere in which Member States are Obliged to Comply with the General Principles of Law and Community Fundamental Rights Principles' (1991/2) *LIEI* 23, 28–9.

96 There is earlier, although less explicit, authority for the proposition that Member States, when implementing EC obligations, are bound by fundamental rights: Joined Cases 201–2/85 *Klensch v Sécrétaire d'Etat* [1986] ECR 3477. See J. Weiler, 'The European Court at a Crossroads: Community Human Rights and Member State Action' in F. Coportorti *et al.*, *Liber Amicorum Pierre Pescatore: Du droit International au droit de l'Integration* (Baden-Baden, Nomos, 1987).

constitutions of those States may not find acceptance in the Community. International treaties concerning the protection of human rights on which the Member States have collaborated or to which they have acceded can also supply guidelines to which regard should be had in the context of Community law.

18. The fundamental rights recognized by the Court are not absolute, however, but must be considered in relation to their social function. Consequently, restrictions may be imposed on the exercise of those rights, in particular in the context of a common organization of a market, provided that those restrictions in fact correspond to objectives of general interest pursued by the Community and do not constitute, with regard to the aim pursued, a disproportionate and intolerable interference, impairing the very substance of those rights.

19. Having regard to those criteria, it must be observed that Community rules which, upon the expiry of the lease, had the effect of depriving the lessee, without compensation, of the fruits of his labour and of his investments in the tenanted holding would be incompatible with the requirements of the protection of fundamental rights in the Community legal order. Since those requirements are also binding on the Member States when they implement Community rules, the Member States must, as far as possible, apply those rules in accordance with those requirements.

Once it was accepted that there were some circumstances in which Member State action falling within the arena of Community law was governed by fundamental rights, it became more difficult to deny the proposition that Member States were bound by fundamental rights whenever they acted within the field of application of EC law. The breakthrough came in *ERT*. ERT, a Greek radio and television company, enjoyed exclusive broadcasting rights under Greek statute. It sought an injunction against an information company and Mr Kouvelas, the Mayor of Thessaloniki, who had set up a rival television station. The respondents argued that ERT's exclusive rights infringed the free movement and competition provisions of EC law. The Greek government invoked Articles 45 and 55 EC which allowed it to impose restrictions for reasons of public policy. ERT counter-argued that these could not be invoked as the conduct violated Article 10 ECHR relating to freedom of expression.

**Case 260/89 *Elliniki Radiophonia Tiléorassi (ERT) v Dimtiki (DEP)* [1991] ECR I-2925**

41. With regard to Article 10 of the European Convention on Human Rights . . . the Court has consistently held, fundamental rights form an integral part of the general principles of law, the observance of which it ensures. For that purpose the Court draws inspiration from the constitutional traditions common to the Member States and from the guidelines supplied by international treaties common to the Member States and from the guidelines supplied by international treaties for the protection of human rights on which the Member States have collaborated or of which they are signatories . . . The European Convention on Human Rights has special significance in that respect . . . It follows that . . . the Community cannot accept measures which are incompatible with observance of human rights thus recognised and guaranteed.

42. As the Court has held . . . it has no power to examine the compatibility with the European Convention on Human Rights of national rules which do not fall within the scope of Community law. On the other hand, where such rules do fall within the scope of Community law, and reference is made to the Court for a preliminary ruling, it must provide all the criteria of interpretation needed by the national court to determine whether those rules are compatible with the fundamental rights the observance of which the Court ensures and which derive in particular from the European Convention on Human Rights.

43. In particular, where a Member State relies on the combined provisions of [Articles 45 and 55] in order to justify rules which are likely to obstruct the exercise of the freedom to provide services, such justification, provided for by Community law, must be interpreted in the light of the general principles of law and in particular of fundamental rights. Thus the national rules in question can fall under the exceptions provided for by the combined provisions of [Articles 45 and 55] only if they are compatible with the fundamental rights the observance of which is ensured by the Court.

44. It follows that in such a case it is for the national court, and if necessary, the Court of Justice to appraise the application of those provisions having regard to all the rules of Community law, including freedom of expression, as embodied in Article 10 of the European Convention on Human Rights, as a general principle of law the observance of which is ensured by the Court.

The application of EU law to acts of national authorities has the potential to recast the European Union's identity in a far-reaching way. Weiler has argued that the European project cannot be expected to replace the nation-state with some identical European construct, as it is, uniquely, the qualities of the nation-state that give individuals a sense of community, identification and cultural differentiation. Its task is to tame and discipline the less attractive pathologies generated by these features: those of xenophobia, exclusionary practices and introspection. The qualities of the European demos would therefore be:

> a commitment to the shared values of the Union as expressed in its constituent documents, a commitment, inter alia, to the duties and rights of a civil society covering discrete areas of public life, a commitment to membership in a polity which privileges exactly the opposites of nationalism – those human features which transcend the differences of organic ethno-culturalism.[97]

The assertion of EU fundamental rights against national authorities would be the central plank of such an identity.[98] European citizenship, on this vision, would be regulated by an interplay between local practices, which would generate feelings of belonging and community, and European values, which would safeguard the individual from the excesses of communitarianism. Such a view is not uncontestable.

---

97 J. Weiler, 'The Reformation of European Constitutionalism' (1997) 35 *JCMS* 97, 119.

98 Advocate General Jacobs in Case C-168/91 *Konstantinidis v Stadt Altemsteig* [1993] ECR I-1191, considered that the status of European citizen could be invoked to oppose any violation of fundamental rights. This suggestion was not taken up by the Court and was even disavowed by Advocate General Gulmann in Case C-2/92 *R v Minister of Agriculture, Fisheries and Food ex parte Bostock* [1994] ECR I-955.

## A. Clapham, 'A Human Rights Policy for the European Community' (1990) *Yearbook of European Law* 309, 311

Talking about human rights may sometimes bestow identity on Community citizens. This has a subjective dimension with citizens finding they have rights in common; as well as containing an objective perspective with the discovery of a common concern about the rights of others (inside or outside the Community). Where these rights move beyond 'God-given' or 'self evident' rights they result in an intense 'contract' or relationship with the right giver. Should the Community realize its role in distributing rights to Community citizens it could expect some increased loyalty. However, such a symbiotic relationship could only occur should the Community respond to the demands of its citizens rather than reinforcing rights which are primarily geared to its own objectives.

Clearly, rights have an important role to play in the process of European integration, but, it must be said that they may well operate as a double-edged sword. Not only are they a cohesive force but they may well be divisive. Should the Community move to tackle questions such as divorce, contraception, abortion, blasphemy, surrogacy, etc., rights might no longer be handy tools for integration but vehicles of division and disintegration. Furthermore, not only will moral diversity have to be tolerated in the move towards unity, but it is clear that effective rights to challenge Community decisions or provisions could well slow up or completely ensnare new initiatives or progress at the Community level.

The double-edged character of fundamental rights grants them a strong political community-building potential. They provide 'utopian promises', which set in motion the dynamic necessary for the development of a political community.[99] For they set out a series of ideals, which individuals can sign up to and which allow the European Union to be identified as a desirable polity. In addition, with their potential for agreement and disagreement they create the political vocabulary through which citizens can discuss and negotiate identity of a political community. Yet this community-building dimension has proved contentious. The Court of Justice has sought to curb fears that it is institution-building, by stating that fundamental rights only govern Member State actions insofar as they fall within the field of EC law.[100]

The most contentious instance of this which has come before the Court of Justice is *SPUC v Grogan*. In 1986, the Irish Supreme Court ruled that it was against the Irish Constitution to help Irish women to have abortions by informing them of the identity and location of abortion clinics abroad. A number of Irish student unions provided the details of abortion clinics in the United Kingdom. The Society for the Protection of the Unborn Child (SPUC) sought an undertaking that the student unions would cease to do this. When SPUC received no reply, it sought an injunction to prevent publication. Grogan argued that the students' right to freedom of expression had been

---

99 F. Rubio Llorente, *La Forma del Poder (Estudios sobre la Constitución)* (Madrid, Centro de Estudios Constitucionales, 1993) 630.

100 Case C-299/95 *Kremzow v Austrian State* [1997] ECR I-2629; Case C-309/96 *Annibaldi v Sindaco del Comune di Guidonia* [1997] ECR I-7493; Case C-94/00 *Roquette Frères SA v Directeur général de la concurrence* [2002] ECR I-9011; Case C-276/01 *Steffensen* [2003] ECR I-3735.

violated. SPUC countered, arguing that the measure fell outside the field of EC law, as it did not constitute a restriction on the freedom to provide services under Article 49 EC.

> ### Case C-159/90 *Society for the Protection of the Unborn Child (SPUC) v Grogan* [1991] ECR I-4685
>
> 22. Having regard to the facts of the case, it must be considered that, in its second and third questions, the national court seeks essentially to establish whether it is contrary to Community law for a Member State in which medical termination of pregnancy is forbidden to prohibit students' associations from distributing information about the identity and location of clinics in another Member State where medical termination of pregnancy is lawfully carried out and the means of communicating with those clinics, where the clinics in question have no involvement in the distribution of the said information . . .
>
> 24. As regards, first, the provisions of [Article 49 EC], which prohibit any restriction on the freedom to supply services, it is apparent from the facts of the case that the link between the activity of the students' associations of which Mr Grogan and the other defendants are officers and medical terminations of pregnancies carried out in clinics in another Member State is too tenuous for the prohibition on the distribution of information to be capable of being regarded as a restriction within the meaning of [Article 49 EC] . . .
>
> 26. The information to which the national court's questions refer is not distributed on behalf of an economic operator established in another Member State. On the contrary, the information constitutes a manifestation of freedom of expression and of the freedom to impart and receive information which is independent of the economic activity carried on by clinics established in another Member State.
>
> 27. It follows that, in any event, a prohibition on the distribution of information in circumstances such as those which are the subject of the main proceedings cannot be regarded as a restriction within the meaning of [Article 49 EC] . . .
>
> 29. . . . the defendants in the main proceedings maintained that fundamental rights and especially freedom of expression and the freedom to receive and impart information, enshrined in particular in Article 10(1) of the European Convention on Human Rights, precluded a prohibition of the kind at issue in the main proceedings.
>
> 30. It was important to bear in mind that when national legislation fell within the field of application of Community law the Court, when requested to give a preliminary ruling, must provide the national court with all the elements of interpretation necessary in order to enable it to assess the compatibility of that legislation with the fundamental rights – as laid down in particular in the European Convention on Human Rights – the observance of which the Court ensures. However, the Court had no such jurisdiction with regard to national legislation lying outside the scope of Community law.

Fundamental rights are treated in a paradoxical manner.[101] On the one hand, EU law stresses the indivisibility of fundamental rights. Civil, political, economic and social rights are to be equally valued and protected. On the other, it does not protect their indefeasibility. Fundamental rights are only to be protected insofar as

---

101 P. Eeckhout, 'The EU Charter of Fundamental Rights and the Federal Question' (2002) 39 *CML Rev.* 945, 957–8. See also G. de Búrca, 'Fundamental Rights and the Reach of EC Law' (1993) 13 *OJLS* 283.

they fall within the field of EC law. Outside that realm, EC law does not protect them. This leads to inequality before the law, with individuals in analogous situations being differently protected. It also provides incentives to cheat. The clear message in *Grogan*, for example, was that the students should offer to advertise, for a nominal fee, on behalf of the British abortion clinics, in order to bring themselves within the field of EC law.

The response to *Grogan* illustrated, however, the contentiousness and difficulty of these types of case and the limited legitimacy of the Court of Justice. Concerned that the abortion debate in Ireland, which had been the subject of numerous heated referenda, would be decided by the Court of Justice, the Irish government obtained a Protocol at Maastricht, ring-fencing the Irish constitutional provisions from EC law.[102] Before the Protocol could enter into effect with the ratification of the Treaty on European Union, the case of *X* occurred.[103] X was a teenager who conceived after being raped. Her parents arranged for her to terminate the pregnancy at a British clinic, but, as she was under sixteen years old, notified the authorities of the reason for her trip abroad. The authorities refused to allow her to travel on the grounds that the Irish Constitution required them not to facilitate abortions. The matter was taken to the Irish Supreme Court, who, arguably, should have referred the matter to the Court of Justice for decision, as the matter fell within the field of EC law: X was going to receive a service, an abortion, in another Member State and was, therefore, covered by Article 49 EC and, as a court against whose decisions there is no judicial remedy, the Irish Supreme Court was bound to refer under Article 234(3) EC. Instead, aware of both the terrible human tragedy of the case and of its considerable political implications for Ireland, the court chose to decide the case itself. It held that, in the circumstances, abortion was compatible with the Irish Constitution, as the danger to the mother's life, as X was suicidal, outweighed the case for protecting the foetus.

Concern also emerged at the Convention on the drafting of the EU Charter on Fundamental Rights with regard to the Court of Justice's gradual expansion of its jurisdiction in this field, to evaluate ever-increasing fields of domestic policy against EU fundamental rights norms. Following a convoluted debate,[104] the eventual provision, Article 51(1), states that the Charter will bind Member States only when 'implementing' EU law. This appears a narrower formulation than the status quo, but in the Declaration concerning the Explanations provided by the Convention, a link is drawn between this provision and the existing case law of the Court of Justice:

---

102 Protocol on Article 40.3.3 of the Constitution of Ireland. A similar protection has been given for Malta: Protocol No. 7 Act of Accession 2003.
103 *Attorney General v X* [1992] 2 CMLR 277.
104 For a discussion of this see G. de Búrca, 'The Drafting of the EU Charter of Fundamental Rights' (2001) 26 *EL Rev.* 126, 136–7.

As regards the Member States, it follows unambiguously from the case law
of the Court of Justice that the requirement to respect fundamental rights
defined in a Union context is only binding on the Member States when they
act in the context of Community law (judgment of 13 July 1989, Case 5/88
*Wachauf* [1989] ECR 2609; judgment of 18 June 1991, *ERT* [1991] ECR I-2925);
judgment of 18 December 1997 (C-309/96 *Annibaldi* [1997] ECR I-7493). The
Court of Justice confirmed this case law in the following terms: 'In addition, it
should be remembered that the requirements flowing from the protection of
fundamental rights in the Community legal order are also binding on Member
States when they implement Community rules . . .' (judgment of 13 April 2000,
Case C-292/97, [2000] ECR I-2737, paragraph 37). Of course this principle, as
enshrined in this Charter, applies to the central authorities as well as to regional
or local bodies, and to public organisations, when they are implementing Union
law.

If the Explanations suggest that the Charter does not alter existing practice, they
also suggest that it should certainly not be expanded. Indeed, there is an overall
concern to divorce the practice of fundamental rights law from any redrawing of the
institutional map:

### Article 51(2)

This Charter does not extend the field of application of Union law beyond the powers of the
Union or establish any new power or task for the Union, or modify powers and tasks in the
other Parts of the Constitution.

It is difficult to know how attainable this will be. The Charter provides a more extensive range of rights than previously existed in EU law. This creates more opportunities
for judicial review and intervention by EU and national courts. The formalisation of
these rights in a Charter also provides the possibility that they will interpret the
provisions more broadly, and therefore, engage in more intensive review.

### Further reading

P. Alston *et al.* (eds.), *The EU and Human Rights* (Oxford, Oxford University Press, 1999)
P. Alston and J. Weiler, '"An Ever Closer Union" in need of a Human Rights Policy' (1998) 9 *EJIL*
658
M. Avbelj, *The European Court of Justice and the Question of Value Choices*, Jean Monnet Working
Paper 6/04
L. Besselink, 'Entrapped by the Maximum Standard: On Fundamental Rights, Pluralism and
Subsidiarity in the European Union' (1998) 35 *CML Rev.* 629
F. Bignami, 'Creating European Rights: National Values and Supranational Interests' (2005) 11
*Columbia Journal of European Law* 241
A. v. Bogdandy, 'The European Union as a Human Rights Organization? Human Rights and the
Core of the European Union' (2000) 27 *CML Rev.* 1307

P. Eeckhout, 'The EU Charter of Fundamental Rights and the Federal Question' (2002) 39 *CML Rev.* 945

T. Hervey and J. Kenner (eds.), *Economic and Social Rights under the EU Charter of Fundamental Rights* (Oxford, Hart, 2003)

K. Lenaerts and E. de Smijter, 'A "Bill of Rights" for the European Union' (2001) 38 *CML Rev.* 273

J. Liisberg, 'Does the EU Charter of Fundamental Rights Threaten the Supremacy of Community Law' (2001) 38 *CML Rev.* 1171

C. McCrudden, *The Future of the EU Charter of Fundamental Rights*, Jean Monnet Working Paper 13/01.

S. Peers and A. Ward (eds.), *The EU Charter of Fundamental Rights* (Oxford, Hart, 2004)

A. Williams, *EU Human Rights Policies: a Study in Irony* (Oxford, Oxford University Press, 2004)

# Judicial relations in the European Union

## 1. Introduction

Granting the possibility for individuals to assert EC legal provisions in national courts in *Van Gend en Loos* transformed the EC legal settlement.[1] The Court of Justice became the guardian of a sovereign legal order, which created new legal subjects and new principles, and was enforceable in domestic courts. The subjects of EC law were also provided with new litigation opportunities. At the apex of all this was the domestic court, for *Van Gend en Loos* was, above all, a judgment about the responsibilities of national courts. These were responsible for the application of EC law and were required by that judgment to provide standing to any individual that asserted directly effective EC rights before them and to disapply any national measures that conflicted with these. Without their cooperation, the whole edifice collapses. This begged the question of why national courts should comply with these pronouncements. We have

---

1 Case 26/62 *Van Gend en Loos v Nederlandse Administratie der Belastingen* [1963] ECR 1.

seen in earlier chapters how they came to accept the authority of EC law. Yet, even if national courts were to be obedient subjects of EC law, further problems arise. There is the danger of their making errors, of courts in different jurisdictions interpreting EC law in different ways, and of illegal EC instruments being allowed to remain in force. More proactively, there was the question of how to develop relations between national courts and the Court of Justice so as to allow the latter to carry out its duties of setting out the content of the EC legal order and of guarding its autonomy.

The instrument for realising this has been the preliminary reference procedure. Set out primarily in Article 234 EC,[2] individuals will litigate a point of EC law before a national court. The national court then considers whether a matter of EC law is necessary to decide the dispute and whether it should refer the question to the Court of Justice. The Court of Justice will then make a judgment on the points of EC law in question and refer the matter back to the national court to apply to the case in hand. Questions of fact, national law and dispute resolution are formally a matter for the national court.

This chapter will consider how the Court of Justice has interpreted the procedure, on the one hand, to realise the central goals of the EC legal order. It will also look at how the Court has developed another agenda through this procedure, which is the creation of an EU court system with its own set of hierarchies and mutual responsibilities. Over time, these two agendas diverged and led to tensions. By the late 1990s, it was clear that the creation of the latter had led to a system whereby too many courts were referring too many questions of EC law for the Court of Justice to be able to realise the goals of the EC legal order effectively. The final part of this chapter considers the reforms that were subsequently introduced at Nice, and how effectively these have resolved the problems.

## 2. Mechanics of the preliminary reference procedure

### (i) EC Treaty provisions

Initially, there was only one provision which provided for direct relations between the Court of Justice and national courts: Article 234 EC.

---

**Article 234 EC**

The Court of Justice shall have jurisdiction to give preliminary rulings concerning:

(a) the interpretation of this Treaty;
(b) the validity and interpretation of acts of the institutions of the Community and of the ECB; . . .

---

2 This was originally Article 177 EEC.

> When such a question is raised before any court or tribunal of a Member State, that court or tribunal may, if it considers that a decision on the question is necessary to enable it to give judgment, request the Court of Justice to give a ruling thereon.
>
> When any such question is raised in a case pending before a court or tribunal of a Member State against whose decisions there is no judicial remedy under national law, that court or tribunal shall bring the matter before the Court of Justice.

At the Treaty of Amsterdam, immigration and asylum law and judicial cooperation in civil matters was transferred from the third pillar, Justice and Home Affairs (JHA), to the first pillar, the EC Treaty. This brought it within the jurisdiction of Article 234 EC. Concern was expressed by the German government that the high number of immigration and asylum cases before national courts would overburden the Court of Justice and would be used by applicants as a way of prolonging the immigration or asylum process. It was, therefore, decided that for matters falling within Title IV of the EC Treaty (Part IV: visas, asylum, immigration and other policies relating to the free movement of persons), only courts against whose decisions there was no judicial remedy should be allowed to refer a question to the Court of Justice.

### Article 68 (1) EC

1. Article 234 shall apply to this Title under the following circumstances and conditions: where a question on the interpretation of this Title or on the validity or interpretation of acts of the institutions of the Community based on this Title is raised in a case pending before a court or a tribunal of a Member State against whose decisions there is no judicial remedy under national law, that court or tribunal shall, if it considers that a decision on the question is necessary to enable it to give judgment, request the Court of Justice to give a ruling thereon.

2. In any event, the Court of Justice shall not have jurisdiction to rule on any measure or decision taken pursuant to Article 62(1) relating to the maintenance of law and order and the safeguarding of internal security.

3. The Council, the Commission or a Member State may request the Court of Justice to give a ruling on a question of interpretation of this Title or acts of the institutions of the Community based on this Title. The ruling given by the Court of Justice in response to such a request shall not apply to courts or tribunals of the Member States which have become res judicata.

The difference between Article 234 EC and Article 68 EC was expressed most vividly in *Georgescu*.[3] Georgescu was a Romanian who entered Germany illegally. At the time of her entry into Germany she had no visa, as was required by EC law at that time. Subsequent EC legislation exempted Romanians from needing a visa to enter the European Union. It was argued, therefore, that the initial legislation did not require Romanians to have a visa, but merely deferred temporarily their exemption from having to have a visa. On this basis Georgescu argued that she was not criminally liable for illegal entry. The local German court sought to refer the matter under Article 234 EC. The Court refused jurisdiction. It observed that visas fell within

---

3 Case C-51/03 *Georgescu* [2004] ECR I-3203.

Title IV of the EC Treaty. In the circumstances, it could not receive a reference from that court, as there was a judicial remedy (e.g. a right of appeal) against it under German law.

It was also felt by some at Amsterdam that it would be helpful if the Court of Justice could give rulings on matters that fell within the third pillar, JHA. This was contentious with a number of Member States who wished to keep the third pillar as intergovernmental as possible. The Treaty of Amsterdam adopted a compromise under which governments could 'opt in' their national judiciaries into the preliminary reference procedure.

### Article 35(1) TEU

1. The Court of Justice of the European Communities shall have jurisdiction, subject to the conditions laid down in this Article, to give preliminary rulings on the validity and interpretation of framework decisions and decisions, on the interpretation of conventions established under this Title and on the validity and interpretation of the measures implementing them.

2. By a declaration made at the time of the signing of this Treaty or any time thereafter, any Member State shall be able to accept a jurisdiction of the Court of Justice to give preliminary ruling as specified in paragraph 1.

3. Where a Member State has made a declaration pursuant to paragraph 2 of this Article:

(a) any court or tribunal of that State against whose decisions there is no judicial remedy under national law may request the Court of Justice to give a preliminary ruling on a question raised in a case pending before it and concerning the validity or interpretation of an act referred to in paragraph 1 if that court considers that a decision on the question is necessary to enable it to give judgment, or

(b) any court or tribunal of that State may request the Court of Justice to give a preliminary ruling on a question raised in a case pending before it and concerning the validity or interpretation of an act referred to in paragraph 1 if that court considers that a decision on the question is necessary to enable it to give judgment.

4. Any Member State, whether or not it has made a declaration pursuant to paragraph 2, shall be entitled to submit statements of case or written observations to the Court in cases which arise under paragraph 3.

5. The Court of Justice shall have no jurisdiction to review the validity or proportionality of operations carried out by the police or other law enforcement services of a Member State or the exercise of the responsibilities incumbent upon Member States with regard to the maintenance of law and order and the safeguarding of internal security.

Austria, Belgium, Finland, Germany, Greece, Luxembourg, Portugal, Sweden, the Czech Republic and the Netherlands have all made Declarations accepting the jurisdiction of the Court of Justice to give a preliminary ruling. Spain also made a Declaration accepting jurisdiction, but only where references are made from national courts of last resort.[4] The optional nature of the procedure protects neither national autonomy nor the EU interest. Judgments of the Court of Justice will presumably bind all

---

4 OJ 1999 L114/56. In the case of the Czech Republic, see Final Act to the Treaty of Accession of European Union 2003, Declaration 25 by the Czech Republic on Article 35 TEU, OJ 2003 L236/957.

Member States, including those which have not made a Declaration. In opting out of the system of preliminary rulings, Member States do not opt out of their obligations under EU law. They merely place the courts of other Member States in a privileged position vis-à-vis their own, by allowing the former to be part of a law-making and law-adjudicating process, whilst denying it to the latter. From a Union perspective, this imbalance is also unsatisfactory as it will result in the courts of some Member States being able to have resort to the expertise of the Court of Justice whilst others are not.

Article 234 EC remains the predominant procedure of the three procedures. Between 2000 and 2004, the Court gave 1,285 judgments on the basis of Article 234 EC,[5] one under Article 68 EC and two under Article 35 TEU.[6] The Constitutional Treaty's intended abolition of the pillar system would have resulted in all three procedures being brought into a single procedure in which the Court would have had jurisdiction to give rulings on immigration, asylum, policing and judicial cooperation in criminal matters in the same manner as matters currently dealt with by the Article 234 EC procedure.

### Article III-369 CT

The Court of Justice of the European Union shall have jurisdiction to give preliminary rulings concerning:

(a) the interpretation of the Constitution;
(b) the validity and interpretation of acts of the institutions, bodies, offices and agencies of the Union.

Where such a question is raised before any court or tribunal of a Member State, that court or tribunal may, if it considers that a decision on the question is necessary to enable it to give judgment, request the Court to give a ruling thereon.

Where any such question is raised in a case pending before a court or tribunal of a Member State against whose decisions there is no judicial remedy under national law, that court or tribunal shall bring the matter before the Court.

If such a question is raised in a case pending before a court or tribunal of a Member State with regard to a person in custody, the Court shall act with the minimum of delay.

Although the changes do not appear radical, criminal justice, immigration and asylum constitute the heartlands of most national judicial systems.[7] The consequence would have been a significant increase in references to the Court of Justice. It would also have led to the Court deciding an increasing number of cases which go to the core

---

5 *Annual Report of the European Court of Justice 2004* (Luxembourg, OOPEC, 2005) 168.
6 Joined Cases C-187/01 and C-385/01 *Gözütok and Brügge* [2003] ECR I-1345; Case C-469/03 *Miraglia*, judgment of 10 March 2005; Case C-105/03 *Pupino*, judgment of 16 June 2005. Recently the Court gave its first judgment under Article 68 EC, Case C-443/03 *Leffler v Berlin Chemie*, judgment of 8 November 2005.
7 In the United Kingdom, 81,725 cases were heard by Immigration Adjudicators, the judicial body of first instance for asylum in the United Kingdom, in 2003: Home Office, *First Quarterly Statistics 2004* (London, 2004) Table 5.

of both civil liberty and public order sensitivities. It would, therefore, have increased the salience of the Court, but also put it under increased pressure, both politically and in terms of its workload.[8]

### (ii) The sequence of the reference procedure

### (a) Making of the reference

If the national court decides to make a reference under Article 234 EC, that reference will take the form of a question or number of questions about EC law. These must be accompanied by a statement setting out the factual and legal context of the dispute.

---

**European Court of Justice, Information Note on References by National Courts for Preliminary Rulings**

6. [The reference] must contain a statement of reasons which is succinct but sufficiently complete to give the Court, and those to whom the decision must be notified (the Member States, the Commission, and in certain cases the Council and the European Parliament), a clear understanding of the factual and legal context of the main proceedings.

In particular, it must include an account of the facts which are essential for understanding the full legal significance of the main proceedings, an account of the points of law which may apply, a statement of the reasons which prompted the national court to refer the question or questions to the Court of Justice and, if need be, a summary of the arguments of the parties. The purpose of all this is to put the Court of Justice in a position to give the national court an answer which will be of assistance to it.

The decision making the reference must also be accompanied by copies of the documents needed for a proper understanding of the case, especially the text of the applicable national provisions. However, as the case-file or documents annexed to the decision making the reference are not always translated in full into the other official languages of the Community, the national court must make sure that its decision includes all the relevant information.

---

This statement frames the dispute. The Court of Justice cannot look behind the reference, but must take it as the basis on which it provides its answer to the questions asked of it.[9] In *WWF*, therefore, a challenge was made to the transformation of the military airport in Bolzano, Italy, into one for commercial use because there had been a failure to carry out an environmental impact assessment.[10] The airport authorities counter-challenged the reference, arguing that the facts presented by the national court were inaccurate and that the national court, being confined to considering questions of law, had exceeded its jurisdiction by considering these questions of fact. The Court dismissed these arguments. It noted that it was for the national court, not itself, to ascertain the facts, and that it was not its role to examine whether the

---

8 D. Chalmers, 'The Court of Justice and the Constitutional Treaty' (2005) 4 *I-CON* 428.

9 T. Tridimas, 'Knocking on Heaven's Door: Fragmentation, Efficiency and Defiance in the Preliminary Reference Procedure' (2003) 40 *CML Rev.* 9, 21–6.

10 Case C-435/97 *WWF v Autonome Provinz Bozen* [1999] ECR I-5613.

reference had been made in accordance with national laws on court jurisdiction and procedure.

The statement of the factual and legal context set out by the national court is so central to the procedure that the Court will sometimes look to it rather than the explicit questions set out by the national court in providing the judgment it gives. In *Lindfors*, a Finnish national moved back to Finland and brought with him his car.[11] In Finland, any person using a car imported from another Member State was liable to pay a consumption tax. The Finnish court asked only whether this violated Directive 83/183, which prohibited tax on personal property imported permanently from another Member State. The Directive was narrowly drafted so it only prohibited tax on importation and not, as was the case in Finland, tax on use. The Court of Justice stated, therefore, that even though the point was not referred, it would examine whether the Finnish law was compatible with Article 18 EC, which provides for free movement of persons. It stated that the Article did not exempt Lindfors from paying tax, but it did require that he not be placed in a less advantageous position than those permanently resident in Finland.

### (b)   Interim measures

The reference procedure is court-to-court, with national courts acting as gate-keepers to the Court of Justice.[12] The Court has characterised the preliminary reference procedure as:

> a non-contentious procedure excluding any initiative of the parties who are merely invited to be heard in the course of this procedure.[13]

Private parties have no direct access to the Court of Justice, nor can they appeal decisions of the national courts to the Court of Justice. The parties to the dispute are not wholly excluded from the procedure, as they may submit written observations to the Court.[14] In this, they may be joined by the Council, the Parliament and any of the Member States, all of whom may intervene. In addition, there are oral hearings at which each of the parties and those intervening may make oral representations of between fifteen and thirty minutes long, depending upon the nature of the proceedings.

There is a lengthy period between the time the reference is made by the national court and the adoption of a judgment by the Court of Justice. In 2004, this period was an average of 23.5 months.[15] National courts are required to consider, therefore, whether to grant interim relief pending final judgment. The circumstances under which interim relief is to be granted varies according to the nature of the dispute. If

---

11 Case C-365/02 *Lindfors* [2004] ECR I-7183.
12 Private parties not allowed to appear before the national court will not, therefore, be allowed to intervene before the Court of Justice: Case C-181/95 *Biogen v Smithkline Beecham* [1996] ECR I-717.
13 Case C-364/92 *Fluggesellschaft v Eurocontrol* [1994] ECR I-43.
14 Statute of the Court of Justice, Article 20.
15 *Annual Report of the European Court of Justice 2004* (Luxembourg, OOPEC, 2005) 174.

the dispute concerns the interpretation of a provision of EC law, the conditions for granting interim relief are very relaxed. The national court must grant interim relief where this is necessary to secure the full effectiveness of the judgment to be given by the Court of Justice. In other words, they must take action, including disapplying national law, to ensure that rights which may be granted by the Court will still be of benefit to the parties.[16] The position is different where the dispute concerns a challenge to the validity of a Community measure. In such cases, there is concern about the possible damage to the EC legal order and uncertainty generated by an EC measure being provisionally declared invalid in one Member State as a consequence of the granting of interim relief. The criteria for granting relief are, therefore, far stricter. Interim relief may only be granted where the referring court has serious doubts as to the validity of the Community act, the validity of the contested act is not already in issue before the Court of Justice, the interim relief is necessary to avoid serious and irreparable damage being caused to the party seeking the relief and the national court takes due account of the Community interest by obtaining all relevant information on the Community act in question. The national court is also required to respect any rulings by the Court of Justice on the issue.[17]

The distinction is not unproblematic. The destabilising effects of interim relief on the EC legal order are equally true for the national legal order; that is to say that if a national court disapplies a national law pending a reference before the Court of Justice, this creates a legal vacuum in that Member State. The status of that law is unclear, as is the authority of the judgment for third parties. It is not clear, therefore, why it should be easier to obtain interim relief against national law than against EC law. The difficulty does not appear to be that the terms for obtaining interim relief against an EC legal measure are too restrictive. The Court identifies the types of consideration that should play a role: namely the severity of the damage to the parties must be weighed against broader questions of public policy. It is rather that the terms of interim relief against national law are too easy to satisfy. This has allowed litigants to play the system. They have sought, using the relatively relaxed criteria, to have national law disapplied knowing full well that whatever the terms of the judgment, it will be difficult for a national government to re-establish the law up to two years after it was last applied.[18]

### (c)   Application of the ruling

The Court of Justice will make a ruling exclusively on points of EC law, which is transmitted back to the national court to apply to the dispute before it. Although the ruling binds the national court,[19] it is free to refer the question back to the Court of

---

16 Case C-213/89 *R v Secretary of State for Transport ex parte Factortame* [1990] ECR 2433.
17 Case C-465/93 *Atlanta Fruchthandelsgesellschaft* [1995] ECR I-3761; Case C-334/95 *Krüger v Hauptzollamt Hamburg-Jonas* [1997] ECR I-4517.
18 For an example of the problem see R. Rawlings, 'The Eurolaw Game: Some Deductions from a Saga' (1993) 20 *JLS* 309. For more discussion see pp. 304–5.
19 Case 52/76 *Benedetti v Munari* [1977] ECR 163.

Justice if it is either dissatisfied with the ruling or is unclear about the meaning of the ruling. In such circumstances, in a form of judicial 'ping pong', the Court has tended to simply reiterate or extrapolate on its prior judgment.[20]

The binding effects of the Court's judgments are, however, paper obligations. There is no meaningful sanction to be applied against national courts that do not follow them. That said, national compliance is very high. A cross-country study found implementation of the Court's rulings in 96.3 per cent of the cases studied.[21] Challenges to the authority of the Court were rarely in the form of direct non-observance, but, since questions of fact, national law and dispute resolution are formally a matter for the national court,[22] it was more common for national courts to use these points to find less direct ways of challenging the ruling. A study of Austrian courts found that a variety of devices were used to evade rulings of the Court of Justice that were unpopular with the local court. These included narrow constructions of EC legal norms, arguing that the ruling does not apply to the facts, weak remedies, *a contrario* reasoning and application of domestic, rather than EU, legal norms if it would lead to the same result.[23] The Court of Justice has tried to circumvent this in some instances by sending back rulings which are so detailed that they leave national courts little room for discretion in how they decide the dispute in hand. By contrast, in other cases, they have sought to diffuse conflict by sending back rulings that are sufficiently vague to allow the national court considerable discretion in deciding how to resolve the dispute.[24]

### 3. Functions of the preliminary reference procedure

At the Treaty of Nice, the institutional role of the Court of Justice was discussed. The Court of Justice submitted a discussion paper to the IGC in which it described its challenges and its role. In this paper the Court described the goal of the preliminary reference procedure as being:

> to guarantee respect for the distribution of powers between the Community and its Member States and between the Community institutions, the uniformity and consistency of Community law and to contribute to the harmonious development of the law within the Union.[25]

---

20  Joined Cases 28–30/62 *Da Costa v Netherlands Inland Revenue Administration* [1963] ECR 37; Case 244/80 *Foglia v Novello* (*No. 2*) [1981] ECR 3045.
21  S. Nyikos, 'The Preliminary Reference Process: National Court Implementation, Changing Opportunity Structures and Litigant Desistment' (2003) 4 *EUP* 397, 410.
22  Case 104/79 *Foglia v Novello* [1980] ECR 745.
23  B. Bepuly, *The Application of EC Law in Austria*, IWE Working Paper 39.
24  The manner in which the Court has done this has been subject to some criticism. J. Snell, 'European Courts and Intellectual Property: a Tale of Zeus, Hercules and Cyclops' (2004) 29 *EL Rev.* 178.
25  European Court of Justice, *The Future of the Judicial System of the European Union* (Luxembourg, 1999) 21. This is accessible at www.curia.eu.int/en/instit/txtdocfr/autrestxts/ave.pdf

Extrapolating from the Court's case law, one can see that the procedure has four central functions. The first is the development of EC law. It enables the Court of Justice to develop new interpretations of EC law, resolve uncertainties, correct injustices and enunciate principles. Secondly, the Court talks of the maintenance of the institutional balance. As the preliminary reference procedure begins with litigation by private parties, it is better to view it as a central avenue for judicial review. Private parties are either unhappy with the constraints imposed by national law and are seeking freedom from these, or alternatively, they are seeking to challenge constraints imposed upon them by the EU institutions. Thirdly, the Court talks of the preliminary reference procedure as being necessary for the uniformity and consistency of EC law.[26] Historically, decisions of the national courts of one Member State do not bind the national courts of other Member States. Without the possibility of access to a court whose authority is accepted by all actors, divergent traditions and interpretations of EC law would arise in the different national jurisdictions. This role is not simply about coordinating the actions of the national judiciaries in order to ensure that unmanageable differences do not emerge. It is also about securing the unity of the EC legal order. The preliminary reference procedure allows litigation in the Netherlands, for example, between two Dutch nationals, as was the case in *Van Gend en Loos*, to have implications for the legal systems of all the other Member States. The judgment of the Court, insofar as it binds all EU courts, makes that litigation central for courts in other Member States, as though the case had occurred in their own national jurisdictions. It makes all courts Community courts; part of a single EU legal system with its own legal identity. Fourthly, the preliminary reference procedure has an administration of justice function. It enables national courts to decide disputes that involve EC law by allowing them to tap into the expertise of the Court of Justice.[27]

### (i)  Development of EC law

The reference procedure accounts for about 45 per cent of the cases that come to the Court of Justice.[28] The significance of the procedure lies not in the proportion of the Court's case law that it provides, but qualitatively, in the type of questions it allows the Court to address. Almost all the significant rulings concerning EC law, other than those concerning the remit of the powers of the EU institutions, have come via the

---

26 This was picked up early on in R. Buxbaum, 'Article 177 of the Rome Treaty as a Federalizing Device' (1969) 21 *Stanford Law Review* 1041. It has also been noted in a number of extra-judicial comments made by members of the Court: G. Mancini and D. Keeling, 'From *CILFIT* to *ERT*: the Constitutional Challenge Facing the Court' (1991) 11 *YBEL* 1, 2–3; G. Tesauro, 'The Effectiveness of Judicial Protection and Co-operation between the National Courts and the Court of Justice' (1993) 13 *YBEL* 1, 17.

27 Although see Case 166/73 *Rheinmühlen-Düsseldorf v Einfuhr- und Vorratstelle für Getreide* [1974] ECR 33.

28 Between 2000 and 2004, the Court gave judgment in 2,632 cases, of which 1,186 were preliminary references. *Annual Report of the European Court of Justice 2004* (Luxembourg, OOPEC, 2005) 168.

preliminary reference procedure, for the procedure allows a much wider variety of issues to come to the Court's attention.

To that end, the Court has construed its powers to interpret EC law under Article 234 EC widely. It will give a ruling on anything which forms part of the EC legal order, even if it is neither an EC Treaty provision nor a piece of secondary legislation. International agreements, such as the GATT, were concluded by the Member States and came into force before the EC's existence and could not, therefore, have been concluded by an act of any of the EC institutions. The Court has ruled, however, that the EC has acceded to them, making them part of the EC legal order.[29] It can, therefore, give preliminary rulings upon their interpretation to ensure the uniform interpretation of Community law.[30] Similarly, it could be argued that the Court of Jsutice has no jurisdiction to give rulings upon general principles of law or fundamental rights, as these do not appear in any EC Treaty provision or piece of secondary legislation. The Court has been willing to accept references on these insofar as they surround the interpretation of the EC Treaty and the interpretation and review of secondary legislation.[31]

The Court has applied  its powers of interpretation widely in another direction. Whilst it has no general power to give rulings on provisions of national law,[32] it will give rulings wherever the latter refers to the contents of provisions of EC law or adopts similar solutions to those found in EC law.[33] In *Dzodzi*, a Togolese woman challenged a decision by the Belgian authorities refusing her a residence permit following the death of her Belgian husband.[34] The situation was, in EC terms, an internal domestic one governed by Belgian law. The Belgian law stated, however, that the spouses of Belgian nationals should be treated in the same way as spouses of other EC nationals. Notwithstanding that the measure was governed by Belgian law, the Court ruled it to be in the Community legal interest that it give a ruling, on the grounds that every Community provision should be given a uniform interpretation, irrespective of the circumstances in which it is to be applied, in order to forestall future  differences in interpretation.

The principle that the Court of Justice has jurisdiction to interpret Community law concepts, whatever the circumstances, has allowed it to extend its jurisdiction in two other ways. The first is where a contract between two private parties incorporates a term of EC law. In *Federconsorzi*, some of AIMA's virgin olive oil had been stolen from Federconsorzi's premises.[35] The contract between the two stated the latter would be

---

29 Joined Cases 21–24/72 *International Fruit Company v Produktschap voor Groenten en Fruit* [1972] ECR 1226.
30 Joined Cases 267–269/81 *Amministrazione delle Finanze dello Stato v SPI* [1983] ECR 801.
31 e.g. Case 11/70 *Internationale Handelsgesellschaft v Einfuhr und Vorratsstelle Getreide* [1970] ECR 1125.
32 Case 75/63 *Hoekstra v Bedrijfsvereniging Detailhandel* [1964] ECR 177.
33 Case C-247/97 *Schoonbroodt* [1998] ECR I-8095; Case C-170/03 *Feron*, judgment of 17 March 2005. For discussion see S. Lefevre, 'The Interpretation of Community law by the Court of Justice in Areas of National Competence' (2004) 29 *EL Rev.* 501.
34 Joined Cases C-297/88 and C-197/89 *Dzodzi v Belgium* [1990] ECR I-3673.
35 Case C-88/91 *Federconsorzi v AIMA* [1992] ECR I-4035.

liable for the losses for the amount stipulated by the EC legislation in force. Once again the Court considered that the Community interest required it to give a uniform interpretation to prevent future differences in interpretation. The second is where the EC and Member States have signed an international agreement which falls partly within EC competencies and partly within national competencies. The Court has ruled that it will give rulings on provisions in these agreements that straddle these competencies as it is in the Community interest to avert future differences of interpretation of a provision, whatever the circumstances in which it is to apply. In *Hermès*, the Court of Justice was asked to rule on Article 50 of the TRIPS Agreement, an agreement on Trade Related Intellectual Property Rights that formed part of the World Trade Organisation.[36] The provision concerned enforcement of intellectual property rights, something that largely fell within national competence. The Court nevertheless held that insofar as the provision could potentially cover situations which fell within the scope of Community law, most notably where intellectual property rights generated by EC law were infringed, the provision required a uniform interpretation.

### (ii)   Judicial review of EU institutions

Article 234 EC allows the Court of Justice not merely to give interpretations of EC law, but also to rule on the validity of EC legislation and administrative acts of the EU institutions.[37] The mechanism for this is that the individual will challenge the national measure implementing the EU act before a national court. In considering the legality of the latter, the national court will refer to the Court of Justice the question of whether the Community measure, which provides the legal authorisation for the national measure, is lawful or not. In this way, it acts alongside the direct action procedures in Articles 230(4) and 241 EC, which provide explicitly for individuals to challenge the acts of EU institutions.[38] Its relationship with these provisions is a complicated one. The Court sees it as part of a system of remedies. In *Jégo-Quéré*, the Commission, concerned about the levels of stocks of the fish hake, adopted a Regulation setting a minimum mesh size for nets to ensure that baby hake were not caught. Jégo-Quéré, a French company, fished for whitebait, a very small fish. The new minimum mesh sizes were now too big to allow it to do so effectively. It could not challenge the measure before a national court, as the Commission Regulation provided for no implementing measures to be taken with the consequence that there was no national law to challenge. They sought to challenge the Regulation directly before the Court of Justice under Article 230(4) EC.[39] The Court held that they lacked standing, but that there were corollary duties on national authorities to allow

---

36  Case C-53/96 *Hermès International v FHT* [1998] ECR I-3603; Joined Cases C-300/98 and C-302/98 *Parfums Christian Dior v Tuk Consultancy* [2000] ECR I-11307.

37  Joined Cases 133–136/85 *Rau v Bundesanstalt für Landswirtschaftliche Marktordnung* [1987] ECR 2289.

38  On these see pp. 418–36.        39  See pp. 430–3.

individuals to challenge these acts before national courts, who could then refer the matter to the Community courts.

> ### Case C-263/02P *Jégo-Quéré v Commission* [2004] ECR I-3425
>
> 29. It should be noted that individuals are entitled to effective judicial protection of the rights they derive from the Community legal order, and the right to such protection is one of the general principles of law stemming from the constitutional traditions common to the Member States. That right has also been enshrined in Articles 6 and 13 of the ECHR . . .
>
> 30. By Articles 230 EC and Article 241 EC, on the one hand, and by Article 234 EC, on the other, the Treaty has established a complete system of legal remedies and procedures designed to ensure review of the legality of acts of the institutions, and has entrusted such review to the Community Courts. Under that system, where natural or legal persons cannot, by reason of the conditions for admissibility laid down in the fourth paragraph of Article 230 EC, directly challenge Community measures of general application, they are able, depending on the case, either indirectly to plead the invalidity of such acts before the Community Courts under Article 241 EC or to do so before the national courts and ask them, since they have no jurisdiction themselves to declare those measures invalid, to make a reference to the Court of Justice for a preliminary ruling on validity . . .
>
> 31. Thus it is for the Member States to establish a system of legal remedies and procedures which ensure respect for the right to effective judicial protection . . .
>
> 32. In that context, in accordance with the principle of sincere cooperation laid down in Article 10 EC, national courts are required, so far as possible, to interpret and apply national procedural rules governing the exercise of rights of action in a way that enables natural and legal persons to challenge before the courts the legality of any decision or other national measure relative to the application to them of a Community act of general application, by pleading the invalidity of such an act . . .
>
> 33. However, it is not appropriate for an action for annulment before the Community Court to be available to an individual who contests the validity of a measure of general application, such as a regulation, which does not distinguish him individually in the same way as an addressee, even if it could be shown, following an examination by that Court of the particular national procedural rules, that those rules do not allow the individual to bring proceedings to contest the validity of the Community measure at issue. Such an interpretation would require the Community Court, in each individual case, to examine and interpret national procedural law. That would go beyond its jurisdiction when reviewing the legality of Community measures . . .
>
> 34. Accordingly, an action for annulment before the Community Court should not on any view be available, even where it is apparent that the national procedural rules do not allow the individual to contest the validity of the Community measure at issue unless he has first contravened it.

*Jégo-Quéré* indicates that the absence of *locus standi* before a national court may prevent an EC act being challenged via Article 234 EC. The other circumstance in which the Court will not allow the preliminary reference procedure to be used to invalidate an EU measure, is where a party had *locus standi* to challenge a measure directly before the Court of Justice under Article 230(4) EC but failed to bring the action within the necessary time limits. In *TWD*, the Commission thus declared a state aid granted by the German government to TWD, a textile company, to be incompatible with the EC law on state aids.[40] TWD had standing to bring an action before the Court of Justice challenging the Commission's Decision. It was required by Article 230(5) EC to bring this within two months of the Decision becoming known to it. The Court refused to rule on the validity of the Commission's Decision in response to a reference sent by a German court in 1992. It stated that once the time limit had expired, legal certainty required that the national court be bound by the Commission Decision and could not, therefore, raise the question of its validity.[41]

### (iii)   Preserving the unity of EC law

In its submission to the Treaty of Nice, the Court of Justice spoke of 'the need to secure the unity of Community law by means of a supreme court'.[42] There had to be one Court, which was accepted as having pre-eminent authority over the interpretation and validity of EC law. This view is not uncontested by national courts,[43] but it has been used to grant the Court of Justice a monopoly over declaring EC acts invalid.[44] In *Fotofrost*, a Commission Decision requiring import duties to be paid on binoculars imported from the eastern part of Germany was challenged before a Hamburg court on the grounds it conflicted with the 1957 Protocol on German Internal Trade, which allowed free trade between the two divided parts of Germany, and was, therefore, illegal. The Hamburg court asked the Court of Justice whether it could declare the Commission Decision invalid.

---

**Case 314/85 *Firma Fotofrost v Hauptzollamt Lübeck-Ost* [1987] ECR 4199**

13. In enabling national courts, against those decisions where there is a judicial remedy under national law, to refer to the Court for a preliminary ruling questions on interpretation or validity, [Article 234] did not settle the question whether those courts themselves may declare that acts of Community institutions are invalid.

14. Those courts may consider the validity of a Community act and, if they consider that the grounds put forward before them by the parties in support of invalidity are unfounded, they may reject them, concluding that the measure is completely valid. By taking that action they are not calling into question the existence of the Community measure.

15. On the other hand, those courts do not have the power to declare acts of the Community institutions invalid. As the Court emphasized in the judgment of 13 May 1981 in Case 66/80 *International Chemical Corporation v Amministrazione delle Finanze* [1981] ECR 1191, the main purpose of the powers accorded to the Court by Article [234] is to ensure that Community

---

40  Case C-188/92 *TWD Textilwerke Deggendorf v Germany* [1994] ECR I-833.
41  D. Wyatt, 'The Relationship between Actions for Annulment and References on Validity after TWD Deggendorf' in J. Lonbay and A. Biondi (eds.), *Remedies for Breach of EC Law* (Chichester, John Wiley, 1997).
42  European Court of Justice, *The Future of the Judicial System of the European Union* (Luxembourg, 1999) 17.
43  See pp. 196–206.
44  G. Bebr, 'The Reinforcement of the Constitutional Review of Community Acts under the EEC Treaty' (1988) 25 *CML Rev.* 667.

law is applied uniformly by national courts. That requirement of uniformity is particularly imperative when the validity of a Community act is in question. Divergences between courts in the Member States as to the validity of Community acts would be liable to place in jeopardy the very unity of the Community legal order and detract from the fundamental requirement of legal certainty.

16. The same conclusion is dictated by consideration of the necessary coherence of the system of judicial protection established by the Treaty. In that regard it must be observed that requests for preliminary rulings, like actions for annulment, constitute means for reviewing the legality of acts of the Community institutions. As the Court pointed out in its judgment of 23 April 1986 in Case 294/83 *Parti Ecologiste 'Les Verts' v European Parliament* [1986] ECR 1339, 'in Articles [230 and 241], on the one hand, and in Article [234], on the other, the Treaty established a complete system of legal remedies and procedures designed to permit the Court of Justice to review the legality of measures adopted by the institutions'.

17. Since Article [230] gives the Court exclusive jurisdiction to declare void an act of a Community institution, the coherence of the system requires that where the validity of a Community act is challenged before a national court the power to declare the act invalid must also be reserved to the Court of Justice.

18. It must also be emphasized that the Court of Justice is in the best position to decide on the validity of Community acts. Under Article 20 of the Protocol on the Statute of the Court of Justice of the EEC, Community Institutions whose acts are challenged are entitled to participate in the proceedings in order to defend the validity of the acts in question. Furthermore, under the second paragraph of Article 21 of that Protocol the Court may require the Member States and institutions which are not participating in the proceedings to supply all information which it considers necessary for the purposes of the case before it.

19. It should be added that the rule that national courts may not themselves declare Community acts invalid may have to be qualified in certain circumstances in the case of proceedings relating to an application for interim measures; however, that case is not referred to in the national court's question.

Such a claim, on its face, is highly radical. It states that national courts are never to challenge the validity of EC legislation or administration, no matter what their concerns are, either under EC law or national law. Commission studies have not suggested any rebellion against *Fotofrost* by national courts. Since 2000, Commission studies have been unable to find a single example of its being challenged. This is, in part, because the practical application of the *Fotofrost* judgment is rather different from its rhetoric. As the last paragraph cited above indicates, national courts are not completely prevented from suspending the application of Community acts. As was mentioned earlier, they may still suspend acts through the granting of interim relief pending a reference to the Court of Justice.[45] A compact is thereby offered, whereby national courts may provisionally suspend the application of an act provided they refer the matter to the Court of Justice for a definitive ruling. They retain their power of review but at the cost of having to make a reference.

---

45 Case C-465/93 *Atlanta Fruchthandelsgesellschaft* [1995] ECR I-3761; Case C-334/95 *Krüger v Hauptzollamt Hamburg-Jonas* [1997] ECR I-4517. See pp. 278–9.

## (iv)   Dispute resolution

The division of duties between national courts and the Court of Justice suggests that dispute resolution is a matter for the national court. However, the Court of Justice will not give a ruling if it considers this ruling will not be used to determine a genuine dispute before the national court. This inevitably means that it will look at the litigation before the national court to verify whether a dispute is taking place. This position was tested for the first time in the *Foglia* saga. Foglia had contracted to sell Italian liqueur wine to Novello in France with the proviso that Novello would reimburse any taxes Foglia incurred, unless these were levied contrary to Community law. Foglia sought to recover the French taxes paid from Novello, equivalent to 148,000 Italian lira (about 140 euros), who refused on the grounds that these had been levied contrary to Community law. The matter was brought before an Italian court which was asked to rule on the compatibility of the French taxes with EC law. The case had all the hallmarks of a test case. Both Foglia and Novello argued that the taxes were illegal, the amount of tax paid was derisory and Foglia indicated that he was participating in this case on behalf of Italian traders of this wine. The Court of Justice refused to give judgment to the initial reference on the grounds that there was no genuine dispute.[46] The Italian court rereferred the matter, asking what the roles of the national court and Court of Justice were in such matters.

### Case 244/80 *Foglia v Novello (No. 2)* [1981] ECR 3045

14. With regard to the first question it should be recalled, as the Court has had occasion to emphasize in very varied contexts, that [Article 234] is based on cooperation which entails a division of duties between the national courts and the Court of Justice in the interest of the proper application and uniform interpretation of Community law throughout all the Member States.

15. With this in view it is for the national court – by reason of the fact that it is seized of the substance of the dispute and that it must bear the responsibility for the decision to be taken – to assess, having regard to the facts of the case, the need to obtain a preliminary ruling to enable it to give judgment.

16. In exercising that power of appraisal the national court, in collaboration with the Court of Justice, fulfils a duty entrusted to them both of ensuring that in the interpretation and application of the Treaty the law is observed. Accordingly the problems which may be entailed in the exercise of its power of appraisal by the national court and the relations which it maintains within the framework of [Article 234] with the Court of Justice are governed exclusively by the provisions of Community law.

17. In order that the Court of Justice may perform its task in accordance with the Treaty it is essential for national courts to explain, when the reasons do not emerge beyond any doubt from the file, why they consider that a reply to their questions is necessary to enable them to give judgment.

46 Case 104/79 *Foglia v Novello* [1980] ECR 745.

18. It must in fact be emphasized that the duty assigned to the Court by [Article 234] is not that of delivering advisory opinions on general or hypothetical questions but of assisting in the administration of justice in the Member States. It accordingly does not have jurisdiction to reply to questions of interpretation which are submitted to it within the framework of procedural devices arranged by the parties in order to induce the Court to give its views on certain problems of Community law which do not correspond to an objective requirement inherent in the resolution of a dispute. A declaration by the Court that it has no jurisdiction in such circumstances does not in any way trespass upon the prerogatives of the national court but makes it possible to prevent the application of the procedure under [Article 234] for purposes other than those appropriate for it.

19. Furthermore, it should be pointed out that, whilst the Court of Justice must be able to place as much reliance as possible upon the assessment by the national court of the extent to which the questions submitted are essential, it must be in a position to make any assessment inherent in the performance of its own duties in particular in order to check, as all courts must, whether it has jurisdiction. Thus the Court, taking into account the repercussions of its decisions in this matter, must have regard, in exercising the jurisdiction conferred upon it by [Article 234], not only to the interests of the parties to the proceedings but also to those of the Community and of the Member States. Accordingly it cannot, without disregarding the duties assigned to it, remain indifferent to the assessments made by the courts of the Member States in the exceptional cases in which such assessments may affect the proper working of the procedure laid down by [Article 234] . . .

28. On the one hand it must be pointed out that the court before which, in the course of proceedings between individuals, an issue concerning the compatibility with Community law of legislation of another Member State is brought is not necessarily in a position to provide for such individuals effective protection in relation to such legislation.

29. On the other hand, regard being had to the independence generally ensured for the parties by the legal systems of the Member States in the field of contract, the possibility arises that the conduct of the parties may be such as to make it impossible for the State concerned to arrange for an appropriate defence of its interests by causing the question of the invalidity of its legislation to be decided by a court of another Member State. Accordingly, in such procedural situations it is impossible to exclude the risk that the procedure under [Article 234] may be diverted by the parties from the purposes for which it was laid down by the Treaty.

30. The foregoing considerations as a whole show that the Court of Justice for its part must display special vigilance when, in the course of proceedings between individuals, a question is referred to it with a view to permitting the national court to decide whether the legislation of another Member State is in accordance with Community law.

*Foglia* was extremely contentious. The power to refuse a reference established a hierarchical element between the Court of Justice and the national court, as it granted a power to the Court of Justice to review the national court's decision to refer. The enquiry into the existence of a genuine dispute by the Court of Justice would also require it to look behind the national court's reference and examine the factual background to the dispute. There was consequently debate about whether this violated the cooperative spirit of Article 234 EC or transgressed unduly on the national court's monopoly over fact-finding.[47] Whatever its merits, there are severe practical difficulties in applying *Foglia*.[48] The finding of an absence of a genuine dispute requires the Court to take a view of the facts of the case and to contradict the national court's view on the need for a reference. Without independent fact-finding powers, and dependent upon the referring court and the intervening parties, the Court has little capacity to second-guess national courts.

Within this context, the Court of Justice has accepted test cases. In *Leclerc Siplec v TF1 Publicité*, Leclerc Siplec challenged a refusal by TF1, one of the major French television broadcasters, to televise an advertisement which sought to persuade viewers to purchase petrol from the forecourts of Leclerc's chain of supermarkets.[49] The reason for the refusal was a French law prohibiting television advertising of the distribution sector. Both parties to the dispute were in agreement about the domestic legal situation and the need for a reference. The Court accepted the reference. It noted that what was being sought was a declaration from the national court that the French law did not comply with EC law. The parties' agreement did not make the need for that declaration any less pressing or the dispute any less real. Whilst resolution of test cases is an important part of the judicial function, it is very difficult to distinguish them from hypothetical cases. In both, there is little conflict between the immediate parties to the dispute.

Since *Foglia*, the Court has also accepted cases where the national law of one Member State is challenged in the courts of another. In *Eau de Cologne, Eau de Cologne*, a cosmetics company, agreed to supply cosmetics to an Italian company, Provide.[50] The contract contained a warranty that the cosmetics would comply with Italian law. Provide repudiated the contract on the grounds that the cosmetics did not comply with Italian labelling laws. Eau de Cologne argued that they complied with the EC Directive regulating the matter. Under a choice of forum provision in the agreement, the matter was brought before a German court which referred a question on the interpretation of the Directive. The Court accepted the genuineness of the dispute despite a number of factors, notably the seemingly trivial nature of the breach and the choice of forum which allowed a German court to adjudicate upon the compatibility of Italian legislation with EC law.

---

47 For differing views see A. Barav, 'Preliminary Censorship? The Judgment of the European Court in *Foglia v Novello*' (1980 ) 5 *EL Rev.* 443, 451–55; H. Rasmussen, *On Law and Policy in the European Court of Justice* (Dordrecht, Martijnus Nijhoff, 1986) 465–97; D. Wyatt, '*Foglia (No. 2)*: The Court Denies it has Jurisdiction to Give Advisory Opinions' (1982) 7 *EL Rev.* 186; C. Gray, 'Advisory Opinions and the Court of Justice' (1983) 8 *EL Rev.* 24.

48 G. Bebr, 'The Existence of a Genuine Dispute: an Indispensable Precondition for the Jurisdiction of the Court under Article 177 EC?' (1980) 17 *CML Rev.* 525, 532.

49 Case C-412/93 *Leclerc Siplec v TF1 Publicité* [1995] ECR I-179. M. O'Neill, 'Article 177 and Limits to the Right to Refer: an End to the Confusion?' (1996) 2 *European Public Law* 375.

50 Case C-150/88 *Eau de Cologne v Provide* [1989] ECR 3891.

The *Foglia* line of reasoning survives. Instead of being used by the Court to review the motives of the parties, it is being used to review the contents of the reference.[51] The national court will be required to explain in detail why the questions are necessary to resolve the dispute. The Court will not look behind the facts provided by the national court, but will refuse to give a reference where, on the basis of these, it is manifestly apparent that the dispute is fictitious. In *Plato Plastik*, Plato Plastik produced plastic bags in Austria which it sold to Caropack, who sold them at supermarkets. Under the contract, Plato Plastik's statutory obligation to participate in a collection and recovery scheme was transferred to Caropack. Following prosecution by the Austrian authorities, Plato Plastik asked for confirmation from Caropack that it was participating in the scheme. Caropack refused, arguing that it could not absolve Plato Plastik of its statutory duties. The Austrian court referred the question whether the Austrian scheme for the collection and recovery of waste complied with Directive 94/62/EC on Packaging Waste. The Commission noted that both parties agreed on the law and were using the case to have the Austrian scheme declared illegal.

---

### Case C-341/01 *Plato Plastik v Caropack* [2004] ECR I-4883

26. It has consistently been held that it is solely for the national court before which the dispute has been brought, and which must assume responsibility for the subsequent judicial decision, to determine in the light of the particular circumstances of the case both the need for a preliminary ruling in order to enable it to deliver judgment and the relevance of the questions which it submits to the Court. Consequently, where the questions submitted by the national court concern the interpretation of Community law, the Court of Justice is, in principle, bound to give a ruling . . .

27. However, the Court has also held that, in exceptional circumstances, it should examine the conditions in which the case was referred to it by the national court . . . The spirit of cooperation which must prevail in the preliminary ruling procedure requires the national court, for its part, to have regard to the function entrusted to the Court of Justice, which is to assist in the administration of justice in the Member States and not to deliver advisory opinions on general or hypothetical questions . . .

28. The Court has accordingly held that it has no jurisdiction to give a preliminary ruling on a question submitted by a national court where it is quite obvious that the interpretation or assessment of the validity of a Community rule sought by that court bears no relation to the facts or purpose of the main action, where the problem is hypothetical or where the Court does not have before it the factual or legal material necessary to enable it to give a useful answer to the questions submitted to it . . .

29. In order that the Court of Justice may perform its task in accordance with the EC Treaty it is essential for national courts to explain, when the reasons do not emerge beyond any doubt from the file, why they consider that a reply to their questions is necessary to enable them to give judgment. Thus the Court has also on various occasions stressed that it is important for the national court to state the precise reasons for which it is in doubt as to the interpretation

---

51 T. Kennedy, 'First Steps Towards a European Certiorari' (1993) 18 *EL Rev.* 121; D. Anderson, 'The Admissibility of Preliminary References' (1994) 14 *YBEL* 179, 186–8.

of Community law and which led it to consider it necessary to refer questions to the Court for a preliminary ruling . . .

30. In the present case, the action before the national court seeks, on an application by Plato Plastik, an order that Caropack must provide the latter with confirmation of its participation in the ARA system relating to the plastic bags delivered to it. It is not manifestly apparent from the facts set out in the order for reference that the dispute is in fact fictitious . . . The fact that the parties to the main proceedings are in agreement as to the interpretation of the Community provisions in question does not affect the reality of the dispute in the main proceedings . . .

31. Consequently, the argument that the dispute is fictitious cannot succeed.

The Court of Justice will also refuse to give a reference where, even though the reference comes from a court or tribunal, the proceedings are not of a 'judicial character'. For proceedings to be of a judicial character, they must be capable of producing binding effects. In *Borker*, a member of the Parisian Bar complained to its Council about the refusal of a German court to allow him to plead before it.[52] The Paris Bar Council only had jurisdiction to rule on matters which related directly to the Paris Bar. It certainly had no jurisdiction to give a ruling on the behaviour of a German court. The Court refused to accept the reference, stating that the proceedings were not of a judicial character. Moreover, the Court will only accept the reference if there is also a legal dispute. In Italy, a company can gain legal personality through registering its articles of association with a civil court. In *Job Centre Coop*, where an undertaking sought to provide manpower services, the question arose whether the Italian public monopoly over the provision of such services breached EC law.[53] The Court of Justice refused to entertain the reference, noting that the national court was carrying out administrative functions, and as the proceedings were not of a judicial character, it was not competent to refer.

## 4. Preliminary references and the European judicial order

### (i)  *Article 234 EC and the creation of a Community judicial order*

The Court of Justice has crafted the preliminary reference procedure to create an autonomous court system with its own system of judicial hierarchies. It has done this by holding that Article 234 EC provides a direct link between itself and all national courts in the European Union. This court structure is different from national systems of administration of justice. These are characterised by compartmentalisation and decentralisation. There are specialised courts for particular areas, such as tax, intellectual property law, labour law and social security, and distinctions may be made between private law courts and administrative ones. Multitiered systems of appeal

---

52  Case 138/80 *Borker* [1980] ECR 1975.
53  Case C-111/94 *Job Centre Coop* [1995] ECR I-3361. See also Case C-178/99 *Salzmann* [2001] ECR I-4421; Case C-182/00 *Lutz* [2002] ECR I-547.

result in only a very small proportion of cases reaching the more senior courts. The preliminary reference procedure, by contrast, allows all courts and tribunals within the European Union, no matter how high or low, to make a reference to a single court: the Court of Justice. The Community court structure is, therefore, a flat court structure of 'first, and then equals', in which all national courts are granted equal possibilities to make a reference to the Court of Justice, and no national law can disenfranchise any national court of the possibility of making a reference.

In *Rheinmühlen*, the question arose as to whether national courts were prevented from being able to refer by rulings on the matter from superior courts, which would normally bind them. Rheinmühlen received a subsidy to export barley outside the European Union. When he failed to do this, the German authorities sought to recover the subsidy. The Hesse Finance Court considered that he was entitled to recover the full subsidy, but, on appeal, the Federal Finance Court ruled that he was entitled only to recover part of the subsidy. The matter was referred back to the Hesse court, which considered that the Federal Court's ruling was inconsistent with the EC Regulation on the matter. It referred the question as to whether it still had a discretion to refer, unfettered by the ruling of the superior domestic court.

### Case 166/73 *Rheinmühlen-Düsseldorf v Einfuhr- und Vorratstelle für Getreide* [1974] ECR 33

2. [Article 234] is essential for the preservation of the Community character of the law established by the Treaty and has the object of ensuring that in all circumstances this law is the same in all States of the Community.

Whilst it thus aims to avoid divergences in the interpretation of Community law which the national courts have to apply, it likewise tends to ensure this application by making available to the national judge a means of eliminating difficulties which may be occasioned by the requirement of giving Community law its full effect within the framework of the judicial systems of the Member States.

Consequently any gap in the system so organized could undermine the effectiveness of the provisions of the Treaty and of the secondary Community law.

The provisions of [Article 234], which enable every national court or tribunal without distinction to refer a case to the court for a preliminary ruling when it considers that a decision on the question is necessary to enable it to give judgment, must be seen in this light.

3. The provisions of [Article 234] are absolutely binding on the national judge and, in so far as the second paragraph is concerned, enable him to refer a case to the Court of Justice for a preliminary ruling on interpretation or validity.

This Article gives national courts the power and, where appropriate, imposes on them the obligation to refer a case for a preliminary ruling, as soon as the judge perceives either of his own motion or at the request of the parties that the litigation depends on a point referred to in the first paragraph of [Article 234].

4. It follows that national courts have the widest discretion in referring matters to the Court of Justice if they consider that a case pending before them raises questions involving interpretation, or consideration of the validity, of provisions of Community law, necessitating a decision on their part.

> It follows from these factors that a rule of national law whereby a Court is bound on points of law by the rulings of a superior court cannot deprive the inferior courts of their power to refer to the Court questions of interpretation of Community law involving such rulings.
>
> It would be otherwise if the questions put by the inferior court were substantially the same as questions already put by the superior court.
>
> On the other hand the inferior court must be free, if it considers that the ruling on law made by the superior court could lead it to give a judgment contrary to Community law, to refer to the court questions which concern it.
>
> If inferior courts were bound without being able to refer matters to the Court, the jurisdiction of the latter to give preliminary rulings and the application of Community law at all levels of the judicial systems of the Member States would be compromised.

The only circumstance in which the Court of Justice will have regard to national hierarchies is where it is clear that the decision of the lower court making the reference has been overturned on appeal by a more senior national court.[54] They do not have to follow earlier interpretations made by the latter if they choose to make a reference, and they have the same rights to make the reference as the latter. The consequence of this new relationship between lower national courts and the Court is to displace existing domestic judicial hierarchies.

### (ii) The subjects of the Community judicial order

The granting of a power to all courts in the European Union to refer throws up a further question: namely what is considered a court or tribunal for these purposes? Throughout the Union, a variety of professional, regulatory and arbitral bodies, which are not formally designated as courts under national law, adjudicate upon EC rights. It would be problematic, in terms of the uniformity of EC law, if some of these bodies were entitled to refer, but not others.

In *Broekmeulen*, therefore, the Court of Justice ruled that the uniformity of EC law required that a Community definition be provided for what constituted a court or tribunal for the purposes of Article 234 EC.[55] It indicated that this should be a broad definition, which should include many bodies that were not formally courts within the national legal system. In *Broekmeulen*, the Court held that an appeal committee within the Dutch professional body, regulating entry of doctors to the profession, constituted a court because it determined individual rights under EC law, acted under governmental legal supervision and employed quasi-legal procedures. Over the years, the Court of Justice has refined the qualities necessary for a body to be a court. In general, bodies must:

---

54 Case 65/81 *Reina v Landeskreditbank Baden-Württemberg* [1982] ECR 33; Case C-309/02 *Radlberger Getränkegesellschaft v Land Baden-Württemberg* [2004] ECR I-11763.
55 Case 246/80 *Broeckmeulen v Huisarts Registratie Commissie* [1981] ECR 2311.

- be established by law;
- be independent;
- have a binding jurisdiction;
- use *inter partes* procedures; and
- apply rules of law.[56]

Immigration adjudicators,[57] professional disciplinary bodies,[58] bodies established to review public contracts[59] and tax adjudicators[60] have all been found to be courts, notwithstanding that they are not part of the formal judiciaries of their Member States. It is not always necessary that the body operate *inter partes* procedures, in which two parties go head to head to be considered a court. Bodies with inquisitorial powers, where the judicial body asks questions of the defendant or applicant, and on that basis makes a decision, can also be considered courts.[61]

The other elements seem central, however. The body must be independent from the parties. It must be operationally independent in that it must have no organisational links with any of the parties appearing before it.[62] There must also be safeguards protecting its independence. In *Gabalfrisa*, the Court considered the Tribunales Ecónomico-Administrativos, which reviewed the decisions of the tax authorities in Spain, to be courts.[63] Although members of these bodies were appointed and dismissed by the minister, there was a clear separation of functions between them and the tax authority. By contrast, in *Syfait*, the Court did not consider the Greek competition authority to be a court even though it was formally independent.[64] There were insufficient guarantees against dismissal of its members by the Minister for Economic Development and there was an operational link between its decision-making part and its fact-finding part. The latter was part of the state and supplied facts to the former.

The body must also have a public status in the sense that it must have a compulsory jurisdiction. This has left a whole host of private bodies, most notably arbitration panels, outside the definition of a court.[65] These decisions indicate the tensions and limits in this area. Uniformity of EC law would grant the power to refer to a body on

---

56 This was first established in Case 61/65 *Vaasen v Beambtenfonds voor het Mijnbedrijf* [1966] ECR 272. See recently, Case C-53/03 *Syfait v Glaxo Smith Kline* [2005] ECR I-4609.

57 Case C-416/96 *El Yassini v Secretary of State for the Home Department* [1999] ECR I-1209.

58 Case 246/80 *Broeckmeulen v Huisarts Registratie Commissie* [1981] ECR 2311.

59 Case C-54/96 *Dorsch v Bundesbaugesellschaft Berlin* [1997] ECR I-4961; Case C-92/00 *HI v Stadt Wien* [2002] ECR I-5553.

60 Case C-17/00 *De Coster v Collège des bourgmestre et échevins de watermael-Boitsfort* [2001] ECR I-9445.

61 Case C-54/96 *Dorsch v Bundesbaugesellschaft Berlin* [1997] ECR I-4961; Joined Cases C-110–147/98 *Gabalfrisa v Agencia Estatal de Administracion Tributaria* [2000] ECR I-1577.

62 Case C-24/92 *Corbiau v Administration des Contributions* [1993] ECR I-1277; Case C-516/99 *Schmid* [2002] ECR I-4573.

63 *Gabalfrisa*, above n. 61.

64 Case C-53/03 *Syfait v Glaxo Smith Kline* [2005] ECR I-4609.

65 Case 102/81 *Nordsee Deutsche Hochseefischerei v Reederei Mond Hochseefischerei* [1982] ECR 1095; Case C-125/04 *Denuit v Transorient-Mosaïque Voyages and Culture*, judgment of 27 January 2005.

the basis of its functions rather than its status, namely whether its decisions affect EC rights or not. Only this would enable the possibility of referral wherever EC rights were being determined. Yet such a wide-ranging definition would have resulted in bodies being recognised as courts which are not recognised as such by any Member State legal system.[66]

### (iii) Docket-control by the Court of Justice

Any court system involves the creation of a judicial hierarchy in which certain courts have authority over others. In national legal systems, appeal procedures allow the appellate court to overturn the decision of the lower court, and, in some jurisdictions, there are systems of precedent, whereby decisions of higher courts constrain lower court discretion more generally. Hierarchy is also maintained through appellate courts deciding which cases they will accept. If a lower court refuses to give leave to the parties to appeal its decision, an appellate court can revisit the matter and allow it to be appealed. Although the preliminary reference contains no system of appeal, hierarchical relations have been developed between the Court of Justice and national courts in four ways.

### (a) The binding effects of judgments on national courts

The doctrines of *stare decisis* and precedent do not formally exist in EC law. Judgments of the Court of Justice only formally govern the dispute before them. For other parties, they only declare the pre-existing state of the law.[67] Clearly, the idea that judgments have no broader effects would be highly unsatisfactory for the development of the Community legal order. It was felt to be particularly problematic where the Court of Justice declared a Community measure to be illegal. If the judgment only bound the parties concerned, it was only invalid for the terms of the dispute, but the principles enunciated by the Court in the judgment could clearly be invoked by others adversely affected by the measure. In *ICC*, therefore, the Court ruled that a judgment declaring an EC measure illegal bound all courts and authorities in the European Union.[68] The binding force of Court judgments which interpreted EC law was unclear for some time. Whilst some Advocates General have asserted that all Court rulings have general *erga omnes* effects,[69] others have asserted that they do not.[70]

---

66 G. Bebr, 'Arbitration Tribunals and Article 177 of the EEC Treaty' (1985) 22 *CML Rev.* 489.
67 T. Koopmans, 'Stare Decisis in European Law' in D. O'Keeffe and H. Schermers (eds.), *Essays in European Law and Integration* (Deventer, Kluwer, 1982); A. Arnull, 'Owning up to Fallibility: Precedent and the Court of Justice' (1993) 30 *CML Rev.* 247.
68 Case 66/80 *International Chemical Corporation v Amministrazione Finanze* [1981] ECR 1191; Case 314/85 *Firma Fotofrost v HZ Lübeck Ost* [1987] ECR 4199.
69 e.g. Advocate General Darmon in Case 338/85 *Pardini v Ministerio del Commercio con L'Estero* [1988] ECR 2041; Advocate General Van Gerven in Case 145/88 *Torfaen Borough Council v B & Q* [1989] ECR 765.
70 e.g. Advocate General Lenz in Case 103/88 *Fratelli Constanzo v Milano* [1989] ECR 1839.

In *Kühne*, the Court resolved this by holding that the authority of its judgments was such as to bind all courts and administrative authorities in the European Union. Kühne exported chicken legs with part of the chicken's back still attached to states outside the European Union. In a judgment involving other parties, the Court of Justice had ruled that these were to be classified as 'chicken legs' for the purposes of customs classification.[71] Kühne then sought reimbursement from the Dutch authorities who had previously placed its goods in a customs classification on which higher customs duties were levied. The Dutch authorities observed that the matter had previously been decided by a Dutch court, which had decided against Kühne, and could not, therefore, be re-opened. Kühne argued that they were bound to reconsider in the light of the earlier Court of Justice judgment.

### Case C-453/00 *Kühne & Heitz v Productschap voor Pluimvee en Eieren* [2004] ECR I-837

21. The interpretation which, in the exercise of the jurisdiction conferred on it by Article 234 EC, the Court gives to a rule of Community law clarifies and defines, where necessary, the meaning and scope of that rule as it must be or ought to have been understood and applied from the time of its coming into force . . .

22. It follows that a rule of Community law interpreted in this way must be applied by an administrative body within the sphere of its competence even to legal relationships which arose or were formed before the Court gave its ruling on the question on interpretation.

23. The main proceedings raise the question whether the above-mentioned obligation must be complied with notwithstanding that a decision has become final before the application for review of that decision in order to take account of a preliminary ruling by the Court on a question of interpretation has been lodged.

24. Legal certainty is one of a number of general principles recognised by Community law. Finality of an administrative decision, which is acquired upon expiry of the reasonable time-limits for legal remedies or by exhaustion of those remedies, contributes to such legal certainty and it follows that Community law does not require that administrative bodies be placed under an obligation, in principle, to re-open an administrative decision which has become final in that way.

25. However, the national court stated that, under Netherlands law, administrative bodies always have the power to re-open a final administrative decision, provided that the interests of third parties are not adversely affected, and that, in certain circumstances, the existence of such a power may imply an obligation to withdraw such a decision even if Netherlands law does not require that the competent body re-open final decisions as a matter course in order to comply with judicial decisions given subsequent to the decision. The aim of the national court's question is to ascertain whether, in circumstances such as those of the main case, there is an obligation to re-open a final administrative decision under Community law.

26. As is clear from the case-file, the circumstances of the main case are the following. First, national law confers on the administrative body competence to re-open the decision in question, which has become final. Second, the administrative decision became final only as a result of a judgment of a national court against whose decisions there is no judicial remedy.

---

71 Case C-151/93 *Voogd Vleesimport en -export* [1994] ECR I-4915.

Third, that judgment was based on an interpretation of Community law which, in the light of a subsequent judgment of the Court, was incorrect and which was adopted without a question being referred to the Court for a preliminary ruling in accordance with the conditions provided for in Article 234 EC. Fourth, the person concerned complained to the administrative body immediately after becoming aware of that judgment of the Court.

27. In such circumstances, the administrative body concerned is, in accordance with the principle of cooperation arising from Article 10 EC, under an obligation to review that decision in order to take account of the interpretation of the relevant provision of Community law given in the meantime by the Court. The administrative body will have to determine on the basis of the outcome of that review to what extent it is under an obligation to re-open, without adversely affecting the interests of third parties, the decision in question.

### (b)   Limiting the circumstances in which the Court of Justice will accept references

It will be clear from the preceding section that there are a number of circumstances in which the Court of Justice will refuse to give a ruling even though a reference has been made by a body that it recognises as a court.[72] The first set of circumstances in which this will occur is where the Court wishes to protect its judicial function. It will not give a reference if it is manifestly apparent that there is no legal dispute, the factual and legal context to the dispute has not been provided in sufficient detail for the Court to be able to give an answer to the question or the question is clearly not relevant to the dispute or is purely hypothetical.[73] The second set of circumstances in which the Court will refuse to give a reference is where it will undermine the *locus standi* conditions set out in other provisions of the EC Treaty. This will be the case where the party challenging the EC act could have brought the matter by direct action before the Court, but the time limits for bringing such an action have elapsed.[74]

### (c)   Setting out the circumstances in which referral is obligatory

National courts act as gate-keepers to the Court of Justice as it is they who decide which cases should be referred. This dilutes the possibility of private parties being able to secure access before the Court. If the national court refuses to refer, there is usually little redress unless they can successfully appeal to another national court. It also makes the Court of Justice strongly dependent on them. If they refer nothing to it, it is deprived of the most important source of its workload. Notwithstanding the power of national courts, there are a number of circumstances in which, formally at least, they are required to refer.

---

72 See pp. 287–91.
73 A good summary of the conditions is set out in Case C-379/98 *PreussenElektra v Schhleswag* [2001] ECR I-2099.
74 Case C-188/92 *TWD Textilwerke Deggendorf v Germany* [1994] ECR I-833.

Article 234(3) EC states that courts against whose decision there is no judicial remedy in national law, are obliged to refer where the point of EC law is necessary to decide the dispute in hand. All other courts fall within Article 234(2) EC and enjoy a discretion whether to refer. There had been discussion for many years as to which courts fell within Article 234(3) EC. The 'abstract' theory stated that it was the highest courts in the land against whose decisions there was never a possibility of appeal. The 'concrete' theory, by contrast, stated that it was the highest court in the case in hand. If a party was denied leave to appeal to a higher court, the court refusing them leave to appeal would be a court against whose decisions there was no judicial remedy for the purposes of Article 234(3) EC. The matter was resolved in *Lyckeskog*, which opted for the concrete theory. In this case, Lyckeskog was prosecuted for importing rice into Sweden without paying customs duties. He appealed to the Swedish Court of Appeal, arguing that the relevant EC Regulation allowed this where the rice was for personal use. The Swedish Court of Appeal, whose decisions could be appealed to the Swedish Supreme Court, referred the question as to whether it fell within Article 234(3) EC if it refused Lyckeskog leave to appeal.

### Case C-99/00 *Lyckeskog* [2002] ECR I-4839

14. The obligation on national courts against whose decisions there is no judicial remedy to refer a question to the Court for a preliminary ruling has its basis in the cooperation established, in order to ensure the proper application and uniform interpretation of Community law in all the Member States, between national courts, as courts responsible for applying Community law, and the Court. That obligation is in particular designed to prevent a body of national case-law that is not in accordance with the rules of Community law from coming into existence in any Member State

15. That objective is secured when, subject to the limits accepted by the Court of Justice . . . supreme courts are bound by this obligation to refer . . . as is any other national court or tribunal against whose decisions there is no judicial remedy under national law.

16. Decisions of a national appellate court which can be challenged by the parties before a supreme court are not decisions of a 'court or tribunal of a Member State against whose decisions there is no judicial remedy under national law' within the meaning of Article 234 EC. The fact that examination of the merits of such appeals is subject to a prior declaration of admissibility by the supreme court does not have the effect of depriving the parties of a judicial remedy.

17. That is so under the Swedish system. The parties always have the right to appeal to the Högsta domstol against the judgment of a hovrätt, which cannot therefore be classified as a court delivering a decision against which there is no judicial remedy. Under Paragraph 10 of Chapter 54 of the Rättegångsbalk, the Högsta domstol may issue a declaration of admissibility if it is important for guidance as to the application of the law that the appeal be examined by that court. Thus, uncertainty as to the interpretation of the law applicable, including Community law, may give rise to review, at last instance, by the supreme court.

18. If a question arises as to the interpretation or validity of a rule of Community law, the supreme court will be under an obligation, pursuant to the third paragraph of Article 234 EC, to refer a question to the Court of Justice for a preliminary ruling either at the stage of the examination of admissibility or at a later stage.

*Lyckeskog* secures the universal jurisdiction of the Court of Justice. In principle, in every case there should be a point at which individuals are able to demand a reference from a national court because there will be a moment where either leave to appeal is refused or the case is decided by the highest court in the land, and that court falls within Article 234(3) EC. There are drawbacks to such an interpretation, as it prevents national courts stopping proceedings becoming too drawn out, or matters not being referred to the Court of Justice because the sums involved are too small or the case is of very limited importance.

To date, the only two circumstances in which national courts have not been required to refer involved the doctrines of *acte éclairé* and *acte clair*. The former allows a court not to refer if a materially identical matter has already been decided by the Court of Justice, whereas the latter states that a question need not be referred if the provision in question is so clear that there is no reasonable doubt about its application. This was decided in *CILFIT*, which concerned a challenge by a group of textile firms to levies imposed by the Italian Ministry of Health on wool imported by them from outside the European Union. The case centred on whether wool was an animal product, as an EC Regulation prohibited levies being imposed on 'animal products'. The dispute went up to the Italian Court of Cassation, the highest civil court in Italy. The Italian Ministry of Health argued that there was no need to make a reference to the Court as the interpretation of EU law in the case, namely the question of whether wool was an animal product, was so obvious.

### Case 283/81 *CILFIT v Ministry of Health* [1982] ECR 341

13. It must be remembered in this connection that in its judgment of 27 March 1963 in Joined Cases 28–30/62 *Da Costa v Nederlandse Belastingadministratie* [1963] ECR 31 the Court ruled that: 'Although the third paragraph of [Article 234] unreservedly requires courts or tribunals of a Member State against whose decision there is no judicial remedy under national law . . . to refer to the Court every question of interpretation raised before them, the authority of an interpretation under [Article 234] already given by the Court may deprive the obligation of its purpose and thus empty it of its substance. Such is the case especially when the question raised is materially identical with a question which has already been the subject of a preliminary ruling in a similar case.'

14. The same effect, as regards the limits set to the obligation laid down by the third paragraph of [Article 234], may be produced where previous decisions of the Court have already dealt with the point of law in question, irrespective of the nature of the proceedings which led to those decisions, even though the questions at issue are not strictly identical.

15. However, it must not be forgotten that in all such circumstances national courts and tribunals, including those referred to in paragraph (3) of [Article 234], remain entirely at liberty to bring a matter before the Court of Justice if they consider it appropriate to do so.

16. Finally, the correct application of Community law may be so obvious as to leave no scope for any reasonable doubt as to the manner in which the question raised is to be resolved. Before it comes to the conclusion that such is the case, the national court or tribunal must be convinced that the matter is equally obvious to the courts of the other Member States and to the Court of Justice. Only if those conditions are satisfied may the national court or

tribunal refrain from submitting the question to the Court of Justice and take upon itself the responsibility for resolving it.

17. However, the existence of such a possibility must be assessed on the basis of the characteristic feature of Community law and the particular difficulties to which its interpretation gives rise.

18. To begin with, it must be borne in mind that Community legislation is drafted in several languages and that the different language versions are equally authentic. An interpretation of a provision of Community law thus involves a comparison of the different language versions.

19. It must also be borne in mind, even where the different language versions are entirely in accord with one another, that Community law uses terminology which is peculiar to it. Furthermore, it must be emphasised that legal concepts do not necessarily have the same meaning in Community law and in the law of the various Member States.

20. Finally, every provision of Community law must be placed in its context and interpreted in the light of the provisions of Community law as a whole, regard being had to the objectives thereof and to its state of evolution at the date on which the provision in question is to be applied.

21. In the light of all those considerations, the answer to the question submitted by the Corte Suprema di Cassazione must be that the third paragraph of [Article 234 EC] is to be interpreted as meaning that a court or tribunal against those decisions there is no judicial remedy under national law is required, where a question of Community law is raised before it, to comply with its obligation to bring the matter before the Court of Justice, unless it has established that the question raised is irrelevant or that the Community provision in question has already been interpreted by the Court or that the correct application of Community law is so obvious as to leave no scope for any reasonable doubt. The existence of such a possibility must be assessed in the light of the specific characteristics of Community law, the particular difficulties to which its interpretation gives rise and the risk of divergences in judicial decisions within the Community.

Read literally, the exception is so narrow so as to be almost meaningless.[75] There will be few national judges who have the capacity to compare the nuances and context of a provision in all languages of the EC.[76] Even the Court of Justice, with all the back-up of its translating services, has struggled to come to terms with the interpretive difficulties posed by the authenticity of all the different language versions of EC law.[77] To concentrate on the formal limits of *CILFIT* is to miss its significance. *CILFIT* encourages national courts to decide matters of EC law for themselves. To some, therefore, it creates a lacuna in judicial protection by providing circumstances where individuals will not have access to the Court of Justice.[78] To others, the doctrine of *acte clair* acts as a valve, defusing potential conflict between the higher national courts and the Court of Justice, by allowing the former to decide matters exclusively by themselves

---

75  H. Rasmussen, 'The European Court's Acte Clair Strategy in *CILFIT*' (1984) 9 *EL Rev.* 242; Mancini and Keeling, above n. 26, 4.

76  For an attempt to do so see *Cunningham v Milk Marketing Board for Northern Ireland* [1988] 3 CMLR 815.

77  For difficulties with the different language versions of EC legislation see Case C-72/95 *Aanemersbedrijf P. K. Kraaijeveld v Gedeputeerde Staten van Zuid-Hooland* [1996] ECR I-5403.

78  A. Arnull, 'Reflections on Judicial Attitudes at the European Court' (1985) 34 *ICLQ* 168, 172; A. Arnull, 'The Use and Abuse of Article 177 EEC' (1989) 52 *MLR* 622, 626.

without engaging in any overt act of judicial rebellion.[79] The practice of most national courts is increasingly to refer primarily only in important and novel cases. Between 1999 and 2002, German,[80] Dutch,[81] French,[82] Swedish,[83] Spanish,[84] Portuguese,[85] Finnish,[86] Austrian[87] and Italian[88] courts of last resort failed to refer questions of EC law necessary to decide a dispute. Furthermore, whilst they are receptive to the authority of EC law, neither the Spanish, Italian, French nor German Constitutional Courts have ever made a reference to the Court of Justice.

If *CILFIT* does perform this role of encouragement of giving national courts some leeway for decision-making, it does so in a highly distorted manner. It requires the highest national court to hide behind semantic grounds as a reason for non-referral, that is, that the matter has already been decided or that the provision is so clear that it does not require interpretation. The Court does permit national courts to put forward the far stronger reasons for non-referral, namely that there are important national constitutional values at stake that they wish to decide, or that to refer might lead to an abuse of the litigation process with one party needlessly drawing out the process.

### (d) The accountability of national judges

The duties of national judges under Article 234 EC have traditionally appeared to be paper duties. There was no sanction in EC law for failure to fulfil their duties under Article 234 EC. Matters changed in *Köbler*.[89] Köbler, it will be remembered, was an Austrian professor who lost bonuses, to which he would otherwise have been entitled for his length of service in the university sector, because he had spent some years working at a German university. The Austrian Administrative Court, a court of last resort, wrongly ruled that this did not breach EC law and that it was not, therefore, obliged to refer. The Court of Justice ruled that the state could be liable to pay damages

79 J. Golub, 'The Politics of Judicial Discretion: Rethinking the Interaction between National Courts and the European Court of Justice' (1996) 19 *WEP* 360, 376–7.

80 Judgment of the Bundesfinanzhof of 21 March 2002, Az VII R 35/01, RIW 2002, 644; judgment of the Bundesfinanzhof of 15 May 2002, Az I R 40/01, Der Betrieb 2002, 1743; judgment of the Bundesgerichtshof of 11 June 2002, I ZR 273/99 (Sportlernahrung) and I ZR 34/01 (Muskelaufbaupräparate).

81 RTL/Veronica, Holland Media Group and CLT-UFA SA/Commissariaat voor de Media (2002) Rechtspraak Bestuursrecht 5; judgment of Hoge Raad of 25 July 2000, Belissingen in belastingzaken, 2000, 307; judgment of Benelux Gerichtshof of 24 June 2002.

82 Conseil d'Etat, judgment of 28 July 2000 Schering-Plough Application 205710; Lilia Milaja, judgment of the Cour administrative d'appel de Nancy, Droit Adminstratif 2000 No. 208.

83 Regeringsrätten, 10 April 2000, RÅ 1999–630.

84 *Gabai Oil v Petronor*, judgment of Tribunal Supremo of 15 March 2001; judgment of the Tribunal Supremo of 7 March 2002 (RJA 2002/3525). See also the judgments of the Tribunal Supremo of 27 March 2002 (RJA 2002/3616), 15 July 2002 (RJA 2002/7724) and 16 November 2002 ( La Ley 28-I-2003, marginal 599).

85 Judgment of the Supremo Tribunal Administrativo of 14 October 1999, Case 31355.

86 Judgment of the Supreme Administrative Court of 20 March 2002.

87 Case C-224/01 *Köbler v Austria* [2003] ECR I-10239.     88 Foro Italiano (2002) I, Col. 3090.

89 Case C-224/01 *Köbler v Austria* [2003] ECR I-10239.

under the *Francovich* principle for the illegal act of the court. One of the illegal acts in this case was a breach of the Article 234(3) EC requirement to refer. The Court held that an action for damages would be available where it was manifestly apparent that a court had failed to comply with its obligations under Article 234(3) EC. This would be the case where it was evident that neither the doctrine of *acte clair* nor that of *acte éclairé* applied. In this instance, the Court ruled it was not obviously apparent, as the Austrian had mistakenly, but in good faith, thought that the matter was covered by a previous ruling of the Court, which had held that the treatment was lawful. It contemplated, therefore, that it fell within the doctrine of *acte éclairé*.

In principle, this adds an incentive for courts to comply with their duties under Article 234 EC. National courts falling under Article 234(2) EC are as subject to appeal when they fail to apply EC law properly, as when they misapply domestic law. There is financial redress against the state if courts against whose decision there is no judicial remedy fail to refer where it is obvious that they should. However, the duty might still only be a paper one.[90] The redress is against the state, not against the court. It is not clear, short of legislation, what the other arms of government could do to redress a decision of a senior court. The incentives do not, therefore, fall directly on the court in question. Such an action would also require a court of first instance to rule negatively on the actions of the senior court. For it would require a new action to be brought before such a court demanding that it rule that the latter had acted illegally. It seems implausible that many lower courts would do this.

*Köbler* is, therefore, more important for what it symbolises. This has been well described by Davies, who states that the implication of this case law is that:

> Thus national court interpretations of Community law, while sometimes creative and purposive, take place in a grey area of semi-legitimacy, a sort of tolerated but not approved practice, where the assumption seems to be that ultimately any point of law will in fact make its way to the Court of Justice. Moreover, national final courts will have no interpretive competence at all.[91]

This view is strongly at odds with that of the judges of national courts, who see themselves as responsible for the administration of all law on their territories. Moreover, as a number of commentators have observed, it obstructs the goal of creating a Community court system in which all courts in the European Union identify themselves both as Community and national courts. By denying the contribution of national judges to the development of EC law, it emasculates and infantilises them.[92]

---

90 J. Komárek, 'Federal Elements in the Community Judicial System: Building Coherence in the Community Legal System' (2005) 42 *CML Rev.* 9, 12–18.

91 G. Davies, 'The Division of Powers between the European Court of Justice and National Courts', *ConWeb* No. 3/2004, 19.

92 *Ibid.*; P. Allott, 'Preliminary Rulings: Another Infant Disease' (2000) *EL Rev.* 538, 542; H. Rasmussen, 'Remedying the Crumbling EC Judicial System' (2000) 37 *CML Rev.* 1071, 1092.

## 5. Reform of the judicial architecture of the European Union

The structure of the Community court system has to be gauged against how effectively it realises the objectives that it has set itself, namely those of the development of EC law, preservation of its unity, judicial review of EU institutional activity and dispute resolution. Over the years, a number of features have emerged, which have thwarted achievement of these objectives.[93]

**Bottlenecking**    At the end of 2004, there were 840 cases pending before the Court of Justice, with the mean wait for a reference being 23.5 months.[94] The delay incurred is in addition to that which has already been incurred before the national courts. The pressures are also growing. The number of cases increased by about 40 per cent during the 1990s. With enlargement kicking in, one estimate suggests that the number of cases arriving at the Court of Justice will go up from about 500 per annum to 700 per annum. The consequences of this for the development of EC law are that important cases get stuck in a queue behind other cases. It also has important side-effects for the question of judicial review. Courts will not allow prima facie illegal behaviour by the European Union to continue for this period, particularly where it violates individuals' rights. The consequence is that, in practical terms, judicial review is decided at the stage of the granting of interim relief by the national court, as it is only at this moment that serious attention can be given to whether the situation should persist. This is deeply unsatisfactory, as it is a national court rather than the Court of Justice deciding these matters and the conditions for granting interim relief are different from those for definitive judicial review.[95] Finally, it is unsatisfactory in relation to dispute resolution. For many litigants, the redress simply arrives too late to be of much use to them. For others, conversely, the length of the procedure is an advantage. The delay becomes a litigation strategy that can be used to exert undue pressure on the other side.[96]

**Legal pollution**    The bottlenecking does not occur because the Court of Justice is a lazy court. It gave 275 judgments in 2004.[97] This compares favourably with national supreme courts. The British House of Lords gave 72 judgments in 2002,[98] the French Conseil Constitutionel gave 28 judgments in 2003,[99] and the Italian Constitutional Court delivered 51 judgments in 2003.[100] This workload places enormous time and

---

93 On the evolution of the system over the year see C. Barnard and E. Sharpston, 'The Changing Face of Article 177 References' (1997) 34 *CML Rev.* 1113; C. Turner and R. Munoz, 'Revising the Judicial Architecture of the European Union' (1999/2000) 19 *YBEL* 1, 1–32.

94 *Annual Report of the European Court of Justice 2004* (Luxembourg, OOPEC, 2005) 167, 174.

95 Case C-465/93 *Atlanta Fruchthandelsgesellschaft v Bundesant für Ernährung und Forstwirtschaft* [1995] ECR I-3761.

96 R. Rawlings, 'The Eurolaw Game: Some Deductions from a Saga' (1993) 20 *Journal of Law and Society* 309.

97 *Annual Report of the European Court of Justice 2004* (Luxembourg, OOPEC, 2005) 169.

98 *Judicial Statistics 2002* (London, Department of Constitutional Affairs, 2003) Table 1.4.

99 See www.conseil-constitutionnel.fr/tableau/tab03.htm

100 See www.cortecostituzionale.it/ita/attivitacorte/novita/ novitaold.asp

organisational pressures on the Court of Justice. Deadlines are tight, translation services stretched and time for judicial debate and reflection limited.[101]

**Expertise**    The Court of Justice is asked to adjudicate on a startling array of cases. Some, such as VAT or agriculture, are highly technical with the Court having to familiarise itself with complex constellations of facts. Others, such as intellectual property law, involve the Court having to delve into highly specialised areas of law with a long intellectual legacy. In other cases, most notably free movement, it is engaging in regulatory review, considering the appropriateness and intelligibility of local regulation. In many areas of EC social law, it is acting as a labour court. Finally, in some cases, it is behaving as a constitutional court, adjudicating on general principles that underpin the EC legal order. In all other jurisdictions, these tasks would be divided between different courts. As a set of generalists, required to do all of them, it is becoming increasingly difficult for the Court to do any of them well, particularly given the time pressures it is under.

**Legitimacy**    The Court of Justice enjoys neither a high level of awareness amongst European citizens, nor strong support. A survey found that only in Luxembourg was there more awareness of the Court than any of the other EU institutions.[102] It also found very little diffuse support for the institution, namely that citizens would support it even where they disagreed with its decisions. In Denmark, for example, such support was as low as 9.3 per cent in the early 1990s.[103] The preliminary reference procedure arguably contributes to this problem through the manner in which it structures the Court's docket. The delays and contingencies of Article 234 EC result in its very rarely being used by litigants who are going to court for compensation. Instead, it is used predominantly by two types of litigant. One type is those interested in judicial politics. This litigant is using the courts to bring about legal reform. She is not interested in compensation, but establishing a new legal principle. The second type of litigant is interested in regulatory or fiscal politics. Where large undertakings have ongoing relations with regulatory or fiscal authorities, one of the parties may use litigation to reconfigure the long-term basis for the relationship. Often the challenge is to a relatively small tax or piece of regulation, but the motive is to change the climate in which business is done. A study found that between 1994 and 1998, these two types of litigation accounted for 66.35 per cent of all references from the

---

101 J. Weiler, 'Epilogue: The Judicial après Nice' in G. de Búrca and J. Weiler (eds.), *The European Court of Justice* (Oxford, Oxford University Press, 2001).

102 On judicial politics, see K. Alter, 'The European Union's Legal System and Domestic Policy: Spillover or Backlash?' (2000) 54 *International Organisation* 489; K. Alter and J. Vargas, 'Explaining Variation in the Use of European Litigation Strategies: European Community Law and British Gender Equality Policy' (2000) 33 *Comparative Political Studies* 452.

103 J. Gibson and G. Caldeira, 'Challenges in the Legitimacy of the European Court of Justice: A Post Maastricht Analysis' (1998) 28 *British Journal of Political Science* 63.

United Kingdom.[104] The difficulty with this is that it leads to an imbalance. Litigation is predominantly about the overturning of national regimes by discontented constituencies, who are, otherwise, too isolated to mobilise change domestically. If the Court accedes to only 10 per cent of these challenges, because of the one-way nature of the case, it still comes across as a body consistently opposed to the domestic status quo.

There has been a corresponding ongoing debate about how to reform the preliminary reference procedure.[105] Earlier suggestions focussed on either creating a system of EC regional courts,[106] which would create a new judicial layer between national courts and the Court of Justice, or developing specialised courts for complex, fact-intensive areas of EC law.[107] Neither of these has found favour.[108] Debate has instead distilled down to two alternatives. One is that national courts decide more cases by themselves.[109] A suggestion was made that national courts submit draft answers with their references. If the Court agrees at an early stage that the draft answer is correct, it would simply state that it did not object to the suggested interpretation.[110] The other is that the Court of Justice decides more by engaging in more efficient case-management. This would involve internal organisation of the Court through increased resort to Chambers, an increase in the jurisdiction of the CFI and an expansion of the translation services.[111]

Both approaches were canvassed in the run-up to the Treaty of Nice where reform of the preliminary reference procedure was considered in the light of the prospect of enlargement. Two reports were to be extremely influential during that period.[112] One

---

104  D. Chalmers, *The Much Ado About Judicial Politics*, Jean Monnet Working Paper 1/2000, 34.

105  A. Arnull, 'Refurbishing the Judicial Architecture of the European Community' (1994) 43 *ICLQ* 296; W. v. Gerven, 'The Role of the European Judiciary Now and in the Future' (1996) 21 *EL Rev.* 211; D. Scorey, 'A New Model for the Communities' Judicial Architecture in the New Union' (1996) 21 *EL Rev.* 224.

106  J.-P. Jacqué and J. Weiler, 'On the Road to European Union: a New Judicial Architecture: an Agenda for the Intergovernmental Conference' (1990) 27 *CML Rev.* 185.

107  P. Kapteyn, 'The Court of Justice of the European Communities after the Year 2000' in D. Curtin and T. Heukels (eds.), *Institutional Dynamics of European Integration: Liber Amicorum Schermers*, vol. 1 (Dordrecht, Martijnus Nijhoff, 1994) 135, 141–5.

108  Court of First Instance, 'Reflections on the Future Development of the Community Judicial System' (1991) 16 *EL Rev.* 175.

109  See Advocate General Jacobs in Case C-338/95 *Wiener v Hauptzollamt Emmerich* [1997] ECR I-6495.

110  S. Strasser, *The Development of a Strategy of Docket Control for the European Court of Justice and the Question of Preliminary References*, Jean Monnet Working Paper 95/3.

111  British Institute of International and Comparative Law, *The Role and Future of the Court of Justice* (London, BIICL, 1996) 126–31. This is not unproblematic as the translation unit at the Court of Justice faces considerable strains. P. Mullen, 'Do You Hear What I Hear? Translation, Expansion and Crisis in the European Court of Justice' in M. Cowles and M. Smith (eds.), *The State of the European Union*, vol. 5, *Risks, Reform, Resistance and Revival* (Oxford, Oxford University Press, 2000).

112  For discussion of these reports see A. Dashwood and A. Johnston (eds.), *The Future of the Judicial System of the European Union* (Oxford Portland, Hart, 2001); P. Craig, 'The Jurisdiction of the Community Courts Reconsidered' in G. de Búrca and J. Weiler (eds.), *The European Court of Justice* (Oxford, Oxford University Press, 2001); H. Rasmussen, 'Remedying the Crumbling EC Judicial System' (2000) 37 *CML Rev.* 1071.

was the Due Report. An independent report, commissioned by the Commission in late 1999, it was written by a group of senior national judges and former judges of the Court of Justice.[113] It proposed both a reform of Article 234 EC to allow national courts to decide more cases and a reform of the Court's organisation to allow it to do so more effectively. The reforms of Article 234 EC were fivefold.

- A provision should be set out expressly stipulating that national courts had full authority to decide questions of EC law. The Due Report felt that their contribution to the EC legal system as Community courts was sometimes lost, and that it had to be reaffirmed symbolically.
- EC courts falling under Article 234(2) EC should be reminded that they are not to refer systematically. Such courts should only refer where there is reasonable doubt as to the meaning of EC law or where the point has real significance for EC law.
- The *CILFIT* conditions should be expanded for Article 234(3) EC courts – those courts against whose decisions there is no judicial remedy. These should only be required to refer on questions that were sufficiently important for EC law and about whose solution there was reasonable doubt.
- A national court should consult the Court of Justice before it declares a measure invalid, even as an interim measure. This is stipulated in *Fotofrost*, but the Due Report felt it should be made an express Treaty requirement.
- The CFI should be given jurisdiction to receive preliminary references in five specified areas. These would be competition, intellectual property, cooperation in police and home affairs, visas, asylum and immigration. In addition, provision should be made for references to a specialised court dealing with judicial cooperation in civil matters and questions of private international law.

The spirit of these reforms was to spread responsibility for the development of EC law more evenly between national courts and the Court of Justice. It was also about elevating the position of the Court of Justice so that its position resembled more that of a traditional constitutional court. The allocation of references to the CFI and the instruction to national courts only to send references on significant matters would have had the combined effect of allowing it to focus its work on a more limited number of cases – those pivotal to the EC legal order – and on enunciating general principles of the EC legal order.

The submissions made by the Court of Justice and the CFI to the IGC placed greater emphasis on preserving the unity of EC law.[114] Any significant reorganisation of the preliminary reference procedures, it was argued, was likely to jeopardise that role. To that end, the Community courts suggested only two changes. One was to allow

---

113 *Report by the Working Party on the Future of the European Communities' Court System* (Brussels, EC Commission, 2000).
114 *Contribution by the Court of Justice and the Court of First Instance to the Intergovernmental Conference* (Luxembourg, OOPEC, 2000). See also the earlier more extensive document, European Court of Justice, *The Future of the Judicial System of the European Union* (Luxembourg, 1999).

the CFI to hear preliminary references in specified areas. The other was to allow the Court of Justice to determine its own rules of procedure in order to enable it to handle its workload more efficiently. At that time, these were decided by the Council acting unanimously, and the Court felt this was too cumbersome to enable creative and flexible management of the docket. The assumptions of the Community courts were that the only real problem was that of delay. Given the division of duties between the courts, and the relatively cumbersome nature of their procedures, the number of references created a heavy burden. If these could be liberalised, then they would be able to provide more case law and the gap between supply and demand would disappear.

A small concession was made to cater for the need for decentralisation. An amendment to the Rules of Procedure of the Court of Justice allows it to dispose of a reference by means of an order, rather than a full judgment where it considers the answer is apparent.

### Article 104(3) Rules of Procedure

Where a question referred to the Court for a preliminary ruling is identical to a question on which the Court has already ruled, where the answer to such a question may be clearly deduced from existing case-law or where the answer to the question admits of no reasonable doubt, the Court may, after informing the court or tribunal which referred the question to it, hearing any observations . . . and hearing the Advocate General, give its decision by reasoned order in which, if appropriate, reference is made to its previous judgment or to the relevant case-law.

The new rule has been used, and, in 2004, ten such orders were given. Yet the circumstances of their use are extremely restricted. They only discourage references which, in the Court's view, are either *acte clair* or *acte éclairé*. The central reforms introduced by the Treaty of Nice, therefore, largely followed the suggestions made by the Community courts.[115] Reforms concentrated on augmenting the capacity of the Community courts to receive references.

Provision was made in the first place for the CFI to hear preliminary references in areas to be specified. Its central place in these fields was to be reinforced by there being no general appeal to the Court of Justice from its rulings and by the Court's only being able to review its decisions in exceptional circumstances.

### Article 225(2) EC

The Court of First Instance shall have jurisdiction to hear and determine questions referred for a preliminary ruling under Article 234, in specific areas laid down by the Statute.
 Where the Court of First Instance considers that the case requires a decision of principle likely to affect the unity or consistency of Community law, it may refer the case to the Court

---

115 A. Johnston, 'Judicial Reform and the Treaty of Nice' (2001) 38 *CML Rev.* 499.

of Justice for a ruling. Decisions given by the Court of First Instance on questions referred for a preliminary ruling may exceptionally be subject to review by the Court of Justice, under the conditions and within the limits laid down by the Statute, where these is a serious risk of the unity or consistency of Community law being affected.

### Declaration 15 on Article 225(2) EC

The Conference considers that, in exceptional case in which the Court of Justice decides to review a decision of the Court of First Instance on a question referred for a preliminary ruling, it should decide by an emergency procedure

It was speculated after the Treaty of Nice that this provision could transform the CFI into the central Community court dealing with references. The possibility also offered by Nice for an increase in the size of the CFI would allow it to establish specialised Chambers to deal with particular types of reference.[116] The Court of Justice would thereby be able to position itself more firmly as a constitutional court, only pronouncing on broad principles which affect the unity and consistency of EC law.[117] To date, however, this has not happened. The CFI has yet to be allocated any concrete functions in the field of preliminary references. This has led to pressure stemming around the other reform that was agreed at the Treaty of Nice. This was not included within the Treaty itself, but in the Statute of the Court of Justice, and provided for greater use of the Chamber system.

### Article 16 Statute of the Court of Justice

The Court shall form Chambers of three or five Judges. The Judges shall elect the Presidents of the Chambers from among their number. The Presidents of the Chambers of five Judges shall be elected for three years. They may be re-elected once.

The Grand Chamber shall consist of thirteen Judges. It shall be presided over by the President of the Court. The Presidents of the Chambers of five Judges and other Judges appointed in accordance with the Rules of Procedure shall also form part of the Grand Chamber.

The Grand Chamber shall sit when a Member State or a Community institution that is party to the proceedings so requests.

The Court of Justice shall sit in plenary session where cases are brought before it pursuant to Articles 195(2), 213, 216 or 247(7) of the EC Treaty . . .

Moreover, where it considers that a case before it is of exceptional importance, the Court may decide, after hearing the Advocate General, to refer the case to the full Court.

The significance of Article 16 lies not so much in the creation of the Grand Chamber. It is rather that it makes clear that preliminary references can only be heard by Chambers of three or five judges. At the end of 2004, of the 260 cases assigned, 226

---

116 The Treaty of Nice confines the Court of Justice to one judge from each Member State. The CFI is to comprise at least one judge from each Member State. See pp. 122–3.
117 Weiler, above n. 101.

(86.2 per cent) were assigned to Chambers of three or five.[118] This gives significant power to individual judges, as in a Chamber of three, only two judges have to agree for a judgment to be reached. Indeed, increasingly important cases are decided by Chambers of three judges. The *RTL* judgment is an example.[119] The judgment was the most important yet given by the Court of Justice on Directive 89/552/EC, the Broadcasting Directive, as it concerned the amount of advertising that could be broadcast on television. It also contained the most detailed examination of the principle of freedom of expression given by the Court of Justice, and the first explicit endorsement of the Charter by the Court. It was decided, however, by a Chambers of three judges.

The jury is still out on whether these changes will reduce the current delays. In 2004, the Court of Justice gave 375 judgments, whilst in the year preceding the ratification of Nice, it gave 269.[120] There was thus a significant rise in output. Part of this was accounted for by the arrival of the ten judges from the new Member States on 1 May 2004. The wait for preliminary references only fell from 24.1 months to 23.5 months in that period, however,[121] and no references from the new Member States have yet arrived. Indeed, immediately after the ratification of Nice, the President of the CFI indicated that these reforms may not be sufficient and that the decentralisation of tasks to national courts may have to be revisited.[122]

If the problem is not one merely of delay, but of a structural imbalance in the type of litigation arriving at the Court, then deciding more cases is likely to exacerbate existing problems. Resolution of more cases involving an ever more eclectic array of issues is both likely to stretch the Court's expertise and dilute its capacity to act as a constitutional court. For it will not only be deciding cases of great principle in amongst fact-intensive, technical areas, but many of these 'constitutionalising' judgments will be decided by as few as three judges. More generally, there are real concerns about the orderly development of EC law, where one has a single court rushing out around 400 judgments per year under increasingly tight deadlines. The potential for error and self-contradiction is considerable, and it will be increasingly difficult for national legal systems to keep up with and reflect on that amount of case law.

The new context places real challenges on the Court of Justice to maintain the quality of its reasoning. If that were not sufficiently worrying for its legitimacy, increasing its output is likely to lead to more 'judicial politics' as it is making itself more available to disgruntled parties to challenge their domestic settlements, with the corresponding backlash against its judgments. It was thus symptomatic that the first case to be referred to the Court from the new Member States was the lawfulness of the ban in Hungary on the display of communist insignia.[123] This is not a run of the mill dispute

118 *Annual Report of the European Court of Justice 2004* (Luxembourg, OOPEC, 2005) 181.
119 Case C-245/01 *RTL v Niedersächsische Landesmedienanstalt für privaten Rundfunk* [2003] ECR I-12489.
120 *Annual Report of the European Court of Justice 2004*, above n. 118, 183.      121 *Ibid.*, 174.
122 B. Vesterdorf, 'The Community Court System Ten Years from Now and Beyond: Challenges and Possibilities' (2003) 28 *EL Rev.* 303, 317–18.
123 Case C-328/04 *Vajnai*, OJ 2004 C262/27.

concerning the opening up of trade between Member States. Instead, it is an attempt to force the Court of Justice to ask Hungary to revisit the politically sensitive question of how it handles its communist past. The Court cannot win from such references. A refusal to rule will be interpreted as appeasing a draconian domestic settlement. By contrast, an external body's ruling that the ban is illegal, given the foreign imposition of communism on Hungary, would be seen as highly inflammatory.

## Further reading

K. Alter, 'The European Union's Legal System and Domestic Policy: Spillover or Backlash' (2000) 54 *International Organisation* 489

D. Anderson and M. Demetriou, *References to the European Court* (London, Sweet and Maxwell, 2002)

G. de Búrca and J. Weiler (eds.), *The European Court of Justice* (Oxford, Oxford University Press, 2001)

D. Chalmers, 'The Court of Justice and the Constitutional Treaty' (2005) 4 *International Journal of Constitutional Law* 428

A. Dashwood and A. Johnston (eds.), *The Future of the Judicial System of the European Union* (Oxford/Portland, Hart, 2001)

J.-P. Jacqué and J. Weiler, 'On the Road to European Union: a New Judicial Architecture: an Agenda for the Intergovernmental Conference' (1990) 27 *CML Rev.* 185

J. Komárek, 'Federal Elements in the Community Judicial System: Building Coherence in the Community Legal System' (2005) 42 *CML Rev.* 9

S. Nyikos, 'The Preliminary Reference Process: National Court Implementation, Changing Opportunity Structures and Litigant Desistment' (2003) 4 *European Union Politics* 397

H. Rasmussen, 'Remedying the Crumbling EC Judicial System' (2000) 37 *CML Rev.* 1071

R. Rawlings, 'The Eurolaw Game: Some Deductions from a Saga' (1993) 20 *Journal of Law and Society* 309

J. Snell, 'European Courts and Intellectual Property: a Tale of Zeus, Hercules and Cyclops' (2004) 29 *EL Rev.* 178

T. Tridimas, 'Knocking on Heaven's Door: Fragmentation, Efficiency and Defiance in the Preliminary Reference Procedure' (2003) 40 *CML Rev.* 9

C Turner and R. Munoz, 'Revising the Judicial Architecture of the European Union' (1999/2000) 19 *Yearbook of European Law* 1

## PART II

## Administrative Law

8

# Accountability in the European Union

| CONTENTS | |
|---|---|

## 1. Introduction

The first part of this book (chapters 1–7) explored what might be termed the constitutional fundamentals of the European legal order. The principal focus was on the powers enjoyed by the institutions and bodies of the European Union. Constitutions, however, perform two main tasks, of which setting out public authorities' powers is but one. The other, equally important, task is to set out the ways in which the exercise of public power may be held to constitutional account. It is with this aspect of the constitutional function that the following three chapters are concerned. First, in this chapter, we explore something of the various 'political' mechanisms that exist in the European Union to secure accountability. In chapters 9 and 10 we turn to what might be termed 'legal accountability', as we consider in detail the ways in which the courts may enforce the rule of European law, first, against and within Member States and, secondly, against the institutions of the EU.

This chapter commences with a brief explanation of what is, and what is not, meant by the term 'accountability'. The various contributions to the search for accountability that have been made by the European Parliament are then outlined. In the third section of the chapter we examine the importance of notions of transparency to accountability within the EU. As we shall see, without transparency there can be little accountability and it is in this context, perhaps, that the EU has progressed furthest. We then examine what has been undoubtedly the greatest crisis, thus far, in the accountability of the European Union, when the entire College of Commissioners was compelled to resign from office in 1999. The reasons for and the institutional reactions to this momentous event are considered in the fourth section. The final part of the chapter concerns the role in securing accountability that is played by the European Ombudsman, an office created in 1995 and one which, over the past decade, has emerged as a valuable force for seeking greater accountability within the EU.

## 2. Nature and importance of accountability

Accountability is a term that has come only relatively recently into legal analysis. The growth in the consideration that is given to it, however, has been little short of explosive, particularly in the context of EU law.[1] Despite the recent attention it has received, 'accountability is not a term of art for lawyers'.[2] This means that it has no fixed or precise meaning, and that it may be used rather loosely as a term covering a variety of processes and purposes.

### R. Mulgan, '"Accountability": an Ever-expanding Concept?' (2000) 78 *Public Administration* 555, 555–6

One sense of 'accountability', on which all are agreed, is that associated with the process of being called 'to account' to some authority for one's actions. Indeed, this sense may fairly be designated the original or core sense of 'accountability' . . . Such accountability has a number of features: it is *external*, in that the account is given to some other person or body outside the person or body being held accountable; it involves *social interaction and exchange*, in that one side, that calling for the account, seeks answers and rectification while the other side, that being held accountable, responds and accepts sanctions; it implies *rights of authority*, in that those calling for an account are asserting rights of superior authority over those who are accountable, including the rights to demand answers and to impose sanctions . . .

But more recently, in academic usage at least, 'accountability' has increasingly been extended beyond these central concerns and into areas where the various features of core 'accountability' no longer apply. For instance, 'accountability' now commonly refers to the sense of individual responsibility and concern for the public interest expected from pub-lic servants ('professional' and 'personal' accountability), an 'internal' sense which goes beyond the core external focus of the term. Secondly, 'accountability' is also said to be a feature of the various institutional checks and balances by which democracies seek to control the actions of governments (accountability as 'control') even when there is no interaction

---

1 See, e.g., C. Harlow, *Accountability in the European Union* (Oxford, Oxford University Press, 2002) and A. Arnull and D. Wincott (eds.), *Accountability and Legitimacy in the European Union* (Oxford, Oxford University Press, 2002).

2 C. Harlow, 'European Governance and Accountability' in N. Bamforth and P. Leyland (eds.), *Public Law in a Multi-Layered Constitution* (Oxford, Hart, 2003) 79.

or exchange between governments and the institutions that control them. Thirdly, 'account-ability' is linked with the extent to which governments pursue the wishes or needs of their citizens (accountability as 'responsiveness') regardless of whether they are induced to do so through processes of authoritative exchange and control. Fourthly, 'accountability' is applied to the public discussion between citizens on which democracies depend (accountability as 'dialogue'), even when there is no suggestion of any authority or subordination between the parties involved in the accountability relationship.

In what follows we shall endeavour to stick to Mulgan's 'core sense' of account-ability, albeit that (unlike him) we do see judicial review and the legal enforcement of European law as being intimately connected to accountability, even if there is not always the 'social interaction and exchange' between courts and other institutions that Mulgan sees as being important. Certainly, all the forms and mechanisms of account-ability we consider comply clearly with the criteria of being 'external' and of implying 'rights of authority'. Thus, forms of internal 'accountability' (which Mulgan terms 'professional responsibility' and which are better understood as functions of manage-ment rather than of accountability) are not considered here. The internal management structures of the Commission and the Council, for example, are not examined. Sim-ilarly, forms of 'accountability' where there is no expectation that those doing the accounting are in a position of authority over those being called to account are not considered. The extent to which the institutions and bodies of the European Union may in this sense be 'accountable' to the media, for example, is excluded from our consideration.

Before proceeding further, it is important to consider the relationship between accountability and democracy and, in particular, between accountability and the alleged democratic deficit of the European Union. The latter has already been dis-cussed twice in this book[3] and it will not be analysed further here, save to say that the search for accountability and the search for democracy should not be confused with one another. Some commentators have allowed the quest for accountability in the European Union to become swallowed up and thereby lost in the broader search for a cure to the alleged democratic deficit.[4] It is important to resist this tendency. Account-ability is concerned with subjecting the decisions and actions of institutions (and, usually, executive institutions such as the Commission and the Council) to ex ante and ex post scrutiny. Building on Mulgan's definition, it comprises three main elements: the institutions must *explain* what they are doing and/or what they are seeking to do, they must make themselves politically *liable* for what they do and pro-pose to do and they must take *responsibility* for what they do.[5] The first element is a *calling* to account; the second and third a *holding* to account. Neither the institutions

---

3 See chapter 2 (where the democratic deficit was considered in the light of arguments about constitutionalism) and chapter 4 (where it was considered in the context of law-making in the European Union).

4 See, e.g., E. Fisher, 'The European Union in an Age of Accountability' (2004) 24 *OJLS* 495.

5 Compare Harlow's analysis, in which she posits that accountability comprises three main elements: 'expla-nation or the giving of an account, blame and censure, and redress': see Harlow, above n. 1, 9.

being called or held to account, nor those to whom they are accountable, need necessarily be democratic. They might be, of course, but they need not be. There is therefore no necessary link between accountability and democracy. They may overlap, for sure, but the securing of accountability within the European Union will not necessarily make the EU more democratic. It is therefore preferable to keep these two ideas – accountability and democracy – separate.

One institution that has (for the most part)[6] tried to take seriously the problem of accountability in the Union is the European Parliament.[7] The Parliament has three sets of powers that seek to enhance accountability in the European Union: powers relating to appointment and dismissal, particularly (but not only[8]) of members of the Commission,[9] powers relating to petitions[10] and powers of inquiry.[11] The substance of these powers was summarised in chapter 3,[12] where the use in 2004 of the Parliament's powers to scrutinise appointments to the Commission was also outlined.[13] As we shall see later in this chapter, when we consider in more detail the resignation of the Santer Commission in 1999, the extent to which the European Parliament is able – and willing – to subject nominees to and members of the Commission to detailed and searching scrutiny is a key component in seeking greater accountability in the European Union.[14] While the Parliament's powers to scrutinise *nominees* to the Commission have developed well – as the 2004 controversy over Rocco Buttiglione and other nominee Commissioners demonstrated – its powers to scrutinise the work of the Commission once the Commissioners are in office have not developed as far as they ought to have done since the mass resignation of 1999.[15]

The right to petition the European Parliament is a broad one in that petitions may be submitted on any matter which 'comes within the EU's fields of activity' and is limited only in that the petitioner must be 'directly' affected by the matter,[16] a constraint that is in practice interpreted relatively generously by the Parliament's

6 For criticisms of the European Parliament's record, see p. 336.

7 Another is the European Court of Auditors, whose powers were briefly outlined in chapter 3. Audit is a form of financial accountability that is of great importance to the practice of government, both within the European Union and the Member States. It is a specialised subject that we cannot consider in detail here. For an excellent overview, see I. Harden, F. White and K. Donnelly, 'The Court of Auditors and Financial Control and Accountability in the EC' (1995) 1 *EPL* 599. See also Harlow, above n. 1, ch. 5 and A. Tomkins, 'Transparency and the Emergence of a European Administrative Law' (1999–2000) 19 *YEL* 217, 247–51.

8 The European Parliament also appoints, e.g., the European Ombudsman (see below) and plays a role in the appointment of members of the European Court of Auditors and members of the Executive Board of the European Central Bank. On the latter, see European Parliament, Rules of Procedure (16th edn, 2005), rules 101–2.

9 See Article 201 EC on dismissal and Article 214 EC on appointment. See further European Parliament, Rules of Procedure (16th edn, 2005), rules 98–100.

10 See Article 194 EC.     11 See Article 193 EC.     12 See pp. 116–19.

13 For extensive discussion of the European Parliament's scrutiny in 2004 of those nominated to serve in the Barroso Commission, see the essays collected at (2005) 1 *European Constitutional Law Review* 153–225.

14 See generally P. Magnette, 'Appointing and Censuring the European Commission: the Adaptation of Parliamentary Institutions to the Community Context' (2001) 7 *ELJ* 292.

15 See pp. 334–7.     16 European Parliament, Rules of Procedure (16th edn, 2005), rule 191(1).

Committee on Petitions.[17] The principal value of petitions, it seems, is to complement the role of the European Ombudsman in affording to aggrieved individuals (and, for that matter, corporations) a low-cost means of having a complaint about the implementation of Community law investigated at a European level. As with the Ombudsman, whose work we shall consider later in this chapter, the subject-matter of petitions tends to cluster around a relatively small number of main issues. For example, failures by Member States to comply with European norms of environmental impact assessment and failures by Member States to recognise the professional qualifications obtained by individuals in other Member States, thereby hindering the free movement of persons, were cited in the committee's report for 2002–03 as generating particularly large numbers of petitions.[18] Whether, in addition to providing a cheap means of facilitating the redress of individuals' grievances, petitions also offer a means whereby the accountability *stricto sensu* of the European Union may be enhanced, however, must be doubted. Certainly there is little evidence in the reports of the Parliament's committee on petitions to suggest this.

At Maastricht, the right of the European Parliament to set up a temporary committee of inquiry to investigate 'alleged contraventions or maladministration in the implementation of Community law' was established in the Treaties: Article 193 EC.

### Article 193 EC

In the course of its duties, the European Parliament may, at the request of a quarter of its members, set up a temporary committee of inquiry to investigate, without prejudice to the powers conferred by this Treaty on other Institutions or bodies, alleged contraventions or maladministration in the implementation of Community law, except where the alleged facts are being examined before a court and while the case is still subject to legal proceedings.

At first, the new committees of inquiry were welcomed as a means of making 'an original contribution to the scrutiny of Community policies' and of bringing the Parliament to the attention of 'a wider public than its traditional activity normally does'.[19] To start with, it seemed that this verdict was likely to be justified, as the second committee of inquiry to be established did indeed make a significant contribution to

17  See, e.g., Committee on Petitions, *Report on the Deliberations of the Committee 2003-04*, A6-0040/2005 and Committee on Petitions, *Report on the Deliberations of the Committee 2002–03*, A5-0239/2003. For an earlier appraisal, see E. Marias, 'The Right to Petition the European Parliament after Maastricht' (1994) 19 *EL Rev.* 169.

18  It is the practice of the European Parliament's Committee on Petitions to refer complaints of this nature to the Commission, which may use such a petition as the basis for commencing an investigation into Member State infringement of Community law under Article 226 EC. The law and practice of Article 226 EC is considered in detail in the next chapter. It is important to recognise the close relationship between this form of legal 'accountability' and the more political mechanisms considered in this chapter.

19  M. Shackleton, 'The European Parliament's New Committees of Inquiry: Tiger or Paper Tiger?' (1998) 36 *JCMS* 115, 116.

scrutiny and raise the popular profile of the Parliament.[20] This was the Parliament's inquiry into BSE, or mad cow disease.

> ## M. Shackleton, 'The European Parliament's New Committees of Inquiry: Tiger or Paper Tiger?' (1998) 36 *Journal of Common Market Studies* 115, 124–5
>
> The coverage of the BSE committee was particularly great with several hundred articles appearing in the press of all Member States of the Union. In some countries individual journalists decided to follow the committee throughout its work and became involved in doing extra research of their own . . .
>
> [The committee] provoked a number of specific changes which would almost certainly not have taken place had [it] not existed, but [it] also acted as a sounding board for more general policy debates about the development of the Union. Thus, although [it was] set up to examine relatively limited domains, [its] work took [it] into much broader territory [of] the shape of the Common Agricultural Policy . . .
>
> [In 1997] Commission President Santer admitted that mistakes had been made and announced a major set of organisational changes in the way the Commission would deal in future with food hygiene. The Directorate-General responsible for consumer affairs (DG XXIV) would see its responsibilities significantly expanded, with its staff of 140 to be almost doubled. It would take control from the DG for agriculture (DG VI) of seven scientific, veterinary and food committees advising on public health, as well as a special unit to evaluate public health risks. This was a major change in direction, particularly in view of the high prestige and influence that DG VI had always enjoyed.
>
> The speed of this response was no doubt influenced by the debate in the Parliament on a possible censure motion against the Commission for its mishandling of the BSE affair.

Westlake's analysis was similarly positive: 'through its tenacious pursuit of officials, documents, scientists and politicians', he argued, the Parliament's committee of inquiry on BSE 'made it clear to the EU institutions that they would, in future, be held fully accountable for their actions'.[21] Unfortunately, however, since the committee of inquiry on BSE, the European Parliament has further established only a tiny number of such inquiries, and none has repeated the successes of either scrutiny or profile that were achieved by the BSE committee.[22] For all the initial excitement at their inclusion in the Treaties, European Parliament committees of inquiry have yet to become the key players in securing greater accountability in the European Union that they were promised to be.

20 The first committee of inquiry concerned the Community transit regime, which relates to tax exemptions on imports into the EC, a scheme in respect of which there were allegations of widespread fraud.

21 M. Westlake, '"Mad Cows and Englishmen": the Institutional Consequences of the BSE Crisis' (1997) 35 *JCMS Annual Review* 11, 23. For further analysis of the impact of the BSE crisis on the European Union, see K. Vincent, '"Mad Cows" and Eurocrats: Community Responses to the BSE Crisis' (2004) 10 *ELJ* 499.

22 Only four such have been established since the BSE committee, dealing, respectively, with the ECHELON interception system, with human genetics, with foot and mouth disease and with improving safety at sea.

## 3. Transparency

As we mentioned in the introduction to this chapter, all forms of accountability require a measure of openness, or transparency. It is plainly impossible to hold anyone to account if you do not first have a sense of what it is you are holding them to account for. Without transparency, there can be no effective accountability.

Transparency is an umbrella term that covers a variety of values.[23] At least five such can be distinguished. The first is *access to documents* or, at least, access to information. Such access can be, but does not necessarily have to be, legally enforceable. The second is *knowledge* about who makes decisions and about how specific decisions were made. Third is the element of transparency that focuses on *comprehensibility and accessibility* as to the framework, structure and procedures of decision-making, so that competences, for example, are as clearly laid out as possible. Perhaps the most notorious illustration of this value of transparency was the renumbering of the Treaty Articles that took place at Amsterdam, although the attempt to catalogue the competences of the European Union in Part I of the Constitutional Treaty is another important example.[24] The fourth aspect of openness which falls within the rubric of transparency is concerned with *consultation*. On this front, the EU's institutions – and especially the Commission – enjoy a relatively good reputation. Indeed, since its inception the Commission has had to rely heavily on external inputs into its policy-making processes, partly because of its small staff, and partly to buttress its own legitimacy and bargaining power in the face of Member States.[25] The final aspect of transparency is the *duty to give reasons*. Such a requirement has a lengthy heritage in the European Union: Article 253 EC provides that 'Regulations, Directives and Decisions . . . shall state the reasons on which they are based'. The Court of Justice ruled on the importance of this obligation as early as 1962.[26]

These various aspects of transparency are important for a variety of reasons. In the literature on open government and freedom of information, five reasons are commonly recited. The first reason might be called the administrative argument: this is that with greater transparency comes greater accuracy and objectivity in record-keeping generally and as regards personal files in particular. Secondly, there is the constitutional argument, which posits that greater transparency supports the legal and constitutional roles of the European Parliament and the European Court of Auditors (as well as national bodies and others) in law-making or in administrative oversight. Thirdly, there is the legal argument: namely, that reasons and openness in decision-making are essential if citizens and others are to be able to determine whether, and if so on what grounds, they might have a right to some form of legal redress against an

---

23 See M. O'Neill, 'The Right of Access to Community Held Documentation as a General Principle of EC Law' (1998) 4 *EPL* 403.

24 See chapter 5.

25 See, e.g., T. Christiansen, 'A Maturing Bureaucracy? The Role of the Commission in the Policy Process' in J. Richardson (ed.), *European Union: Power and Policy-Making* (London, Routledge, 1996).

26 See Case 24/62 *Germany v Commission* [1963] ECR 63, 69. The duty to give reasons is considered further in chapter 10.

allegedly disproportionate or procedurally unfair decision. Fourthly, there is the policy argument. This posits that greater openness leads to better decision-making – that mistakes will be fewer or smaller if decisions and the decision-making process are opened up to greater public and media scrutiny, and that fraud will be harder to conceal. Finally, the popular or political argument has it that greater transparency enhances the ability of informed citizens meaningfully to participate in a democracy. Some of these arguments might be said to require rather more research before they can safely be assumed to be correct. In particular, there is a marked shortage of empirical evidence to support the administrative argument or the policy argument. Even the legal argument seems to lack the force of the constitutional and the political arguments: is there any reliable evidence to support the view that litigants really need greater transparency before knowing whether to commence legal action or not? That said, however, even though not all of the arguments commonly made in favour of greater openness are as solid as they might be, the constitutional and the political arguments alone surely provide all the justification which is required to take transparency seriously.

Despite the range of issues covered by transparency, the recent focus in the European Union has been on access to documents. The EU's journey towards a regime of access to documents has been a long one. Its starting point lies in a Declaration attached to the Treaties at Maastricht. As Dyrberg has suggested, 'before the Maastricht Treaty secrecy was the norm in the Institutions'.[27] Declaration 17 provided that:

> transparency of the decision-making process strengthens the democratic nature
> of the institutions and the public's confidence in the administration. The Con-
> ference accordingly recommends that the Commission submit to the Council
> no later than 1993 a report on measures designed to improve public access to
> the information available to the institutions.

This Declaration set in motion a series of consultation and position papers emanating from the Commission, setting out both existing practices and possible reforms.[28] Over the course of the first half of 1993 it emerged that the preferred way forward lay in the promulgation of a code of conduct on access to documents. Proposals for such a code were set out in the Commission paper *Openness in the Community*.[29] These proposals were then discussed by the European Council at its meeting in Copenhagen. This ongoing dialogue between the Commission and the Council produced the Code which came into force in early 1994.[30]

---

27 P. Dyrberg, 'Accountability and Legitimacy: What is the Contribution of Transparency?' in Arnull and Wincott, above n. 1, 86.
28 See, e.g., European Commission, *Increased Transparency in the Work of the Commission*, OJ 1993 C63/8 and European Commission, *Public Access to the Institutions' Documents*, OJ 1993 C156/5.
29 COM(93)258; OJ 1993 C166/5.
30 See Council Decision 93/731 of 20 December 1993, OJ 1993 L340/43; and Commission Decision 94/90 of 8 February 1994, OJ 1994 L46/58.

The Code provided that as a 'general principle', the public 'will have the widest possible access to documents held by the Commission and the Council'. Anyone could for any reason (or for none, presumably) apply to the Council or to the Commission for access to documents. There were no standing restrictions. There was no requirement to show just cause. Applications had to be made in writing and in a sufficiently precise manner so as to enable the document(s) concerned to be identified. The institution had one month in which to inform the applicant whether her application had been approved. If the institution informed the applicant that it intended to refuse the application, the applicant then had one month in which to make what the Code referred to as a 'confirmatory application'. The Code then provided that:

> if a confirmatory application is submitted, and if the Institution concerned decides to refuse to release the document, that decision, which must be made within one month of submission of the confirmatory application, will be notified in writing to the applicant as soon as possible. The grounds for the decision must be given, and the decision must indicate the means of redress that are available, i.e. judicial proceedings and complaints to the Ombudsman.

The Code then provided for a series of circumstances which would justify the institutions refusing to release documents. There were five mandatory reasons and one discretionary reason. As to the first, the Code provided that:

> the Institution *will* refuse access to any document whose disclosure could undermine: (1) the protection of the public interest (public security, international relations, monetary stability, court proceedings, inspections and investigations); (2) the protection of the individual and of privacy; (3) the protection of commercial and industrial secrecy; (4) the protection of the Community's financial interests; (5) the protection of confidentiality as requested by the natural or legal persons that supplied the information or as required by the legislation of the Member State that supplied the information.

The Code then concluded by stating that the institutions '*may* also refuse access in order to protect the Institution's interest in the confidentiality of its proceedings'.

The formal Decisions implementing the Code were both judicially reviewable (with most of the cases being decided by the Court of First Instance, only a few going on to the Court of Justice) and subject to the jurisdiction of the European Ombudsman. As a result, both the Courts and the Ombudsman have built up a considerable volume of case law on access to documents.

At Amsterdam, a new Article (Article 255) was added to the EC Treaty. Article 255 EC elevates access to documents to the status of a Treaty right. It provides that 'any citizen of the Union, and any natural or legal person residing or having its registered office in a Member State, shall have a right of access to European Parliament, Council and Commission documents'. It further provides that 'general principles and limits on grounds of public or private interest governing this right of access to documents' are to be enshrined in law.[31] After much debate, this was eventually achieved when Regulation 1049/2001 regarding public access to European Parliament, Council and Commission documents came into force in December 2001.[32] While the Regulation replaced the Code of Conduct, the Courts' case law and the Ombudsman's decisions under the Code continue to be important in a number of respects. The most significant cases to be decided under the Code will be examined before we move on to discuss the Regulation.

The first case on access to documents to reach the CFI was *Carvel v Council*.[33] Despite the attention it received at the time, however, the case turned out to be rather disappointing. Carvel sought disclosure of the minutes, attendance and voting records of the Social Affairs Council and of the Justice Council. The former were released to him whereas the latter were not. The ground on which the EC Council sought to rely in deciding to withhold the documents relating to the Justice Council was the discretionary ground provided for in the Code: that is to say, the protection of the institution's interest in the confidentiality of its proceedings. Carvel mounted five arguments to the effect that the Council's decision was unlawful. He alleged: breach of 'the fundamental principle of Community law' of access to documents; breach of the principle of legitimate expectation; infringement of Decision 93/731 (i.e. the Council Decision bringing into legal effect the provisions of the Code), infringement of Article 253 EC and 'misuse of powers'. The CFI focused in its judgment only on the third of these arguments, and said nothing as to the other four. Thus, the case turned on the narrow point of how the discretionary exception should properly be interpreted. Carvel argued that the Council's decision to deny him access to the documents amounted to a 'blanket refusal to grant access' and that this violated the Council's implied duty to balance carefully the interests involved before deciding whether access should in any particular case be granted or not. The CFI agreed. The significance of the case was therefore limited. It provided authority for the important proposition that the institutions may not lawfully merely assert that confidentiality trumps openness, and that if they are to be successful in so arguing, they must specifically balance the respective interests of confidentiality and openness with regard to each document to which access is sought. While this was a valuable clarification of an aspect of the procedure which was not spelt out in the Code, the judgment in *Carvel* was nonetheless a disappointment. The CFI was presented with an opportunity to trumpet the new-found privileging of openness and transparency in the European legal order, but it did not do so. The judgment was minimalist and

---

31 The CFI held in Case T-191/99 *Petrie v Commission* [2001] ECR II-3677 that Article 255 EC is not directly effective.

32 Regulation 1049/2001 regarding public access to European Parliament, Council and Commission documents, OJ 2001 L145/43.

33 Case T-194/95 *Carvel and Guardian v Council* [1995] ECR II-2765.

narrow, and contained no ringing endorsement of the central importance of freedom of information.

The same could be said of the first decision of the Court of Justice in this field. *Netherlands v Council*[34] concerned an action for annulment brought by the Dutch government to seek to have the Code of Conduct on access to documents set aside. The Netherlands argued that for the Council to have introduced the Code under Article 207 EC (which allows the Council to 'adopt its rules of procedure') constituted an abuse of power, for the reason that a matter as important as transparency could not lawfully be reduced to the level of internal organisation. This argument failed to find favour with the Court of Justice, which held that actions for annulment are available only in respect of measures adopted by the institutions which are intended to have legal effects, and the Code was not such a measure. While the Code itself was a voluntary agreement, the Council Decision (93/731) which brought the provisions of the Code into legal effect was not, of course. Yet neither was this annulled, on the ground that despite the fact that this Decision *does* have legal effects vis-à-vis third parties, this fact could not in the Court's view question its categorisation as a measure of internal organisation. As with the CFI in *Carvel*, the Court of Justice in the *Netherlands* case refrained from making any grand statement about the general importance of transparency.

There followed a series of cases on access to documents, which focused on the same procedural point: namely, whether the institution refusing access had given sufficient reasons justifying its decision.[35] It was not until the *Hautala* case, decided by the CFI in 1999[36] and on appeal by the Court of Justice in 2001,[37] that the full potential of the Code of Conduct began to be realised.[38] Heidi Hautala, a Member of the European Parliament, sought from the Council clarification of the criteria for control of arms exports as defined by the EC Council in 1991–92. In its response, the Council referred to a 1996 report of a body called the Working Group on Conventional Arms Exports, stating that this group had been charged with the responsibility of giving particular attention to the criteria with a view to reaching a common interpretation of them, and further stating that the Political Committee of the Council had approved recommendations thus far made by the group. Hautala then submitted a request for access to the Working Group's 1996 report, access which the Council denied on the ground that the report contained 'highly sensitive information disclosure of which would undermine the public interest as regards public security'. Hautala argued that this decision was unlawful.

---

34 Case C-58/94 *Netherlands v Council* [1996] ECR I-2169.
35 The series of cases is discussed by A. Tomkins, 'Transparency and the Emergence of a European Administrative Law' (1999–2000) 19 *YEL* 217, 226–30.
36 Case T-14/98 *Hautala v Council* [1999] ECR II-2489.
37 Case C-353/99 P *Council v Hautala* [2001] ECR I-9565.
38 See also Case C-353/01 P *Mattila v Council and Commission* [2004] ECR I-1073.

## Case T-14/98 *Hautala v Council* [1999] ECR II-2489[39]

41. The fact that the contested report comes under Title V of the Treaty on European Union has no effect on the jurisdiction of the Court . . . Decision 93/731 applies to all Council documents, irrespective of their content . . .

42. Thus . . . documents relating to Title V of the Treaty on European Union are covered by Decision 93/731 in the absence of provisions to the contrary. The fact that under . . . that Treaty the Court of First Instance does not have jurisdiction to assess the lawfulness of acts falling within Title V thus does not exclude its jurisdiction to rule on public access to those acts.

43. The applicant puts forward three pleas in law to support her application: first, infringement of Article 4(1) of Decision 93/731; second, infringement of Article 253 EC; third, breach of the fundamental principle of Community law that citizens of the European Union must be given the widest and fullest possible access to documents of the Community institutions, and of the principle of protection of legitimate expectations . . .

65. The three arguments put forward by the applicant in support of her first plea in law should be considered in turn. It should thus be determined, first, whether the confirmatory application was given adequate consideration by the Council; second, whether access to the contested report could be refused by reference to the public interest concerning international relations; and third, whether the Council was obliged to consider whether it could grant partial access, authorising disclosure of the parts of the document not covered by the exception on grounds of protection of the public interest . . .

[The CFI then examined and dismissed the first and second of these arguments.]

75. As regards the third argument, which is supported by the Swedish Government, namely that the Council infringed Article 4(1) of Decision 93/731 by refusing to grant access to the passages in the contested report which are not covered by the exception based on protection of the public interest, it should be observed that the Council considers that the principle of access to documents applies only to documents as such, not to the information contained in them.

76. It is thus for the Court to verify whether the Council was obliged to consider whether partial access could be granted. Since this is a question of law, review by the Court is not limited.

77. Decision 93/731 is a measure of internal organisation adopted by the Council . . . In the absence of specific Community legislation, the Council determines the conditions for dealing with requests for access to its documents (see, to that effect, Case C-58/94 *Netherlands v Council* [1996] ECR I-2169). Consequently, if the Council so wished, it could decide to grant partial access to its documents, under a new policy.

78. Decision 93/731 does not expressly require the Council to consider whether partial access to documents may be granted. Nor, as the Council accepted at the hearing, does it expressly prohibit such a possibility . . .

82. Furthermore, the Court of Justice stressed in *Netherlands v Council* the importance of the public's right of access to documents held by public authorities. The Court of Justice noted that Declaration No 17 links that right with 'the democratic nature of the institutions' . . .

---

[39] The judgment of the CFI was approved on appeal to the Court of Justice: see above n. 37.

83. The Court of First Instance recently held, referring to *Netherlands v Council*, that: 'The objective of Decision 93/731 is to give effect to the principle of the largest possible access for citizens to information with a view to strengthening the democratic character of the institutions and the trust of the public in the administration'.

84. Next, it should be noted that where a general principle is established and exceptions to that principle are then laid down, the exceptions should be construed and applied strictly, in a manner which does not defeat the application of the general rule . . . In the present case, the provisions to be construed are those of Article 4(1) of Decision 93/731, which lists the exceptions to the above general principle.

85. Furthermore, the principle of proportionality requires that 'derogations remain within the limits of what is appropriate and necessary for achieving the aim in view' . . . In the present case, the aim pursued by the Council in refusing access to the contested report was, according to the reasons stated in the contested decision, to 'protect the public interest with regard to international relations'. Such an aim may be achieved even if the Council does no more than remove, after examination, the passages in the contested report which might harm international relations.

86. In that connection, the principle of proportionality would allow the Council, in particular cases where the volume of the document or the passages to be removed would give rise to an unreasonable amount of administrative work, to balance the interest in public access to those fragmentary parts against the burden of work so caused. The Council could thus, in those particular cases, safeguard the interests of good administration.

87. Accordingly, Article 4(1) of Decision 93/731 must be interpreted in the light of the principle of the right to information and the principle of proportionality. It follows that the Council is obliged to examine whether partial access should be granted to the information not covered by the exceptions.

88. As appears from paragraph 75 above, the Council did not make such an examination, since it considers that the principle of access to documents applies only to documents as such and not to the information contained in them. Consequently, the contested decision is vitiated by an error of law and must therefore be annulled.

Two bold moves were made in this judgment. First, it contained a clear statement recognising a legally enforceable principle of a right to information in the Community legal order that went beyond, and was not limited to, the provisions of the Code. Equally importantly, it imposed a duty on the institutions to the effect that before they decide to withhold a document, they must first consider whether any part(s) of that document could safely be disclosed. No duty to consider 'redacting' documents (as it is called) was to be found in the Code itself, and thus in this respect the CFI took the law beyond the framework of the Code and began to develop a jurisprudence of transparency that may be independent of it. *Hautala* was not the only case decided in relation to the Code in which the CFI showed itself to be bold in the enforcement and development of rights to transparency. In *British American Tobacco v Commission*,[40] the CFI overturned the Commission's assessment of whether the applicant's interest in access to particular documents outweighed the institutions' interest in safeguarding

---

40 Case T-111/00 *British American Tobacco v Commission* [2001] ECR II-2997.

the confidentiality of their proceedings. In *Kuijer v Council*,[41] the CFI overturned a decision of the Council in which it had refused to disclose documents drawn up in connection with asylum and immigration policy in which the human rights situation in various non-Member States was discussed.

These cases show that by the time Regulation 1049/2001 came into force, the Courts had moved some distance towards creating a valuable jurisprudence of transparency. The Regulation has in some respects strengthened that jurisprudence, but in other respects has weakened it.[42]

### Regulation 1049/2001 regarding public access to European Parliament, Council and Commission documents

*Article 2: Beneficiaries and scope*

1. Any citizen of the Union, and any natural or legal person residing or having its registered office in a Member State, has a right of access to documents of the institutions, subject to the principles, conditions and limits defined in this Regulation.

2. The institutions may, subject to the same principles, conditions and limits, grant access to documents to any natural or legal person not residing or not having its registered office in a Member State.

3. This Regulation shall apply to all documents held by an institution, that is to say, documents drawn up or received by it and in its possession, in all areas of activity of the European Union . . .

*Article 4: Exceptions*

1. The institutions shall refuse access to a document where disclosure would undermine the protection of:

(a) the public interest as regards:
   • public security,
   • defence and military matters,
   • international relations,
   • the financial, monetary or economic policy of the Community or a Member State;
(b) privacy and the integrity of the individual, in particular in accordance with Community legislation regarding the protection of personal data.

2. The institutions shall refuse access to a document where disclosure would undermine the protection of:

• commercial interests of a natural or legal person, including intellectual property,
• court proceedings and legal advice,
• the purpose of inspections, investigations and audits, unless there is an overriding public interest in disclosure.

---

41 Case T-211/00 *Kuijer v Council* [2002] ECR II-485.
42 For a detailed account of the implementation of the Regulation, see European Commission, *Report on the Implementation of the Principles in Regulation 1049/2001*, COM(2004)45.

3. Access to a document, drawn up by an institution for internal use or received by an institution, which relates to a matter where the decision has not been taken by the institution, shall be refused if disclosure of the document would seriously undermine the institution's decision-making process, unless there is an overriding public interest in disclosure.

Access to a document containing opinions for internal use as part of deliberations and preliminary consultations within the institution concerned shall be refused even after the decision has been taken if disclosure of the document would seriously undermine the institution's decision-making process, unless there is an overriding public interest in disclosure.

4. As regards third-party documents, the institution shall consult the third party with a view to assessing whether an exception in paragraph 1 or 2 is applicable, unless it is clear that the document shall or shall not be disclosed.

5. A Member State may request the institution not to disclose a document originating from that Member State without its prior agreement.

6. If only parts of the requested document are covered by any of the exceptions, the remaining parts of the document shall be released . . .

*Article 6: Applications*

1. Applications for access to a document shall be made in any written form, including electronic form, in one of the languages referred to in Article 314 of the EC Treaty and in a sufficiently precise manner to enable the institution to identify the document. The applicant is not obliged to state reasons for the application.

2. If an application is not sufficiently precise, the institution shall ask the applicant to clarify the application and shall assist the applicant in doing so, for example, by providing information on the use of the public registers of documents.

3. In the event of an application relating to a very long document or to a very large number of documents, the institution concerned may confer with the applicant informally, with a view to finding a fair solution.

4. The institutions shall provide information and assistance to citizens on how and where applications for access to documents can be made.

*Article 7: Processing of initial applications*

1. An application for access to a document shall be handled promptly. An acknowledgement of receipt shall be sent to the applicant. Within 15 working days from registration of the application, the institution shall either grant access to the document requested and provide access in accordance with Article 10 within that period or, in a written reply, state the reasons for the total or partial refusal and inform the applicant of his or her right to make a confirmatory application in accordance with paragraph 2 of this Article . . .

*Article 11: Registers*

1. To make citizens' rights under this Regulation effective, each institution shall provide public access to a register of documents. Access to the register should be provided in electronic form. References to documents shall be recorded in the register without delay.

It will be seen that, while the broad thrust of the Regulation is the same as the Code, there are a number of differences of detail between the two regimes.[43] First,

43 See M. De Leeuw, 'The Regulation on Public Access to European Parliament, Council and Commission Documents in the European Union: Are Citizens Better Off?' (2003) 28 *EL Rev.* 324.

the scope of the Regulation is wider, in principle, in that it applies not only to the Council's and Commission's documents (as the Code did), but to all documents in the possession of the Council, the Commission or the European Parliament, irrespective of their origin. The practical effect of this broadening, however, will depend heavily on the interpretation that is given to the controls that are built into the Regulation to limit access to documents emanating from third parties (Article 4(4)) and from Member States (Article 4(5)). The apparent veto that has been accorded to Member States is particularly striking – and has been much criticised by commentators.[44] Secondly, the exceptions have been reworked substantially, with the old scheme of mandatory and discretionary exceptions being replaced by two tiers of imperative exceptions, the first tier being absolute (Article 4(1)) and the second, relative (Article 4(2)). It is to be noted that the absolute exceptions apply notwithstanding any 'public interest' in the disclosure of the relevant documents. It is also to be noted that nowhere is the notion of 'public interest' (Article 4(2)) defined – this is a matter that will have to be developed through the practices of the institutions and through judicial review. Additional changes include the shortening of the time limits within which the institutions must respond to applications (down from one month to fifteen working days) and the provision requiring the establishment of registers of documents (Article 11). The Code contained no such requirement, and this was a much criticised flaw in its scheme.[45]

The Regulation has begun to generate a degree of case law. Thus far, all the cases have been decided by the CFI. None is spectacular, but several highlight particular points of detail. *Turco v Council*,[46] for example, shows that the exception in Article 4(2) relating to 'court proceedings and legal advice' is significantly broader than the equivalent exception in the Code, which referred only to 'court proceedings' and not to legal advice. This is a respect in which the regime under the Regulation allows for less openness than that under the Code. Interestingly, the European Ombudsman (see below) had earlier decided that the Council's legal position on this matter was incorrect, and that it should not be able to rely on Article 4(2) to withhold disclosure of its legal opinions when such opinions had been given in the context of law-making. Only legal opinions given in the context of litigation should be withheld under this provision, according to the Ombudsman. After the CFI's ruling in *Turco*, the Ombudsman recognised that his position could no longer be maintained.[47]

---

44 See, e.g., the views of Statewatch, the pressure group which monitors civil liberties in the European Union: www.statewatch.org/. The reach of the veto is illustrated by Case T-168/02 *IFAW v Commission*, judgment of 30 November 2004, discussed below.

45 The European Ombudsman decided in 2001 that the Council's failure to maintain a register of its documents amounted to maladministration, notwithstanding the fact that the Code (which was in force at the time of the Ombudsman's decision) contained no such requirement: see further p. 345.

46 Case T-84/03 *Turco v Council*, judgment of 23 November 2004.

47 See European Ombudsman, *Special Report to the European Parliament in Complaint 1542/2000/(PB)SM* and European Ombudsman, *Draft Recommendation to the Council in Complaint 2371/2003/GG*, both available from the Ombudsman's website: www.euro-ombudsman.eu.int

In *IFAW v Commission*,[48] the applicant, a German NGO concerned with nature conservation, sought disclosure of certain documents relating to the reclaiming of part of an estuary for the construction of a runway. A number of the documents originated from Germany, bringing Article 4(5) of the Regulation into play. The applicants argued that Article 4(5) should be interpreted as meaning that, while national authorities may request the institutions not to disclose a document originating in a Member State without its prior agreement, the final decision concerning disclosure remains with the institutions and must be based on one of the exceptions listed in Article 4. The CFI disagreed.

---

**Case T-168/02 *IFAW v Commission*, judgment of 30 November 2004.**

55. . . . with respect to third-party documents, Article 4(4) of the Regulation places the institutions under an obligation to consult the third party concerned with a view to assessing whether an exception in Article 4(1) or (2) is applicable, unless it is clear that the document should or should not be disclosed. It follows that the institutions are under no obligation to consult the third party concerned if it is clearly apparent whether the document should or should not be disclosed. In all other cases, the institutions must consult the relevant third party. Accordingly, consultation of the third party is, as a general rule, a precondition for determining whether the exceptions to the right of access provided for in Article 4(1) and (2) of the Regulation are applicable in the case of third-party documents.

56. Moreover, as the applicant rightly points out, the Commission's duty to consult third parties under Article 4(4) of the Regulation does not affect its power to decide whether one of the exceptions provided for in Article 4(1) and (2) of the Regulation is applicable.

57. However, it follows from Article 4(5) of the Regulation that the Member States are subject to special treatment. That provision confers on a Member State the power to request the institution not to disclose documents originating from it without its prior agreement . . . The power conferred on the Member States by Article 4(5) of the Regulation is explained by the fact that it is neither the object nor the effect of that Regulation to amend national legislation on access to documents . . .

58. Article 4(5) of the Regulation places the Member States in a different position from that of other parties and lays down a *lex specialis* to govern their position. Under that provision, the Member State has the power to request an institution not to disclose a document originating from it without its 'prior agreement'. The obligation imposed on the institution to obtain the Member State's prior agreement, which is clearly laid down in Article 4(5) of the Regulation, would risk becoming a dead letter if the Commission were able to decide to disclose that document despite an explicit request not to do so from the Member State concerned. Thus, contrary to what the applicant argues, a request made by a Member State under Article 4(5) does constitute an instruction to the institution not to disclose the document in question.

59. The Member State is under no obligation to state the reasons for any request made by it under Article 4(5) of the Regulation and, once it has made such a request, it is no longer a matter for the institution to examine whether non-disclosure of the document in question is justified in, for example, the public interest.

---

48 Case T-168/02 *IFAW v Commission*, above n. 44.

In contrast with the tough line taken by the CFI in *IFAW*, *Verein für Konsumenten-information*[49] demonstrates that, in appropriate cases, the CFI will continue with the more robust approach familiar from its earlier decisions such as *Hautala*. In this case, the CFI ruled that the Commission had failed to give adequate consideration to whether it could disclose to an Austrian office for consumer protection some 47,000 pages of documents relating to the Commission's finding that several Austrian banks had operated an illegal cartel. The CFI held that the quantity of the documents requested did not justify the Commission's failure to carry out a 'concrete, individual' examination of the documents in order to assess whether they should be disclosed.[50] Such an examination is required, the CFI held, for the purpose of enabling the institutions 'to assess, on the one hand, the extent to which an exception to the right of access is applicable and, on the other, the possibility of partial access'.[51] It is only where it is 'obvious' that access either should or should not be granted that such an examination of the documents in question is not required.

Requests for access to documents have grown exponentially, particularly as regards requests for Commission documents. In each of the last three years of the Code of Conduct, there were around 450 requests to the Commission for access to documents. Under the Regulation, there were 991 such requests in 2002, 1,523 requests in 2003 and 2,600 requests in 2004.[52] In about 68 per cent of cases the documents requested are disclosed, in almost all cases completely (in only about 3 per cent of cases is partial disclosure made). The grounds for refusal most frequently relied on by the Commission are the protection of inspections, investigations and audits (31 per cent of refusals in 2004) and protection of the Commission's decision-making processes (25 per cent of refusals in 2004). The breakdown by area of interest has remained broadly constant over the years of the Regulation: competition, indirect taxation, the internal market and the environment arouse most interest, accounting between them for about 40 per cent of requests. Perhaps more interesting is the identity of those who make use of the Regulation. On this matter, the Commission reported for 2004 that:

> As in previous years applications were made largely by companies, NGOs, law firms and various interest groups . . . [A] significant proportion . . . relate to Commission activities regarding the monitoring of Community law. In many cases, the purpose is to obtain documents which could support the requester's position in connection with a complaint, relating for example to a presumed infringement of Community law, or an administrative or legal appeal.[53]

---

49 Case T-2/03 *Verein für Konsumenteninformation v Commission*, judgment of 13 April 2005.
50 *Ibid.* para. 74.    51 *Ibid.* para. 75.
52 The statistics in this paragraph are taken from the Commission's *Annual Reports on the application of Regulation 1049/2001*: see COM(2003)216, COM(2004)347 and COM(2005)348.
53 European Commission, *Report on the Application in 2004 of Regulation 1049/2001*, COM(2005)348, 7.

This is consistent with the Commission's previous statements on the use of the Regulation. In a paper published early in 2004, for example, the Commission stated that:

> It emerges from the statistics on those who benefited from the right of access to the documents of the Institutions that citizens exercising this right mainly belong to very specific groups. Applications for access to the Institutions' documents generally come from the academic world (for research purposes) or professional sectors (such as lobbies trying to influence decision-making or lawyers wanting to find information to defend the interests of their clients). Since applicants are not required to justify their applications and since only copying and postal charges can be invoiced to them, the Regulation paves the way for commercial applications. Thus the Commission has had to process applications for access to documents that could have a commercial value (lists of addresses or of contact points) or documents that normally have to be paid for, but of which the Commission holds copies.[54]

This is a healthy reminder that when we think about transparency as a means of accountability, we have to bear in mind the question of *to whom* transparency makes the institutions accountable. It appears from the evidence of the Commission's reports that Regulation 1049/2001 succeeds in making the European Union accountable only to a small range of largely self-interested professionals. This is likely to be less the fault of anything in the Regulation itself and more a general, and perhaps inescapable, feature of freedom of information laws. At the least, however, it suggests that accountability, if it is to be widespread, should not be limited to ensuring transparency alone. Transparency is an important first step towards, and not a substitute for, accountability.

### 4. Responsibility and resignation: governance and the Commission

The greatest crisis (thus far) in the accountability of the European Union came in 1999 when the twenty members of the Santer Commission were ignominiously required to resign. Their resignation was triggered by a report of a Committee of Independent Experts, which had been appointed by the European Parliament to examine a series of allegations of 'fraud, mismanagement and nepotism' in the Commission.[55] In this section we shall examine first the background to the 1999 resignation and secondly, its consequences for accountability.

---

54 European Commission, *Report on the Implementation of the Principles in Regulation 1049/2001*, COM(2004)45, 10–11.

55 For commentary, see A. Tomkins, 'Responsibility and Resignation in the European Commission' (1999) 62 *MLR* 744; P. Craig, 'The Fall and Renewal of the Commission: Accountability, Contract and Administrative Organisation' (2000) 6 *ELJ* 98; and V. Mehde, 'Responsibility and Accountability in the European Commission' (2003) 40 *CML Rev.* 423.

The Committee of Independent Experts was established in January 1999 on the insistence of the European Parliament and with the consent of the Commission. It was appointed as a compromise measure in the heat of a ferocious battle between the Commission and the Parliament over the European Union's budget. Concern had been growing for several years that all was not well with the budget. In November 1995, the European Court of Auditors had refused to certify the EU's annual accounts after discovering that the equivalent of nearly £3 billion had not been properly accounted for. The following year, concern in the European Parliament as to the Commission's slow rate of response to allegations of fraud led to the Parliament threatening to freeze 10 per cent of the Commissioners' salaries. In 1998, the Commission's own anti-fraud unit disclosed that £600 million of the Commission's humanitarian aid budget for the years 1993–95 could not be accounted for. One of the responsibilities of the European Court of Auditors is to draw up an annual report in respect of the European Union's budget for each financial year.[56] This report forms the basis of the European Parliament's 'discharge' of the budget. Discharge is a formal process that marks the final closure of the accounts for the financial year in question and serves as a political verdict on the performance of the Commission.[57] In its report for the financial year 1997, published in November 1998, the Court of Auditors stated that some £3 billion (5 per cent of the EU's budget) could not be accounted for. The report was replete with criticism: on structural funds, for example, the Commission's financial planning was described as 'unrealistic and subject to amendments', the Commission's monitoring and controls were said to be 'insufficient, especially as regards checks on the reality of operations'. The Court of Auditors concluded by declaring that:

> the incidence of errors affecting the transactions underlying the Commission's payments is too high for the Court to provide assurance about their legality and regularity. Many of the errors found in the payments provide direct evidence of failure to implement the control mechanisms . . . or to apply requisite checks before payments are made.

Just as the European Parliament was about to debate the report, in January 1999, one of the Commission's internal auditors, Paul van Buitenen, passed to it a dossier in which he made a number of allegations to the effect that repeated efforts had been made by senior Commission officials to suppress investigations into fraud. He also made a number of claims that officials in the Santer Commission were in the habit of awarding lucrative contracts to family contacts and associates.

The European Parliament adopted a Resolution on 14 January 1999 on improving the financial management of the Commission. The Resolution called for a 'committee of independent experts to be convened under the auspices of the Parliament and the

---

56  Articles 246–248 EC.
57  See I. Harden, F. White and K. Donnelly, 'The Court of Auditors and Financial Control and Accountability in the European Community' (1995) 1 *EPL* 599, 620.

Commission with a mandate to examine the way in which the Commission detects and deals with fraud, mismanagement and nepotism, including a fundamental review of Commission practices in the awarding of all financial contracts'. Five people were appointed to the Committee: three auditors and two lawyers. Its terms of reference stated that its first report should seek to establish the extent to which 'the Commission, as a body, or Commissioners individually, bear specific responsibility for the recent examples of fraud, mismanagement or nepotism raised in parliamentary discussions, or in the allegations which have arisen in those discussions'. When its first report was published in March 1999, the entire College of Commissioners resigned. While, in the event, they remained in office for a further six months (allowing for the 1999 election to the European Parliament to take place before a new Commission was sworn in), the resignation nonetheless marked the most dramatic single event in the European Union's institutional history. The cause of the resignation was the Committee's now notorious finding that 'it is becoming increasingly difficult to find anyone [in the Commission] who has even the slightest sense of responsibility'.[58]

Upon the publication of its first report, the Committee was immediately asked by the European Parliament to draw up a second, the terms of reference for which were that the Committee was mandated to concentrate on 'formulating recommendations for improving: procedures for the awarding of financial contracts and of contracts for interim or temporary staff to implement programmes; [and] the co-ordination of Commission services responsible for detecting and dealing with fraud, irregularities and financial mismanagement (and, particularly, internal auditing departments, and financial control)'. The Committee's second (and final) report was published in September 1999. Its most important contribution, for present purposes, was its treatment of notions of what it called political and ethical responsibility – or of what we are referring to in this chapter as accountability. In its first report, the Committee had noted that while the Treaties do mention responsibility/accountability, they do so only rather briefly. Article 216 EC provides for the legal responsibility of individual members of the Commission to the Court of Justice, and Article 201 EC provides that the European Parliament may secure the resignation of the entire College of Commissioners by passing a motion of censure with the requisite two-thirds majority. In that report the Committee had been keen to develop the view that these Treaty provisions should not be seen as exhausting the Commission's responsibilities. To this end, the Committee introduced the notion of what it called 'ethical responsibility', or 'responsibility for not behaving in accordance with proper standards in public life'.[59]

While the Committee introduced this theme in its first report, it left many questions unanswered as to the nature of ethical responsibility. These questions were made

---

58 Committee of Independent Experts, *First Report on Allegations Regarding Fraud, Mismanagement and Nepotism in the European Commission* (15 March 1999) para. 9.4.25. Both this report and the Committee's second report (see below) are available at www.europarl.eu.int/experts/
59 *Ibid.* para. 1.6.2.

more complicated by the outgoing Santer Commission which, upon its resignation, published two Codes of Conduct: one on Commissioners, and the other on Commissioners and Departments. Both of these Codes described various legal, political and ethical responsibilities on the part of Commissioners, but they did so in largely unsatisfactory ways. They stated, for example, that Commissioners were responsible only for matters of policy, and not for questions of implementation. They further stated that Commissioners were principally responsible to themselves through a peculiar notion of collective responsibility. Collective responsibility, for the Santer Commission, appeared to revolve around the notion of each Commissioner minding her own business, not rocking the boat, and not querying the work of (or any allegations of wrongdoing in) any other Commissioner.

The Committee of Independent Experts took the opportunity in its second report to revisit these issues, and to flesh out in a little more detail what it meant by ethical responsibility. The first thing to note is that the Committee unreservedly rejected the Santer Commission's views. It stated that the purported distinction between responsibility for policy and responsibility for implementation was 'tenable neither in law nor in fact'.[60] In the Committee's view, Commissioners should be responsible for policy and for the 'sound implementation' of their policies.[61] The Committee also stated, *contra* the Santer Commission, that collective responsibility should require each and every Commissioner to keep herself 'informed as to the activities of every other Commissioner . . . One Commissioner should not be able to evade responsibility for decisions which have been taken by the Commission as a college – whether nominally or in reality – by passing it to another Commissioner'.[62]

All of this is to the good. The Committee's vision of what the Commission should be responsible for is both more mature and more appropriate than was the rather blinkered and self-serving approach of the Santer Commission. A more testing issue, however, is the related one of to whom the Commission's obligations of responsibility should be owed. It is all very well setting out what the Commission should be 'ethically' (a better word might be 'constitutionally') responsible for, it is quite another to develop the institutional framework necessary for turning such aspirations into *realpolitik*. To whom should the Commission be responsible, and what should whosoever that is be able to do in the event that the Commission fails to abide by its standards of responsibility? What should the sanctions be, and who should be empowered to implement them? While these questions were considered by the Committee in its second report, it was, unfortunately, not entirely clear what the Committee considered the most helpful way forward to be.

The Committee suggested that the Commission should be responsible in three main ways: legally responsible to the Court of Justice, politically responsible to the

---

60 Committee of Independent Experts, *Second Report on Reform of the Commission: Analysis of Current Practice and Proposals for Tackling Mismanagement, Irregularities and Fraud* (10 September 1999) para. 7.9.1. Available at www.europarl.eu.int/experts/
61 *Ibid.* para. 7.9.3.      62 *Ibid.* para. 7.10.2.

European Parliament and ethically responsible. There are two points of difficulty here: first, it is unclear whether the Commission's political responsibility is confined to the collective responsibility provided for in Article 201 EC. Is there to be some notion of individual political responsibility to the European Parliament in addition to Article 201? Secondly, it is unclear what the relationship is between ethical and political responsibility. This is what the Committee suggested:

> ethical responsibility is about (non-) compliance, intentional or negligent, with ethical, professional, legal rules of conduct on the part of an individual to whom blame can be attributed, individually or collectively. Political responsibility, on the other hand, is about (i) the political consequences arising from ethically, professionally, or legally reprehensible conduct, (ii) the nature of those consequences, and (iii) the authority by which the consequences are decided.[63]

Elsewhere in its second report, the Committee recommended the establishment of a new Standing Committee on Standards in Public Life. This new, permanent committee should first draw up standards of ethical responsibility and then also update them regularly, monitor their application and implementation and give advice on specific issues or particular questions which are brought to its attention.[64] It is curious that in the paragraphs of the report dealing with ethical responsibility and its enforcement, this proposed new Committee on Standards is not mentioned. One can only assume that the Committee of Independent Experts intended this new Committee on Standards to be the body which should oversee and enforce ethical responsibility. Quite where the Ombudsman would fit into this picture is, again, unclear. The Committee of Independent Experts ignored the Ombudsman completely. For these reasons, 'ethical responsibility', even after the Committee's second report, remained somewhat of a mess.

The Committee seemed to assume that both Commissioners and officials would have obligations of ethical responsibility, whereas only Commissioners themselves would be politically responsible. At least we know who enforces political responsibility: that is the role of the European Parliament. Beyond this basic starting-point, however, the Committee's recommendations as to political responsibility were as hard to comprehend as they were in relation to ethical responsibility. The Committee commenced its discussion of political responsibility by dividing it into two themes: first, it stated that the Parliament has a right to be *informed* by the Commission, which must give an account of its actions to the Parliament. This the Committee labelled 'accountability'. Secondly, the Committee continued, the Parliament also *judges* the ultimate political responsibility of the Commission and draws the political consequences. This is 'political responsibility'.[65] As to the first, the Committee recommended that the Commission 'make it clear that it will give the widest interpretation possible to its duty of accountability towards Parliament and that any member of the Commission who knowingly misleads Parliament, or omits to correct at the

---

63 *Ibid.* para. 7.8.3.     64 *Ibid.* paras. 7.7.3–7.7.4.     65 *Ibid.* para. 7.14.1.

earliest opportunity any inadvertent error in information given to Parliament, will be expected to offer his/her resignation'.[66] But to whom should the offer of resignation be made: to the President of the Commission, to the new Committee on Standards, or to the European Parliament? On this question the Committee's report was silent. As to 'political responsibility', the Committee seemed to suggest that collective political responsibility should continue to be enforced by the European Parliament (in accordance with Article 201 EC), and that the political responsibility of individual Commissioners should be enforced 'through a significant strengthening of the hand of the Commission President'.[67] To this end, the Committee called for Treaty amendments, lamenting that 'it is inconsistent with the need to strengthen the sense of responsibility of all persons working in the Commission, starting at the top, that no more specific provisions regarding the political responsibility of the Commission as a body, and no provisions at all regarding the political responsibility of individual Commissioners, are to be found in the Treaties'.[68]

It is clear from the various questions that were left unresolved by the Committee of Independent Experts that, even after its two reports, there remained a considerable way to go before the extent of the Commission's various responsibilities could be crystallised. What happened following the work of the Committee was that the incoming Prodi Commission published a series of Codes of Conduct and consultation papers. Depressingly, these documents largely replicated the depleted version of responsibility articulated by the Santer Commission. Even Vice-President Kinnock's consultation papers on reform of the Commission failed to recognise the complexity – or the importance – of accountability. While his consultation papers paid lip-service to the labels 'accountability' and 'responsibility', the analysis was thin, the definitions were disappointingly restrictive, and the scope seemed as limited as ever. Responsibility, in particular, seemed once again to have been reduced to the level of managerial responsibility (that is to say, the idea that each official should 'feel comfortable' about taking responsibility for his or her own actions). Any grander ideal of ethical, constitutional or political responsibility was left out of the account.[69]

The Prodi Commission's series of consultation documents and White Papers culminated in its White Paper on European Governance, published in July 2001.[70] From the outset this was regarded, both within the EU institutions and by academic commentators, as being a document of the utmost significance.[71] It received a great deal of

---

66 *Ibid.* para. 7.14.14.      67 *Ibid.* para. 7.14.21.      68 *Ibid.* para. 7.14.19.

69 See, e.g., European Commission, *Commission Reform: Strategic Options Paper*, CG3(1999) 10/6; *Reforming the Commission: Consultative Document*, CG3(2000) 1/17; and *Reforming the Commission: A White Paper*, COM(2000)200.

70 European Commission, *European Governance: A White Paper*, COM(2001)428.

71 As may be seen by comparing its text with that of the Laeken Declaration (considered in detail in chapter 2), the White Paper on Governance made a significant contribution to the construction of the debate on the future of Europe.

attention, much of it critical.[72] Reading the White Paper, it is easy to forget that it was born out of the scandal of 1999. By the time of its publication, the Prodi Commission had moved – and had been permitted to move – the debate on from the outstanding questions of political accountability or responsibility that had been left unresolved by the Committee of Independent Experts, to issues of internal management structures, priority-setting, and better regulation and law-making. The White Paper was amazingly self-serving, presenting the European Union as being in a 'real paradox' in which, while European citizens wanted it to solve 'major problems', they simultaneously regarded the EU's institutions with 'increasing distrust'.[73] The Commission was presented as the only institution that could rescue the European Union from such popular distrust. It was this citizen dissatisfaction with the EU generally – as represented in the Irish 'no' vote on the Nice Treaty, cited by the Commission on the opening page of the White Paper – and not the scandal of 1999 that was presented as being the main impetus behind the reforms which the White Paper advocated. These were reforms designed not to enhance the accountability of the Commission, but to streamline its effectiveness, to bolster its position with regard to the other institutions and to augment its power. As Follesdal has argued, the White Paper was based on the assumptions that:

> The Commission, and it alone, can find solutions without conflict . . . The Commission alone reliably acts in the general European interest, which should dominate all other concerns. The Commission should enjoy broad executive discretion under broad legislation, and be free from detailed scrutiny.[74]

This is not to say that there was nothing of value in the White Paper: on the contrary, there was. Its remarks about opening up the policy-making process, about improving the European Union's international representation, and about enhancing the implementation of EU policies, are all to be welcomed. As we saw above, greater participation in the policy-making process may help to secure an improved level of transparency, and it may even go some way to meeting the challenge of the alleged democratic deficit, but it will not, of itself, secure greater accountability.[75] And this was the great problem with the White Paper: it said so little about accountability. Indeed, what the White Paper did say about accountability seemed to concern the accountability of others, not that of the Commission. It stated, for example, that if

---

72 See, e.g., the Symposium: *Mountain or Molehill? A Critical Appraisal of the Commission White Paper on Governance*, Jean Monnet Working Papers 6/01.

73 European Commission, *European Governance: A White Paper*, COM(2001)428, 3.

74 A. Follesdal, 'The Political Theory of the White Paper on Governance: Hidden and Fascinating' (2003) 9 *EPL* 73, 74.

75 On participation in the policy and law-making process, see chapter 4. See further, European Commission, *General Principles and Minimum Standards for Consultation of Interested Parties by the Commission*, COM(2002)704; P. Magnette, 'European Governance and Civic Participation: Beyond Elitist Citizenship?' (2003) 51 *Political Studies* 144 and D. Curtin, 'Private Interest *Representation* or Civil Society *Deliberation*? A Contemporary Dilemma for European Union Governance' (2003) 12 *Social and Legal Studies* 55.

civil society was to have a greater input into the policy-making process, it should be more accountable![76] (To whom, one may wonder?) As Follesdal has suggested, the Commission seems not to have noticed that accountability is also a requirement that it should face. Yet:

> on this issue, the White Paper has problematic suggestions diminishing rather than enhancing accountability. It proposes that the European Parliament should not carry out a detailed scrutiny of the Commission but rather should maintain broad oversight. A second proposal is that legislation by the European Parliament and the Council should be made more flexible, and be limited to essential principles and frameworks regarding implementation. The two suggestions combine to give more discretion to the Commission, with less scrutiny of how that discretion is used.[77]

The response of the European Parliament was disappointing in the extreme. It held two plenary debates on the White Paper[78] and one of its committees – the Committee on Constitutional Affairs – produced a report on it.[79] It would not be true to say that this report meekly accepted the entirety of the White Paper: it did say, for example, the reform of European governance 'must be based on a fundamental critical analysis of the democratic deficit' which would require consideration of legitimacy, parliamentary scrutiny, open government and participation, and it also said that 'the concept of administrative efficiency must not jeopardise democratic legitimisation'. But nowhere did it discuss the importance of political accountability, and nowhere did it make any reference to the reports of the Committee of Independent Experts. In the two plenary debates there was, likewise, broad support for the White Paper and no mention at all of the work or the findings of the Committee of Independent Experts. It was as if the scandal of 1999 had never happened.

Two years later, in 2003, the Commission published a follow-up report on European governance,[80] in which lessons to be drawn from reactions to the White Paper and from the public consultation exercise were outlined. This report said nothing at all about political accountability. It was concerned with transparency, with participation through the regions and through civil society, and with the 'better regulation' agenda. By 2003, of course, the popular and institutional focus of the European Union had moved on – the Convention on the Future of Europe and its Draft Constitutional Treaty had well and truly overshadowed the disgrace and mass resignation of 1999. The Constitutional Treaty continued the trend set by the Commission's White Paper

---

76 European Commission, *European Governance: A White Paper*, COM(2001)428, 15.
77 Follesdal, above n. 74, 79.     78 On 4 September and 2 October 2001.
79 Committee on Constitutional Affairs, *Report on the Commission White Paper on Governance*, A5-0399/2001.
80 European Commission, *Report on European Governance* (2003), available at http://europa.eu.int/comm/governance/docs/index_en.htm

on Governance: its provisions would have done nothing to enhance the political accountability of the Commission. Given the level of mismanagement that the events of 1999 revealed, this was a remarkable omission and it stands as testament to the Prodi Commission's success in effectively closing down the debate on political accountability in the European Union which the reports of the Committee of Independent Experts had seemed, for a short while, to have started.

## 5. The European Ombudsman

The office of the European Ombudsman (EO) was created at Maastricht. The first European Ombudsman, Jacob Söderman, took office in 1995 and retired in 2003, since which time the Ombudsman has been Nikiforos Diamandouros. The EO's powers are set out in Article 195 EC.[81]

### Article 195(1) EC

The European Parliament shall appoint an Ombudsman empowered to receive complaints from any citizen of the Union or any natural or legal person residing or having its registered office in a Member State concerning instances of maladministration in the activities of the Community Institutions or bodies, with the exception of the Court of Justice and the Court of First Instance acting in their judicial role.

In accordance with his duties, the Ombudsman shall conduct inquiries for which he finds grounds, either on his own initiative or on the basis of complaints submitted to him direct or through a Member of the European Parliament, except where the alleged facts are or have been the subject of legal proceedings. Where the Ombudsman establishes an instance of maladministration, he shall refer the matter to the Institution concerned, which shall have a period of three months in which to inform him of its views. The Ombudsman shall then forward a report to the European Parliament and the Institution concerned. The person lodging the complaint shall be informed of the outcome of such inquiries.

The Ombudsman shall submit an annual report to the European Parliament on the outcome of his inquiries.

The right to complain to the EO is recognised in the EC Treaty as one of the basic rights of European citizenship (Article 21 EC). It is also included in the Charter of Fundamental Rights (Article 43 of the Charter).[82]

As Article 195 EC makes plain, the Ombudsman's main task is to investigate complaints of 'maladministration'.[83] This term is not defined in the Treaty. Rather, it was left to the EO to develop a working understanding of what maladministration would mean in the context of the European Union.

---

81 See also the Statute of the Ombudsman: European Parliament Decision 94/262, OJ 1994 L113/15.
82 These various provisions would all have had equivalents in the Constitutional Treaty: see Articles I-10, II-103 and III-335.
83 A secondary task is to undertake 'own initiative inquiries', on which see further below.

### European Ombudsman, *Annual Report 1995*, 17

Clearly, there is maladministration if a Community Institution or body fails to act in accordance with the Treaties and with the Community acts that are binding upon it, or if it fails to observe the rules and principles of law established by the Court of Justice . . .

For example, the European Ombudsman must take into account the requirement of [Article 6 TEU] that Community Institutions and bodies are to respect fundamental human rights.

Many other things may also amount to maladministration, including:

* administrative irregularities;
* administrative omissions;
* abuse of power;
* negligence;
* unlawful procedures;
* unfairness;
* malfunction or incompetence;
* discrimination;
* avoidable delay;
* lack or refusal of information.

This list is not intended to be exhaustive. The experience of national Ombudsmen shows that it is better not to attempt a rigid definition of what may constitute maladministration. Indeed, the open-ended nature of the term is one of the things that distinguishes the role of the Ombudsman from that of a judge.

In his Annual Report for 1997, the European Ombudsman supplemented what he had stated in his first Annual Report, by stating that 'the fundamental notion [of maladministration] can be defined as follows: maladministration occurs when a public body fails to act in accordance with a rule or principle which is binding upon it'.[84]

The EO's initial approach to the concept of maladministration was disappointingly narrow and legalistic. It left little room for the Ombudsman that was not already occupied by the courts of law – there was very little included within the 1995 and 1997 definitions of maladministration that was not also unlawful. The EO's understanding of maladministration may be contrasted with the altogether broader approach that had been adopted by the United Kingdom's Parliamentary Ombudsman. By 1993, the British Ombudsman had included the following within his list of instances of maladministration: rudeness, refusal to answer reasonable questions, neglecting to inform complainants of their rights, knowingly giving advice which is misleading or inadequate, offering manifestly disproportionate redress, failure by management to monitor compliance with adequate procedures, cavalier disregard of advice and failure to mitigate the effects of rigid adherence to the letter of the law where that produces manifestly inequitable treatment.[85] By contrast with the EO's definition of

---

84 European Ombudsman, *Annual Report 1997*, 23.
85 See Cabinet Office, *The Ombudsman in your Files* (London, HMSO, 1995).

maladministration, there is plenty that is here regarded as falling within the Ombudsman's remit while not being judicially reviewable. You cannot take an official to court simply for being rude, for example, nor can you do so when the official fails to 'mitigate the effects of rigid adherence to the letter of the law'. The European Ombudsman was well aware of the narrow and legalistic approach he had chosen to adopt. As he argued in his Annual Report for 1997:

> The starting point for the work of all the Institutions and bodies created by, or under, the EU Treaties is law. As the Court of Justice has emphasised on many occasions, the European Community is a Community of law. Therefore, when the European Ombudsman investigates whether a Community Institution or body has acted with[in] the rules and principles which are binding upon it, his first and most essential task must be to establish whether it has acted lawfully.[86]

Amplifying the point, the EO went on to state that '[t]he Ombudsman does not seek to question discretionary administrative decisions, provided that the Institution or body concerned has acted within the limits of its legal authority'.[87] Adopting this strict line severely restricted the early impact of the EO, as we shall see, and it appears that in recent years the Ombudsman has moved some distance away from this position.

To return to the basic definition of maladministration: it occurs, we are told, when a public body fails to act in accordance with a rule or principle which is binding upon it. In the application of this definition, much will clearly depend on the meaning given to the phrase 'rule or principle'. For all the EO's early insistence that 'principle', in effect, meant 'legal principle', the European Parliament's Committee on Petitions, which works closely with the Ombudsman, suggested that a Code of Good Administrative Behaviour be drawn up, in which further principles of good administration could be enshrined – principles that the Ombudsman could enforce, but that need not be strictly legal. Accordingly, the Ombudsman drafted a Code and placed it before the European Parliament which, after some amendment, adopted it by Resolution in 2001. The Code is neither legally binding nor judicially enforceable. In adopting it, however, the European Parliament called on the Ombudsman to apply it when examining whether there was maladministration. This the Ombudsman now does.[88] As the Code includes a number of provisions that go some way beyond the requirements of the law, this has led to the partial decoupling of principles of maladministration from principles of law, albeit without the formal 1997 definition of maladministration having been amended. The Code, which is available from the Ombudsman's

---

86 European Ombudsman, *Annual Report 1997*, 24.     87 *Ibid.* 26.
88 See, e.g., the statement in the Ombudsman's *Annual Report 2004* (at 34) that '[t]he Ombudsman . . . takes account of the rules and principles contained in the Code when examining complaints and in conducting own-initiative inquiries'.

website,[89] includes provisions covering all the main legal requirements as to good administration. There are, accordingly, provisions on discrimination, proportionality, abuse of power, impartiality, legitimate expectation, the right to be heard, giving reasons for decisions, and so forth.[90] But the Code also provides, for example, that officials shall be 'service-minded, correct, courteous and accessible in relations with the public', that they should 'try to be as helpful as possible', and that 'if an error occurs which negatively affects the rights or interests of a member of the public, the official shall apologise for it and endeavour to correct' it (Article 12). Similarly, Article 19 of the Code provides that '[a] decision of the Institution which may adversely affect the rights or interests of a private person shall contain an indication of the appeal possibilities available for challenging the decision'. None of these principles is a rule of law, yet breach of any of them may now constitute an instance of maladministration.[91] The Ombudsman's use of the Code marks a welcome departure from his initial (and unnecessary) insistence that maladministration effectively meant illegal administration and that reviewing administrative discretion was beyond his jurisdiction.

The mandate of the EO remains limited in two main ways: the complainant must be either a citizen of or residing in the European Union or, if it is a corporation or association, it must have its registered office in a Member State, and the complaint must be against a Community institution or body (other than the Court of Justice or the CFI acting in their judicial role).[92] The latter is a particularly important limitation to the work of the Ombudsman, as he receives each year large numbers of complaints – all inadmissible – which relate to the application of Community law by national or regional authorities. Such 'indirect' (i.e. national or regional) administration of Community law falls outwith the Ombudsman's mandate (although, by contrast, petitions to the European Parliament as to the 'indirect' administration of Community law may be made). It is to be noted that there is no standing requirement for a complaint to the EO to be admissible: that is to say, complainants do not have to show that they are 'directly and individually concerned' in the matter[93] or that the matter 'affects' them 'directly', as those who seek to petition the European Parliament must.[94]

89 See www.euro-ombudsman.eu.int/default.htm
90 On EU law as it pertains to these principles, see chapter 10.
91 See, e.g., the statement in the Ombudsman's *Annual Report 2003* (at 11) that maladministration 'includes respect for human rights, for the rule of law *and for principles of good administration*' (emphasis added).
92 In addition, the Statute of the Ombudsman, above n. 81, provides that the author and subject of the complaint must be identified, that the complaint must be made within two years of the events complained of and that the complaint must have been preceded by appropriate administrative approaches to the institution or body concerned: see European Ombudsman, *Annual Report 2004*, 35.
93 This is the test for standing for 'non-privileged' applicants seeking judicial review under Article 230 EC: see chapter 10.
94 See Article 194 EC.

## European Ombudsman, *Annual Report 2004*, 36–7

During 2004 the Ombudsman received 3,726 new complaints, an increase of 53% compared to 2003. Of this 53% overall increase, 51% (657 complaints) is accounted for by complaints from the ten new Member States that joined the Union on 1 May 2004. The remaining 49% represents an increase in complaints sent from the fifteen old Member States and from elsewhere in the world . . .

Complaints were sent directly by individual citizens in 3,536 cases and 190 came from associations or companies . . .

Of all the complaints examined, 25% were within the mandate of the Ombudsman.[95] Of these, 490 met the criteria of admissibility, but 147 did not provide grounds for an inquiry.[96] Inquiries were therefore begun in 343 cases.

Most of the complaints that led to an inquiry were against the Commission (69%). As the Commission is the main Community Institution that makes decisions having a direct impact on citizens, it is normal that it should be the principal object of citizens' complaints. There were 58 complaints against the European Communities Personnel Selection Office, 48 against the European Parliament and 22 against the Council of the European Union.

The main types of maladministration alleged were lack of transparency, including refusal of information (127 cases), discrimination (106 cases), avoidable delay (67 cases), unsatisfactory procedures (52 cases), unfairness or abuse of power (38 cases), failure to ensure fulfilment of obligations, that is failure by the European Commission to carry out its role as 'Guardian of the Treaties' vis-à-vis Member States (37 cases), negligence (33 cases) and legal error (26 cases).

If a complaint is outside the mandate or inadmissible, the Ombudsman always tries to advise the complainant of another body that could deal with the complaint, especially if the case involves Community law . . .

[Such] advice was given in 2,117 cases. In 906 of these, the complainant was advised to turn to a national or regional Ombudsman and 179 complainants were advised to petition the European Parliament. In 359 cases, the advice was to contact the European Commission . . . In 613 cases, the complainant was advised to contact other bodies, mostly specialised Ombudsmen or complaints-handling bodies in a Member State.

The last point made here is important: since its inception in 1995 the office of the EO has worked hard to construct a pan-European network of Ombudsmen which, in the view of the current European Ombudsman, has now 'developed into a powerful collaboration tool . . . compris[ing] almost 90 offices in 29 countries'.[97] The network provides an 'effective mechanism for co-operation on case-handling',[98] which is particularly important given the large numbers of complaints that the EO receives each year that concern national, regional or local administration, rather than European

---

95 The vast majority (91 per cent) of complaints which fell outside the mandate did so because they were not against a Community institution or body.
96 The most common reason for a complaint falling at this hurdle (i.e. a complaint being within the EO's mandate but nonetheless inadmissible)was that prior administrative approaches had not been made: this was true for 57 per cent of such cases.
97 European Ombudsman, *Annual Report 2004*, 25.      98 *Ibid.* 25–26.

institutions or bodies. Many such complaints can now be directly transferred from the EO to the appropriate national Ombudsman.[99]

So much for the use that is made of the European Ombudsman, and of his powers. What remains to be examined is what the Ombudsman actually does. While, as we saw above, the Ombudsman's main task is the investigation of complaints, this is not his only function. The EO also has the power to conduct 'own initiative inquiries'. In practice, the Ombudsman makes use of this power in two main instances: first, he uses it to investigate possible cases of maladministration when a complaint has been submitted by a non-authorised person (such as when the complainant is not a citizen or a resident of the European Union), secondly, and more importantly perhaps, he uses the power to tackle what appear to him to be 'systemic' problems in the institutions.[100] Into the second category fall some of the most significant investigations carried out by the Ombudsman, including the first two own initiative inquiries, which took place in 1996–97. These concerned, respectively, transparency and access to documents, and Commission procedures governing the handling of complaints, made to it by individuals, of Member State infringement of Community law.[101]

Significant as own initiative inquiries may sometimes be, however, it is the investigation of complaints that consumes the bulk of the Ombudsman's resources. The way in which complaints are investigated, and the Ombudsman's various means of taking action in respect of them, are outlined in the following extract.

### European Ombudsman, *Annual Report 2004*, 19–23

In 2004 113 cases were closed with a finding of no maladministration. This is not necessarily a negative outcome for the complainant, who at least receives the benefit of a full explanation from the Institution or body concerned of what it has done, or receives an apology . . . Even if the Ombudsman does not find maladministration, he may identify an opportunity for the Institution or body to improve the quality of its administration in the future. In such cases, the Ombudsman makes a further remark, as he did, for instance in the following . . .:

- The Ombudsman confirmed that, on the basis of the exceptions provided for in its rules on access to documents, the Commission was right to refuse access to certain documents about World Trade Organisation (WTO) negotiations. The documents had been requested by the environmental organisation, 'Friends of the Earth'. Given the expectations of many citizens for greater openness in this important policy area, however, he encouraged the Commission to consider additional means that might render these negotiations more transparent . . .

Whenever possible, the Ombudsman tries to achieve a positive-sum outcome that satisfies both the complainant and the Institution complained against. The co-operation of the Community Institutions and bodies is essential for success in achieving such outcomes, which help enhance relations between the Institutions and citizens and can avoid the need for expensive

---

99 *Ibid*. 26.      100 *Ibid*. 23.
101 The former is considered below. The latter is considered in chapter 9.

and time-consuming litigation. During 2004 65 cases were settled by the Institution or body itself following a complaint . . .

When the Ombudsman finds maladministration, he always tries to achieve a friendly solution if possible. In some cases, a friendly solution can be achieved if the Institution or body concerned offers compensation to the complainant. Any such offer is made ex gratia: that is, without admission of legal liability and without creating a precedent . . .

When a friendly solution is not possible, the Ombudsman may close the case with a critical remark or make a draft recommendation. A critical remark is normally made if it is no longer possible for the Institution concerned to eliminate the instance of maladministration, the maladministration appears to have no general implications and no follow up action . . . seems necessary. A critical remark . . . indicates to the Institution or body concerned what it has done wrong, so as to help avoid maladministration in the future. In 2004 the Ombudsman made 36 critical remarks . . . It is important for the Institutions and bodies to follow up critical remarks from the Ombudsman, taking action to resolve outstanding problems and avoid maladministration in the future . . .

In cases where maladministration is particularly serious, or has general implications, or if it is still possible for the Institution concerned to eliminate the maladministration, the Ombudsman normally makes a draft recommendation. The Institution or body concerned must respond to the Ombudsman with a detailed response within three months. During 2004 17 draft recommendations were made . . .

If a Community Institution or body fails to respond satisfactorily to a draft recommendation, the Ombudsman may send a special report to the European Parliament. This constitutes the Ombudsman's ultimate weapon and is the last substantive step he takes in dealing with a case, since the adoption of a resolution and the exercise of Parliament's powers are matters for the political judgement of the Parliament. There was one special report made in 2004 . . . [which concerned the Commission's failure] to provide a coherent and convincing explanation for differences in the grading of press officers in its delegations in third countries . . .

It is clear from the preceding extract that the Ombudsman sees one of his principal tasks as being to secure improvements in future public administration. Even when he is investigating individual claims as to the administrative wrongs of the past, he pays at least as much regard to trying to improve administrative practices for the future as he does to securing compensation or apology for the complainant. In this respect, Ombudsmen are quite unlike courts. Courts are concerned only with resolving disputes between parties. They have no particular concern with seeking to improve institutional practice. Ombudsmen are not so confined. This is a theme which has been highlighted in the work of the European Ombudsman, particularly since Nikiforos Diamandouros replaced Jacob Söderman in 2003. The current Ombudsman has declared his 'guiding philosophy . . . to be both "reactive", i.e., responding to complainants, and "proactive", that is, reaching out to the Ombudsman's various constituencies through a variety of initiatives designed to maximise service to users'.[102] In 2005, he argued that the work of the European Ombudsman:

102 European Ombudsman, *Annual Report 2004*, 9.

> has a dual dimension. On the one hand, the Ombudsman acts as an external mechanism of control, investigating complaints about maladministration and recommending corrective action where necessary. On the other hand, the Ombudsman serves as a resource to the Institutions, helping them to better their performance by directing attention to areas for improvement. The ultimate goal in both instances is to improve the service provided to European citizens.[103]

Mr Söderman did not emphasise this aspect of the EO's role. We saw above that Mr Söderman adopted a narrow and legalistic interpretation of maladministration. This was consistent with his general approach as Ombudsman, particularly in his first years in post, which was often legalistic, seeing the EO more as a surrogate court and much less as the sort of proactive office that his successor advocates.[104] This is not necessarily inappropriate – even if it is somewhat limited. After all, complaining to an Ombudsman is always going to be considerably cheaper than embarking on litigation. More importantly perhaps, even an Ombudsman who conceives of his role as being little more than that of a surrogate court may be in a better position than are the courts of law to use the complaints he receives as a resource with which he can seek to encourage improvements in administrative practices. This is something which courts are not well placed to do. Once a court has given judgment it has disposed of the issue. A court rules, for example, that the Commission has failed to supply adequate reasons for refusing access to documents. Judgment is given for the applicant, and the court closes the case. There is no mechanism within the structure of litigation for the courts, once judgment has been given, to pursue the matter further to encourage the decision-maker to give effect to the court's judgment in a way which leads to better administration for the future. For Ombudsmen, by contrast, this is (or should be) an essential aspect of their role. Ombudsmen do not merely announce their rulings and move on to the next case. Ombudsmen can follow up, can engage the decision-maker in dialogue about how administration should be improved, can thereby learn from the decision-maker more about the ways in which the administration works and can thus become better informed, more expert and begin to contribute more meaningfully (more helpfully and more directly) to the ongoing conversation between administrators and citizens, understanding and mediating the various interests of both. As such, Ombudsmen may be said to engage in the process of accountability in its purest sense, bringing to the fore what Mulgan saw as the essential element of 'interaction and exchange' between the body calling to account and the body being held accountable.[105]

---

103 N. Diamandouros, *Foreword to the European Code of Good Administrative Behaviour* (2005). See above n. 89.

104 This stance is neatly illustrated by Mr Söderman's treatment of complaints concerning access to documents: see A. Tomkins, 'Transparency and the Emergence of a European Administrative Law' (1999–2000) 19 *YEL* 217, 240–4.

105 See the discussion of Mulgan's argument at pp. 312–13.

It should be said that the narrower, more legalistic approach that Mr Söderman adopted in his first years as European Ombudsman gradually softened as his office grew in confidence. The development in his approach may be seen by contrasting two decisions he made concerning transparency, one in 1997 and the other in 2001. The Ombudsman's first own initiative inquiry was conducted from June 1996 to December 1997, its subject-matter being access to documents.[106] Its results were very disappointing. The Ombudsman's inquiry was limited to investigating whether the various institutions and bodies of the European Union possessed rules on access to documents. The task the Ombudsman set himself was to discover whether such rules *existed*. At no point did he inquire into the matter of what the rules actually provided as to access. As long as there were rules – rules, apparently of any description – that would be sufficient. Even if the rules turned out to provide for exceedingly limited access, or access only on the payment of a large sum of money, no matter. Good administration, it seems, was concerned with having rules and following them, regardless of their substance.

Such early minimalism may be compared with the more adventurous spirit shown by the EO's decision in 2001 that the Council's failure to maintain a list, or register, of all the documents put before it constituted maladministration. What is striking about this decision, in comparison with the 1997 own initiative inquiry, is that the Code of Conduct, which was in force at the time, contained no requirement that any such register be maintained.[107] The Ombudsman's reasoning in this decision is instructive.

---

### European Ombudsman, *Special Report to the European Parliament in Complaint 917/2000/GG* (2001)[108]

The complainant claimed that by failing to provide a list of all the documents concerned or by failing systematically to register and file those documents, the Council had contravened the principles of good administration.

The Council argued that it is not necessary or appropriate to keep a complete, centralised record and register of each paper which is circulated to its members or their representatives, however preliminary or transitory it may be. In the view of the Council, this would impose a heavy administrative burden on its General Secretariat . . .

[T]he Ombudsman took the view that . . . Community law grants citizens a right of access of documents held by the Council . . . It is obvious, however, that the exercise of this right could be seriously impaired or even thwarted if a citizen does not even know which documents are held by the Council . . .

In these circumstances, the Ombudsman considered that the principles of good administration require that in order to allow citizens to make proper use of their right of access to

---

106 See European Ombudsman, *Annual Report 1996*, 81.

107 Compare Regulation 1049/2001, Article 11: see p. 325.

108 As with all the EO's special reports, the full text is available from the Ombudsman's website: www.euro-ombudsman.eu.int. A summary was published in *Annual Report 2002*, 195.

> documents, all the documents that are put before the Council are listed in a document or register that is accessible to all citizens. The additional administrative work that this will entail for the Council would have to be accepted in view of the fundamental importance which the right of citizens to have access to documents held by the Council has in order to guarantee openness and transparency in the latter's decision-making.

Since he took office, Mr Diamandouros has continued in this more robust vein. Many of his decisions could be cited by way of illustration, but just one will have to suffice for present purposes. In October 2005, the Ombudsman presented to the European Parliament a special report in which he explained his decision that the Council refusing to meet in public when it is acting in its legislative capacity, without giving reasons for this refusal, was an instance of maladministration. The Ombudsman's reasoning was as follows.

### European Ombudsman, *Special Report to the European Parliament in Complaint 2395/2003/GG* (2005)

At present, the extent to which the Council's meetings in its legislative capacity are public is limited by the Council's own internal Rules of Procedure. All that needs to be done in order to open all such meetings to the public would therefore be for the Council to amend its Rules of Procedure. In the Ombudsman's view, the Council's failure to do so constitutes an instance of maladministration. This finding is based on the following considerations: (a) Article 1(2) of the Treaty on European Union establishes a general principle that the Council and other Community Institutions and bodies must take decisions 'as openly as possible' and (b) the Council has not submitted any valid reasons as to why it should be unable to amend its Rules of Procedure with a view to opening up the relevant meetings to the public.

As the Ombudsman acknowledged, opening up such meetings to the public was a move that would have been accomplished by the Constitutional Treaty, had it come into force.[109] That the Constitutional Treaty was not in force at the time the Ombudsman issued his special report was evidently no bar to his holding that the Council was guilty of maladministration by meeting in private when exercising legislative power. It is clear from decisions such as this that the European Ombudsman has come a long way from the excessive caution of his first years and that he is likely to play an ever greater role in seeking the full accountability of the European Union.

### Further reading

A. Arnull and D. Wincott (eds.), *Accountability and Legitimacy in the European Union* (Oxford, Oxford University Press, 2002)

P. Craig, 'The Fall and Renewal of the Commission: Accountability, Contract and Administrative Organisation' (2000) 6 *ELJ* 98

---

109 See Article I-50(2) CT.

M. De Leeuw, 'The Regulation on Public Access to European Parliament, Council and Commission Documents in the European Union: Are Citizens Better Off?' (2003) 28 *EL Rev.* 324

V. Deckmyn (ed.), *Increasing Transparency in the European Union?* (Maastricht, EIPA, 2002)

I. Harden, F. White and K. Donnelly, 'The Court of Auditors and Financial Control and Accountability in the EC' (1995) 1 *European Public Law* 599

C. Harlow, *Accountability in the European Union* (Oxford, Oxford University Press, 2002)

P. Magnette, 'Appointing and Censuring the European Commission: the Adaptation of Parliamentary Institutions to the Community Context' (2001) 7 *ELJ* 292

V. Mehde, 'Responsibility and Accountability in the European Commission' (2003) 40 *CML Rev.* 423

M. O'Neill, 'The Right of Access to Community Held Documentation as a General Principle of EC Law' (1998) 4 *European Public Law* 403

S. Peers, *The New Regulation on Access to Documents: a Critical Analysis*, Queen's Papers on Europeanisation 6/2002

A. Tomkins, 'Responsibility and Resignation in the European Commission' (1999) 62 *MLR* 744

# The enforcement of European law

## 1. Introduction

This chapter is concerned with the enforcement of EU law against Member States, against national and domestic authorities within Member States, and against private parties.[1] The next chapter is concerned with the enforcement of EU law against the

---

1 The bulk of the chapter is concerned with the enforcement of *Community* law. The judicial enforceability of measures adopted under the second and third pillars is considerably weaker than is the case with regard to the EC. There is, for example, no equivalent in the TEU to Article 226 EC and the direct effect of Framework

institutions and bodies of the European Union. This chapter and the next are, as such, concerned with legal accountability in the European Union and should accordingly be read in the light of what was said about accountability in the previous chapter. In this chapter we shall consider, first, the enforcement of EU law by the European Court of Justice and, secondly, its enforcement by national courts and tribunals. The former is governed principally by Articles 226–228 EC and the latter by principles of Community law developed by the Court of Justice – principles such as direct effect, indirect effect and state liability. As will be recalled from chapter 2, it is principles of EU law such as these that mark the European Union out as being so different from other international organisations.

## 2. Enforcement by the Court of Justice: Articles 226–228 EC

When the original Treaty of Rome was drafted it was envisaged that the principal means by which Community law would be enforced would be those set out in what was then Article 169 of the Treaty and what is now Article 226 EC. This provides as follows:

### Article 226 EC

If the Commission considers that a Member State has failed to fulfil an obligation under this Treaty, it shall deliver a reasoned opinion on the matter after giving the State concerned the opportunity to submit its observations.

If the State concerned does not comply with the opinion within the period laid down by the Commission, the latter may bring the matter before the Court of Justice.

In addition, Article 227 EC provides that '[a] Member State which considers that another Member State has failed to fulfil an obligation under this Treaty may bring the matter before the Court of Justice'. Use of Article 227 has, in practice, been rare, Member States preferring to leave it to the Commission to take action rather than to institute legal proceedings themselves.[2] As well as Articles 226 and 227 EC, the Treaties contain further provisions allowing legal proceedings to be brought against Member States for breach of particular rules of Community law: see, for example, Article 88 EC on state aids and Article 104 EC on excessive deficit procedure. Important as these provisions are, it is Article 226 that has played the leading role in the 'centralised enforcement' of EU law.[3]

Decisions and Decisions adopted under the third pillar is expressly excluded by force of Article 34(2) TEU. By contrast, the duty of consistent interpretation (also known as 'indirect effect') has been extended to the third pillar: see Case C-105/03 *Pupino*, judgment of 16 June 2005 (see below n. 96).

2 For examples see Case 141/78 *France v United Kingdom* [1979] ECR 2923 and Case C-388/95 *Belgium v Spain* [2000] ECR I-3123.

3 The phrase is Ian Harden's and may be used to distinguish Article 226 from the enforcement of EU law by national courts (on which see below). See I. Harden, 'What Future for the Centralised Enforcement of Community Law?' (2002) 55 *CLP* 495.

## (i)   Article 226 EC procedure

Article 226 proceedings comprise two main elements, known as the administrative stage and the judicial stage. The usual process is that the Commission initiates matters with an informal letter to the Member State government in which the Commission sets out the reasons it suspects an infringement. The Member State government is invited to reply and to supply further information. This will be followed by a formal request to the Member State to submit observations (known as the 'letter of notice'). The aim throughout these early stages is to negotiate an agreement. Only if no agreement can be reached will the Commission reach the final phase of the administrative stage and deliver a reasoned opinion. Only if there continues, in the Commission's view, to be a failure to comply will the matter be referred to the Court of Justice. As would be expected, cases are settled or withdrawn at every stage of the process, so that only a minority of investigations reach the Court of Justice. Thus, of the 3,927 cases that were current at the end of 2003, 1,855 were at the first, informal administrative stage, in 999 a reasoned opinion had been given, and 411 had been referred to the Court of Justice. In 2002, 995 letters of formal notice were given, 487 reasoned opinions were delivered, and 180 cases were referred to the Court. The figures for 2003 were 1,552, 533 and 215, respectively.[4] The Commission estimated in 2003 that over 89 per cent of the cases were settled before being formally referred to the Court.[5]

Thus, the heart of the enforcement procedure under Article 226 EC is an administrative process, with the judicial proceedings acting as a backdrop to structure the negotiations between the Commission and the Member States. This impression is confirmed not only by the relatively small number of cases that arrive at the Court, but also by what happens when cases get there. Out of the 256 Article 226 proceedings to reach it between 2001 and 2003, for example, the Court held for the Commission in 240 cases and for the Member State in only 16.[6] This suggests that matters arrive at the Court only where the Commission believes it has a cast-iron case, and that the primary function of the Court in most cases is simply to ratify the Commission's decision.

There is a marked contrast in the judicial approach to the two stages of the Article 226 process. The administrative stage – in both its informal and formal phases – is regarded as an almost entirely non-judicially reviewable matter of Commission discretion. Once a reasoned opinion has been delivered, on the other hand, the Court of Justice has laid down a series of procedural rules designed to safeguard the interests of the Member States. The extent of the Commission's discretion in the

---

4 See European Commission, *21st Annual Report on the Application of Community Law*, COM(2004)839.
5 European Commission, *20th Annual Report on the Application of Community Law*, COM(2003)669, Annex I, 8.
6 On these statistics, which are derived from the Annual Reports of the Court of Justice, see D. Chalmers, 'Judicial Authority and the Constitutional Treaty' (2005) 4 *I-CON* 448, 452–3.

administrative stage is illustrated by the early case of *Lütticke v Commission*.[7] Lütticke complained to the Commission that Germany had violated Community law in respect of a particular tax regime it had adopted. The Commission investigated the complaint, came to the view that Germany had not infringed Community law, and decided not to take further action. Lütticke sought judicial review of the Commission's decision. The Court held that the application for judicial review was inadmissible, ruling that:

> the part of the [Article 226] procedure which precedes reference of the matter to the Court constitutes an administrative stage intended to give the Member State concerned the opportunity of conforming with the Treaty. During this stage, the Commission makes known its view by way of an opinion only after giving the Member State concerned the opportunity to submit its observations. No measure taken by the Commission during this stage has any binding force. Consequently, an application for the annulment of the measure by which the Commission arrived at a decision on the application is inadmissible.

In a similar vein, the Court ruled in *Commission v United Kingdom* that the matter of the Commission's motives in commencing infringement proceedings was not an issue that a Member State could challenge by way of judicial review[8] and in *Commission v Netherlands*, that even protracted delays in the Commission's dealing with the administrative stage are not judicially reviewable unless they are so extreme that they would infringe the Member State's procedural rights by making it more difficult for the state concerned to refute the Commission's arguments.[9]

On the other hand, the Court of Justice has ruled that the Commission has less room for manoeuvre once it comes to the reasoned opinion. As early as in 1961, the Court ruled that the reasoned opinion must contain a sufficiently 'coherent exposition of the reasons which led the Commission to the conviction that the State concerned failed to fulfil an obligation under the Treaty'.[10] In *Commission v Italy*, the Court ruled that the reasoned opinion must reflect its views as set out in its earlier letter of notice: if a change occurs that requires the Commission to alter its view, it has to start over.[11] The following extract summarises, in the Court's words, the current position.[12]

---

7 Case 48/65 *Lütticke v Commission* [1965] ECR 19.
8 See Case 416/85 *Commission v United Kingdom* [1988] ECR 3127.
9 See Case C-96/89 *Commission v Netherlands* [1991] ECR I-2461.
10 See Case 7/61 *Commission v Italy* [1961] ECR 317.
11 Case 7/69 *Commission v Italy* [1970] ECR 111. That said, the Court will allow some account to be taken of changes in circumstances: see Case C-11/95 *Commission v Belgium* [1996] ECR I-4115.
12 See, to similar effect, Case 293/85 *Commission v Belgium* [1988] ECR 305 and Case C-439/99 *Commission v Italy* [2002] ECR 305.

### Case C-350/02 *Commission v Netherlands* [2004] ECR I-6213

18. In . . . an action for failure to fulfil obligations the purpose of the pre-litigation procedure is to give the Member State concerned an opportunity, on the one hand, to comply with its obligations under Community law and, on the other, to avail itself of its right to defend itself against the charges formulated by the Commission . . .

19. The proper conduct of that procedure constitutes an essential guarantee required by the Treaty not only in order to protect the rights of the Member State concerned, but also so as to ensure that any contentious procedure will have a clearly defined dispute as its subject-matter . . .

20. It follows that the subject-matter of proceedings under Article 226 EC is delimited by the pre-litigation procedure governed by that provision. The Commission's reasoned opinion and the application must be based on the same grounds and pleas, with the result that the Court cannot examine a ground of complaint which was not formulated in the reasoned opinion . . . which for its part must contain a cogent and detailed exposition of the reasons which led the Commission to the conclusion that the Member State concerned had failed to fulfil one of its obligations under the Treaty . . .

21. It should also be emphasised that, whilst the formal letter of notice which comprises an initial succinct résumé of the alleged infringement, may be useful in construing the reasoned opinion, the Commission is none the less obliged to specify precisely in that opinion the grounds of complaint which it already raised more generally in the letter of formal notice and alleges against the Member State concerned, after taking cognizance of any observations submitted by it under the first paragraph of Article 226 EC. That requirement is essential in order to delimit the subject-matter of the dispute prior to any initiation of the contentious procedure provided for in the second paragraph of Article 226 and in order to ensure that the Member State in question is accurately apprised of the grounds of complaint maintained against it by the Commission and can thus bring an end to the alleged infringements or put forward its arguments in defence prior to any application to the Court by the Commission.

A long line of case law shows that the Commission must afford Member States sufficient time to respond to the views it sets out in its reasoned opinions.[13] This matter was recently – and fiercely – contested in *Commission v France*, a bitter dispute that arose out of the BSE (or 'mad cow disease') crisis in British agriculture. In 1996 the Commission adopted a Decision, the effect of which was to prohibit the export of beef and other bovine products from the United Kingdom. Two years later the Council and Commission decided to relax this prohibition in relation to beef that could be certified to come from herds in Northern Ireland. France refused to comply and continued to ban the import of all bovine products from anywhere in the United Kingdom, basing its decision on the advice of government veterinary experts. After seeking a negotiated solution, the Commission took action against France under Article 226. In its defence, France raised a range of procedural matters, among which was a concern that the Commission had failed to give sufficient time for the French authorities to respond to the Commission's views. The Commission initially gave France five working days to respond to its reasoned opinion. At France's request this was extended to two weeks (albeit that the two-week period included the Christmas

---

13  See, e.g., Case 211/81 *Commission v Denmark* [1982] ECR 4547.

break). When the case came before the Court of Justice, it was unsympathetic to France's complaints.

---

### Case C-1/00 *Commission v France* [2001] ECR I-9989

61. ... the French Government argues that the Commission required it to reply both to the letter of formal notice and to the reasoned opinion within urgent time-limits which it did not justify with regard to either traders' economic interests or protection of consumers' health. In so doing, the Commission infringed the *audi alteram partem* rule.[14] It also committed an abuse of process by substituting a shortened pre-litigation procedure for proceedings for interim relief, in order to put pressure on the French Government, without observing the procedural and substantive conditions governing proceedings for interim relief.

62. The Commission responds to this complaint by stating that the period which a Member State is allowed for replying to a letter of formal notice must be reasonable and that, in order to determine whether it is, account must be taken of all the circumstances of the case ... Here, the French authorities were well aware of the Commission's standpoint before the letter of formal notice was sent but had made clear their intention not to implement the decisions at issue and, moreover, announced that intention to the press before notifying the Commission. Furthermore, the present case did not involve a subtle and new interpretation of a provision of the Treaty or of secondary Community legislation, but a failure to implement Community measures benefiting from the presumption of legality against which no action for annulment had been brought within the time-limit laid down for that purpose. The Commission also points out that it granted the extension of time sought by the French Government.

63. In addition, the Commission denies the existence of an obligation to state reasons for the brevity of the periods in question and contests the argument that, to avoid committing an abuse of process, it should have applied for interim relief in parallel with the proceedings dealing with the merits of the case.

64. As to those arguments, it should be noted that the purpose of the pre-litigation procedure is to give the Member State concerned an opportunity to comply with its obligations under Community law or to avail itself of its right to defend itself against the complaints made by the Commission.

65. That dual purpose requires the Commission to allow Member States a reasonable period to reply to letters of formal notice and to comply with reasoned opinions, or, where appropriate, to prepare their defence. In order to determine whether the period allowed is reasonable, account must be taken of all the circumstances of the case. Thus, very short periods may be justified in particular circumstances, especially where there is an urgent need to remedy a breach or where the Member State concerned is fully aware of the Commission's views long before the procedure starts ...

66. ... the French Republic had been informed as early as 10 September 1999 of the Commission's concern that it should implement [the relevant Community law] within a short time, failing which infringement proceedings would be brought.

---

### (ii)   Complainants and Article 226 EC

These cases show that certain procedural guarantees have been built into the Article 226 process in order to seek to protect the interests of Member States. The guarantees may not always be enforced as robustly as the Member States would like, but at least

---

14 i.e., the duty to hear the other side, an elemental aspect of procedural fairness: see further chapter 10.

there is some judicial recognition that the Member States have interests which require the Commission to act fairly. The position is markedly different, however, for other potentially interested parties. It must always be remembered that the Commission is relatively small. It has neither the resources nor the personnel to police the implementation of every piece of Community law in every Member State. It is heavily reliant on private parties alerting the Commission that a Member State is committing an infringement. In 2002, for example, the Commission commenced 2,356 infringement cases, of which 1,290 (55 per cent) arose out of complaints by private parties. In 2003 it commenced 2,709 cases, of which 1,431 (53 per cent) arose out of complaints.[15] Complainants are therefore central in the Commission's enforcement of European law through Article 226. Yet the only interests to have received judicial protection in the Article 226 process are those of the Member States. Complainants, by contrast, are frozen out – notwithstanding the key role which, in practice, they play. This is illustrated by the *Star Fruit* case.[16] A Belgian banana trader alleged that it had been prejudiced by the organisation of the French banana market which it believed was contrary to EC law. The trader complained to the Commission but the latter did not commence proceedings against France. Star Fruit sought to take the Commission to court for failure to act.[17] The Court of Justice ruled that the action was inadmissible.

### Case 247/87 *Star Fruit v Commission* [1989] ECR 291

11. . . . it is clear from the scheme of Article [226] of the Treaty that the Commission is not bound to commence the proceedings provided for in that provision but in this regard has a discretion which excludes the right for individuals to require that institution to adopt a specific position.

12. It is only if it considers that the Member State in question has failed to fulfil one of its obligations that the Commission delivers a reasoned opinion. Furthermore, in the event that the State does not comply with the opinion within the period allowed, the institution has in any event the right, but not the duty, to apply to the Court of Justice for a declaration that the alleged breach of obligations has occurred.

13. It must also be observed that in requesting the Commission to commence proceedings pursuant to Article [226] the applicant is in fact seeking the adoption of acts which are not of direct and individual concern to it within the meaning of the second paragraph of Article [230] and which it could not therefore challenge by means of an action for annulment in any event.[18]

14. Consequently, the applicant cannot be entitled to raise the objection that the Commission failed to commence proceedings against the French Republic pursuant to Article [226] of the Treaty.

15 See European Commission, *21st Annual Report on the Application of Community Law*, above n. 4.

16 Case 247/87 *Star Fruit v Commission* [1989] ECR 291. See also Case C-87/89 *Sonito v Commission* [1990] ECR I-1981, in which the Court ruled that 'it is clear from the scheme of Article [226] that the Commission has no obligation to commence proceedings under that Article; it has a discretionary power precluding the right of individuals to require it to adopt a particular position and to bring an action for annulment against its refusal to take action' (para. 6).

17 For the action for failure to act, see Article 232 EC.

18 The law of 'direct and individual concern' is considered in detail in chapter 10.

This discretion has been widely criticised in academic literature as diminishing the effectiveness of EC law.[19] Attempts to oblige the Commission to take action, however, have all been turned down by the Court.[20] Accordingly, complainants have turned instead to the European Ombudsman. In his first year of operation the Ombudsman received a series of complaints about the Commission's handling of certain Article 226 cases. Among the highest profile of these were two complaints originating in the United Kingdom. Both concerned environmental impact. In one, the 'Newbury Bypass' case, the complaint concerned the Commission's refusal to commence infringement proceedings against the UK government for its failure to conduct an environmental impact assessment.[21] The complainants were aggrieved, in particular, at the Commission's failure to inform them of its decision and of its failure to give reasons. In the second, the 'M40' case, which also concerned the alleged failure of the British authorities to conduct a full environmental impact assessment in the context of its road-building programme in the 1990s, the principal complaint against the Commission was one of excessive delay.[22] The Ombudsman found no maladministration in either case, but closed both with critical remarks. In the former he stated that, 'as a matter of good administrative behaviour, the Commission should have informed the . . . complainants of its decision before . . . announcing the decision publicly through a press release'.[23] In the latter he stated that 'there was no justification for the delay in this case'.[24]

The Ombudsman was sufficiently concerned about the Commission's handling of Article 226 cases that he decided to launch an own-initiative inquiry into the process. As he stated in his report on the 'Newbury Bypass' case:

> it appears that the procedure currently used by the Commission causes considerable dissatisfaction amongst European citizens, some of whom regard the Commission's approach to the discharge of its responsibilities under Article [226] as arrogant and high-handed. Furthermore, the procedure appears not to promote the degree of transparency which European citizens increasingly expect in the functioning of Community institutions and bodies.[25]

---

19 See, e.g., R. Mastroianni, 'The Enforcement Procedure under Article 169 of the EC Treaty and the Powers of the European Commission: *Quis Custodiet Custodes?*' (1995) 1 *EPL* 535. See also Harden, above n. 3.

20 To this end the Court of Justice has overturned judgments of the Court of First Instance that sought to strengthen the position of third party complainants. All Article 226 cases are heard by the Court of Justice and not by the CFI, but the CFI does have jurisdiction in enforcement actions in competition law. It held in Case T-54/99 *max.mobil v Commission* [2002] ECR II-313 that the 'principle of sound administration' required third party complainants to be able to seek judicial review of Commission decisions not to take action against Member States under Article 86(3) EC. The Court of Justice allowed the Commission's appeal, insisting that 'the Commission is not required to bring proceedings' and that 'individuals cannot require the Commission to take a position on a specific issue': see Case C-141/02 P *Commission v T-Mobile* [2005] ECR I-1283, para. 69.

21 European Ombudsman, *Annual Report 1996*, 59.      22 *Ibid.* 67.

23 *Ibid.* 65.      24 *Ibid.* 73.      25 *Ibid.* 66.

**European Ombudsman, *Own-initiative Inquiry into the Commission's
Administrative Procedures for Dealing with Complaints under Article [226],*
EO Annual Report 1997, 270–4**

[T]he Ombudsman has received many complaints concerning the administrative procedures used by the Commission in dealing with complaints lodged by private citizens concerning Member States' failure to fulfil their Community law obligations. The object of these complaints was . . . the administrative process which takes place before judicial proceedings may begin. The allegations . . . concerned, in particular, excessive time taken to process complaints, lack of information about the ongoing treatment of the complaints and not receiving any reasoning as to how the Commission had reached a conclusion that there was no infringement . . .

The Ombudsman . . . suggested that the Commission might communicate to registered complainants a provisional conclusion that there was no breach of Community law and its findings in support of that conclusion, with an invitation to submit observations . . . He pointed out the two advantages of such a procedure. Firstly, it would most likely contribute to a more effective administration . . . Secondly, it would enhance the citizens' trust in the Commission by allowing them to participate more fully . . .

In its comments, the Commission stated that complaints from individuals remain the most important source on which the Commission bases its task of monitoring the application of Community law . . .

[I]t appeared from the Commission's comments that: (1) the receipt of complaints is acknowledged; (2) the complainant is kept informed about the action taken by the Commission; (3) under the Commission's internal rules, a decision to close the file without taking any action or a decision to initiate official infringement proceedings must be taken within a maximum period of one year from the date when the complaint was registered, except in special cases, the reasons for which must be stated . . .

The observance of these rules appears to be an adequate means for ensuring both that the citizen is kept informed about the processing of his complaint and that the complaint will be processed without undue delay . . . The Ombudsman therefore found that the inquiry had not revealed any instance of maladministration in this respect.

The Commission has taken note of suggestions made to it with regard to improving citizens' procedural rights in the Article [226] procedure . . . It appeared that in future the Commission would, in all cases, inform the complainant of its intention to close the file with the reasons why the Commission finds that there is no infringement of Community law, except where a complaint is manifestly unfounded or where the complainant appears to have lost interest in the complaint.

This is a valuable step in the process to which the Commission has committed itself . . . [C]itizens will thereby have the possibility to put forward views and criticisms concerning the Commission's point of view before it commits itself to a final conclusion that there is no infringement of Community law.

While these conclusions resulted in a degree of improved procedural protection for complainants, the Ombudsman's work received a mixed reception. Most critical was Rawlings.

**R. Rawlings, 'Engaged Elites: Citizen Action and Institutional Attitudes in Commission Enforcement' (2000) 6 *European Law Journal* 4, 18**

The own-initiative inquiry has been much trumpeted by the Ombudsman. Yet, it was largely a wasted opportunity. One feature is the way in which Mr Soderman, impressed by the 'constructive and service minded' approach of the Commission to the inquiry, took its assurances at face value. There was, for example, no statistical analysis of the treatment of complaints, nor any apparent probing of 'special cases'. Remarkable as it may seem, it has not always been the case that complaints to the Commission are registered. Again, a promise of citizen participation, once a provisional conclusion has been reached, is of limited value. Experience teaches that, for such input to be effective, it would have to happen much earlier in the decision-making process, as, indeed, is the case in the Ombudsman's own investigation of admissible complaints. Nor should the narrow focus of the inquiry on the preliminary stages of the 'complaint pyramid' be overlooked. Take the internal time limit for closing a file. As anyone with experience of waiting lists knows, such a requirement hardly guarantees speedy action elsewhere in a decision-making chain. In sum, the quality of the procedural change produced was tepid.

In 2002, the Commission published a Communication on how it would treat complainants. The Communication indicated that anybody may bring a complaint – the complainant does not have to show an interest in the proceedings to do so.[26] A complaint will be disregarded only if it is sent anonymously, if it fails to refer to a particular Member State, if it focusses exclusively on private practices or if it either refers to something outside the field of Community law or to something on which the Commission has taken a clear position. The Commission undertakes to consider the matter within twelve months and to keep the complainant informed of the steps taken and the outcome. Whilst all this brings some transparency to the processes, the Commission makes it clear that it still has complete discretion as to whether to initiate proceedings, and that any enforcement action is a bilateral matter between it and the Member State concerned. In this, the complainant is left as little more than a messenger rather than an active participant in the process.


### (iii)   Scope of Member States' responsibilities

One feature of the Article 226 process is that it may be used only against Member States. The question arises therefore as to what is considered to be state action for the purposes of Article 226. Although formally actions are brought against the state, in practice it is the central government which is proceeded against. The Court of Justice has held that the central government of a Member State is responsible for the acts and omissions of all state agencies 'even in the case of a constitutionally independent

---

26 European Commission, *On Relations with the Complainant in respect of Infringements of Community Law*, COM(2002)141.

institution'.[27] The central government is thus responsible not only for all of its own acts but also for those of local and regional government. It may also be held indirectly responsible for the actions of private parties, as in the 'Spanish Strawberries' case.

### Case C-265/95 *Commission v France* ('Spanish Strawberries') [1997] ECR I-6959

2. The Commission states that for more than a decade it has regularly received complaints concerning the passivity of the French authorities in face of violent acts committed by private individuals and by protest movements of French farmers directed against agricultural products from other Member States. Those acts consist, inter alia, in the interception of lorries transporting such products in France and the destruction of their loads, violence against lorry drivers, threats against French supermarkets selling agricultural products originating in other Member States, and the damaging of those goods when on display in shops in France.

3. The Commission has noted that as from 1993 certain groupings of French farmers, including an organization known as 'Coordination Rurale', launched a systematic campaign to restrict the supply of agricultural products from other Member States, which takes the form in particular of threats to wholesalers and retailers in order to induce them to stock exclusively French products, the imposition of a minimum selling price for the products concerned, and the organisation of checks to verify whether those traders are complying with the instructions given.

4. Thus, from April to July 1993 that campaign was directed particularly at strawberries originating in Spain. In August and September 1993 tomatoes from Belgium were treated in the same way.

5. In 1994 the same type of action, involving threats against shopping centres and destruction of goods and means of transport, was directed against Spanish strawberries in particular. Violent incidents took place on two occasions at the same place within a period of two weeks but the police who were present took no action to provide effective protection for the lorries and their loads . . .

8. . . . the French Government replied that it had always strongly condemned the acts of vandalism committed by French farmers. It stated that the preventive measures which it had taken by way of surveillance, protection and the gathering of information had brought about a notable reduction in incidents between 1993 and 1994. Moreover, the fact that public prosecutors had systematically conducted criminal investigations showed the French authorities' determination to bring prosecutions in respect of all criminal conduct aimed at obstructing imports of agricultural products from other Member States . . .

10. . . . the Commission therefore delivered a reasoned opinion under the first paragraph of Article [226] EC. In that opinion it stated that, by failing to take all necessary and proportionate measures in order to prevent the free movement of fruit and vegetables from being obstructed by actions by private individuals, the French Republic had failed to fulfil its obligations under the common organizations of the markets in agricultural products and Article[s] [28] and [10] EC.

The Court of Justice agreed with the Commission and declared that France had infringed Community law.

27  See Case 77/69 *Commission v Belgium* [1970] ECR 237. See also Case 1/86 *Commission v Belgium* [1987] ECR 2797.

This approach creates problems of compliance. It is surely otiose to hold central government responsible for the acts of bodies which are constitutionally independent of it. This very constitutional independence may prevent central government from taking effective measures to curtail the breach. In many jurisdictions, notably federal ones, national authorities have no powers to sanction the actions of local or regional authorities. In all Member States, the area in which this is most apparent is in relation to acts of the judiciary. An enforcement action brought against a Member State in such circumstances would risk asking it to compromise the independence of the judiciary and perhaps even to provoke a constitutional crisis. The Court of Justice and the Commission were initially ambivalent on this matter. Advocate General Warner suggested in *Bouchereau* that Article 226 could not be used in cases of simple judicial error but would be available in circumstances where a national court deliberately disregarded or ignored EC law.[28] In turn, while the Commission initiated proceedings against Germany in 1974 in relation to the *Internationale Handelsgesellschaft* decision of the German Constitutional Court,[29] those proceedings were subsequently dropped. More recently, the Court held in the important case of *Commission v Italy* that enforcement proceedings could be brought in respect of settled judicial practices that conflict with Community law, even where to do so would be to implicate a Member State's highest court.[30] The case concerned a series of decisions of the Italian Court of Cassation in which the national court had consistently interpreted Italian law on customs duties in a way that conflicted with EC law.

> **Case C-129/00 *Commission v Italy* [2003] ECR I-14637**
>
> 29. A Member State's failure to fulfil obligations may, in principle, be established under Article 226 EC whatever the agency of that State whose action or inaction is the cause of the failure to fulfil its obligations, even in the case of a constitutionally independent institution . . .
>
> 30. The scope of national laws, regulations or administrative provisions must be assessed in the light of the interpretation given to them by national courts . . .
>
> 31. In this case what is at issue is Article 29(2) of Law No 428/1990 which provides that duties and charges levied under national provisions incompatible with Community legislation are to be repaid, unless the amount thereof has been passed on to others. Such a provision is in itself neutral in respect of Community law in relation both to the burden of proof that the charge has been passed on to other persons and to the evidence which is admissible to prove it. Its effect must be determined in the light of the construction which the national courts give it.
>
> 32. In that regard, isolated or numerically insignificant judicial decisions in the context of case law taking a different direction, or still more a construction disowned by the national supreme court, cannot be taken into account. That is not true of a widely-held judicial construction which has not been disowned by the supreme court, but rather confirmed by it.
>
> 33. Where national legislation has been the subject of different relevant judicial constructions, some leading to the application of that legislation in compliance with Community

28 Case 30/77 *R v Bouchereau* [1979] ECR 1999, 2220.
29 *Internationale Handelsgesellschaft v Einfuhr- und Vorratsstelle für Getreide und Futter mittel* [1974] 2 CMLR 540.
30 Compare Case C-224/01 *Köbler v Austria* [2003] ECR I-10239, discussed below.

law, others leading to the opposite application, it must be held that, at the very least, such legislation is not sufficiently clear to ensure its application in compliance with Community law.

There is an element of disingenuity in the Court of Justice's judgment. It framed the problem as one of the Italian legislature drafting bad laws rather than as one of poor judicial practice. In this way, it avoided directly confronting national courts whilst holding them accountable under Community law. It may be, however, that this has merely postponed the day of reckoning, which will come when the Court has to rule on national interpretations either of Community legal instruments or of a national constitution.

### (iv) Sanction: Article 228 EC

As it was originally drafted, Article 171 [now 228] of the EC Treaty provided that: 'If the Court of Justice finds that a Member State has failed to fulfil an obligation under this Treaty, the State shall be required to take the necessary measures to comply with the judgment of the Court of Justice'. Commentators (especially legal commentators) routinely criticised this provision as constituting an enforcement machinery with no real bite – as having no effective sanction. Szyszczak, for example, argued that even if the outcome of an Article 226 process is 'successful' (that is, even if the Member State is found to be in breach of Community law), 'there is no genuine sanction against a Member State which refuses to abide by the Court's ruling'.[31] Steiner agreed, taking the argument further: 'no sanctions were provided to compel States to fulfil their obligations . . . This omission posed a real threat to the uniform application of Community law, indeed to the Community's very existence'.[32] At Maastricht, the provision was amended to read as follows:[33]

**Article 228 EC**

If the Court of Justice finds that a Member State has failed to fulfil an obligation under this Treaty, the State shall be required to take the necessary measures to comply with the judgment of the Court of Justice.

If the Commission considers that the Member State concerned has not taken such measures it shall, after giving that State the opportunity to submit its observations, issue a reasoned opinion specifying the points on which the Member State concerned has not complied with the judgment of the Court of Justice. If the Member State concerned fails to take the

---

31 E. Szyszczak, 'EC Law: New Remedies, New Directions?' (1992) 55 *MLR* 690, 691.
32 J. Steiner, 'From Direct Effects to *Francovich*: Shifting Means of Enforcement of Community Law' (1993) 18 *EL Rev.* 3.
33 The Constitutional Treaty, had it come into force, would have modified the procedure under Article 228, eliminating the need for a second reasoned opinion: see Article III-362 CT.

necessary measures to comply with the Court's judgment within the time-limit laid down by the Commission, the latter may bring the case before the Court of Justice. In doing so it shall specify the amount of the lump sum or penalty payment to be paid by the Member State concerned which it considers appropriate in the circumstances. If the Court of Justice finds that the Member State concerned has not complied with its judgment it may impose a lump sum or penalty payment on it.

Predictably, lawyers warmly welcomed the new remedy of the penalty payment. Here, at last, was a 'genuine sanction'. The effectiveness of the penalty payment, however, should not be assumed. Consider, for example, the following extract, in which Harlow and Rawlings examine the impact of the first Article 228 case to reach the Court of Justice after the Maastricht amendment, *Commission v Greece*.[34]

### C. Harlow and R. Rawlings, 'Accountability and Law Enforcement: the Centralised EU Infringement Procedure' (*mimeo*)

Initiated on the basis of five years of non-implementation of non-compliance with an ECJ ruling concerning a toxic waste dump at Kouroupitos (Chania) in Crete, it ended in the imposition of a daily penalty payment of €20,000 coupled with an order to close the dump. Although Article 228 does not specify the period within which a judgment must be complied with, 'the importance of immediate and uniform application of Community law means that the process of compliance must be initiated at once and completed as soon as possible'.[35] Yet the penalty itself proved to be only a first step towards compliance. Six months later, when Greece began payment under threat that the Commission would otherwise withhold its aid payments, nothing had been done to remove the offending dump that was the subject of the proceedings. Six months later again, when the European Parliament's Environment Committee met in Brussels, it heard that Greece, which by now owed €4.20 million, had paid off €2.98 million, though otherwise the position had not changed; the fines were now remitted with a promise of rehabilitation. By keeping the matter as a constant agenda item, the Committee helped to secure closure of the dump.[36] But the Committee had to return to Kouroupitos in 2005, when it learned from the Commission that the new site was not functioning properly and that a formal notice had been served on the Greek authorities.[37] Shortly afterwards, a press notice announced new Article 226 proceedings against Greece.[38]

The case, it appears, is a healthy reminder to lawyers that a problem is not necessarily cured just because there is a court judgment ruling that it is cured. Court judgments

---

34 Case C-387/97 *Commission v Greece* [2000] ECR I-5047. For further analysis, see M. Theodossiou, 'An Analysis of the Recent Response of the Community to Non-compliance with Court of Justice Judgments: Article 228(2) EC' (2002) 27 *EL Rev.* 25.

35 *Commission v Greece*, above n. 34, para. 82.

36 R. Corbett *et al.*, 'The European Parliament at Fifty: a View from the Inside' (2003) 41 *JCMS* 353, 371.

37 European Parliament Environment Committee, 3 February 2005, PE 350.283, 2.

38 IP/05/418 (12 April 2005).

are not self-executing and the judicial enforce*ability* of the law can sometimes be a quite different thing from its judicial enforce*ment*.

That said, however, Article 228 EC is generally seen to have sharpened and improved the Commission's centralised enforcement of EU law. Certainly, the penalties imposed under Article 228 can be significant. The basic fine is 500 euros per day. This is but a minimum, however. To calculate the applicable fine, this minimum is multiplied by a series of coefficients:

- a coefficient on a scale of 1 to 20 to mark the seriousness of the infringement;
- a coefficient on a scale of 1 to 3 for the duration of the infringement;
- a coefficient reflecting the Member State's ability to pay, ranging from 1 for Luxembourg to 26.7 for Germany.[39]

Each of these is multiplied on top of one another, with the consequence that the potential daily fines are enormous. The largest would involve Germany, for a serious and long-standing infringement, and would come to 801,000 euros per day or around 292 million euros per year.

It seems that the Court of Justice has now started to wield its power to impose penalty payments against Member States quite aggressively. *Commission v France*[40] concerned what Harlow and Rawlings have described as the 'persistent and possibly deliberate violations' by France of EU fisheries policy on drift-net trawling.[41] As Harlow and Rawlings explain, 'It was established by the Commission on the strength of evidence from its own inspectors that France had never properly enforced the relevant regulations since they had come into force in the 1980s and had in fact been found to be in default as long ago as 1991.'[42] The Commission brought proceedings under Article 228, recommending that France be required to make a penalty payment:

> What happened next is of great significance. Clearly concerned that France would escape too lightly, Advocate General Geelhoed advised departing from the Commission recommendations by adding a lump sum payment in respect of the period of infringement between the two judgments – a change of such magnitude that it was found to merit an adjournment for re-argument.[43] The phrase 'lump sum or penalty payment' in Article 228, maintained the Advocate General, need not be read disjunctively.[44]

The Court of Justice agreed with its Advocate General.

---

39 OJ 1997 C63/2. These have not yet been calculated for the new Member States.
40 Case C-304/02 *Commission v France*, judgment of 12 July 2005.
41 See C. Harlow and R. Rawlings, 'Accountability and Law Enforcement: the Centralised EU Infringement Procedure' (mimeo).
42 Case C-64/88 *Commission v France* [1991] ECR I-272.
43 See Opinion of 29 April 2004; Order for Reopening of Case C-304/02 of 16 June 2004; and Opinion of 18 November 2004.
44 Harlow and Rawlings, above n. 41.

## Case C-304/02 *Commission v France*, judgment of 12 July 2005

75. To punish the failure to comply with the judgment in Case C-64/88 *Commission v France*, the Commission suggested that the Court should impose a daily penalty payment on the French Republic from delivery of the present judgment until the day on which the breach of obligations is brought to an end. In light of the particular features of the breach that has been established, the Court considers that it should examine in addition whether imposition of a lump sum could constitute an appropriate measure.

76. When invited to give their views on whether, in proceedings brought under Article 228(2) EC, the Court may, where it finds that the Member State concerned has not complied with the Court's judgment, impose both a lump sum and a penalty payment on it, the Commission and the Danish, Netherlands, Finnish and United Kingdom Governments answered in the affirmative.

77. Their reasoning is based, essentially, on the fact that those two measures are complementary, in that each of them respectively seeks to achieve a deterrent effect. A combination of those measures should be regarded as one and the same means of achieving the objective laid down by Article 228 EC, that is to say not only to induce the Member State concerned to comply with the initial judgment but also, from a wider viewpoint, to reduce the possibility of similar infringements being committed again.

78. The French, Belgian, Czech, German, Greek, Spanish, Irish, Italian, Cypriot, Hungarian, Austrian, Polish and Portuguese Governments have put forward a contrary view.

79. They rely on the wording of Article 228(2) EC and on the use of the conjunction 'or', to which they accord a disjunctive sense, and on the objective of this provision. The provision is not punitive in nature, since Article 228(2) EC does not seek to punish the defaulting Member State, but only to induce it to comply with a judgment establishing a breach of obligations. It is not possible to distinguish several periods of a breach of obligations; only its entire duration is to be taken into consideration. The imposition of more than one financial penalty is contrary to the principle prohibiting the same conduct from being punished twice. Furthermore, in the absence of Commission guidelines concerning the applicable criteria for calculating a lump sum, imposition of such a sum by the Court would conflict with the principles of legal certainty and transparency . . .

80. The procedure laid down in Article 228(2) EC has the objective of inducing a defaulting Member State to comply with a judgment establishing a breach of obligations and thereby of ensuring that Community law is in fact applied. The measures provided for by that provision, namely a lump sum and a penalty payment, are both intended to achieve this objective.

81. Application of each of those measures depends on their respective ability to meet the objective pursued according to the circumstances of the case. While the imposition of a penalty payment seems particularly suited to inducing a Member State to put an end as soon as possible to a breach of obligations which, in the absence of such a measure, would tend to persist, the imposition of a lump sum is based more on assessment of the effects on public and private interests of the failure of the Member State concerned to comply with its obligations, in particular where the breach has persisted for a long period since the judgment which initially established it.

82. That being so, recourse to both types of penalty provided for in Article 228(2) EC is not precluded, in particular where the breach of obligations both has continued for a long period and is inclined to persist.

83. This interpretation cannot be countered by reference to the use in Article 228(2) EC of the conjunction 'or' to link the financial penalties capable of being imposed. As the Commission and the Danish, Netherlands, Finnish and United Kingdom Governments have

submitted, that conjunction may, linguistically, have an alternative or a cumulative sense and must therefore be read in the context in which it is used. In light of the objective pursued by Article 228 EC, the conjunction 'or' in Article 228(2) EC must be understood as being used in a cumulative sense.

The Court of Justice broadly followed the methodology suggested by the Commission, and France was ordered to make penalty payments of 57,761,250 euros for each six-month period of future non-compliance and – in the light of 'the public and private interests in issue' – a lump sum payment of 20,000,000 euros. Whether the Court's robust approach will yield fuller compliance it is, at the time of writing, too soon to tell. Whatever the outcome, France's reaction will surely be fascinating – and may go some distance in determining the shape of both the Commission's and the Court's future use of Article 228.

Such evidence as we have suggests that Member States do take Article 228 proceedings seriously, and that it sharpens their attitudes in a way that Article 226 proceedings may not. The Commission has started to use Article 228 more actively. At the end of 2002, for example, twenty-eight Article 228 proceedings had been brought, in twenty-three of which Member States had brought their law into line with Community law.[45] While Article 228 appears to bring a rate of compliance greater than that achieved by Article 226, it is hampered by its being available only after an initial judgment of non-compliance has already been made by the Court. A lengthy procedure has to be undergone before it can be instigated. This was recognised at the Convention on the Future of Europe, at which proposals were made to the effect that the Commission should be able to commence actions for a fine simultaneously with the commencement of infringement actions under Article 226 EC.[46] These recommendations were only partially adopted. It was agreed that in cases where states failed to transpose a Directive, proceedings could be started simultaneously.[47] For other proceedings, there had first to be a ruling of infringement and only then could Article 228 proceedings begin.

### (v)   Conclusions

The Court of Justice's record in cases brought before it under Articles 226 to 228 EC is mixed. On the one hand, it has sought to protect what it views as the administrative discretion of the Commission, shielding it from judicial review in all the various aspects of the procedure that lead up to the issuing of a reasoned opinion. The Court has done very little to seek to advance the procedural protections accorded to private parties who complain to the Commission, notwithstanding the Commission's

---

45 On this, see Chalmers, above n. 6, 453–4.
46 See Final Report of the Discussion Group on the Court of Justice, CONV636/03.
47 Article III-362(3) CT.

self-confessed reliance on such complainants. To the (still limited) extent that complainants' interests are protected, it is the Ombudsman rather than the Court of Justice that has played the key role. The Court has been more concerned, by contrast, with the procedural protections designed to safeguard the interests of the Member States, albeit that the Court has been conscious of the importance of not allowing Member States improperly to use their procedural protections in order to escape effective Commission investigation. On the other hand, the Court has taken an expansive view of the scope of Member States' responsibilities under Article 226 and it has, in recent case law, started to use its jurisdiction under Article 228 in a remarkably aggressive way. Even if the Court has not always seen Articles 226 to 228 as being the principal means by which Community law should be enforced (on which, see below), its recent case law on Article 228, at least, suggests that Commission enforcement of Community law may be about to come out of the shadows, somewhat, and play a more prominent part.

## 3. Enforcement through the national courts: direct effect

As we saw in the previous section, when the EC Treaty was drafted it was envisaged that the procedure as set out in what is now Article 226 EC would be the primary means by which Community law is enforced against the Member States. One of the most notable features of all European law is that such a vision has only rarely been shared by the Court of Justice. Indeed, from its earliest case law until the present day, the Court has engaged in a prolonged and radical programme that has resulted in the judicial creation of a series of ways in which national courts, rather than the Court of Justice, are expected to play the lead role in the enforcement of Community law against the Member States, national authorities and private parties. Three principal means have been established:

- the creation and subsequent expansion of the law of direct effect (*Van Gend en Loos*[48] and its progeny);
- the creation and subsequent expansion of the duty of consistent interpretation (also known as 'indirect effect') (*Von Colson*[49] and *Marleasing*[50]);
- the creation and subsequent expansion of the principle of state liability (*Francovich*[51] and *Brasserie du Pêcheur/Factortame III*[52]).

The cases that have established and developed these principles are among the most important – and the most revolutionary – ever decided by the Court of Justice. The

---

48 Case 26/62 *Van Gend en Loos v Nederlandse Administratie der Belastingen* [1963] ECR 1.
49 Case 14/83 *Von Colson and Kamann v Land Nordrhein-Westfalen* [1984] ECR 1891.
50 Case C-106/89 *Marleasing SA v La Comercial Internacionale de Alimentacion SA* [1990] ECR I-4135.
51 Joined Cases C-6 and 9/90 *Francovich and Bonifaci v Italy* [1991] ECR I-5357.
52 Joined Cases C-46 and 48/93 *Brasserie du Pêcheur v Germany* and *R v Secretary of State for Transport ex parte Factortame (No. 3)* [1996] ECR I-1029.

law that has been created in these decisions is, to a large extent, what marks the European Union out as being so different from other international organisations.[53] The remainder of this chapter considers each of these three means in turn.

### (i)   Establishment of direct effect

The first, of course, was the Court's invention of direct effect in *Van Gend en Loos*. As will be recalled from chapter 2,[54] the question in this case was whether as a matter of Community law an importer (Van Gend en Loos) could plead before a Dutch national court (the Tariefcommissie) that Article 25 [formerly 12] EC had been infringed, and more specifically whether the importer could as a matter of Community law claim the protection of rights conferred on it by Community law, rights which the national court was under a duty to protect. Article 25 provides that 'customs duties on imports and exports and charges having equivalent effect shall be prohibited between Member States'. The Tariefcommissie referred these questions to the Court of Justice under Article 234 EC.

It is noteworthy that in this case, which was decided when the EC comprised only six Member States, three of those Member States intervened in the proceedings, all of them submitting arguments against the importer. The Dutch and Belgian governments argued that the Court of Justice did not have the jurisdiction to answer the questions referred to it. They submitted that the solution to the problem posed by the importer fell within the exclusive jurisdiction of the national court, 'subject to an application in accordance with the provisions laid down by Articles [226 and 227] of the Treaty'. In other words, in the view of the Dutch and Belgian governments, the enforcement of Article 25 was as a matter of Community law governed by Article 226 – it was a question for the Commission. If the Commission considered that the (in this instance) Dutch authorities had failed adequately or properly to implement the aspects of the free movement of goods which were required by Article 25, then it could bring infringement proceedings before the Court of Justice. If an importer such as Van Gend en Loos was unhappy with the Dutch authorities' compliance with Article 25, then its remedy in Community law was not to sue in the national courts, but was to take the much cheaper route of complaining to the Commission, so that the Commission could take the necessary legal action under Article 226. It is important to note here that it was not the view of the Dutch and Belgian governments that this would necessarily be the only remedy available to the importer. This would be the remedy available as a matter of Community law, but there may in addition be a domestic or national legal remedy open to the importer, but if there were that would be a question for the national legal authorities (in this instance for the Tariefcommissie), and not for the

---

53 See chapter 2.
54 The following discussion of *Van Gend en Loos* should be read alongside the analysis of the constitutional importance of the case in chapter 2.

Court of Justice to determine. What role provisions of Community law could play in national legal proceedings was in their view a national issue, not one for the Court of Justice to decide.

While Advocate General Roemer agreed with the tenor of these submissions, the Court chose not to follow his advice. It rejected out of hand the submission that it lacked jurisdiction, stating that the Dutch and Belgian governments' argument had 'no legal foundation'. The Court's reasoning in support of this ruling was terse and cryptic. The Court stated that it was not being asked to adjudicate on the application of the Treaty according to the principles of national law – a matter which it conceded remained a question for national courts. Rather, in the Court's view, it was being asked 'to interpret the scope of Article [25] . . . within the context of Community law and with reference to its effect on individuals'.[55] For the Court, it followed immediately from this observation that the argument of the Dutch and Belgian governments was without legal foundation. It is difficult to see how this reasoning addresses the issue at the heart of the Dutch and Belgian objections: namely, that the question of the 'individual' or 'private' enforcement[56] of Community law was a question for the national court to determine, and not for the Court of Justice. Just because the provision of Community law has an effect on 'individuals' (or, in this instance, on a multinational corporation) this does not justify the claim – which the Court made – that the issue is therefore necessarily one for the Court of Justice to determine. The conclusion simply does not follow from the reasoning. As for the argument that Article 25 should be enforced only through the machinery laid out in the Treaty (i.e., in Articles 226 to 227), the Court dismissed the suggestion as 'misconceived'. The Court ruled that '[t]he fact that these Articles of the Treaty enable the Commission and the Member States to bring before the Court a State which has not fulfilled its obligations does not mean that individuals cannot plead these obligations, should the occasion arise, before a national court'.

What happened next is well known. The Court found that while the EC Treaty contained no specific textual authority in support of the view that provisions of Community law could be directly effective, authority for such a view could nonetheless be gleaned from 'the spirit, the general scheme and the wording' of the Treaty. Having established that the notion of direct effect was recognised in Community law, the Court then proceeded to consider whether Article 25 was sufficiently 'clear and unconditional' to be capable of bearing direct effect. This aspect of the Court's ruling is actually rather narrow. Article 25 was found to be capable of bearing direct effect only because it satisfied a number of specific criteria: that it was a clear, unconditional and negative prohibition which was not dependent upon any further implementing measures at either EC or national level. These criteria imply a restrictive vision

---

55 Describing Van Gend en Loos as an individual is rather odd. It is a company which was founded in 1796 and which by 2002 employed over 4,100 people in 27 offices located in three states.

56 As opposed to the 'centralised' enforcement under Articles 226 to 228 EC.

of the range of provisions of Community law that may be invoked before national courts.

### (ii)   Liberalisation and expansion of direct effect

In practice, however, they have been interpreted liberally. The requirement that provisions contain a negative prohibition was dropped in *Reyners*[57] and the law of direct effect was further liberalised in the important case of *Defrenne v Sabena*. Under Belgian law, female air stewards were required to retire at the age of forty, unlike their male counterparts. Gabrielle Defrenne had been forced to retire from the Belgian national carrier, Sabena, on this ground in 1968. She brought an action claiming that the lower pension payments this entailed breached the principle in Article 141 EC that 'each Member State shall ensure and maintain the principle that men and women should receive equal pay for work of equal value'. On its face there appeared to be a number of obstacles to Article 141 being directly effective. The principle seemed to be neither clear nor unconditional, as complete implementation of the principle would require elaboration of further criteria for recognising discrimination and implementing measures to abolish it.

### Case 43/75 *Defrenne v Sabena* [1976] ECR 455

16. Under the terms of the first paragraph of Article [141], the Member States are bound to ensure and maintain 'the application of the principle that men and women should receive equal pay for equal work'.

17. The second and third paragraphs of the same Article add a certain number of details concerning the concepts of pay and work referred to in the first paragraph.

18. For the purposes of the implementation of these provisions a distinction must be drawn within the whole area of application of Article [141] between, first, direct and overt discrimination which may be identified solely with the aid of the criteria based on equal work and equal pay referred to by the Article in question and, secondly, indirect and disguised discrimination which can only be identified by reference to more explicit implementing provisions of a Community or national character.

19. It is impossible not to recognise that the complete implementation of the aim pursued by Article [141], by means of the elimination of all discrimination, direct or indirect, between men and women workers, not only as regards individual undertakings but also entire branches of industry and even of the economic system as a whole, may in certain cases involve the elaboration of criteria whose implementation necessitates the taking of appropriate measures at Community and national level . . .

21. Among the forms of direct discrimination which may be identified solely by reference to the criteria laid down by Article [141] must be included in particular those which have their origin in legislative provisions or in collective labour agreements and which may be detected on the basis of a purely legal analysis of the situation.

22. This applies even more in cases where men and women receive unequal pay for equal work carried out in the same establishment or service, whether public or private.

---

57 Case 2/74 *Reyners v Belgium* [1974] ECR 631.

23. As is shown by the very findings of the judgment making the reference, in such a situation the court is in a position to establish all the facts which enable it to decide whether a woman worker is receiving lower pay than a male worker performing the same tasks.

24. In such situation, at least, Article [141] is directly [effective] and may thus give rise to individual rights which the courts must protect.

In the 1970s, following judgments such as *Defrenne*, the strict criteria set out in *Van Gend en Loos* were relaxed in favour of a more flexible test, namely whether the provision was sufficiently precise and unconditional to be invoked in national courts.[58] In the eyes of one judge, the invocability of EC Treaty provisions had been reduced to a simple question of justiciability.[59] It seems now that only the most open-ended and aspirational of provisions in the EC Treaty will be held not to be directly effective – Article 2 EC, for example.[60]

*Defrenne v Sabena* marked a significant liberalisation of the law of direct effect, in that it brought provisions of Community law that were less than 'clear and unconditional' within the scope of the doctrine. The case is important, in addition to this, for a second reason. In *Van Gend en Loos* the party against whom the trader wished to have EC law enforced was the Dutch customs authorities – that is, a part of the Dutch state. Defrenne, by contrast, was taking action against a private company – the Belgian airline, Sabena. Could Community law be invoked before a national court in proceedings against a private party? And, in particular, could this be done in the context of legal proceedings that sought the enforcement of a provision (Article 141 EC) that specifically provided that 'each *Member State* shall ensure and maintain the principle that men and women should receive equal pay for work of equal value'?

### Case 43/75 *Defrenne v Sabena* [1976] ECR 455

30. It is . . . impossible to put forward arguments based on the fact that Article [141] only refers expressly to 'Member States'.

31. Indeed, as the Court has already found in other contexts, the fact that certain provisions of the Treaty are formally addressed to the Member States does not prevent rights from being conferred at the same time on any individual who has an interest in the performance of the duties thus laid down.

32. The very wording of Article [141] shows that it imposes on States a duty to bring about a specific result to be mandatorily achieved within a fixed period.

33. The effectiveness of this provision cannot be affected by the fact that the duty imposed by the Treaty has not been discharged by certain Member States and that the joint institutions have not reacted sufficiently energetically against this failure to act.

---

58 See, e.g., Case 148/78 *Publico Ministero v Ratti* [1979] ECR 1629 and Case 8/81 *Becker v Finanzamt Münster-Innenstadt* [1982] ECR 53.

59 P. Pescatore, 'The Doctrine of "direct effect": an Infant Disease of Community Law' (1983) 8 *EL Rev.* 155, 176–7.

60 See Case 126/86 *Zaera v Institutio Nacionale de la Seguridad Social* [1987] ECR 3697.

34. To accept the contrary view would be to risk raising the violation of the right to the status of a principle of interpretation, a position the adoption of which would not be consistent with the task assigned to the Court by Article [220] of the Treaty.

35. Finally, in its reference to 'Member States', Article [141] is alluding to those States in the exercise of all those of their functions which may usefully contribute to the implementation of the principle of equal pay.

36. Thus, contrary to the statements made in the course of the proceedings this provision is far from merely referring the matter to the powers of the national legislative authorities.

37. Therefore, the reference to 'Member States' in Article [141] cannot be interpreted as excluding the intervention of the courts in direct application of the Treaty.

38. Furthermore it is not possible to sustain any objection that the application by national courts of the principle of equal pay would amount to modifying independent agreements concluded privately or in the sphere of industrial relations such as individual contracts and collective labour agreements.

39. In fact, since Article [141] is mandatory in nature, the prohibition on discrimination between men and women applies not only to the action of public authorities, but also extends to all agreements which are intended to regulate paid labour collectively, as well as to contracts between individuals . . .

69. The Governments of Ireland and the United Kingdom have drawn the Court's attention to the possible economic consequences of attributing direct effect to the provisions of Article [141], on the ground that such a decision might, in many branches of economic life, result in the introduction of claims dating back to the time at which such effect came into existence.

70. In view of the large number of people concerned such claims, which undertakings could not have foreseen, might seriously affect the financial situation of such undertakings and even drive some of them to bankruptcy.

71. Although the practical consequences of any judicial decision must be carefully taken into account, it would be impossible to go so far as to diminish the objectivity of the law and compromise its future application on the ground of the possible repercussions which might result, as regards the past, from such a judicial decision.

72. However, in the light of the conduct of several of the Member States . . . it is appropriate to take exceptionally into account the fact that, over a prolonged period, the parties concerned have been led to continue with practices which were contrary to Article [141], although not yet prohibited under their national law . . .

74. In these circumstances, it is appropriate to determine that, as the general level at which pay would have been fixed cannot be known, important considerations of legal certainty affecting all the interests involved, both public and private, make it impossible in principle to reopen the question as regards the past.

75. Therefore, the direct effect of Article [141] cannot be relied on in order to support claims concerning pay periods prior to the date of this judgment, except as regards those workers who have already brought legal proceedings or made an equivalent claim.

Direct effect in the context of legal proceedings against a Member State is known as 'vertical direct effect'. Direct effect in the context of legal proceedings against a private party is known as 'horizontal direct effect'. The importance of the Court's ruling in *Defrenne* was its recognition that Treaty provisions such as Article 141 were capable of bearing both vertical and horizontal direct effect: that is, they may be invoked, relied on and enforced in domestic legal proceedings whether the party proceeded against is the state or a private party.

It may be added that the socio-economic consequences of the finding of horizontal direct effect in *Defrenne* were considerable. On the one hand, protection for women in the workplace was significantly enhanced. On the other, the financial implications were significant, as the immediate burden of compliance fell upon all parties against whom the right could be asserted. The Irish government argued that the costs of compliance would exceed Irish receipts from the European Regional Development Fund for the period 1975–77 and the British government argued that it would add 3.5 per cent to labour costs – a considerable admission, it might be thought, on the part of those two governments as to the degree of exploitation of women in their respective jurisdictions! With such large adjustment costs, the only manner through which the Court of Justice could feel confident about securing compliance with its judgment was through limiting its temporal effects. Individuals would therefore not be able to bring actions for such discrimination as had occurred since the EC Treaty had come into force (which would have been the normal position). Instead, except with regard to proceedings which had already been commenced, Article 141 was to have direct effect only in relation to discrimination which occurred after the judgment. Rulings that limit the temporal effects of the Court's judgments are rare. Their symbolism is considerable, however. For, as Rasmussen has observed, they destroy the illusion that the Court is engaging in a neutral exercise of merely giving life to the text, as it is impossible 'to maintain this myth while ruling that Article [141] was deprived of direct effects until the day of pronouncement of the Court's decision; only to produce such effects from that day onwards'.[61]

*Van Gend en Loos* and *Defrenne v Sabena* were concerned with direct effect of Treaty provisions. The vast bulk of EC law, however, is contained not in the EC Treaty but in secondary legislation. Regulations were held to be capable of bearing direct effect in *Leonesio* in 1972.[62] This is neither surprising nor especially controversial, particularly given Article 249 EC, which provides that '[a] Regulation shall have general application. It shall be binding in its entirety and directly applicable in all Member States'. If Treaty provisions could be directly effective there seems no reason why Regulations should not likewise be directly effective.[63]

### (iii)  Direct effect of Directives

The position of Directives is more complicated. Article 249 EC provides that '[a] Directive shall be binding, as to the result to be achieved, upon each Member State to which it is addressed, but shall leave to the national authorities the choice of form and methods'. A number of objections were posited to the notion that Directives could be capable of direct effect. It was stated, first, that the discretion given by

---

61  H. Rasmussen, *On Law and Policy in the European Court of Justice* (Dordrecht, Martinus Nijhoff, 1986) 441.

62  Case 93/71 *Leonesio v Italian Ministry of Agriculture* [1972] ECR 293. See also Case 39/72 *Commission v Italy* [1973] ECR 101.

63  Decisions have also been held to be capable of bearing direct effect: see Case 9/70 *Grad v Finanzamt Traustein* [1970] ECR 838.

Article 249 EC to Member States to implement Directives resulted in individuals being able to derive rights only from the executory acts of national authorities, and not from the Directives themselves. Secondly, it was argued that to give direct effect to Directives would blur the distinction between Directives and Regulations, a distinction which was so clearly spelt out in Article 249. Thirdly, and perhaps most importantly, it was pointed out that, in numerous fields, the EC enjoys a competence to adopt Directives but not Regulations and that, according to Directives, full direct effect would amount to a blurring of the distinction between the two legal forms, allowing the EC in effect to legislate through the back door in areas that the Treaty had not permitted through the front. We will return to this argument below. Lastly, it was also argued that, as there was no formal requirement that Directives be published, legal certainty would be prejudiced by according them direct effect. This last argument, however, was rendered nugatory by the amendment to Article 254(2) EC at Maastricht, which now requires all Directives to be published in the *Official Journal.*

Notwithstanding these various arguments, the Court of Justice ruled in *Van Duyn* that, in certain circumstances, Directives could bear direct effect. Van Duyn was refused leave to enter the United Kingdom in order to take up an offer of a secretarial post at the Church of Scientology, as the UK government had imposed a ban on foreign scientologists entering the United Kingdom. Ms van Duyn challenged the ban on the ground, inter alia, that it breached Directive 64/221/EEC, which required that any ban be based upon the personal conduct of the individual. The Court of Justice considered that her association with the Church of Scientology met the requirements of the Directive. It considered, first, whether the Directive was capable of direct effect.

### Case 41/74 *Van Duyn v Home Office* [1974] ECR 1337

12. . . . It would be incompatible with the binding effect attributed to a Directive by Article [249] to exclude, in principle, the possibility that the obligation which it imposes may be invoked by those concerned. In particular, where the Community authorities have, by Directive, imposed on Member States the obligation to pursue a particular course of conduct, the useful effect of such an act would be weakened if individuals were prevented from relying on it before their national courts and if the latter were prevented from taking it into consideration as an element of Community law. Article [234], which empowers national courts to refer to the Court questions concerning the validity and interpretation of all acts of the Community institutions, without distinction, implies furthermore that these acts may be invoked by individuals in the national courts. It is necessary to examine, in every case, whether the nature, general scheme and wording of the provisions in question are capable of having direct effects on the relations between Member States and individuals.

This reasoning is remarkably weak. For one thing it starts from an *a contrario* position of whether there is any good reason why Directives should not have direct effect. No less a figure than Federico Mancini, a former judge at the Court of Justice, has admitted that 'this judgment goes beyond the letter of Article

[249]'.[64] More significantly, the ruling provoked a strong counter-reaction from both French and German courts. The view of the French Conseil d'Etat, the highest court of administrative law in France, can be seen in its judgment in the *Cohn-Bendit* case. Cohn-Bendit was a German national who had been a leader of the student disturbances in 1968. He was offered a job as a broadcaster in France. The French Minister of the Interior sought to deport him. Cohn-Bendit invoked Directive 64/221/EC, stating that it required both that any decision be formally reasoned and that the grounds for the decision be made known to the immigrant. As this had not happened, the decision was illegal, he argued.

### *Minister of the Interior v Cohn-Bendit* [1980] 1 CMLR 543

it appears clearly from the provisions of Article [249] of the Treaty that if Directives bind Member States 'with regard to the result to be achieved' and if, in order to achieve the results which they define, the national authorities of Member States are under an obligation to adapt their legislative and regulatory provisions to the Directives which are addressed to them, these authorities remain the only competent authorities to determine the form to give to the implementation of these Directives and to determine themselves, under the control of the national judicial authorities, their own method for producing their effect in internal national law . . .

Directives cannot be invoked by persons within the jurisdiction of those Member States in order to support a legal action undertaken against any administrative action with regard to an individual . . .

It follows from the foregoing that M. Cohn-Bendit cannot hope to succeed in his argument . . . to annul the decision of the Minister of the Interior.

The German Bundesfinanzhof took the same view of the direct effect of Directives,[65] until the German Constitutional Court intervened 'to put its resistance to an end'.[66]

### P. Figueroa Regueiro, *Invocability of Substitution and Invocability of Exclusion: Bringing Legal Realism to the Current Developments of the Case Law of Horizontal Direct Effect of Directives*, Jean Monnet Working Paper 7/02

The reasoning of [the French Conseil d'Etat and the German Bundesfinanzhof] ran along similar lines. They considered that Article [249] expressly distinguished Regulations from Directives and, as only the former were described as 'directly applicable', the latter seemed to be intended to take effect within the national order only via national implementing measures.

---

64 G. Mancini and D. Keeling, 'Language, Culture and Politics in the Life of the European Court of Justice' (1995) 1 *Colum. J European Law* 397, 401.

65 See *Re Value Added Tax Directives* [1982] 1 CMLR 527.

66 P. Figueroa Regueiro, '*Invocability of Substitution and Invocability of Exclusion: Bringing Legal Realism to the Current Developments of the Case Law of Horizontal Direct Effect of Directives*, Jean Monnet Working Paper 7/02.

> The development of the doctrine of direct effect of Directives was considered by the national courts to push the Treaty too far. The Court of Justice realised that the fact that its arguments were perceived by national courts to be an implausible interpretation of the Treaty could undermine the co-operation of national courts, so a new argument was introduced in support of direct effect of Directives . . . the so-called 'estoppel' argument.

The 'estoppel' argument, adopted by the Court of Justice to justify the extension of direct effect to Directives, was first employed in *Ratti*.[67] The argument runs as follows: Directives impose a duty upon Member States to adopt the appropriate implementing measures by a certain date; it would be wrong for Member States to be able to rely upon and gain advantage through their failure to carry out this obligation; they are thus 'estopped' or prevented from denying the direct effect of Directives once the time limit for their implementation into national law has expired. Thus, in *Ratti*, a trader was prosecuted for not labelling his solvents in accordance with Italian law. He sought to rely upon two Directives. Whilst the transitional period for one of these had expired, it had not for the other. The Court held that he could rely only upon the first Directive. The Member State was estopped by its failure to take the necessary implementing measures from denying this Directive's direct effect. The other Directive was not directly effective, however, as the Member State was still within its period of grace. Directives will be directly effective, therefore, only from the end of the transposition period and, even then, will be capable of direct effect only if the Member State has failed to implement them or has not implemented them correctly. Where Directives are correctly implemented, individual rights flow from the national implementing provisions and not from the Directives themselves.

The estoppel argument has one very important implication. As the direct effect of Directives is predicated on the 'fault' of the Member State in failing to implement the Directive, it follows that parties may invoke and rely on the terms of such Directives in national legal proceedings against the state. But it does not follow from the estoppel argument that parties may invoke and rely on Directives in national legal proceedings against other private parties. In other words, the estoppel argument may be used to justify the vertical direct effect of Directives, but not their horizontal direct effect. This limitation was graphically illustrated in the *Marshall* case. Ms Marshall, a dietician employed by a British health authority, was dismissed at the age of sixty-two on the ground that she had reached pensionable age. A man would not have been dismissed at that age but Ms Marshall had no redress under the Sex Discrimination Act 1975 because of a blanket exclusion in that Act relating to terms and conditions relating to death and retirement. Ms Marshall claimed that there had been a breach of Article 5 of the Equal Treatment Directive 76/207/EEC.

---

67 Case 148/78 *Ratti* [1979] ECR 1629. See also Case 8/81 *Becker v Finanzamt Münster-Innenstadt* [1982] ECR 53.

### Case 152/84 *Marshall v Southampton and SW Hampshire Area Health Authority* [1986] ECR 723

48. With regard to the argument that a Directive may not be relied upon against an individual, it must be emphasised that according to Article [249 EC], the binding nature of a Directive, which constitutes the basis for the possibility of relying on the Directive before a national court, exists only in relation to 'each Member State to which it is addressed'. It follows that a Directive may not of itself impose obligations on an individual and that a provision of a Directive may not be relied upon as such against such a person.

49. In that respect it must be pointed out that where a person involved in legal proceedings is able to rely on a Directive as against the State he may do so regardless of the capacity in which the latter is acting, whether employer or public authority. In either case it is necessary to prevent the State from taking advantage of its own failure to comply with Community law . . .

51. The argument submitted by the United Kingdom that the possibility of relying on provisions of the Directive against the respondent *qua* organ of the State would give rise to an arbitrary and unfair distinction between the rights of State employees and those of private employees does not justify any other conclusion. Such a distinction may easily be avoided if the Member State concerned has correctly implemented the Directive in national law.

If *Marshall* was an attempt to assuage some of the criticism which had been levelled at the Court of Justice since *Van Duyn*, it also created problems of its own. For one thing, the Court's reliance on the textual reference to Member States in Article 249 sits uncomfortably with the Court's treatment in *Defrenne v Sabena* of the reference to Member States in Article 141 EC. For another, the rule in *Marshall* creates illogical outcomes – Marshall could rely on the Directive because she was employed by a public authority, a part of the state. Had she been employed by a private hospital she would not have been able to rely on the Directive. Thus, a somewhat arbitrary, two-tier legal system has been created in which parties have greater protection against public bodies than against private ones, notwithstanding the fact that their functional relationship with the two may be the same. Thirdly, it is difficult to see how the estoppel argument can justify reliance on a Directive against a public health authority. Certainly, the state is responsible for implementing Directives and, certainly, public health authorities are a part of the state, but there is no sense in which public health authorities are responsible for transposing the terms of equal pay Directives into national law – yet here the Directive was held to be enforceable as against the authority. For these reasons the rule in *Marshall* (that Directives may have vertical but not horizontal direct effect) has come under withering attack, from academic commentators and Advocates General alike.[68]

---

68 See, e.g., Advocate General Van Gerven in Case C-271/91 *Marshall v Southampton and South West Hampshire Area Health Authority (Marshall II)* [1993] ECR I-4367, Advocate General Jacobs in Case C-316/93 *Vaneetveld v Le Foyer* [1994] ECR I-763 and Advocate General Lenz in Case C-91/92 *Faccini Dori v Recreb* [1994] ECR I-3325.

The Court of Justice, however, has stood firm and reconfirmed its position in the constitutionally significant case of *Faccini Dori*. Ms Dori concluded a contract at Milan railway station with Interdiffusion Srl for an English-language correspondence course. She then had second thoughts and cancelled her contract, relying upon the provisions of Directive 85/577/EC, concerning the protection of the consumer in respect of contracts negotiated away from business premises. Italy had not taken any steps to implement the Directive. The Court was asked whether the Directive could be invoked against another private party. Six Member States intervened to argue against horizontal direct effect, with only the Greek government intervening in favour.

---

### Case C-91/92 *Faccini Dori v Recreb* [1994] ECR I-3325

20. As the Court has consistently held since its judgment in *Marshall*, a Directive cannot of itself impose obligations on an individual and cannot therefore be relied upon as such against an individual.

21. The national court observes that if the effects of unconditional and sufficiently precise but untransposed Directives were to be limited to relations between State entities and individuals, this would mean that a legislative measure would operate as such only as between certain legal subjects, whereas, under Italian law as under the laws of all modern States founded on the rule of law, the State is subject to the law like any other person. If the Directive could be relied on only as against the State, that would be tantamount to a penalty for failure to adopt legislative measures of transposition as if the relationship were a purely private one.

22. . . . the case law on the possibility of relying on Directives against State entities is based on the fact that under Article [249] a Directive is binding only in relation to 'each Member State to which it is addressed'. The case law seeks to prevent 'the State from taking advantage of its own failure to comply with Community law'.

24. The effect of extending that case law to the sphere of relations between individuals would be to recognise a power in the Community to enact obligations for individuals with immediate effect, whereas it has competence to do so only where it is empowered to adopt Regulations.

25. It follows that, in the absence of measures transposing the Directive within the prescribed time-limit, consumers cannot derive from the Directive itself a right of cancellation as against traders with whom they have concluded a contract or enforce such a right in a national court.

---

The reasoning in paragraph 24 of the Court's judgment is significant. As was mentioned above, the effect of granting full (i.e. horizontal) direct effect to Directives would be to blur the constitutionally important distinction between Regulations and Directives. This distinction is constitutionally important because it goes to the question of where the line should be drawn between the law-making powers of the EC and those of the Member States. The constitutional significance of this was discussed in detail in chapter 5. The EC has the power to make law that applies directly to private parties – that is, law that takes effect without the need for any intervention or implementing measures by Member States – only where the EC has the competence to adopt Regulations. Where the EC has the competence only to adopt Directives, it has no constitutional authority to make law that can directly apply to private parties: for such law to apply, it requires the participation (through the passage of implementing measures) of the Member States. The Court's robust judgment in *Faccini Dori* is an important reminder that, whatever the illogicalities and unfortunate consequences of the rule in *Marshall*, the solution to the problems posed by that rule cannot be found by unconstitutionally enlarging the EC's law-making powers.

The clarity of the position taken in *Faccini Dori* has been muddied by a number of cases in which the Court of Justice has held that, whilst a private party may not found an action against another private party on the basis of a Directive, a Directive may in certain circumstances be invoked as a 'shield' in a dispute between private parties to prevent a provision of national law being invoked by one against the other. This phenomenon, sometimes known as 'incidental direct effect', has arisen particularly in the context of Directive 83/189/EC.[69] Both the issue in general and the leading case, *Unilever Italia SpA v Central Food SpA*[70] are expertly analysed by Weatherill.

### S. Weatherill, 'Breach of Directives and Breach of Contract' (2001) 26 *European Law Review* 177, 177–81, 182–3

Directive 83/189, which is now replaced by Directive 98/34, requires Member States to notify draft technical regulations to the Commission and to refrain from applying the measures pending Commission examination of their compatibility with EC law. The duration of the initial 'standstill' obligation imposed on national authorities is defined in the Directive, and can be extended by the Commission . . . The Commission's inquiry into the compatibility of the draft national measures with Community law will typically focus on their compatibility with the Treaty provisions governing the free movement of goods. [The] Directive is in short an early warning system. It is designed to forestall the introduction of trade restrictions rather than having to tackle them ex post facto . . . [It] forms an important component of the Commission's emphasis on effective market management, which includes a quest for transparency in proposed national activity that may hinder the stabilisation of the process of European market-building . . .

Nothing in the notification Directive makes any provision for consequences that might flow before national courts from State failure to abide by the obligations of notification and suspension of draft measures. Beginning in the mid-1980s the Commission, eager to hold Member States to their promise to co-operate with it under Directive 83/189, consistently expressed the view that State default deprived the relevant measures of enforceability in proceedings before national courts involving third parties. This view was by no means uncontroversial, but it eventually received confirmation from the Court in its 1996 ruling in *CIA Security International SA v Signalson SA and Securitel Sprl*.[71] Breach of the procedural obligation to notify robs the [national] measure of enforceability in proceedings before national courts

---

69 The substance of this Directive is analysed in more detail in the chapter on the single market: see *EUL*, chapter 11. Some commentators consider 'incidental direct effect' also to have arisen in other contexts: see, e.g., Case C-129/94 *Ruiz Bernáldez* [1996] ECR I-1829. It is to be noted, however, that this case (like *Lemmens*, below n. 72, considered by Weatherill) was concerned with criminal proceedings and was not therefore directly a dispute between two private parties.

70 Case C-443/98 *Unilever Italia SpA v Central Food SpA* [2000] ECR I-7535.

71 Case C-194/94 *CIA Security International SA v Signalson SA* [1996] ECR I-2201.

involving third parties. Accordingly a trader was unable to rely on Belgian law to secure a court order against another trader dealing in products that were not in conformity with a Belgian technical regulation that had not been notified to the Commission in accordance with Directive 83/189 . . .

The most remarkable attempt to exploit the ruling in *CIA Security* arrived in *Johannes Martinus Lemmens*.[72] The Court ruled that a conviction for driving while drunk could not be challenged on the basis that the equipment for recording the level of intoxication was designed according to standards that had not been notified under Directive 83/189. This was a step too far. Although a general argument based on the '*effet utile*' of the notification Directive which had found favour with the Court in *CIA Security* might have encouraged the Court to uphold the offender's submission . . . one may assume that the Court was of the view that improving effective market management could not safely be regarded as a trump card such as to override other important interests in society, such as the effective suppression of drunken driving. The Court, provoked by the ingenious submissions presented to it in *Lemmens* to realise that caution was called for, took the opportunity to fix a limit to the scope afforded to private parties to escape obstructive national technical rules. In *Lemmens* it adopted a legal formula that is noticeably more precise than that found in *CIA Security*. The Court observed that failure to notify rendered regulations inapplicable only inasmuch as they hindered the use or marketing of non-conforming products. This pins down the key distinction between *CIA Security*, where the private individual was able to evade the obstructive but non-notified rules, and *Lemmens*, where he was not. *Unilever Italia SpA v Central Food SpA*,[73] the latest case in this series . . . adheres explicitly to the rationale made precise in *Lemmens* . . .

Unilever had supplied Central Food with a quantity of virgin olive oil. Central Food rejected the goods on the basis that they were not labelled in accordance with a relevant Italian law. This law had been notified to the Commission but Italy had not observed the Directive's 'standstill' obligation. Unilever submitted that the law should not be applied and sued Central Food for the price of the goods. The Court pointed out that were the Italian rules applied they would have the effect of hindering trade in a product not complying with the rules. The Court acknowledged that its own case law denies that a Directive can of itself impose obligations on an individual, but flatly stated that that case law does not apply where violation of the obligations arising under Directive 83/139 renders a national measure inapplicable . . . The Court asserted that the Directive 'does not in any way define the substantive scope of the legal rule on the basis of which the national court must decide the case before it. It creates neither rights nor obligations for individuals'.[74] So, it seems, Central Food would have to accept the goods.

The Court of Justice is correct in *Unilever* to point out that were the Italian rules applied they would have the effect of hindering trade in a product not complying with the rules. This repeats the core of the Court's reasoning in *Lemmens* which was evidently directed at identifying precisely when the Directive bites in national proceedings. The striking element of the ruling in *Unilever* is the Court's readiness to adopt this reasoning even in a case where the impact of the unenforceability of the State measure was felt directly in a contractual dispute between private parties. The Court makes light of this novelty. It observes that in *CIA Security* it has already held State default under the Directive to be capable of impinging on a dispute between private parties. It is submitted that this underplays the differences between the cases. There was no contract in *CIA Security*. In fact the Belgian law at stake was a form of quasi-regulatory power, placing in private hands the possibility of taking court action

---

72 Case C-226/97 *Lemmens* [1998] ECR I-3711.     73 Above n. 70.     74 *Ibid.* para. 51.

to secure the withdrawal from the market of a product not in conformity with the Belgian law (which had not been notified). In many States this type of power would be exercised by a public body. In Belgium it so happened that a private party performed this function. The Court's brisk assumption that the factual background of *CIA Security* was materially similar to that which arose in *Unilever* because both cases involved a pair of private litigants is not persuasive and it seems that the Court has embraced the application of the notification Directive in a contractual dispute between private parties without fully considering the size of the leap beyond existing case law which it is thereby making . . .

So what is the justification for extending the impact of State default under a Directive into the private sphere in this way? The Court states clearly that it is not overturning its longstanding refusal to accept that Directives are capable of horizontal direct effect. The Court insists that its decision in *Unilever* is not formally incompatible with the denial of horizontal direct effect to Directives. The Directives did not impose an obligation on Central Food. The contract imposed the obligation. At this level the Court is therefore perfectly justified in treating *Unilever* as disclosing a quite different issue from those at stake in key cases such as *Faccini Dori* . . . in which the Court was pressed to accept, but firmly denied, that an obligation drawn from a Directive could be directly imposed on a private party. The question, however, is the extent to which the Court's approach in *Unilever* has the effect of subverting its stated opposition to granting horizontal direct effect to Directives. Although one may accept the Court's analysis that the Directive did not impose an obligation directly on Central Food, nevertheless the injection into the proceedings of the consequences of Italy's failure to suspend its law as required by Directive entirely changed the circumstances in which the pattern of rights and obligations arising under the contract fell to be judged. Goods which could have been refused under domestic law now had to be accepted. This is not horizontal direct effect according to its classic meaning, but it is not so very far away in its effect on the legal position of private parties. An unimplemented Directive has exerted a powerful impact on a private party; it has altered Central Food's contractual position. It is troubling that the Court of Justice feels justified in loading immense constitutional significance on to such a narrow distinction.

Weatherill is right to identify the ways in which *Unilever* adds difficulty to the clarity and constitutional robustness of the Court of Justice's ruling in *Faccini Dori*. But, as he emphasises, while *Unilever* may make the position more subtle, it does not alter the fundamental principle in *Faccini Dori*: Directives cannot have full horizontal direct effect. It would, in particular, be a mistake to see *Unilever* and the other cases on Directive 83/189 as constituting any new legal principle on the basis of which private parties, by way of exception to the general rule laid down in *Faccini Dori*, may seek the horizontal enforcement of Directives in proceedings before national courts.[75] As Prechal has noted, the fact that Directives may on occasion entail horizontal 'side-effects' may have attracted renewed attention following the judgment in *Unilever*, but the phenomenon itself is by no means new, having first been discussed by legal commentators as long ago as 1979.[76]

75 For a contrary view, see D. Colgan, 'Triangular Situations: the Coup de Grâce for the Denial of Horizontal Effect of Community Directives' (2002) 8 *EPL* 545.

76 See S. Prechal, 'Case-note' (2005) 42 *CML Rev.* 1445, 1446, citing C. Timmermans, 'Directives: their Effect within the National Legal Systems' (1979) 16 *CML Rev.* 533.

### (iv)  Vertical direct effect and the extension of the state

While it remains the case that Directives cannot and do not have full horizontal direct effect, the Court of Justice has found a number of ways of limiting the consequences of this rule. Two such methods – the duty of consistent interpretation (or 'indirect effect') and state liability – will be considered in detail below. But there is one such method which needs to be considered here: namely, the expansive understanding that the Court has shown of the notion of the state. This is most clearly, and most famously, illustrated in the case of *Foster v British Gas*.[77] Ms Foster was forced to retire at sixty, whereas men could continue working until sixty-five. She and four other women invoked the Equal Treatment Directive against her former employer, British Gas. The latter was at the time a nationalised industry – the facts of this case took place before British Gas was privatised. At the material time the board members of British Gas were appointed by a minister in the UK government (the Secretary of State), who could also issue to the board various directions and instruments. In addition, the board was required to submit periodic reports to the Secretary of State.

### Case C-188/89 *Foster v British Gas* [1990] ECR I-3313

16. As the Court has consistently held . . . where the Community authorities have, by means of a Directive, placed Member States under a duty to adopt a certain course of action, the effectiveness of such a measure would be diminished if persons were prevented from relying upon it in proceedings before a court and national courts were prevented from taking it into consideration as an element of Community law. Consequently, a Member State which has not adopted the implementing measures required by the Directive within the prescribed period may not plead, as against individuals, its own failure to perform the obligations which the Directive entails. Thus, wherever the provisions of a Directive appear, as far as their subject-matter is concerned, to be unconditional and sufficiently precise, those provisions may, in the absence of implementing measures adopted within the prescribed period, be relied upon as against any national provision which is incompatible with the Directive or insofar as the provisions define rights which individuals are able to assert against the State.

17. The Court further held in . . . *Marshall* that where a person is able to rely on a Directive as against the State he may do so regardless of the capacity in which the latter is acting, whether as employer or as public authority. In either case it is necessary to prevent the State from taking advantage of its own failure to comply with Community law.

18. On the basis of those considerations, the Court has held in a series of cases that unconditional and sufficiently precise provisions of a Directive could be relied on against organisations or bodies which were subject to the authority or control of the State or had special powers beyond those which result from the normal rules applicable to relations between individuals.

19. The Court has accordingly held that provisions of a Directive could be relied on against tax authorities . . . local or regional authorities . . . constitutionally independent authorities responsible for the maintenance of public order and safety . . . and public authorities providing public health services . . .

---

77 Case C-188/89 *Foster v British Gas* [1990] ECR I-3313.

> 20. It follows . . . that a body, whatever its legal form, which has been made responsible, pursuant to a measure adopted by the State, for providing a public service under the control of the State and has for that purpose special powers beyond those which result from the normal rules applicable in relations between individuals, is included . . . among the bodies against which the provisions of a Directive capable of having direct effect may be relied upon.

It is to be noted that the Court's judgment in *Foster* contains no formal definition, as such, of 'the state', of 'organs of the state' or of 'emanations of the state'. Rather, the Court of Justice has preferred to leave it to national courts to determine, on a case-by-case basis, whether the general approach outlined in *Foster* applies or not.[78]

## 4. Duty of consistent interpretation ('indirect effect')

According direct effect to measures of Community law is far from the only way of enabling their enforcement by national courts and tribunals. It is important not to overlook this. The Court of Justice, of course, may enforce a provision of Community law whether it has direct effect or not: see the discussion of Articles 226 to 228 EC, above. In addition, national courts may enforce measures of EU law, even where they do not have direct effect, through two additional means: namely, through the duty of consistent interpretation (or 'indirect effect') and through the doctrine of state liability.

### (i) Establishment of the duty

The former was first developed in *Von Colson*.[79] Two female social workers, Von Colson and Kamann, sought employment in a German prison which was administered by the Land Nordrhein-Westfalen (i.e. by the regional government). The prison catered exclusively for male prisoners. Von Colson and Kamann were refused employment on the ground, it appears, of their sex. They sued in the German labour court relying on the German law which had purported to implement the terms of Directive 76/207/EC, the Equal Treatment Directive. Under that national law, the German court could order by way of remedy that Von Colson and Kamann be compensated only for such losses as they had suffered as a result of applying for the positions which had been denied them. No broader compensation or damages for discrimination were permitted. The national court referred to the Court of Justice the question of whether such a restriction in the availability of compensation was compatible with Community law. Von Colson and Kamann could not rely on the Directive itself in their

---

78 For cases in the English courts to have addressed this issue see, e.g., *Doughty v Rolls Royce* [1992] 1 CMLR 1045 and *NUT v St Mary's Church of England Junior School* [1997] 3 CMLR 630.

79 Case 14/83 *Von Colson and Kamann v Land Nordrhein-Westfalen* [1984] ECR 1891. See also Case 79/83 *Harz v Deutsche Tradax* [1984] ECR 1921, decided by the Court of Justice on the same day as *Von Colson*.

proceedings before the German labour court, as its terms were insufficiently clear and unconditional to satisfy the test for direct effect.[80] However, the Court of Justice ruled that this did not necessarily mean that the Directive could be of no assistance to the claimants.

### Case 14/83 *Von Colson and Kamann v Land Nordrhein-Westfalen* [1984] ECR 1891

16. It is . . . necessary to examine Directive 76/207 in order to determine whether it requires Member States to provide for specific legal consequences or sanctions in respect of a breach of the principle of equal treatment regarding access to employment.

17. The object of that Directive is to implement in the Member States the principle of equal treatment for men and women, in particular by giving male and female real equality of opportunity as regards access to employment. With that end in view, Article 2 defines the principle of equal treatment and its limits, while Article 3(1) sets out the scope of the principle specifically as regards access to employment. Article 3(2)(a) provides that Member States are to take the measures necessary to ensure that any laws, Regulations and administrative provisions contrary to the principle of equal treatment are abolished.

18. Article 6 requires Member States to introduce into their national legal systems such measures as are necessary to enable all persons who consider themselves wronged by discrimination 'to pursue their claims by judicial process'. It follows from the provision that Member States are required to adopt measures which are sufficiently effective to achieve the objective of the Directive and to ensure that those measures may in fact be relied on before the national courts by the persons concerned. Such measures may include, for example, provisions requiring the employer to offer a post to the candidate discriminated against or giving the candidate adequate financial compensation, backed up where necessary by a system of fines. However the Directive does not prescribe a specific sanction; it leaves Member States free to choose between the different solutions suitable for achieving its objective . . .

22. It is impossible to establish real equality of opportunity without an appropriate system of sanctions. That follows not only from the actual purpose of the Directive but more specifically from Article 6 thereof which, by granting applicants for a post who have been discriminated against recourse to the courts, acknowledges that those candidates have rights of which they may avail themselves before the courts.

23. Although . . . full implementation of the Directive does not require any specific form of sanction for unlawful discrimination, it does entail that that sanction be such as to guarantee real and effective judicial protection. Moreover it must also have a real deterrent effect on the employer. It follows that where a Member State chooses to penalize the breach of the prohibition of discrimination by the award of compensation, that compensation must in any event be adequate in relation to the damage sustained . . .

24. In consequence it appears that national provisions limiting the right to compensation of persons who have been discriminated against as regards access to employment to a purely nominal amount, such as, for example, the reimbursement of expenses incurred by them in submitting their application, would not satisfy the requirements of an effective transposition of the Directive . . .

26. . . . The Member States' obligation arising from a Directive to achieve the result envisaged by the Directive and their duty under Article [10 EC] to take all appropriate measures,

---

80 See para. 27 of the Court's judgment.

whether general or particular, to ensure the fulfilment of that obligation, is binding on all the authorities of Member States including, for matters within their jurisdiction, the courts. It follows that, in applying the national law and in particular the provisions of national law specifically introduced in order to implement Directive 76/207, national courts are required to interpret their national law in the light of the wording and purpose of the Directive . . .

28. . . . It is for the national court to interpret and apply the legislation adopted for the implementation of the Directive in conformity with the requirements of Community law, insofar as it is given a discretion to do so under national law.

The Court's reasoning in support of this conclusion is instructive and is, in some respects, reminiscent of its reasoning in *Van Gend en Loos*. In particular, the fact that the EC Treaty contains no explicit authority for the proposition that national courts are required to interpret and apply provisions of national law in conformity with Community law did not stop the Court of Justice making such a proposition. The Court explicitly relied on two sources of law in support of its establishment of the doctrine of indirect effect: Article 6 of Directive 76/207/EC and Article 10 EC. The latter, which contains the 'fidelity principle', was discussed in detail in chapter 5.[81] What should be noted here is the central role played in *Von Colson* by Article 6 of the Directive. Article 6 provides that 'Member States shall introduce into their national legal systems such measures as are necessary to enable all persons who consider themselves wronged by failure to apply to them the principle of equal treatment within the meaning of [this Directive] to pursue their claims by judicial process'. As Arnull has suggested, the 'seemingly innocuous terms' of this provision have been interpreted by the Court of Justice 'with great boldness and creativity and have provided the basis for a principle of effective judicial protection' which the Court has, in a series of cases, expanded into a general principle of EU law.[82] We shall return to this point below.

At first, it was possible to interpret the Court's ruling in *Von Colson* as being limited to the specific context of the interpretation by a national court of national law whose explicit purpose was the transposition of Community law (and in particular of Directives) into national law. However, any such limited interpretation was scotched by the Court in its ruling in *Marleasing*.[83] Marleasing brought an action against La Comercial in order to have the latter's articles of association declared void as having been created for the sole purpose of defrauding and evading creditors. The Spanish Civil Code stated that contracts made with 'lack of cause' were void. Directive 68/151/EC contained an exhaustive list of reasons under which companies could be declared void. Avoidance of creditors was not on that list.

---

81 See p. 193.
82 A. Arnull, *The European Union and its Court of Justice* (Oxford, Oxford University Press, 1999), 153.
83 Case C-106/89 *Marleasing SA v La Comercial Internacional de Alimentacion SA* [1990] ECR I-4135.

### Case C-106/89 *Marleasing SA v La Comercial Internacionale de Alimentacion SA* [1990] ECR I-4135

8. . . . as the Court pointed out in its judgment in *Von Colson* . . . the Member States' obligation arising from a Directive to achieve the result envisaged by the Directive and their duty under Article [10 EC] to take all appropriate measures, whether general or particular, to ensure the fulfilment of that obligation, is binding on all the authorities of Member States including, for matters within their jurisdiction, the courts. It follows that, in applying national law, whether the provisions in question were adopted before or after the Directive, the national court called upon to interpret it is required to do so, as far as possible, in the light of the wording and the purpose of the Directive in order to achieve the result pursued by the latter and thereby comply with the third paragraph of Article [249 EC].

#### (ii)  Extent of the duty

Notwithstanding the qualifying words 'as far as possible', *Marleasing* expanded the law of indirect effect in two ways: first, by giving it a more wide-ranging content, requiring *all* national legislation to be interpreted in the light of EC law, irrespective of whether it is implementing legislation or not and irrespective of whether it was enacted prior or subsequent to the provision of EC law in question; and secondly, by strengthening the national courts' interpretive duty. As Docksey and Fitzpatrick have observed:

> it is no longer sufficient for a national court to turn to Community law only if the national provision is 'ambiguous'. Its first priority must be to establish the meaning of the Community obligation and only then to conclude whether it is possible to achieve the necessary reconciliation with the national law.[84]

It is to be noted also that, unlike *Von Colson*, *Marleasing* concerned a dispute between two private parties. Directives may have horizontal indirect effect even while they may not have horizontal direct effect.

While *Marleasing* allows for Directives to be involved in the adjudication of private law and of relations between private parties, the judgment does not go so far as to insist that Directives should govern such relations in an exclusive manner. Instead, it creates a new form of what might be termed 'inter-legality', in which a mix of national and Community law regulates a dispute, with the Community law element opening up adjudication to wider norms and concerns whilst the national law element ensures that the local traditions and trajectories surrounding the dispute are not overlooked.

---

84 C. Docksey and B. Fitzpatrick, 'The Duty of National Courts to Interpret Provisions of National Law in accordance with Community Law' (1991) 20 *ILJ* 113, 119.

> ## M. Amstutz, 'In-between Worlds: *Marleasing* and the Emergence of Interlegality in Legal Reasoning' (2005) 11 *European Law Journal* 766, 781–2
>
> The internal culture-specific 'constraints' on national adjudication remain unaffected by the requirement for interpretation in conformity with Directives; local specificities of the various legal discourses are not pushed aside, say, by rational arguments that in the end are always weaker than the constraints of organically grown legal cultures. For ultimately it is the legal policies present in the private law of the individual Member States that act as 'regulators' in the process of incorporating Community private-law positions into the national legal discourses. They are ensuring that two separate sets of norms do not emerge in Member States' civil legal systems – one deriving from the historical trajectory of the State concerned, the other dictated by the Community. They alone can offer guarantees for a Community private law integrated into the national legal culture, and this fact immediately makes it clear how they ensure the evolutionary capacity of national law in the biotope of the European Community: by on the one hand – as artful combinations of 'flexible' and 'fixed' control parameters – blocking the propagation of the 'perturbations' from European law throughout the national private law, without on the other losing the national law's responsiveness to EC law.

Although some have argued that *Marleasing* creates a skilful new balance between Community and national law, others have suggested that, at its widest, it would come close to requiring national judges to read national law as giving effect to EC law, almost irrespective of the wording of the provision of national law. Such an interpretation would be tantamount to granting Directives horizontal effect in all circumstances except where there was no national legislation to interpret. Further, such a strong interpretive obligation would pose considerable problems for legal certainty.[85]

The risks posed to legal certainty have been recognised in two ways by the Court of Justice. First, the Court has held that indirect effect does not require *contra legem* interpretations of national law, that is to say, the strength of the interpretive obligation is not so strong as to require a provision of national law to be given a meaning that contradicts its 'ordinary' meaning.[86] Secondly, the Court has been particularly wary of using the doctrine in the field of criminal law, where legal certainty is particularly important for safeguarding the liberties of the individual. In *Arcaro*,[87] the Court stated that the:

> obligation of the national court to refer to the content of the Directive when interpreting the relevant rules of its own national law reaches a limit where such an interpretation leads to the imposition on an individual of an obligation laid down by a Directive which has not been transposed or, more

---

85 See G. de Búrca, 'Giving Effect to European Community Directives' (1992) 55 *MLR* 215.
86 Most notably, Case C-334/92 *Wagner-Miret v Fondo de Garantia Salarial* [1993] ECR I-6911.
87 Case C-168/95 *Arcaro* [1996] ECR I-4705.

especially, where it has the effect of determining or aggravating, on the basis of the Directive and in the absence of a law enacted for its implementation, the liability in criminal law of persons who act in contravention of that Directive's provisions.[88]

Notwithstanding these qualifications, the Court forcefully restated the importance of the duty of consistent interpretation in its judgment in *Pfeiffer*. The case arose out of a dispute concerning the correct interpretation of Article 6 of Directive 93/104/EC, which provides that 'Member States shall take the measures necessary to ensure that, in keeping with the need to protect the safety and health of workers . . . the average working time for each seven-day period, including overtime, does not exceed 48 hours'.

> ### Joined Cases C-397–403/01 *Pfeiffer and others v Deutsches Rotes Kreuz* [2004] ECR I-8835
>
> 114. The requirement for national law to be interpreted in conformity with Community law is inherent in the system of the Treaty, since it permits the national court, for the matters within its jurisdiction, to ensure the full effectiveness of Community law when it determines the dispute before it . . .
>
> 115. Although the principle that national law must be interpreted in conformity with Community law concerns chiefly domestic provisions enacted in order to implement the Directive in question, it does not entail an interpretation merely of those provisions but requires the national court to consider national law as a whole in order to assess to what extent it may be applied so as not to produce a result contrary to that sought by the Directive . . .
>
> 116. In that context, if the application of interpretative methods recognised by national law enables, in certain circumstances, a provision of domestic law to be construed in such a way as to avoid conflict with another rule of domestic law or the scope of that provision to be restricted to that end by applying it only insofar as it is compatible with the rule concerned, the national court is bound to use those methods in order to achieve the result sought by the Directive . . .
>
> 119. Accordingly, it must be concluded that, when hearing a case between individuals, a national court is required, when applying the provisions of domestic law adopted for the purpose of transposing obligations laid down by a Directive, to consider the whole body of rules of national law and to interpret them, so far as possible, in the light of the wording and purpose of the Directive in order to achieve an outcome consistent with the objective pursued by the Directive. In the main proceedings, the national court must thus do whatever lies within its jurisdiction to ensure that the maximum period of weekly working time, which is set at 48 hours by Article 6(2) of Directive 93/104, is not exceeded.

*Pfeiffer* is the latest of a series of cases to suggest that the duty is regarded by the Court of Justice as being as important as ever.[89] The judgment in *Pfeiffer* also illustrates

88 *Ibid.* para. 42.
89 Other cases to have pointed in the same direction, albeit not quite as clearly as *Pfeiffer*, perhaps, include Case C-185/97 *Coote v Granada Hospitality* [1998] ECR I-5199 and Cases C-240–244/98 *Océano Grupo*

the extent to which the Court has developed what it sees as the basis of the doctrine. Effective judicial protection may have *originated* with the terms of Article 6 of Directive 76/207/EC, but it is no longer so confined. On the contrary, it is now 'inherent within the system of the Treaty', we are told. A more resounding echo of the radical constitutionalism of *Van Gend en Loos* would be difficult to imagine. As such, *Pfeiffer* underscores what, for the Court, is the constitutional importance of the duty of consistent interpretation.

As well as being constitutionally important, the duty is also of enormous *practical* significance. Despite the greater academic attention that is generally given to direct effect, it is indirect effect that 'is currently the main form of ensuring effect of Directives whether correctly, incorrectly or not transposed at all'.[90] That said, however, its impact has not been uniform. Perhaps its most far-reaching application has been in the context of the Equal Treatment Directive (Directive 76/207) – the measure with which *Von Colson* was concerned, of course.[91]

### (iii)   When does the duty arise?

One matter on which the Court of Justice has not been clear is the question of when the duty of consistent interpretation arises. The Court gave a rather cryptic ruling in *Kolpinghuis Nijmegen*, one interpretation of which was that the duty may arise from the date a Directive is published.[92] On one reading, this would seem odd: we saw above that a Directive may have (vertical) direct effect only after the date has passed by which Member States are required to transpose it into national law. It might be thought desirable for the same to be true for indirect effect. The Court addressed this issue in *Centrosteel*, where it ruled that:

> Where it is seised of a dispute falling within the scope of the Directive *and arising from facts postdating the expiry of the period for transposing the Directive*, the national court, in applying provisions of domestic law or settled case law . . . must . . . interpret that law in such a way that it is applied in conformity with the aims of the Directive.[93]

---

*Editorial v Rocio Murciano Quintero* [2000] ECR I-4491. For analysis, see S. Drake, 'Twenty Years after *Von Colson*: the Impact of "Indirect Effect" on the Protection of the Individual's Community Rights' (2005) 30 *EL Rev.* 329.

90 G. Betlem, 'The Doctrine of Consistent Interpretation: Managing Legal Uncertainty' (2002) 22 *OJLS* 397, 399.

91 *Ibid.* 401. Drake similarly argues that this Directive has 'enjoyed a preferential and generous approach to enforcement by the Court of Justice'. See Drake, above n. 89, 335–6.

92 Case 80/86 *Kolpinghuis Nijmegen* [1987] ECR 3969. See Betlem, above n. 90, 403–5.

93 Case C-456/98 *Centrosteel v Adipol* [2000] ECR I-6007, para. 17, emphasis added. It is curious to note that the judgment has not removed all uncertainty, for the reason that the italicised words are not repeated in the operative part of the judgment. See Betlem, above n. 90.

However, in a recent Opinion in *Adeneler*,[94] Advocate General Kokott indicated a preference for the duty of interpretation to begin from the moment of publication. Her argument was that the direct effect of Directives derives from Article 249 EC, which binds Member States at the moment of transposition. By contrast, indirect effect, in her opinion, is based on Article 10 EC, which imposes a positive obligation on all national bodies, including courts, to take all appropriate measures to ensure compliance with Community law. This duty, she argues, arises in the context of Directives from the moment of their publication. Whether the Court of Justice will follow this reasoning remains to be seen.

### (iv)   Range of measures that national courts must take into account

A final issue to be addressed is the question of which instruments of European law national courts are required to consider. It might have been thought, in the wake of *Von Colson*, that national courts would be required to consider only such instruments of European law as may be directly enforceable in national courts (i.e., Treaty provisions, Regulations, Decisions and Directives). As early as 1989, however, the Court established that the duty of consistent interpretation was a free-standing principle in its own right. It may have been *developed* in the context of seeking ways to make Directives effective before national courts, but from as early as 1989 that has not been its sole purpose. In *Grimaldi*,[95] the Court of Justice held that national courts were to take account not just of 'hard law' but also of legally non-binding recommendations. More dramatic, perhaps, was the Court's ruling in *Pupino*, which controversially extended indirect effect to the third pillar of the European Union.[96] This judgment was discussed briefly in chapter 5,[97] where the Court's 'supranationalisation' of the third pillar was addressed, but its practical importance justifies its reiteration here. *Pupino* arose out of a dispute relating to the interpretation by an Italian criminal court of Council Framework Decision 2001/220/JHA, concerning the safeguards afforded to vulnerable victims when they appear as witnesses in criminal proceedings. The Framework Decision had been adopted under Article 34(2)(b) TEU, which provides that 'Framework Decisions shall be binding upon the Member States as to the result to be achieved but shall leave to the national authorities the choice of form and methods. They shall not entail direct effect'. Article 35 TEU provides that 'The Court of Justice shall have jurisdiction, subject to the conditions laid down in this Article, to give preliminary rulings on the validity and interpretation of Framework Decisions'.

---

94 Case C-212/04 *Adeneler v Ellinikos Organismos Galaktos*, Opinion of 27 October 2005, paras. 47–50.
95 Case 322/88 *Grimaldi v Fonds des Maladies Professionelles* [1989] ECR 4407.
96 Case C-105/03 *Pupino*, judgment of 16 June 2005.        97 See p. 194.

## Case C-105/03 *Pupino*, judgment of 16 June 2005

33. It should be noted at the outset that the wording of Article 34(2)(b) EU is very closely inspired by that of the third paragraph of Article 249 EC. Article 34(2)(b) EU confers a binding character on framework decisions in the sense that they 'bind' the Member States 'as to the result to be achieved but shall leave to the national authorities the choice of form and methods'.

34. The binding character of framework decisions, formulated in terms identical to those of the third paragraph of Article 249 EC, places on national authorities, and particularly national courts, an obligation to interpret national law in conformity with Community law.

35. The fact that, by virtue of Article 35 EU, the jurisdiction of the Court of Justice is less extensive under Title VI of the Treaty on European Union than it is under the EC Treaty, and the fact that there is no complete system of actions and procedures designed to ensure the legality of the acts of the institutions in the context of Title VI, does nothing to invalidate that conclusion.

36. Irrespective of the degree of integration envisaged by the Treaty of Amsterdam in the process of creating an ever closer union among the peoples of Europe within the meaning of the second paragraph of Article 1 EU, it is perfectly comprehensible that the authors of the Treaty on European Union should have considered it useful to make provision, in the context of Title VI of that Treaty, for recourse to legal instruments with effects similar to those provided for by the EC Treaty, in order to contribute effectively to the pursuit of the Union's objectives.

37. The importance of the Court's jurisdiction to give preliminary rulings under Article 35 EU is confirmed by the fact that, under Article 35(4), any Member State, whether or not it has made a declaration pursuant to Article 35(2), is entitled to submit statements of case or written observations to the Court in cases which arise under Article 35(1).

38. That jurisdiction would be deprived of most of its useful effect if individuals were not entitled to invoke framework decisions in order to obtain a conforming interpretation of national law before the courts of the Member States.

39. In support of their position, the Italian and UK Governments argue that, unlike the EC Treaty, the Treaty on European Union contains no obligation similar to that laid down in Article 10 EC, on which the case law of the Court of Justice partially relied in order to justify the obligation to interpret national law in conformity with Community law.

40. That argument must be rejected.

41. The second and third paragraphs of Article 1 of the Treaty on European Union provide that that Treaty marks a new stage in the process of creating an ever closer union among the peoples of Europe and that the task of the Union, which is founded on the European Communities, supplemented by the policies and forms of co-operation established by that Treaty, shall be to organise, in a manner demonstrating consistency and solidarity, relations between the Member States and between their peoples.

42. It would be difficult for the Union to carry out its task effectively if the principle of loyal co-operation, requiring in particular that Member States take all appropriate measures, whether general or particular, to ensure fulfilment of their obligations under European Union law, were not also binding in the area of police and judicial co-operation in criminal matters, which is moreover entirely based on co-operation between the Member States and the institutions . . .

43. In the light of all the above considerations, the Court concludes that the principle of interpretation in conformity with Community law is binding in relation to framework

decisions adopted in the context of Title VI of the Treaty on European Union. When applying national law, the national court that is called upon to interpret it must do so as far as possible in the light of the wording and purpose of the framework decision in order to attain the result which it pursues and thus comply with Article 34(2)(b) EU.

44. It should be noted, however, that the obligation on the national court to refer to the content of a framework decision when interpreting the relevant rules of its national law is limited by general principles of law, particularly those of legal certainty and non-retroactivity.

45. In particular, those principles prevent that obligation from leading to the criminal liability of persons who contravene the provisions of a framework decision from being determined or aggravated on the basis of such a decision alone, independently of an implementing law.

The significance of *Pupino* is twofold. First, there is no equivalent in the Treaty on European Union of Article 10 EC, the one provision of the EC Treaty on which the Court of Justice had expressly relied in support of its creation of the duty in *Von Colson*. As indicated in *Pfeiffer*, the duty is now seen by the Court as one which, as direct effect has always been, requires no textual justification. It is, rather, a duty that inheres 'within the system' of the Treaties. Secondly, the judgment is significant for its decoupling of indirect effect from direct effect. Article 34 TEU makes it plain that Framework Decisions under the third pillar cannot entail direct effect, yet *Pupino* shows that, despite this, they can have indirect effect.

Before we move on to state liability, there is one further point about the duty of consistent interpretation that needs to be made. We saw above that the Court of Justice developed the doctrine of direct effect in the face of objections from several Member States that it was through Articles 226 to 228 EC that Community law should be enforced, and not through the national courts. Such arguments were rehearsed, but dismissed, in *Van Gend en Loos*. By contrast, Articles 226 to 228 were not even mentioned in the Court's judgments in *Von Colson* and *Marleasing*. Thus, whereas the law of direct effect was developed notwithstanding the Court's recognition of the Article 226 alternative, the law of indirect effect was developed as if Article 226 simply did not exist. Nowhere in its consideration in these cases of the importance of 'effective judicial protection' is the judicial protection that may be afforded through Articles 226 to 228 EC even recognised, never mind evaluated. It is an extraordinary omission – and it is a point to which we shall have cause to return later in this chapter.

## 5. State liability

### (i) 'National procedural autonomy' and its (partial) erosion

The principle of national procedural autonomy governs the procedures that national courts must follow when enforcing rights conferred under Community law. The principle was laid down by the Court of Justice in a series of important constitutional cases in the 1970s. The principle provides that 'it is for the domestic legal system of each Member State to designate the courts having jurisdiction and to determine the procedural conditions governing actions at law intended to ensure the protection of the rights which citizens have from the direct effect of Community law'.[98] This principle was always subject to two conditions, known as the condition of equivalence and the condition of effectiveness. The first of these states that procedural circumstances required by national law may not be less favourable in the context of the enforcement of Community norms than they are with regard to norms deriving from domestic law. The second states that procedural circumstances required by national law will not be applicable if their effect is to make it impossible in practice to exercise the rights derived from Community law which national courts are obliged to enforce.

The principle of national procedural autonomy was never something about which the Court of Justice appeared to be entirely content. While a constitutional lawyer would recognise it as a cornerstone of federalism – clearly demarcating the boundaries of responsibilities as between the Court of Justice and the various national legal systems – the Court repeatedly urged the Community legislature to adopt legislation harmonising aspects of procedural law, such as causation, remoteness, interim relief, limitation periods, quantum in damages and so forth.[99] This invitation, however, was not taken up.

In the early 1990s, the Court of Justice decided two extraordinary cases which caused the principle of national procedural autonomy to be substantially rewritten. The first of these cases is *Factortame*[100] and the second is *Francovich*,[101] the case in which the doctrine of state liability was established. Before we can come to *Francovich*, we need more clearly to appreciate the importance of *Factortame*. This famous case concerned a challenge to the validity of certain provisions of the United Kingdom's Merchant Shipping Act 1988. Factortame argued that the provisions of the Act were contrary to Community law in that they effectively prevented several Spanish-owned fishing vessels from fishing against the United Kingdom's quota under the terms of the common fisheries policy, contrary to Article 43 EC. The national court referred the matter to the Court of Justice. In the meantime, Factortame sought an interim order from the national court, the effect of which would have been to order the UK government to suspend the operation of the relevant provisions of the Act. In proceedings before the English courts, the House of Lords found that the applicants would suffer irreparable damage if the interim relief which they sought was not granted. However, the House of Lords ruled that, notwithstanding this finding, English courts had no jurisdiction to grant such relief, as the remedy sought was barred by statute.[102] The

---

98 See Case 39/73 *Rewe-Zentralfinanz v Direktor der Landwirtschaftskammer Westfalen-Lippe* [1973] ECR 1039, para. 5. See also Case 45/76 *Comet BV v Produktschap voor Siergewassen* [1976] ECR 2043.

99 See A. Arnull, *The European Union and its Court of Justice* (Oxford, Oxford University Press, 1999) 151.

100 Case C-213/89 *R v Secretary of State for Transport ex parte Factortame Ltd* [1990] ECR I-2433.

101 Joined Cases C-6 and 9/90 *Francovich and Bonifaci v Italy* [1991] ECR I-5357.

102 The relevant provision was the Crown Proceedings Act 1947, s. 21(2), which provided that 'the court shall not in any civil proceedings grant any injunction or make any order against an officer of the Crown'.

House of Lords then referred to the Court of Justice the question of whether this rule of national law should, as a matter of Community law, be set aside in circumstances where (as here) its application would deprive a party of the enjoyment of rights which were derived from Community law. The Court of Justice had little difficulty in answering in the affirmative.

### Case C-213/89 *R v Secretary of State for Transport ex parte Factortame Ltd* [1990] ECR I-2433

18. [I]n Case 106/77 *Amministrazione delle finanze dello Stato v Simmenthal SpA* [1978] ECR 629 the Court held that directly applicable rules of Community law 'must be fully and uniformly applied in all the Member States from the date of their entry into force and for so long as they continue in force' (paragraph 14) and that 'in accordance with the principle of the precedence of Community law, the relationship between provisions of the Treaty and directly applicable measures of the institutions on the one hand and the national law of the Member States on the other is such that those provisions and measures . . . by their entry into force render automatically inapplicable any conflicting provision of . . . national law' (paragraph 17).

19. In accordance with the case law of the Court, it is for the national courts, in application of the principle of cooperation laid down in Article [10 EC], to ensure the legal protection which persons derive from the direct effect of provisions of Community law . . .

20. The Court has also held that any provision of a national legal system and any legislative, administrative or judicial practice which might impair the effectiveness of Community law by withholding from the national court having jurisdiction to apply such law the power to do everything necessary at the moment of its application to set aside national legislative provisions which might prevent, even temporarily, Community rules from having full force and effect are incompatible with those requirements, which are the very essence of Community law . . .

21. It must be added that the full effectiveness of Community law would be just as much impaired if a rule of national law could prevent a court seised of a dispute governed by Community law from granting interim relief in order to ensure the full effectiveness of the judgment to be given on the existence of the rights claimed under Community law. It follows that a court which in those circumstances would grant interim relief, if it were not for a rule of national law, is obliged to set aside that rule.

22. That interpretation is reinforced by the system established by Article [234 EC] whose effectiveness would be impaired if a national court, having stayed proceedings pending the reply by the Court of Justice to the question referred to it for a preliminary ruling, were not able to grant interim relief until it delivered its judgment following the reply given by the Court of Justice.

23. Consequently, the reply to the question raised should be that Community law must be interpreted as meaning that a national court which, in a case before it concerning Community law, considers that the sole obstacle which precludes it from granting interim relief is a rule of national law must set aside that rule.

In reaching this conclusion, the Court of Justice did not even mention its case law on national procedural autonomy. What is most extraordinary about this case, however, is not that the principle of national procedural autonomy was ignored: rather, it is what the case suggests about the relationship between the enforcement of Community law by the national courts and its enforcement (through Article 226 EC) by the Court of Justice. There is a sense in which the Court's entire decision in *Factortame* was unnecessary. Before the case was decided, the Commission had brought an action under Article 226 for a declaration that, by imposing the nationality requirements laid down in the Merchant Shipping Act 1988, the United Kingdom had failed to fulfil its obligations under, inter alia, Article 43 EC. While this Article 226 case had not, at the time *Factortame* was decided, been heard by the Court, at the same time as the Commission had lodged its Article 226 action with the Court's registry, it had also applied to the Court for an interim order requiring the United Kingdom to suspend the application of the nationality requirements of the 1988 Act. By an order of 10 October 1989, the President of the Court granted the application for an interim order,[103] following which the United Kingdom made an Order in Council amending the relevant provision of the Merchant Shipping Act 1988 with effect from 2 November 1989. All of this occurred well before *Factortame* was decided by the Court of Justice (judgment was handed down on 19 June 1990) or even before the case was argued before the Court (the oral hearing took place on 5 April 1990). Thus, Community law had already been enforced by the Court of Justice in *Commission v United Kingdom*. Why, then, did the Court decide that it needed to be enforced all over again, this time by the national courts? Why especially in a case of unusual political sensitivity raising the most acute constitutional questions in the country concerned?[104]

At the heart of *Factortame* lies the same principle that motivated the Court of Justice in *Von Colson*: namely, the notion of effective judicial protection. We saw above that the source of this principle, in *Von Colson*, was Article 6 of Directive 76/207/EC. That is a Directive of no direct application to the *Factortame* case, of course (*Factortame* being concerned with fishing quotas and nationality requirements, not with equal treatment in employment). This was no bar to the Court for the reason that, by the time *Factortame* was decided, the Court had taken the principle of effective judicial protection from the context of Directive 76/207 and had elevated it to a general principle of law, applicable across the range of Community law. This move occurred in *Johnston*, in which the Court stated that the 'requirement of judicial control stipulated by [Article 6 of Directive 76/207] reflects a general principle of law which underlies the constitutional traditions common to the Member States. That principle is also laid down in Articles 6 and 13 of the European Convention on Human Rights'.[105] The Court's expansion of and reliance on the principle of effective judicial protection as a general principle of law has not meant the complete demise of the earlier principle

---

103 See Case 246/89 R *Commission v United Kingdom* [1989] ECR 3125.

104 That is to say, questions pertaining to the 'sovereignty of Parliament'. See A. Tomkins, *Public Law* (Oxford, Oxford University Press, 2003) ch. 4.

105 Case 222/84 *Johnston v Chief Constable of the Royal Ulster Constabulary* [1986] ECR 1651, para. 18. See also Case 222/86 *UNECTEF v Heylens* [1987] ECR 4097. For discussion, see A. Arnull, *The European Union and its Court of Justice* (Oxford, Oxford University Press, 1999) ch. 5.

of national procedural autonomy, but it has required its considerable rethinking. The Court has, for example, felt it necessary in some cases to intervene to eliminate the adverse effects of limitation periods,[106] although in others it has not intervened.[107] Similarly with procedural rules that constrain parties in their ability to raise new points of law on appeal: sometimes the Court has intervened in the interests of effective judicial protection,[108] other times it has resisted intervention in the interests of national procedural autonomy.[109] The case law is sometimes difficult to reconcile and seems closely dependent upon the facts and the complex procedural rules at stake in each case. Fortunately, the details need not detain us here. What is important for present purposes is simply an understanding of the extent of and the reasons for the dilution of the principle of national procedural autonomy in *Factortame*. The reason why this is important lies in how the way was left open for the creation of state liability in *Francovich*.

## (ii)   Establishment of state liability

*Francovich* concerned Italy's persistent failure to implement the terms of Directive 80/987/EC, a measure that was intended to guarantee to employees a minimum level of protection under Community law in the event of the insolvency of their employer. The Directive provided in particular for specific guarantees of payment of unpaid wage claims. The Court of Justice found that the terms of this Directive were not in their entirety sufficiently precise and unconditional for it to be directly effective.

---

**Joined Cases C-6 and 9/90** *Francovich and Bonifaci v Italy* **[1991] ECR I-5357**

31. It should be borne in mind at the outset that the EEC Treaty has created its own legal system, which is integrated into the legal systems of the Member States and which their courts are bound to apply. The subjects of that legal system are not only the Member States but also their nationals. Just as it imposes burdens on individuals, Community law is also intended to give rise to rights which become part of their legal patrimony. Those rights arise not only where they are expressly granted by the Treaty but also by virtue of obligations which the Treaty imposes in a clearly defined manner both on individuals and on the Member States and the Community institutions [citing *Van Gend en Loos* and *Costa v ENEL*].

32. Furthermore, it has been consistently held that the national courts whose task it is to apply the provisions of Community law in areas within their jurisdiction must ensure that

---

106  Case C-208/90 *Emmott v Minister for Social Welfare* [1991] ECR I-4269.
107  Case C-338/91 *Steenhorst-Neerings v Bestuur van de Bedrijfsvereniging voor Detailhandel* [1993] ECR I-5475 and Case C-410/92 *Johnson v Chief Adjudication Officer* [1994] ECR I-5483.
108  Case C-312/93 *Peterbroeck v Belgium* [1995] ECR I-4599.
109  Joined Cases C-430–31/93 *Van Schijndel v Stichting Pensioenfonds voor Fysiotherapeuten* [1995] ECR I-4705.

those rules take full effect and must protect the rights which they confer on individuals [citing *Simmenthal*].

33. The full effectiveness of Community rules would be impaired and the protection of the rights which they grant would be weakened if individuals were unable to obtain redress when their rights are infringed by a breach of Community law for which a Member State can be held responsible.

34. The possibility of obtaining redress from the Member State is particularly indispensable where, as in this case, the full effectiveness of Community rules is subject to prior action on the part of the State and where, consequently, in the absence of such action, individuals cannot enforce before the national courts the rights conferred upon them by Community law.

35. It follows that the principle whereby a State must be liable for loss and damage caused to individuals as a result of breaches of Community law for which the State can be held responsible is inherent in the system of the Treaty.

36. A further basis for the obligation of Member States to make good such loss and damage is to be found in Article [10 EC], under which the Member States are required to take all appropriate measures, whether general or particular, to ensure fulfilment of their obligations under Community law. Among these is the obligation to nullify the unlawful consequences of a breach of Community law . . .

37. It follows from all the foregoing that it is a principle of Community law that the Member States are obliged to make good loss and damage caused to individuals by breaches of Community law for which they can be held responsible.

38. Although State liability is thus required by Community law, the conditions under which that liability gives rise to a right to reparation depend on the nature of the breach of Community law giving rise to the loss and damage.

39. Where, as in this case, a Member State fails to fulfil its obligation under the third paragraph of Article [249 EC] to take all the measures necessary to achieve the result prescribed by a Directive, the full effectiveness of that rule of Community law requires that there should be a right to reparation provided that three conditions are fulfilled.

40. The first of those conditions is that the result prescribed by the Directive should entail the grant of rights to individuals. The second condition is that it should be possible to identify the content of those rights on the basis of the provisions of the Directive. Finally, the third condition is the existence of a causal link between the breach of the State's obligation and the loss and damage suffered by the injured parties.

41. Those conditions are sufficient to give rise to a right on the part of individuals to obtain reparation, a right founded directly on Community law.

42. Subject to that reservation, it is on the basis of the rules of national law on liability that the State must make reparation for the consequences of the loss and damage caused. In the absence of Community legislation, it is for the internal legal order of each Member State to designate the competent courts and lay down the detailed procedural rules for legal proceedings intended fully to safeguard the rights which individuals derive from Community law . . .

43. Further, the substantive and procedural conditions for reparation of loss and damage laid down by the national law of the Member States must not be less favourable than those relating to similar domestic claims and must not be so framed as to make it virtually impossible or excessively difficult to obtain reparation.

Unlike in *Factortame*, in *Francovich* the Court of Justice did refer to its earlier case law on national procedural autonomy. Paragraphs 42–43 of the Court's judgment in

*Francovich* may be read as an attempt to accommodate the new remedy the Court established in that case within the framework of national procedural autonomy. The new remedy of state liability may be 'founded directly on Community law', but it is to be applied by national courts and 'on the basis of the rules of national law on liability'. What the Court's judgment in *Francovich* notably omits is any reference to Articles 226 to 228 EC. Yet, as in *Factortame*, so too in *Francovich* there had been an earlier action brought by the Commission under Article 226. It will be recalled that when *Factortame* was decided by the Court of Justice, the Article 226 case had not at that stage been heard, although interim relief had been granted. With regard to *Francovich*, however, the full Article 226 case had not only been heard, but decided, by the Court. Its judgment in *Commission v Italy* was handed down in February 1989: that in *Francovich* nearly three years later, in November 1991.[110] In *Commission v Italy*, the Commission ran three arguments: that Italy had violated Community law in failing to implement Articles 3 and 5 of Directive 80/987/EC (concerning the setting up of guarantee institutions), Article 7 (concerning the guarantee of payment of benefits due to employees under statutory social security schemes) and Article 8 (concerning the guarantee of payment of old-age benefits). The Court of Justice agreed fully with the Commission with regard to all three claims and granted a declaration accordingly. The Court justified its creation of state liability in *Francovich* on the basis, in part, that without it the 'full effectiveness' of Community law would be impaired. As with its decision in *Factortame*, so too here has the Court, it seems, lost sight of the fact that to be effective the enforcement of Community law does not have to come about at the instigation of private parties but could – *and moreover in both of these cases actually did* – come about at the instigation of the Commission, just as the EC Treaty had always imagined it would.

Be that as it may, *Francovich* is clearly a decision of major importance. As Craig has suggested, 'In any legal system there will always be certain judicial decisions which stand out as being of seminal importance for the development of a particular body of law. The judgment . . . in *Francovich* undoubtedly warrants inclusion in any list of such cases in the European Community.'[111] *Francovich* is right up there with cases such as *Van Gend en Loos* in its contribution to the judge-made constitutional law of the European Union. All the Court's favourite tricks are employed once again in *Francovich*: the references to individual rights (paragraph 33), the notion of constitutional principles being 'inherent in the system of the Treaty', rather than being spelled out in its text (paragraph 35) and the use of the fidelity clause in Article 10 EC (paragraph 36). *Francovich* is another example of the Court's (in)famous and by now well-established techniques of constitution-making. As such, the literature on *Francovich* is enormous. All the major legal periodicals in European law have carried numerous articles analysing various aspects of the case. Indeed, considerable

---

110 Case 22/87 *Commission v Italy* [1989] ECR 143.
111 P. Craig, '*Francovich*, Remedies and the Scope of Damages Liability' (1993) 109 *LQR* 595.

attention was paid to *Francovich* not only in the European law reviews, but also in legal journals that only relatively rarely devote detailed consideration to matters of EU law.[112] Almost all commentators broadly welcomed the Court's decision, most frequently on the ground of its alleged citizen empowerment.[113] The Court of Justice itself, of course, sought to rely on this notion in support of its decision (see paragraph 33 of its judgment). For all the urgency of the rhetoric, however, the reality of *Francovich* is that it has precious little to do with either citizen empowerment or the protection of individual rights. State liability is concerned principally with *sanction*, not rights.[114] As Caranta has observed, 'effective judicial protection' is used 'more to exact obedience from Member States than to protect citizens'.[115]

A notable feature of the Court's judgment in *Francovich* is the law-making it undertakes. Whatever may be argued about the rights and wrongs of *Francovich*, one thing is undeniable: this is a judgment in which much more than mere adjudication takes place. The Court of Justice engages in the course of its judgment in an undisguised exercise in legislation. The establishment in paragraph 40 of its judgment of the three criteria that must be satisfied before the state will be liable can be described as nothing else.

One of the most powerful critiques of *Francovich* was offered by Harlow. She objected to the ruling on two main grounds: first, that as a technique of administrative law enforcement, state liability was ill thought through and secondly, that it was constitutionally problematic. Harlow's first ground can be broken down into three arguments: that there was no thought given to the issue of who would actually benefit from the imposition of state liability, that no thought was given to the issue of how (or even whether) national courts would be able to apply the new remedy, and that in any case, the doctrine of state liability does not solve the problem it was designed to address.

### C. Harlow, ' *Francovich* and the Problem of the Disobedient State' (1996) 2 *European Law Journal* 199, 204–7

At the outset we should dismiss the vision of a squad of citizen policemen engaged in law enforcement. There are, of course, actions fought by individuals or groups of individuals. *Marshall* falls into this category; *Francovich* . . . and *Faccini Dori* may. In the field of

---

112 See, e.g., Craig, *ibid.* See also R. Caranta, 'Governmental Liability after *Francovich*' [1993] *CLJ* 272 and M. Ross, 'Beyond *Francovich*' (1993) 56 *MLR* 55.

113 See, e.g., E. Szyszczek, 'Making Europe More Relevant to its Citizens' (1996) 21 *EL Rev.* 35; J. Steiner, 'From Direct Effects to *Francovich*: More Effective Means of Enforcement of Community Law' (1993) 18 *EL Rev.* 3.

114 A point made powerfully by Harlow: see C. Harlow, *State Liability: Tort Law and Beyond* (Oxford, Oxford University Press, 2004) 56–8.

115 R. Caranta, 'Judicial Protection against Member States: a New *Jus Commune* Takes Shape' (1995) 32 *CML Rev.* 703, 710.

environmental law, we find a developing pattern derived from human rights law, where a number of specialist organisations (NGOs) dedicated to the enforcement of human rights through courts operate; in Article [141] cases, their place has largely been assumed by State-funded agencies. Whether or not these groups and agencies can be said to represent 'citizens' is a moot point but they do embody the private enforcement machinery to which the ECJ apparently aspires. This is not to imply, however, that the model of 'politics through law' espoused by the ECJ is best pursued through the medium of the action for damages . . . there is much to be said in favour of judicial review as the standard procedure, with annulment or declaratory orders as the standard remedy, in this type of citizen enforcement. In other areas, citizen enforcement is in any event a fantasy . . . [A]n overwhelming majority of actions against the Community are brought by corporations . . . [in litigation that] typically involves licences and other economic interests . . .

It is probable that French administrative law, in which liability undoubtedly contains an element of sanction, provided the pattern for the ECJ's sanctions theory of liability. Before this road was travelled however, attention should have been paid to the special position of the French Conseil d'Etat. The Conseil is something more than a court; it is both the conscience of the executive, responsible for determining equitable claims . . . and possesses regulatory functions in respect of administrative authorities. A partial explanation for its sanctions theory of administrative liability undoubtedly lies in its lack of mandatory remedies. Its legendary problem with delay and with implementation of judgments, especially by local authorities, are also relevant . . . Although the temptation to disregard the rulings of a court without mandatory remedies is fairly obvious, no widespread problem of disobedience has been identified [notwithstanding the fact that] at the time of *Francovich* . . . Italy certainly had a bad record for transposing Directives . . .

[A]t the end of the day, no system of State liability can be truly mandatory. The problem is circular: unenforceable or unenforced rulings bring the legal system into disrepute (the problem of *Francovich*); mandatory orders or punitive damages are substituted; the slur is greater from unenforced commands than from platonic, declaratory judgments; thus the problem simply escalates.

Harlow's constitutional ground of objection was not that the Court of Justice had no constitutional authority to rule as it did in *Francovich*. That, for her, should be treated as 'water under the bridge', as it should in respect of *Van Gend en Loos*.[116] Rather, her constitutional objection was to the Court's privileging the rule of law over political systems of accountability. 'The rule of law', she wrote, 'is a noble ideal but one which, unrestrained, is capable of degenerating into an ideology of law courts'.[117] It must also be remembered, she insisted, that 'its maturation in modern constitutional theory took place during a period before the flowering of fully representative democracy'. 'Unrestrained,' she warned, 'it is capable of blocking democratic evolution'.[118] What Harlow is concerned with in these remarks is the sense that pervades both the *Francovich* judgment itself and the bulk of legal commentary on it, that no constitutional problem is solved until it is judicially solved and that there is no constitutional problem that cannot be satisfactorily solved by the judiciary. If and

---

116 C. Harlow, '*Francovich* and the Problem of the Disobedient State' (1996) 2 *ELJ* 199, 201.
117 *Ibid.* 222.        118 *Ibid.* 223.

insofar as there was a 'problem of the disobedient state' prior to *Francovich*, it was not a problem, in Harlow's view, that ought to have been addressed judicially. It was a problem of political enforcement that should have been addressed politically. If a state persistently refuses to transpose Directives into its national law, there is likely to be a reason for that. It may be due to administrative turmoil within the state, or it may be because there are political or legal problems in tying the 'result to be achieved' by the Directive into the fabric of national law. Whatever the difficulties may be, they call for discussion and deliberation – and perhaps also bargaining and negotiation – at the political level. It is through such political means that the European Union may further its 'democratic evolution'. *Francovich* short-circuits this route, allowing legal remedies to replace what the European Union actually needs: namely, open political discussion about the tensions which exist between European law and national law.

It is unsurprising, perhaps, that Member State governments have not exactly rushed to welcome the principle of state liability. Indeed, shortly before *Francovich* was decided the Member States considered, in the IGC that led to Maastricht, whether to write into the Treaties some notion of state liability – it was at Maastricht, it will be recalled, where Article 228 EC was redrafted so as to introduce into Community law the new remedy of a penalty payment. While the Member States agreed to the new Article 228, however, they drew the line at the notion that national courts should be able to award damages against the state for breach of Community law.[119]

---

### J. Tallberg, 'Supranational Influence in EU Enforcement: the ECJ and the Principle of State Liability' (2000) 7 *Journal of European Public Policy* 104, 115–16

When the ECJ introduced the principle of State liability, it was the obligation of Member States to ensure that individuals actually could rely on this remedy. If the substantive and procedural conditions for State liability laid down in national law were sufficient to satisfy the ECJ's standards, these were to be relied on. If not, national legal systems would have to be adjusted; either through governments legislating to the effect that appropriate remedies were created, or through courts recognising a new cause of action or adjusting existing remedies.

Most national legal systems did not, however, provide a corresponding remedy against the State in matters of national law, and where they did not, this seldom permitted actions against the legislative and judicial branches of government. *Francovich* . . . therefore introduced something which was partially or completely new, and which required that appropriate remedies be created through judicial or legislative action. Yet, by 1997, no Member State had taken legislative action to accommodate the development in Community law. A Swedish

---

119 See J. Tallberg, 'Supranational Influence in EU Enforcement: the ECJ and the Principle of State Liability' (2000) 7 *JEPP* 104, 114–15. Harlow has suggested that 'the case for State liability is now greatly reduced by the introduction of the "penalty payment" procedure' in Article 228 EC: see C. Harlow, *State Liability* (Oxford, Oxford University Press, 2004) 63.

legal investigator, who has mapped the reception of the new principle in co-operation with the Ministries of Justice in the other Member States, describes the prevailing approach in most governments as being the ostrich strategy of burying the head in the sand. Rather than duly initiating the legislative measures required to give full effect to the EC rules on State liability, national governments have confidently refrained from any action and accepted the often less-than-optimal fit resulting from the existing order or the modifications that national courts may undertake . . .

It is difficult to assess the extent to which national procedures have been sufficiently adjusted, de facto or de jure. But while certain legal systems, such as the French and the Dutch, have had few difficulties accommodating the new European rules on State liability, others, such as the Italian, are known to have deterred litigants through procedural incertitude, that is, by not clearly specifying what legal procedures to use . . .

Of the cases that indeed have been decided by national courts, the dominant, but by no means exclusive, picture is one of hesitancy or even reluctance. In relatively few cases have the claimants actually been awarded compensation; more often, their claims have been dismissed on procedural or substantive grounds.

It is to be noted that among those claimants whose eventual claims for compensation have been dismissed is Mr Francovich himself. Even in the case in which the principle of state liability was established, was the state, in the end, found not to be liable![120]

### (iii)  Conditions for, and expansion of, state liability

As we saw above, the principle of state liability was introduced into Community law as a means of enhancing the ability of national courts to enforce Directives without giving them full direct effect. It was not long, however, before the principle of state liability was extended beyond this context, such that the state could be held liable by national courts for a variety of different types of breach of Community law, breaches that did not necessarily have to relate to Directives at all. The leading authority is now the Court of Justice's judgment in Joined Cases *Brasserie du Pêcheur* and *Factortame III*. Brasserie du Pêcheur, a French firm, had been forced to discontinue exports of beer to Germany in 1981. This was due to a German 'purity law' which did not allow beers lawfully marketed according to different rules in other Member States to enjoy the designation 'Bier' and did not allow the marketing of beer which contained additives. This law was declared illegal in 1987 on the ground that it contravened Article 28 EC, the provision outlawing quantitative restrictions or measures having equivalent effect on the free movement of goods.[121] Brasserie du Pêcheur sought compensation of DM1,800,000 for the loss of sales between 1981 and 1987. The facts of *Factortame* were given above.[122] After the system of

---

120  Case C-479/93 *Francovich v Italy (Francovich II)* [1996] ECR I-3843.

121  This rule is a key component of the free movement of goods and is, as such, considered in detail in *EUL*, chapter 15.

122  See p. 391.

registration contained in the United Kingdom's Merchant Shipping Act 1988 had been declared illegal, the applicants claimed for damages against the British government.

> ### Joined Cases C-46 and 48/93 *Brasserie du Pêcheur v Germany* and *R v Secretary of State for Transport ex parte Factortame (No. 3)* [1996] ECR I-1029
>
> 31. . . . the Court held in *Francovich* that the principle of State liability for loss and damage caused to individuals as a result of breaches of Community law for which it can be held responsible is inherent in the system of the Treaty.
>
> 32. It follows that that principle holds good for any case in which a Member State breaches Community law, whatever be the organ of the State whose act or omission was responsible for the breach . . .
>
> 35. The fact that, according to national rules, the breach complained of is attributable to the legislature cannot affect the requirements inherent in the protection of the rights of individuals who rely on Community law and, in this instance, the right to obtain redress in the national courts for damage caused by that breach . . .
>
> 38. Although Community law imposes State liability, the conditions under which that liability gives rise to a right to reparation depend on the nature of the breach of Community law giving rise to the loss and damage . . .
>
> 39. In order to determine those conditions, account should first be taken of the principles inherent in the Community legal order which form the basis for State liability, namely first, the full effectiveness of Community rules and the effective protection of the rights which they confer and, second, the obligation to cooperate imposed on Member States by Article [10 EC] . . .
>
> 40. In addition . . . it is pertinent to refer to the Court's case law on non-contractual liability on the part of the Community.[123]
>
> 41. First . . . Article [288 EC] refers as regards the non-contractual liability of the Community, to the general principles common to the laws of the Member States, from which, in the absence of written rules, the Court also draws inspiration in other areas of Community law.
>
> 42. Second, the conditions under which the State may incur liability for damage caused to individuals by a breach of Community law cannot, in the absence of particular justification, differ from those governing the liability of the Community in like circumstances. The protection of the rights which individuals derive from Community law cannot vary depending on whether a national authority or a Community authority is responsible for the damage.
>
> 43. The system of rules which the Court has worked out with regard to Article [288 EC], particularly in relation to liability for legislative measures, takes into account, inter alia, the complexity of the situations to be regulated, difficulties in the application or interpretation of the texts and, more particularly, the margin of discretion available to the author of the act in question.
>
> 44. Thus, in developing its case law on the non-contractual liability of the Community, in particular as regards legislative measures involving choices of economic policy, the Court has had regard to the wide discretion available to the institutions in implementing Community policies.

---

123 Non-contractual liability on the part of the EC is governed by Article 288(2) [formerly 215(2)] EC. The law relating to Article 288(2) EC is considered in chapter 10: see p. 457. It will be seen that one of the features of the Court's judgment in *Brasserie du Pêcheur/Factortame III* was its attempt to harmonise the conditions governing state liability with those governing the EC's liability.

45. The strict approach taken towards the liability of the Community in the exercise of its legislative activities is due to two considerations. First, even where the legality of measures is subject to judicial review, exercise of the legislative function must not be hindered by the prospect of actions for damages whenever the general interest of the Community requires legislative measures to be adopted which may adversely affect individual interests. Second, in a legislative context characterised by the exercise of a wide discretion, which is essential for implementing a Community policy, the Community cannot incur liability unless the institution concerned has manifestly and gravely disregarded the limits on the exercise of its powers . . .

46. That said, the national legislature – like the Community institutions – does not systematically have a wide discretion when it acts in a field governed by Community law. Community law may impose upon it obligations to achieve a particular result or obligations to act or refrain from acting which reduce its margin of discretion, sometimes to a considerable degree. This is so, for instance, where, as in the circumstances to which the judgment in *Francovich* relates, Article [249 EC] places the Member State under an obligation to take, within a given period, all the measures needed in order to achieve the result required by a Directive. In such a case, the fact that it is for the national legislature to take the necessary measures has no bearing on the Member State's liability for failing to transpose the Directive.

47. In contrast, where a Member State acts in a field where it has a wide discretion, comparable to that of the Community institutions in implementing Community policies, the conditions under which it may incur liability must, in principle, be the same as those under which the Community institutions incur liability in a comparable situation.

48. In the case which gave rise to the reference in Case C-46/93, the German legislature had legislated in the field of foodstuffs, specifically beer. In the absence of Community harmonization, the national legislature had a wide discretion in that sphere in laying down rules on the quality of beer put on the market.

49. As regards the facts of Case C-48/93, the United Kingdom legislature also had a wide discretion. The legislation at issue was concerned, first, with the registration of vessels, a field which, in view of the state of development of Community law, falls within the jurisdiction of the Member States and, secondly, with regulating fishing, a sector in which implementation of the common fisheries policy leaves a margin of discretion to the Member States.

50. Consequently, in each case the German and United Kingdom legislatures were faced with situations involving choices comparable to those made by the Community institutions when they adopt legislative measures pursuant to a Community policy.

51. In such circumstances, Community law confers a right to reparation where three conditions are met: the rule of law infringed must be intended to confer rights on individuals; the breach must be sufficiently serious; and there must be a direct causal link between the breach of the obligation resting on the State and the damage sustained by the injured parties.

52. Firstly, those conditions satisfy the requirements of the full effectiveness of the rules of Community law and of the effective protection of the rights which those rules confer.

53. Secondly, those conditions correspond in substance to those defined by the Court in relation to Article [288] in its case law on liability of the Community for damage caused to individuals by unlawful legislative measures adopted by its institutions.

54. The first condition is manifestly satisfied in the case of Article [28] of the Treaty, the relevant provision in Case C-46/93, and in the case of Article [43], the relevant provision in Case C-48/93 . . .

55. As to the second condition, as regards both Community liability under Article [288] and Member State liability for breaches of Community law, the decisive test for finding that a breach of Community law is sufficiently serious is whether the Member State or,

the Community institution concerned manifestly and gravely disregarded the limits of its discretion.

56. The factors which the competent court may take into consideration include the clarity and precision of the rule breached, the measure of discretion left by that rule to the national or Community authorities, whether the infringement and the damage caused was intentional or involuntary, whether any error of law was excusable or inexcusable, the fact that the position taken by a Community institution may have contributed towards the omission, and the adoption or retention of national measures or practices contrary to Community law.

57. On any view, a breach of Community law will clearly be sufficiently serious if it has persisted despite a judgment finding the infringement in question to be established, or a preliminary ruling or settled case law of the Court on the matter from which it is clear that the conduct in question constituted an infringement . . .

65. As for the third condition, it is for the national courts to determine whether there is a direct causal link between the breach of the obligation borne by the State and the damage sustained by the injured parties.

66. The aforementioned three conditions are necessary and sufficient to found a right in individuals to obtain redress, although this does not mean that the State cannot incur liability under less strict conditions on the basis of national law.

67. As appears from . . . *Francovich*, subject to the right to reparation which flows directly from Community law where the conditions referred to in the preceding paragraph are satisfied, the State must make reparation for the consequences of the loss and damage caused in accordance with the domestic rules on liability, provided that the conditions for reparation of loss and damage laid down by national law must not be less favourable than those relating to similar domestic claims and must not be such as in practice to make it impossible or excessively difficult to obtain reparation . . .

82. Reparation for loss or damage caused to individuals as a result of breaches of Community law must be commensurate with the loss or damage sustained so as to ensure the effective protection for their rights.

83. In the absence of relevant Community provisions, it is for the domestic legal system of each Member State to set the criteria for determining the extent of reparation. However, those criteria must not be less favourable than those applying to similar claims based on domestic law and must not be such as in practice to make it impossible or excessively difficult to obtain reparation.

At the heart of the Court's judgment in *Brasserie du Pêcheur/Factortame III* lay the ruling that Member States will be liable in damages for breaches of Community law (and not only for failures to transpose Directives) wherever three conditions are met: where the rule of law infringed is 'intended to confer rights on individuals', where the breach is 'sufficiently serious', and where there is a 'direct causal link' between the breach of the obligation resting on the state and the damage sustained by the injured parties.[124] What the case also established is that such liability may arise even in the context of national legislation. Both *Brasserie du Pêcheur* and *Factortame III*

---

124 These criteria are similar, but not absolutely identical, to those set out in *Francovich*. The Court of Justice subsequently made it clear that there is not intended to be any material difference between the two sets of criteria: see Joined Cases C-178–9 and 188–90/94 *Dillenkofer and others v Germany* [1996] ECR I-4845, paras. 21–8.

concerned challenges to the compatibility of national legislation with superior norms of Community law. The Court of Justice ruled that state liability may arise in this context where the state concerned has 'manifestly and gravely disregarded the limits on its discretion' (paragraph 55).[125] It is to be noted that, as in *Francovich*, the Court continued to state that the determination, in any particular case, of whether the conditions for liability are met is a matter principally for the national courts.[126] When *Brasserie du Pêcheur* returned to the German courts the Bundesgerichtshof ruled that, on the facts, the claimants in that case were not entitled to reparation.[127] After many years of struggle the claimants in *Factortame* were more fortunate.[128]

We have seen that state liability will arise only where there is a 'sufficiently serious' breach of Community law. The Court of Justice has ruled that not every breach of Community law will be sufficiently serious to give rise to liability. The latitude of the Court's approach is illustrated by the following case, in which the Court ruled that the UK government had misconstrued a Directive and had, thereby, failed to transpose it adequately into national law. The Court went on to hold, however, that as the United Kingdom's interpretation was both plausible and in good faith, its breach of Community law was not sufficiently serious to merit liability.

### Case C-392/93 *R v HM Treasury ex parte British Telecommunications plc* [1996] ECR I-1631

39. . . . Community law confers a right to reparation where three conditions are met: the rule of law infringed must be intended to confer rights on individuals; the breach must be sufficiently serious; and there must be a direct causal link between the breach of the obligation resting on the State and the damage sustained by the injured parties.

40. Those same conditions must be applicable to the situation . . . in which a Member State incorrectly transposes a Community Directive into national law. A restrictive approach to State liability is justified in such a situation, for the reasons already given by the Court to justify the strict approach to non-contractual liability of Community institutions or Member States when exercising legislative functions in areas covered by Community law where the institution or State has a wide discretion: in particular, the concern to ensure that the exercise of legislative functions is not hindered by the prospect of actions for damages whenever the general interest requires the institutions or Member States to adopt measures which may adversely affect individual interests . . .

---

125 This test is derived from the law relating to the liability of the EC under Article 288(2) EC.

126 See, to similar effect, Case C-392/93 *R v HM Treasury ex parte British Telecommunications plc* [1996] ECR I-1631, Case C-5/94 *R v Ministry of Agriculture, Fisheries and Food ex parte Hedley Lomas* [1996] ECR I-2553 and Joined Cases C-283, 291 and 292/94 *Denkavit International and others v Bundesamt für Finanzen* [1996] ECR I-5063.

127 The Bundesgerichtshof ruled that, as to the second and third conditions set out by the Court of Justice, no sufficiently serious breach had been established which could be the direct cause of the damage claimed. See E. Deards, '*Brasserie du Pêcheur*: Snatching Defeat from the Jaws of Victory' (1997) 22 *EL Rev.* 620.

128 See the judgment of the House of Lords in *R v Secretary of State for Transport ex parte Factortame (No. 5)* [1999] 3 CMLR 597.

41. Whilst it is in principle for the national courts to verify whether or not the conditions governing State liability for a breach of Community law are fulfilled, in the present case the Court has all the necessary information to assess whether the facts amount to a sufficiently serious breach of Community law.

42. According to the case law of the Court, a breach is sufficiently serious where, in the exercise of its legislative powers, an institution or a Member State has manifestly and gravely disregarded the limits on the exercise of its powers . . . Factors which the competent court may take into consideration include the clarity and precision of the rule breached . . .

43. In the present case, [the relevant provision of the Directive concerned] is imprecisely worded and was reasonably capable of bearing, as well as the construction applied to it by the Court in this judgment, the interpretation given to it by the United Kingdom in good faith and on the basis of arguments which are not entirely devoid of substance . . . That interpretation, which was also shared by other Member States, was not manifestly contrary to the wording of the Directive or to the objective pursued by it.

Since *Brasserie du Pêcheur/Factortame III*, the most significant expansion of state liability occurred in *Köbler v Austria*, in which the Court of Justice controversially ruled that the state could, under certain circumstances, be liable in damages in respect of rulings by national courts that were in breach of Community law. Köbler was a professor employed in an Austrian university. Part of his salary was based on length of service, but periods of employment in universities in Member States other than Austria did not count towards this aspect of his salary. When the Austrian court held this to be compatible with Community law,[129] Köbler brought an action in damages, arguing that the state was liable in respect of the court's ruling.

### Case C-224/01 *Köbler v Austria* [2003] ECR I-10239

33. In the light of the essential role played by the judiciary in the protection of the rights derived by individuals from Community rules, the full effectiveness of those rules would be called in question and the protection of those rights would be weakened if individuals were precluded from being able, under certain conditions, to obtain reparation when their rights are affected by an infringement of Community law attributable to a decision of a court of a Member State adjudicating at last instance.

34. It must be stressed, in that context, that a court adjudicating at last instance is by definition the last judicial body before which individuals may assert the rights conferred on them by Community law. Since an infringement of those rights by a final decision of such a court cannot thereafter normally be corrected, individuals cannot be deprived of the possibility of rendering the State liable in order in that way to obtain legal protection of their rights.

35. Moreover, it is, in particular, in order to prevent rights conferred on individuals by Community law from being infringed that under the third paragraph of Article 234 EC a court against whose decisions there is no judicial remedy under national law is required to make a reference to the Court of Justice.

---

129 In so ruling, the Austrian court sought to rely on the Court of Justice's ruling in Case C-15/96 *Schöning-Kougebetopoulou* [1998] ECR I-47.

36. Consequently, it follows from the requirements inherent in the protection of the rights of individuals relying on Community law that they must have the possibility of obtaining redress in the national courts for the damage caused by the infringement of those rights owing to a decision of a court adjudicating at last instance . . .

37. Certain of the governments which submitted observations in these proceedings claimed that the principle of State liability for damage caused to individuals by infringements of Community law could not be applied to decisions of a national court adjudicating at last instance. In that connection arguments were put forward based, in particular, on the principle of legal certainty and, more specifically, the principle of *res judicata*, the independence and authority of the judiciary and the absence of a court competent to determine disputes relating to State liability for such decisions.

38. In that regard the importance of the principle of *res judicata* cannot be disputed . . . In order to ensure both stability of the law and legal relations and the sound administration of justice, it is important that judicial decisions which have become definitive after all rights of appeal have been exhausted or after expiry of the time limits provided for in that connection can no longer be called in question.

39. However, it should be borne in mind that recognition of the principle of State liability for a decision of a court adjudicating at last instance does not in itself have the consequence of calling in question that decision as *res judicata*. Proceedings seeking to render the State liable do not have the same purpose and do not necessarily involve the same parties as the proceedings resulting in the decision which has acquired the status of *res judicata*. The applicant in an action to establish the liability of the State will, if successful, secure an order against it for reparation of the damage incurred but not necessarily a declaration invalidating the status of *res judicata* of the judicial decision which was responsible for the damage. In any event, the principle of State liability inherent in the Community legal order requires such reparation, but not revision of the judicial decision which was responsible for the damage.

40. It follows that the principle of *res judicata* does not preclude recognition of the principle of State liability for the decision of a court adjudicating at last instance.

41. Nor can the arguments based on the independence and authority of the judiciary be upheld.

42. As to the independence of the judiciary, the principle of liability in question concerns not the personal liability of the judge but that of the State. The possibility that under certain conditions the State may be rendered liable for judicial decisions contrary to Community law does not appear to entail any particular risk that the independence of a court adjudicating at last instance will be called in question.

43. As to the argument based on the risk of a diminution of the authority of a court adjudicating at last instance owing to the fact that its final decisions could by implication be called in question in proceedings in which the State may be rendered liable for such decisions, the existence of a right of action that affords, under certain conditions, reparation of the injurious effects of an erroneous judicial decision could also be regarded as enhancing the quality of a legal system and thus in the long run the authority of the judiciary.

44. Several governments also argued that application of the principle of State liability to decisions of a national court adjudicating at last instance was precluded by the difficulty of designating a court competent to determine disputes concerning the reparation of damage resulting from such decisions.

45. In that connection, given that, for reasons essentially connected with the need to secure for individuals protection of the rights conferred on them by Community rules, the principle of State liability inherent in the Community legal order must apply in regard to decisions

of a national court adjudicating at last instance, it is for the Member States to enable those affected to rely on that principle by affording them an appropriate right of action. Application of that principle cannot be compromised by the absence of a competent court . . .

51. As to the conditions to be satisfied for a Member State to be required to make reparation for loss and damage caused to individuals as a result of breaches of Community law for which the State is responsible, the Court has held that these are threefold: the rule of law infringed must be intended to confer rights on individuals; the breach must be sufficiently serious; and there must be a direct causal link between the breach of the obligation incumbent on the State and the loss or damage sustained by the injured parties . . .

52. State liability for loss or damage caused by a decision of a national court adjudicating at last instance which infringes a rule of Community law is governed by the same conditions.

53. With regard more particularly to the second of those conditions and its application with a view to establishing possible State liability owing to a decision of a national court adjudicating at last instance, regard must be had to the specific nature of the judicial function and to the legitimate requirements of legal certainty, as the Member States which submitted observations in this case have also contended. State liability for an infringement of Community law by a decision of a national court adjudicating at last instance can be incurred only in the exceptional case where the court has manifestly infringed the applicable law.

54. In order to determine whether that condition is satisfied, the national court hearing a claim for reparation must take account of all the factors which characterise the situation put before it.

55. Those factors include, in particular, the degree of clarity and precision of the rule infringed, whether the infringement was intentional, whether the error of law was excusable or inexcusable, the position taken, where applicable, by a Community institution and non-compliance by the court in question with its obligation to make a reference for a preliminary ruling under the third paragraph of Article 234 EC.

56. In any event, an infringement of Community law will be sufficiently serious where the decision concerned was made in manifest breach of the case law of the Court in the matter.

The Court of Justice went on to rule that, on the facts of the case, the breach of Community law committed by the Austrian court was not sufficiently serious to merit reparation under the principle of state liability. Nonetheless, the decision is an important one, which, if it is followed, is likely to have a number of consequences for domestic legal systems.[130]

### H. Scott and N. Barber, 'State Liability under *Francovich* for Decisions of National Courts' (2004) 120 *Law Quarterly Review* 403, 404–5

The extension of *Francovich* liability to courts of final decision has profound implications for the domestic legal hierarchy. After *Köbler* the English High Court could find itself compelled to pass judgment on a decision of the English House of Lords. A litigant disappointed by the House of Lords' decision could start a fresh action against the United Kingdom. The High Court, a few months later, would then be called on to assess whether the House of Lords

---

130 *Köbler* may also have consequences for the relationship between national courts and the Court of Justice under Article 234 EC: see, on this issue, P. Wattel, '*Köbler*, *CILFIT* and *Welthgrove*: We Can't Go on Meeting Like This' (2004) 41 *CML Rev.* 177.

had made an error of law that was sufficiently serious to warrant damages. The High Court would, almost certainly, refer the question to the ECJ under Article 234 if it thought there was any doubt as to the correctness of the Lords' ruling. In response to such a reference the ECJ would give a ruling on the content of European law . . .

This prospect raises a number of problems for domestic legal systems. First, and most superficially, it reduces legal certainty. This is not, as some in *Köbler* tried to argue, because it allows the reopening of concluded cases. Once the State's highest court has ruled, the judgment is definitive between the parties and cannot be challenged; the principle of *res judicata* is not affected. The *Francovich* action is a separate legal right and is directed against the State; a body which, ordinarily, would not have been a party to the original action. However, *Köbler* does have the effect of allowing litigants a second chance to raise the legal question apparently resolved in the primary action: frustrated in the House of Lords, the litigant could re-start the process through *Francovich* in the High Court. Secondly, the decision upsets the domestic legal hierarchy. The High Court would be obliged to question the correctness of a decision of the House of Lords made a few months earlier: it would have to decide whether there was a sufficient chance of error to warrant a reference to the ECJ, and, when this ruling was returned, how severe the error had been. Further problems might arise as this secondary action progressed up the legal order, perhaps ending with one group of Law Lords ruling on the judgment of their colleagues. Thirdly, the decision has the potential to create serious constitutional conflict within the domestic legal order. The German Constitutional Court has ruled that in exceptional cases it might refuse to accept rulings of the ECJ (see *Brunner* [1994] 1 CMLR 57). If such a decision was then challenged under *Francovich*, a first instance judge might be forced to choose between loyalty to the final court of appeal and to the ECJ.

## Further Reading

M. Accetto and S. Zleptnig, 'The Principle of Effectiveness: Rethinking its Role in Community Law' (2005) 11 *European Public Law* 375

G. Betlem, 'The Doctrine of Consistent Interpretation: Managing Legal Uncertainty' (2002) 22 *Oxford Journal of Legal Studies* 397

R. Caranta, 'Judicial Protection against Member States: a New *Jus Commune* Takes Shape' (1995) 32 *CML Rev.* 703

P. Craig, 'Once More unto the Breach: the Community, the State and Damages Liability' (1997) 113 *LQR* 67

M. Dougan, 'The *Francovich* Right to Reparation: Reshaping the Contours of Community Remedial Competence' (2000) 6 *European Public Law* 103

M. Dougan, *National Remedies before the Court of Justice* (Oxford, Hart, 2005)

S. Drake, 'Twenty Years after *Von Colson*: the Impact of "Indirect Effect" on the Protection of the Individual's Community Rights' (2005) 30 *EL Rev.* 329

I. Harden, 'What Future for the Centralised Enforcement of Community Law?' (2002) 55 *Current Legal Problems* 495

C. Harlow, '*Francovich* and the Problem of the Disobedient State' (1996) 2 *ELJ* 199

S. Prechal, *Directives in EC Law* (2nd edn, Oxford, Oxford University Press, 2005)

R. Rawlings, 'Engaged Elites: Citizen Action and Institutional Attitudes in Commission
  Enforcement' (2000) 6 *ELJ* 4
J. Tallberg, 'Supranational Influence in EU Enforcement: the ECJ and the Principle of State
  Liability' (2000) 7 *Journal of European Public Policy* 104
M. Theodossiou, 'An Analysis of the Recent Response of the Community to Non-compliance
  with Court of Justice Judgments: Article 228(2) EC' (2002) 27 *EL Rev.* 25
W. van Gerven, 'Bridging the Unbridgeable: Community and National Tort Laws after *Francovich*
  and *Brasserie*' (1996) 45 *ICLQ* 507

# 10

## Judicial review: the legal accountability of the Community institutions

## 1. Introduction

We saw in chapter 5 that Community law imposes a series of limits on the law-making powers of the European Union. The principles of conferred powers, subsidiarity and proportionality as introduced into the Treaties and developed by the courts may be seen to provide a developing jurisprudence of legislative review. In this chapter we consider the principal ways in which Community law has fashioned a body of administrative law in which the legality of the decisions and actions taken by the Community institutions may be judicially reviewed. It must immediately be emphasised that there is no bright line to be drawn in EC law between constitutional or legislative review, on the one hand, and administrative or executive review, on the other. In this sense, the materials considered in this chapter should be read alongside and in the light of those considered in chapter 5.

The most important provisions of the EC Treaty as regards judicial review are Articles 230 and 288(2) (before renumbering, these were Articles 173 and 215(2), respectively). Unlike some aspects of constitutional review under Article 5 EC, the core provisions of these Articles have been enshrined in Community law since its earliest days. Both are considered in some detail in this chapter.[1] The former concerns the action for annulment and the latter, the principle of non-contractual liability; that is to say, the former is used when an applicant wishes to argue that a Community institution has acted unlawfully and the latter is used to sue a Community institution for compensatory damages. These are the Articles of the EC Treaty that empower the Community courts to enforce the rule of law as against the institutions and bodies of the European Union. In the previous chapter we were concerned with the enforcement of Community law against the Member States and national or domestic authorities; here, we are concerned with its enforcement against the EC itself. An immediate and pressing question is whether the Community courts enforce the rule of EC law against the institutions and bodies of the EC as vigorously and rigorously as we saw, in the previous chapter, they do against the Member States.

Before we proceed: one word of warning. It is not the case that all judicial review actions aimed at the institutions of the EC arrive in the Court of Justice (or the Court of First Instance) directly, through Article 230 EC. Many arrive indirectly, as a preliminary reference under Article 234 EC. Suppose, for example, that a national authority applies a measure of Community law in a way which adversely affects a party's interests. The party thinks it has been dealt with unlawfully and so commences a legal action against the national authority in a national court. Suppose further that, in the course of such action, the applicant wishes simultaneously to run two parallel arguments: the first challenges the way in which the national authority has applied a measure of Community law and the second challenges the legality of the Community measure itself. The second argument may well be referred by the national court to the Court of Justice.[2] Indeed, the Court has ruled that if a national court considers that a measure of Community law is invalid, a reference will be *required*, on the basis that it is only the European courts (and not national courts) which have the jurisdiction to hold that measures adopted by the Community are unlawful.[3] A good number of the cases which have developed various of the grounds of review available in European administrative law have arrived in the Court of Justice via this route – such cases are considered below.[4]

---

1 In addition to these, Article 232 EC (review of omissions, or failure to act) and Article 241 EC (the plea of illegality) feature in some cases, but neither has been central to the enforcement of Community law and neither is considered in depth here. For analysis, see K. Lenaerts and D. Arts, *Procedural Law of the European Union* (London, Sweet and Maxwell, 1999) chs. 8–9.

2 It should be noted that this course of action will not be open to all parties. Parties who clearly have standing to seek review of a Community measure under Article 230 EC may be required to use that direct route if they wish to launch a challenge – they may not be able to use the indirect route via Article 234. See, on this point, Case C-188/92 *TWD Textilwerke Duggerdorf v Germany* [1994] ECR I-833 but cf. Case C-408/95 *Eurotunnel SA v Sea France* [1997] ECR I-6315.

3 See Case 314/85 *Firma Foto-Frost v Hauptzollamt Lübeck-Ost* [1987] ECR 4199.

4 Whether such cases arrive in the Court of Justice through Article 230 or through Article 234 makes no difference to their authority in terms of their substantive rulings.

### Article 230 EC

The Court of Justice shall review the legality of acts adopted jointly by the European Parliament and the Council, of acts of the Council, of the Commission and of the ECB, other than
recommendations and opinions, and of acts of the European Parliament intended to produce
legal effects vis-à-vis third parties.

It shall for this purpose have jurisdiction in actions brought by a Member State, the
European Parliament, the Council or the Commission on grounds of lack of competence,
infringement of an essential procedural requirement, infringement of this Treaty or of any
rule of law relating to its application, or misuse of powers.

The Court of Justice shall have jurisdiction under the same conditions in actions brought
by the Court of Auditors and by the ECB for the purpose of protecting their prerogatives.

Any natural or legal person may, under the same conditions, institute proceedings against
a decision addressed to that person or against a decision which, although in the form of a
regulation or a decision addressed to another person, is of direct and individual concern to
the former.

The proceedings provided for in this article shall be instituted within two months of the
publication of the measure, or of its notification to the plaintiff, or, in the absence thereof, of
the day on which it came to the knowledge of the latter, as the case may be.

There are three sets of issues that must be addressed in order to understand the way in
which this provision operates in practice. These are (1) the range of acts which may
be judicially reviewed, (2) the standing of various parties to seek judicial review, and
(3) the grounds of review. Most academic commentary on Article 230 EC, at least
most of the commentary written in English, has focussed overwhelmingly on the
second of these – standing – and has left the others relatively underexamined. In
this chapter, while the law of standing is considered at some length, we will focus at
least as much on the question of what the courts will actually do once an action for
annulment is held to be admissible, that is, once standing has been granted. After all,
there is little point in understanding in great detail the law of 'direct and individual
concern' without knowing in equal detail what the courts will and will not hold to be
lawful under the grounds of review set out in Article 230(2).

## 2. Scope of judicial review under Article 230 EC

In order to be judicially reviewable under Article 230 EC, the act under review must
be 'intended to produce legal effects vis-à-vis third parties'. Mere recommendations
and opinions are not reviewable. Unfortunately, there is no authoritative list of acts
intended under Community law to bind third parties. It is obvious that the forms of
legislation listed under Article 249 EC (that is, Regulations, Directives and Decisions)
are reviewable. But the Court of Justice has ruled that these forms do not constitute an
exclusive list of reviewable acts for the purposes of Article 230.[5] What does, and what
does not, 'count' as a reviewable act has proved contentious and controversial. This

---

5 See Case 22/70 *Commission v Council* ('ERTA') [1971] ECR 263.

is especially so in three contexts: in competition policy, in infringement proceedings under Article 226 EC, and in matters of political sensitivity.

As we shall see more clearly later in this chapter, competition has provided the context in which a good deal of European administrative law has been developed. This is partly because it is one of the relatively few areas of European policy which is *directly* administered by the EC's institutions. The vast bulk of European policy is administered indirectly, by Member States, domestic authorities and national intervention agencies. In competition, by contrast, it is the Commission itself which is the principal executive actor. Another reason why cases concerned with competition have made such a significant contribution to the development of EC administrative law is that the (usually corporate and frequently multinational) parties involved in competition disputes are often extremely well resourced and are able to bear the high costs of litigation more readily than may be the case in other sectors. A third reason is that since the very early days of the EC, the Commission's actions in its enforcement of competition have been regulated by legislation which has conferred on interested parties a series of procedural and substantive rights. The impact of the legislation is examined in more detail below.[6] The processes through which the Commission enforces competition policy are complex. Some stages of the process involve the Commission making decisions that produce binding legal effects on third parties and others do not. This has resulted in a patchwork, whereby some aspects of the Commission's decision-making in competition cases are judicially reviewable, whereas others are not. The Court of Justice has held, for example, that a letter from the Commission informing a company that the Commission is intending to initiate proceedings against it, and setting out a series of objections, is not a reviewable act.[7] In contrast, where the Commission has the power to investigate or to impose a fine, a letter from it indicating that it does not intend to pursue the matter has been held to be a reviewable act.[8] For an undertaking involved in competition proceedings, the economic consequences of both sorts of act may be enormous, yet in the one, the Commission has virtually unchecked discretion subject to no judicial review whereas, in the other, the undertaking has considerable legal protection.

In the law relating to Article 226 EC (the action for infringement), the Court of Justice has, as we saw in the previous chapter, granted an exceptionally wide margin of discretion to the Commission, in terms of its motivation for commencing or discontinuing proceedings,[9] in terms of time limits[10] and in terms of the Commission deciding whether to proceed with an action.[11] In addition, the Court has held that the Commission's reasoned opinions cannot be the subject of annulment actions, as they

---

6 See p. 441.    7 Case 60/81 *IBM v Commission* [1981] ECR 2639.

8 Case 39/93 P *SFEI v Commission* [1994] ECR I-2681. See C. Kerse and N. Khan, *EC Antitrust Procedure* (5th edn, London, Sweet and Maxwell, 2005), paras 8-031–8-036 for further analysis.

9 Case 416/85 *Commission v United Kingdom* [1988] ECR 3127.

10 Case C-96/89 *Commission v Netherlands* [1991] ECR I-2461.

11 Case 247/87 *Star Fruit v Commission* [1989] ECR 291.

have no binding effects.[12] As a result, the extent to which the Commission's actions in preparation for litigation under Article 226 may be judicially reviewed is extremely limited, the consequences of which were explored in chapter 9.

The third context in which the scope of judicial review may give rise to issues of concern is where cases are politically sensitive. There is no direct equivalent in EC law to the 'political question' doctrine in American constitutional law. This doctrine allows the American courts effectively to bypass having to decide certain politically sensitive issues on the basis that, as a matter of constitutional interpretation, they are regarded as being suitable for resolution in a political forum rather than in the courts.[13] Many commentators thought, for example, that, instead of ruling in its infamous decision in *Bush v Gore*[14] that the electoral recounts in Florida should be halted, effectively handing the US Presidency to George W. Bush, the US Supreme Court would have been better advised to employ the political question doctrine, leaving the matter for the political branches to resolve.[15] In the United Kingdom, the courts employ notions of 'justiciability' to similar effect, holding, for example, that government decisions as to how troops should be deployed are, in principle, non-justiciable.[16]

The Court of Justice, by contrast, has not (yet) developed an equivalent doctrine, enabling it to avoid having to pass judgment on politically sensitive matters. This may be, at least in part, because the TEU excludes from the jurisdiction of the Court most of the politically sensitive matters that are dealt with under the second and third pillars: see Article 46 TEU. Whether the Court will be inclined to develop such a doctrine as (or if) more cases come before it concerning the area of freedom, security and justice, we shall have to wait and see. For the time being, what the Court tends to do when it is anxious to avoid a politically controversial matter is to rule that the act under challenge is not intended to produce legal effects and is therefore beyond the scope of judicial review. This is illustrated in two recent cases. In *Le Pen v Parliament*,[17] the CFI ruled that a declaration of the President of the European Parliament 'taking note' of the notification of the French government that the leading Front National politician, Jean-Marie Le Pen, was, under French law, disqualified from holding office, was not capable of being the subject of an action for annulment.[18] This was notwithstanding the fact that the effect of such 'taking note' was that Le Pen, who had been elected an

---

12  Case 48/65 *Lütticke v Commission* [1966] ECR 19.

13  See *Marbury v Madison* (1803) 5 US (1 Cranch) 137 and *Baker v Carr* (1962) 369 US 186; for analysis, see R. Barkow, 'More Supreme than Court? The Fall of the Political Question Doctrine and the Rise of Judicial Supremacy' (2002) 102 *Colum. L Rev.* 237.

14  *Bush v Gore* (2000) 531 US 98.

15  See, e.g., B. Ackerman (ed.), *Bush v Gore: The Question of Legitimacy* (New Haven, Yale University Press, 2002).

16  See *Council of Civil Service Unions v Minister for the Civil Service* [1985] AC 374.

17  Case T-353/00 *Le Pen v Parliament* [2003] ECR II-1729.

18  The case was unsuccessfully appealed to the Court of Justice. See Case C-208/03 P *Le Pen v Parliament*, Judgment of 7 July 2005.

MEP in 1999, could neither assume the rights nor perform the functions of a Member of the European Parliament.

*Commission v Council*[19] ('Stability and Growth Pact') was, if anything, even more politically contentious. This case concerned certain provisions of the stability and growth pact, the formal agreement among those Member States of the European Union to have adopted the euro as their currency, which requires those states, among other matters, to maintain fiscal discipline and to avoid excessive government deficits.[20] The Member States' obligations under the stability and growth pact are monitored by the Commission. The Commission may report defaulting states to the Council and may make recommendations to the Council as to the action which should be taken. The actual enforcement of the stability and growth pact, however, is a matter for the Council. All of this is enshrined in Article 104 EC. The Commission reported both France and Germany to the Council for running excessive budgetary deficits. In late 2003, the Council decided not to follow the Commission's recommendations to impose sanctions on France and Germany. The Council's decision was clearly politically motivated. While the Member States inside the eurozone have agreed *in principle* that the fiscal management of their domestic economies may be constrained at the European level, when it came to the crunch, the national governments in the Council shied away from imposing sanctions. Such an interference with an issue traditionally regarded as being so deeply embedded within national sovereignty was, evidently, a step too far for the Council.[21] The Commission sought judicial review of the Council's decisions.

The Court of Justice ruled, on the one hand, that the Council's failure to adopt the formal measures which the Commission had recommended it adopt was not judicially reviewable but, on the other, that the Council's decision to hold in abeyance the ongoing deficit procedures against France and Germany was intended to produce legal effects and was, therefore, reviewable. (On the substance, the Court ruled that the Council had acted unlawfully in holding the deficit procedures against France and Germany in abeyance, as this was a course of action that the Council was not empowered under Article 104 EC to take in the circumstances which prevailed in these particular cases.) For present purposes, what is interesting about the judgment is the holding that the Council's failure to follow the Commission's recommendations was not intended to produce legal effects. This ruling does not sit altogether comfortably with the Court's ruling, handed down only a year previously in *Eurocoton*, an important case concerning administrative procedure in anti-dumping (an issue to which

---

19 Case C-27/04 *Commission v Council* [2004] ECR I-6649.

20 Legally, the stability and growth pact consists of two Regulations and a Resolution of the European Council: Council Regulation 1466/97/EC, OJ 1997 L209/1, Council Regulation 1467/97/EC, OJ 1997 L209/6 and Resolution of the European Council (Amsterdam), 17 June 1997.

21 See B. Dutzler and A. Hable, 'The European Court of Justice and the Stability and Growth Pact: Just the Beginning?' (2005) 9 *European Integration Online Papers* No. 5, available at http://eiop.or.at/eiop/texte/2005-005a.htm

we return below).[22] In *Eurocoton*, the Court held that the Council's failure to adopt a proposal submitted to it by the Commission for a regulation imposing an anti-dumping duty produced legal effects for individuals and constituted an act open to challenge under Article 230 EC.[23] What is the difference between the Council's failure to follow the Commission's recommendations in an anti-dumping case (a failure that is judicially reviewable) and its failure to follow the Commission's recommendations with regard to the stability and growth pact (a failure that is not judicially reviewable)? The Court in *Commission v Council* attempted to distinguish *Eurocoton*, on the basis that the Council's decision-making in anti-dumping is time-limited whereas this is not true with regard to the stability and growth pact, but the Court's reasoning on the point is not entirely persuasive and one is left with the suspicion that the real distinction between the cases is one of politics, not legal doctrine. That said, it is to be noted that the Court (perhaps surprisingly) did not use the 'intended to produce legal effects' test to exclude judicial review entirely from the stability and growth pact. Even if the Court is sometimes understandably reluctant to enter overtly political territory, it is not so timid that it will always seek to avoid bringing matters of political sensitivity within the reach of judicial review.

### 3. Standing to seek judicial review under Article 230 EC

Article 230 EC divides potential applicants into three groups. First, Member States, the Council, the Commission and the European Parliament are privileged applicants: all are *entitled* to bring eligible actions under Article 230. Secondly, the European Court of Auditors and the European Central Bank are what might be called semi-privileged applicants, who are entitled to bring actions but only where they do so 'for the purpose of protecting their prerogatives'. Thirdly, there is everyone else: ordinary people and corporations may bring actions under Article 230 only where they have a 'direct and individual concern' in the matter. This last is probably the most famous aspect of judicial review in EC law. Since the 1960s, the Court of Justice has interpreted 'direct and individual concern' very narrowly, effectively closing the doors of the European courts to the vast majority of potential applicants, restricting the availability of judicial review to all but a handful. As we shall see, there has been the odd case in which a more inclusive approach has been suggested, but the general picture for non-privileged applicants is one of very restrictive standing rules. Lawyers and commentators have been vociferous in their criticism of this area of the law, but the argument is in reality more complex than the critics often make out. In this section we will explore the typical lawyerly reaction and set out some of the reasons why it might be seen to be unjustified. First, however, we must consider the position of privileged and semi-privileged applicants.

---

22 See pp. 425 and 443.    23 See Case 76/01 P *Eurocoton and others v Council* [2003] ECR I-10091.

### (i)   Privileged and semi-privileged applicants

Member States, the Commission and the Council have always been privileged applicants. The European Parliament, by contrast, has enjoyed this status only since the Treaty of Nice. Until the TEU came into being (at Maastricht) the Parliament was accorded no formal status to seek judicial review at all. Prior to Maastricht, however, the Court of Justice considered the standing of the European Parliament in two constitutionally significant cases, known as 'Comitology'[24] and 'Chernobyl'.[25] In both, the Parliament sought to bring judicial review proceedings under Article 173 EC (now Article 230 EC). In the first, the Court ruled that it had no standing to do so, as the Treaty did not include the European Parliament among the institutions that were expressly accorded standing. In the latter, however, the Court changed its mind and, notwithstanding the strong textual argument on which it had relied in the earlier case, held that the Parliament did have standing to bring actions under Article 173 'for the purpose of protecting its prerogatives'. In its judgment in Chernobyl, the Court noted that the various alternative remedies available to the European Parliament may be 'ineffective or uncertain' and held that, as a result, the law should be reformed.

---

### Case C-70/88 *European Parliament v Council* ('Chernobyl') [1990] ECR I-2041

20. . . . [Current remedies are] not sufficient to guarantee, with certainty and in all circumstances, that a measure adopted by the Council or the Commission in disregard of the Parliament's prerogatives will be reviewed.

21. Those prerogatives are one of the elements of the institutional balance created by the Treaties. The Treaties set up a system for distributing powers among the different Community institutions, assigning to each institution its own role in the institutional structure of the Community and the accomplishment of the tasks entrusted to the Community.

22. Observance of the institutional balance means that each of the institutions must exercise its powers with due regard for the powers of the other institutions. It also requires that it should be possible to penalize any breach of that rule which may occur.

23. The Court, which under the Treaties has the task of ensuring that in the interpretation and application of the Treaties the law is observed, must therefore be able to maintain the institutional balance and, consequently, review the observance of the Parliament's prerogatives when called upon to do so by the Parliament, by means of a legal remedy which is suited to the purpose which the Parliament seeks to achieve . . .

25. However, it is the Court's duty to ensure that the provisions of the Treaties concerning the institutional balance are fully applied and to see to it that the Parliament's prerogatives, like those of the other institutions, cannot be breached without it having available a legal remedy, among those laid down in the Treaties, which may be exercised in a certain and effective manner.

---

24 Case 302/87 *European Parliament v Council* [1988] ECR 5615.
25 Case C-70/88 *European Parliament v Council* [1990] ECR I-2041. For commentary, see J. Weiler, 'Pride and Prejudice: *Parliament v Council*' (1989) 14 *EL Rev.* 334 and K. Bradley, 'Sense and Sensibility: *Parliament v Council* Continued' (1991) 16 *EL Rev.* 245.

26. The absence in the Treaties of any provision giving the Parliament the right to bring an action for annulment may constitute a procedural gap, but it cannot prevail over the fundamental interest in the maintenance and observance of the institutional balance laid down in the Treaties establishing the European Communities.

27. Consequently, an action for annulment brought by the Parliament against an act of the Council or the Commission is admissible provided that the action seeks only to safeguard its prerogatives and that it is founded only on submissions alleging their infringement. Provided that condition is met, the Parliament's action for annulment is subject to the rules laid down in the Treaties for actions for annulment brought by the other institutions.

The reform effected by the Court of Justice in this case was written into Article 173 EC as it was amended at Maastricht. The European Central Bank and (after Amsterdam) the Court of Auditors were accorded the same, semi-privileged, standing to seek judicial review, i.e. they were permitted to bring actions in order to protect their prerogatives, meaning that they could challenge those acts which deprived them of the possibility of exercising a power conferred by Community law (but that they could challenge only such acts). Only at Nice in 2001 was the European Parliament finally elevated to the status of a fully privileged applicant. The European Central Bank and the Court of Auditors remain semi-privileged.

What is most interesting about this story is the active role played in it by the Court of Justice. The Court did not wait for the EC Treaty to be amended before according standing to the European Parliament. On the contrary, despite the fact that the Treaty was silent on the matter and notwithstanding the fact that the Court had ruled to opposite effect less then two years previously, in 'Chernobyl' the Court rewrote the law. We shall have reason to revisit this aspect of the Court's activism later in this chapter, when we consider its – rather different – stance on non-privileged applicants.

### (ii) Non-privileged applicants: direct concern

Article 230 EC makes it clear that private parties – non-privileged applicants – may seek judicial review where the act under review is expressly addressed to them. This will classically be the case with Decisions (see Article 249 EC). Where a Decision is not expressly addressed to the applicant, however, or where the applicant wishes to challenge the legality of some other form of enactment, such as a Regulation, private parties will have standing to seek judicial review only where they meet the criteria of being both 'directly' and 'individually' concerned in the matter. The test of direct concern is relatively straightforward, and is not especially controversial. That of individual concern, by contrast, is widely perceived to be one of the most problematic features of the European courts' case law in judicial review.

Direct concern means simply that the measure which the applicant wishes to challenge must affect the applicant's legal position directly. There must be a direct link between the measure of Community law that is challenged and the damage or loss that the applicant has suffered.[26] It is akin to a test of causation. If the measure in question leaves to the national authorities of a Member State a degree of discretion as to how the measure should be implemented, this may be sufficient to break the chain of causation, such that the applicant is not directly concerned. In such a case, the applicant's remedy will lie in the national court, the action being taken against the national authority, not against the measure of Community law itself, with the national court having the opportunity, where appropriate, to refer any question of the validity or interpretation of Community law to the Court of Justice under Article 234 EC.

It is to be noted that it is the applicant's *legal* position that must be directly concerned. If a measure of Community law affects an interest which is not recognised by the Court of Justice as being legally protected, the applicant will not be directly concerned. This is neatly illustrated in the dispute between the Front National and the European Parliament. Most MEPs are members of a political group, for example, the Socialist group, or the Green group. A few independent MEPs, including a number of far-right Front National MEPs, belonged to no group, meaning that they suffered some disadvantages in the European Parliament, particularly with regard to secretarial support. Accordingly, they sought to establish a 'Groupe Mixte', also known as the 'TDI Group'. Other political groups objected to this, on the basis that, under the rules of the European Parliament, a political group should contain MEPs who shared political affinities. The decision not to allow the TDI Group was challenged by a number of MEPs individually and by the Front National. The Court of First Instance held that both sets of applicants were directly concerned, but that the applicants' substantive arguments (that the European Parliament's decision was unlawful) were not made out.[27] The Front National appealed to the Court of Justice.

> **Case C-486/01 P *Front National v European Parliament* [2004] ECR I-6289**
>
> 34. . . . the condition that the decision forming the subject-matter of [annulment] proceedings must be of 'direct concern' . . . requires the Community measure complained of to affect directly the legal situation of the individual and leave no discretion to the addressees of that measure, who are entrusted with the task of implementing it, such implementation being purely automatic and resulting from Community rules without the application of other intermediate rules . . .
>
> 35. In this instance there is no question that the contested act – to the extent to which it deprived the Members having declared the formation of the TDI Group, and in particular the Members from the Front National's list, of the opportunity of forming . . . a political group . . . – affected those Members directly. As the Court of First Instance rightly pointed out . . . those Members were in fact prevented, solely because of the contested act, from forming themselves into a political group and were henceforth deemed to be non-attached Members . . .; as a result, they were afforded more limited parliamentary rights and lesser material and financial advantages than those they would have enjoyed had they been members of a political group . . .

---

26  See, e.g., Cases 41–44/70 *International Fruit Company v Commission* [1971] ECR 411.

27  See Joined Cases T-222/99, T-327/99 and T-329/99 *Martinez and others v Parliament* [2001] ECR II-2823.

36. Such a conclusion cannot be drawn, however, in relation to a national political party such as the Front National . . . [A]lthough it is natural for a national political party which puts up candidates in the European elections to want its candidates, once elected, to exercise their mandate under the same conditions as the other Members of the Parliament, that aspiration does not confer on it any right for its elected representatives to form their own group or to become members of one of the groups being formed within the Parliament . . .

39. . . . the Court of First Instance admittedly found that, since the contested act deprived the Members concerned, particularly those elected from the Front National's list, of the opportunity to organise themselves into a political group, it directly impinged on the promotion of the ideas and projects of the party which they represented in the European Parliament and, hence, on the attainment of that political party's stipulated object at European level, the reason why the Front National was directly affected by the act.

40. Such effects, however, cannot be regarded as directly caused by the contested act.

The Court of Justice held, therefore, that while the MEPs were directly concerned, the Front National was not.

### (iii)   Non-privileged applicants: individual concern

### (a)   The *Plaumann* formula

The Court of Justice defined 'individual concern' in its seminal ruling in *Plaumann*. The case concerned the import of clementines. The German authorities wished to suspend a duty on the fruit, but the Commission refused them permission to do so. The applicant company was an importer of clementines who sought judicial review of the Commission's Decision (which had been addressed to the German authorities, not to the applicant). The Court of Justice ruled that the applicant lacked standing.

### Case 25/62 *Plaumann & Co v Commission* [1963] ECR 95, 107

Persons other than those to whom a Decision is addressed may only claim to be individually concerned if that Decision affects them by reason of certain attributes which are peculiar to them or by reason of circumstances in which they are differentiated from all other persons and by virtue of these factors distinguishes them individually just as in the case of the person addressed. In the present case the applicant is affected by the disputed Decision as an importer of clementines, that is to say, by reason of a commercial activity which may at any time be practised by any person and is not therefore such as to distinguish the applicant in relation to the contested Decision as in the case of the addressee.

The *Plaumann* formula constitutes a very restrictive law of individual standing. Private parties will be able to seek judicial review of Decisions not expressly addressed to them only if they can distinguish themselves from all other persons, not only actually but potentially.[28] Even though not many of us are in fact engaged in the business of

---

28  It is to be noted that the Commission argued in the case that the law of individual standing should be even more restrictively drawn than this. The Commission's position is analysed at some length in the Opinion of Advocate General Roemer, at 112–16.

importing clementines, any of us may in theory be or become clementine importers. Even though the Plaumann company did in fact have an explicit interest in whether the duty was payable on imports of clementines, and even though all those not engaged in the business of importing clementines lacked such an interest, Plaumann's interest was nonetheless deemed insufficient to give it standing to seek judicial review of the Commission's Decision, on the basis that anyone in the EC *could* import clementines, even if most of us do not in fact do so.

This ruling may be criticised on at least three grounds. First, it is practically unnecessary. One function of standing rules in any jurisdiction is to keep unmeritorious applicants away from the courts of law. No court wants to be swamped with tendentious or vexatious litigants. All courts are concerned with the so-called 'floodgates' opening, drowning the court with tidal waves of cases to decide. Even if, for the sake of argument, we concede that courts are right to be so concerned (and it is not self-evident that they are), this is no justification for the *Plaumann* formula. The Court of Justice could surely have safely accorded standing to all those who were actually engaged in the business of importing clementines without being overwhelmed by a flood of applications for judicial review.

Secondly, it is doctrinally problematic. It makes it excessively difficult for interested parties to seek judicial review. Plaumann was, after all, specifically affected by the Commission's decision. Its legal interest in the decision should therefore have been recognised by the Court holding it to be individually concerned. Plaumann was not a consumer who wanted to be able to buy cheaper fruit. It was not a grocery store that wanted to maximise its profits. It was not a farmer who wanted the price of domestic fruit to be protected. Persons in any of these positions would have been *indirectly* interested in whether the duty was payable – all of these, one may argue, would have been interested in the outcome, but not sufficiently so as to be able to seek judicial review. But Plaumann was in none of these positions. Plaumann was one of a relatively small number of parties who were themselves directly affected by and interested in whether the duty was payable.

Thirdly, the *Plaumann* formula is textually unjustified. The text of Article 230 [formerly 173] EC clearly does not *require* the Court's ruling. The Court could plausibly and sensibly have interpreted the words of the Treaty in a number of ways. In itself, this is not a criticism of the Court's decision – large numbers of judicial decisions concern the interpretation of Treaty or legislative texts which may be construed and applied in a variety of ways. The problem is not that the Treaty did not *require* the outcome in *Plaumann*, but that it does not justify it. There is nothing in the Treaty to imply that the phrase 'direct and individual concern' should be interpreted as narrowly as the Court chose to in *Plaumann*.

Further, the contrast with the Court's early statements in cases such as *Van Gend en Loos*, concerned with the enforcement of Community law, at the instigation of private parties, before national courts and tribunals, could hardly be more stark.[29] As we saw

---

29  See Case 26/62 *Van Gend en Loos v Nederlandse Administratie der Belastingen* [1963] ECR 1.

in chapter 9, in *Van Gend en Loos*, decided only five months before *Plaumann*, the Court went out of its way to enhance the ways, indeed arguably to invent new ways, in which the 'non-privileged' could gain access to and could secure remedies from the courts of law. It is as if there are two versions of the rule of law for the Court of Justice – a classic case, if you will, of double standards. Where a private party wishes to enforce Community law against a national authority or a Member State, the Court will not merely help, but rewrite Community law to create new protections. But where a private party wishes to enforce the rule of law against one of the EC's institutions, the Court closes its doors in all but the most exceptional of situations.

This is not to say that non-privileged applicants can never gain access to the Court of Justice under Article 230 EC. One situation in which standing has been accorded to private parties is where applicants are able to establish that they belong to a class of persons that is completely closed. This is illustrated by the following two cases. In the first, *Piraiki-Patraiki*, seven Greek cotton traders sought judicial review of a Commission Decision that authorised France to impose a three-month quota on imports into France of Greek cotton yarn. The Decision was addressed to the French and Greek governments, not to the traders.

---

### Case 11/82 *Piraiki-Patraiki v Commission* [1985] ECR 207

12. The applicants argue that they fulfil the conditions set out [in *Plaumann*] since they are the main Greek undertakings which produce and export cotton yarn to France. They argue that they therefore belong to a class of traders individually identifiable on the basis of criteria having to do with the product in question, the business activities carried on and the length of time during which they have been carried on. In that regard the applicants emphasize that the production and export to France of cotton yarn of Greek origin requires an industrial and commercial organization which cannot be established from one day to the next, and certainly not during the short period of application of the decision in question.

13. That proposition cannot be accepted. It must first be pointed out that the applicants are affected by the Decision at issue only in their capacity as exporters to France of cotton yarn of Greek origin. The Decision is not intended to limit the production of those products in any way, nor does it have such a result.

14. As for the exportation of those products to France, that is clearly a commercial activity which can be carried on at any time by any undertaking whatever. It follows that the Decision at issue concerns the applicants in the same way as any other trader actually or potentially finding himself in the same position. The mere fact that the applicants export goods to France is not therefore sufficient to establish that they are individually concerned by the contested Decision.

15. The applicants argue however that their situation may be distinguished from that of any other exporter to France of cotton yarn of Greek origin inasmuch as they had entered into a series of contracts of sale with French customers, to be performed during the period of application of the Decision and covering quantities of cotton yarn in excess of the quotas authorized by the Commission. The applicants state that those contracts could not be carried out because of the quota system applied by the French authorities . . .

17. If that argument were held to be well founded, it would only avail those applicants who could show that before the date of the contested Decision they had entered into contracts with

French customers for the delivery of cotton yarn from Greece during the period of application of that Decision . . .

19. With regard to [such] applicants, it must be held that the fact that, before the adoption of the Decision at issue, they had entered into contracts which were to be carried out during the months to which the decision applied constitutes a circumstance which distinguishes them from any other person concerned by the Decision, in so far as the execution of their contracts was wholly or partly prevented by the adoption of the Decision.

*Sofrimport* is to similar effect. Here, a French fruit-trading company sought judicial review of Commission Regulation 962/88 and other related measures suspending the issue of import licences for dessert apples originating in Chile.

### Case C-152/88 *Sofrimport v Commission* [1990] ECR I-2477

9. The applicant is directly concerned by the contested measures because Regulation No 962/88 requires the national authorities to reject pending applications for import licences and thus leaves them no discretion.

10. With regard to the question whether the applicant is individually concerned, it must be determined whether the contested measures affect it by reason of certain attributes which are peculiar to it or by reason of circumstances in which it is differentiated from all other persons . . .

11. It should be observed first of all that the applicant is in the position referred to in Article 3(3) of Council Regulation No 2707/72 laying down the conditions for applying protective measures for fruit and vegetables which requires the Commission, in adopting such measures, to take account of the special position of products in transit to the Community. Only importers of Chilean apples whose goods were in transit when Regulation No 962/88 was adopted are in that position. Those importers thus constitute a restricted group which is sufficiently well defined in relation to any other importer of Chilean apples and cannot be extended after the suspensory measures in question take effect.

12. Secondly, since Article 3 of Regulation No 2707/72 gives specific protection to those importers, they must therefore be able to enforce observance of that protection and bring legal proceedings for that purpose.

13. Importers whose goods were in transit when the contested regulations came into force must therefore be considered to be individually concerned by those regulations in so far as they concern those goods. The application for annulment is therefore admissible only in so far as it challenges the application of protective measures to products in transit.

Note the role played in the Court's decision here by Regulation 2707/72. The Court specifically relied on the existence of protections which had been afforded in legislation to traders in the applicant's position. This is significant as it raises the issue of the origin, or source, of the rights which European administrative law may recognise. Do we have such rights because of the creativity of the European courts, or because they are provided for in legislation? This is a thorny issue in the European law of judicial review, which we shall consider in more detail when we turn, below, to the grounds on which judicial review may be sought under Article 230 EC.

## (b)    Individual concern and Regulations

Cases such as *Plaumann* and *Piraiki-Patraiki* concern challenges to Decisions which are addressed to persons other than the applicant. We have seen that the Court has made it difficult enough for such challenges to proceed. Where a non-privileged applicant wishes to challenge, not a Decision but a Regulation, even greater hurdles must be overcome. As will be recalled from chapter 4, a Regulation is defined in Article 249 EC as a measure having 'general application'. How can applicants show that they are *individually* concerned by a measure that is of *general* application? The Court of Justice addressed this problem in *Calpak*, a case in which a number of Italian companies wished to challenge measures contained in Commission Regulations that concerned production aids for pears.

> ### Cases 789 and 790/79 *Calpak and others v Commission* [1980] ECR 1949
>
> 6. The Commission's main contention is that as the disputed provisions were adopted in the form of Regulations their annulment may only be sought if their content shows them to be, in fact, Decisions . . .
>
> 7. [Article 230 EC] empowers individuals to contest, inter alia, any Decision which, although in the form of a Regulation, is of direct and individual concern to them. The objective of that provision is in particular to prevent the Community institutions from being in a position, merely by choosing the form of a Regulation, to exclude an application by an individual against a Decision which concerns him directly and individually; it therefore stipulates that the choice of form cannot change the nature of the measure.
>
> 8. By virtue of [Article 249 EC] the criterion for distinguishing between a Regulation and a Decision is whether the measure at issue is of general application or not . . .
>
> 9. A provision which limits the granting of production aid for all producers in respect of a particular product to a uniform percentage of the quantity produced by them during a uniform preceding period is by nature a measure of general application . . . In fact the measure applies to objectively determined situations and produces legal effects with regard to categories of persons described in a generalized and abstract manner. The nature of the measure as a Regulation is not called in question by the mere fact that it is possible to determine the number or even the identity of the producers to be granted the aid which is limited thereby.
>
> 10. . . . the applicants have not established the existence of circumstances such as to justify describing that choice . . . as a Decision adopted specifically in relation to them and, as such, entitling them to institute proceedings . . .
>
> 11. It follows that the objection raised by the Commission must be accepted.

Since *Calpak*, the Court of Justice has not been entirely consistent in keeping to the tough line set out in that case. Numerous commentators have observed that, in a number of particular policy areas, the Court has permitted challenges to proceed even where, on a strict interpretation, *Calpak* would suggest that they were inadmissible.[30]

---

30 See, e.g., A. Arnull, 'Private Applicants and the Action for Annulment under Article 173 of the EC Treaty' (1995) 32 *CML Rev.* 7.

This is most notably the case in the context of anti-dumping.[31] Dumping is where a producer from outside the EC sells goods within the EC at such a low price that traders within the EC cannot compete. Where this occurs, traders will complain to the Commission who will investigate and who may require Member States to impose anti-dumping duties. Community legislation provides that, in anti-dumping cases, the Commission must act only by Regulations addressed to the Member States, not by Decisions.[32] Deciding to impose, or not to impose, such duties can have a very considerable economic impact on traders who will, from time to time, wish to challenge the Commission's decision-making. In a series of cases, the Court of Justice has allowed such challenges to be made, notwithstanding the fact that the legal measure under review is a legislative one – a Regulation – that is addressed not to the traders concerned, but to the Member States. Thus, in *Allied Corporation*, the Court held that measures imposing anti-dumping duties are liable to be of direct and individual concern to producers and exporters who are identified in those measures or who were involved in the Commission's investigations.[33] In *Timex*, the Court held that a Regulation introducing an anti-dumping duty is of direct and individual concern to an undertaking if it is established that the objectives of that undertaking, being the only manufacturer of the product in question in one Member State and the leading manufacturer in the EC, lay at the origin of the complaint made to the Commission; that the undertaking's views were heard during the Commission's investigation; and that the duty was fixed in the light of the injury caused to that undertaking.[34] In *Extramet*, decided by the full Court, it was held as follows:

> ### Case C-358/89 *Extramet Industrie SA v Council* [1991] ECR I-2501
>
> Although . . . Regulations imposing anti-dumping duties are in fact, as regards their nature and their scope, of a legislative character inasmuch as they apply to all the traders concerned, taken as a whole, their provisions may none the less be of individual concern to certain traders.
>
> That is the case, in general, with regard to producers and exporters who are able to establish that they were identified in the measures adopted by the Commission or the Council or were concerned by the preliminary measures, and with regard to importers whose retail prices for the goods in question have been used as a basis for establishing the export price.
>
> A trader who is both the largest importer and the end-user of the product forming the subject-matter of the anti-dumping measure and who demonstrates that his business activities depend to a very large extent on his imports and are seriously affected by the contested Regulation in view of the limited number of manufacturers of the product concerned and of the difficulties which he encounters in obtaining supplies from the sole Community producer, his main competitor for the processed product, must also be deemed to be individually concerned.

31 But see also some aspects of competition policy (e.g. Case 26/76 *Metro v Commission (No. 1)* [1977] ECR 1875) and state aids (e.g. Case 169/84 *Cofaz v Commission* [1986] ECR 391).
32 See Council Regulation 384/96 of 22 December 1995, OJ 1996 L56/1.
33 See Joined Cases 239 and 275/82 *Allied Corporation and others v Commission* [1984] ECR 1005, especially at paras. 12–15.
34 See Case 264/82 *Timex v Commission* [1985] ECR 849, especially at paras. 13–16.

(c)    A more generous approach?

*Allied Corporation, Timex* and *Extramet* were each concerned with challenges to anti-dumping Regulations. None overrules or even casts doubt upon the basic rulings in *Plaumann* and *Calpak.* The anti-dumping cases do not represent a modification of the basic position, but an exception to it. In 1994, however, the full Court of Justice handed down a judgment (in *Codorníu*) that applied the approach taken in the anti-dumping cases in the altogether different arena of agriculture, the very arena in which the *Plaumann* and *Calpak* rulings had been developed. Could it be that the Court was heralding that its formerly restrictive approach had passed its use-by-date? Codorníu was a Spanish producer of sparkling wines that had, since the 1920s, used the term 'Gran Cremant' as a trade mark to describe one of its quality wines. When a 1989 Council Regulation provided that the term 'crémant' could only be used to describe certain sparkling wines from France and Luxembourg, Codorníu sought judicial review. In its judgment, the Court of Justice rehearsed its established case law, including the *Plaumann* formula, but nonetheless held that Codorníu's application was admissible. Its reasoning was unusually laconic (normally taken as a sign that there was significant disagreement among the judges).

> ### Case C-309/89 *Codorníu SA v Council* [1994] ECR I-1853
>
> 21. Codorníu registered the graphic trade mark 'Gran Cremant de Codorniu' in Spain in 1924 and traditionally used that mark both before and after registration. By reserving the right to use the term 'crémant' to French and Luxembourg producers, the contested provision prevents Codorníu from using its graphic trade mark.
>
> 22. It follows that Codorníu has established the existence of a situation which from the point of view of the contested provision differentiates it from all other traders.

*Codorníu* was enthusiastically welcomed by lawyers and commentators across Europe, who had long argued that the Court's approach to individual concern should be liberalised. At the time the case was decided, jurisdiction to hear Article 230 annulment actions was passed from the Court of Justice to the Court of First Instance. *Codorníu* was interpreted as the senior court's signal to its junior partner that it should feel free to redevelop the law of standing along more liberal lines. The days of the *Plaumann* formula, it seemed, were numbered. In an essay which may be taken as representative of the typical lawyers' response, Arnull urged a less restrictive approach to be taken to individual concern and offered the following comments on *Plaumann*, which may be read almost as an attempt to write its obituary.

> ### A. Arnull, 'Private Applicants and the Action for Annulment under Article 173 of the EC Treaty' (1995) 32 *Common Market Law Review* 7, 44–6
>
> What is the explanation for the Court's . . . unwillingness to allow private applicants to bring actions for annulment other than in exceptional cases? That question is very difficult

to answer. It seems likely that the Court's approach was the product of a number of factors, some connected with the perceived intentions of the authors of the Treaty, some with the Court's own view of the needs of the Community system . . . The limited standing conferred by Article [230] on natural and legal persons has also been seen as a reflection of the liberal economic philosophy which underpins much of the Treaty . . . One other consideration seems worth mentioning. This is that a proliferation of direct challenges to Community acts by natural and legal persons, perhaps accompanied by applications for interim measures, could have seriously disrupted the proper functionings of the Community system . . . The most progressive of the Court's decisions have been concerned principally with making the Community work. Where, as in cases on direct effect, this has meant protecting the rights of the individual under Community law against encroachment by national authorities, the Court has not hesitated to uphold the rights of the individual. Where the conflict was between the rights of the individual and those of the Community's still immature institutions, however, the Court initially tended to give precedence to the latter.

However, it was not to be. The CFI did not take up the Court of Justice's offer. This is clear from a series of its decisions, of which the *Greenpeace* case is representative.[35] In *Greenpeace*, three environmental campaigning groups and several individuals resident on the Canary Islands challenged the legality of a series of Commission Decisions granting aid from the European Regional Development Fund (ERDF) to assist with the construction of two power stations, one on Gran Canaria and the other on Tenerife. The CFI ruled that neither the associations nor the individuals had standing.

### Case T-585/93 *Greenpeace and others v Commission* [1995] ECR II-2205

30. In order to establish that they are individually concerned, the applicants submit, primarily, that all individuals who have suffered or potentially will suffer detriment or loss as a result of a Community measure which affects the environment have standing to bring an action under Article [230] and, in the alternative, that all individuals who have suffered or potentially will suffer 'particular' detriment or loss as a result of such a measure have that standing.

31. They add that the requirement that in order to establish *locus standi* an applicant must show that he is affected in the same way as the addressee of a decision is not borne out by the case law of the Court of Justice . . .

32. The applicants ask the Court to adopt a liberal approach on this issue and recognize that, in the present case, their *locus standi* can depend not on a purely economic interest but on their interest in the protection of the environment . . .

37. As regards the *locus standi* of the applicant associations, the applicants point out that the relevant case law of the Court of Justice appears to deny standing to such organizations only where their members are not themselves individually concerned by the Community

---

35 See also Case T-298/94 *Roquette Frères v Council* [1996] ECR II-1531 and Case T-100/94 *Michailidis v Commission* [1998] ECR II-3115, among others. For analysis, see A. Arnull, 'Private Applicants and the Action for Annulment since *Codorníu*' (2001) 38 *CML Rev.* 7. Arnull states (at 51) that 'recent case law shows that the optimism with which some commentators (including this one) greeted the ruling in *Codorníu* was largely misplaced' and that, if anything, 'the test of individual concern seems to have become even stricter, particularly where a legislative act is being challenged'.

measure challenged. Where one or more members of an association are entitled to bring annulment proceedings, therefore, the association representing their interests should also be so entitled.

38. The applicants consider that those two conditions are met in the present case . . .

39. In the alternative, the applicants submit that the representative environmental organizations should be considered to be individually concerned by reason of the particularly important role they have to play in the process of legal control by representing the general interests shared by a number of individuals in a focused and coordinated manner . . .

54. The applicants are 16 private individuals who rely either on their objective status as 'local resident', 'fisherman' or 'farmer' or on their position as persons concerned by the consequences which the building of two power stations might have on local tourism, on the health of Canary Island residents and on the environment. They do not, therefore, rely on any attribute substantially distinct from those of all the people who live or pursue an activity in the areas concerned and so for them the contested Decision, in so far as it grants financial assistance for the construction of two power stations on Gran Canaria and Tenerife, is a measure whose effects are likely to impinge on, objectively, generally and in the abstract, various categories of person and in fact any person residing or staying temporarily in the areas concerned.

55. The applicants thus cannot be affected by the contested Decision other than in the same manner as any other local resident, fisherman, farmer or tourist who is, or might be in the future, in the same situation . . .

56. Nor can the fact that [certain of the] applicants have submitted a complaint to the Commission constitute a special circumstance distinguishing them individually from all other persons and thereby giving them *locus standi* to bring an action under Article [230]. No specific procedures are provided for whereby individuals may be associated with the adoption, implementation and monitoring of decisions taken in the field of financial assistance granted by the ERDF. Merely submitting a complaint and subsequently exchanging correspondence with the Commission cannot therefore give a complainant *locus standi* to bring an action under Article [230] . . .

59. . . . [S]pecial circumstances such as the role played by an association in a procedure which led to the adoption of an act within the meaning of Article [230] may justify holding admissible an action brought by an association whose members are not directly and individually concerned by the contested measure . . .

60. The three applicant associations . . . claim that they represent the general interest, in the matter of environmental protection, of people residing on Gran Canaria and Tenerife and that their members are affected by the contested Decision; they do not, however, adduce any special circumstances to demonstrate the individual interest of their members as opposed to any other person residing in those areas. The possible effect on the legal position of the members of the applicant associations cannot, therefore, be any different from that alleged here by the applicants who are private individuals. Consequently, in so far as the applicants in the present case who are private individuals cannot, as the Court has held, be considered to be individually concerned by the contested Decision, nor can the members of the applicant associations, as local residents of Gran Canaria and Tenerife . . .

62. In the present case . . . the Commission did not, prior to the adoption of the contested Decision, initiate any procedure in which Greenpeace participated; nor was Greenpeace in any way the interlocutor of the Commission with regard to the adoption of the . . . Decision. Greenpeace cannot, therefore, claim to have any specific interest distinct from that of its members to justify its *locus standi*.

The judgment of the Court of First Instance was affirmed on appeal to the Court of Justice.[36] As well as marking a clear return to *Plaumann*, *Greenpeace* raises two further issues of interest. The first is the relationship between direct actions under Article 230 EC and indirect challenges to the legality of Community law that may come before the Court of Justice via the preliminary reference procedure under Article 234 EC. In its judgment on appeal, the Court noted that the CFI's ruling that Greenpeace and the other applicants lacked direct and individual concern under Article 230 did not mean that the substantive issues which the applicants wished to raise went unchallenged.[37] Greenpeace had also brought actions challenging the legality of using moneys from the ERDF to construct the two power stations before the national courts in Spain. As the Court of Justice noted, this meant that closing off the Article 230 route did not mean that the environmental interests on which Greenpeace and the other applicants had relied would receive no 'effective judicial protection' at all. The second issue raised by *Greenpeace* is the fact that this was an action brought (at least in part) by a pressure group. This gives rise to the question of whether the law of standing should be any different for political interest groups such as Greenpeace, or whether the law should be blind as to the nature of the natural or legal person bringing the action. Both of these issues were brought sharply into focus in the *UPA* case.[38]

### (d) Reform?

*UPA* is well known for the robust way in which Advocate General Jacobs challenged the *Plaumann* formula. The Advocate General argued strongly that it should be abolished and replaced by a new approach. His arguments were, in the event, not accepted by the Court of Justice, although they did find favour with the Court of First Instance.[39] They are nonetheless worthy of detailed consideration. The Unión de Pequeños Agricultores (UPA) is a major Spanish trade association that represents the interests of Spanish farmers. It sought judicial review of a Council Regulation concerning olive oil. The common organisation of the European market in oils and fats had been regulated by the EC since the mid-1960s, with a complex system of various forms of aid and price caps. In the late 1990s, the Council sought to revise the scheme, its Regulation 1638/98 abolishing the earlier price intervention scheme (replacing it with a system of aid for storage), abolishing consumption aid and the specific allocation of aid to small producers, and excluding from the various aid schemes olive groves planted after 1998. UPA sought to challenge the 1998 Regulation on the basis, inter alia, that it did not contribute to the goals of the common agricultural policy and that it violated the principle of equal treatment. The Court of First Instance dismissed the application for the reason that UPA lacked standing. UPA appealed to the Court of Justice.

---

36 See Case C-321/95 P *Greenpeace and others v Commission* [1998] ECR I-1651.  37 *Ibid.* at paras. 32–3.

38 Case C-50/00 P *Unión de Pequeños Agricultores v Council* [2002] ECR I-6677.

39 See Case T-177/01 *Jégo-Quéré SA v Commission* [2002] ECR II-2365. The judgment of the CFI was overturned on appeal to the Court of Justice: see Case C-263/02 P *Commission v Jégo Quéré SA* [2004] ECR I-3425.

In his Opinion, Advocate General Jacobs set out a series of reasons why, in his view, the current law was in need of reform. Underlying the Advocate General's analysis were two basic principles: first, that any test of standing must comply with what he called 'the principle of effective judicial protection' and, secondly, that the alternative avenue of review (that is, of commencing an action in the national court and hoping for a preliminary reference to the Court of Justice under Article 234 EC) is an altogether inadequate option. The principle of effective judicial protection, which was mentioned by the Court of Justice in its judgment in *Greenpeace*, is not a creation of the Court's or of the Advocate General's imaginations, but is found in the constitutional traditions common to the Member States, in Articles 6 and 13 of the ECHR, and in Article 47 of the European Union's Charter of Fundamental Rights, all of which were expressly relied on by Advocate General Jacobs.[40] Having explained this, the Advocate General set out a series of reasons why, in his view, proceedings before national courts are incapable of guaranteeing that non-privileged applicants seeking to challenge the validity of Community measures are granted fully effective judicial protection.

---

### Case C-50/00 P *Unión de Pequeños Agricultores v Council* [2002] ECR I-6677
### Advocate General Jacobs

41. It may be recalled, first of all, that the national courts are not competent to declare measures of Community law invalid. In a case concerning the validity of a Community measure, the competence of the national court is limited to assessing whether the applicant's arguments raise sufficient doubts about the validity of the impugned measure to justify a request for a preliminary ruling from the Court of Justice. It seems to me, therefore, artificial to argue that the national courts are the correct forum for such cases. The strictly limited competence of national courts in cases concerning the validity of Community measures may be contrasted with the important role which they play in cases concerning the interpretation, application and enforcement of Community law. In such cases, the national courts may, as the Commission stated at the hearing, be described as the ordinary courts of Community law. That description is, however, not appropriate for cases which do not involve questions of interpretation, but raise only issues of the validity of Community measures, since in such cases the national courts do not have power to decide what is at issue.

42. Second, the principle of effective judicial protection requires that applicants have access to a court which is competent to grant remedies capable of protecting them against the effects of unlawful measures. Access to the Court of Justice via Article 234 EC is however not a remedy available to individual applicants as a matter of right. National courts may refuse to refer questions, and although courts of last instance are obliged to refer under the third paragraph of Article 234 EC, appeals within the national judicial systems are liable to entail long delays which may themselves be incompatible with the principle of effective judicial protection and with the need for legal certainty. National courts – even at the highest level – might also err in their preliminary assessment of the validity of general Community measures and decline to refer questions of validity to the Court of Justice on that basis. Moreover, where

---

40 See Case C-50/00 P *Unión de Pequeños Agricultores v Council* [2002] ECR I-6677, Opinion of Advocate General Jacobs, para. 39.

a reference is made, it is in principle for the national court to formulate the questions to be answered by the Court of Justice. Individual applicants might thus find their claims redefined by the questions referred. Questions formulated by national courts might, for example, limit the range of Community measures which an applicant has sought to challenge or the grounds of invalidity on which he has sought to rely.

43. Third, it may be difficult, and in some cases perhaps impossible, for individual applicants to challenge Community measures which – as appears to be the case [here] – do not require any acts of implementation by national authorities. In that situation, there may be no measure which is capable of forming the basis of an action before national courts. The fact that an individual affected by a Community measure might, in some instances, be able to bring the validity of a Community measure before the national courts by violating the rules laid down by the measures and rely on the invalidity of those rules as a defence in criminal or civil proceedings directed against him does not offer the individual an adequate means of judicial protection. Individuals clearly cannot be required to breach the law in order to gain access to justice.

44. Finally, compared to a direct action before the Court of First Instance, proceedings before the national courts present serious disadvantages for individual applicants. Proceedings in the national courts, with the additional stage of a reference under Article 234 EC, are likely to involve substantial extra delays and costs. The potential for delay inherent in proceedings brought before domestic courts, with the possibility of appeals within the national system, makes it likely that interim measures will be necessary in many cases. However, although national courts have jurisdiction to suspend a national measure based on a Community measure or otherwise to grant interim relief pending a ruling from the Court of Justice, the exercise of that jurisdiction is subject to a number of conditions and is – despite the Court's attempts to provide guidance as to the application of those conditions – to some extent dependent on the discretion of national courts. In any event, interim measures awarded by a national court would be confined to the Member State in question, and applicants might therefore have to bring proceedings in more than one Member State. That would, given the possibility of conflicting decisions by courts in different Member States, prejudice the uniform application of Community law, and in extreme cases could totally subvert it . . .

46. The procedure [under Article 230] is more appropriate because the institution which adopted the impugned measure is a party to the proceedings from beginning to end and because a direct action involves a full exchange of pleadings . . . The availability of interim relief under Articles 242 and 243 EC, effective in all Member States, is also a major advantage for individual applicants and for the uniformity of Community law . . .

48. Of even greater importance is the point that it is manifestly desirable for reasons of legal certainty that challenges to the validity of Community acts be brought as soon as possible after their adoption. While direct actions must be brought within the time limit of two months laid down in the fifth paragraph of Article 230 EC, the validity of Community measures may, in principle, be questioned before the national courts at any point in time . . .

49. I consider, for all of those reasons, that the case law on the *locus standi* of individual applicants . . . is incompatible with the principle of effective judicial protection . . .

By way of reform, Advocate General Jacobs then recommended the following:

60. In my opinion, it should therefore be accepted that a person is to be regarded as individually concerned by a Community measure where, by reason of his particular circumstances, the measure has, or is liable to have, a substantial adverse effect on his interests.

61. A development along those lines of the case law on the interpretation of Article 230 EC would have several very substantial advantages.

62. First . . . [it avoids] what may in some cases be a total lack of judicial protection – a *déni de justice*.

63. Second, the suggested interpretation of the notion of individual concern would considerably improve judicial protection. By laying down a more generous test for standing for individual applicants than that adopted by the Court in the existing case law, it would not only ensure that individual applicants who are directly and adversely affected by Community measures are never left without a judicial remedy; it would also allow issues of validity of general measures to be addressed in the context of the procedure which is best suited to resolving them, and in which effective interim relief is available.

64. Third, it would also have the great advantage of providing clarity to a body of case law which has often, and rightly in my view, been criticised for its complexity and lack of coherence, and which may make it difficult for practitioners to advise in what court to take proceedings, or even lead them to take parallel proceedings in the national courts and the Court of First Instance.

65. Fourth, by ruling that individual applicants are individually concerned by general measures which affect them adversely, the Court of Justice would encourage the use of direct actions to resolve issues of validity, thus limiting the number of challenges raised via Article 234 EC. That would, as explained above, be beneficial for legal certainty and the uniform application of Community law . . .

66. A point of equal, or even greater, importance is that the interpretation of Article 230 EC which I propose would shift the emphasis of judicial review from questions of admissibility to questions of substance. While it may be accepted that the Community legislative process should be protected against undue judicial intervention, such protection can be more properly achieved by the application of substantive standards of judicial review which allow the institutions an appropriate margin of appreciation in the exercise of their powers than by the application of strict rules on admissibility which have the effect of blindly excluding applicants without consideration of the merits of the arguments they put forward.

Shortly after this opinion was handed down, the Court of First Instance applied its reasoning in the *Jégo-Quéré* case.[41] But when *UPA* was considered by the Court of Justice, it chose not to follow the advice of its Advocate General. The Court insisted on the continuing force of the *Plaumann* formula, stating that any reform to the law of standing must come not from the Court, but from the Member States. To Advocate General Jacobs' detailed arguments that the alternative route via national courts and Article 234 EC was inadequate, the Court responded in one line: 'it is for the Member States to establish a system of legal remedies and procedures which ensure respect for the right to effective judicial protection'.[42] This is nonsense. If, as in *UPA* itself, an applicant wishes to challenge a Regulation or some other form of Community law that is directly applicable (that is, a form of Community law which is automatically

41 See above n. 39.     42 At para. 41 of its judgment.

effective, without the need for any intervening act by a national authority), it may very well be that there is simply no cause of action available in a national court. This is not the fault of any national authority. It is a direct result of the *European* law, with the EC Treaty, on the one hand, having created forms of European law (such as Regulations) which are directly applicable (see Article 249 EC) and the Court of Justice, on the other, having held that only itself, and no national court, has the jurisdiction to rule that a measure of Community law is unlawful.[43]

The Court suggested that, if the *Plaumann* formula needs to be reformed, such reform must come from Treaty revision rather than from judicial decision-making. This again is disingenuous. The *Plaumann* formula is not contained in the text of the Treaties: it is the Court's interpretation of the Treaty phrase 'direct and individual concern'. That phrase, of course, cannot be altered by the Court of Justice. But, as we saw above, the *Plaumann* formula is far from the only plausible interpretation of the words contained in the Treaty. The problem, insofar as there is one, is not with the words 'direct and individual concern', but with the restrictive interpretation that the Court of Justice has given to those words. Changing that is not something that needs to be left to those with authority to rewrite the Treaties, but is the Court's own responsibility. The buck-passing it attempted in its judgment in *UPA* is disreputable. It also stands in marked contrast to the proactively reformist attitude the Court adopted in the 'Chernobyl' case with regard to the standing of the European Parliament.[44]

The Constitutional Treaty, had it come into force, would have reformed the law of standing for private parties. Article III-365 of the Constitutional Treaty (the equivalent in that Treaty of Article 230 EC) would have provided as follows:

> (4) Any natural or legal person may . . . institute proceedings against an act addressed to that person or which is of direct and individual concern to him or her, and against a regulatory act which is of direct concern to him or her and does not entail implementing measures.

While adopting a different form of words from that proposed by Advocate General Jacobs, this provision would have had the effect of liberalising standing for private parties seeking judicial review of Regulations.[45]

### (e)   Nature of applicants: private parties and interest groups

Before we leave the law of standing and move, as Advocate General Jacobs urged all EU lawyers to do, from questions of access to issues of substance, there is one final

---

43 See Case 314/85 *Foto-Frost v Hauptzollamt Lübeck-Ost* [1987] ECR 4199.    44 See p. 417.

45 For commentary on the discussion on standing in the Convention on the Future of Europe, see M. Varju, 'The Debate on the Future of Standing under Article 230(4) EC in the European Convention' (2004) 10 *EPL* 43.

point to address. This concerns the nature of the applicants who brought the two cases we have considered in these last pages: Greenpeace and UPA. Both are interest groups. The established case law of the Court of Justice provides that interest groups and trade associations may bring applications under Article 230 EC under three sets of circumstances: when a legal provision expressly grants a series of procedural powers to trade associations; when the association represents the interests of undertakings which would, themselves, be entitled to bring applications under Article 230; and when the association is distinguished individually because its own interests as an association are affected, in particular because its negotiating position has been affected by the measure whose annulment is being sought.[46] As we have seen, none of these circumstances prevailed in *Greenpeace* or *UPA*. Beyond these sets of circumstances, why *should* interest groups be permitted to seek judicial review? After all, it is not as if such groups lack alternative means of putting their viewpoints across. Advocate General Jacobs talked at length in his Opinion in *UPA* about the relationship between judicial review before the Court of Justice and the legal protection afforded by national courts. But nowhere in his Opinion, or for that matter in the judgment of the Court, was there any analysis of the broader question of the relationship between judicial review and political accountability. What is it that should be made accountable in the courts and what is it that should be reviewed within the political process?

This question is too infrequently addressed by lawyers. There is a lazy (and arrogant) assumption in much legal literature that if an applicant is denied a judicial remedy, the applicant is denied justice. A moment's reflection will show that such an assumption is often misplaced, particularly so where the applicant is an interest group. Both pressure groups such as Greenpeace and trade associations such as UPA possess extraordinary opportunities to intervene in and, indeed, to shape the political process, both within Member States and in the European Union itself. The following extract focusses on the roles such groups play with regard to policy-making in the Commission.

> ### S. Mazey and J. Richardson, 'Interest Groups and the Brussels Bureaucracy' in J. Hayward and A. Menon (eds.), *Governing Europe* (Oxford, Oxford University Press, 2003) ch. 13, 209–10, 215, 217–18
>
> Wherever policy is initiated, it is Commission officials who are charged with the task of drafting legislative proposals that are acceptable to affected interests and governments within (and beyond) the Union. The result is an often symbiotic . . . relationship between the Commission and groups. Groups are, of course, drawn to Brussels by a desire to defend and promote the interests of their members in the context of EU policy making. The Commission is, however, equally dependent on groups. Not only do they provide Commission officials with technical information and advice, the support of cross-national advocacy coalitions of groups is essential to the successful introduction of Commission proposals. These functional incentives to consult groups are buttressed by the Commission's political need to be able to

---

46 See, e.g., Case T-38/98 *Associazione Nazionale Bieticoltori v Council* [1998] ECR II-4191, para. 25, and the cases cited therein.

demonstrate openness and thus enhance its own legitimacy. It is unsurprising, therefore, that the Commission is the focus of so much lobbying by interest groups, independent experts, national administrations, QUANGOs and NGOs . . .

Whilst some interests – for example, in agriculture and IT – have managed to become part of an identifiable 'policy community', many – for example, in social policy and environment – are involved in loose 'issue networks' . . . [Such] groups rarely find it difficult to gain access to officials . . .

There is a very strong commitment within the Commission to consult widely with groups [such that there is an] organisational ideology favouring consultation . . . Moreover, this consultation culture has been reinforced in recent years by the increasing political salience of the EU's democratic deficit, which has prompted the introduction of new procedures and guidelines designed to increase the transparency and effectiveness of Commission–group relations.

There are two reasons, sadly overlooked in the opinions and judgments delivered in the *Greenpeace* and *UPA* cases, to be cautious about extending standing to interest groups. The first is that such groups may very well already have intervened in the law-making or policy-making process that has resulted in the measure the groups subsequently seek to have reviewed judicially. Why should a party that has already been able to make such a contribution be permitted another bite in court? (As such, perhaps there is an argument for reversing the current law: interest groups should *not* be permitted standing when they have already participated?) Secondly, we need to be careful not to substitute judicial review for political accountability. Take the *Greenpeace* case, for example: why should it be characterised as being a *legal* concern to decide whether European funds should be allocated to the environmentally controversial construction of a new power station? Is this not precisely the sort of question which is best resolved politically, not by judges? One of the few lawyers to have grappled with these (far from straightforward) questions is Carol Harlow.[47]

### C. Harlow, 'Public Law and Popular Justice' (2002) 65 *Modern Law Review* 1, 13

In public interest litigation, campaigning groups can be treated as experts provided their hidden agenda is overtly recognised. Alternatively, they can be treated as single issue political parties, in which case their presence as advocates in the legal process needs a different justification. Otherwise . . . the triumph of pressure groups or factions or special interests will mark a corruption of the legal process. To put this important point differently, too close a relationship between courts and campaigning groups may result in a dilution of the neutrality and objectivity of law.

Adopting Harlow's position does not mean that Advocate General Jacobs was necessarily wrong to have argued for a liberalisation of the law of individual concern. It

---

47 As well as the piece extracted here, see also C. Harlow, 'Towards a Theory of Access for the European Court of Justice' (1992) 12 *YEL* 213 and C. Harlow and R. Rawlings, *Pressure Through Law* (London, Routledge, 1992).

may well be that he was right, albeit that he may have been better advised to have advocated his preferred liberalisation in a case brought by an individual rather than by a powerful trade association. Harlow's point is a more profound one: it asserts that whatever position one adopts on the law of standing, whether you think (as the Commission did in the 1960s) that the *Plaumann* formula is insufficiently restrictive, or whether you join the likes of Arnull and so many others who applaud every move away from *Plaumann*, everyone's desired law of standing must take fully into account *who* the applicant is, *why* they are seeking to challenge the measure under review, and *whether* their goal is to protect their *legal* rights and interests or to advance their *political* objectives.

## 4. Grounds of review under Article 230 EC

Four grounds of review are listed in Article 230 EC: lack of competence; infringement of an essential procedural requirement; infringement of the EC Treaty or of any rule of law relating to its application; and misuse of power. While the list is exhaustive, infringement of the Treaty constitutes a general ground into which others are subsumed. The Court of Justice has not insisted on a strict classification and has recognised several 'general principles of Community law', breaches of which may be classed as infringements of the Treaty. There are five main general principles: fundamental rights, proportionality, legal certainty (from which the doctrine of legitimate expectation stems), non-discrimination and transparency. Of these, two will be considered in this chapter (proportionality and legal certainty); the others are considered elsewhere in this book.[48]

### (i)  Intensity of review

When considering the various grounds of review, there is one overall issue which should be borne in mind throughout. This is the intensity of review. While, as we shall see, there are exceptions, the general picture is one of the Court allowing the institutions to enjoy considerable discretion in carrying out their activities. The following extract, taken from a case concerning the common agricultural policy, is illustrative.

### Case T-13/99 *Pfizer Animal Health v Council* [2002] ECR II-3305

166. As to the scope of judicial review, it is settled case law that in matters concerning the common agricultural policy the Community institutions enjoy a broad discretion regarding definition of the objectives to be pursued and choice of the appropriate means of action. In that regard, review by the Community judicature of the substance of the relevant act must be confined to examining whether the exercise of such discretion is vitiated by a manifest error or a misuse of powers or whether the Community institutions clearly exceeded the bounds of their discretion . . .

48 Fundamental rights were considered in chapter 6; non-discrimination is considered in *EUL*, chapter 20; transparency was considered in chapter 8.

167. . . . the Community institutions enjoy a broad discretion, in particular when determining the level of risk deemed acceptable for society.

168. Furthermore, it is settled case law that where a Community authority is required to make complex assessments in the performance of its duties, its discretion also applies, to some extent to the establishment of the factual basis of its action.

The same basic approach applies also in the context of competition policy, where the Court of Justice has held that as the Commission is involved in making complex economic assessments, review by the Community judicature must take account of the discretionary margin implicit in the relevant provisions.[49] Commercial policy is, again, treated in the same way.[50] In all of these areas, the courts will find Community measures to be invalid only where the EC has made a 'manifest error', such that the institution concerned has 'clearly exceeded' the bounds of its discretion. Such an approach results in the threshold of illegality being placed very high, meaning that even when applicants are granted standing, they still have significant hurdles to jump if they are to win their cases. The contrast between the position of private parties in proceedings before the domestic courts against national authorities, and their position in proceedings before the European courts against the institutions of the EC is, once again, notable. All of this said, however, the following extract shows that notwithstanding the extent of the deference shown by the European courts to the Commission and Council, it is not the case that judicial review under Article 230 EC can never be successful.

### Case C-12/03 P *Commission v Tetra Laval* [2005] ECR I-987

39. Whilst the Court recognises that the Commission has a margin of discretion with regard to economic matters, that does not mean that the Community courts must refrain from reviewing the Commission's interpretation of information of an economic nature. Not only must the Community courts, inter alia, establish whether the evidence relied on is factually accurate, reliable and consistent but also whether that evidence contains all the information which must be taken into account in order to assess a complex situation and whether it is capable of substantiating the conclusions drawn from it.

With this in mind, we can now proceed to examine each of the grounds of review in turn.

### (ii)   Lack of competence

As we saw in chapter 5, it is an elemental principle of EU constitutional law that the institutions and bodies of the European Union have only those powers to act

---

49 See, e.g., Joined Cases C-68/94 and C-30/95 *France and others v Commission* ('Kali and Salz') [1998] ECR I-1375, paras. 220–24.

50 See, among many examples, Case C-284/94 *Spain v Council* [1998] ECR I-7309, at para. 33 and the cases cited therein.

which are provided for in the Treaties and in the legislation which is properly made
under them (see Article 5 EC, the principle of conferred powers). Where an institution acts in a way which goes beyond those powers, it is acting unlawfully. In
some legal systems this is known as the doctrine of 'ultra vires'. In terms of judicial
review and Article 230 EC, this is a relatively straightforward ground of review. Its
more controversial applications concern legislative review – particularly, in recent
years, in the context of legislation purportedly adopted under Article 95 EC, the
relevant case law concerning which was explored in chapter 5. Lack of competence for the purposes of administrative law is illustrated by the following case,
*Commission v Council*. Portugal had granted certain financial aid to pig farmers,
which the Commission had found to be incompatible with the common market
and, therefore, in breach of Community law on state aids (see Articles 87–89 EC).
Article 88(2) EC provides that in 'exceptional circumstances' a Member State may
apply to the Council for a ruling that aid, which would ordinarily be in breach of
Community law, may be regarded as being compatible with the common market.
Portugal availed itself of this provision with the result that the Council effectively overturned the Commission's decision. The Commission challenged the Council's actions
under Article 230, arguing that the Council lacked the legal competence to act as
it had.

### Case C-110/02 *Commission v Council* [2004] ECR I-6333

29. . . . the intention of the Treaty, in providing through Article 88 EC for aid to be kept
under constant review and supervised by the Commission, is that the finding that aid may be
incompatible with the common market is to be arrived at, subject to review by the Community
judicature, by means of an appropriate procedure which it is the Commission's responsibility
to set in motion . . .

30. As is clear from its very wording, the third subparagraph of Article 88(2) EC covers an
exceptional case. According to that provision, the Council acting unanimously, 'on application
by a Member State', may decide that aid which that State is granting or intends to grant must
be regarded as compatible with the common market 'in derogation from the provisions of
Article 87 or from the regulations provided for in Article 89', if such a decision is justified
by 'exceptional circumstances'. . .

44. . . . where a decision finding an aid incompatible with the common market has been
adopted by the Commission, the Council cannot paralyse the effectiveness of that decision
by itself declaring the aid compatible with the common market . . .

47. It follows . . . that, on a proper interpretation of the third subparagraph of Article
88(2) EC, the Council cannot, on the basis of that provision, validly declare compatible with
the common market an aid which allocates to the beneficiaries of an unlawful aid, which
a Commission decision has previously declared incompatible with the common market, an
amount designed to compensate for the repayments which they are required to make pursuant
to that decision . . .

51. It follows that the Commission's first plea in support of its action, arguing that the
Council lacked the competence to adopt the contested decision, is well founded, and that the
latter must therefore be annulled.

An aspect of administrative law which is closely related to this ground of review is the doctrine concerning delegation of powers. The rule is that, where powers are given to an institution, that institution may delegate the powers to another body only where such delegation is (a) legally possible and (b) properly executed. The leading authority on this point in Community law is the very old case of *Meroni*, decided in 1958.[51]

---

### Case 9/56 *Meroni v High Authority* [1957–58] ECR 133, 152

The consequences resulting from a delegation of powers are very different depending on whether it involves clearly defined executive powers the exercise of which can, therefore, be subject to strict review in the light of objective criteria determined by the delegating authority, or whether it involves a discretionary power, implying a wide margin of discretion which may, according to the use which is made of it, make possible the execution of actual economic policy.

A delegation of the first kind cannot appreciably alter the consequences involved in the exercise of the powers concerned, whereas a delegation of the second kind, since it replaces the choices of the delegator by the choices of the delegate, brings about an actual transfer of responsibility.

---

### (iii)   *Infringement of an essential procedural requirement*

The case law on infringement of an essential procedural requirement is rather more difficult than that on lack of competence. What constitutes an 'essential procedural requirement' is something that the courts have been slow to articulate. Even where the courts have been active, they have not always been consistent. There is no general *legal* code of administrative procedure to which we can turn in order to discover what European administrative law requires or permits by way of procedural fairness. The only general principle provided for in the Treaties is found in Article 253 [formerly 190] EC, which requires the institutions to give reasons for their decisions. This provision is considered below. In many areas, procedural requirements have been laid down principally by legislation rather than by case law. Such legislation tends to be subject-area specific, with the result that procedural protections may be conferred by legislation in some areas but not in others. As Tridimas has observed, Community law:

> does not provide for a general right to a fair hearing in administrative proceed-
> ings. Recognition of such a right in Community legislation seems to be coinci-
> dental rather than principled. A right to a hearing is recognised, for example, in
> competition, anti-dumping and trade mark proceedings but not in proceedings
> for state aids or the common customs tariff. Those differences are not based on
> any objective reasons but are rather due to historical happenstance.[52]

---

51  Compare Case C-154/04 *R (Alliance for Natural Health) v Secretary of State for Health*, Opinion of Advocate General Geelhoed, 5 April 2005.

52  T. Tridimas, *The General Principles of EC Law* (Oxford, Oxford University Press, 1999) 244 (notes omitted).

Consequently, infringement of an essential procedural requirement is a ground of review that varies considerably from context to context.

The European Ombudsman has endeavoured to change this by developing general principles of administrative procedure but, at least as far as the law is concerned, his efforts have met with only limited success. The Petitions Committee of the European Parliament suggested to the Ombudsman in 1998 that he develop a code of practice on good administrative behaviour. This the Ombudsman did, and he presented his code to the Parliament, which adopted a resolution approving it in September 2001. At the same time, a 'right to good administration' was included in the Charter of Fundamental Rights.

---

### Article 41 EU Charter of Fundamental Rights

1. Every person has the right to have his or her affairs handled impartially, fairly and within a reasonable time by the institutions and bodies of the Union.
2. This right includes:

- the right of every person to be heard, before any individual measure which would affect him or her adversely is taken;
- the right of every person to have access to his or her file, while respecting the legitimate interests of confidentiality and of professional and business secrecy;
- the obligation of the administration to give reasons for its decisions.

3. Every person has the right to have the Community make good any damage caused by its institutions or by its servants in the performance of their duties, in accordance with the general principles common to the laws of the Member States.
4. Every person may write to the institutions of the Union in one of the languages of the Treaties and must have an answer in the same language.

---

As the law stands, of course, the Charter of Fundamental Rights is not judicially enforceable. The Ombudsman, however, uses both Article 41 of the Charter and his Code of Good Administrative Behaviour in investigating complaints of maladministration. The Ombudsman sees his Code as a document that 'explains in more detail what the Charter's right to good administration should mean in practice'[53] and regards a breach of the principles contained in Article 41 or the Code of Behaviour as prima facie evidence of maladministration.

### (a) Right to be heard

To turn now from the 'soft law' of codes and guidelines to the 'hard law' of legislation and cases, it is in the arena of competition where much of the law of administrative procedure has been developed. In some instances, rules first made in competition cases have been extended and applied elsewhere; in other instances, not. Where procedural guarantees first articulated in connection with competition law have been

---

53 European Ombudsman, *The European Code of Good Administrative Behaviour*, 3. The text of the Code is available from the Ombudsman's website: see www.euro-ombudsman.eu.int/code/en/default.htm

extended and applied beyond that context, their extension beyond competition has not been uniform. As we shall see, rules which have, for example, been extended to anti-dumping have not been further extended to the law of state aids, and so on. There are two main reasons why competition law has formed the starting point for much of the law of procedural fairness: first, because it is in competition law that the EC's institutions (or, at least, the Commission) most clearly engage in direct administration, making decisions that have immediate impacts upon private parties (particularly on large corporations which, being well-financed, have the resources for litigation). The vast bulk of the EC's policies are administered not by the institutions themselves, but indirectly by national and regional authorities within Member States. Competition is a major exception.

> ## C. Kerse and N. Khan, *EC Antitrust Procedure* (5th edn, London, Sweet and Maxwell, 2005) para. 1–031
>
> In practice most Community policies are implemented by national agencies. So national customs authorities enforce the common customs tariff and control the import and export of goods. National intervention boards operate the mechanisms of the Common Agricultural Policy (CAP), administering quotas, making grants and support payments and purchasing and storing surpluses. Moreover, though the Treaty imposes on the Commission the duty to ensure that the provisions of the Treaty are applied (Article 211 EC) it is rare that the Commission itself has direct inspection and enforcement powers. A major exception is the enforcement of the Community competition rules where . . . the Commission has powers to carry out investigations and, if necessary, fine undertakings found to have contravened [the Treaty].

The second reason is that, since the early 1960s, Community legislation has set out in some detail the procedures according to which the Commission should act in competition matters. This legislation (formerly Regulation 17 but, with effect from May 2004, Regulation 1/2003)[54] provides for a number of procedural safeguards and rights that are afforded to undertakings subject to investigation by the Commission.[55] Thus, in the competition context, Community law has long recognised certain 'rights of defence', or procedural protections, which the Commission must observe. These rights include the right to be heard, the right of access to the file and the principle of sound administration. The right to be heard, in this context, encompasses two principles: an obligation on the Commission to make its case known to the undertaking(s) concerned, and the right of the undertaking(s) to reply.[56] Undertakings involved in competition procedures before the Commission are entitled to see all the evidence on which the Commission bases its case, but the Commission's obligations of disclosure are not limited to the evidence on which it expressly bases its case.

54 Council Regulation 1/2003/EC of 16 December 2002 on the implementation of the rules on competition laid down in Articles 81 and 82 EC, OJ 2003 L1/1 (4 January 2003).
55 See especially Regulation 1/2003, Article 27.
56 See Cases 56 and 58/64 *Consten and Grundig v Commission* [1966] ECR 299. See now Regulation 1/2003, Article 27.

**Joined Cases C-204–5/00 P, C-211/00 P, C-213/00 P, C-217/00 P and C-219/00 P *Aalborg Portland v Commission* ('Cement') [2004] ECR I-123**

64. The rights of the defence are fundamental rights forming an integral part of the general principles of law, whose observance the Court ensures . . . drawing inspiration for that purpose from the constitutional traditions common to the Member States and from the guidelines supplied by international treaties for the protection of human rights on which the Member States have collaborated or to which they are signatories, such as the European Convention for the Protection of Human Rights and Fundamental Freedoms . . .

65. Thus, when requesting information, the Commission may not compel an undertaking to provide it with answers which might involve an admission on its part of the existence of an infringement which it is incumbent upon the Commission to prove . . .

66. Equally, respect for the rights of the defence requires that the undertaking concerned must have been afforded the opportunity, during the administrative procedure, to make known its views on the truth and relevance of the facts and circumstances alleged and on the documents used by the Commission to support its claim that there has been an infringement of the Treaty . . .

67. In that sense, Regulation No 17 provides that the parties are to be sent a statement of objections which must set forth clearly all the essential facts upon which the Commission is relying at that stage of the procedure. However, that may be done summarily and the decision is not necessarily required to be a replica of the Commission's statement of objections . . . since the statement of objections is a preparatory document containing assessments of fact and of law which are purely provisional in nature . . .

68. A corollary of the principle of respect for the rights of the defence, the right of access to the file, means that the Commission must give the undertaking concerned the opportunity to examine all the documents in the investigation file which may be relevant for its defence . . . Those documents include both incriminating evidence and exculpatory evidence, save where the business secrets of other undertakings, the internal documents of the Commission or other confidential information are involved . . .

69. It may be that the undertaking draws the Commission's attention to documents capable of providing a different economic explanation for the overall economic assessment carried out by the Commission, in particular those describing the relevant market and the importance and the conduct of the undertakings acting on that market . . .

70. The European Court of Human Rights has none the less held that, just like observance of the other procedural safeguards enshrined in Article 6(1) of the ECHR, compliance with the adversarial principle relates only to judicial proceedings before a tribunal and that there is no general, abstract principle that the parties must in all instances have the opportunity to attend the interviews carried out or to receive copies of all the documents taken into account in the case of other persons . . .

71. The failure to communicate a document constitutes a breach of the rights of the defence only if the undertaking concerned shows, first, that the Commission relied on that document to support its objection concerning the existence of an infringement . . . and, second, that the objection could be proved only by reference to that document.

While the right to be heard has been recognised in competition law since the early 1960s, it was not enforced in an anti-dumping case until *Al-Jubail* in 1991.[57] In

---

57 See Case C-49/88 *Al-Jubail v Council* [1991] ECR I-3187. Even then, however, the CFI has not always been keen to follow the line that the Court of Justice sought to establish in *Al-Jubail* (see, e.g., Case T-167/94 *Nölle v Council* [1995] ECR II-2589).

*Al-Jubail*, the Court of Justice annulled an anti-dumping Regulation for infringement of the right to a fair hearing. The Court ruled that the institutions had not discharged their duty to place at the applicants' disposal all the information which would have enabled them to defend their interests. Two contextual differences seem to have motivated the courts in distinguishing the procedural protections available in competition cases from those available in anti-dumping: on the one hand, the Commission enjoys coercive powers in the former but not in the latter, and on the other, the EC proceeds by way of Decisions in the former and Regulations in the latter. In *Al-Jubail*, however, the Court of Justice appeared to acknowledge that both factors were differences more of form than of substance. In anti-dumping, as in competition, the Commission acts as an independent investigative regulator; in both contexts, secondary legislation confers rights on interested parties to participate in Community decision-making (albeit to different degrees); in anti-dumping, as in competition, the EC's decisions may have a critical economic impact on the activities of business undertakings; and while formally the EC adopts Regulations rather than Decisions in the context of anti-dumping, they are Regulations that 'normally affect only a distinct number of sufficiently individualised producers, exporters and importers which, furthermore, are entitled to participate during the investigation'.[58]

*Al-Jubail* is one of a number of authorities for the proposition that parties may enjoy procedural protections in Community law even without Community legislation expressly conferring them. This had first been suggested by the Court in the early 1970s in *Transocean Marine Paint*, where the Court referred to the right to be heard as a 'general rule'.[59] However, the Court has not been entirely consistent on this point, refining its position in *Hoffmann-La Roche*, where it held that 'observance of the right to be heard is *in all proceedings in which sanctions, in particular fines or penalty payments, may be imposed* a fundamental principle of Community law'.[60] This is a significantly narrower formulation than that found in *Transocean Marine Paint*. In *Al-Jubail*, the Court spoke in the following terms.

### Case C-49/88 *Al-Jubail v Council* [1991] ECR I-3187

15. ... the right to a fair hearing ... must be observed not only in the course of proceedings which may result in the imposition of penalties, but also in investigative proceedings prior to the adoption of anti-dumping Regulations which, despite their general scope, may directly and individually affect the undertakings concerned and entail adverse consequences for them.

16. It should be added that, with regard to the right to a fair hearing, any action taken by the Community institutions must be all the more scrupulous in view of the fact that, as they stand at present, the rules in question do not provide all the procedural guarantees for the protection of the individual which may exist in certain national legal systems.

---

58 See H. Nehl, *Principles of Administrative Procedure in EC Law* (Oxford, Hart, 1999) 74.
59 Case 17/74 *Transocean Marine Paint v Commission* [1974] ECR 1063.
60 Case 85/76 *Hoffmann-La Roche v Commission* [1979] ECR 461.

In *Technische Universität München*, the Court of Justice further extended the right to be heard in the context of customs law.[61] The case concerned the import of an electronic microscope from Japan by the applicant, the Technical University of Munich. Its application for an exemption from customs duties had been transferred by the competent national customs authorities to the Commission which, having consulted a group of experts, rejected it on the ground that an 'apparatus of equivalent scientific value' was manufactured and available in the EC. The case is particularly significant given that customs law is executed not by the Community institutions alone, but by the Community institutions and national authorities acting together.[62] It is also significant in that in earlier case law, the Court had minimised the extent to which procedural protections could be granted in the face of the exercise of broad administrative discretion. The opposite of this approach was taken here (contrary, it might be added, to the advice offered by Advocate General Jacobs in his Opinion in the case).

---

### Case C-269/90 *Technische Universität München v Hauptzollamt München-Mitle* [1991] ECR I-5469

13. It must be stated first of all that, since an administrative procedure entailing complex technical evaluations is involved, the Commission must have a power of appraisal in order to be able to fulfil its tasks.

14. However, where the Community institutions have such a power of appraisal, respect for the rights guaranteed by the Community legal order in administrative procedures is of even more fundamental importance. Those guarantees include, in particular, the duty of the competent institution to examine carefully and impartially all the relevant aspects of the individual case, the right of the person concerned to make his views known and to have an adequately reasoned decision. Only in this way can the Court verify whether the factual and legal elements upon which the exercise of the power of appraisal depends were present.

15. The Court must therefore examine whether the disputed decision was adopted in accordance with the principles mentioned above. . .

23. . . . it must be stated that Regulation No 2784/79 does not provide any opportunity for the person concerned, the importer of scientific apparatus, to explain his position to the group of experts or to comment on the information before the group or to take a position on the group's recommendation.

24. However, it is the importing institution which is best aware of the technical characteristics which the scientific apparatus must have in view of the work for which it is intended. The comparison between the imported apparatus and the instruments originating in the Community must, consequently, be made according to the information about the intended research projects and the actual intended use of the apparatus provided by the person concerned.

25. The right to be heard in such an administrative procedure requires that the person concerned should be able, during the actual procedure before the Commission, to put his own case and properly make his views known on the relevant circumstances and, where necessary, on the documents taken into account by the Community institution. This requirement was not met when the disputed decision was adopted.

---

61 Case C-269/90 *Technische Universität München v Hauptzollamt München-Mitle* [1991] ECR I-5469.

62 On this matter, see further Case T-346/94 *France Aviation v Commission* [1995] ECR II-2843 and Case T-42/96 *Eyckeler and Malt v Commission* [1998] ECR II-401. For discussion, see H. Nehl, *Principles of Administrative Procedure in EC Law* (Oxford, Hart, 1999) 78–81.

In his masterly account of the development of principles of administrative procedure in Community law, Hanns Peter Nehl has suggested that 'this principled finding constitutes a turning point in the philosophy hitherto underlying both judicial review of administrative discretion and, more specifically, judicial control on procedural grounds' and that the 'conceptual revolution' contained in it calls for detailed analysis which, as he goes on to show, reveals that the Court of Justice's judgment was the direct result of 'the forceful intervention of the referring national court'.[63]

> **H. Nehl, *Principles of Administrative Procedure in EC Law* (Oxford, Hart, 1999) 133–5**
>
> [T]he German Federal Court of Finance (Bundesfinanzhof), which was of the opinion that the Commission decision was substantively wrong, asked the ECJ under Article [234 EC] to give a preliminary ruling on its validity. At this point a very interesting discourse between the Bundesfinanzhof and the ECJ about the concept of judicial review ... began ... The Bundesfinanzhof questioned whether the hitherto fairly restrictive stance of the ECJ in reviewing discretion involving the assessment of complex technical issues is compatible with the 'constitutional principle of effective legal protection recognised in Community law'. The crucial point in this invitation addressed to the Court to reconsider its case law was that under German doctrine, as required by Article 19(1) of the Basic Law laying down the principle of 'effective judicial protection', such a restrained review of administrative discretion is to be regarded as 'unconstitutional'. The Bundesfinanzhof thereby implicitly threatened to engage once again in a 'constitutional' or 'supremacy' quarrel with the ECJ by involving the Federal Constitutional Court (Bundesverfassungsgericht). The ECJ was therefore faced with a strong 'argument' in favour of a more intense scrutiny of the Commission's conduct ... The ECJ thus annulled the Commission decision on the grounds of a range of procedural defects ... Unsurprisingly, the ECJ's ruling has come to live a life of its own [particularly] in litigation before the CFI.

In *Lisrestal*, this general approach was applied in the context of the administration of the European Social Fund.[64] In its judgment (confirmed by the Court of Justice), the Court of First Instance ruled that:

> the respect of the rights of the defence in all proceedings which are initiated against a person and are liable to culminate in a measure adversely affecting that person is a fundamental principle of Community law which must be guaranteed, even in the absence of any specific rules concerning the proceedings in question.[65]

That there are limits to the courts' extension of procedural guarantees, however, can be shown from recent case law in the field of state aids. A recent decision of the CFI in this area sets out the established law.

---

63 Nehl, above n. 58, 133.    64 Case C-32/95 P *Commission v Lisrestal* [1996] ECR I-5375.

65 See Case T-450/93 *Lisrestal v Commission* [1994] ECR II-1177, para. 42. See also in this context Case C-462/98 P *Mediocurso v Commission* [2000] ECR I-7183.

### Case T-198/01 *Technische Glaswerke Ilmenau v Commission*, judgment of 8 July 2004

192. In the procedure for reviewing State aid, interested parties other than the Member State responsible for granting the aid . . . cannot themselves claim a right to debate the issues with the Commission in the same way as may that Member State . . . Therefore, essentially, they play the role of a source of information for the Commission . . .

193. None of the provisions on the procedure for reviewing State aid reserves a special role, among the interested parties, to the recipient of aid. Moreover, the procedure for reviewing State aid is not a procedure initiated 'against' the recipient of the aid that entails rights on which it may rely and which are as extensive as the rights of the defence as such . . .

194. In that connection, it should be pointed out that the Community Court cannot, on the basis of the general legal principles relied on by the applicant, such as those of the right to due process, the right to be heard, sound administration or equal treatment, extend the procedural rights which the Treaty and secondary legislation confer on interested parties in procedures for reviewing State aid. Similarly, it is inappropriate to refer to the case law on, inter alia, the application of Articles 81 EC and 82 EC and the control of concentrations, which concern procedures initiated against undertakings – which therefore enjoy specific procedural rights – and not against a Member State . . .

197. . . . since the interested parties other than the Member State concerned cannot rely on a right to participate in an adversarial procedure with the Commission, it cannot be held that the applicant ought to have been granted access to the non-confidential part of the file on the administrative procedure or that the Commission necessarily had to send it the comments or replies to the Commission's questions . . .

198. Moreover, it has already been held that neither the provisions on State aid nor the case law require the Commission to hear the views of the recipient of State resources on its legal assessment of the measure in question or to inform the Member State concerned – or, *a fortiori*, the recipient of the aid – of its position before adopting its decision, where the interested parties and the Member State concerned have been given notice to submit their comments.

It may be seen, then, that Community law offers only patchy legal protection in the context of guaranteeing fair administrative procedures. In the main, such protection as exists has been created by legislation rather than through case law, legislation which is subject-area specific and which does not seek to lay down general principles applicable across the range of European administration. There are exceptions, where the Court of Justice has extended the reach of particular protections but, as we have seen, even where the Court has acted in this way it has sometimes done so only because of intense pressure placed upon it from elsewhere. Whether the European Ombudsman's desire (as reflected in Article 41 of the Charter of Fundamental Rights), to see introduced into EU law a general right to good administration, comes to fruition, we shall have to wait and see. For the time being, the law of 'essential procedural requirements' remains a rather patchwork affair, with the courts seeking to advance only intermittently.

### (b)   Duty to give reasons

As mentioned at the beginning of this section, the only procedural guarantee contained in the EC Treaty itself is the duty to give reasons enshrined in Article 253 [formerly 190] EC. This provides that 'Regulations, Directives and Decisions adopted jointly by the European Parliament and the Council, and such acts adopted by the Council or the Commission, shall state the reasons on which they are based'. The scope of the duty to give reasons in Community law is comparatively broad: it applies not only to legislative acts, but also to administrative decisions taken by the Commission or the Council. The duty to give reasons is one aspect of transparency, which was considered in detail in chapter 8.[66] The obligation to give reasons is a legal requirement which is fully justiciable. Failure to comply with the duty may be classed as an infringement of an essential procedural requirement and may, therefore, lead to the court quashing the relevant measure. Exactly what kind and what detail of reasons must be given varies, but at a minimum, the Court of Justice will require that sufficient reasons have been furnished so as to allow parties to understand their legal position.

### Case 24/62 *Germany v Commission* [1963] ECR 63

In imposing upon the Commission the obligation to state reasons for its decisions, Article [253] is not taking mere formal considerations into account but seeks to give an opportunity to the parties of defending their rights, to the Court of exercising its supervisory functions and to Member States and to all interested nationals of ascertaining the circumstances in which the Commission has applied the Treaty. To attain these objectives, it is sufficient for the decision to set out, in a concise but clear and relevant manner, the principal issues of law and of fact upon which it is based and which are necessary in order that the reasoning which has led the Commission to its decision may be understood.

Beyond this minimum, what precisely will be required, in terms both of the quantity and the quality of reasons given, will depend on a number of factors. The following formula is frequently repeated in the Courts' case law.

### Case C-76/01 P *Eurocoton and others v Council* [2003] ECR I-10091

88. According to settled case law, the statement of reasons required by Article [253 EC] must be appropriate to the act at issue and must disclose in a clear and unequivocal fashion the reasoning followed by the institution which adopted the measure in question in such a way as to enable the persons concerned to ascertain the reasons for the measure and to enable the competent Community Court to exercise its power of review. The requirements to be satisfied by the statement of reasons depend on the circumstances of each case, in particular the content of the measure in question, the nature of the reasons given and the interest which the addressees of the measure, or other parties to whom it is of direct and individual concern, may have in obtaining explanations. It is not necessary for the reasoning to go into all the relevant facts and points of law, since the question whether the statement of reasons meets the requirements of Article [253] must be assessed with regard not only to its wording but also to its context and to all the legal rules governing the matter in question.

---

66 Breach of other transparency rules, such as failure to allow access to documents, may also be held to constitute infringements of an essential procedural requirements: see, e.g., Case T-124/96 *Interporc v Commission* [1998] ECR II-231.

*(iv)   Infringement of the EC Treaty or of any rule of law relating to its application*

As mentioned above, it is on this ground that applicants may argue that a general principle of Community law has been violated. Two such general principles will be considered here: proportionality and legal certainty. Along with fundamental rights and non-discrimination, these are the principal doctrines against which the *substance* of the EC's administration and decision-making may be judicially reviewed. If the first ground of review (lack of competence) is concerned with the EC's *powers* and the second with its *procedures*, here we move into the territory of substantive review.

(a)   Proportionality[67]

Proportionality, which is a central theme of German public law, has been recognised as a principle of Community law since the 1950s. The Court of Justice expressly relied on it, and treated it as a general principle of Community law, in the important constitutional case of *Internationale Handelsgesellschaft*.[68] The Advocate General in that case opined that 'the individual should not have his freedom of action limited beyond the degree necessary in the public interest'.[69] This early formulation captures the essence of the notion of proportionality, but it has since been expanded upon, as is exemplified by *Fedesa*, which concerned a challenge to a Directive that prohibited the use of certain hormonal substances in livestock farming.

---

### Case C-331/88 *R v Minister of Agriculture, Fisheries and Food ex parte Fedesa* [1990] ECR I-4023

12. It was argued that the Directive at issue infringes the principle of proportionality in three respects. In the first place, the outright prohibition on the administration of the five hormones in question is inappropriate in order to attain the declared objectives, since it is impossible to apply in practice and leads to the creation of a dangerous black market. In the second place, outright prohibition is not necessary because consumer anxieties can be allayed simply by the dissemination of information and advice. Finally, the prohibition in question entails excessive disadvantages, in particular considerable financial losses on the part of the traders concerned, in relation to the alleged benefits accruing to the general interest.

13. The Court has consistently held that the principle of proportionality is one of the general principles of Community law. By virtue of that principle, the lawfulness of the prohibition of an economic activity is subject to the condition that the prohibitory measures are appropriate and necessary in order to achieve the objectives legitimately pursued by the legislation in question; when there is a choice between several appropriate measures recourse must be had to the least onerous, and the disadvantages caused must not be disproportionate to the aims pursued.

---

67 For detailed analysis and commentary, see N. Emiliou, *The Principle of Proportionality in European Law* (Deventer, Kluwer, 1996) and E. Ellis (ed.), *The Principle of Proportionality in the Laws of Europe* (Oxford, Hart, 1999).

68 Case 11/70 *Internationale Handelsgesellschaft v Einfuhr- und Vorratsstelle Getreide* [1970] ECR 1125.

69 Advocate General de Lamothe, *ibid.* 1147.

From this formulation it may be seen that proportionality consists of numerous, related principles: measures must be appropriate; they must be necessary in order to achieve legitimate objectives; when there is a choice between several appropriate measures, recourse must be had to the least onerous; and the disadvantages caused must not be disproportionate to the aims pursued. De Búrca has argued that, in effect, the doctrine of proportionality entails a three-part test: (1) is the measure suitable to achieve a legitimate aim; (2) is the measure necessary to achieve that aim (i.e., are there other, less restrictive means available), and (3) does the measure have an excessive effect on the applicant's interests?[70] Tridimas has argued that, while de Búrca's analysis is supported by a number of Advocate General Opinions, the bulk of the case law suggests that the courts do not really distinguish between the second and third of de Búrca's three tests.[71] His view is as follows.

> **T. Tridimas, *The General Principles of EC Law* (Oxford, Oxford University Press, 1999) 91**
>
> [P]roportionality requires that a measure must be appropriate and necessary to achieve its objectives. According to the standard formula used by the Court, in order to establish whether a provision of Community law is consonant with the principle of proportionality, it is necessary to establish whether the means it employs to achieve the aim correspond to the importance of the aim and whether they are necessary for its achievement. Thus, the principle comprises two tests: a test of suitability and a test of necessity. The first refers to the relationship between the means and the end . . . The second is one of weighing competing interests.

Considerably more important than determining whether, analytically, the doctrine of proportionality properly consists of two, three or more tests, is understanding what the doctrine actually enables the courts to do in judicial review cases. On this issue, Tridimas is refreshingly clear.

> **T. Tridimas, *The General Principles of EC Law* (Oxford, Oxford University Press, 1999) 93**
>
> The application of the tests of suitability and necessity enable the Court to review not only the legality but also, to some extent, the merits of legislative and administrative measures. Because of that distinct characteristic, proportionality is often perceived to be the most far-reaching ground of review, the most potent weapon in the arsenal of the public law judge. It will be noted, however, that much depends on how strictly a court applies the tests of suitability and necessity and how far it is prepared to defer to the choices of the authority which has adopted the measure in issue . . . [I]n Community law, far from dictating a uniform test, proportionality is a flexible principle which is used in different contexts to protect different interests and entails varying degrees of judicial scrutiny.

---

70 See G. de Búrca, 'The Principle of Proportionality and its Application in EC Law' (1993) 13 *YEL* 105, 113.
71 T. Tridimas, *The General Principles of EC Law* (Oxford, Oxford University Press, 1999) 92.

Two important points are made here. The first is to alert us to the fact that proportionality review, unlike the previous grounds of review considered in this chapter, may allow the judiciary to quash administrative decisions which they consider to be simply unmeritorious, misguided or wrong. This raises the issue, familiar to all constitutional and administrative law students, of whether the judges should have such apparently broad powers to quash what are often political decisions. It is one thing to argue that the courts ought to be able to quash decisions which bureaucrats have no legal power to make (lack of competence) or that administrators have made unfairly (infringement of an essential procedural requirement). Courts would seem well placed to perform both of these functions, as they are staffed by people who, on the whole, have considerable training and experience in distinguishing the lawful from the unlawful and in insisting on rigorous decision-making procedures. This is not to say that either of these grounds of review are free of problems – as we have seen, the European Courts have at best a patchy record, particularly as regards developing a coherent law of fair procedures. But it is to say that we may legitimately expect courts to be able to perform their reviewing functions well when measures are challenged on these grounds. Proportionality, however, is different. As a ground of review, it invites the courts to engage in a task for which there is no particular reason to believe they are especially well suited. Determining whether or not public policy is 'suitable' or 'necessary' is a matter that requires expertise in public administration, not necessarily in law. It is a task that one could imagine being well performed by a good Ombudsman, but it is not self-evident that it should be a matter for the courts of law.

The second issue highlighted by Tridimas is the variable intensity of review under the doctrine of proportionality. There is a marked contrast in the case law of the Courts between the application of proportionality with regard to the Member States and its application with regard to the EC's institutions. The Court of Justice's attitude in the latter context is, again, exemplified by its judgment in *Fedesa*.[72]

---

### Case C-331/88 R v Minister of Agriculture, Fisheries and Food ex parte Fedesa [1990] ECR I-4023

14. . . . with regard to judicial review . . . it must be stated that in matters concerning the common agricultural policy the Community legislature has a discretionary power which corresponds to the political responsibilities given to it by . . . the Treaty. Consequently, the legality of a measure adopted in that sphere can be affected only if the measure is manifestly inappropriate having regard to the objective which the competent institution is seeking to pursue . . .

15. On the question whether or not the prohibition is appropriate in the present case, it should first be stated that even if the presence of natural hormones in all meat prevents detection of the presence of prohibited hormones by tests on animals or on meat, other control methods may be used and indeed were imposed on the Member States by [other legislation].

---

72 See p. 448.

It is not obvious that the authorization of only those hormones described as 'natural' would be likely to prevent the emergence of a black market for dangerous but less expensive substances. Moreover, according to the Council, which was not contradicted on that point, any system of partial authorization would require costly control measures whose effectiveness would not be guaranteed. It follows that the prohibition at issue cannot be regarded as a manifestly inappropriate measure.

16. As regards the arguments which have been advanced in support of the claim that the prohibition in question is not necessary, those arguments are in fact based on the premise that the contested measure is inappropriate for attaining objectives other than that of allaying consumer anxieties which are said to be unfounded. Since the Council committed no manifest error in that respect, it was also entitled to take the view that, regard being had to the requirements of health protection, the removal of barriers to trade and distortions of competition could not be achieved by means of less onerous measures such as the dissemination of information to consumers and the labelling of meat.

17. Finally, it must be stated that the importance of the objectives pursued is such as to justify even substantial negative financial consequences for certain traders.

18. Consequently, the principle of proportionality has not been infringed.

As this extract makes clear, when proportionality is raised by an applicant as an argument against the legality of an aspect of Community policy, the Court of Justice will intervene only where the Community institution has acted in a way which is 'manifestly inappropriate'.[73] This is not the case where proportionality is used as an argument to challenge the legality of Member State action. Suppose, for example, that a party considers that a national authority has restricted its access to the free movement of goods and argues that the restriction is disproportionate. In a case such as this, the Court will hold that the national measure is unlawful unless the Member State can establish that it is necessary to achieve a legitimate aim and that no less restrictive alternative exists.[74] As Tridimas puts it, 'the function of the principle in this context is to promote market integration. For that reason, the degree of scrutiny employed by the Court is much stricter and the "manifestly inappropriate" test gives way to a test of necessity'.[75]

Principles of review such as proportionality place courts in a precariously difficult position. Too robust an application, and they will be accused of political activism – of substituting their own discretion for that of the political institutions whose measures are under review. Too timid an application, and they will be accused of complacency – of showing such excessive deference to the policy choices made elsewhere that judicial review becomes an ineffectual check on the exercise of power. On the whole, the Court of Justice has tended to veer in the first direction when it comes to reviewing the actions of Member States, and in the second direction when it comes to reviewing

---

73 Where an applicant argues not that Community *discretion* has been disproportionately applied, but that a Community law *right* has been disproportionately interfered with, the Courts may subject the measure under challenge to more intense scrutiny. This is exemplified in the Courts' case law on access to documents, considered in chapter 8.

74 See *EUL*, chapter 19.     75 Tridimas, above nn. 71, 124.

Community policy. Helping to steer both courses is the Court's own commitment to European integration: where national authorities obstruct the path of integration, the Court's instinct is to wield proportionality as a sword, but where a challenge is made to the suitability or necessity of a Community measure, its instinct is to use proportionality as a shield to protect the institutions.

That said, the next extract illustrates the extent to which proportionality may be used to subject the Community institutions to searching scrutiny, even under the 'manifestly inappropriate' test. The *Jippes* case was brought by the Netherlands Association for the Protection of Animals, who argued that Community policy with regard to tackling foot-and-mouth disease was disproportionate in that, in prohibiting the use of preventive vaccination, it failed to take sufficiently into account the legitimate interests of animal welfare. The Court of Justice repeated its standard formulation that, given the wide discretionary power enjoyed by the EC in matters concerning the Common Agricultural Policy, 'judicial review must be limited to verifying that the measure in question is not vitiated by any manifest error or misuse of powers and that the authority concerned has not manifestly exceeded the limits of its power of assessment'.[76] In this light, the Court proceeded to examine the parties' arguments. The application was, in the end, unsuccessful, but the Court's considered treatment of the applicants' arguments shows how detailed proportionality review can be, even where the context is one of broad discretionary powers.

### Case C-189/01 *Jippes and others v Minister van Landbouw, Natuurbeheer en Visserij* [2001] ECR I-5689

85. When considering the constraints attaching to different possible measures, it is necessary to verify that the Community legislature has taken full account of the requirements of animal welfare.

86. In that connection, as regards the information available to the Council at the time when the non-vaccination policy was adopted, it is apparent [that the legislation] was adopted following a study by the Commission. That study, which was carried out in 1989, took into consideration the sanitary and financial aspects of the different methods of combating foot-and-mouth disease and the effect which they would have on exports and the realisation of the internal market. Having weighed the cost against the advantages offered by the various options, the Commission decided in favour of a non-vaccination policy, and that conclusion was endorsed by the Council . . .

87. As appears from the study in question and was stated in the proceedings before the Court, where outbreaks of foot-and-mouth disease are established, preventive vaccination does not enable the disease to be eradicated, particularly since vaccinated animals may continue to carry the virus and may contaminate healthy animals. Moreover, given that the current state of scientific knowledge is such that it is impossible to distinguish between vaccinated animals and infected animals, the development of the disease cannot be effectively monitored.

---

76 Case C-189/01 *Jippes and others v Minister van Landbouw, Natuurbeheer en Visserij* [2001] ECR I-5689, para. 80, citing *Fedesa*.

88. The Court has also been told that, according to that study, it is impossible, even where no outbreaks occur, to guarantee that the virus is not present in a vaccinated herd. For that reason, the Code lays down stricter control standards for animals and animal products originating in a country or zone free from foot-and-mouth disease where vaccination is practised than for animals and products originating in a country or zone where vaccination is not practised.

89. Irrespective of those sanitary justifications, the study also showed that a preventive vaccination policy aimed at protecting all animals in the Community would involve significantly greater expense and drawbacks in terms of controls than a non-vaccination policy, having regard to the number of animals to be vaccinated, the multiplicity of the types of virus and the frequency with which the vaccination would have to be carried out.

90. The Council could also take account of the economic repercussions of a vaccination policy in terms of exports of animals and animal products to third countries. Numerous third countries comply with the recommendations contained in the Code; consequently, if a State were to opt for a vaccination policy, that would limit the export possibilities open to stockfarmers and producers in that State.

91. Lastly, the non-vaccination policy jointly adopted by all the Member States was designed to guarantee, on the basis of a high level of health, the free movement of goods in the internal market.

92. By contrast, it has not been established that a preventive vaccination policy would have the effect of reducing the number of outbreaks of foot-and-mouth disease.

93. By the same token, it has not been established that such a policy would have reduced the need, upon the occurrence of outbreaks of the disease, to have recourse to sanitary slaughter and to restrict movements of animals, humans and goods. According to well-established scientific opinion, such measures remain the most effective way of combating foot-and-mouth disease, whether or not vaccination has been carried out. It should be noted in that regard that restrictions on movement and the prompt slaughtering of infected animals on the spot are measures which had already been introduced by [earlier Community legislation].

94. Consequently, the risk of disruption to the economy and to society as a whole, as referred to by the national court, would not necessarily have been less great if a preventive vaccination policy had been adopted rather than a non-vaccination policy.

95. It follows from the foregoing that, when instituting the policy of non-vaccination, the Council carried out a global assessment of the advantages and drawbacks of the system to be established and that that policy, corresponding to . . . the practice followed by numerous countries worldwide, was not on any view manifestly inappropriate in the light of the objective of controlling foot-and-mouth disease.

96. In addition, it is necessary to take into consideration the fact that the ban on a general system of preventive vaccination does not preclude recourse, where the circumstances so require, to selective emergency vaccination in accordance with the requirements of a particular situation.

97. It is not correct to claim that such a policy fails to take into account the protection and health of animals. On the contrary, it was aimed at improving the health of all the animals concerned by safeguarding them against a particularly frightening disease.

98. Moreover, the fact that the Community legislature took account of the Community interest when establishing its policy for combating foot-and-mouth disease did not prevent it from having regard to the particular situation prevailing in certain Member States, such as the density of the animal population in the Netherlands . . .

99. By contrast, although the effect of such a policy is to preclude the possibility of preventive vaccination of animals belonging to an individual or to a specific group of stockfarmers,

and whilst that may be regrettable, it does not follow that the policy must be called in question on account of the particular situation of the individual or group concerned. The Council was obliged to have regard to the general state of health of all livestock rather than that of certain individual animals. In the present case, the requirements to be taken into consideration for the purposes of weighing the interests at stake were such as to justify a global assessment of the advantages and drawbacks of the measures contemplated . . .

100. Consequently, having regard to the wide discretionary power conferred on the Council in matters concerning the common agricultural policy, it must be concluded that the ban on preventive vaccination . . . does not exceed the limits of what is appropriate and necessary in order to attain the objective pursued by the Community rules.

## (b)  Legal certainty and legitimate expectation[77]

The principle of legal certainty is protected, in one form or another, in all European legal systems and has been recognised as a principle of Community law since the early 1960s.[78] At its most basic level, it requires that Community law is clear and that its consequences are foreseeable. This is a principle that will be particularly strictly applied in the context of Community law that imposes financial burdens on private parties.[79] The principle of legal certainty prohibits retroactive laws, meaning that measures should not take effect before they are published.[80] It also requires that sufficient information is made public to enable parties to know clearly what the law is, so that they may comply with it. This is illustrated by *Opel Austria*. The European Economic Area came into force on 1 January 1994, and prohibited the imposition of tariffs on trade between the EC and Austria. On 20 December 1993, eleven days before the entry into force of the Agreement, the Council adopted a Regulation which imposed a 4.9 per cent tariff on gearboxes produced by General Motors Austria (which subsequently became Opel Austria). The Regulation was published in the *Official Journal* on 31 December 1993. Opel was not notified of the Regulation until 6 January 1994 and the Regulation was not made available to the public until 11 January 1994. The Court of Justice ruled that the Regulation did not come into effect until the last date. Opel brought an action claiming the Regulation violated the principle of legal certainty.

### Case T-115/94 *Opel Austria v Council* [1997] ECR II-39

124. . . . Community legislation must be certain and its application foreseeable by individuals. The principle of legal certainty requires that every measure of the institutions having legal effects must be clear and precise and must be brought to the notice of the person concerned in such a way that he can ascertain exactly the time at which the measure comes into being and starts to have legal effects. That requirement of legal certainty must be observed all the more strictly in the case of a measure liable to have financial consequences in order

---

77 See generally, S. Schonberg, *Legitimate Expectations in Administrative Law* (Oxford, Oxford University Press, 2000).
78 See Joined Cases 42 and 49/59 *SNUPAT v High Authority* [1961] ECR 109.
79 See Case 169/80 *Administration des Douanes v Gondrand Frères* [1981] ECR 1931.
80 See Case 63/83 *R v Kent Kirk* [1984] ECR 2689.

that those concerned may know precisely the extent of the obligations which it imposes on them . . .

125. By adopting the contested regulation on 20 December 1993 when it knew with certainty that the EEA Agreement would enter into force on 1 January 1994, the Council knowingly created a situation in which, with effect from January 1994, two contradictory rules of law would co-exist, namely the contested Regulation, which is directly applicable in the national legal systems and re-establishes a 4.9% import duty on F-15 gearboxes produced by the applicant; and Article 10 of the EEA Agreement, which has direct effect and prohibits customs duties on imports and any charges having equivalent effect. Consequently, the contested Regulation cannot be regarded as Community legislation which is certain and its operation/application cannot be regarded as foreseeable by those subject to it. It follows that the Council also infringed the principle of legal certainty.

126. . . . those two infringements of general legal principles must be regarded as being in themselves sufficiently serious to warrant the annulment of the contested Regulation.

A further manifestation of the principle of legal certainty is the doctrine of legitimate expectation. This doctrine has roots both in the principle of legal certainty and in the concept of good faith. It requires that if a Community institution induces a party to take a particular course of action, the institution may not then renege on its earlier position where to do so would cause the other party to suffer loss. As Tridimas has observed, this is a principle that 'has found fertile ground for its application particularly in agriculture and staff cases'.[81] The leading case is *Mulder*, concerned with milk quotas.[82] In order to attempt to reduce overproduction of milk, Community law offered dairy farmers a series of incentives temporarily to cease milk production. Mulder took advantage of one such scheme and agreed to cease production for a five-year period, commencing in 1979. In the early 1980s, it became clear that such temporary schemes were insufficient, and Council Regulation 856/84 sought to impose a levy on those farmers who produced more than a certain quota. The quota was to be calculated by reference to a farmer's production for 1981, 1982 or 1983. When Mulder recommenced milk production in 1984, he was charged the levy. He argued that this breached his legitimate expectations derived from the agreement he had made in 1979. The Court of Justice agreed, ruling that:

> where a producer . . . has been encouraged by a Community measure to suspend marketing for a limited period in the general interest . . . he may legitimately expect not to be subject, upon the expiry of his undertaking, to restrictions which specifically affect him precisely because he availed himself of the possibilities offered by the Community provisions.[83]

We shall return to the *Mulder* case below, where we consider questions of liability.

---

81 See Tridimas, above n. 71, 169.

82 Case 120/86 *Mulder v Minister van Landbouw en Visserij* [1988] ECR 2321. See also Case C-152/88 *Sofrimport v Commission* [1990] ECR I-2477 and Case C-51/95 *Unifruit Hellas v Commission* [1997] ECR I-727.

83 *Mulder, ibid.* para. 24. After the judgment in *Mulder*, the EC relegislated with a view to accommodating the interests of those who, like Mulder, had voluntarily suspended milk production for a certain time. The revised scheme was also challenged – successfully – on the basis that it also breached legitimate expectations: see Case C-189/89 *Spagl v Hauptzollamt Rosenheim* [1990] ECR I-4539. There followed an

### *(v) Misuse of powers*

The final ground of review, misuse of powers, can be mentioned almost as a postscript, such is its relative insignificance. It is concerned with the exercise of a lawful power for a purpose other than that for which it was conferred. 'The test is a strict one. A decision is vitiated by a misuse of power only if it appears, on the basis of objective, relevant and consistent evidence, to have been adopted with the exclusive or main purpose of achieving ends other than those stated. It is only in exceptional circumstances that the Court will accept this plea.'[84] Kerse and Khan report, for example, that there have to date been no competition cases where the Court of Justice has annulled a decision of the Commission on this ground. For a rare example of the Court annulling a decision on this ground, see the staff case, *Giuffrida v Commission*.[85]

### *(vi) Consequences of annulment*

The consequences of a finding of illegality are set out in Article 231 [formerly 174] EC.

---

**Article 231 EC**

If the action is well founded, the Court of Justice shall declare the act concerned to be void.
In the case of a Regulation, however, the Court of Justice shall, if it considers this necessary, state which of the effects of the Regulation which it has declared void shall be considered as definitive.

---

A finding of invalidity has *erga omnes* effect by binding all national courts in the European Union.[86] In *BASF*, the Court of Justice ruled that 'acts of the Community institutions are in principle presumed to be lawful and accordingly produce legal effects, even if they are tainted by irregularities, until such time as they are annulled or withdrawn'.[87] The Court went on to add the following rider:

> by way of exception to that principle, acts tainted by an irregularity whose gravity is so obvious that it cannot be tolerated by the Community legal order must be treated as having no legal effect, even provisional, that is to say that they must be regarded as legally non-existent. The purpose of this exception is to maintain a balance between two fundamental, but sometimes conflicting, requirements with which a legal order must comply, namely stability of legal relations and respect for legality.[88]

---

action for damages under Article 288 EC (Joined Cases C-104/89 and C-37/90 *Mulder v Council and Commission ('Mulder II')* [1992] ECR I-3061) which is considered at p. 461.

84 Kerse and Khan, above n. 8, para. 8–051.

85 Case 105/75 *Giuffrida v Commission* [1976] ECR 1395.

86 See Case 66/80 *International Chemical Corporation v Amministrazione delle Finanze* [1981] ECR 1191.

87 See Case C-137/92 P *Commission v BASF* [1994] ECR I-2555, para. 48.

88 *Ibid.* para. 49.

A ruling to that effect will have the consequence of releasing all parties from any obligation to which they might have thought themselves subject under the measure. Otherwise, the effects will vary according to the measure declared invalid. A Regulation declared invalid is void not just between the parties to the dispute, but also in respect of third parties. While the presumption in the first paragraph of Article 231 EC is that it is void *ab initio*, considerable discretion is given to the Court under the second paragraph of Article 231, enabling it to determine the effects of its ruling. Accordingly, the Court may declare that only part of a measure is void, maintaining in place other aspects of it. Temporal limitations may also be placed upon an annulment, meaning that the legislation will remain in force until new legislation is passed to replace it.[89]

Article 233 [formerly 176] EC provides that an institution 'whose act has been declared contrary to this Treaty shall be required to take the necessary measures to comply with the judgment of the Court'. This provision requires such institutions not simply to remedy their position with regard to the other parties to the dispute, which led to the finding of invalidity, but to examine all the legal implications of the judgment and to adjust their position accordingly. This duty does not, however, extend so far as to allow the Court to require an institution to adopt a specific course of action. The principles contained in Articles 231 and 233 EC have been made to apply by the Court of Justice whether the finding of invalidity has come about through a direct action under Article 230 or indirectly via a preliminary reference under Article 234.

### 5. Liability under Article 288(2) EC

We saw in chapter 9 that the Court of Justice has developed a doctrine of state liability in Community law under which Member States will be liable to pay compensatory damages when (1) a rule of European law intended to confer rights on individuals (2) has been sufficiently seriously breached and (3) where that breach directly causes damage.[90] Since long before the Court introduced the doctrine of state liability, the EC Treaty has contained within it a provision governing the liability of the institutions. This is Article 288(2) [formerly 215(2)] EC.

---

**Article 288(2) EC**

In the case of non-contractual liability, the Community shall, in accordance with the general principles common to the laws of the Member States, make good any damage caused by its institutions or by its servants in the performance of their duties.

---

89  See, e.g., Case C-392/95 *Parliament v Council* [1997] ECR I-3213.
90  This is the formulation contained in the Court of Justice's judgment in Joined Cases C-24 and 48/93 *Brasserie du Pêcheur/Factortame III* [1996] ECR I-1029, para. 51, discussed in chapter 9.

Despite early suggestions to the contrary,[91] it is now established that Article 288(2) EC creates a separate cause of action in the Community Courts: an action for liability under this provision does not have to be based on a prior finding of invalidity under Article 230.

Where an institution of the EC has acted illegally, causing damage to a party,[92] Article 288(2) will, prima facie, be engaged. That said, a distinction must be made between those areas in which Community institutions are engaged in policy-making and enjoy a margin of discretion, and those where they are not. In the case of the latter, three essential ingredients must be present to found an action under Article 288(2): illegality, causation and damage. With the former, liability will arise only when there has been, in the words of the Court of Justice, 'a sufficiently flagrant violation of a superior rule of law for the protection of the individual'. This important phrase is known as the *Schöppenstedt* formula.[93] General principles of Community law and fundamental rights have been held to be superior rules of law for the purposes of the *Schöppenstedt* formula, as has the doctrine of misuse of powers.[94] The duty to give reasons, on the other hand, is not regarded as a superior rule of law and so a failure to give reasons cannot give rise to an action under Article 288(2).[95]

To trigger liability, the Community institution concerned must have behaved in a way that 'manifestly and gravely disregarded' the legal limits imposed on it.[96] In its early years, the Court was far from clear on what this meant, with everything appearing to depend on the facts of the case. In *Brasserie du Pêcheur (Factortame III)*, aware of the inconsistencies that might otherwise arise, the criteria delimiting state liability, set out in that case,[97] were held also to apply to the liability of Community institutions under Article 288(2).[98] This has resulted in the Court having to reconsider its earlier case law in this field. A leading case is *Bergaderm*, which concerned a Commission Decision that had banned the use of a particular chemical, bergapten, in sun oil on the ground that it was carcinogenic. Bergaderm was the only company that produced sun oil using this chemical. Following the Decision, it went into liquidation. It sued the Commission, claiming that the latter had misinterpreted the scientific evidence. The application failed, but the Court set out new parameters for Article 288(2).

91  See, e.g., Case 25/62 *Plaumann v Commission* [1963] ECR 95.
92  On the difficulties that may be experienced in seeking to prove causation, see, e.g., Joined Cases 64 and 113/76, 167 and 239/78, 27–28 and 45/79 *Dumortier Frères v Council* [1979] ECR 3091 and Case T-168/94 *Blackspur DIY v Council and Commission* [1995] ECR II-2627. It is generally the case that only specific and quantifiable loss is recoverable – that is to say, losses actually sustained. However, there are some cases in which the Court of Justice has awarded damages for lost profits: see, e.g., Joined Cases C-104/89 and C-37/90 *Mulder v Council and Commission ('Mulder II')* [1992] ECR I-3061, considered below.
93  See Case 5/71 *Aktien-Zuckerfabrik Schöppenstedt v Council* [1971] ECR 975.
94  For a summary of the position, see Joined Cases T-481 and 484/93 *Vereniging van Exporteurs in Levende Varkens v Commission* [1995] ECR II-2941.
95  See, e.g., Case C-76/01 P *Eurocoton v Council* [2003] ECR I-10091, para. 98 and the case law cited therein.
96  Joined Cases 83 and 94/76, 4, 15 and 40/77 *HNL v Council and Commission* [1987] ECR 1209.
97  See p. 401.
98  See Case C-352/98 P *Laboratoires Pharmaceutiques Bergaderm SA v Commission* [2000] ECR I-5291.

## Case C-352/98 P *Laboratoires Pharmaceutiques Bergaderm v Commission* [2000] ECR I-5291

39. [Article 288(2) EC] provides that, in the case of non-contractual liability, the Community is, in accordance with the general principles common to the laws of the Member States, to make good any damage caused by its institutions or by its servants in the performance of their duties.

40. The system of rules which the Court has worked out with regard to that provision takes into account, inter alia, the complexity of the situations to be regulated, difficulties in the application or interpretation of the texts and, more particularly, the margin of discretion available to the author of the act in question . . .

41. The Court has stated that the conditions under which the State may incur liability for damage caused to individuals by a breach of Community law cannot, in the absence of particular justification, differ from those governing the liability of the Community in like circumstances. The protection of the rights which individuals derive from Community law cannot vary depending on whether a national authority or a Community authority is responsible for the damage . . .

42. As regards Member State liability for damage caused to individuals, the Court has held that Community law confers a right to reparation where three conditions are met: the rule of law infringed must be intended to confer rights on individuals; the breach must be sufficiently serious; and there must be a direct causal link between the breach of the obligation resting on the State and the damage sustained by the injured parties . . .

43. As to the second condition, as regards both Community liability under Article [288(2)] of the Treaty and Member State liability for breaches of Community law, the decisive test for finding that a breach of Community law is sufficiently serious is whether the Member State or the Community institution concerned manifestly and gravely disregarded the limits on its discretion . . .

44. Where the Member State or the institution in question has only considerably reduced, or even no, discretion, the mere infringement of Community law may be sufficient to establish the existence of a sufficiently serious breach . . .

46. In that regard, the Court finds that the general or individual nature of a measure taken by an institution is not a decisive criterion for identifying the limits of the discretion enjoyed by the institution in question.

Although *Bergaderm* does not overturn older case law, it does suggest a spectrum of cases, ranging from situations where the Community institutions are faced with complex choices and where they enjoy a fair degree of discretion, to more straightforward scenarios where they have little or no discretion. Liability will attach to the former where the institution has acted not merely illegally, but egregiously, whereas mere lack of care may be sufficient in the case of the latter. Questions of complexity and discretion have thus been made central to determining the standard of liability. Legislative action may be subject to the lower standard if the Court of Justice feels the action required from the institutions is relatively straightforward. In *Fresh Marine*, the Commission had instigated anti-dumping proceedings against a Norwegian undertaking, Fresh Marine, which farmed salmon, alleging that it had sold salmon on the Community market at a price below that at which it was sold on the Norwegian market. Fresh Marine offered a price undertaking, accepted by the Commission, that it would sell salmon on the Community market at an average price of ECU 3.25/kilo. It sent quarterly reports to the Commission setting out its sale and prices. In 1997, the Commission adopted a Regulation imposing anti-dumping duties on Fresh Marine. Fresh Marine argued that this was based on a negligent misreading of its report. The Court agreed, and found the Commission liable in damages.

### Case T-178/98 *Fresh Marine v Commission* [2000] ECR II-3331

57. Although the measures of the Council and Commission in connection with a proceeding relating to the possible adoption of anti-dumping measures must in principle be regarded as constituting legislative action involving choices of economic policy, so that the Community can incur liability by virtue of such measures only if there has been a sufficiently serious breach of a superior rule of law for the protection of individuals . . . the special features of the present case must be pointed out. In the present case, the damage at issue arose from the allegedly unlawful conduct of the Commission when it examined the October 1997 report with the intention of checking whether the applicant had complied during the third quarter of 1997 with the undertaking, the acceptance of which had brought to an end the anti-dumping and anti-subsidy investigation in regard to it. That allegedly unlawful conduct led the Commission to believe that the applicant had broken its undertaking. It took place in the course of an administrative operation which specifically and exclusively concerned the applicant. That operation did not involve any choices of economic policy and conferred on the Commission only very little or no discretion.

58. It is true that the alleged unlawfulness of the Commission's conduct caused the alleged damage only when, and because, it was confirmed by the adoption of provisional measures against imports of the applicant's products within the framework of Regulation No 2529/97. However, the Commission, in that Regulation, did no more with regard to the applicant than draw the appropriate provisional conclusions from its analysis of the abovementioned report, in particular from the level of the average price of exports charged by the applicant during the period covered by that report . . .

61. In conclusion, mere infringement of Community law will be sufficient, in the present case, to lead to the non-contractual liability of the Community . . . In particular, a finding of an error which, in analogous circumstances, an administrative authority exercising ordinary care and diligence would not have committed will support the conclusion that the conduct of the Community institution was unlawful in such a way as to render the Community liable.

There remains the question of when the Court of Justice will regard the Community institutions to have manifestly and gravely disregarded the limits of their discretion. This has not happened in recent times, and we must go back to 1992 for such a case. To reduce overproduction of milk, Community law offered dairy farmers a series of incentives temporarily to cease milk production. Mulder took advantage of one such scheme and agreed to cease production for a five-year period, commencing in 1979. In the early 1980s, the Community institutions sought to curb these schemes through the introduction of quotas limiting the amount of milk that could be produced. The calculation of the quotas was based on previous milk production, and Mulder was penalised because of his temporary cessation of milk production under the scheme.

As we saw above, Mulder successfully argued before the Court of Justice that this breached his legitimate expectations. After the EC's revised scheme was also found to be invalid, Mulder and others in his position sought damages under Article 288(2) EC.

---

**Joined Cases C-104/89 and C-37/90 *Mulder v Council and Commission* [1992] ECR I-3061[99]**

12. Article [288] of the Treaty provides that, in the case of non-contractual liability, the Community, in accordance with the general principles common to the laws of the Member States, is to make good any damage caused by its institutions in the performance of their duties. The scope of that provision has been specified in the sense that the Community does not incur liability on account of a legislative measure involving choices of economic policy unless a sufficiently serious breach of a superior rule of law for the protection of the individual has occurred . . . More specifically, in a legislative field such as the one in question, which is characterized by the exercise of a wide discretion essential for the implementation of the Common Agricultural Policy, the Community cannot incur liability unless the institution concerned has manifestly and gravely disregarded the limits on the exercise of its powers . . .

13. The Court has also consistently held that, in order for the Community to incur non-contractual liability, the damage alleged must go beyond the bounds of the normal economic risks inherent in the activities in the sector concerned . . .

14. Those conditions are fulfilled [here].

15. In this regard, it must be recalled in the first place that, as the Court held in [*Mulder I*] regulations were adopted in breach of the principle of the protection of legitimate expectations, which is a general and superior principle of Community law for the protection of the individual.

16. Secondly, it must be held that, in so far as it failed completely, without invoking any higher public interest, to take account of the specific situation of a clearly defined group of economic agents, that is to say, producers who, pursuant to an undertaking . . . delivered no milk during the reference year, the Community legislature manifestly and gravely disregarded the limits of its discretionary power, thereby committing a sufficiently serious breach of a superior rule of law.

17. That breach is all the more obvious because the total and permanent exclusion of the producers concerned from the allocation of a reference quantity, which in fact prevented them from resuming the marketing of milk when their non-marketing or conversion undertaking expired, cannot be regarded as being foreseeable or as falling within the bounds of the normal economic risks inherent in the activities of a milk producer.

---

Central to the Court of Justice's reasoning in *Mulder* was the fact that the illegal behaviour impacted upon a defined group of producers. It would seem, therefore, that there may be a two-fold test for liability in such cases. The Community institutions must be seriously at fault, and the claimant must be part of a group which is particularly at risk from such behaviour. This test may be criticised as being excessively restrictive. Normally, regimes of government liability adopt one test or the other:

---

99 For further proceedings in the same joined cases, see also [2000] ECR I-203.

one can sue either where an institution is at fault or where institutional behaviour exposes one to a particularly high risk of loss, whether or not the institution has behaved illegally. The dual test makes Community institutions highly unaccountable for the financial consequences of their actions.[100]

There has been some slight acknowledgment of this by the Court in that it has held open the possibility of a 'risk-based' test whereby Community institutions may be liable for damages even where they have acted legally. *Afrikanische Frucht* concerned a change in the regime, formerly under Regulation 404/93, governing the importation of bananas into the EC. Regulation 2362/98 imposed new overall limits and allocated quotas between importers. Afrikanische Frucht claimed that these changes bore down particularly heavily on traditional operators.

---

**Joined Cases T-64/01 and T-65/01 *Afrikanische Frucht v Council and Commission*, judgment of 10 February 2004**

150. It should be recalled that, in the event of the principle of non-contractual liability as a result of a lawful act being recognised in Community law, a precondition for such liability would in any event be the cumulative satisfaction of three conditions: the reality of the damage allegedly suffered, the causal link between it and the act on the part of the Community institutions, and the unusual and special nature of that damage (Case C-237/98 P *Dorsch Consult v Council and Commission* [2000] ECR I-4549).

151. In its judgment in Case T-184/95 *Dorsch Consult v Council and Commission*, cited above, the Court of First Instance stated that damage is special when it affects a particular class of economic operators in a disproportionate manner by comparison with other operators, and unusual when it exceeds the limits of the economic risks inherent in operating in the sector concerned, the legislative measure that gave rise to the damage pleaded not being justified by a general economic interest.

152. Those two conditions are clearly not satisfied in this case.

153. First, the reference quantity of each of the applicants for 1999 was determined on the basis of objective criteria contained in Regulation No 2362/98 and applicable without distinction to all economic operators in the same situation as the applicants. In particular, the applicants are concerned by the provisions of that Regulation which they criticise in the same manner as any other traditional operator who supplied bananas to the new Member States in 1994 and/or during the first three quarters of 1995. There can thus be no question of a particular sacrifice made by them alone.

154. Second, the economic and commercial risks inherent in operating in the banana sector were not exceeded. In that regard, it is sufficient to observe that the Community institutions enjoy a margin of discretion in the choice of the means needed to achieve their policy, especially in a sphere such as that of the common organisation of the markets, whose purpose involves constant adjustments to meet changes in the economic situation. The applicants' activities entailed, in particular, the risk that the arrangement for trade with third States introduced by Title IV of Regulation No 404/93 might be changed.

---

Whatever the rhetoric, however, there is not a single instance of Community liability yet being imposed under this heading.

---

100  See generally, P. Craig, 'Compensation in Public Law' (1980) 96 *LQR* 413.

A final issue to consider is that of joint or concurrent liability – that is to say, situations where both a Community institution and a Member State may be liable. There are two sets of situations where this may occur.[101] The first, and more common, is where a national authority implements or administers an unlawful Community measure, such as the transposition of a Directive or the collection of agricultural levies. The second is where a decision is taken jointly by a Member State and an institution, such as in the field of external trade, where Member States are permitted to restrict imports of third country goods once they have received the permission of the Commission. The most equitable solution would be to establish a system of joint and several liability in these circumstances. The applicant could choose whom to sue under such a system, with unsuccessful defendants recovering contributions from each other afterwards. Such a scheme, however, has not been established in the European Union. Instead, the Court of Justice presumes that parties should first exhaust remedies in domestic courts,[102] although the presumption is rebuttable where it would be impossible for an applicant to obtain a remedy in a national court.[103] This has resulted in unsatisfactory and needless complexity, requiring, in some instances, that applicants simultaneously commence actions in both the domestic and the European courts.[104]

### Further reading

A. Arnull, 'Private Applicants and the Action for Annulment under Article 173 of the EC Treaty' (1995) 32 *CML Rev.* 7

A. Arnull, 'Private Applicants and the Action for Annulment Since *Codorniu*' (2001) 38 *CML Rev.* 7

K. Bradley, 'Sense and Sensibility: *Parliament v Council* Continued' (1991) 16 *EL Rev.* 245

G. de Búrca, 'The Principle of Proportionality and its Application in EC Law' (1993) 13 *Yearbook of International Law* 105

E. Ellis (ed.), *The Principle of Proportionality in the Laws of Europe* (Oxford, Hart, 1999)

N. Emiliou, *The Principle of Proportionality in European Law* (Deventer, Kluwer, 1996)

European Ombudsman, *The European Code of Good Administrative Behaviour*, www.euro-ombudsman.eu.int/code/en/default.htm

C. Harlow, 'Towards a Theory of Access for the European Court of Justice' (1992) 12 *Yearbook of International Law* 213

C. Harlow, 'Public Law and Popular Justice' (2002) 65 *MLR* 1

C. Harlow and R. Rawlings, *Pressure Through Law* (London, Routledge, 1992)

C. Kerse and N. Khan, *EC Antitrust Procedure* (5th edn, London, Sweet and Maxwell, 2005)

H. Nehl, *Principles of Administrative Procedure in EC Law* (Oxford, Hart Publishing, 1999)

S. Schonberg, *Legitimate Expectations in Administrative Law* (Oxford, Oxford University Press, 2000)

---

101 See W. Wils, 'Concurrent Liability of the Community and a Member State' (1992) 17 *EL Rev.* 191, 194–8.

102 See, e.g., Case 96/71 *Haegeman v Commission* [1972] ECR 1005.

103 See, e.g., Case 281/82 *Unifrex v Commission and Council* [1984] ECR 1969.

104 See, e.g., Case T-167/94 *Nölle v Council and Commission* [1995] ECR II-2589.

T. Tridimas, *The General Principles of EC Law* (Oxford, Oxford University Press, 1999)

T. Tridimas, 'Liability for Breach of Community Law: Growing up and Mellowing Down?' (2001) 38 *CML Rev.* 301

W. van Gerven, 'Non-contractual Liability of Member States, Community Institutions and Individuals for Breaches of Community Law with a View to a Common Law for Europe' (1994) 1 *Maastricht Journal of European and Comparative Law* 6

M. Varju, 'The Debate on the Future of Standing under Article 230(4) EC in the European Convention' (2004) 10 *EPL* 43

J. Weiler, 'Pride and Prejudice: *Parliament v Council*' (1989) 14 *EL Rev.* 334

W. Wils, 'Concurrent Liability of the Community and a Member State' (1992) 17 *EL Rev.* 191